Alternatives to Economics

Christian Socio-Economic Perspectives

Clive Beed
Cara Beed

UNIVERSITY PRESS OF AMERICA, ® INC.
Lanham • Boulder • New York • Toronto • Oxford

4501 Forbes Boulevard
Suite 200
Lanham, Maryland 20706
UPA Acquisitions Department (301) 459-3366

PO Box 317
Oxford
OX2 9RU, UK

Printed in the United States of America
British Library Cataloging in Publication Information Available

Library of Congress Control Number: 2006921856
ISBN-13: 978-0-7618-3398-7 (paperback : alk. paper)
ISBN-10: 0-7618-3398-6 (paperback : alk. paper)

∞™ The paper used in this publication meets the minimum requirements of American National Standard for Information Sciences—Permanence of Paper for Printed Library Materials, ANSI/NISO Z39.48-1992.

Contents

List of Tables vii

Acknowledgements ix

Preface xi

1 Christian Belief as Relevant to Modern Socio-Economic Life **1**
Social Science's Disregard of Christian Thought 5
Objections Concerning the Primary Source of Christian Belief 8
Objections Concerning Fundamentalism 15
Judeo-Christian Sources of Socio-Economic Intentions 20

2 Christian Principles for the Organization of Employment **25**
Catholic Social Thought 26
Protestant Evangelical Thought 31
Applying the Principles to Employment Organization 40
Making Work Ownership Effective 49

3 Biblical Exegesis-Based Principles for Economic Distribution **56**
Deriving Normative Intentions for Economic Distribution 57
Economic Distributional Intentions of the Mosaic Law 64
Jesus' Teachings Relating to Distribution and the Intentions of the Law 76
James Barr on Jesus and the Law 84
Further Implications of Distributional Intentions of the Law 90

4 Christian Explanations for Unemployment **95**
A Christian Explanation for Unemployment 97

Comparison of Orthodox Economics' and Christian Reasons for Unemployment 107
Conclusion 113

5 Socio-Economic Principles in Contemporary Christian and Islamic Thought 115
Normative Economic Principles in Contemporary Islamic and Judeo-Christian Thought 120
Economic Implications of Two Common Principles 127
Conclusion 132

6 A Christian Perspective on Economics 134
The Christian Worldview and Economic Questions 138
Human Life Has Inseparable Spiritual and Material Dimensions 140
God Has Normative Intentions for Human Spiritual and Material Life 144
Humankind Strives for Coherence in Understanding Personal and Social Behavior Through Modes of Interpretation Outside of God 147
Conclusion 151

7 Christians and the Autonomy of Economics 154
From Interdependence to Autonomy: J. David Richardson on Economics 157
From Interdependence to Autonomy: Richardson on Economic Implications of Christian Thought 163
The Autonomous Views of Anthony Waterman 169
Conclusion 175

8 Science and Contemporary Economics 178
Background to the Traditional View of Science 179
Anti-Positivism 182
Anti-Positivism and the Physical Sciences 183
Anti-Positivism and the Social Sciences 191
In What Sense is Economics Regarded as Science? 196
Conclusion 206

9 Naturalism and Contemporary Economics 210
Naturalism 211
Naturalism in Social Science 216
Non-naturalism in Social Science 219
The Reflection of Non-Naturalism and Naturalism in Contemporary Economics 224
Conclusion 234

10 Causal Explanation and Laws in Naturalistic Social Science **237**
The Identification and Behaviour of Social Kinds 239
Causal Explanation and Mechanisms 245
Domain Restrictions and Mechanisms 247
Openness and Mechanisms 249
An Example of a Social Science Law 253
Conclusion 256

11 The Status of Economics as a Naturalistic Social Science **259**
The Weak Stance on Naturalism 261
Assessing the Claims of Competing Theories in Economics 263
Assessing the Claims of Any one Theory in Social Science and Economics 267
The Innovative Value of Predictive Claims of Naturalistic Economic Theory 270
Policy Implications From (Naturalistic?) Economic Theory 274
Conclusion 278

12 Intellectual Progress and Academic Economics **280**
The Meaning of Intellectual Progress in Social Science and Economics 281
Mainstream Economic Theory and Attributes of Intellectual Progress 287
Examples From Rational Choice Theory 287
Examples From Game Theory 291
Rational Choice and Game Theory Use Outside Academic Economics 296
Conclusion 298

13 A Christian Response to Naturalistic Social Science **301**
A Christian Response to Naturalistic Social Science 303
Christian Belief and the Development of Physical and Social Science 309
Worldviews and Metaphysical Frameworks in Physical and Social Science 313
The Normative Purpose of Christian Socio-Economic Analysis 318
Conclusion 325

14 The Methodology of Christian Socio-Economic Analysis **328**
The Christian Worldview as an Alternative Organizing Framework 334
The Methodology of Christian Socio-Economic Analysis 342

Holism and Circular Causation in Christian Socio-Economic Analysis 345
Christian Methodological Connections With Holism 347
Further Methodological Features of Christian Socio-Economic Analysis 352
Conclusion 358

Bibliography **361**

Index **403**

About the Authors **415**

List of Tables

Table 2.1.	Normative Principles from Three Papal Encyclicals Governing Work	30
Table 2.2.	Evangelical Principles Governing Employment Organization and Opportunity	33
Table 3.1.	Mosaic Law Measures Encouraging Economic Equality in Ancient Israel	66
Table 3.2.	Normative Socio-economic Principles Derived from Ten Mosaic Law Measures	75
Table 5.1.	Selected Economic Principles Common to Islam and Judeo-Christianity	126
Table 9.1.	Polarities between Non-naturalistic and Naturalistic Economics	228
Table 11.1.	Kincaid's (1996) Characteristics of Social Science Naturalism	262
Table 13.1.	Characteristics of Naturalism	304
Table 13.2.	Socio-economic Phenomena and Their Relation to Naturalism	309
Table 14.1.	Methodological Characteristics of Christian Socio-economic Analysis	344

Acknowledgements

The chapters of this book are based on revisions of our earlier papers, previously published in refereed academic journals. We thank the editors and publishers of the following journals for their kind permission to reproduce here revised versions of material that earlier appeared in their pages.

By kind permission of Taylor & Francis Group Ltd. (http://www.tandf.co.uk/), chapter 2 includes work based on 'Work ownership implications of recent Papal social thought', *Review of Social Economy* (2002) 60, 1: 47–69.

By kind permission of Elsevier, chapter 2 includes work based on 'Judeo-Christian principles for employment organization', *Journal of Socio-Economics* (2002) 31, 5: 457–468.

By kind permission of Emerald Group Publishing Ltd. (http://www.emeraldinsight.com/ijse.htm), chapter 3 includes work based on 'Distributional implications of Judeo-Christian thought', *International Journal of Social Economics* (2004) 31, 10: 903–922.

By kind permission of the Editor, Professor I. Howard Marshall and Paternoster Periodicals, chapter 3 includes work based on 'Jesus and equity in material distribution', *Evangelical Quarterly* (2005) 77, 2: 99–118.

By kind permission of the Editor, Professor Ruth Taplin, and AB Academic Publishers, chapter 4 includes work based on 'A Judeo-Christian theory of unemployment', *Journal of Interdisciplinary Economics* (2005) 16, 2: 121–143.

By kind permission of the Editor, Professor Ruth Taplin, and AB Academic Publishers, chapter 5 includes work based on 'Socio-economic principles in contemporary Christian and Islamic thought', *Journal of Interdisciplinary Economics* (2003) 14, 3: 227–248.

By kind permission of Taylor & Francis Group Limited (http://www.tandf.co.uk/), chapter 6 includes work based on 'A Christian perspective on economics', *Journal of Economic Methodology* (1996) 3, 1: 91–112.

By kind permission of Emerald Group Publishing Ltd. (http://www.emeraldinsight.com/ijse.htm), chapter 7 includes work based on 'The autonomy of economics from Judeo-Christian thought: a critique', *International Journal of Social Economics* (2003) 30, 9: 942–966.

By kind permission of M. E. Sharpe Inc., chapter 8 includes work based on 'Philosophy of science and contemporary economics: an overview', *Journal of Post Keynesian Economics* (1991) 13, 4: 459–494.

By special and kind permission of the copyright holder, the Association for Evolutionary Economics, chapter 9 includes work based on 'Polarities between naturalism and non-naturalism in contemporary economics: an overview', *Journal of Economic Issues* (1996) 30, 4: 1077–1104.

By kind permission of Blackwell Publishers, chapter 10 includes work based on 'Is the case for social science laws strengthening?', *Journal for the Theory of Social Behaviour* (2000) 30, 2: 131–153.

By kind permission of Oxford University Press, chapter 11 includes work based on 'The status of economics as a naturalistic social science', *Cambridge Journal of Economics* (2000) 24, 4: 417–435.

By kind permission of M. E. Sharpe Inc., chapter 12 includes work based on 'Intellectual progress and academic economics', *Journal of Post Keynesian Economics* (2000) 22, 2: 163–185.

By kind permission of the copyright holder, the *Christian Scholar's Review*, chapter 13 includes work based on 'An evangelical Christian response to naturalistic social science', *Christian Scholar's Review* (2004) 34, 1: 21–41.

Our thanks go to Charles Clark for his encouraging and informative preface to this book, and to John Milbank and John Tiemstra for their supportive endorsements. We thank academic colleagues who have encouraged us in our continued research and writing, including Charley Clark, and also Bruce Duncan, Kim Sawyer, Gordon Preece, Paul Oslington, Jeremy Galbreath and Ray Wyatt. Thanks go also to the anonymous referees whose advice has come to us via the academic journal editors, and to Warwick Dunbar, Elva Board and Ricardo Luz for their assistance with computing. David Chao, University Press of America, has been of great assistance, as has our proofreader, Edward Caruso and our indexer, Margaret Findlay. We value the interest and constant support of our family and friends.

Preface

Economic theory, as an intellectual discipline, has its origins in the Scholastic idea that faith and reason both reflect the same reality; they are two ways to understanding God's creation. Understanding the world started with understanding the creator of the world, and then understanding the plan of the creator. The plan of the creator, in terms of economic analysis, revolves around how individuals and communities should carry out their economic activities (those that relate to the material reproduction of the community) in a manner that best promotes human happiness (with the ultimate happiness coming from union with God). By emphasizing the end or purpose of economic activity we come to a better understanding of what promotes, and what retards, that end. Economic inquiry consisted of starting with the economic wisdom in the Bible and applying it to the specific economic circumstances.

The complementary approach of faith and reason to social inquiry begins to change in the Enlightenment period. The Enlightenment accepted the basic principles of Christian Ethics, yet they change the relationship between faith and reason. Instead of placing faith in God as He has been revealed to us through revelation, faith was placed in the abilities of human reason to discover all things. This change in attitude is best expressed in Rene Descartes' "I think, there for I am" pronouncement. Thus instead of an interaction of faith and reason, where both inform and enlighten each other (best demonstrated in the work of St. Thomas Aquinas) we were left with reason alone, grounded in itself, with no check or humility. While this was a slow process, by the early 20th century the break with a values grounded economic analysis (with the values loosely grounded in Christian Ethics) was complete. Neoclassical economic theory is purely a rationalistic explanation of economic activity, in which neither historical nor social context plays a significant role in either the creation of economic theories and explanations, or in the confirmation or refutation of existing theories. Furthermore, market values became the only important values. We see this best in the highest level of neoclassical economic theory, axiomatic general equilibrium theory, where the analysis has no real world grounding. The proofs of the various theorems are independent of the actual phenomenon being explained. As Gerard Debreu stated in his classic *Theory of Value*: "Allegiance to rigor dictates the axiomatic form of the analysis where the theory, in the strict sense, is logically entirely disconnected from its interpretation. Such a dichotomy reveals all the assumptions and logical structure of the analysis" (1959, p. x). Yet at no time is the realism or empirical validity of the assumptions brought into question, such that, in the end, one is left with merely an ideological defense of free market capitalism and not a reason based understanding of economic activity or even more important, a values based evaluation of how well existing economic institutions and practices promote human happiness.

While the economics profession happily continued along the rationalist lines of the Vienna Circle, Modernism morphed into Post Modernism, and the foundation upon which the unlimited faith in human reason was based began to crumble. By the 1970s many commentators wrote about the "crisis in economic theory." This crisis existed at many levels. At the surface it was clear that the standard neoclassical model could not explain the stagflation (high unemployment coupled with high inflation) of the 1970s (and thus offer good advice on how to counter it), nor could they explain the boom of the 1990s, where both unemployment and inflation fell below their so-called "natural levels." At a deeper level, deconstruction and the other intellectual fades of Post Modernism, called into question the "scientific" credentials of economic analysis. The claim that economics was a science on par with the natural sciences became laughable (and a bit embarrassing). The final straw, however, came with the logical conclusion of the Post Modern agenda, moral relativism. Now not only could economics not say anything meaningful about the actual state of the economy, it couldn't say anything meaningful about the ideal state of the economy, where it should be heading. Economics, as an intellectual discipline, had gone from studying the actual economy in order to help move it towards normative goals, to studying a hypothetical economy in the hope that it yields insights that will help up promote normative goals, to studying an imaginary economy in order to justify the imaginary economy. We should be fair to economists and mention that the same problem exists in most of the social sciences. We should also note that the majority of economists are blissfully ignorant of this state of affairs, as most graduate programs no longer teach the history of economic thought, much less the philosophical and methodological foundations of economics. In most graduate programs economics as an intellectual discipline has ceased to exist. Instead these are merely practitioner training programs churning out mindless technicians. This, of course, is a sorry state for the once great "Worldly Philosophy." The tradition of Adam Smith, John Stuart Mill, Karl Marx, Thorstein Veblen, Alfred Marshall, Joseph Schumpeter and John Maynard Keynes centered on economics as a moral science, addressing real issues from ethical perspectives.

It should not surprise anyone that one of the responses to Post Modernism and moral relativism has been a revival in faith based investigations into social issues. Just as all our actions are based on values and value jugdments, so too are our efforts to understand and explain human actions. Value-neutral is not only value-less, it is impossible. Theorists need values to guide their research, and tolerance (the only value Post Modernism accepts) isn't enough. We need the substance, not the shadow (actually Post Modernism is a reflection of the shadow). This revival started at the policy level, often with religious groups releasing statements on pressing economic and social issues, statements that combined empirical analysis of the problems with solutions grounded in their faith traditions. These documents were answering Leo XIII's 1890 call to understand "the world as it really is," and look elsewhere for solutions to its problems (*Rerum Novarum*, 14). At the academic level, we see this reaction in the rise of articles and books on Christianity and Economics. While some of the writings in this field consist of economic analyses of religion, there is also a noticeable attention to economic issues important to Christians (such as wealth and poverty). That is, a good number of economists have allowed their faith tradition to influence their scholarly work as economists, usually by determining what topics to apply their economic skills and knowledge. These efforts, however, completely miss the Post Modern criticism. In many ways, while faith is brought back into the picture, it is still kept separate from reason. This is only a half step in the right direction, one that does not deal at all with the essential challenge of Post Modernism and moral relativism.

The way to retrieve this once great tradition is to return to the roots of economics as a social science, back to the time where values (supported by faith and reason) guided intellectual efforts, and where faith and reason were not kept separate from each other. What is needed to save economic and social analysis from total irrelevance is a Christian economic analysis, that is, one that is grounded in the Truths (and values) of Christian ethics (truths learned though faith and reason): that the world exists; that everything that exists was brought into existence (was created); that everything that is created (by a creator), is created for a reason; and that everything that is created reaches its highest perfection when it fulfills the purpose for which it is created. In more simple terms: God created the world; God has a plan for the world; His plan is revealed in the Divine law and we can discover it in the natural law; and human happiness is best promoted when we follow God's plan.

Thus the starting point of economic analysis has to be Genesis: God created man and woman in His likeness and image. This means we need to adopt a Christian Anthropology which states: that all persons have the ability to reason and free will and thus are moral actors; that as children of God, all persons have an inherent human dignity that cannot be violated; that humans are necessarily social in that they need to live in communities in order to reach their potential, and that happiness comes from giving one self to others in love. The starting point is grounded in both faith and reason and provides the necessary moral and philosophical foundations upon which we can proceed to investigate economic actions and the economy (it is worth noting that this is a much more fruitful starting point than the "rational economic man" fiction).

At the vanguard of these efforts to develop a Christian understanding of the economy has been Clive and Cara Beed. In various articles, and now in the book you have before you, they have developed both a critique of neoclassical economic analysis based on its weak philosophical and methodological foundations as well as the foundations of an alternative approach to understanding the economy. Part of the success of the Beeds on these issues must stem from their interdisciplinary collaboration. An economist working with a sociologist helps to avoid the overly narrow view of neoclassical economics (although the trend in sociology, and in political science, seems to be in the direction of neoclassical economics and its reliance on mathematical formalism and empty empiricism). A look at Cara Beed's research shows that these are topics (such as the effects of abuse) that one cannot abstract from the particulars and hope, through reason alone, to find the universal. Even more importantly, one cannot abstract from the humanity of each person (which neoclassical economics does). Another reason for the success of the Beeds rests in the high level of philosophical and methodological analysis that grounds their critique of neoclassical economics. In fact, one can get a full overview of the past thirty years of research and debate in the area of economic methodology from this book, encyclopedic in its coverage and profound in its insights.

Yet the real gem in *Alternatives to Economics*, the reason it will become the seminal book on viewing the economy from a Christian perspective, is the Beeds' insistence to ground the analysis of economic questions in a Biblical perspective. From the beginning (especially Chapters 2 and 4 on employment issues), we see that the sacred scriptures that form the heart and soul of Western Civilization are still relevant as a starting point for addressing the human condition. The Beeds remind us that economics involves human activities, economics is a human science, and thus all economics is normative (grounded in values). Our ultimate values (values upon which all legitimate values are based) are the values of the ultimate; the source for universal values is the universal. This doesn't mean that the Bible necessarily answers all economic questions. It does mean that if our goal is to promote human happiness, then we need to keep in mind the source of that happiness, and the rules for living in community that have been given to us to promote human happiness. *Alternatives to Economics* is an important and necessary step in the effort to create an economy worthy of God's children, an economy which, as we say in the Catholic social thought tradition, protects human dignity and promotes the common good. Anything that can get economists to seriously address this goal is sorely needed and greatly appreciated.

Charles M. A. Clark
Senior Scholar, Vincentian Center for Church and Society
Professor of Economics, Tobin College of Business
St. John's University
New York

Chapter One

Christian Belief as Relevant to Modern Socio-Economic Life

This book presents two propositions based on current orthodox Judeo-Christian thought. One details a framework for contemporary socio-economic analysis contained in Judeo-Christian belief. This framework is intended to be used both as a tool of analysis and for altering forms of socio-economic organization. The second proposition is that, for Christians, the framework is meant to take precedence over the theories of secular social science because of the limitations inherent in social science. Both these claims seem implausible, and are not accepted by non-Christians. Even some Christians believe that the cultural, social and technological distance separating the time when Judeo-Christian thought was first articulated is too great to allow the transposition of Christian ideas to the contemporary socio-economic world. Promoting this view, Novak (1982, 335) holds that 'writers of the biblical era did not envisage questions of political economy such as those we face today.' This type of belief is usually tied to the rejection of the second proposition above, that Judeo-Christian-based analysis is primary to the social sciences (economics, sociology, psychology, anthropology, political science). After all, these fields of study, especially economics, constitute 'science,' and 'so few theologians or religious leaders understand economics' (Novak, 1982, 18, 336). This second proposition of our argument appears all the more improbable for the theories of secular social science have been proffering socio-economic advice for the last three hundred years, steadily usurping Christian socio-economic thought. A thriving social science industry has developed in which Christian ideas are ignored.

Against these trends, the case here utilizes orthodox interpretations of Judeo-Christian thought to show that theories of social science are subordinate to understanding revealed by Judeo-Christian belief. Economics is taken as the main social science example, and the Judeo-Christian framework is shown to constitute a theoretical alternative for understanding socio-economic phenomena.

This applies even though social science methods and data have a useful role in describing the sources and historical context of Judeo-Christian belief, in outlining socio-economic conditions, and partially explaining them at any historical juncture. Christian socio-economic analysis, or social theology as it could also be called, can use data, concepts and findings from social science for its purposes, but it is not intrinsic to the collection and manipulation of socio-economic data that only the social sciences can provide them (Beed, 2003a).

The argument, therefore, does not suggest that economics/social science is vacuous in revealing reality. Instead, it is argued that Christian thought takes precedence. While the grace of God, His blessings and presence, are available to all—unbelievers and believers—the Christian system is taken to expose reality in greater degree than do the theories of non-Christian-based social science. The life of Christ and the Holy Spirit dwelling within individual Christians is held to assist them see reality and truth more clearly. 'The inner illumination of the mind is strengthened,' as Milbank (1990, 248) puts it.

Secular social scientists do not accept the subordinacy of social science to Christian understanding. If confronted with it, they respond with incredulity and 'missionary zeal' (see p. 15) to defend their position. Their education and socialization lead them to believe that social science is far more important than Christianity for explaining and prescribing for human socio-economic behavior. Most social scientists would not take seriously that Christianity is intended to inform socio-economic life, let alone compete with social science. Some social and educational justifications exist in the reasons they hold for this view. These reasons are evaluated from the Christian perspective progressively developed through subsequent chapters.

The case, therefore, is controversial even within Christian circles. In all likelihood, its components will be contested by Christians holding different views, and some of these views are assessed throughout the book. The first proposition of the book is unwrapped via three contemporary orthodox sources of Judeo-Christian thought. These are recent Papal social thought, a selection of Protestant theologians and economists who loosely might be described as 'evangelical' (defined in later chapters), and a cross-section of modern academic Biblical exegesis, non-evangelical and evangelical. Three different sources are taken to investigate their common ground in relation to the propositions illustrated, and to ascertain their extent of support. Chapters 2–4 give three different illustrations of the first proposition above: the framework for contemporary socio-economic analysis contained in Judeo-Christian belief, and its purpose to be so used. The implication from the three examples is that the framework or system can be used to analyze diverse socio-economic phenomena. Chapter 5 shows that contemporary interpreters of Islam also claim to possess such a framework, and that distinct similarities exist between the

Judeo-Christian and the Islamic systems in this area. Thus, two major religions of the world—'the people of the Book'—maintain their primary relevance to socio-economic application.

Chapters 2–4 are prerequisites for examining the second proposition, the primacy of the Judeo-Christian system over secular social science for explaining and prescribing for socio-economic life. Chapter 6 offers the first demonstration by outlining specific philosophical differences between the Judeo-Christian framework and that embodied in secular economics, while Chapter 7 argues that economists who are Christians, and who currently accord autonomous standing to economics are mistaken in terms of Christian belief. This and the following chapters argue against the view held by some economist Christians that economics is a set of neutral tools that can be used to reveal reality reliably, and to devise real-world policy. Concepts such as opportunity costs, scarcity, and trade-offs, for example, are not discoveries by economics, but have been used for aeons consistently with Christian thought, while the distinction between positive and normative economics is untenable. The argument of this book is that such concepts can only be defined in terms of values, and cannot be used independently from the purposes inherent to the contexts in which they are applied, and the values underlying those contexts. It is these values and purposes that distinguish Christian thought from that of secular economics. The five chapters (8–12) traverse particular limitations encased in contemporary economic theory that render it of limited use for understanding reality. These chapters argue that mainstream economic theories have been singularly unsuccessful in helping people understand the world and prescribe for its improvement. The final two chapters return to the first proposition discussed in Chapters 2–4, by showing how the Judeo-Christian system differs from that manifest in the claims of naturalistic social science to explain reality, including all forms of secular economic theory.

Thus, the second proposition of the book is pursued in two ways. One is by assessing how the worldview inherent in the orthodox Judeo-Christian thought systems of Chapters 2–4 compares with worldviews underlying secular social science, emphasizing that embodied in contemporary orthodox economics. The second way is by assessing the innovative nature and reliability of explanations or theories in social science. The overall conclusion from these Chapters 6–14 is that the Judeo-Christian worldview differs dramatically from those typically underlying social science, and that explanations or theories in social science do not have a high degree of applicability to the real world or represent innovative explanatory gain over what can be obtained from Judeo-Christian explanation. This conclusion is consistent with the overall challenge canvassed—that thematic intentions, principles, and bases for action derive from orthodox Judeo-Christian interpretations, relating to the personal and social life of all peoples at all times. These intentions serve as a basis for describing, explaining and prescribing for socio-economic life. The concluding chapter (14) draws these themes together, and presents a methodology that could be practiced for a Judeo-Christian form of socio-economic analysis.

Chapters 2 and 3 provide examples from the three selected Judeo-Christian orthodoxies alleging consistent socio-economic intentions and principles from their interpretations of Christian thought. The three streams hold that the triune God intends humankind to apply these intentions to its own contexts and situations. The intentions or principles are meant explicitly to apply to fallen humanity, even though trade-offs would be necessary in their application. If this reasoning is valid, God has placed an awesome responsibility on humans. From interpreting the Bible, from prayer, theological reflection, and church tradition, the task for people is to ascertain what these intentions and principles might be. People are also expected to work out how they might relate to their own situations and be applied in them. Here, assessment of the empirical reality confronting people is crucial. None of these are straightforward tasks. A direct, one-to-one connection between Biblical text or message, theological proposition, church tradition, and unraveling God-given intention does not necessarily occur, especially as the Biblical text has probably been redacted over a long period of time. The original autographs, if they ever existed, have long disappeared. Hermeneutical skills are prerequisites for this interpretive undertaking, although the lengthy experience of application of these skills shows that consensus among Christians is not achieved by the process. However, if God is setting this interpretive task for people, He has assigned a strategic role to human intellect (as well as to spiritual discernment) in the exercise, but its application is not unproblematic. With the unique personalities God gives each person, a believer will not necessarily interpret the same theme or principle as another Christian. Nor will all agree how any one socio-economic precept should be applied. At the least, their application might differ depending on empirical and cultural context. Although a way to resolve these dilemmas might be to seek agreement among Christian believers, this may not yield determinate conclusions. Hay (1989, 309–313) provides a helpful discussion of these problems.

Two examples in Chapters 2 and 3 suggest how principles or intentions educed by the three currents of contemporary orthodox Christian thought might relate to socio-economic thinking current today in well-developed countries. Chapter 2 delineates propositions from the selected Catholic and Protestant interpretations that might be applied to the organization of paid employment. Indeed, these interpreters argue they are *meant* to be applied in today's world. Chapter 3 does a similar thing for intentions allegedly guiding the distribution of wealth and income, but engaging directly with recent academic Biblical commentary to derive the principles. The two contrasting approaches (secondary theological reflection and direct Biblical interpretation) are taken to show that consistent results can be developed from them. It will also become clear in both Chapters 2 and 3 that few of the necessary principles are followed nowadays. If the elucidation of the intentions or principles in Chapters 2 and 3 is persuasive, the two topics—foundations for organization of paid work and priorities for distribution of wealth (and income) appear to be vitally important to the triune God. The topics have weighed heavy long on the minds of secular thinkers. For instance, the two issues of employment and distribution were uppermost in the thinking of the economist, J. M. Keynes. To him, 'the outstanding faults of the economic society in which we live are its failure to provide full employment and its arbitrary and inequitable distribution of wealth and income' (Keynes, 1936, 372). In the time since Keynes wrote, these dual problems have preoccupied theoreticians and policy makers. It is ironic that God is reported as recognizing the importance of the problems and proposing solutions to them three thousand years before Keynes. Yet, few economists know or are interested in what God, via the interpreters ancient and modern, is supposed to have said about the questions. Most economists are likely to view such concepts with disdain. What Keynes and other secular economists have said since is far more relevant to them.

SOCIAL SCIENCE'S DISREGARD OF CHRISTIAN THOUGHT

This manner of ignoring Christian thought about socio-economic questions is typical of social science today. In their writing, the overwhelming majority of secular social scientists appear to be uninterested in Christian belief, do not understand it, are unsympathetic to it, and, when faced with it, act as though Christians lack thinking ability. If religious belief is mentioned to social science students at all, it is likely they will receive a distorted and simplistic version, even a caricature, at least as far as Christians perceive their religion.

For instance, sociology students have religious belief introduced to them by unreferenced scriptural quotations in Giddens' widely-used text (1993, 455; 1997, 434). No more is said about the one New Testament quotation (Rom. 12:10–14, 18) than it conveys 'a sense of universal love and of God's goodness.' This is valid as far as it goes, but is inadequate because nothing further is stated about the responsibility believers have to each other and are meant to practice in the wider world. A main reason for the quote in Giddens is to compare it with a previous one from the Koran, and to suggest that Islam and Christianity reject 'the God of the other.' The content of religious beliefs is even less explored in Giddens' fourth edition (Giddens with Birdsall,

2001) in so far as scriptural quotations are no longer included. Students reading the chapter would gain only the slightest understanding of the content of Christian religious belief, and how it might relate to the world. Adequate sociological analysis of the major belief system of the world cannot be undertaken without examining the content of its beliefs.

Another symptom of social science's disregard is that Christian academic writing on socio-economic matters, such as Catholic social thought, is near totally ignored in the secular academic literature. Aside from a few exceptional secular journals, social scientists submitting Christian-based papers to secular social science journals are likely to have editors decline to referee them because they are thought by the editors to be more suitable to theological journals. Accordingly, Christians interested in the socio-economic implications of their beliefs talk mainly to themselves, as does theology to itself.

Secular social science studiously avoids confronting the content of religious beliefs, as distinct from religious institutional organization and affiliation. The ways this occurs could be extended, but this is not the purpose of this book. Nevertheless, it is not exaggerating to suggest that secular social science has a 'totalitarian impulse' (see p. 15) when confronted with the socio-economic implications of Christian belief, that it exhibits fundamentalist tendencies in ignoring Christian socio-economic thought. These are harsh words for which a justification is attempted in Chapters 6 and 7. Secular social science thinks it knows much better than Christianity why socio-economic dislocation exists, and what should be done about it. Economics is taken in this book as the main example from the social sciences because it may be the social science from which most practical socio-economic guidance is sought by policy makers today, and economics is prone to want to see itself as such. As well, the sophisticated formalistic edifice of contemporary economics presents the appearance of a formidable science, and can serve as a barrier to its evaluation. Lay and Christian thinkers can be intimidated by the scientific appearance of economics, and end up being inveigled into its thrall and propensity to appropriate segments of the other social sciences. Contemporary economics enjoys a supreme self-confidence so that it thinks itself as the queen of the social sciences—'the most "scientific" of the social sciences' (Hands, 2001b, 390), and a highly important guide to assessing and prescribing for humankind's material state, with moral or spiritual considerations (if they exist) of secondary importance. Needless to say, these latter propositions are not accepted by diverse currents of Christian thought. Rejecting them is not exclusively a fundamentalist propensity. Even Pope John Paul II claimed that 'the whole way of looking at the question of economics is marked by the premises of materialistic economism.' This economistic perspective contains a 'fundamental error . . . of considering human labour solely according to its economic purpose.' It 'includes a conviction of the primacy and superiority of the material,' subordinating the spiritual and also moral values to material reality (*Laborem Exercens*, LE, 1981, 31, 55).

From the Christian interpretations surveyed and advocated here, Christianity can be viewed as the most important guide, far more important than economic theory, for the material, moral and spiritual dimensions of human life, dimensions that cannot be separated according to these Christian perspectives. Chapter 6 traverses these ideas showing how the Christian worldview and viewpoint promoted here can be understood as differing dramatically from the viewpoint of modern economic theory. Some economist Christians do not accept the contention that Judeo-Christian thought should take precedence over economics, and their stand is evaluated in Chapter 7. Chapters 8 to 12 argue that the claims of economic theory and models for unraveling reality are exaggerated anyway. Economics does not constitute a practical or coherent system of explanation or prediction even on its own terms. Given the starting point of this book, these conclusions should not be surprising. The three Christian modes can be interpreted to regard Christianity, not secular social science, as providing the necessary socio-economic guidance for humankind to pursue its optimal development. One of the ideas that social science cannot get its head around, and therefore does not discuss, is that 'optimal development' in Christianity means something different from the same words in secular thought. It includes, for example, each person developing and maintaining an intimate personal relationship with God, Jesus, and the Holy Spirit. Secular thinkers would ridicule this idea having any importance to socio-economic life, or even to people's personal lives.

Thus, one contemporary reason for the rejection of Christian thought from social science is that non-religious social scientists think it is totally irrelevant to humankind's social material condition. To them, 'Christian' means personal, private, individualistic, pietistic belief. Unfortunately, and as well, Christian belief may be conflated in the minds of non-religious social scientists with powerful institutional churches pursuing their vested interests at times with (and an historical legacy of) little relation to the foundation beliefs of Christianity. The teachings of the triune God reported in the Bible do emphasize the qualities of personal spiritual belief. The spiritual interrelationships between God and individual people are vitally important. But, the socio-economic dimensions of Christian belief, as elaborated in the Bible for example, can be construed as of equal importance. God's dealings with people, as reported, emphasize how believers are intended to live in relation to other people, how they should behave in particular ways in principle toward them—and not just to fellow believers. These intentions are taken to stem from the spiritual interrelationships between the triune God and humans. The love God has for people cannot be divorced from the love people are meant to show each other. God's love for humans in Jesus Christ is intended to flow through each person to other people. The 'love' in question has crucial practical dimensions, involving not just vague, abstract feelings. The relationships people are encouraged to practice with each other cannot be divorced from the relationships in love people are designed to have with the triune God. The case here is that intentions or principles instigated by God to govern human socio-economic life derive from and are inseparable from those aiming to guide people's spiritual life, the relationships in love people are designed to have with God. Whether those intentions were transmitted directly by God to the named authors of the Biblical texts, whether they were redacted over a long time period via the traditions of believing communities, or whether some mixture of both processes occurred, is not crucial to the argument, as long as the intentions can be shown to be consistent between different interpretations, and different source segments, of Judeo-Christian thought.

All the God-based intentions or requirements provide the mould for the social and economic dimension of the normative behavior to which God calls all humankind. Normative here means providing norms or precepts of behavior for people to interpret and follow. The Bible, for instance, reports that God expects already committed Christians to seek and observe the required guides. This is no easy job because each believer probably has a different understanding from every other, which is another potential source of disagreement between Christians. But the Bible also proposes that God calls *all* people, not just existing believers. God earnestly desires all people to commit themselves to Him. Clearly, He prefers all people to become believers, and follow His normative guidelines for human personal and socio-economic development. The Bible has a message to offer and there is a job to do. Some Christians might object that a God- and Biblically-based mode of socio-economic analysis is not relevant to a fallen world. However, God and Jesus have always been calling people to return to Them, both individuals and social groups. The task of Christians is to initiate the Kingdom of God on earth, with God's assistance, even though it will never be complete on earth until Jesus' second coming.

OBJECTIONS CONCERNING THE PRIMARY SOURCE OF CHRISTIAN BELIEF

Various objections to the approach canvassed are discussed throughout the book. Conceivable objections, for example, could emanate from sundry schools of theology, and from practitioners of particular theological methodologies and philosophies. Since so many competing trends exist in academic theology today, it is not feasible to consider criticism that could arise from all these sources. Therefore, just one representative of one current is emphasized, although a range of theologians is cited who dissent from the line promoted here. This section endeavors to show that what is being proposed is not theologically simplistic. The representative critic stressed is James Barr, exponent of the historical critical method, or Biblical research. Barr's views here are taken only from eight of his most recent books (1973, 1977, 1980, 1982, 1983, 1984, 1999, 2000). Barr is selected because he is a prominent Christian advocate of an alternative viewpoint from that advocated here, and he has been a specifically-vocal critic of one of the lines of Christian interpretation illustrated (evangelicalism) that favors application of Christian principles to the modern world.

At this point in the argument, just one pertinent objection is considered against the methodology of the three orthodox Christian forms of interpretation. This concerns the function for Christians and the world of the primary documentary source of Judeo-Christian belief, the Bible. The three Christian modes can be construed as upholding the importance of the Bible as the fount of intentions or principles for application to the world. This claim is illustrated further in Chapters 2 and 3, and for the moment is posed as an assumption. It is reflected, for instance, in recent encyclicals of the former Pope of the Roman Catholic Church, John Paul II. He claimed that 'the Church's social teaching finds its source in Sacred Scripture, beginning with the Book of Genesis and especially in the Gospel and the writings of the Apostles' (LE, 1981, 17). Thus, in this Papal encyclical analyzing and prescribing ethical stances for human work, there are over four times as many citations to Biblical texts as to official statements of the Catholic Church, but to no other sources. This is an unusual balance in recent encyclicals between citations to the Bible and to the Roman Catholic magisterium, but is indicative of greater explicit attachment to scripture since Vatican II.

Barr has a different view of the Bible from that implied in such a direct reliance on scripture. He notes reasonably (1980, 62; original emphasis) that because so many contemporary questions are 'not directly treated by the Bible,' 'some people think we should derive from the Bible *principles* which can then be applied to decision [*sic*] about these matters.' This is one component of the methodology of the three Christian interpretive forms on which the arguments of this book are based. Barr rejects the approach and instead proffers his own explanation and guidelines for how Christians do form, and should form, their ethical positions. First, he explains what he believes the Bible does not do: 'We do not derive from the Bible information that in itself authorizes or gives the foundation for such and such a doctrinal or ethical position' (1980, 62). Instead, the doctrinal and ethical positions of Christians 'have as their point of origin a total vision, a conception of what Christian life, action and society should be like. These visions come from Christian men, informed by the Bible but also informed by all sorts of other influences which play upon their lives.' Similar thoughts are expressed in Barr (1999, 607): To enable Christians to make up their minds about 'the burning issues of the day,' 'we begin with the present day and then consider the Bible, not alone, but as part of the mixture of relevant factors . . .' These 'relevant factors' include knowledge from 'modern sciences' (Barr, 1973, 38), in which Barr presumably includes economics, and certainly, sociology (1973, 110).

In both his 1980 and 1999 statements above, Barr discusses together the normative basis of Christian belief—the conception of what Christian life should be like—with how Christians actually do form their ethical (and doctrinal) positions. But prescription is different from description. Two different and potentially contradictory sets of influences can be at work. Barr concedes that the conception of what Christian life should be like is informed by the Bible, and should be so. This is similar but not identical to claiming that the Christian ethical position derives from Biblical information serving as the foundation for this position—an approach Barr rejects above. However, in both accounts of the process of forming ethical stances—the position Barr (1980) rejects and the position he accepts—the Bible is taken to be at least one foundational normative influence. In the position Barr rejects, one stressed by the three forms of Christian interpretation represented in subsequent chapters here, the Bible is taken to be a major, if not *the,* foundational influence.

Barr (1980) then adds on a different set of contributors affecting the ethical and doctrinal positions of Christians—'all sorts of other influences which play upon' their lives. Nobody need doubt this is so, but these influences can be good or bad, they can conform to Christian belief or they can deviate from it. Some evaluative framework or sorting mechanism is needed by Christians to determine whether these 'other influences' are consistent with the 'conception of what Christian life, action and society should be like.' After all, this conception is to be 'informed by the Bible,' and Barr offers no other normative conceptual framework outside the Bible by which evaluation of these 'other influences' can be made. The approach advocated in the three Christian strands examined here is for Christians to make a normative assessment of these 'other influences' in terms of the foundational information provided in the Bible—expressed in this book as its intentions or principles. To suggest that the Bible is merely to be 'part of the mixture of relevant factors' enabling Christians to form judgements about 'the burning issues of the day' (Barr, 1999, 607) is to leave aside the question of what these 'relevant factors' might be. About these, little consensus has been achieved even among social scientists in their theorizing on the reasons for the existence of such burning issues. (This assertion is illustrated for particular issues in economics in later chapters). If this is the case, Christians are no better placed than anyone else to assess what this 'mixture of relevant factors' might be.

Toward the end of his 1980 (62–63) treatment, Barr appears to move to the line advocated here (that dependent on the three forms of orthodox Christian interpretation). To exemplify the 'vision' of what Christian life and society should resemble, 'the Bible exercises a critical role: it questions what people think, it queries the basis of their judgements, it asks whether the tradition which modern men form is really in continuity with its biblical origins.' Barr does not assign 'a critical role' to any other framework for Christians, except for some unspecified 'mixture of relevant factors.' If the critical role Barr attributes to the Bible embodies the evaluative questions he suggests Christians have to ask—'what people think,' and so on—they cannot avoid assessing how the characteristics of modern society conform to Biblical intention, to assess whether modern traditions are 'in continuity' with biblical foundations. From claiming fourteen lines earlier that Biblical information gives no 'foundation' for any ethical (or doctrinal) position, Barr moves to advocate normatively that the Bible is intended to be used to ask whether modern social traditions are continuous with biblical origins. Barr concedes also that the individual Christian is similarly affected by the Bible. A Christian's actions cannot avoid being influenced by 'the biblical material,' for this 'bears upon the whole man, his total faith and life.' In taking 'his decisions as a free agent,' the Christian acts 'out of that total faith and life' that bears upon his whole (Barr, 1973, 142). He is moulded, influenced, guided, and affected by that faith on which the Biblical material bears.

One of the reasons Barr holds to the relegation of the Bible as a basis for ethical behavior—that it does not serve as 'the foundation for such and such a doctrinal or ethical position'—is that he thinks human nature is not constant, that it changes depending on the cultural and historical milieu in which humans find themselves. Barr (1973, 40–41) criticizes, for instance, 'the idea that human nature in essence remains unchanged through time and through the vicissitudes of cultural change. This we now know to be untrue. There is no universal human nature.' Accordingly, 'a work like the Bible, which is the product of one particular cultural situation . . . cannot therefore be authoritative in any decisive sense for other cultures.' Cultural relativism is a popular facet of postmodernism, but its propositions about human nature are speculative rather than factual. This is not the place to rehearse the arguments about the changeability of human nature—which Barr has not done either. All we need note here is that an opposite viewpoint from Barr's is still held, a perspective on which the arguments of this book depend. Thus, the Christian realist philosopher, Trigg (1999, 3, 4), in the second edition of his historical review of ideas of human nature, argues 'for a culture-transcendent view of human nature.' Trigg writes 'in the conviction that human life has remained the same in its essentials through recorded history . . . people have remained the same.' Similarly, the philosopher of history and Christian, McCullagh (1998, 26) believes 'that cultural variation of people's perceptions of the everyday world is not great' even though it does exist.

Between the functions attributed to the Bible in the three Christian currents examined here, and in those of Barr, a gulf exists. The three Christian modes rest on the assumption that the Bible is meant to serve as the source of God's intentions for humanity. As noted above, it is not crucial to this viewpoint whether those intentions are regarded as having been mediated by the understanding of communities who, over time, redacted these intentions, believing they were being guided by God, or whether the intentions are regarded as having been transmitted directly by God to the men (or communities) who penned the words of the Biblical texts, or a mixture of both. Irrespective of its background compilation, the Bible is seen as functioning as the source book via which God's worldview can be discerned, and through which human activity can be described, explained and improved. This is a normative position rejected by Barr (1973, 110) who suggests correctly for most people that 'the framework through we see the world' is no longer a biblical one. Instead the framework is 'furnished by science, sociology and so on.' There is an implication here that the Biblical framework may even be contradictory to the framework through which people now see the world. An assumption of this book is that the Biblical framework is not contrary to natural science (an assumption not debated here), but that it can be contrary to the social sciences because, as the case of economics illustrates, the scientific achievements of economic theory in terms of increasing the understanding of the world have been minor. Calling the social sciences 'science' does nothing to elevate their ability to explain and prescribe for human behavior.

Barr does not reach his position by reviewing the alleged achievements of social science. Rather, he reaches it by presenting a particular interpretation of the Bible. In Barr's view, the role of the Bible has become diminished normatively because 'what was once taken as God's truth is now seen as Hebrew or early Christian customs and folklore' (Barr, 1973, 110). An implication of this view is that this folklore might be more a human construction than God's. It has not been possible throughout Christian history to demonstrate incontrovertibly which of these two paths (the traditional orthodox or Barr's) for devising 'a total orientation for life,' as Barr puts it, is the more valid. Rather than delving into this inconclusive argument, Barr's position on the Bible can be scrutinized more closely.

Barr evidently believes the Bible has a message, for he advocates that 'the message of the Bible' be 'more highly regarded' (Barr, 1973, 112), and he is gratified that interpretation has 'rightly caught the broad outlines of the biblical message' (Barr, 1977, 181). What *'the'* message of the Bible is does not become sufficiently clear. Nevertheless, the Bible has objectified 'the classic model of understanding God' (Barr, 1973, 128). Again, this 'understanding God' requires elaboration. The nearest Barr comes to specifying either the message of the Bible of the 'understanding God' is via his discussion of Christian theology (1973, 114). The meaning of theology is not pursued, but Christian theology 'must give some central place to Jesus of Nazareth' and 'its God must be the God who was already known in Israel' (1973, 114). As Barr admits, the main sources of information about both these topics is the Bible (e.g., 1973, 18–19; 1984, 52), but he claims above that this information is now seen as Hebrew or early Christian folklore. If it is no more than custom or folklore, it might not be very reliable information about Jesus or the God of Israel. A circular argument might be lurking here in so far as the main source of knowledge of Jesus and the God of Israel is the Bible, but this is just ancient custom and folklore.

Despite this position, Barr proposes that the Bible has a broader function than as the main source of knowledge about Jesus and the God of Israel. The Bible also looks to the future. This is because 'the tradition' of Jesus 'in its classic and received form,' that is via the Bible, 'now becomes the framework within which events to come can be perceived and understood' (Barr, 1973, 122). Again, a document just based on custom and folklore, in contradistinction to revealing God's truth (Barr, 1973, 110), would seem to be an unreliable framework via which future events might be understood. Barr does float the idea that the traditions on which the Bible is based could be regarded as 'inspired' (1973, 131) by those who want to associate the Bible with the word of God. But he takes no stance on this possibility.

The three sources of orthodox Christian interpretations on which the Christian arguments of this book rely can accept that parts of the Bible might be described as 'Hebrew or early Christian customs and folklore' (Barr, 1973, 110). The intentions of God and Jesus nevertheless are taken to reflect or shine through those expressions. If, for example, Christian redactors of the first century believed they were compiling and recounting under the guidance of the Holy Spirit, the words of Jesus as they were remembered, and that a reasonable degree of consistency ended up between the four Gospel accounts, it is immaterial to God's truth as reported that these words be described as 'early Christian customs and folklore.' Wells (1980, 338) puts it that 'contact with the Spirit is not susceptible of historical proof.' If God's and Jesus' consistent intentions are capable of being discerned through interpretation, then of course the Bible provides the framework through which events as they occur 'can be perceived and understood' (Barr, 1973, 122). One purpose of this book is to argue that such consistent intentions exist, and that three strands of orthodox Christianity hold that such beliefs, principles, and intentions can be used to help explain and prescribe for socio-economic life in the present and future, and help explain the past. They are emphatically not trying 'to drag [Biblical] texts out of their ancient setting and make them applicable to the modern world' (Barr, 1973, 141). They *are* trying to drag God's intentions out of the texts and make *them* applicable to the world. It is in this sense that the Bible 'feeds and illuminates the understanding of modern men in their modern situation' (Barr, 1973, 141).

In Barr's thinking, a risk in the three orthodox Christian interpretations is that they could be assigning too high a status to the Bible as the source of correct information about God. Barr worries if there might be 'an element in the Bible of distortion of the ultimate truth about God.' If this distortion exists, it does not attach to particular passages in the Bible, but 'to the Bible as a whole' (Barr, 1973, 130). Only the *possibility* of distortion is raised. Barr's argument at this point, his repeated assertions of the likelihood of theological error in the Bible (e.g., 1973, 14–15, 127), and therefore his skepticism that a document based on 'Hebrew or early Christian customs and folklore' (Barr, 1973, 110) can yield 'the ultimate truth about God,' would carry more weight had he given examples where this distortion might have occurred in the Bible 'as a whole.' It is not difficult to point to individual passages of the Bible seemingly inconsistent with one another. They would need to be assessed via the tools of exegesis whether this is so, and how they relate to 'the message of the Bible,' its teleology (neither of which Barr, 1984, Ch. 12, does). Barr expounds his belief about distortions in 'the ultimate truth about God' for 'the Bible as a whole' only as undemonstrated hypothesis. It would require further analysis to substantiate the hypothesis. Certainly, others of diverse theological standpoints have pursued the matter for particular issues discussed in the Bible (e.g., Wright, 1990, 2004, in relation to the status of women and slaves in the Old Testament Mosaic Law), but no more than Barr have their conclusions pointed to distortions attaching to 'the Bible as a whole' as 'the ultimate truth about God.'

If the Bible is no more than a human 'communication' recounting 'a struggle, a conflict, a controversy, in which men came into combat with one another over their God,' yielding no uniform resolution to these struggles, it is unlikely to reflect 'the unity of the one God' (Barr, 1973, 181), let alone have any unity in the text itself. Struggle, conflict, controversy and combat connote disagreement and contradiction rather than unity about anything. One cannot have it both ways. If the Bible is 'the classic model of understanding God' (Barr, 1973, 128), it should exhibit the characteristics of a model. These are constituted by internal consistency, the principles underlying the model's construction should be able to be copied, the model should be an example for imitation, and may even function as an exemplary case, it should be possible to draw deductions or implications from the model, and depending on the assumptions underlying the model, it should be possible to make non-temporal predictions from the model. The three orthodox Christian interpretations on which the arguments of this book are based, hold that the Bible indeed does serve as such a model.

OBJECTIONS CONCERNING FUNDAMENTALISM

Two of the orthodox Christian streams used in this book, evangelicalism and official Roman Catholic thought, have been identified with fundamentalism by Barr (1977, 105), although a more careful assessment of Catholic thought labels only Catholic integralism as fundamentalist (Coleman, 1992, 76). 'Fundamentalism' has received wide unfavorable press in recent years, and the term has often been used loosely as an abbreviated form of contempt by unfriendly Christian and non-Christian critics to discredit anybody with whom they disagree. But the word, 'fundamentalist,' is used also without specification, as shown below. Further, numerous definitions of fundamentalism have been employed (a review of some of these is in Harris, 1998). Marty and Appleby (1991, 819–827), for example, provide an extended definition of fundamentalism. According to them, religious fundamentalists:

- Believe in a unified, revealed truth.
- Separate themselves from outsiders.
- Identify, dramatize, and even mythologize an enemy.
- Possess missionary zeal.
- Want to institute a comprehensive system to replace existing structures.
- Believe the new system takes the form of law from sacred texts.
- Have a sense of righteousness about the law.
- Reject different interpretations of the sacred text, and insist their interpretation is the only correct one.
- Interpret particular historical events in terms of the sacred texts.
- Frequently have a totalitarian impulse.

Interestingly, no mention is made in this list of the inerrancy of the sacred texts. Nevertheless, all Christians follow some of the items in the list in some degree; for instance, they believe in a unified, revealed truth, but not that the entire truth has been revealed to humankind by God. They also have some degree of missionary zeal, and some sense of righteousness about the Bible. But all Christians, including the viewpoints considered here and we ourselves, do not follow all the features above, or any one absolutely. For example, in the secular academic journal publications on which large parts of this book are based, no attempt has been made to separate from outsiders, for the publications were subject to prior secular refereeing before being published in the journals. The arguments of this book do not identify an enemy, despite the criticism of secular social science. They do not propose a system 'to replace existing structures' in 'the form of law from sacred texts,' although the application of principles from the sacred text of the Bible is promoted. As pointed out above, different interpretations of the Bible are inevitable among Christians, even though one might hope they could be reduced by dialogue between Christians. No historical event is interpreted in terms of the Bible in this book, and, hopefully, no totalitarian impulse is reflected either. Nevertheless, the Christian approach advocated in this book may be described by even its Christian adversaries as 'fundamentalist' because this is a common way of reducing 'opponents by imposing the word as a term of opprobrium' (Marty and Appleby, 1991, 815). At the least, the book's arguments might be classed as theologically naive by those who disagree with them.

Usually, the term 'fundamentalism' is used loosely without reference to such characteristics as Marty and Appleby's list above. Two economists who have written about religious matters illustrate this contention. One is Kuran, an orthodox economist contributor to another of Marty and Appleby's books on fundamentalism. Kuran (1993a, 290) describes 'fundamentalist economics' as a 'cluster of doctrines' that 'share a professed . . . opposition to secular economic ideals and practices—an opposition based, moreover, on a common aspiration to ground economic prescriptions in normative religious sources.' Defined like this, anybody who criticizes secular economics and derives economic guidelines from a faith that rests on scriptural foundations could be labeled unfavorably as 'fundamentalist.' Thus, the books by the Christians and economists, Hay (1989), and Tiemstra et al. (1990) could be construed in this category, although we would not describe them as 'fundamentalist,' and Kuran does not mention them. In fact, Kuran uses 'fundamentalism' as a catchall, without naming any 'fundamentalist economist' or analyzing their work. Unnamed 'fundamentalist economists' are his enemies, in which he uses the term with little relation to Marty and Appleby's list above.

Iannaccone (1993) is another orthodox economist in Marty and Appleby (1993) who uses an equally loose but different meaning of fundamentalism from Kuran (whose main target of criticism continues to be Islamic economics). Iannaccone, a Christian, defines fundamentalists as 'theologically conservative Protestants' (1993, 342) but does not explain what 'theologically conservative' means, or why Catholics are let off the hook. Iannaccone initially defines fundamentalism by quoting Averill (1989) that fundamentalists believe:

- The Bible is inerrant and errorless.
- History will end utter disaster.
- Christ will return at this point.
- They must 'anathematize' and separate themselves from anybody who takes a different view.

Iannaccone decides this definition is too narrow, so subsumes 'fundamentalism' under the heading of 'evangelicalism.' 'Evangelicalism' (1993, 343) refers to Christians who believe that 'salvation comes only through personal faith in Jesus Christ as Savior,' in 'the need to proselytize,' and 'the Bible as the inerrant Word of God.' (Iannaccone does not state his own position on these criteria). Most Christians probably believe in the first criterion absolutely, and in the second partially. As to the third, it depends what is meant by 'inerrant,' which Iannaccone does not discuss. The impression he gives is that its meaning is unproblematic.

This assumption has been questioned ever since the word 'inerrant' came into popular usage. For instance, the evangelical, Erickson (1998, 248–250) points out that at least six different meanings of inerrancy can be posed. Thus, absolute 'inerrancy' means that each word in the Bible is to be interpreted literally, that the earth was made in six days, and that women have to remain silent in church. 'Inerrant' is often taken to mean that the Bible is without error, as per Iannaccone above. However, 'without error' is also capable of various meanings. It could be taken, as per Barr (1977, 51), that each statement in the Bible corresponds to 'external reality or to historical events.' This is akin to applying a correspondence theory of truth (Kirkham, 1992; Schmitt, 1995) to each sentence in the Bible. Using this correspondence notion of inerrancy still requires that each statement in the Bible be interpreted to discern its meaning in relation to 'external reality or to historical events.' One difficulty with Barr's (1977) ascription of the practice of correspondence inerrancy to fundamentalists/conservative evangelists is that he does not show any of them systematically using this notion of inerrancy. All Barr points to are particular instances where theologians have taken individual Biblical texts or books and alleged their historicity (e.g., Barr, 1977, 136–137; 141–142). Other 'conservative evangelical works' being 'quite similar' are criticized accordingly (Barr, 1977, 139). Harris' (1998) basically sympathetic review of Barr's work repeats the correspondence idea of inerrancy without considering alternative meanings of inerrancy that have been posed. She points out (1998, 63–64) that Barr has evinced little interest in alternative theories or explanations of inerrancy, but neither does she; except that Harris does admit inerrancy to be 'a loose concept' (1998, 178).

The problem that neither Barr nor Harris explores is that meanings of 'inerrancy' in the likes of Erickson's (1998) list above can contradict each other. For instance, unlike correspondence to 'external reality or to historical events,' 'without error' can be interpreted that God's purposes for humankind as reported in the Bible are the only correct purposes for humanity to follow. This position holds the Bible overall to be doctrinally without error irrespective of its historical or scientific errors, and even of doctrinal errors that might be contained in particular texts. Nonetheless, God's purposes or intentions still have to be interpreted from the text overall. This idea of inerrancy is more akin to a coherence theory of truth (Kirkham, 1992; Schmitt, 1995) that need bear no resemblance to a correspondence theory of truth. Whether each statement in the Bible corresponds to external reality or to historical events is not necessarily relevant to this undertaking. On Barr's version of 'inerrant' above, that some Biblical texts do not equate to external reality or to historical experience would not necessarily undermine the didactic message the text was purportedly promoting, or imply that God's purposes could not be derived from it. The poetry, songs and parables in the Bible, for example, were surely not intended to correspond to external reality or historical events, but were probably trying to show something about God's dealings with people. Whether Emmaus was an actual village near Jerusalem to which two of the apostles were going after the Resurrection (Lk. 24. 13–35), or whether the story is a redactional construction designed to teach certain lessons about how the risen Jesus can be recognized by people, is not crucial to those looking for God's purposes in the Biblical text or the Bible as a whole.

The latter idea above of 'inerrancy' or 'without error' is probably closer to the issue of what it means to ask if the Bible is 'true.' As the philosopher of religion, Tilghman (1994, 126–127) puts it:

> When people ask 'Is the Bible true?' they are invariably asking 'Is the Bible the true record of God's relation with mankind and does it tell me what I must do in order to live properly or to achieve salvation or something of that sort?' Historical criticism can evaluate the validity of the historical portions of scripture, but we have no comparable methods for answering the latter question, the one that is really on people's minds.

It is to the latter concerns that this book is addressed, in which it is admitted that no categorical, absolute or foolproof methods exist by which the question can be answered. All that is attempted here is a particular interpretation, one based on three streams of reputedly orthodox Judeo-Christian thought that collectively can hardly be dismissed as fundamentalist.

Nevertheless, interpretative and hermeneutical issues in relation to Judeo-Christian belief have been debated for aeons and some may never be resolved. But in keeping with those Christian critics above who want to dismiss fundamentalists or evangelicals, the debate about inerrancy (outlined in various theological texts) is not acknowledged. Instead, they opt for a simple definition of 'fundamentalist/evangelical' on the basis of an undefined conception of 'inerrancy.' An additional confusion arises in using 'inerrancy' as a criterion for defining 'fundamentalism/evangelicalism,' as Iannaccone, Barr and Harris do. For as Bray (1996, 542) points out, 'support for "inerrancy" as a defining exegetical or hermeneutical principle is not great among evangelical biblical scholars.' The confusion in Iannaccone (1993) is compounded, for unlike Kuran, Iannaccone lists many names he classifies as 'fundamentalists/evangelicals.' For none of them does he show that they follow any of his three criteria.

Since this book criticizes secular economics from a Judeo-Christian perspective, perhaps some economist Christians may describe the approach here as 'fundamentalist.' This is because they are skeptical of attempts to develop what might be called 'religious economics,' that is, investigations of the socio-economic content of religious belief, with which this book is concerned. Economist Christians of this ilk believe in the veracity of orthodox secular economics and do not adopt a critical attitude to it. To them, specifically Christian-based socio-economic investigation can carry little weight in the secular arena. If economist Christians believe this, no wonder non-Christians ignore Christian socio-economic thought. One result of this disregard is that conventional economists and social scientists eschew religious belief in their professional work, more so than natural scientists (Stark et al., 1996; Wuthnow, 1985). Another result of the neglect of Christian socio-economic thought is that secular academic economists and students of economics in Western countries get barely any exposure today to the socio-economic content of Christian belief. (Ironically, they may get more about Islamic belief). There are hardly any courses examining the socio-economic implications of Christian belief in secular universities. Secular academic economics and social science journals rarely publish papers exploring the socio-content of Christian belief, and as mentioned above, Christian books are not reviewed in these journals. Academic economics journals are more likely to consider less threatening religious-related issues like analyzes of religious behavior, church attendance or church-sect distinctions using orthodox economics frameworks.

Iannaccone (1998) offers an introduction to this latter area in a flagship journal of the American Economic Association. This area he calls the economics of religion, that is, interpreting religious behavior via an orthodox microeconomic theoretical system. Iannaccone does not analyze religious economics, but explains what is meant by it, as we noted above. He states that an extensive religious economics literature exists, but a reader would not get the impression that this occurs currently in relation to Christian belief. Iannaccone cites only two economist Christian authors in this area (Waterman and Elzinga) whose papers date from the late 1980s. Both these authors are orthodox economists, like Iannaccone, and therefore skeptical of religious economics (and non-orthodox economics). The Iannaccone-type review paper on the economics of religion gives little insight into contemporary religious economics, Christian or otherwise. Secular academic economists would be left thinking of its insignificance and irrelevance to modern life. Fortunately, this imbalance has been redressed somewhat in Oslington (2003).

Another reason why the methodology underlying the Christian interpretations promoted in this book might be described by unfriendly critics as 'fundamentalist' is that it violates the canons of Enlightenment and post-Enlightenment secular rationality embodied in Western thought over the past three hundred years. However, Biblical Christianity rationality was never equivalent to secular rationality (McGrath, 1997, 216–219). For economics, some of the differences between the Biblical understanding of rationality and its use in orthodox secular academic economics are explored elsewhere (Beed and Beed, 1999; Beed, 2004). As we shall see in later chapters, one of the persistent criticisms of orthodox economics is that it 'seems to be just an exercise in deducing all of the possible mathematical implications of a particular abstract definition of rationality' (Hands, 2001b, 339). We would amend this quotation to 'particular abstract *definitions* of rationality.' Certainly, the idea of secular rationality itself has been scrutinized thoroughly in the last few decades and found to have no consistent meaning (e.g., Hindess, 1988; Trigg, 1998; Dennis, 1998; Schwartz, 1998). None of this is to detract from the importance of using reason, as distinct from any particular definition of rationality, in the pursuit of knowledge.

JUDEO-CHRISTIAN SOURCES OF SOCIO-ECONOMIC INTENTIONS

The three orthodox Christian bases for this book take their primary source of Judeo-Christian thought about human behavior and relationships from the Old and New Testaments of the Bible. In these latter documents, reports (however derived) are taken to be expressed by God, by God's Son, Jesus Christ, by the Old Testament (OT) prophets, the New Testament (NT) apostles, and sundry other writers. The three orthodox bases have also developed or incorporated secondary sources of Christian thought, such as the teaching of the Church (as with Catholic Social Thought), and derivative theological systems (like Protestant evangelical theology). A mixture of history, myth and metaphor, the Biblical texts embrace an extensive canvass of human behavior ranging from people's relations with God in His trinitarian conception, through personal relations between people (e.g., sexual conduct), to social and economic contact. The secondary sources that have evolved throughout the history of the institutional church develop interpretations of these themes. The dominant realm covered by writers in all these fields concerns the interrelationships of God and Jesus Christ with people that are held to be inseparable from the relationships people have (and are expected to have) with each other. Both the primary sources of Christianity and its secondary interpreters seek an explanatory symbiosis of and prescriptive, paradigmatic guide in principle for human behavior, not a blueprint to carry out the precepts of Christian belief. Each person and society has to interpret the themes and grapple with applying them in their day and age.

Much of the Bible deals with the normal course of people's lives on earth, with their daily tasks, as they existed when and where the texts were written. Given this framework, it is to be expected that people would be described in activities nowadays defined as 'economic'. These include people in their work, in their productive activities seeking to meet material needs, in their buying and selling, in the prices they faced for goods, in their wealth acquisition, in their material indigence and poverty, in their material (and other) oppression, and so on. All these and related activities encompass what is today called economics, for which no uniformly agreed secular definition exists. Often, the economic details of people's lives in the Bible are described in the context of God (or His agent) laying down prescriptive norms for how economic behavior should differ from that people were practicing and experiencing. Given this mode of representation, the chief form of explanation for the nature of the given behavior was people not following the norms God had established.

This form of analysis in the Bible starts from a description of where people are; indeed, God and Jesus always seem to take each person where they are now. Nevertheless, the description is invariably within the holistic framework of where people are in their relation to God and Jesus e.g., Adam and Eve are described in the Garden of Eden, but only in the relation they have to God. They do not exist independently, autonomously from God and His requirements for them. So important is this principle that it is presented at the beginning of the whole ethical prologue to the Bible, the book of Genesis. Genesis is of crucial importance in suggesting principles for how human life and nature are intended by God to be throughout all history (aspects of which are explored in Beed and Beed, 1998). Its relevance to economic matters is in highlighting 'that physical and material delightfulness (superfluity) is needful for healthy human well-being everywhere' (Schneider, 2002, 61).

The criterion of human interrelationship with God is the overriding theoretical framework or teleology proposed in the Bible to clarify the purpose of human life, and its events. The activities of people are described and explained in terms of norms God established independently of the people themselves. The postulates do not stem from the activities of people; human behavior as it exists is not the source of these principles (unlike the approach taken by the secular social sciences). Instead, the description of people's activities is already theory-laden—that is, described in relation to the requirements God and Jesus have for them.

There is no precedent in the Bible for the idea that underlies all the contemporary social sciences, that human behavior can be described and analyzed as though it were autonomous empirical data existing independently of the normative intentions God has for human existence. The 'autonomous' view derived from a transposition of natural science concepts by eighteenth century 'weak,' non-Biblically-committed Christians or Deists such as Adam Smith, and non-Christians like David Hume, into the newly emerging human sciences. No hint exists in any of the different forms of expression in the Bible that behavioral frameworks explicitly ignoring God's purposes for humankind can provide adequate explanations for human action or correct prescriptions for it. If such an enterprise were achievable, human behavior could be explained outside God's provenance. Judeo-Christian thought would have little relevance to this explanation. The teleology reflected throughout the Bible rejects that searching for this approach would succeed. It does not accept that sinful human action is to be understood outside the framework of God's normative guidelines, or that stable second best solutions can be devised for fallen humankind.

It is a false analogy to suggest that these same limitations apply to physical science. The varied modes of expression in the Bible do not purport to explain the nature of the physical world, but they do claim to explain human behavior, which is also the aim of secular social science. The Bible proposes that human action can only be understood in relation to God's normative purposes for humankind. Human behavior is only to be comprehended in relation to God that is inseparable from relations between people themselves. Social science, including economics, rejects these assumptions. The history of the development of social science is the shedding over time of anything to do with the triune Christian God (often for the good reason that the institutional church stifled the exploration of the relation of Biblical teaching to spiritual and material life). The irony is that secular social science is on an unproductive road because it eschews the triune Christian God.

There are other helpful examples than this book of social science, economist, and social theologian Christians deriving and using Biblical principles pertaining to socio-economic issues, and relating them to contemporary life. One is Mason's (1987, 1996) use and development of Wright's (1990, 1995) principles derived from the latter's Old Testament Law interpretations. Another is Hay (1989), as is Tiemstra et al.'s (1990) joint economist-theologian attempt to devise an alternative paradigm for economic theory's way forward against its modern orthodox impasse. Other Protestant evangelical examples relating Biblical principles to modern socio-economic life are in Gushee (1999). In the Catholic tradition, Alford et al. (2005) fits comfortably with these approaches. All these enterprises possess the positive quality of assigning pre-eminence to Biblical intention, and ascertaining how modern socio-economic life compares, and should conform, to that. Other important authors, such as Douglas Vickers, Gary North and Robert Black, each with distinctive approaches different from that of this book, have related Christian belief to economics. Yet, because of the stranglehold orthodox economics has on academic organization, and its disinclination to accommodate even secular competitors, the Christian attempts are few and far between, and ignored in the secular literature. Anything colored with a Christian connotation in secular academic economics (or social science) is viewed with disdain, at most regarded as the province of theology not social science. Accordingly, the resources devoted to academic Christian socio-economic investigation are minuscule. If, throughout its history, Christianity had been pursuing the full extent of its vocation, academia would be overflowing with such attempts. This is not to overlook the long history of Christian socio-economic discussion, although this book does not rehearse that process. Today, however, Christianity finds itself in a hostile secular academic environment. Accordingly, Christian socio-economic investigation has to emanate from Christian and theological colleges, and the few Christian universities, because the secular universities are unsympathetic to such ventures.

The first proposition this book demonstrates, then, is that according to three strands of orthodox Christian interpretation, the Christian Bible and Judeo-Christian thought embody paradigms, intentions or principles meant by the triune God to be applicable to contemporary socio-economic organization, and to all past human societies. This is compatible with holding that the Biblical message was expressed originally to its ancient hearers and readers in their socio-cultural contexts (Beed, 2003b). If this depiction were a valid representation of Christian thought, it would not be difficult to show (although it is not done here) that these principles have often been ignored in the organization of human society in all history both by Christians and non-Christians. Partly because of this disregard, a non-Christian tradition took form from the eighteenth century seeking alternative non-Christian explanations and prescriptions for human behavior. Thus was born secular social science, priding itself on applying scientific methods to the study of human behavior. Yet, social science's attempts to discover socio-economic principles of comparable validity to physical scientific principles have come to little. This is the second proposition we seek to demonstrate. The great disappointment to social science over the last three hundred years is that its exercises have not produced enduring theories or explanations for human behavior, or principles that might be applied to 'improve' this behavior. This is despite the enormous quantity of data and theorizing undertaken by social science. From an orthodox Christian perspective, the failure is not surprising. Attempts to discover principles underlying the description and explanation of human disorder, or prescribing for the organization of human society outside of the triune God's framework are not sustainable. These are not fundamentalist or theologically naive arguments. However, they are an affront to secular social science because they question the practical relevance of its theoretical propositions.

Chapter Two

Christian Principles for the Organization of Employment

This chapter shows how two mainstream Christian approaches develop principles from their Christian interpretations applicable to contemporary socio-economic life. The assertion emanates from orthodox Christian traditions that the Christian system has a primary bearing on social and economic life, as well as personal life. It is not just a figment of the imagination of fundamentalists or divergent non-orthodox Christian groups. The aspect of economic life under scrutiny is the organization of employment. The aim of the chapter is to show that two different streams of orthodox Christian belief hold that the Judeo-Christian system is designed to yield principles relevant to ways in which employment should be organized in economically advanced countries. Getting work organized correctly is a pre-requisite for optimizing wealth creation and its appropriate distribution. The first example in the first section of the chapter is from Catholic Social Thought. The second example in the second section is from Protestant evangelical authors. A selection of principles is outlined from each of these sources respectively, relating to the organization of employment. It becomes apparent that a high degree of common ground occurs in the socio-economic principles each system promotes. In the third section of this chapter, one common principle from both Christian systems of belief is taken to illustrate how it might be applied to the organization of employment and work in advanced industrial societies today. The fourth and final section of the chapter canvasses selected suggestions for implementing the common Christian principle. Employment is taken to mean remunerated or paid work in the conventional sense of these terms. However, the Biblical concept of work is not exhausted by these specifications and could incorporate, for example, traditionally unpaid work of mothers caring for children.

CATHOLIC SOCIAL THOUGHT

The first example of contemporary Christian socio-economic principles is from Catholic Social Thought (CST), specifically from three recent encyclicals of Pope John Paul II (Beed and Beed, 2002a). CST is taken as the first example because the Catholic tradition has long promoted its interpretation of the socio-economic implications of Christian belief (this history is outlined in Duncan, 1991, and Charles, 1998). To successive Popes, the notion of drawing out principles intended to relate to socio-economic life is part of the necessary practice of the Christian church. The encyclicals discussed here are *Centesimus Annus* (CA) (1991), *Sollicitudo Rei Socialis* (SRS) (1987), and *Laborem Exercens* (LE) (1981). These continue the rich and long tradition of CST, and especially that loosely termed 'modern Catholic social teaching' (Kammer, 1991, 6), taken usually to have originated with Pope Leo XIII's 1891 social encyclical, *Rerum Novarum (The Condition of the Working Class)*. It is not possible to consider John Paul II's writing on work without acknowledging its dependence on earlier CST. Nevertheless, no previous Pope of the twentieth century has written as much about work and employment as John Paul II. According to one economist, John Paul II's views on work 'constitute the most modern and progressive stance expressed by the Church since its early years' (Wisman, 1998, 1663).

The argument here is that implications for policy toward employment can, and are intended to be derived from the three encyclicals. Until recently, limited attention has been given to these topics in commentaries by Catholic clergy, academics and other supportive church writers. These reactions from outside the official Church are designated here as non-Church CST response. (Official Church statements by Conferences of National Bishops and the like are not discussed here). Non-Church CST (e.g., Baum, 1982; Houck and Williams, 1983; Gaburro and Cressotti, 1998; Tondini, 1998) has explored employment-related matters but has not been strongly oriented to drawing policy conclusions (although note the exceptions of Naughton, 1992, and Alford and Naughton, 2001). In this chapter, employment-related principles are argued to be dominant in the three encyclicals, and employment policy deductions can be drawn from them.

According to John Paul II, 'there is something wrong with the organization of work and employment' (LE, 1981, 77). In common with Biblical teaching and Christian tradition, John Paul II holds 'there can be *no genuine solution of the "social question" apart from the Gospel*' (CA, 1991, 12; all emphases are original). In CST, work and employment as they are meant to be organized in Gospel terms play a crucial role in resolving social problems. In keeping with CST and much Christian writing, the approach of this chapter is to pursue the principles for employment as guidelines (SRS, 1987, 89), rather than as blueprints or technical solutions applicable to contemporary Western society. As John Paul II put it, 'the Christian faith does not presume to imprison changing socio-political realities in a rigid schema, and it recognizes that human life is realized in history in conditions that are diverse and imperfect' (CA, 1991, 65–66).

Below, selected principles are classified from the three encyclicals relating to the desirable organization of work. Although such an exercise has been undertaken for individual encyclicals (e.g., by Gruenberg, 1998 for LE), no collation has been assembled for all three. The principles are well known in Catholic Church and non-Church CST (e.g., Massaro, 1998) so the review is very brief, but each principle could be discussed more thoroughly than here. Each is presented only as revealed in the three encyclicals, no reference is made to secondary comment on them, and no evaluation is proposed of how they might derive from Biblical texts. The principles are derived from the encyclicals as they are expressed, and no critical or theological reflection is made on them here, although great potential exists for this to be done.

A first principle that can be educed from the three encyclicals is that all able persons have a duty and right to work, applying human abilities to the resources provided by God (LE, 1981, 67–68). A second principle is the priority of the subjective nature of work over its objective nature. This means that 'the proper subject of work continues to be man' whereby he realizes his humanity; 'work is "for man" and not man "for work"' (LE, 1981, 24, 29). Third is the linkage between human work and the original Act of Creation, for 'work is a way of sharing in the activity of the Creator.' Man is co-worker and co-creator with God (LE, 1981, 94, 98). Fourth, the right to private property ownership is assured (CA, 1991, 12, 43). However, this right is constrained, for private property 'is under a "social mortgage", which means that it has an intrinsically social function, based upon and justified precisely by the principle of the universal destination of goods' (SRS, 1987, 95). The right to private property is 'not an absolute value' but is constrained by other 'necessary complementary principles, such as the *universal destination of the earth's goods*' (CA, 1991, 12–13), meaning that 'the goods of this world are *originally meant for all*' (SRS, 1987, 94, 84). The universal destination of the earth's goods is related closely to a fifth principle, that both the nature of work and its products should be directed to the common good. Common good means 'the full development "of the whole individual and of all people",' a 'concern for the "spiritual and human development of all"' (SRS, 1987, 81, 24). The five principles above relating to work are listed as numbers 1 to 5 in Table 2.1 below.

The principle of solidarity (number 6 in Table 2.1) affirms that the weakest should be defended. In a work context, application of solidarity may take various forms. For instance, limits should be placed 'on the autonomy of the parties who determine working conditions, and by ensuring in every case the necessary minimum support for the unemployed worker' (CA, 1991, 24). The principle of solidarity is related closely to the principle of the Church's preferential option for the poor (SRS, 1987, 93), in which the poverty of the poor is 'not only economic but cultural and spiritual poverty as well' (CA, 1991, 17, 79). Like the constrained right to private property, the 'duty of solidarity' embodies '*a firm and persevering determination* to commit oneself to the *common good*; that is to say to the good of all and of each individual, because we are *all* really responsible *for all*' (SRS, 1987, 21, 82–83).

Closely related to the principle of solidarity is a seventh principle, cooperation in work. This means that 'human work, by its very nature, is meant to unite peoples, not divide them' (CA, 1991, 39), that 'it is a characteristic of work that it first and foremost unites people' (LE, 1981, 83). Here is an emphasis on collaboration and unity in work where '*people work with each other*, sharing in a "community of work" which embraces ever widening circles.' '*Initiative and entrepreneurial ability*', and 'prudence in undertaking reasonable risks' (CA, 1991, 45, 46) are vital ingredients to the process of work, but these are the nearest qualities to advocating competition between workers or companies. Rather, what is required is 'the cooperation of many people in working towards a common goal,' and 'disciplined work in close collaboration with others' (CA, 1991, 46).

An eighth long-standing CST principle affecting work is re-emphasized. This is '*the principle of the priority of labour over capital*', 'a postulate of the order of social morality,' and another aspect of '*the primacy of man over things*' (LE, 1981, 49, 64, 52–53). Capital cannot be allowed to dominate people. Rather, domination should proceed the other way; human needs should dominate the use of capital. In this reasoning, for example, capital use cannot be permitted to reduce people to involuntary unemployment. This precept reflects also application of the principle of the universal destination of the earth's goods. In so far as capital is privately owned, '*the right to private property is subordinated to the right to common use*, to the fact that goods are meant for everyone' (LE, 1981, 59). Private ownership rights to the means of production are subordinate to the principle of the universal destination of the earth's goods and to 'the principle of respect for work' (LE, 1981, 61).

A ninth principle might be termed the principle of moral scrutiny of work. The ways work is organized and the rights workers are meant to enjoy in its exercise are not to be divorced from the uses to which the products of work are applied. A '*continual reappraisal of man's work*' (LE, 1981, 75) is necessary in all these areas. For instance, 'the decision to invest in one place rather than another, in one productive sector rather than another, is always *a moral and cultural choice*' (CA, 1991, 53). This choice in CST is not just an economic one. What is required are investments and jobs that contribute to 'authentic human development' (SRS, 1987, 55) because 'of itself, an economic system does not possess criteria for correctly distinguishing new and higher forms of satisfying needs from artificial new needs which hinder the formation of a mature personality' (CA, 1991, 52). The deleterious effects of relying purely on narrow economic criteria can be reflected in jobs and products that inhibit the development of human personality, and of the family, itself a 'community of work and solidarity' (CA, 1991, 70). The '*phenomenon of consumerism*' (CA, 1991, 52; SRS, 1987, 57) is one such example of harmful human ecological purpose, as is damage to natural ecological systems (CA, 1991, 54).

The tenth principle is the right of and necessity for workers to form associations such as trade unions (and for employers similarly). This principle relates to the principle of solidarity. The principle exists also partly because 'the right of association is a natural right of the human being' (CA, 1991, 13). In CA, the positive historical role and importance of trade unions are emphasized, as is the contribution of Christians to their development. Trade unions are crucial in negotiating contracts between employees and employers and 'as "places" where workers can express themselves'; they 'defend workers' rights and protect their interests as persons, while fulfilling a vital cultural role' (CA, 1991, 24, 50). Trade unions are an 'indispensable *element of social life*, especially in industrialized societies,' and '*a mouthpiece for the struggle for social justice*' (LE, 1981, 82, 83). The right to strike is recognized as a legitimate trade union tool, and workers should not be 'subjected to personal penal sanctions for taking part in a strike.' At the same time, the strike weapon is to be used cautiously, for it is 'an extreme means' (LE, 1981, 85).

The concept of, and right of workers to, a just wage (number 11 in Table 2.1) has a long history in Roman Catholic thought. To John Paul II, 'a just wage is the concrete means of *verifying the justice* of the whole socioeconomic system.' Not only is '*just remuneration* for work done' 'the key problem of social ethics,' but a just wage is a '*practical means*' of meeting the principle of the universal destination of the earth's goods (LE, 1981, 78, 77, 78). Wages cannot be set 'without taking into account the bare minimum required for the support of the individual and his family' (CA, 1991, 8). This concept of wages assumes a particular familial context, and highlights the necessary reward for full-time work, for 'a workman's wages should be sufficient to enable him to support himself, his wife and his children,' with 'a certain amount of savings' (CA, 1991, 15, 23). Without a guarantee of a just wage, John Paul II approvingly quotes *Rerum Novarum* that the workman 'is made the victim of force and injustice' (CA, 1991, 15). Since employees are usually in a weaker power position than employers in relation to wage setting, the determination of the just wage 'cannot be left to the "free consent of the parties"' (CA, 1991, 14). Here, the role of the State as 'indirect employer' is instrumental in exercising 'a determining influence' on the 'direct employer' (LE, 1981, 70, 69).

Principle twelve in Table 2.1 is that where workers are subject to the scourge of unemployment, they must be ensured a right to unemployment benefits. This is 'a duty springing from the fundamental principle of the moral order in this sphere . . . the right to life and subsistence' (LE, 1981, 73). As well, workers have a right to retraining, workers' compensation, health insurance and pensions (CA, 1991, 23–24). Principle thirteen means that workers should be entitled also to limitation of their working hours, a 'right to legitimate rest,' and for 'children and women to be treated differently' from men re work duration. 'Humane' working hours and adequate free-time are important guarantees (CA, 1991, 14, 24). These requirements are justified on various grounds, but an important one is to enable workers to blend work and non-work life. Indeed, 'the whole labour process must be organized and adapted in such a way as to respect the requirements of the person and his or her forms of life, above all life in the home . . .' (LE, 1981, 80).

Number fourteen in Table 2.1 is an example of the principle of subsidiarity. In LE (1981, 63) and SRS (1987, 83), John Paul II employs this principle in relation to 'intermediate' bodies. 'Intermediate' means units of society between the small and weak individual and family, and the large and powerful

Table 2.1. Normative Principles from Three Papal Encyclicals Governing Work

1. All able persons have a duty and right to work.
2. The subjective nature of work has priority over its objective nature.
3. Work is a way of sharing in the activity of God.
4. The right to private property is guaranteed but subordinate to the principle of the universal destination of the earth's goods.
5. The common good should be pursued.
6. The weakest should be defended (the principle of solidarity).
7. Cooperation in work is emphasized.
8. Labor has priority over capital.
9. The content and products of work must be scrutinized morally.
10. Workers have a right to association e.g., in trade unions.
11. A just wage is required.
12. Rights to unemployment benefits, workers' compensation, retraining and pensions are necessary.
13. The right to rest is guaranteed.
14. Intermediate bodies are crucial to ensuring that the above principles are met (the principle of subsidiarity).

Source: Developed from LE (1981); SRS (1987); CA (1991)

state. Whenever possible, these intermediate bodies rather than the state should render assistance to the needy individual and family because they are closer to those in need and more likely to understand that need. Table 2.1 above is a summary of the fourteen normative principles discussed above governing the organization of work. The list is not absolute; each principle could be expressed differently and additional items could be added, such as workers' rights to employment security.

PROTESTANT EVANGELICAL THOUGHT

The second example of an orthodox Christian tradition developing socio-economic principles related to employment organization from its interpretations of Judeo-Christianity is from Protestant evangelical belief (Beed and Beed, 2002b; further developed in Beed, 2005c). 'Evangelical' is a prominent Protestant cross-denominational strain, whose theology is exemplified by the likes of Spykman (1992), Grudem (1994), McGrath (1997), and Erickson (1998). In this system, the Christian Bible constitutes the supreme authority for two purposes: as the source of knowledge of the triune God, and as 'a guide to Christian living' (McGrath, 1994, 51). There are further features of evangelicalism, but its reliance on the Bible for these two purposes is the relevance here for the derivation of its principles. Evangelicalism holds that the Christian Bible contains mandates in principle applicable to all aspects of contemporary personal and social life, including the economic. This view is contained in the evangelical economist Hay's (1989, 16) method, for example, of deriving 'a set of principles for economic life which are universal in their application . . . [and which] . . . are powerful in application to economic problems.'

One illustration of evangelical thought deriving principles for the economic and the social is shown here. The example uses a particular paradigmatic starting point to ascertain socio-economic principles allegedly relevant to modern society. The principles are those interpreted to underlie the organization of the state of Israel in the Old Testament, a line of thought with which all Christians do not agree. But, as with the approach adopted above for Catholic Social Thought, no evaluation is made at this point about the veracity of this methodology in question. Some appraisal is made of it in the next chapter. For the moment, it is accepted for the purposes of the argument that this starting point is valid, that it does represent a theological approach consistent with orthodox Christian belief. Its theological rationale is canvassed by the likes of Kaiser (1983), Goldingay (1995), Wright (1990, 1995, 2004), Ballard (1994), Mason (1996) and others. The theological paradigm these authors discern is held to reveal the will of God, as expressed in principles underlying the Old Testament Mosaic Law (sometimes just called the Law), consistent with the Genesis mandate, and outlined in three books of the Old Testament, but extending into the New Testament.

A typical instance underlying this approach is Bauckham (1989, 38) who held that 'Jesus, as in all his ethical teaching, presses the fundamental intention of the law to the absolute limit, as the standard at which his followers must aim.' For the evangelicals under scrutiny here, the principles, norms or standards of organization underlying the Old Testament Law are held to be relevant to contemporary society, not the detail. This section does not show the Old Testament Biblical exegesis by which the principles are derived. Instead, a selection of principles taken to be relevant to employment organization is drawn from existing Old Testament academic evangelical Biblical interpretation. In this thinking, 'it must be conceded that in the mind of God at least there is a set of principles for the social and economic life of his creatures' (Hay, 1989, 68). The problem arises that different interpretations or exegeses of the Biblical text might produce different principles. This is why the argument in this section can be suggested only as a particular evangelical Christian interpretation. Among evangelicals themselves, different interpretations exist, and therefore so does their relation to contemporary socio-economic life (a useful review of these is Gay, 1991). If this approach is accepted as legitimate, some principles that can be construed as relevant to private sector job organization are discussed below. A few evangelical economists have already produced lists of related principles. For instance, Hay (1989, 72–79) proposes eight principles derived from the Old and New Testaments relating to contemporary economic life. These are of broader socio-economic connotation than those depicted here that relate specifically to employment organization. Hay's list (and Tiemstra et al.'s, 1990, 109–110) can be regarded as background complementary principles to those enumerated here, although absolute identity does not exist between them. Thus, Hay (1989,78) specifically excludes private property rights that are interpreted here as integral to a consensus of evangelical interpretation. Comparable principles to those of Hay and Tiemstra et al. are summarized in Table 2.2, and the evangelical sources from which they derive are listed at the end of the table.

No one source author would necessarily subscribe to all the items of the table, and the different sources do not attach comparable importance to each item (thus, only some authors in the Schlossberg et al. compendium might actually subscribe to them). The table lists normative standards from the Old Testament Law that can be derived from the evangelical sources specified, and that can be assessed as relevant to the contemporary organization of work and employment. No absolute truth attaches to the way each principle is ex-

Table 2.2. Evangelical Principles Governing Employment Organization and Opportunity

1. Mutual interrelationships exist between economic, social and religious considerations.
2. Pursuing optimal development depends on the people of the society maintaining active, voluntary, individual relationships with the triune God in the community of Judeo-Christian social organization, and on following all the items below.
3. Work requires the stewardship of land, animals, people and property.
4. God is the ultimate owner of property that is the source of human work and capital.
5. Property rights are constrained by specific responsibilities to other people, animals and the environment.
6. Property is to be protected in and by family units to preserve them.
7. The family unit retains ownership and control of the financial capital that provides its remunerated work.
8. Property and financial capital is to be distributed equitably among family units.
9. Locally-based social mechanisms are required to oversee and safeguard administration of the above principles.
10. Subject to all the above, remunerated work capable of supporting family units should become available to all who seek it.

Sources: Kaiser, 1983; Griffiths, 1984; Mason, 1987, 1996; Hay, 1989, Mason and Schaefer, 1990; Tiemstra et al., 1990; Schlossberg et al., 1994; Wright, 1990, 1995; Sider, 1997; Blomberg, 1999.

pressed. It is possible to describe each one differently, and additional principles could be formulated. How each principle relates to particular sources for the table, and to specific Old Testament Law texts are discussed below.

The first three principles of Table 2.2 provide the background context for employment opportunity and organization. They are by way of general statements applicable in every circumstance, not just the issue under consideration here. In the Old Testament Law texts (and throughout the Bible), these evangelical sources hold that no divide is drawn between economic, social or religious considerations, specified as item 1 in Table 2.2. This is because an holistic conception pervades its view of human behavior. In evangelical theological interpretation (e.g., Tiemstra et al., 1990; Wright, 1995; Sider, 1997; Blomberg, 1999), economic practice is viewed as affecting social and religious practice, and vice versa. This can be put another way to say that the whole condition of each person is uppermost in Biblical thought. The situation of people in their economic roles, as in work, cannot be separated from maintaining their welfare in other sectors of their life, as in the family (illustrated in the Old Testament Law texts of Ex. 20:1–17; Dt. 4:1–8; 25–31; 5:6–21; 7:1–26). Item 2 in Table 2.2 also relates to the holistic nature of God's socio-economic strategy (exemplified in Lev. 26:3–45; Dt. 29:1–29), but differs from item 1 in specifying the necessity for people to maintain active relationships with the triune God and the community of like-minded people. An instance of employment-related implication of items 1 and 2 is that job-generating investments involve not just technical financial concerns but ethical and moral ones as well. These latter concerns refer to the content of the investment itself, and to the ways jobs are organized. Thus, investments contributing to the suffering of human beings and animals, or to the destruction of the physical environment would be censured. The recent growth of the ethical investment field is a reflection of these matters (Sparkes, 1995). From this perspective, all investments are to be weighed up in terms of their effects on the battery of interrelated economic, social and personal principles that constitute God's normative purposes for humankind. Although humankind might not acknowledge the principles, God seeks to persuade all humankind of their veracity.

Item 3, that work requires the stewardship of land, animals, people and property, is closely related to the above. Work was intimately attached to the concept of nurture and care for creation in Old Testament Law thought. Stewardship is human responsibility in relation to God's creation (the natural environment and people) for the exercise of abilities God entrusts to people (Hay, 1989, 71; Schlossberg et al., 1994, 13–14). This orientation is reflected in Old Testament Law texts such as Lev. 19:9–17; 23–25; 33–37; 22: 26–28; 25:1–7; and Dt. 20:19–20. The stewardship norm mirrors a much older Genesis-based concept than contained in the Mosaic Law. Humans are to care in their work, as in all else, for the perfect creation God had made; to be co-workers, carers, and developers with God of this ideal environment. The abilities or attributes God makes available to people for this task are more commonly called gifts or talents in the Bible. People are responsible to God both individually and socially for the performance of stewardship. Work is one way in which people exercise stewardship and use these talents. How work is organized can strongly affect the degree to which people are able to exercise stewardship.

Item 4 of Table 2.2 maintains that property, of which God is the ultimate owner, is the source of financial capital and employment. Human capital is another important component of capital, but is not discussed here, given the importance of financial capital. Financial capital and social capital are essential to the development of human capital. Without these two counterparts, human capital is fettered. Property, in the evangelical interpretation under focus here, is taken to mean financial capital. Property is 'that which one owns, one's wealth or goods' (Soane, 1993, 507), and is a necessary prerequisite for work. This definition does not require the prefix 'private' before the term 'property,' and is compatible with Catholic Social Thought use of the term (e.g., in O'Neill, 1994, 785, who does use the term 'private property'). (Private) property also has a relational quality, referring to the relationship between persons and tangible objects. Private property in the Law consisted mainly of domestic family housing, land, animals and implements. This property with its labor input was the source of (financial) capital through the economic activity of farming. Private property is interpreted to be a gift in stewardship from God who retains its absolute ownership (Wright, 1990, 116). The inviolability of private property (subject to particular constraints raised in item 5) is accepted widely by many strains of evangelical interpretation in their exegesis of the Old Testament Law texts (such as Lev. 25:8–10; 13–16; 23–28; and also Num. 26:52–56; 33:54). It is upheld from the radical position of Sider (1977, 1997), through the middle ground of Tiemstra et al. (1990), to the conservative of Griffiths (1984)—positions as interpreted by Gay (1991).

In item 5, property rights are constrained by specific responsibilities to other people, animals and the environment. The rights have sanctity or inviolability only if they are used consistently with all of God's principles. For instance, property rights used for personal enrichment not shared with others, or for activities undermining other of the Table 2.2 principles have no place in God's program. Leviticus 19:18 summarizes the stewardship responsibilities to people as 'you shall love your neighbor as yourself: I am the Lord.' The love in question involved practical measures affecting one's personal property rights and with the added potential to generate employment for other people. Examples were that harvest gleanings must be left 'for the poor' to gather (Lev. 19: 10), interest-free loans should be extended to the poor (Ex. 22:25–27; Lev. 25:35–38; Dt.15: 1–11, 23; 19–23), and the outstanding balances of loans were to be cancelled every seventh year (Dt. 15:1–4). A cornucopia of regulations governed how the ancient Israelites could use their personal property in relation to other people. Rules applied also to animals (e.g., Dt. 25:4, 'you shall not muzzle an ox when it treads out the grain'), and to the natural environment (e.g., Dt. 20.19, in besieging a city not to destroy its fruit trees). Again, these responsibilities carry implications for how contemporary employment should be organized. For example, property rights used to restrict the time employees have for family life or rest, or to minimize the control employees have over the content of their work would be highly questionable.

As the above Old Testament Law texts indicate, protection of private property was to be exercised in the context of preserving the family unit (Wright, 1990, 44–70). The family unit in the Old Testament Law context referred to the extended family, but it might be reasonable to extend the principle to contemporary family forms—extended, nuclear and single persons. The significance of the Law, according to Rogerson (1996, 41), was that it provided principles to counteract external forces that might undermine the family. Maintaining the family unit is an important task God sets for people, and a precondition for facilitating work—the application of human labor to resources God has provided. Since maintaining the family is crucial, it cannot be separated from the importance of maintaining the family basis of property

(Mason, 1996). As becomes clearer below, this criterion is also important to the organization of employment. The emphasis on the family unit as the basic social element has implications for contemporary social, as distinct from, economic policy, but, as noted above, an holistic conception pervades Biblical thought. These ideas are summarized as item 6 in Table 2.2.

In the evangelical Old Testament Law interpretation, private property and financial capital were to be owned and controlled by those who worked with it (Kaiser, 1983, 153–157, 210–221; Wright, 1995, 190–192, 197–208; Blomberg, 1999, 40–46). The extended family unit worked with and controlled its own financial capital (as in Dt. 15:1–18; 23:19–20; 24:10–13; Ex. 22:25–27; Lev. 25:8–16; 25–28; 47–54). A separation between ownership and control of financial capital was foreign to the practice of work. This consideration did not apply to aliens and slaves in the Israelite society who had no share in the initial land distribution, and who were required to be supported in work by Israelite families. Evangelical Christians believe that Jesus the Messiah redeemed this situation by extending His reinterpretation of the principles of the Mosaic Law to all people. The Christian-led anti-slavery movement of the nineteenth century, for instance, relied on Jesus extending God's redemption to all people equally. However, in the context of an Israelite society based on the Law, wage labor was a fall back position for Israelite family members who had lost their land, but was not intended to be a permanent state. This individualistic (family) control of the social structures of work had older precedents in the Old Testament than the Mosaic Law. It did not exist just because of the extended-family-based nature of self-sufficient peasant farming in the early state of Israel. God had enshrined personal independence and responsibility, self-management and freedom for humans in all aspects of life (not just work) from the first book of the Bible, Genesis. Each person was designed to have a personal relationship with God, but human free will was able to voluntarily disobey God as well as obey Him. Continuing those underlying principles of human existence, the personal autonomy each Israelite possessed in relation to God was the precondition on which God's socio-economic program was based. In the work context, the Israelites in extended family units were to be their own masters of the factors of production. These views are summarized as item 7 of Table 2.2, and they have clear implications for contemporary employment organization.

In the Old Testament Law, this postulate that those engaging in remunerated work should possess ownership and control rights over the private financial capital with which they worked was accorded to the family unit. Kaiser (1983, 152–158, 181–190, 204–208), Wright (1990, 183–221) and others have argued that decision making in relation to remunerated work within the extended family was intended to be shared between husband and wife. In their view, no Biblical basis exists for misconstruing the planned organization of remunerated work within the Israelite family as reflecting patriarchal dominance (whatever else might have been patriarchal elements in the Law). A reasonable contemporary extension of this implication is that both family heads in intact nuclear families have rights to work ownership and control of financial capital, as do single family heads. This does not mean that remunerated work outside the home is necessarily desirable for both family heads of intact nuclear families. All it means is that where family heads have ownership and control rights of the financial capital with which they work, decision making in relation to that capital is intended to be shared between both heads of intact nuclear families. It does not mean that both heads are meant to engage in paid work with this capital.

Not only was the sanctity or inviolability of ownership and control of private property and financial capital protected, so was the sanctity of its distribution (item 8 of Table 2.2). When the tribes of Israel arrived in the promised land, allotments of land were distributed to each tribe and extended family according to its size, and the location of the plots was determined by lot (Num. 26:52–56; 33:54. Jos. Chaps. 13–21). Thereafter, numerous regulations aimed to ensure that this proportional distribution of land, and therefore, capital, was maintained (Mason, 1987, 1996). For example, temporary sale of land between families was abrogated, without additional compensation, every forty-nine years (the Jubilee) to reinstate the original distributional pattern (Lev. 25:8–17).' The major purpose of these laws,' according to Griffiths (1984, 57), 'was to put a sharp brake on the ownership of land being concentrated in a small number of families.' Many disincentives applied therefore against an increasing concentration of ownership of private property and financial capital. So important was the function of private property and financial capital, that each family was to be maintained with a proportional and equitable share in it. As Kaiser (1983, 95) put it, 'the unnatural accumulation of wealth was kept in fairly balanced check' because the land 'was the base line for the whole economy and this was shared equally.'

Items 6 and 8 of Table 2.2 imply the protection and equitable distribution of private property and financial capital as a prerequisite for optimal socio-economic development. This conforms with recent exploration in economics where highly concentrated distributions of wealth are postulated to be inimical to the productive abilities of individuals (e.g., Solimano, 1998b; Hoff, 1998; Blanchflower and Oswald, 1998). However, the Mosaic Law does not suggest that the constraint of wide social distribution of productive financial capital and economic power would apply at the cost of economic growth. Neither is there any implication that efficiency or wealth creation takes precedence over social or spatial equity. A mutual interrelation exists between the achievement of both conditions. Through its provisions to encourage the able-bodied to possess remunerated work, the Law was intended to facilitate a higher rate of economic growth than if unemployment occurred (Mason, 1992, 17).

The dispersed private property distributional pre-conditions for optimal socio-economic development have been re-echoed repeatedly throughout history. They are emphasized by evangelical interpretation of the Old and New Testaments, by other Protestant streams, by Catholic Social Thought (e.g., Simons, 1995), Jewish social thought (Novak, 1992), and Islamic economics (e.g., Chapra, 1992). An example is the 1990 ecumenical Oxford Declaration on Christian Faith and Economics that pointed to links between the optimal development of democracy and dispersion of ownership of the means of production (Schlossberg et al., 1994, 27). An older example is British distributism in the late nineteenth and early twentieth century, associated with Catholic Social Thought and writers like Belloc and the Chestertons. This asserted 'the core distributist truth that only work and property—as opposed, for example, to consumption and saving- were so central in the lives of ordinary people as to provide the foundations on which an enduring distributist social order could be built' (Mathews, 1999, 10). Similar advocacy of wide-based financial capital ownership for maintaining entrepreneurial vibrancy persists also in contemporary more populist secular literature (e.g., Gates, 1998, 2000).

Item 9 of Table 2.2 points out that political mechanisms were prescribed in the Old Testament Law for ensuring the previous principles were practiced (as in the texts of Ex. 21:22; 22:9–10; Lev. 24:10–23; Dt. 15:22–27; 16:18–20; 17:9; 19:17). These were local elders and judges who adjudicated on civil matters, and local priests (Levites) who decided on religious matters; 'what we have in Israel therefore is a centralized (yea universal) ethical/legal canon, but the absence of a centralized state or temple to enforce and interpret it' (Mason, 1992, 13). A localized or decentralized state existed in the planned Israelite society (Mason and Schaefer, 1990, 53)—an instrument for interpreting and applying the Law, including maintaining social control over financial capital, and for organizing such social infrastructure as necessary. This principle infers, for instance, that local community agencies are jointly responsible with private initiative for maintaining and organizing employment, subject to all the previous principles. Since this chapter focuses on employment organization within the firm, this item is not discussed further.

Item 10 of Table 2.2 implies that the combined effect of all the above principles of the Law should be to push toward widespread employment opportunity, functioning within specific forms of employment organization. There is a strong implication that work in a context of economic independence would be available for everyone if all the requirements of the law were followed (which they were not). As Hay (1989, 34) puts it, 'if the allocation of land by families is protected there should be no lack of work opportunities for the individual.' Maintaining each extended family with its own means of production was paramount, in which direct rather than indirect laws were prescribed to achieve this outcome. For the able-bodied disadvantaged, for instance, it was not a case of providing indirect welfare support or subsidy disconnected from a remunerated work role. Rather, a paid job guarantee was provided. Thus, if an Israelite family could not support itself in extreme circumstance, the destitute family head became a hired servant (Lev. 25:39–40)—a work context was provided for support. If the impoverished Israelite sold his land, as noted above, it could remain in other hands only for a maximum period of forty-nine years, at which time it reverted free of charge to the original trustee-owner (Lev. 25:8–17). Even before this time, the land could be compulsorily repurchased by kin of the impoverished. These are mechanisms pushing directly toward maintaining and restoring remunerated work opportunities, and of re-establishing self-managed work for the family (Wright, 1995; Mason, 1996). These work opportunities were to be of such a nature that the family would be able to maintain itself sufficiently to participate in the collective life of the community. Remunerated work was seen as integral to this process. There has been little simultaneous occurrence of the first nine principles of Table 2.2 throughout history. If the principles had occurred concurrently, a starkly different content of socio-economic organization would long have been evident. For example, 'it would have been impossible for "labour" to be in conflict with "capital"' unlike the situation Marx addressed, 'where capital was owned by a few, but the majority were without access to that capital' (Griffiths, 1984, 57).

If the intentions of the paragraph above are taken to apply to contemporary industrialized society, they imply the ready availability of equivalent full-time jobs. This idea contradicts current trends where remunerated work sufficient to maintain the socio-economic stability of families is not available to all who seek it. The idea contradicts also post-industrial forecasters such as Reich (1991) and Rifkin (1995) who acquiesce to the disappearance of paid work for segments of the population, in the extreme envisaging an 'end of work' scenario (explicitly rejected by Papal social thought). However, equivalent full-time jobs are socially defined, and could mean shorter working hours than occurs currently. Some secular researchers also contend against the post-industrial forecasts, with a similar rationale to the Christian expressions above. For instance, Pixley (1993, 302) maintains that the 'only progressive solution to contemporary joblessness lies in genuine employment opportunities for all who want them.' The issue of appropriate means of job generation is not pursued further here. If a concerted attempt was made to apply an interrelated battery of Table 2.1 and 2.2-type principles, there is every likelihood of greater availability of equivalent full-time jobs even in post-industrial societies. A helpful Christian discussion of aspects of such issues is Massaro (1998, 227–245).

APPLYING THE PRINCIPLES TO EMPLOYMENT ORGANIZATION

Each of the principles in Tables 2.1 and 2.2 above is capable of being related to the contemporary organization of employment. This section discusses just one employment-related implication of three principles similar in both tables. One Catholic principle selected is number 4 in Table 2.1, the right to private property ownership. This section does not review all applications of the private property principle in work or elsewhere. Diverse employment-related implications of the principle exist (a selection of these is reviewed by Alford and Naughton, 2001). O'Boyle (1998), for instance, discusses supra-firm alliances and inter-firm partnerships in the US, examples of 'intermediate bodies with economic, social and cultural purposes' advocated by John Paul II in LE (1981, 63), via the principle of subsidiarity (item 14 in Table 2.1). These would be crucial to overseeing and coordinating work in an economy conforming to CST-type principles. The employment-related implication of principle 4 in Table 2.1 explored in this section concerns the relation of private property rights to company organization affecting the division between ownership and control. The evangelical principles closest to this particular implication of the Catholic principle are numbers 6 and 7 in Table 2.2. These are that property is to be protected in and by family units to preserve them, and that family units retains ownership and control of the financial capital providing their remunerated work. Compared with CST, little evangelical discussion has occurred about how such principles might be translated into the contemporary organization of work (but see Storkey, 1986, 111–113, 185–187; Hay, 1989, 167–168, 173–174, 213–215, and Tiemstra et al., 1990, 196–201), so that the discussion below is slanted to CST. This imbalance is redressed in the next chapter where evangelical interpretation receives more attention.

The three Catholic encyclicals reviewed above make it clear that if the principles of Table 2.1 are disregarded, distortions from the true nature of work intended by God are bound to occur. One example of distortion is 'that many people, perhaps the majority today, do not have the means which would enable them to take their place in an effective and humanly dignified way within a productive system in which work is truly central' (CA, 1991, 47). The 'means' here to which John Paul II refers is the 'basic knowledge' or human capital necessary to enable them to become productive workers. The context of which John Paul II speaks here is a Third World one, in which it might be argued that lack of private property or physical capital is a greater impediment to employment than lack of knowledge. A second example of distortion in relation to work is alienation (CA, 1991, 58–59), and unemployment might be regarded as third.

Where the private property principle is subverted in the employment organizational context, distortions also occur. Given the social nature of work, each worker should be 'fully entitled to consider himself a part-owner of the great workbench at which he is working with every one else. A way towards that goal could be found by associating labour with the ownership of capital, as far as possible . . .' (LE, 1981, 63). This latter sentence is taken here to mean that John Paul II's preference is for labor to own capital in the company or firm in which the labor works. It seems less likely that an implication of the first sentence in John Paul II's statement above is that each worker in a company should consider himself part-owner of the means of production ('the great workbench') of that company with absentee capital providers, such as stockholders. This is because the part-owner goal is to be found by associating labor with the ownership of capital, as far as possible. That is, within the company, each worker is to be part-owner with everyone else with whom he is working, not with absentee part-owners. Given that the 'part-owner' sentence immediately precedes John Paul II's preference for 'associating labor with the ownership of capital, as far as possible,' the 'part-owner' expression is more than just metaphorical relating to the subjective nature of work. It means literally what it says: Each worker should be joint owner of his work station.

Another statement by John Paul II encouraging this interpretation of workers owning in part or whole the means of production of the companies in which they are employed occurs in the same section of LE (1981, 61–62). This is his advocacy of '*proposals* for *joint ownership of the means of work*, sharing by the workers in the management and/or profits of businesses, so-called shareholding by labour, etc.' These express 'recognition of the proper position of labour and the worker in the production process' and they demand 'various adaptations in the sphere of the right to ownership of the means of production.' John Paul II does not say they demand adaptations merely in the sphere of control or management, but in ownership. That joint ownership is cited first and emphasized in this quotation suggests it is the most important approach. Admittedly, John Paul II does not specify joint ownership with whom—it could be among workers themselves, or it could be between workers and absentee stockholders. However, later in the same section of LE, John Paul II qualifies this uncertainty by the quotation in the paragraph above—labor is to be associated 'with the ownership of capital, as far as possible.' The claim here is not that total or partial worker ownership/control within companies is the only desirable approach, but it does seem to be an important option favored by John Paul II in LE. Obviously, other forms of shared participation within the company in the balance between ownership and control are embodied in John Paul II's advocacy of 'sharing by the workers in the management and/or profits of businesses, so-called shareholding by labour, etc.'

Support can be found from other quotations in the three encyclicals that labor is intended to own in part or whole its capital in its work or employment context. No one of them on its own substantiates the interpretation adopted here, but their joint effect trends in this direction. Some of these are that work should depend on '"something"' the worker can 'call "his own",' and on 'the possibility of earning a living through his own initiative' (CA, 1991, 21). In 'a certain sense,' the aim is to enable workers to '"work for themselves"' (CA, 1991, 61). These quotations do reflect the subjective nature of work, but they also have an objective meaning. Without owning the capital with which he works, a worker cannot achieve these ends. A more metaphorical expression of these aims is the personalist argument that a worker needs to express his deep desire to be working '*for himself*,' and every effort has to be made to preserve this awareness (LE, 1981, 64, 65). Ideas of personal freedom, autonomy, initiative, self-control, self-management and low alienation by those doing work are uppermost in this thinking. Each of these qualities relates to the degree to which workers have ownership of the private property with which they work, as well as to the control they have over their work.

One major barrier to achieving the above qualities within the company format, and the similar evangelical principles numbers 6 and 7 of Table 2.2, is that private property or capital ownership by its workers is not typically met in the contemporary Western (or any other) company. Most people working do not own the private property with which they work, self-employment aside. They are working with someone else's property, and have limited say in its utilization. Usually, workers are directed by representatives of the (absentee) property owners. In this situation, workers may even have restricted control over other principles in Tables 2.1 and 2.2, such as wages and hours. Indirectly, workers may have some influence on these through their trade unions (steadily experiencing diminishing membership in Western countries) and the State. (Of course, there is no guarantee that either employees or employers need take cognizance of any of the Tables 2.1 and 2.2 principles. For instance, the products of work need not have a universal destination or be oriented to the common good, but can be directed to sectional interests.)

Thus, limitation of private property ownership in work in the Catholic and evangelical thinking can be regarded as another example of distortion from the correct nature of work. This distortion can manifest itself in 'the inefficiency of the economic system' due to 'the violation of the human rights to private initiative, to ownership of property and to freedom in the economic sector' (CA 1991, 34). These rights have been violated systemically and historically in all countries, and still are. In the remunerated work context of Western capitalism, most employees have never owned the property with which they work. Accordingly, the 'rights to private initiative' of the majority of the working population have been hampered in the employment context, and their 'freedom in the economic sector' curtailed. The efficiency of the economic system has suffered because of this distortion. Many studies have shown, for example, that in firms where workers do not own and control the property with which they work, productivity is lower than in firms where they do (e.g., Ben-Ner et al., 1996).

The typical private property imbalance in the work context exhibits itself more acutely in less developed economies. The three encyclicals often emphasize comparisons between these countries and those more developed. For instance, SRS (1987, 20) notes for the world context the 'serious problem of *unequal distribution* of the means of subsistence originally meant for everybody, and thus also an unequal distribution of the benefits deriving from them.' A low occurrence of widespread private ownership of the means of subsistence (here understood as the means of production) results in work producing insufficient for those who perform it. In lesser degree, this scenario characterizes developed countries also, although it is not an emphasis on which the three encyclicals focus in relation to work. Rather, John Paul II highlights the unequal distribution of private property as the cause of poverty, a problem of significant proportion in developed countries. Poverty is defined 'more precisely' as 'hindrances to private ownership' (CA, 1991, 13) that even in the developed world appears to be increasing (SRS 1987, 94). There are 'bands of great or extreme poverty in countries of medium and high income' (SRS 1987, 29), and 'social inequalities down to the level of poverty exist in rich countries' (CA 1991, 27). If poverty is regarded in this encyclical thinking as due to the lack of private ownership, the way to overcome it is to extend private ownership. If this occurred, 'the goods of this world . . . *originally meant for all*' (SRS, 1987, 94, 84), consumer and capital goods alike, would become more widely available. How this might apply to capital goods or assets within a company context is examined below.

John Paul II's quotation above, '*joint ownership of the means of work*, sharing by the workers in the management and/or profits of businesses, so-called shareholding by labour, etc.' (LE 1981, 61) is the only means of articulating the private property principle within companies specified in the three encyclicals. Baum (1982, 42) put it for LE that 'the Pope praises all experiments in joint ownership, workers co-shareholding, workers' participation in decision-making, representation of workers on policy boards, and so forth . . .' The three encyclicals do not provide operational examples of these approaches (noted also by Wisman, 1998, 1666). Therefore, first below is considered work reform discussed in recent non-Church CST. (Other Church CST documents are not considered in keeping with the focus of this chapter on Papal CST).

This discussion highlights the first of two reasons in this section for focusing on the private property ownership principle in the company, providing the rationale for the contemporary importance of the principle in CST and evangelical thought. The first reason is that, in general, non-Church CST (or evangelical thought) has not explored the relevance of the private property principle in the company. The existing pattern of private property ownership is assumed, and moulded around this are reform ideas for greater worker participation. The pertinence of the underlying private property principle is ignored. For example, Fitzgerald (1983) reviewed work reform in half a dozen countries in the light of principles in LE (1981). He approved the progress of collective bargaining between unions and employers to achieve 'higher wages, reduced hours and improved working conditions.' Yet, he conceded also that 'management control has not been shifted to workers to any great extent' (Fitzgerald 1983, 261), and was skeptical that worker minority representation on boards of directors or co-determination had contributed to greater say by labor in company decision making. Fitzgerald (1983, 276) concluded that the goal 'whereby capital should be at the service of labor' was far from becoming a reality. All the reforms examined by Fitzgerald contributed little to changing the structure of ownership of private work property in companies. More recent non-Church CST discussing the private property principle does not pursue its implications for the relation between ownership and control in a work context (e.g., Keating and Keating, 1998).

Since Fitzgerald (1983), the formal organization of work has changed markedly. For instance, Gianaris (1996, 127) noted that 'at present, there is a trend toward employee ownership and participation in enterprise decision making, mainly in America and Europe.' Descriptions of these phenomena abound. One example is Durand et al. (1999) analyzing teamwork in the automobile industry in Japan, America and Europe. As such descriptions and evaluations show (e.g., Heller et al., 1998; Levine, 1995), some of the participatory changes conform with aspects of CST-type and evangelical principles, and explicitly with John Paul II's advocacy (e.g., LE, 1981, 61). For instance, greater participation by workers in decision making accords with the principle of cooperation in work, item 7 in Table 2.1 above. Participation can also potentially encourage growth of the development and freedom of workers, and of their dignity—the subjective nature of work highlighted by item 2 in Table 2.1. Indeed, every type of work is to be judged 'above all by *the measure of the dignity* of the subject of work, that is to say the person, *the individual who carries it out*' (LE, 1981, 29). Greater worker participation has strong roots in CST and in secular democratic theory (Chmielewski, 1997).

One of the forms of company organization with potential for worker participation is the ESOP (Employee Stock Ownership Plan). In the United States, ESOPs have grown rapidly (NCEO, 2001). Nevertheless, in most ESOP companies, employees own a small minority of shares. 'About 1, 500 [US] companies,' for example, 'have an average of 15 percent employee ownership' (compared with near 7,000 firms on the three major stock exchanges) (Gianaris, 1996, 109). Although 90 percent of US ESOPs are unlisted, 62 percent of listed ESOP companies have less than 10 percent employee ownership (Gates, 1998, 61). Currently, the median ownership rate of the 11, 500 US ESOPs is 10–15 percent (NCEO, 2001). Therefore, most ESOP boards have few worker-part owner-directors; less than 1 percent of the top 1000 ESOPs have nonmanagerial workers on their boards (Blasi and Kruse, 1991, 216). Indeed, Blasi and Kruse's comprehensive survey of US ESOPs found that less than 5 percent of the top 1000 ESOPs, 'are actively finding ways to encourage employee participation in the company and to train and empower employees to be involved in joint problem-solving teams' (1991, 216). According to Levine (1995, 1, 51, 8), 'substantive employee involvement remains the exception in the US work force,' most US ESOPs 'have little or no employee participation' and 'corporate tyranny' still reigns. Appelbaum and Batt (1994, 69) express it that 'significant changes are affecting only a relatively small group of employees in any one firm.'

Perhaps the situation is improving. Logue and Yates' (1999, 228) survey of Ohio ESOPs found that 'about one-quarter combine ownership with significant employee participation.' Nevertheless, a fair summary to date is that current ESOPs involve minority worker ownership (5–20 percent) and highly restricted workers' participatory decision making. Partly, the latter occurs in the US because of great variation in ESOP-types and because 'while federal ESOP legislation carefully specifies employees' financial rights, it makes only minimal provision for rights to participate' (Logue and Yates, 1999, 227). The point made by Fitzgerald (1983) remains: Worker-directors in ESOPs have little influence on company decision-making (even though ESOPs typically show higher productivity than conventional joint stock companies; see Ben-Ner et al., 1996).

ESOPs are formed for a variety of reasons, only in a small minority of which is the desire for greater worker participation instrumental (Logue and Yates, 1999). The US National Center for Employee Ownership (NCEO) (2001) points out that 'the number of participants [in US ESOPs] is shrinking because the average size of companies with ESOPs has been shrinking . . . This is happening largely because many large public companies who set up ESOPs years ago for purely financial and accounting reasons are terminating those plans as time goes on.' Aside from some well-publicized US ESOP exceptions with majority worker ownership, like Weirton Steel (73 percent), there is no guarantee that ESOPs translate democratic decision making onto the workplace floor more strongly than non-ESOPs. Where trade unions are involved in the formation of ESOPs in the US and UK, however, greater worker participation is produced (Logue and Yates, 1999; McHugh et al., 1999). This phenomenon characterizes Spanish ESOPs (known as SALs), 'a democracy of small capitalists,' strongly encouraged by trade unions (Holstrom, 1993, 148). The potential for ESOPs to achieve greater worker participation is clear (Gates, 2000). As Rosen (NCEO, 2001) explains, 'more and more, companies are asking employees to play a larger role in making decisions about their work. Work teams, total quality programs, job enhancement, re-engineering, and other developments increasingly ask employees to take on the role of business people. If companies want employees to think and act like owners, the best way to do it is to make them owners.' Other variants of employee ownership/control also have potential for expansion. Some of these exist already in joint stock companies, such as commonwealth or foundation-owned firms, like the UK Scott Bader chemical company and the John Lewis retailing partnership, both originally started by Christians. John Lewis, for instance, is a telling case of worker participation and high productivity (Sparkes, 1995, 239), consistent with an economy-wide positive relationship between these two variables (e.g., Ben-Ner et al., 1996).

Other than ESOPs (on which see Naughton, 1992, 103–106), some of the more recent reforms in work have been reviewed in non-Church CST. Chmielewski (1997), for instance, discussed worker participation in US and European companies. Again, the relevance of the private ownership principle to the intra-company context is ignored. It is also significant that Chmielewski did not examine how participation actually functions (except for Germany) or assess how widespread it is. Participation is a matter of degree, and can mean different things in different places, so that any consultation can be construed as participation irrespective of decision outcomes. The more participation that occurs in decision making within the company, the more workers enhance their dignity, freedom and cooperation (the subjective nature of work). With a complete realization of the private ownership principle in work—near 100 percent ESOPs, producers' cooperatives and self-employment—workers own their jobs and, theoretically, have complete control over their work within the company. In lesser situations, participation can possess ill-defined meaning. Worker participation and democracy are strengthened by worker ownership.

Workers potentially can maximize participation, solidarity and community, and minimize 'subjugation' (Chmielewski 1997, 494) if they totally own the property with which they work. Total private job ownership enables workers to potentially realize other CST principles of Table 2.1. Examples include ensuring workers retain control of their employment and of extending employment to others, maintaining the priority of labor over capital, potentially cooperating voluntarily with fellow workers, paying just wages, and limiting work hours. Worker ownership is the only necessary (but not sufficient) condition in Table 2.1 to ensure that all the principles can be rendered operational. This is why private ownership of work within the company context is a principle of major importance in Table 2.1.

The second reason for focusing on private property ownership in work in this section is as follows. It can be accepted that valuable growth in employee ownership and participation in enterprise decision making has occurred in Western countries. Yet, it seems to be doing little to extend private property ownership, in and out of work, at least in the United States. If anything, changes in private property ownership in the United States appear to be going in the opposite direction from those advocated in the three encyclicals above and in the Table 2.2 principles of the evangelicals. For instance, despite the rapid growth of ESOPs in the United States, they have contributed little to changing inequalities in the distribution of private property ownership. In part, this is because 'total employee-held assets in public and closely held corporations now constitute only 3 percent of the value of all corporate stock' (Blasi and Kruse 1991, 253). The worker-participatory ESOP sector is even more minuscule representing 'about 1 percent of the American economy' (Logue and Yates, 1999, 243). In spite of all the moves encouraging labor into business as part owners, and into decision making with management and owners, ownership of private property both in and out of a work context is becoming more concentrated among fewer people in the United States. Wolff (1998, 131) showed that 'by the 1980s, the United States had become the most unequal society in terms of wealth among the advanced industrial nations,' leaving behind a comparability in the 70s. By 1995, the richest 1 percent of US families (defined precisely by Wolff) owned 47 percent of total financial wealth (excluding net equity in owner-occupied housing), the top 20 percent, 93 percent. These figures rose since 1983 from 43 percent and 91 percent respectively. Investments with work- and employment-related effects for other people than the investors were highly important for the rich. For the top 1 percent in 1995, business-related equity made up 67 percent of gross assets (including principal residence), but only 7 percent for the bottom 80 percent. So important were these investments, that the top 10 percent owned around 90 percent of direct 'stock, shares, bonds, trusts, and business equity'

(Wolff, 1998, 139). Even though 41 percent of US households owned stocks and shares through mutual funds, pension accounts etc., the top 10 percent still owned 82 percent of these investments. The 'democratization' of stock ownership and growth of ESOPs seem to have made little inroad. Democratization of the workplace and worker participation have not established the priority of labor over capital in content as distinct from form. Baum's (1982, 42) contention that 'only through such a democratization of the workplace that the priority of labor over capital can be protected' has not prevented the growing concentration of capital ownership. Capital still owns labor. Workplace democratization is a necessary but insufficient condition to establish the priority of labor. Causation goes mainly the other way, from ownership to control. The democratization of capital ownership in work is even more necessary to develop the priority of labor.

The existing pattern of property ownership in the United States (and in most other nation states as described by Wolff, 1996 and Schneider, 2004) is yet another distortion of Table 2.1 and 2.2–type principles; in this case at the least, of the private property ownership principle, including the universal destination of goods, and of solidarity. It is a paradigm instance of a phenomenon long condemned by successive Popes, 'the injustice of the poor distribution of the goods and services originally intended for all' (SRS 1987, 58). ('Goods' include private property and capital for productive enterprise, for most physical capital is "goods" of some kind.) Secular commentators echo this criticism. Gates (1998, 217) comments that 'today's disparities in wealth mock the moral and ethical foundations on which free-enterprise democracies are built' (reemphasized in Gates, 2000). He is supported by Blasi and Kruse (1991, 254) who argue that 'the widespread exclusion of the population from the capitalist system is nothing short of feudalism, and it threatens to turn the American capitalist system into a cruel hoax.' In the United States, the overwhelming majority of population probably does not have access to sufficient private capital to siphon into job producing enterprises in which they retain capital ownership and control. This is not something applying only to the 'poor,' regardless of the disparate definitions of the 'poor.' It probably applies to the 90 percent of US households who own around 10 percent of business assets.

Rerum Novarum (1891) had castigated 'the enormous wealth of a few as opposed to the poverty of the many' (CA 1991, 10). This still exists, except that not all the 'many' in Western countries might be defined as living in absolute 'poverty.' Nevertheless, the 'having' of a few is still 'to the detriment of the "being" of many others' (SRS, 1987, 68). These 'many others' have no financial capacity to provide for their own employment by running or participating in the running of their own businesses. Encouraging wider private ownership of work also articulates more effectively the principles of the universal destination of goods, of solidarity, and of the priority of labor over capital. For example, the universal destination of goods and of solidarity (SRS, 1987, 83) encourages that 'those who . . . have a greater share of goods and common services, should feel *responsible* for the weaker and be ready to share with them all they possess.' Sharing 'all' is consistent with what Jesus taught (e.g., Mt. 19:21; Lk. 18:22).

MAKING WORK OWNERSHIP EFFECTIVE

This section considers how the private property principle within the employment context might be rendered more operational than currently in the Western developed economy. Encouraging private work ownership could be achieved in diverse ways. In keeping with the three Papal encyclicals and the Protestant evangelical thought, all depend on the maintenance of market mechanisms and preservation of a supervisory role for the state. Whether for self-employment or for shared employee work ownership, funds are necessary to facilitate enterprise start-up or worker buy-out of existing enterprises. The Catholic commentator, Novak (1993, 164) advocated the US government 'issue matching grants to IRA [individual retirement account] funds begun by poor persons, by matching one-for-one every dollar saved. These funds would grow tax-free until put to use for capital investments in new businesses . . .' The disadvantages of Novak's approach are that poor people are unlikely to have appreciable IRAs, and he favors the matching grants at the expense of traditional welfare support ('instead of issuing welfare checks'). Both traditional welfare and grants are needed, for removing public income support potentially condemns the poor to destitution, and puts all the responsibility on the non-supported poor to come up with feasible ideas for business ventures. This is unacceptable in terms of the principles of universal destination of goods, and of solidarity. A job generation strategy could not necessarily replace an income maintenance strategy in its entirety.

As Novak noted (1993, 164), extending private work ownership requires that enterprise instigators have access to start-up funds. Extended-family-based capital is an important source for self-employed start-ups, particularly as unemployment can be the immediately previous experience of newly self-employed people. Arum and Muller (2004, 430, 444) summarized empirical findings for advanced economies that 'societies with higher levels of family based social capital have higher rates of self-employment,' applying to all socio-economic groups. Other sources of start-up capital can be local associations advocating work ownership from which start-up loans or grants could be obtained. Another source of funds for such enterprise could devolve from government. Gates (1998, 214–220), for example, listed ten potential fund sources involving government, including a wealth tax that he described 'as a "user fee" charged for the privilege of utilizing the nation's private property tradition as a vehicle for accumulating assets totally disproportionate to any conceivable notion of need' (1998, 217–218). Wolff (1995) also proposed a modest wealth tax based on the Swiss system. Comparing the eleven OECD countries that have direct taxes on wealth (as distinct from estate and capital gains taxes) with the United States that does not, Wolff (1995, 54) found no strong evidence that a wealth tax inhibits savings. Another risk with a wealth tax is capital flight. But Wolff argued that flight depends on influences stronger than tax systems (e.g., political instability), and that both Switzerland and the United States are safe havens for international wealth.

Novak (1993, 163) also advocated local community support for his above proposal. He proposes 'an emphasis on local and 'neighborly' assistance, through family, neighbors, churches, unions, fraternal societies, or other associations.' But the principle of subsidiarity would need to be extended beyond these bodies. At the least, these 'intermediate communities' (CA, 1991, 70) would need to work with the unemployed and with decentralized and local State agencies, with existing employers and private welfare agencies, to develop business plans, partially fund new enterprises, and guide their development. Balkin (1989, 1992) showed that poor people starting businesses depend on extensive local networks even though diverse models exist to help them. Private employment-generating ventures for the unemployed (poor and other) require intimate local knowledge and initiative, mechanisms for mandatory cooperation from government employment agencies, effective on-the-job training, and sufficient funding for both the enterprise and support services (e.g., reading and numerate skills' tuition for disadvantaged people). The latter is especially important as the unemployed poor in advanced Western countries experience composite personal and social disadvantage (summarized for the United States, for example, by Massaro, 1998, 156). In all probability, the unemployed would be able to make little financial contribution to secure their ownership in a new enterprise in which they started work. However, if the business venture succeeded, deductions could be made from their wages, or loans raised from specially created sources. Some such sources exist, like credit unions, rotating credit associations, private foundations and churches with economic funding arms—again, access to cheap government loans could be promoted for these agencies.

The ideas above have little to do with current workfare, enterprise or empowerment zones in the United States, or with recent welfare reform initiatives (outlined in Massaro, 1998). Nevertheless, cases exist partially embodying features above. For instance, the originally-Christian-inspired Center for Employment Training has become a pace setter for skills training for low income people (Giloth, 1998). The Co-operative Home Care Associates employs over 500 mainly colored women most of whom were formerly on public assistance (Dawson, 1998). The City of Seattle has its Ready to Earn Fund that can be tapped by both employers and workers to pay for child care and even emergency housing for new workers (Rice, 1998), and so on. These initiatives share common ground with the Neighborhood Networks overseen by the Department of Housing and Urban Development (HUD) since 1995, and the over 500 microenterprise development organizations represented in the Association for Enterprise Opportunity. The limitation of all these types of schemes is that they are not part of an holistic strategy for private ownership (or any other type of) job creation, such as envisaged in CST. Nor is there explicit advocacy of such a 'bottom-up/top-down' approach by poverty experts (much less of job ownership). For instance, even such an enlightened poverty analyst (and acknowledged Christian) as Rebecca Blank (1997, 2000) provides little explanation of non-government-initiated job creation ventures or proposals (even if partially government funded). Her emphasis is on describing existing US government(s) poverty cash support, job training and placement, and proposing its reform to make it more effective. Public sector job creation might be the 'jobs of last resort' (Blank, 1997, 277) in a comprehensive strategy, as could short-term employer wage subsidies. But neither of these approaches, or enterprise and empowerment zones (not considered to be particularly successful e.g., Mueller and Schwartz, 1998) substitute for the holistic compendium of CST- and evangelical-type private ownership job proposals, or even for secular programs of worker-owned capitalism (e.g., Haslett, 1994).

A better picture of what a more holistic strategy for job ownership might look like on the ground is provided by Spain and Italy, the two Northern hemisphere countries with the largest self-owned/managed sectors. They are also the two most developed countries where CST has had the greatest impact. Workers both owning and controlling directly the capital with which they personally work encompasses producers' or workers' cooperatives (where the scale of activity is beyond the scope of self-employment and partnerships). Workers here are part-private owners of their work. CA (1991, 25) specifies cooperatives as examples of application of the principle of solidarity in 'the numerous efforts to which Christians made a notable contribution in establishing producers,' consumers' and credit cooperatives . . .' Christians have long played an important role in the growth of the international cooperative movement, especially in countries with a strong Catholic tradition (Spain, Italy, and France) and/or those influenced by Protestant and Catholic distributism, like Britain and Canada. Evangelical Christians (e.g., Roels, 1995) have been drawn to cooperatives because this form of organization has the potential to conform more closely to its Christian evangelical principles of self-management and private ownership than joint stock companies or state enterprises, and than small business employing non-owner workers. Cooperative members provide equal contributions of financial capital from their private property or as a lien on it for the cooperative's operation (as per item 8 of Table 2.2); they become part-private owners of the enterprise. In so far as family units provide this financial capital (and legally can receive it back), as per item 7 of Table 2.2, a contributing family's private property may be protected (item 6), but this is subject to the profitable operation of the cooperative. Only in producer cooperatives, however, do financial capital-contributing family unit-representatives as workers retain partial control of their contributed capital (item 7 of Table 2.2). Partial control only is retained with each worker sacrificing complete control to the collective. Producer or worker cooperatives constitute a minority of cooperatives in operation in the world today. More typically, cooperatives (as in retailing, banking and insurance) employ workers who are not necessarily members of the cooperative, and who therefore do not meet the constraints of item 7 of Table 2.2. Nevertheless, cooperatives are becoming more interested in providing employment for their members, so that producer/worker cooperatives are the fastest growing segment of the international cooperative movement (Hurp, 1998). Producer cooperatives also have potential to be one form of government-sponsored (including formerly government-privatized) employment in the West, although this is uncommon to date.

Most cooperatives have not sought explicitly to meet the remaining (holistic) items of Tables 2.1 or 2.2. There are a few examples, however, of Christian-inspired cooperative development that at least in their instigation attempted to meet some of the more encompassing tenets of the Tables. One was the Canadian Antigonish movement, at its peak strength from the 1920s to 1950s. Its initiators were Catholic priests endeavoring to apply their Christian beliefs to redress the poverty among which they lived in the fishing-based provinces of Nova Scotia. Associated with and assisted by the local university, these priests encouraged adult education and cooperative development throughout the fishing and mining villages of Nova Scotia. Credit unions and consumer cooperatives of all kinds (housing, libraries, retailing) were part of an overall strategy seeking to enable residents to tackle their own problems with their own resources, stimulating great international interest in the 1930s (MacLeod, 1997).

Consumer cooperation alone has never been the answer to increasing employment within a region. As the principles of Tables 2.1 and 2.2 above show, production cooperation is more basic because consumption depends on ownership of a job. The Antigonish developers failed to act on this requirement so that many of their positive initiatives came undone by the 1950s. This impasse is sometimes called the Rochdale cul-de-sac, akin to the principal-agent problem. This means cooperative members confine themselves to consuming products but play no part in their production that is delegated to non-member employees (as with modern credit unions and mutual insurance societies). The extreme of this process can be that directors assume control of the cooperative enterprise, and sell it off to private owners, like the demutualization of large mutual assurance societies in Western countries.

A newer Christian-inspired cooperative program sought to mitigate the principal-agent problem, while retaining (at least in its initiation) more of the holistic tenets in the Tables 2.1 and 2.2 above. This venture was facilitated by yet another Catholic priest, from the 1950s, and is the most strikingly holistic example of workers' cooperatives existing internationally—the Mondragon (Basque Spanish) system. Although this has been described exaggeratedly as a case of living Catholic social teaching (Jones, 1993, 68), Mondragon is probably the nearest example to it in the world today. There is no doubt that 'Church social teaching . . . was one of the fonts from which the designers of the Mondragon system drew their inspiration' (Chmielewski, 1994, 236).

Whyte and Whyte (1991, 273–277) point out that specific of the CST Table 2.1–type principles above were explicit guides to the formation of the Mondragon cooperatives; for example, solidarity, the dignity of labor, employment security. The operation of the cooperatives has been well documented from their inception in 1956, but only in the English language since 1973 (some of the more recent analyses are Cheney, 1999; Mathews, 1999; Lutz, 1998; MacLeod, 1997; Kasmir, 1996; Morrison, 1991; Whyte and Whyte, 1991). The Mondragon Cooperative Corporation (MCC) is now the seventh largest business conglomerate in Spain (MCC, 2005), involving over 100 cooperating cooperatives in manufacturing, banking, insurance, welfare, retailing, education (preschool to tertiary), agriculture and fishing. Whereas the Basque region lost 150,000 jobs since 1975, MCC employment in that region has grown steadily to over 33,000 by 2003 (MCC, 2005). Although only half of total MCC employees (68, 000) are cooperators, in the Basque Country, where nearly half of the MCC workforce is located, eighty percent of MCC workers are cooperators. Whereas 60 percent of new businesses started since the 70s in the Basque region failed, only 10 percent of the cooperatives have (Mathews, 1999, 180). MCC firms show higher productivity, lower absenteeism, and greater wage equality than private firms in the region. According to Bonin et al. (1993, 1236), no worker has ever been retrenched from an MCC organization (although they have been moved between them). Thus, the unemployment rate among MCC workers hovered below 1 percent in the early nineties, compared with a region-wide unemployment rate over 20 percent (Morrison, 1991, 200; Whyte and Whyte, 1991, 155–156). None of this implies perfection in MCC companies; they are harmed by problems including maintaining workshop floor democracy *and* managerial efficiency, competition between workers, widening pay differentials, gender discrimination, a traditional employee status for some workers, operating local and overseas firms as conventional capitalist enterprises, and coping with effects of globalization (Cheney, 1999; Lutz, 1998; Kasmir, 1996). From the CST and evangelical perspectives of this chapter, they now lack any explicit Christian-type input, and formal trade union involvement.

One potential objection to the expansion of workers cooperatives as a form of private work ownership is that the scale of operation of modern business is beyond capital funds available to cooperatives or potential members of cooperatives. To the extent this is true, it underlines the importance of the Caja Laboral credit union as the main engine for development of the Mondragon system so that (in the words of its Catholic priest founder) it did 'not condemn itself to the sole alternative of self-financing' (Whyte and Whyte, 1991, 265). However, it may be that scale economies are assuming diminishing importance in contemporary work operations. In any case, economic considerations are only one criterion guiding the organization of work in CST and evangelical thinking. They have to be assessed against at least a battery of Tables 2.1 and 2.2–type principles above. Thus, continual education of cooperative workers and managers in the philosophy and culture of cooperation both at a secular and religious level would seem to be a necessary ingredient for cooperative success. To some extent this is done in the MCC, but by now, the explicit legacy of its CST origins are not emphasized (Cheney, 1999, 55–56). Without this type of education, cooperatives can become just another form of mutual enterprise, the selling of which to private capital in the Western world (demutualization) is now endemic.

Antigonish and Mondragon are but two examples where Christians (with others) have been at the forefront in trying to foster sets of interrelated principles comparable to Tables 2.1 and 2.2 above, via cooperative development. Another case is Italy with the oldest and largest cooperative sector in the world, early encouraged by the trade union movement, left political parties and the Catholic Church.

Many of its producer cooperatives, employing over half a million workers, appear to be as successful as Mondragon's, although they are less integrated and each is smaller than in the regionally-based MCC (Earle, 1986). Although the size of Italian coops varies greatly, most employ less than twenty workers (Bonin et al., 1993, 1294) but show higher productivity, lower wage differentials, more tranquil industrial relations, and more labor-intensive production methods than matched conventionally-organized private firms (Jones and Svejnar, 1985; Bartlett et al., 1992, 116). As with Spanish cooperatives, profit-sharing, participation and individual worker ownership of assets have positive effects on productivity, One newer development is the Italian Social Co-operative Societies stimulated by Catholic Church and left-wing political organizers. These provide employment for the otherwise unemployable disabled, employ the able-bodied also, receive low public subsidy in a wide variety of industries, and are experiencing rapid growth (Mattioni and Tranquilli, 1998). The work ownership policies of these Societies are consistent with those advocated for disabled people in LE (1981, 88–90). Mutual strengthening has long existed between Italian cooperatives (concentrated in northern Italy) and the existence of civic tradition and community, virtues prized in CST and evangelical thought. Putnam (1993, 181) showed that in the north, 'norms of reciprocity and networks of civic engagement have been embodied in tower societies, guilds, mutual aid societies, cooperatives, unions,' undergirding 'levels of economic and institutional performance generally much higher than in the South.' Which came first—mutual aid or tradition—is hard to establish, but there is no doubt they fostered each other. In the Italian case, private work ownership via cooperatives and other forms of mutual companies appears to have had beneficial community effects.

Cooperatives *per se* are not the sole solution to pursuing the CST and evangelical principles above in relation to work organization. Further, sizeable difficulties exist in the way of their encouragement in Western capitalist economies (Dow, 2003). Nevertheless, they and their variants like commonwealth-owned firms may be the best chance of achieving certain of the principles (beyond the scale of self-employment/partnerships and 100 percent ESOPs). Being potentially subject to a wider control base than conventional joint stock companies, they may also be able to emphasize a greater range of decision making variables, including ethical considerations related to workplace conditions and types of products (Sparkes, 1995, 233–253). Further, these forms of cooperative enterprise fit comfortably with contemporary employment trends emphasizing demand for private and community services, such as the Co-operative Health Care Network mentioned above, and also including information technology. At the least, cooperative employment forms (including 100 percent ESOPs) have more potential than conventional joint stock companies to approach the CST and evangelical principles above of encouraging a wider dispersion of financial capital and economic power throughout society. To date, however, both cooperatives and ESOPs are but a shadow of their potentials, and do not find a fertile breeding ground in the contemporary socio-economic ethos of English-speaking capitalist countries. Nevertheless, as we have argued elsewhere (Beed and Beed, 2005c), the joint stock company does not accord with Biblical notions of personal responsibility in private property ownership or paid employment.

Chapter Three

Biblical Exegesis-Based Principles for Economic Distribution

Recent Papal Social Thought and Protestant evangelical interpretation were given a fair airing in the previous chapter, specifically concerning their principles for employment organization. This chapter focuses on a somewhat different stream of orthodox Christian thought, and a different topic, the distribution of wealth and income. As will become apparent, the sought-after distributional pattern depends on the correct organization of employment. Distribution cannot be considered independently from production. Ameliorating poverty requires appropriately organized means of wealth creation. Nevertheless, the purpose of this chapter is the same as Chapter 2: To show that particular streams of orthodox Christianity promote Biblically-based intentions or principles allegedly applicable to contemporary socio-economic life. This chapter explains the methodology for the given economic issue by which a selection of orthodox Christians who are either Biblical exegetes, theologians or economists derive principles of universal application from one Biblical component of Judeo-Christian belief, affecting the distribution of wealth and income (Beed and Beed, 2004a, 2005b; Beed, 2005e).

Some evaluation is made of this methodology, unlike Chapter 2, where no comment was made on the methodologies underlying the Christian examples. This review includes assessment of the principal author-example taken in this book of a Christian theologian critical of the approach underlying the methodology promoted here, James Barr. The Biblical exegetes on whom the case of this chapter rests are mainly a random Protestant group, plus four Jewish examples, while the theologians and economists in question who rely on this exegesis are Protestant evangelicals, as per the Chapter 2 meaning. The latter are mainly evangelical because this seems to be the only Protestant Christian stream (fundamentalists aside) that seeks to relate principles derived from Biblical exegesis directly to contemporary life. Catholic economists and social commentators, by contrast, are more likely to rely on their church's magisterium for real-world application. The economic principles under scrutiny here relate to the direction in which distributional policy should trend, how it relates to production, gauging how the poor might be identified and assisted, assessing the promotion of 'equal opportunity' versus 'equal outcome,' and considering the relationship between distribution and economic growth. As shown below, all these ideas are being rekindled in the recent revival of interest in distributional issues in economics. This chapter does not extend to showing how society might work today if the Judeo-Christian derivative social precepts relating to distribution were pursued. Developing a tentative overall picture of how the principles might be applied to contemporary society is a separate exercise, in which the study of empirical reality is crucial. Specifically, the chapter does not purport to be a comprehensive discussion of Christian-based redistributional policy oriented to alleviating the position of the economically poor, undertaken elsewhere (e.g., Carlson-Thies and Skillen, 1996; Massaro, 1998; Anderson, 1999).

The project of deriving socio-economic intentions or principles from Christian thought, allegedly relevant to existing society has a long history in Christianity. For instance, in the last half century or so, two proponents of the approach were the Protestant English cleric, William Temple (1942), and the Oxford economist, Denys Munby (1956). However, neither explained how their particular principles were interpreted from any theological system or from the primary source of Christian belief, the Bible, and neither provided close analysis how any principle(s) affected given economic issues. Later exponents of the approach, such as the Oxford evangelical economist, Donald Hay (1989), have made their own interpretations of Biblical texts without the input of academic Biblical commentary. Again, Hay was not able to provide *detailed* analysis in his general and helpful overview of the matter, of how his particular principles related to given economic issues (although more thorough than Temple or Munby). The exercise of this chapter fills in some of these gaps, showing how particular socio-economic intentions can be derived from a particular subset of Biblical texts, as interpreted by the selection of Biblical exegetes. This chapter also fills in earlier gaps in the likes of Temple and Munby by focusing on the analytical detail by which principles for a particular economic issue, the distribution of wealth and income, can be obtained from the Biblical sources.

DERIVING NORMATIVE INTENTIONS FOR ECONOMIC DISTRIBUTION

The discussion below has a similar methodological approach to extracting principles from the early luminaries of economics to ascertain what they meant. Nonetheless, exposing normative precepts in the Bible is an undertaking unfamiliar even to most Christians. Aside from fundamentalists, exegetes and evangelicals do not view the Bible as containing details of principles intended to inform material life. Themes or intentions contained in the Biblical text are important, not the minutiae of detail. The postulates, principles or paradigms emerge from the detail established for particular historico-cultural contexts that therefore have to be examined. A variety of these contexts exist in the Bible. In the Old Testament, for example, the themes are revealed by God's actions such as in the book of Genesis, by didactic teaching of the Mosaic Law (in the Jewish Torah) intended to apply to the original state of Israel, and by the proclamations of the prophets during and after the disintegration of that state. In the New Testament, Jesus' words and actions are the model, and the writings of the apostles reveal how these were applied after Jesus' death.

This section illustrates how themes or intentions governing an aspect of the form of socio-economic organization can allegedly be derived from just one of these sources: the Old Testament (OT) Mosaic Law, an involved set of rules intended to guide life in the promised land of Israel, but rarely followed. In a later section of the chapter, the teachings of Jesus are examined to assess whether they conform with distributional intentions contained in the Mosaic Law. Sections of three chapters of the thirty-nine in the Old Testament detail most of the Mosaic Law. Although the Law is treated as an entity here, the Book of the Covenant (Ex. 20–23), the Deuteronomic Code (Dt. 4–31), and the Holiness Code (Lev. 17–26) were developed at different times by different authors. The Law in Exodus is described in the Bible as revealed by God through Moses on Israel entering the promised land (perhaps around 1250 BC). In Deuteronomy, the Law is reported by the form in which it was rediscovered in approximately 620 BC, and in Leviticus the Law is probably a somewhat later expression than in Deuteronomy. However, no unanimity exists among Biblical scholars about when different components of the Law were developed or redacted, or how the different distributional provisions blend with each other. Further discussion of these topics is in Hartley (1992, 430–433), Chirichigno (1993, 18–29, 186–357), Tigay (1996, 466–467), and Pleins (2001, 49–75). Contemporary academic Biblical commentaries specified below, relating specifically to the OT Law, were used to establish the interpretations. They are mainly Protestant (evangelical and non-evangelical), except for the Jewish commentaries of the Jewish Publications Society by Sarna, Milgrom, Levine, and Tigay.

Two prior theological questions arise for which no answer consensus has been achieved throughout the history of Christianity (Rogerson, 2001). First, why should thematic principles embodied in the Mosaic Law be regarded as relevant in any way to contemporary life, even by Christians? Second, even assuming the first question can be answered, why should the particular set of principles relating to distribution unwrapped below be those relevant for today and all time? On the first question, the relevance of the Mosaic Law to Christians for contemporary life is justified by the evangelical theologian, Wright (1995, 114, 176; original emphasis) when he asserts that Israel's:

> Overall social shape, with its legal and institutional structures, ethical norms and values and theological undergirding, thus becomes the model or paradigm *intended* to have a relevance and application beyond the geographical, historical and cultural borders of Israel itself. The particularity of Israel then does not hinder universal application, but serves it . . . what God required of Israel as a fully human society is *morally consistent* with what God requires of all human societies.

This contention is similar to Stuhlmacher's (1986, 111) that 'the question of the law is the question of the way of life (*Lebensordnung*) revealed and set down by God for Israel and the nations of the world.' These views are held despite the immense socio-cultural gulf between ancient Israelite and contemporary society. Principles from the above Biblical texts, independent of the particular context of those texts, are sought that fit into the theological framework of Christian belief, such as the themes of creation, fall and judgement (Hay, 1993a, 126). This claim assumes that Jesus Christ in the New Testament (NT) held the principles of the Mosaic Law to apply in this sense (as supported by Jesus' statements in Mt. 5:17–19; Lk. 16:17, of which more below), and that comparable principles were meant to govern mutual relationships in the NT church. The evangelical economist, Hay (1989, 51, 48; original emphasis), giving examples of Jesus as presupposing the Law in his teaching, puts it that Jesus' teaching has 'definite continuity with the Law', but that it also expresses '*new* authoritative emphases, not just interpretations.' Another evangelical economist, Griffiths , argues (1984, 49) that Jesus thought of the Old Testament 'law as a divinely given rule of life, which has an enduring validity.' It is certainly clear that Jesus and the NT authors often cited OT Law texts as divinely authoritative (Grudem, 1994, 57). The implicit theological assumption in this type of thinking is that the ethics embodied in the OT Law are universal and eternal, 'embracing the same standard of righteousness for all the nations of the earth as it does for Israel' (Kaiser, 1983, 11). For the evangelical theologian, Blomberg (1999, 242), 'the New Testament carried forward the major principles of the Old Testament and intertestamental Judaism.' In this approach, Israel was intended to be 'a model of what a redeemed community would look like, living in obedience to God's will' (Wright, 1995, 165). Since God seeks to redeem all people, the thematic principles inherent in Israel's organization are important to this enterprise. The principles are not meant solely for a religious community, but are applicable also to secular societies. The above views are shared in varying degree by evangelical Protestant Christians—theologians and economists (e.g., Mott, 1982; Birch, 1991; Hamilton, 1992; Brett, 1992; Cramp, 1994; Mason, 1996), although other Protestants disagree with the idea of deriving or applying social principles from the Bible (e.g., Barr, 1980; Preston, 1990, 1991).

Thus, a different view on the matter from the evangelical one above can be proposed by Christians—that socio-economic principles contained in the Mosaic Law are not intended to be applied today. This view holds that the Mosaic Law described how people at the time responded to what they understood to be God's view on socio-economic matters in their particular context. For some contemporary Christians, the issue might be how to do this today rather than seeking to apply principles contained in the Mosaic Law. However, this latter view still leaves open the question of how and on what basis this is to be done. The economist, Hay (1993a, 126) proposes a theological basis for the presupposition that the intentions of the Mosaic Law extend throughout the Bible, and have universal and timeless application. This is 'that the Bible bears witness to a consistent God, and it would indeed be strange if it turned out to be full of contradictions.' Nevertheless, issues of interpreting derivative social principles from the original Biblical texts remain a problem, even though general interpretive guidelines can be proposed (Williams, 1996).

The second question above regarding relevance relates to the *particular* set of principles affecting equity, exposed below. For instance, the Mosaic Law accepts the institution of slavery, even though it set striking limits to that institution for its time. Some judgement is needed to decide what principle is truly in the spirit of Biblical social precepts. How is this judgement to be made? One criterion used by the evangelical authors above is whether Jesus and the other New Testament writers re-emphasize the distributional criteria exposed in the Mosaic Law below. Two evangelical theologians who have examined Jesus' teachings illustrate this approach. On the issue of release from debt so emphasized in the Law, Wright (1992, 229) argues that Jesus 'takes the themes of release and restoration and applies them both in the economic sense in which they originally functioned, and also with "value added" spiritual dimension.' On the matter of equitable distribution similarly stressed in the Law, Blomberg (1999, 145) contends 'there is a clear message in Jesus' ministry and teaching on meeting the needs of the outcasts and have-nots of this world.' Following this thinking, the theologians and economists cited above emphasize the distinction between socio-economic organization promoted by the OT Law, and those described as characteristics of ancient Israelite society, to features of which the Law's precepts were not directed. Examples of the latter include aspects of slavery and patriarchy. Elsewhere in the OT, the Israelites were called periodically to modes of behavior anathema to Christians, such as massacring heathen peoples who practiced child sacrifice, ritual prostitution and the like. This behavior is justified outside the regulations of the Law, and therefore is not germane to the argument about the Law below.

The theological basis for the justification of the enduring relevance of distributional intentions contained in the Mosaic Law can be assessed further. Just one instance of this is canvassed here. Much debate has occurred about what Jesus meant (assuming He did say it) in His Matthew 5:17–19 (and Luke 16:17) statements. In Matthew's version, Jesus is reported as saying, 'think not that I have come to abolish the law and the prophets; I have come not to abolish them but to fulfil them . . .' One economist Christian, Smith (1993, 177, 178), interprets this to mean that 'Jesus fulfilled the law and prophets in the sense that they point to him.' Therefore, Christians are to interpret the Old Testament Christologically. On this basis, he does not think it is 'necessarily terribly interesting' that 'an Old Testament law (or model) can be demonstrated to be consistent with the New Testament.' The evangelicals considered above (as distinct from theonomists) might agree with all of Smith's claims except his last. It is not that the 'details of Israel's social and political life [that] are binding' (Smith, 1993, 178), but that underlying the detail lies a model, and specific intentions, principles, paradigms, precepts and themes that may be intended for both the church and pagan society, in so far as Israel was to be a light to the world. Thus, if Jesus is reported as teaching precepts relating to economic distribution consistent with those contained in the Mosaic Law, this may be fair warrant that those precepts are meant for believers and for humankind at large. This view conforms with regarding Jesus as the 'sole authoritative interpreter' of 'the Old Testament law,' as per Smith (1993, 177).

It might appear that Jesus' sayings in this chapter are cited without attempting to discern their meaning within the context of the Biblical books from which they come. They are addressed only as the message of Jesus, and therefore might appear ahistorical and acontextual. It can be agreed that their meaning for the original audiences in the contexts in which Jesus made the statements has a bearing on interpreting them today. Yet, these meanings need not be dissimilar from the relevance of those statements today. For instance, Matthew may well be using certain of Jesus' sayings to berate the autocratic structure of the synagogue from which his group is splitting. Undoubtedly, this purpose is significant in trying to determine the relevance of Jesus' critique of status and hierarchy. It does not follow, however, that Jesus' critique has little relevance to matters of status and hierarchy today. On the contrary, the position taken in this book, and by the authorities we cite, is to assert exactly such a continuing relevance to a wider body of organizational structures than only to the synagogue nearly three millennia ago.

Most Biblical exegetes can be construed as interpreting Mt. 5:17–19 at least in the terms advocated above or more strongly, for the continuing relevance of the Law's intentions, as interpreted by Jesus, to both Christians and the world. For instance, one Catholic commentary on Matthew (Senior, 1998, 75) contends that to Jesus the 'Jewish law, as definitively taught by Jesus' remains 'valid for all time and offering the way of true righteousness before God.' Another (Harrington, 1991, 81, 83) suggests that 'the Law and the Prophets remain in force until' the 'coming of the Kingdom in its fullness' when heaven and earth pass away, that there is 'an organic relation between Jesus' teaching and the Torah.' What remains eternally valid to the Presbyterian, Long (1997, 53), is the 'true intent' of the details of the Law as interpreted by Jesus. Thus, 'the church is to ask of every piece of the law, "What is the will of God that lies behind this commandment, and how may we be obedient to that will?"' Six examples (sometimes described as antitheses) revealing the true intentions of God's will and greater righteousness are reported of Jesus following the Mt. 5:17–19 texts. Nevertheless, most contemporary Protestant exegetes seem to hold to the enduring applicability of the intentions of the Law as interpreted by Jesus (e.g., Bruner, 1987; Patte, 1987; Hagner, 1993; Keener, 1999). The Protestant, Hare (1993, 47) suggests that the prophets' interpretation of the law as interpreted by Jesus remains valid also, for he proposes a paraphrase of Mt. 5:17: 'do not suppose that my mission is to abrogate the law or the prophets' interpretation of the law; my mission is not to abrogate but rather to confirm the law and prophets by interpreting Scripture in terms of God's ultimate will.' Gardner (1991, 104; original emphasis), a Brethren, holds even more strongly that 'for Matthew, *the law remains valid until all that the law intends is fully revealed in Jesus' teaching and fully reflected in Jesus' community*.' This sense is echoed by Luz (1989, 266) that '"until all takes place"' [v. 18] means '"until all that which is commanded in the law is done".'

None of these orthodox Christian interpretations accord comfortably with Smith's (1993, 178) conclusion above of the uninteresting nature of Old Testament laws or models conforming with the New Testament. Nor do they conform with Barr's claim (1983, 15) that Jesus' teaching immediately after Mt. 5:17 'is about to range far beyond anything that could be justified as an interpretation of these laws.' On the contrary, all the commentators above assert that Jesus was interpreting the intentions of the Law, even though He was not 'controlled by the actual text of the laws' which to Barr seems a criterion for interpretation (Barr, 1983, 15). To argue, as per Rogerson (2001, 36), that the value of the Old Testament [Law] is 'in terms of example rather than precept' is to overlook that examples reveal precepts or rules for action and conduct. An example is a specimen or instance illustrating a general rule, precept or principle. The general rules pertinent here are the intentions or principles embedded in the Mosaic Law which modern society has to imitate 'in ways appropriate to today's world.' Contra Rogerson, ascertaining the precepts or maxims underlying the Law does not involve 'applying Old Testament laws directly to modern society' (Rogerson, 2001, 37).

Nor is it a telling objection to the intention-based principle approach to note, as per Preston (1994, 129), that movement has to be made from Biblical principle to the complicated empirical reality of the modern world. Nobody supposes that Biblical principles can be applied straightforwardly without taking cognizancc of 'empirical evidence not obtainable from the Bible (or doctrine).' Such evidence is always 'contestable' because even its very description is theory-laden. Principles have to be applied in empirical contexts that can diverge wildly from each other. Preston has long opposed the project of deriving Biblically-based socio-economic principles for application to the modern world. But his opposition does not seem to depend either on academic Biblical commentary or supportive academic analysis of the particular Biblical phenomena in his purview. For example, take Preston's (1994, 131–132) treatment of the Jubilee and his rejection that this embodies principles that might be applied today. His description of the Jubilee depends only on his particular interpretation of the Leviticus 25 text with no supporting secondary references. No historical or cultural background is provided by Preston to place the Jubilee in context. Nevertheless, he concludes that the Jubilee is 'clearly an attempt to translate the ethical teaching of the pre-exilic prophets into a social order after the exile' (1994, 131), despite the arguments of North (1954), Gottwald (1979), Fager (1993), Wright (1995), and Biblical exegetes, such as Hartley (1992) that the Jubilee had its origins long before the pre-exilic prophets, and that its redaction showed slow, gradual development. Fager (1993, 29), for instance, raises the possibility that 'attitudes toward the land which are reflected in the jubilee reach back to the very beginning of Israel.' Preston also holds the Jubilee to be 'unsatisfactory in detail' in differentiating between Israelites and others, and 'in one overall feature; it presupposes a static economy, returning to base every fifty years' (1994, 131–132). In what sense these are 'unsatisfactory' qualities, Preston does not explain. Nor does he explain why the Jubilee is held to presuppose a 'static economy.' The eight features by which Preston summarizes the Jubilee from Leviticus 25 could just as well apply to a growing as to a static economy. In a growing economy, the return 'to base every fifty years' might mean a return to a more wealthy base. Preston concludes his (two paragraph) discussion of the Jubilee by questioning what principle underlies the Jubilee. He fails to delineate that a number of principles do underlie the Jubilee, particularly when it is regarded as part of a system of interrelated socio-economic and religious regulations intended to apply to ancient Israel. Overall, Preston's analysis of the Jubilee is unpersuasive. His discussion of the Jubilee cannot be used as evidence of the invalidity of searching for underlying Biblical principles, and of relating such (allegedly dubious) principles to the modern world.

Nevertheless, the two problems remain. Few Christians suppose that applying any Biblical intention to the modern world is unproblematic; few suggest (fundamentalists aside) that deriving Biblically-based principles is straightforward. The difficulty is compounded because general principles may have to be qualified in certain circumstances, as Jesus' practice in Mt. 5:21–48 indicates (Keener, 1999, 184). Christians can agree with Barr (1999, 607) that 'the Bible does not, in most cases, give in itself a decision' on 'the burning issues' of our day. Disagreement is bound to arise among Christians on both the scores of deriving and applying. But the probability of disagreement does not preclude that this might be the correct methodology for seeking out and using the Bible's intentions in the modern world, as far as Christian believers are concerned. The next section examines the deductions in principle that might be made from the Law relating to economic distribution. After that, some of Jesus' teachings relating to distribution are considered to ascertain if they conform with the Law's intentions.

ECONOMIC DISTRIBUTIONAL INTENTIONS OF THE MOSAIC LAW

If it is the intentions of the Law that are relevant to contemporary Christians, the church and secular society, these need to be assessed. Only one example of the general intent underlying the Law is discussed below, concerning only its content related to economic distribution. The overall conclusion of the analysis following is that the Law aimed to ensure in perpetuity a relatively equal distribution of wealth- and income-generating potential among the extended families of Israel. How is this conclusion derived?

The main forms of potential to generate increments of wealth and income in the newly-settled rural society of Israel were land and labor. Since ownership of the land remained with God or Yahweh (Lev. 25:23), reinforcing a principle first established in the book of Genesis, no land could be sold permanently between families. As Wright (1990, 63; original emphasis) put it, 'Yahweh's ownership of the land is affirmed to ensure the security of *individual families* by preventing permanent alienation of *their land* . . . The primary feature of this system was preservation of multiple family holdings in relative equality and freedom.' To the extent that these objectives succeeded, Mott and Sider (1999, 34) point out that 'the picture of land ownership in the time of the judges suggests some approximation of equality of land ownership . . .' Ensuring the stability of the nation before God was inseparable from maintaining conditions for family economic independence. The aim was a reasonably egalitarian society in which each extended family was guaranteed minimum economic security sufficient to participate responsibly in the social and religious life of the community. In terms of economic equity, this egalitarian exemplar was a revolutionary aspect of the Law, both for the time when it was formulated, and for all history since. Nonetheless, by feudal and medieval times throughout the world where Judaism or Christianity had been influential, despite and because of the influence of the institutional church, the Mosaic Law principles had become totally disregarded; landlordism, extremes of land ownership and wealth, and hierarchical distinctions were entrenched endemically.

Ten measures of Table 3.1 below (akin to Mason, 1987) were enshrined in the Mosaic Law by which the Bible suggests that Israel was to strive for a relatively equal family distribution of wealth and income. Derivation of the ten measures is explained below. Measure 1 ensured that on specific equity criteria, the original land holders, or more correctly, trustees of the land, were given their perpetual leases to enjoy their usufructs from God on entering the promised land (Num. 26:52–56; 33:54. Jos. chaps. 13–21 detail the allotments). There is no strict agreement among Biblical scholars on the precise rendering of the Numbers' texts. However, from a consensus of Milgrom (1990), Harrison (1990), Ashley (1993), and Sakenfeld (1995), the area of land allocated to each tribe was proportional to its population, and the location of each tribe's holding was determined by lot. As per Sakenfeld (1995, 144–145), 'it seems sensible to suppose that general regions were to be determined by casting lots, while specific borders would be drawn to take account of relative numbers of people.' These particular issues are explored further in Beed (2005e), including possible differences between the Numbers and Josiah specifications.

Once the Israelites had settled on their allotted land, the Mosaic Law recognized that, because of inadequate management, differential land fertility, accidents and death, or other arbitrary circumstances, some families might not be able to maintain economic solvency. No criteria defined these poor, any more than it defined equality, but widows and orphans, and aliens (who had no share in the initial land allotment) were singled out for special help. The term, 'poor' in the Bible is not confined to those poor economically, as such from Stegemann (1984) to Hoppe (2004) have pointed out. Nevertheless, the term usually does encompass those who *are* materially indigent, and is so used in the discussion below.

Measures 2 to 4 were relatively minor in their wealth and income transfer effects. In measure 2, anyone could go into someone else's vineyard or crop

Table 3.1. Mosaic Law Measures Encouraging Economic Equality in Ancient Israel

1. The initial free distribution of land was on specific equity criteria.
2. Anyone could eat/gather free food from others' land any time.
3. A produce tax was available free to the poor every third year.
4. Every seven years, land was to remain fallow, and its produce available freely to the poor.
5. Loans were required to the poor.
6. Limits were placed on the collateral the poor were to offer for a loan.
7. Loans were interest-free to Israelites.
8. The outstanding balance of a loan was cancelled every seven years.
9. Land transfers reverted to original holders every forty-nine years (the Jubilee).
10. Fallback provisions were available to the destitute poor, such as bond-servitude.

Sources: Biblical text: May and Metzger, 1977. Commentaries for Exodus: Clements, 1972; Cole, 1973; Childs, 1974; Hyatt, 1980; Davies, 1983; Durham, 1987; Sarna, 1991; Jacob, 1992. Leviticus: Noth, 1965; Wenham, 1979; Levine, 1989; Demarest, 1990; Hartley, 1992; Gerstenberger, 1996; Budd, 1996; Rooker, 2000. Numbers: Milgrom, 1990; Harrison, 1990; Ashley, 1993; Sakenfeld, 1995. Deuteronomy: von Rad, 1966; Weinfeld, 1972, 1995; Craigie, 1976; Mayes, 1979; Maxwell, 1987; Cairns, 1992; Hamilton, 1992; Merrill, 1994; Mann, 1995; Tigay, 1996; Wright, 1996.

field, and eat as much food as he could then and there. But no food could be taken away (Dt. 23:24–25). Some commentators suggest this measure related to travelers (e.g., Craigie, 1976, 304), but most put no constraint on it. As Tigay (1996, 219) points out, fields were laid out so that people often had to pass through those of others. Similarly, farmers had to leave part of their crops unharvested in the fields for widows etc. to gather freely at harvest time (Lev. 19:9–10; 23:22; Dt. 24:19–21). Wright (1996, 261) emphasizes the gleanings *belonged* to these poor, who also had to work to gain the free food. Measure 3 made the proceeds of the ten percent produce tax (the tithe) at the end of every third year available to the aliens, orphans and widows. It was available also to its yearly recipients, the Levitical administrators of the Law (Dt. 14:28–29; 26:12–13) who had no share in the initial land distribution above. The produce collected in these (third) years might have lasted partially until the next collection (Tigay, 1996, 144, 369). Measure 4 completed the sequence of free food available to the poor. All land was to be left fallow every seventh or sabbath year. The trustee-farmer could eat whatever his land produced in this year, but it was also freely available to the poor, as well as to domestic stock and wild animals (Ex. 23:11; Lev. 25:1–7). One suggestion is that individual farmers set their own sabbath year in the earlier Exodus text situation to fit in with their own cultivation plan. In this case, free food would be available continuously to the poor and wild animals, but by the time of Leviticus this had changed to a uniform year for the whole land (Wright, 1990, 145–146). To calm the Israelites' worry that there would not be enough food for them during this sabbath year, God promised that the produce of the sixth year would be equivalent to three years. This would be enough to last during the sixth year, the seventh, and the eighth while sowing was in progress (Lev. 25:20–22).

Measures 2 to 4 may not seem to amount to much, guaranteeing regular minimum food for the poor, for some of which they had to work by gathering the food. The effect of the measures on wealth and income transfer from the prosperous to the poor would have been relatively modest. The next five measures, however, imposed more rigorous requirements on the well-off to share their prosperity with those less fortunate economically.

Measures 5 to 8 list obligations on the well-off lending to the poor (Ex. 22:25–27; Lev. 25:35–38; Dt. 15:1–11, 23:19–20). The Law was adamant in measure 5 that the Israelites had to be open-handed toward the poor, and 'lend him sufficient for his need, whatever it may be' (Dt. 15:7–9). There was no discussion in the Law about whether these poor were to be deserving, able-bodied or economically viable; the fact of being poor was enough to warrant help. Nor was there any discussion about the purpose of loans; for instance, no distinction was made between commercial and non-commercial loans.

In Measure 6, strict limits were placed on the collateral the poor were to offer for a loan. For instance, no lender could take necessities of life such as cloaks or millstones as collateral (Ex. 22:26–27; Dt. 24:6, 12–13, 17). The aim of the Torah's laws of distraint (taking items as collateral) was to ensure that 'the creditor's legitimate right to repayment is subordinated to the survival and dignity of the debtor . . . to considerably reduce the creditor's leverage in securing repayment' (Tigay, 1996, 223). Measure 7 forbad interest on loans, to a poor person or to any fellow Israelite, whatever the purpose of the loan (Ex. 22:25; Lev. 25:35–37; Dt. 23:19–20), although interest was allowed on loans to foreigners. The economist, Mason (1987, 4) holds that 'the zero-interest loan was probably a short-term business loan without collateral to the able-bodied land owner.' He suggests that 'it seems rather unlikely that such a loan would have been available to anyone other than an economically viable (propertied) *beth'ab*, since otherwise there would be little means to raise the money to repay it' (a *beth'ab* was the extended family in which most Israelites lived).

Mason's scriptural citations following do not conclusively underline these claims. Ex. 22:25 specified only the interest-free nature of loans, and Lev. 25:35–37 dealt with the extreme case of an Israelite who could not support himself. He might put up his land as collateral and was required to be maintained by a fellow Israelite (Measure 10). Dt. 15:1–11 provided for sabbatical debt-release and generosity in lending. There is no mention in the Law of whether collateral was required for loans (except for the case of land discussed below), and the sabbatical debt-release implied that obtaining repayments were not uppermost as a motivation for making loans (perhaps not even a consideration). There is no reason in the Law to suppose that economically-dependent Israelite poor, such as hired laborers, orphans, the sick and disabled, would not be eligible for loans, at least as far as Ex. 22:25 and Dt. 23:19–20 were concerned.

Relying on the interpretations of Cairns (1992, 208), Tigay (1996, 145), and Wright (1996, 251), the risks of extrapolating into potential scenarios can be illustrated by some of Mason's reconstructions (1987, 4–5). These latter suggest a scenario for a society dominated more by secular modes than by the Law's intentions. The OT says little about the way the Law was actually used, but the *aim* of the Law measures is the prime consideration here. The Law's specifications give no indication (Mason, 1987, 4) that 'only rarely would any balance [of a loan] remain unpaid beyond six years' (thereby accounting for the absence of OT comment about loans' experience). Nor do the specifications suggest that debtors would have difficulty is getting an additional loan if they were unable to repay it within the seven years, and therefore would be inclined to sell themselves into bond-slavery. Nor do the Law texts suggest a distinction in motivation between 'the zero-interest loan'—a 'compassionate loan without collateral'—and a loan secured by land or bond-slavery collateral (with Mason suggesting that bond-slavery might have been the preferred option). Mason envisages foreclosure occurring if 'repayment of a land-secured loan were not possible' but the Law only distinguished 'a loan secured by land collateral' from other loans only as per item 9 discussed below. Temporary land sale was possible (Lev. 25:35–38), but this was differentiated from the loan provisions in Ex. 22:25–27 and Dt. 15:1–11, 23.

Also questionable is Barr's (1980, 92–93) dismissal that Dt. 23:19–20 (as noted above, similar to Ex. 22:25, and Lev. 25:35–37) really forbad lending at interest. Barr cannot accept that an economy could actually function 'in which credit could be obtained without the payment of interest.' Such an economy would be 'a paradise for debtors,' one totally 'different from our own civilization.' Since Barr cannot conceive of such an economy, he seems to imply it could not exist, especially as neighboring ancient Near Eastern societies had interest rates from twenty to sixty per cent. If Dt. 23:19–20 had ever operated in ancient Israel, what 'a strange sort of society' it would have been (Barr, 1980, 93).

Barr seems to be influenced by the experience of actual economic systems in which interest rates are pervasive. But, the model of economic organization to which ancient Israel was called via the Law was totally unlike anything that existed then, or since. It is feasible that this type of economy could have operated without interest rates (a model on comparable lines is Mills and Presley, 1999). With the other measures of Table 3.1, debtors would not have existed or persisted, for the overall purpose of Table 3.1 was to maintain and restore the extended families of Israel in and to private property-based economic independence. Flows of capital would occur only as long as their products were shared more or less equally throughout the society as a whole, and therefore were undertaken in the interests of the society as a whole. Interest rates would not be obligatory in this situation because interest in the type of societies with which we (and Barr) are familiar functions as a premium accruing to those who have a partial monopoly over capital ownership and/or control. There is no evidence that individual decision making for private capital on the basis of equally distributed private property is less capable than unrestricted markets to arrive at economically rational results. Conventional economists would dispute this assertion, but aside from abstract models, they have no real-world evidence from which to conclude otherwise, because no society containing anything like the economic provisions of the Law has ever existed. Interestingly, secular models are starting to be promoted embodying elements of the Law-type socio-economic arrangements, including low reliance on interest rates (e.g., Albert and Hahnel, 1991a and b; Hirst, 1994). Of course, ancient Israel would have been 'a strange sort of society,' 'different from our own civilization.' But that was precisely God's intention. Israel was to stand apart from the rest of the world, and serve as a model for emulation. Further, abstracting from God's economic strategy for Israel, there has been no relation historically between the levels of interest rates and the ability of the economies of countries to function. Nations have been able to function over long periods of time with low interest rates, while high long-term interest rates, say, above ten per cent, have usually been evidence of pathological economic conditions (Homer and Sylla, 1991; Broersma, 1992; Fry, 1995).

Barr is right on one point. The socio-economic organization, including the interest law, that God is reported as planning for Israel, never came to pass. Barr attributes this to the self-contradictory nature of the implications of Dt. 23:19–20. Perhaps he would see the rest of God's socio-economic strategy for Israel in this vein. The orthodox Judeo-Christian explanation for the failure is Israel's disobedience to the total spiritual-social strategy devised by God. Irrelevant to this explanation is the interest rate experience of adjacent Near Eastern societies to ancient Israel. It is irrelevant because of the great internal socio-economic strength of Israel that would have been generated by God's strategy. There is no doubt that certain attributes of the Table 3.1 measures were similar to those of ancient Near Eastern societies near Israel (e.g., Chirichigno, 1993), but interest rates were not one of them, any more than features of their religious life were intended to be, like ritual prostitution and child sacrifice (Ezekiel 20:25–26 notwithstanding—on which see Greenberg, 1983, 369). That God encouraged ancient Israel to emulate and modify beneficial economic practices of surrounding countries might be no more than an indication that God deals with people in the context of where they are at the time.

Barr goes on to pose an unusual argument that the supply of credit on interest not only existed but was 'recognized and recommended by the law' (Barr, 1980, 93; disputed by Ballard, 1994, 214–217). 'A probable example' is the provision relating to the purchase of Hebrew slaves in Ex. 21:2–6 where the slave was to serve for 'six years, and in the seventh he shall go out free, for nothing.' According to Barr, 'behind this there may lie a complete system combining elements of credit, interest and poor relief.' As the measures of Table 3.1 show, a complete system did lie behind each provision of the Law, including those relating to slaves, but it did not include interest. If, instead, Barr had been referring to actual practices in ancient Israel in contradistinction to the Law (which he was not), it is clear that the Law's provisions were flouted in all directions. It is also clear in the Law's provisions relating to Hebrew slaves that they may well produce more in the six years than the slave and his family consumed, so that the slave owner can be construed as making a net gain from temporarily owning the slave. Only by stretching the meaning of 'interest' beyond the use of the word in the Law would it be reasonable to regard this net gain as 'interest.' This meaning or application is not that intended by the word 'interest' or 'usury' in Dt. 23:19–20, Ex. 22:25, or Lev. 25:35–37 that related to loan provisions affecting only free, non-slave Israelites.

Not only were loans interest free, but by Measure 8 in Table 3.1, the outstanding balance of a loan to a fellow-Israelite was to be cancelled every seventh or sabbath year, irrespective of whether the borrower could repay the balance (Dt. 15:1–4). All commonly used translations of the Bible and most commentaries on Deuteronomy translate Dt. 15:1–4 in this sense (e.g., *The New International Version* of the Bible, 'at the end of every seven years you must cancel debts'). Some commentators (e.g., Wright, 1990, 172; 1996, 188, 196) raise the possibility that only the payment due in the seventh year was cancelled. However, Wright (1990, 173) concludes that 'one cannot finally be dogmatic on this question, and total cancellation of the debt and release of the pledge may not have been impossible.'

The disagreement about one year or permanent debt release can be illustrated. The economist, Beisner (1988, 58–62) holds Dt. 15:1–2 to mean remission only during the seventh (sabbatical) year. His exegesis depends on the Hebrew word in the text, *shamat*, meaning 'to let drop.' Beisner (p. 59) cites one other instance of the use of *shamat* elsewhere in the Mosaic Law, in Exodus 23:11. By analogy from this text specifying the one year land fallow rest, Beisner contends that *shamat* in Dt. 15:1–3 means one year. Beisner (p. 60) offers a further use of *shamat* in the OT to bolster his case. The word is used in Jer. 17.4 in an apparently unrelated sense (e.g., *RSV*: 'you shall loosen your hand . . . '). Beisner's reasoning is that since Jeremiah used the word metaphorically, and since God promised Israel would be brought back to its country in seventy years (Jer. 29:10), the use of *shamat* in Jer. 17.4 implied a temporary letting go. Arguments could be made against each of Beisner's contentions, e.g., that *shamat* does not have an absolute etymological meaning in the OT, but means what its grammatical and social context conveys; that the idea of 'temporary' extending from one to seventy years is to stretch meaning too far. Emphasizing permanent debt release, Mayes (1979) notes the conjunction of Dt. 15:1–3 with the (permanent) law of release from bond servitude in Dt. 15:12ff. Blomberg (1999, 44) holds that the 'Deuteronomy 15 passage does not refer to any point after the seven years at which repayment resumes.' He suggests 'the concern that some might not grant a loan to a needy person because the sabbatical year loomed near (15:9) makes little sense if the debt repayment was merely postponed rather than cancelled.' Tigay (1996) points to the consistency of (permanent) debt forgiveness with the general intention of the Torah to maintain families in economic independence, and to parallels in permanent debt remission in other contemporary ancient Near Eastern societies. This latter situation is emphasized also by Hamilton (1992) and Chirichigno (1993). As to the relevance of Ex. 23:11, Tigay (1996, 145) suggests that the common use of the word, *shamat*, 'may also imply that the agricultural "sabbatical" . . . is to be observed in the same year,' but that 'temporary' versus 'permanent' cannot be read from that into Dt. 15:1–2. On the basis of the evidence in favor of permanent debt release, that interpretation is adopted here.

In Deuteronomy (15:7–9), God is described as warning the Israelites not to be hard-hearted in their application of the loan rules that were probably designed to keep land within the extended family groups. The terms of the loans were so generous in Measures 6 to 8 that more appropriately they might be called grants. The emphasis was not so much of a lender profiting from a loan. Instead an opposite motive from personal gain was involved, embodied in the Law—'you shall love your neighbour as yourself' (Lev. 19:18). The obligation was to help those less fortunate without thought of personal gain.

In Measure 9 of Table 3.1, families who did not prosper after the initial allotment of land, for whatever reason, could temporarily sell all or part of their land in a 'distress sale' (Gerstenberger, 1996, 381), subject to price rules dependent on the land's harvests (Lev. 25:25–28). Thereupon, the temporary buyers derived income from the land's harvests, and the sellers (if necessary) were to be given work by the more prosperous as hired laborers (Lev. 25:35—Measure 10 below). But if the sellers recovered financially after selling, they or their relatives had the right to repurchase their land any time, again according to the price rules. However, land could remain in other ownerships only for a maximum period. The temporary sale of land between families was reassembled without further compensation in Measure 9, to the original land holdings every forty-nine years through the Jubilee (Lev. 25:8–17)—an override to the seven year loan redemptions. The aim of the Jubilee was 'to restore the tenure of land to the smaller household units within the "kinship group" . . . an attempt to preserve, or periodically to restore, the economic viability and independence of the smaller family-plus-land units' (Wright, 1990, 124).

The temporary land sales can be interpreted (Beisner, 1988, 63) 'as collateral for an emergency loan to provide for a family's immediate needs.' The lender would work the land and derive the income from it during the term of the loan (up to forty-nine years). According to the price rules, the income derived from the loan of the land would be no more than the proceeds of the loan. When the Jubilee arrived, the collateral land was returned to its original trustee-owner. The income to the lender from using the land during the term of the loan is equivalent to complete repayment by the borrower for the loan, in so far as the borrower lost the use of the land during the term of the loan (Beisner, 1988, 63). In the long run, therefore, the relative advantage of the lender in distributional terms would not increase. Nor would the relative disadvantage of the borrower increase. The relative position over time of borrower vis-à-vis lender would not alter so far as the requirements of the Law were concerned.

Four features of the Jubilee year emerge: land holdings reverted to their original trustee holders (Measure 9); land remained fallow (Measure 4); debts were cancelled (Measure 8); and debt-bondsmen were freed (Measure 10). The Jubilee returned to the poor their opportunity to regain economic independence, to make a fresh self-managed/self-owned work start, avoiding the creation of a permanently disadvantaged and dependent caste who did not work. It represented 'a serious attempt to maintain the integrity of the socio-economic ground of the nation's theological identity,' being based 'on the importance of preserving the socio-economic viability of the household and, therewith, the stability of the nation's relationship with God' (Wright, 1990, 125, 127). The Jubilee aimed over the long run to maintain a relatively equal distribution of the major source of capital (land), prevent latifundism, and forestall monopolization of land and other forms of capital. The economist Christian, Wilson (1997a, 29) expresses the Jubilee as 'not so much a matter of redistribution, but rather one of creating a level playing field for each generation so that material advantages acquired through one generation's acquisition of wealth are not handed down.'

Fallback provisions afforded additional protection for the poor who could not derive economic independence from the nine measures above. Chief among these (Measure 10 in Table 3.1) was the opportunity noted above to temporarily sell land and be employed as residential laborers (with family) by the better off. They were to have the status of 'hired servant' and were not to be treated 'with harshness' (Lev. 25:35–55). Although not detailed here, up to three stages could apply for these particular support provisions (Wright, 1990, 121–123; Chirichigno, 1993, 351). The measure is expressed differently in Dt. 15:12–18 (and, again, in Ex. 21:1–11) that a Hebrew (probably in debt) could be sold to the better-off, the debtor having the option for redemption after six years, or staying permanently with his employer as a 'bondman.' Differences between the Leviticus, Deuteronomy and Exodus expressions of these provisions might reflect the different times and contexts in which the measures were formulated (Hartley, 1994, 431–433). Alternatively, the laws might refer to different groups of people (Wright, 1990, 249–259), or they might reflect different theological underpinnings but be capable of simultaneous application (Chirichigno, 1993, 354–357). Along different lines, hired laborers (presumably non-residential) had to be paid their wages every day (Lev. 19:13; Dt. 24:14–15). God is reported as recognizing that hired workers were likely to live from hand to mouth, unlikely to have any surplus to carry over for a longer period.

Thus, ten measures of varying importance in the Mosaic Law assisted the economically disadvantaged, and pushed in the direction of relatively (but not absolutely) egalitarian results in the distribution of wealth and income between extended families. The measures did not imply sharing in precisely equal amounts per family, worker or person, or according to the work or skill contribution of people making up extended family units. Rather, the measures meant sharing according to the needs of the family each worker(s) supported. The needs of differing family situations, and responsibilities (such as religious ones), were recognized. Thus, for single people, like orphans, it meant sharing to meet their particular needs. Had the measures ever been practiced fully, a minimum standard of living would have been established for each person, Israelites and resident aliens alike. Opportunity existed for some farmers to prosper more than others, in which differing abilities might have been relevant, but the more prosperous were enjoined as a matter of loyalty to God to siphon a proportion of their extra prosperity in kind and/or work to help the struggling attain reasonable living standards. In Wright's view (1995, 155), 'the economic system was geared institutionally and in principle towards the preservation of a broadly based equality and self-sufficiency on the land, and to the protection of the weakest, the poorest and the threatened—and not to the interests of a wealthy, land-owning elite minority.' This contention conforms generally with that of a variety of modern Old Testament scholars, such as Albertz (1994, 76) and Pleins (2001, 54, 70), although it is not one accepted by Barr (1999, 237) who gives little credence to the Law's intentions for Israel to function as 'a primitive economic democracy.'

The aim of the Table 3.1 measures was not so much a strict quantitative economic equality as working toward 'an egalitarian bias' in the midst of inequality, a socio-economic program labeled 'compassionate stewardship' (Mason, 1987, 7, 2, 9). No one criterion can capture all the dimensions of equality that might be conceptualized or measured. Therefore, at any time inequalities would exist, but the measures were intended to mitigate some qualities of existing distributional inequities. Each extended family was meant to remain economically viable, enabled to participate as much as possible in the social and religious life of the society. 'Distribution according to needs' as well as 'guaranteeing basic needs' is how Mott and Sider (1999, 45) summarize the position. Preventing debt, 'the greatest internal threat to the social foundation of the equality of all the Israelites' (Hartley, 1992, 424), received great emphasis.

One feature of the Table 3.1 measures not discussed above is that economic blessings of abundance were attached to their obedience. Time and again for each measure, God promised explicitly that society's prosperity would be maximized *only* if all the measures (plus religious regulations not discussed here) were followed. Otherwise, economic and social disaster would ensue. The Catholic economist Gordon (1989) calls this the OT solution to the economic problem by observance of the Law. Obedience to God and just standards of equity were preconditions for optimizing material prosperity. This is yet another example of the indissoluble links between the spiritual and material realms of reality in OT (and NT) thought. It underlines the impossibility of 'desupernaturalizing' Judeo-Christian thinking; in this case, the infeasible idea that the Israelites could succeed without obedience to Yahweh and His directions of how to organize their socio-economic and spiritual life (Milbank, 1990, 112–113).

The measures of Table 3.1 demonstrate a 'deeply practical mutual responsibility,' a 'concern for the poor and needy . . . the same ideal of equality among God's people, both economically . . . and socially.' This is held to pervade both OT and NT ethics (Wright, 1990, 113), and therefore to provide enduring justification for the particular set of principles exposed in Table 3.1. For the illustration here, these principles derive from OT Law-type thinking. In this thinking, 'social, economic, and theological realms were . . . bound together inextricably, all three having the family as the basic focal point at which the conjunction of the three realms issued in ethical responsibilities and imperatives . . .' (Wright, 1990, 104). An indissoluble link is postulated in the OT to have existed between the destruction of the socio-economic/familial structure in Israel between c. 800 to 600 BC, and the disintegration of the nation's relationship with God.

From Table 3.1, themes, standards, intentions or norms emerge that the Protestant theologians and economists above suggest are reasonable to be regarded as universal and eternal. In this thinking, all societies are expected to apply such principles in their socio-economic life. For instance, Wright claims (1995, 210) that 'the moral principles of the jubilee' are 'universalizable on the basis of the moral consistency of God.' Confidence in deriving the principles is consolidated by a host of less formal exhortations to assist the poor found in the Mosaic Law, but not examined here. Even so, the expression of norms from Biblical measures such as those enshrined in Table 3.1 is a matter of interpretation (e.g., Kaiser, 1994). However, Table 3.2 below proposes twelve principles that might be derived from the detail of the OT Mosaic Law measures discussed above. Additional themes could also be deduced, and it would be possible to express each of the principles below differently. A case can be made that analogous norms are paralleled elsewhere in the Old Testament, and are reiterated or accepted in the New Testament (Kaiser, 1983; Tiemstra et al., 1990; Birch, 1991; Blank, 1992; Brett, 1992; Sider, 1997; Blomberg, 1999). Given the detailed exposition for each of the Table 3.1 measures above, the derivation of each of the Table 3.2 principles should be clear. For instance, the overall tenor of the ten Table 3.1 measures was argued above to be trending in the direction of greater equality of opportunity and outcome, item 1 of Table 3.2. Since the transposition from Table 3.1 to 3.2 should be self-evident, no further discussion is provided on this matter.

Table 3.2. Normative Socio-economic Principles Derived from Ten Mosaic Law Measures

1. Distributional encouragement is toward greater equality of opportunity and outcome.
2. Market processes are to be modified by regulatory constraint.
3. Prevention of poverty takes precedence over relief of poverty or welfare.
4. The poor are to be assisted to economic independence via loans and jobs.
5. The able-bodied poor achieve their socio-economic independence through self-owned jobs.
6. The disabled are to be supported in reasonable lifestyle, incorporating jobs where appropriate.
7. Poverty is to be eliminated formally and socially, not only by voluntary charity.
8. The family is to act as a protective base against its members' poverty.
9. The private capital of families is protected subject to all the above principles.
10. Socio-economic principles derive from religious principles.
11. The coterminous application of religious and socio-economic norms is not to be imposed authoritarianly, but depends on voluntary personal adoption.
12. Optimal development depends on adherence to socio-economic and religious principles.

JESUS' TEACHINGS RELATING TO DISTRIBUTION AND THE INTENTIONS OF THE LAW

At this point, some of the sayings attributed to Jesus in the Bible, interpreted by a range of Biblical exegetes, are considered to ascertain if they conform with the principles of Table 3.2 (Beed and Beed, 2005b). No discussion is offered here about the authenticity of the sayings ascribed to Jesus. The assumption underlying the discussion below is that Jesus did make them. Even if the Jesus Seminar and some historical critical scholars are right that Jesus did not express some of His statements in the New Testament but that 'early Christians made Jesus into the spokesman for their own beliefs about him' (Miller, 1999, 23), this does not alter the substance of the argument below. The question then becomes whether the early Christian church rather than Jesus expressed intentions or principles consistent with those of the Law, as encapsulated for particular issues in Table 3.2. This different orientation from the one assumed here might alter the degree of commitment contemporary Christians might be expected to adopt toward the principles of Table 3.2, but they do not alter the substance of that commitment.

Only one principle in Table 3.2 is discussed in this section, number one, that distributional encouragement is toward greater equality of opportunity and outcome. The reason for discussing only this one principle is that it forms the substance of this chapter. The issue under particular scrutiny below is whether Jesus' teachings and actions conformed with, and illustrated the need for, greater equality in the distribution of material goods, that is, greater equality in outcome. Many instances in Jesus' mission would seem to support this contention, even though in each case, Jesus is advocating much more than just greater material equity. For example, Matthew 19:21 has Jesus extolling the rich young man to perfection by selling all he had and giving it to the poor. Of course, Jesus' main message here is not commending enhanced material equity (e.g., Keener, 1999, 475; Hare, 1993, 227), but it includes that advocacy nevertheless. For Luke 18:22 and Mark 10:21, selling all and giving to the poor is a condition for gaining treasure in heaven. In Lk. 12:33, Jesus instructs His disciples to 'sell your possessions, and give alms.' In all these cases, selling all, and distributing it to the poor point in the direction of greater equality in material distributional outcome than would prevail otherwise. This orientation is apparent also in the case of Zacchaeus, the rich chief tax collector in Lk. 19:1–10 who gave half of his goods to the poor, and was prepared to restore fourfold anything he had defrauded. This gesture was extolled by Jesus as salvation on Zacchaeus' house. Certainly, Zacchaeus would still have remained a rich man, but Jesus praises Zacchaeus' action that is consistent with encouraging greater equality in material distribution—even though the story says a great deal more than this (Just, 1997, 715–724; Stein, 1992, 465–470). For instance, in giving part of his wealth to the poor, Zacchaeus was showing repentance for his past sins. By demonstrating his faith in Christ, Zacchaeus was gaining his salvation and eternal life. But Zaccheus' decision involved action and works. As Jesus said in Jn. 14:21 and 14:23, the decision to love Jesus involves following His commands and word. In this case, Zacchaeus acted consistently with Jesus' commands encouraging greater material equality. Jesus' emphasis on the need for greater sharing of material goods is also crucial to criteria that will be applied to people for entering the kingdom of God at the Day of Final Judgement (Mt. 25:31–46). Here humankind will be divided into two groups, with those on Jesus' right hand entering the kingdom, 'for I was hungry and you gave me food, I was thirsty and you gave me drink, . . .' The righteous on Jesus' right hand would wonder when they had ever done these things for Jesus; 'And the King will answer them, "Truly, I say to you, as you did it to one of the least of these my brethren, you did it to me."' Biblical exegetes disagree over who the 'least of these my brethren' were: the disadvantaged, outcast and persecuted generally, or just Jesus' disciples (e.g., Patte, 1987, 352; cf. Harrington, 1991, 358), but this does not alter the substance of the case here. The 'necessary compassionate action toward the weak and the poor' (Malina and Rohrbaugh, 1992, 151) would result in greater equality in material distribution. That Jesus advocated greater equality in material distributional outcomes is consistent with accepting that poverty in both the Old and New Testaments can be caused by oppression, laziness, misfortune and voluntary choice.

All the examples above of Jesus' behavior and teaching so self-evidently advocate greater material equality that it hardly seems necessary to dissect further their content via the interpretations of Biblical exegetes. In any case, no Biblical exegete contradicts the claim that Jesus was advocating greater material equality in the texts above, irrespective of other differences in interpretation. Each of those texts has Jesus saying a great deal more than merely advocacy of greater equity, but they do say that. As is clear from the texts, Jesus was extolling the intentions of the Law concerning economic distribution, but He was also opening up new dimensions to those intentions. He was amplifying and extending them, applying them in new contexts, and teaching them with a new spirit. Of course, Jesus did far more than this. His main message was that *He* was the path to personal salvation. Whoever believed and had faith in Him was on the road to eternal life. But to open the gate to eternal life required two things. One was to have faith in Him as God's Son, as the Messiah. The other was to obey and carry out His commands, and these commands reflected God's age-old intentions for human living, applicable to both the individual person and to the social whole. Under scrutiny here is that the existence of wide disparities between rich and poor is contrary to those intentions. There is no implication in Jesus' teaching that the creation of wealth is undesirable, and indeed it was extolled in the Law. Unshared wealth was the problem. But Jesus also taught this particular intention in new directions and with new implications from both the Law and the prophets. He showed that the pursuit of unshared riches diverted people from seeking the kingdom of God, that it contradicted the care people should exercise for their less fortunate fellows, and that it produced a society rent by covetousness and greed.

Throughout His ministry, Jesus stressed these latter messages in many ways. One was His cautioning that the rich would find it difficult to enter the kingdom of God, that 'it is easier for a camel to go through the eye of a needle than for a rich man to enter the kingdom of God' (Mk. 10:25; Mt. 19:24; Lk. 18:25). Jesus said this after telling a rich young man how to win eternal life. Jesus told the man to sell all his possessions and give the proceeds to the poor so he could follow Jesus. The man could not bring himself to do this and went away with a heavy heart. Again, the implications of this story go far beyond relative riches and encouraging greater material equality (Keener, 1999, 477–478; Hagner, 1993, 562). The choice to follow Jesus invariably involves giving up things people value, be they riches, family, fishing, collecting taxes, burying the dead, or saying goodbye to those left behind.

Jesus agonized over the unsharing rich because their wealth was a barrier against pursuing the kingdom of God. His pity and compassion extended across all economic groups, even to those with great wealth, as in 'woe to you that are rich, for you have received your consolation' (Lk. 6:24). Jesus was showing that excessive, and therefore unshared, relative wealth produces a myopic self-oriented worldly contentment that gets in the way of commitment to God and of following God's intentions for living. In this way, Jesus was teaching the principles of the Law in a new spirit. He was not merely denouncing the rich as the prophets had done. He was lamenting that their relative riches obstructed His calling to them. Thus, Jesus did not go around condemning the rich, or tax-collectors, or any others sinners. Instead, He called them to return to God and His ways, and to believe in Himself as the Son of God.

The ways in which unshared riches undermine God's intentions are explained by Jesus in the parable of the rich man and the poor man (Lk. 16:19–31). Here, the rich man ends up suffering everlasting torment in Hades, while the poor man, Lazarus, is received into heaven. The evil of unsharing is one point of the parable (Green, 1997, 604–610; Ringe, 1995, 216–218). As Abraham explains to the rich man, 'remember that you in your lifetime received your good things, and Lazarus in like manner evil things.' Realizing that he cannot be saved, the rich man appeals to Abraham: 'send him

[Lazarus] to my father's house, for I have five brothers, so that he may warn them, lest they also come into this place of torment.' Abraham does not agree to this request because the brothers 'have Moses and the prophets; let them hear them . . . If they do not hear Moses and the prophets, neither will they be convinced if some one should rise from the dead.' The relevance of Moses and the prophets is as discussed earlier in this chapter, the rules laid down in the Law about the responsibilities each man had for the wellbeing of his fellows. In this particular parable, the rich man suffers his fate because he did not ameliorate the material state of the poor man on earth. Both the lack of action by the rich man to relieve the suffering of the poor man, and the suffering of the poor man, are condemned by Jesus. Jesus was teaching that differential riches and poverty were only produced by ignoring God's norms in the Law. The unsharing rich, in the process of becoming and remaining rich, are not able to behave consistently with the intentions of the Law. Getting rich with others remaining poor contradicts these intentions, for it does not allow the rich to practice piety, humility and uplift of the poor. The parable suggests far more than the rich man suffering his fate only because he did not give alms to the poor man. Nor does it mean that only the 'evil' rich will suffer, those who have gained their riches through robbery or fraud. Similarly, it does not suggest that only the 'deserving,' 'moral' or 'status' poor will be rewarded. Lazarus is taken into heaven only because he was poor (irrespective of status) and had a life of suffering.

There is a clear theme throughout Jesus' teaching that giving is more important than receiving, that the main purpose in life is to love others as much as oneself. This love is to be action oriented, helping others practically. This message is reflected repeatedly in Jesus' sayings, from His encouragements toward greater material equity, to rendering practical aid, as in the story of the good Samaritan (Lk. 10:29–37). Even Jesus' adage, 'you cannot serve God and mammon' (Mt. 6:24; Lk. 16:13) reflects this orientation, for the pursuit of unshared wealth runs the high risk of fostering self-centered greed and the worship of money, at the expense of one's fellows (Keener, 1999, 233–234; Blomberg, 1992, 124). It can so easily lead to a denial of the Old Testament Law norm, 'you shall love your neighbor as yourself.' Giving back and sharing with the poor is a message also in Jesus' teaching on inviting guests to a party (Lk. 14:12–14). Do not invite your friends, brothers, relations or rich neighbors. No! Ask the poor, the maimed, the lame, the blind, and so find happiness. Again, in the parable of the feast (Lk. 14:16–24), the host instructs his servant to go out and invite 'the poor and maimed and blind and lame' when the invited guests refused to come. All the texts above encourage greater equality in material distribution than would exist otherwise, even though they have much more to say than this. For example, the last parable implies Israel as the invited guests who refused to come, and the outcasts as the Gentiles who were belatedly invited (e.g., Fitzmyer, 1985, 1053; Bock, 1996, 395).

Jesus practiced what He preached about unshared wealth. He and His disciples lived with little personal property. What they did have, they shared with each other and the poor. They survived from a common purse (Jn. 12:6; 13:29), which, at times, was provided by the money of people who traveled with them (Lk. 8:3). There is disagreement about whether Jesus came from a poor or a middle income tradesman's family. But there is no question that He lived a lifestyle meant to show God's compassion for the economically unfortunate, as well as for those oppressed in other ways, like illness. Jesus administered to all groups in society, including the impoverished and socially outcast. He sought out those despised by the conventional secular and religious establishment, lived in a way with which they could identify, and healed them. The oppressed saw no social barrier between themselves and Jesus. Clearly, Jesus' lifestyle aimed to show God's love for all people who were created of equal worth in His eyes. The idea of equality in economic distribution is only one aspect of the care and love God intends for all people. Jesus demonstrated all aspects of God's love for all people. By His life and ministry to the oppressed, Jesus embodied God's care for humankind. He was the living witness as God on earth to *all* God intends for people. Again, this is the application of God's intentions in the Law but in a new spirit.

Potential inconsistencies in Jesus' teaching on material equity can be considered. One possible discrepancy in Jesus condemnation of excessive relative wealth and of unsharing behavior is in the parable of the talents and the pounds (Mt. 25:14–30; Lk. 19:11–27). Here, the master berates the lazy servant for not investing the master's money with the bankers so the master could receive it back with interest. The servant had not done this, and further angers his master by claiming that the master is a hard man, reaping what he does not sow and gathering what he does not winnow. This 'worthless' servant is accordingly cast into 'the outer darkness' where 'men will weep and gnash their teeth' (Mt. 25:30). Ostensibly, this parable has Jesus praising personal enrichment, and rewarding those who reap what they have not sown (as well as accepting the payment of interest). The parable seems to punish those who do not enrich their masters, and reward those who do. It looks like a contradiction of Jesus other teachings advocating greater equality in material distribution, and concern for one's fellows.

Neither in conventional exegesis (e.g., Blomberg, 1992, 375; Hagner, 1993, 737; Fitzmyer, 1985, 1232–1233; Bock, 1996, 487–488) or in non-standard 'peasant' exegesis (reviewed in Wohlgemut, 1997, 103–120) is the message of this parable focused on money, interest or personal enrichment, any more than the parable of the sower and the seed (Mt. 13:1–23; Mk. 4 :3–20; Lk. 8:4–15) is on seed, sowing or farming. Conventionally, the parable of the pounds and the talents is taken to mean that each person is to use her talents or gifts for the master God's purposes rather than for personal glorification. If one does this, one's gifts expand through doing God's work. If people hide their talents and do not use them for God's work, they will be taken away, perhaps ossifying or decaying through lack of correct use, or misdirected into incorrect purpose. People's talents expand in their correct manner as they are used for God's work, which is up to each person to discover in cooperation with God. This interpretation also implies that when a person is asked to do something by God, she is expected to carry it out to the best of her ability. God's criterion of judgement is not the extent to which the person succeeds in the task, but the motive or spirit with which she undertakes it.

A parable reveals its message under the guise of another suggestively similar situation, it explains something in terms of something else (Jones, 1999, 21–22; Shillington, 1990, 16). The actual descriptive narrative of the parable need be no more than a vehicle for the real message that may be a moral or spiritual argument (e.g., Sider, 1995, 84). Moreover, the person telling a parable may even describe situations or use terms he does not like to get his message across. They are merely situations and terms with which his listeners are familiar. Jesus Himself did this at times. For example, in the parable of the waiting householder, Jesus likens God to a 'thief' who comes when he is not expected (Mt. 24:43; Lk. 12:39). In the parable of the unjust steward, 'the master commended the dishonest steward for his shrewdness' (Lk. 16:8). Again, in Luke's version of the parable of the talents (Lk. 19:11–27), the master was 'hated' by his citizens. They were ultimately rewarded by being slain in the master's presence. It would be mistaken to conclude that Jesus approved of hard men, slaughter, burglary, dishonesty, torture (in the New English Bible's version of Mt. 18:34), beating (Lk. 12:48), or self-mutilation (Mt. 5:29; Mt. 18:8–9), just because Jesus does not condemn, and therefore appears to implicitly approve, these modes of behavior. Jesus was not moralizing on the detail making up the narratives of His parables. The point of Jesus' parables is not to interpret them at face value but to discern their underlying message or moral; they are a challenge to understanding, to organizing and transforming situations (Gowler, 2000). So, when Jesus has the master in the parable of the talents (Mt. 25:27) admonishing the 'wicked' servant for not having invested his money at interest, Jesus was not implicitly accepting the morality of interest, any more than He accepted it for human slaughter or burglary. To use this particular Matthean text as evidence that Jesus encouraged the payment of interest, as Barr (1980, 92) does, is to misread the purpose of Jesus' parables.

Jesus used parables to challenge people's established modes of thinking, to confront minds that had become gross, ears dulled and eyes closed. As He said of such people (Mt. 13:13–15), 'seeing they do not see, and hearing they do not hear, nor do they understand.' To those who did understand the meaning of the parables, however, the path to the kingdom of God was revealed. Repeatedly, people did not want to accept Jesus' message, or were not able to. Jesus recognized this (Mt. 13:14; Jn. 12:40) as the fulfillment of Isaiah's prophecy where God is reported as saying, 'Go and say to this people: Hear and hear, but do not understand; see and see, but do not perceive.' In like vein, Jesus asked the Jews in Jerusalem, 'why do you not understand what I say? It is because you cannot bear to hear my word.' Precisely the same message was reiterated by Paul after Jesus' death (Acts 28:26–28).

A second possible inconsistency in Jesus' teachings advocating greater material equality might be seen in Jesus' reported statement, 'you always have the poor with you' (Mt. 26:11; Mk. 14:7; Jn. 12:8). Jesus might seem to be inferring that there will always be rich and poor, even when the kingdom of God comes, or irrespective of any measures taken to rectify the material situation of the poor. In this sense, Jesus' statement 'has paradoxically become a watchword of callousness' (Sloyan, 1988, 153). However, it is possible Jesus' statement suggests something different. The alternative reading might be reflected in most widely-used translations of the Bible, such as the Revised Standard Version, the New Jerusalem, the King James, and the New English. None of these render the texts above as 'you *will* always have the poor with you,' akin to the New International Version. The present tense of 'you have' is the correct translation from the original Greek. Jesus may well be talking in the present tense, relating to the social environment of His day. He may well be saying to His disciples that the poor are with you always 'and whenever you will, you can do good to them' (Mk. 14:7). In a somewhat related manner, Mann (1986, 557) suggests 'the possibility exists that this was a Markan contribution in the distress of his own times and of his own community.' The expression in Jn. 12:8 of the Revised Standard Version captures this intent well: 'the poor you have always with you . . .' The 'always' cannot be interpreted in the context of the above texts to mean that the poor *will* exist forever. The Greek word translates as 'always,' 'at each moment,' habitually,' 'continuously.' (Miranda, 1982, 59–61). The meaning of Jesus' statement is that the poor are all around Jesus and His disciples constantly, all the time, habitually, they are everywhere. Admittedly, most exegetes do not interpret Mt. 26:11, Mk. 14:7, and Jn. 12:8 in these terms. They apply the 'always' to the future when Jesus' disciples will not have his physical presence (e.g., Whitacre, 1999). Mally (1986, 53) puts it that Jesus contrasts His own fleeting presence among men with the inevitable continuance of poverty. However, in so far as Jesus was extolling the need to help the poor materially in these texts, this interpretation does not tell against the idea that Jesus was still encouraging greater material equality.

The similarity of Jesus' statement in Mt. 26:11 to that of Dt. 15:11 is sometimes used as evidence against our interpretation above. Dt. 15:11 has God saying that 'the poor will never cease out of the land,' apparently contradicting Dt. 15:4–5 in which 'there will be no poor among you . . . if only you will obey the voice of the Lord your God . . .' Contemporary Biblical commentators do not view the two Deuteronomy texts as contradictory. For McConville (2002, 259–261) and Christensen (2001, 313), Dt. 15:4–5 sets out the ideal that would be achieved if God's commands were followed, while Dt. 15:11 describes the imperfect reality that is achieved. Even if Jesus were citing Dt. 15:11, the permanent existence of an economically poor stratum this side of the kingdom of God on earth as the imperfect reality can coexist with Jesus promoting God's commands, as per Dt. 15:4–5. As this chapter argues, those commands in the Law would enhance material equality.

Another indirect and tortured interpretation against Jesus' encouragement of greater material equality on earth might be inferred from His aphorism, 'render to Caesar the things that are Caesar's, and to God the things that are God's' (Mt. 22:21; Mk. 12:17; Lk. 20:25). This might be portrayed as Jesus making a distinction between people's activities on earth and their obligations to God. Perhaps these are two separate and disconnected spheres of human behavior. In this viewpoint, as long as people paid their taxes and fulfilled their obligations to their earthly rulers, and their spiritual obligations to God, the equity basis of people's economic situation on earth is of no concern to God. This is a far-fetched interpretation of Jesus' saying that would be inconsistent with the case advocated in this chapter.

Standard exegesis of Mt. 22:21, Mk. 12:17 and Lk. 20:25 (e.g., Keener, 1999, 525–526; Patte, 1987, 309–310; Fitzmyer, 1985, 1293; Just 9:51–24:53, 1997, 773) supports the case made in this chapter. In the saying about Caesar, Jesus is emphasizing the need to give to God all that comes from God: people's lives, talents, commitment, priorities, time and fruits of production. Caesar can have what is left—which, to Jesus, should be nothing of any value to God. The issue is between two separate kingships. Money and coinage are used by Jesus as a metaphor to represent one of the things of little value to God. Produced by Caesar, money and coinage can be returned to him. Jesus had already taught that no man can serve two masters in 'you cannot serve God and mammon' (Mt. 6:24; Lk. 16:13). To Him, there was only one master, God, and all competing masters were of lesser account, whether Caesar, money, possessions or family. This interpretation does not deny that people have duties to both God and man. There is no question that people have spiritual and earthly responsibilities, but they are dependent on each other rather than mutually exclusive. Being a Christian does not excuse people from having responsibilities to one's fellows.

Given the context where Jesus is reported to have stated the text in question, it could even be regarded as an insult to Caesar, but so profound that no action could be taken against Him. Jesus is shown a coin by Pharisees and Herod's men who, it is emphasized in the text, are trying to trap Him. If Jesus rejects that the tax should be paid to the Roman emperor, He will be arrested (which He is not yet ready to be). If He agrees that the tax should be paid, He runs the risk of alienating the people of Jerusalem, a majority of whom was probably opposed to Rome's rule over them. Jesus avoids both traps set by His enemies. He sidesteps the issue and turns it back on his adversaries. Those who had been sent to trap Him do not know what to make of the answer, another case of their hearing but not understanding. Jesus was being more than just ironic in His reply. He had already singled out money as one of God's major competitors in the world, if not *the* major competitor. On being shown a piece of money, Jesus says give back this false god to where it came from—the civil government.

JAMES BARR ON JESUS AND THE LAW

All the above discussion on Jesus' teaching leads to a reasonable presumption that Jesus taught and lived the intentions of the Law relating to economic distribution, even though He interpreted them in completely new ways. These included expounding the potential dangers inherent in excessive relative wealth. It would have been totally meaningless to Jesus' listeners in the context of His day for Him to berate people for not practicing the Law's measures relating to economic distribution, as expounded in this chapter via Table 3.1. By Jesus' time, none of those measures were followed, and most had probably been long forgotten by most people. The socio-economic structures of Jesus' day were totally inimical to the practice of those measures, and they could not have been applied without enormous social, economic and religious reform. Nevertheless, the argument of the previous section is that Jesus proclaimed the intentions or principles underlying those Mosaic Law measures, namely, the necessity for greater equality in material distribution. Jesus promoted the intentions and principles inherent in the Law relating to economic distribution. We do not, therefore, agree with the contention of the economist Christian, Wilson (1997a, 72) that 'questions of wealth distribution are not addressed in the teaching of Christ.'

Not all Christians are convinced that Jesus unswervingly promoted the intentions of the Law *per se*. Barr (1983, 17), for instance, holds that in contradistinction to the 'strong eudaemonistic element' in 'many parts of the Old Testament'—one certainly upheld in the Law—in Jesus' ethical teaching 'these considerations are greatly minimized.' This section examines this contention in more general terms than just relating to economic distribution. Barr illustrates his claim above with examples relating to the emphasis on family cohesion in the Old Testament, and to the reward of wealth to great men like Abraham and Job. If these are taken to be underlying intentions of the Old Testament, then, according to Barr, Jesus did not uphold them. However, the reward of wealth to particular God-fearing men cannot be regarded as a normative intention or principle of the Old Testament as a whole, and much less of the Law itself. More examples than Abraham and Job are reported in the Old Testament of wealth accruing to those who did *not* follow God. For instance, the psalmists and the early prophets frequently lament of the rich who both ignore God and persecute the poor. The psalmists and prophets cry for God's deliverance of these poor. Again, there are God-fearing men in the Old Testament, such as Moses or Joshua, who are never reported as becoming rich. Further, God-fearing men like David and Solomon became rich by flouting the Law's precepts. There is just no consistency in the Old Testament of the relation between acquiring wealth and fearing God. A theological prosperity doctrine applied in the Law only to the whole Israelite society, rather than to individuals within it, in so far as that society was obedient to God. As the discussion above of the distributional content of the Law showed, the eudaemonistic or welfare-enhancing nature of the Law discriminated against the rich and in favor of the poor. Like the Law, Jesus taught that individual riches can become a stumbling block to obedience to God, but they were not in themselves intrinsically so as long as they were shared.

The second of Barr's examples above of Jesus' ethical teaching supposedly contradicting the eudaemonistic element of the Old Testament Law is in relation to the family. Evidence for this is that Jesus taught that 'the family is a threat to one's obedience to God' and 'one has to be ready to drop one's obligations to it' (Barr, 1983, 17). Barr does not cite the Biblical texts to which he is referring, but presumably, he implies Mt. 10:34–37, Lk. 12:51–53, and perhaps Lk. 21:16. Nor does Barr provide exegetical analysis or evidence to support his judgements. Like the wealth of Abraham and Job, Barr gives only his own interpretations. By taking individual texts at their face value, rather than assessing them in relation to other texts, one could cite Mt. 7:9–11 as evidence that Jesus underlined the necessity for good parental care, Mk. 14.36 and Mt. 21:28–31 that Jesus stressed the necessity of obedience of sons to fathers, and Lk. 18:15–17 that Jesus valued children. Each of these texts is saying much more than these things alone. According to common Biblical exegesis of Mt. 10:34–37, for instance, (e.g., Hagner, 1993, 291–293; Blomberg,

1992, 181)—one text to which Barr presumably refers—Jesus was showing that anything could become a barrier to commitment to God. Any form of idolatry could perform this function, including the family. Jesus was not commenting on the welfare-enhancing or eudaemonistic value of family life so emphasized in the Old Testament. He was showing, contrary to any surface meaning of the words of the relevant Old Testament Laws concerning the value of family, that loyalty to the triune God came first—which is exactly what the Law said anyway. As a standard Catholic commentary puts it for Mt. 10:34–37 (McKenzie, 1986, 81), 'if the gospel introduces a division into families, then the disciple has no choice except to prefer the new community to the community of blood.' Jesus was not saying that 'the family is a threat to one's obedience to God,' but that it could be. There is no contradiction between Jesus' message and the Law. Far from claiming that 'the family is a threat to one's obedience to God,' Jesus held the family in high regard. Francis (1996, 81) points out that a pattern emerges in Jesus teaching 'whereby the obligations of family life . . . are both affirmed and transformed' implying 'a certain radical critique of normative patriarchal structures.' From another perspective, a feminist theologian (Jacobs-Malina, 1993, 2) suggests that Jesus actually embodies the lynch pin of family life, that 'the image of Jesus presented in the gospels finds as its closest analogy the idealized role of the wife/mother as was established in the world of Jesus.'

There is no doubt that Jesus reinterpreted the Law, but the question is whether His re-interpretations changed the intentions of the Law. Barr (1983, 15) thinks that Jesus did so. In a third example here, Barr points to Jesus (in Mt. 5:21) emphasizing that judgement falls on those who kill as well as on those who are angry. Since the Law is silent about God's judgement falling on those who are angry with another person, Barr takes this as evidence 'that Jesus in his teaching is not bound and controlled by these laws and goes far beyond them; the law does not constitute the basis and authority of his teaching . . .' (1983, 15). Contra Barr, it is not hard to read into Jesus' Mt. 5:21 statement a correct understanding of the Law's purposes, because numerous regulations of the Law condemned that to which anger leads, including killing. People do not murder (wars and pathology aside) unless they are angry; they do not fight physically and injure unless they are angry, a son does not strike his father except in anger, nor curse him, and so on. The list of such rules in the Law is extensive, but they all presuppose anger on the part of the offender. An underlying or implicit motive being condemned in these regulations is anger toward another person. It is not the case, as Barr argues, that Jesus proclaims 'a spiritual meaning' of the Law while denying its 'literal meaning' (1983, 15), or that Jesus 'spiritualized' the Law's commands (1984, 121). In Mt. 5:21, Jesus is proclaiming one of the Law's intentions which is to avoid becoming angry with another person. There is no need to hold with Barr that 'a new factor, other than the scriptural text, has gained authority and begun to determine the meaning' (1983, 15). Any text, scriptural or otherwise, has to be interpreted to discern its meaning. In the context where Jesus lived, the motive of anger in killing was clear-cut. Jesus is concerned with the motive of people's actions more than with their result. It is curious Barr takes this line in relation to the interpretation of Mt. 5 :21, because elsewhere (1973, 55–57), he illustrates for many texts in the Bible that their 'purport . . . is something quite other than its surface meaning' implies.

The mode of interpretation advocated here for Mt. 5:21 is supported by a variety of Biblical exegetes. For instance, Keener (1999, 181) objects to the depiction of Jesus' sayings in Mt. 5:21–48 as antitheses; rather Jesus is 'interpreting as a good Jewish scholar of his day would,' a view supported by Gundry (1994, 83). In Keener's view, describing them as antitheses indicates that 'prior theological commitments rather than solid exegesis' serve as the interpretive criterion. (Interestingly, the 5:21–48 'passage uses a weak form of "but" that often even means "and".') The motive or intention of the act of killing is the essential point of Mt. 5:21. Keener (1999, 182–183) puts it that 'this text addresses not just how one acts but who one is, that is, one's character . . . the kind of heart that generates such behavior.' The intention of the Law is crucial, for 'God never wanted people merely to obey rules; he wanted them to be holy as he is, to value what he values.' Just as the Law eschewed anger, so 'Jesus' prohibition of acting in anger is a general principle.' Similarly to Hagner (1993, 116), the point of Mt. 5:21 'is that anger, as the root of murder, deserves in principle the same penalty' as murder. Thus, 'Jesus' teachings . . . penetrate to the divinely intended (i.e. the teleological) meaning of the law,' so that 'the ethical teaching of Jesus the Messiah . . . is nothing other than the true meaning of the Torah' (Hagner, 1993, 106, 109).

A fourth example of Jesus supposedly going beyond the Law's underlying intentions is given by Barr (1984, 9). This is Jesus' statement in Mt. 5:38, 'You have heard that it was said, "An eye for an eye and a tooth for a tooth." But I say to you, Do not resist one who is evil . . .' (Jesus was citing the expressions of *lex talionis* from Ex. 21:23–24, Lev. 24:19–20, and Dt. 19:21.) According to Barr, 'the ancient law says one thing, but Jesus says another; what he says is not identical with what the ancient law had said.' Only on a surface reading can it be said that Jesus' statement differs from the intention of the *lex talionis* expression in the context of the Law as a whole. Certainly, Jesus' statement is 'not identical' with the *lex talionis* expressed in Ex. 21:23–24, Lev. 24:19–20, and Dt. 19:21. However, it can be debated whether Jesus actually contradicts the intentions of the Law underlying those expressions. At the least, the exegetical discussion that has ranged over this issue needs to be reviewed, which Barr does not do, and its modern version is surveyed briefly below. The problem with Barr's judgement is that the *lex talionis* expressed in the Law texts above cannot necessarily be regarded as a summary of the Law's approach to wrongdoing, much less of its intentions governing rectification where the Law's regulations were broken. Barr has not analyzed the content, intentions or principles of the Law, and appears to assume that the *lex talionis* expression expresses the mode of dealing with people who broke the Law. Barr has taken one text (Ex. 21:23–24, Lev. 24:19–20, and Dt. 19:21) from the umpteen that constitute 'the ancient law,' and presented it as though it were some sort of summation of the Law's method of dealing with wrongdoing, against which to pit Jesus' Mt. 5:38 statement.

The problems in Barr's rendition above revolve around the intentions of the Law affecting wrongdoing or breaking the Law's codes. It is not the place here to analyze those intentions in general. Biblical exegetes and a long line of analysts, from Daube (1947) through Kaiser (1983) to Wright (1990; 1995) have pursued this task. All that has been attempted in this book so far is to depict some of the intentions of the Law relating to particular aspects of socio-economic life. However, something needs to be said about the intentions of the Law relating to dereliction because Barr's claim above either stands or falls by it. A starting point is to note the numerous instances in the Law where the *lex talionis* expressions of Ex. 21:23–24, Lev. 24:19–20, and Dt. 19:21 did not apply. For example, in Ex. 21:18, when men quarrel and one injures the other but the injured party recovers, the perpetrator was to pay for the loss of the injured man's time. There was no 'wound for wound' of Ex. 21:23–24. Again, in Ex. 21:12, if a man kills another man via God letting the victim 'fall into' the murderer's hand, the murderer could flee to a place of safety. There was no 'life for life' of Ex. 21:23–24. So many exceptions existed in the Law to the *lex talionis* statements of Ex. 21:23–24, Lev. 24:19–20, and Dt. 19:21 that it is hardly worth listing them. This raises the question why all the exceptions occurred. Was the Law self-contradictory, or did the exceptions reflect some other motive?

The *lex talionis* principle was not unique to ancient Israel, but existed in the Code of Hammurabi, Middle Assyrian Laws, and Roman Law, although its application varied widely between these states. Most Biblical exegetes argue that the purpose of dealing with infringements to the Mosaic Law was to ensure 'commensurate punishment for a crime,' that 'retribution was to be fair, not arbitrary' (Rooker, 2000, 297, 298). Accordingly, the *lex talionis* of Ex. 21:23–24, Lev. 24:19–20, and Dt. 19:21 is often regarded by exegetes as having functioned as a guide, was not applied literally (except for murder) or intended for personal vengeance, and operated only in the legal sphere where restitution was usually met by some form of compensation (Gerstenberger, 1996, 366), the latter view reinforced by practice of *lex talionis* in other ancient Near Eastern societies (Levine, 1989, 269).

On the basis of these types of views, Jesus, as the sole authoritative interpreter of the Law, is seen by a variety of Biblical exegetes in Mt. 5:38 as taking the intentions of *lex talionis* one step further. From its origin as unbridled extra-legal revenge, through literal legal retribution, to legal non-literal compensation, Jesus takes *lex talionis* further in a positive direction (that for which it was intended) to the 'overcoming of force' (Luz, 1989, 330). Hare (1993, 55) expresses it that *lex talionis,* having moved from a 'strict' or literal interpretation to money compensation, is taken by Jesus in Mt. 5:38 to a 'love' compensation. Jesus' substitution is by far the more radical. Even Jesus' statement elsewhere (Lk. 6:31; Mt. 7:12), 'as you wish that men would do to you, do so to them,' might be thought of as reinterpreting *lex talionis* from the negative to the positive context. Jesus' inversion (exemplified in Mt. 5:38 and following) places the emphasis on rightdoing to others, not retaliating to wrongdoing. In this, Jesus was only reiterating an underlying intention of the Law; 'you shall love your neighbor as yourself' (Lev. 19:18). As this book so far has shown, specific socio-economic institutional constraints were contained in the Law in an effort to articulate the Lev. 19:18 intention in one sphere of Israel's life. Returning to Mt. 5:38, however, Jesus is interpreted by Keener (1999, 198) as calling on his followers to transcend the previous modes of expression of *lex talionis* because they 'must be so secure' in their 'status before God' that they 'can dispense with human honor.' In similar vein, Long (1997, 62) puts it that the Law 'set human society on a trajectory of moderation and restraint, and, now, Jesus brings that curve to its logical destination.' Although Jesus formally abrogates *lex talionis* in a literal sense, He actually intensifies its application, for Jesus 'is establishing a new covenant in which God's law is internalized in a way that prevents it from being fully encapsulated in a list of rules and that precludes perfect obedience' (Blomberg, 1992, 113). In this manner, Jesus' antitheses of Mt. 5:21–48 oppose 'not so much the law itself but a shallow and inadequate understanding of what the commandment entails' and 'penetrates to the deeper spirit of the law' (Hagner, 1993, 112). Certainly, it might be possible to contend with all these exegetical interpretations of Mt. 5:38 above, but they have to be argued with, not ignored, as per Barr (1984, 9), in relation to exegetical discussion of the issue at the time when he wrote.

The four examples given by Barr above of Jesus allegedly going well outside the intentions of the Law are not persuasive. Barr's exegesis of each of the relevant texts is debatable in so far as little analytical apparatus is used to establish his interpretations, nor are Biblical exegetes cited to support these interpretations. It is not being argued here that all Jesus' teachings represent His re-interpretations of the Law, as though the Law controlled Jesus' teachings absolutely. This issue is not the purpose of this book and has not been examined here—nor has it by Barr. (Nor, indeed, by Barton, 1997, 103 when he claims that 'the teachings of Jesus in the Gospels are for the most part not an interpretation of Old Testament texts at all, not even ostensibly so.') What is claimed here (and by Kaiser et al., 1996) is that where Jesus dealt with the Law, He reinterpreted its underlying intentions in completely new ways but consistently with those intentions. To note that Jesus 'seldom' took 'an Old Testament passage' and expounded it (Barr, 1984, 12), as though this demonstrates that Jesus overlooked the intentions of the Law, is to diverge from the point of Jesus' teachings. Jesus used all sorts of approaches, including parables, to get His message across. Despite Barr's assertion (1984, 12) that 'pre-existing scripture is not the criterion for the truth of a parable,' he does not demonstrate this contention which is debatable anyway. For example, what does Jesus' parable of the good Samaritan illustrate if not Lev. 19:18, 'you shall love your neighbor as yourself'?

Nevertheless, it is still the case that any intention or principle embodied in the Law or reinterpreted by Jesus has to be applied in specific contexts, today's being different from Old and New Testament times. Some examples are provided in the New Testament showing how Jesus applied the intentions to certain concrete situations of His time. But there was no way Jesus could illustrate how all the intentions might be applied in all contexts that face people. It is here that the empirical detail confronting people at the time becomes relevant. It is up to people themselves to make the interpretation and application, in which, say, Christians (and anybody else) might disagree among themselves about appropriate mechanisms. Part of the freedom in Christ available to Christians is to exercise free will, in cooperation with the triune God, discerning the intentions God has for human life and then trying to apply them in the empirical context faced by people. Many Christians probably believe that in some basic degree, these intentions are reflected with reasonable consistency throughout the Bible, that they reflect its teleology, rather than being stated in one or few texts.

FURTHER IMPLICATIONS OF DISTRIBUTIONAL INTENTIONS OF THE LAW

The discussion so far in this chapter supports the following claim: The socio-economic intentions of the Mosaic Law, as distinct from their wording or detail, are relevant to contemporary Christians and the world. Jesus' encouragement of one such distributional intention, discussed above, underlines this claim. In this case, further comment can be made on the relevance to Christians of the universality of the Law's distributional intentions in principle. Each of the Table 3.2 principles above has further implications than as merely revealed in the table. Thus, items 1, 2 and 4 imply that market processes are subject to social control over the distribution of productive assets (in the same way that social constraints, via the Law's administrators, were required to effect the constellation of Table 3.1 measures). Indeed, the tenor of Tables 3.1 and 3.2 is to push toward material equality through control over the distribution of assets more than over the distribution of income. Disparities could remain in income distribution although forces would be operating to diminish them. This latter tendency is comparable to some contemporary secular normative views of distribution. For example, Miller (1999, 249–250) suggests that 'a just distribution of income would be substantially unequal, but the range of inequality would be considerably smaller than the range that now exists in almost all capitalist economies.' The emphasis on asset distribution as distinct from income distribution, occurs in some current economics' discussion. Thus, Bowles and Gintis (1998, 10) construct a case that an implementable class of asset distributions exists that is 'both more egalitarian and more efficient than the concentrations of asset holding observed in most capitalist economies.' On a different tack, item 4 of Table 3.2 does not connote just a non-institutional response to the needs of the less privileged. Formal, direct, social (e.g., governmental) arrangements are consistent with this aim, and item 5 proposes that the able-bodied, poor unemployed are to be provided with productive self-owned and self-managed paid jobs, not workfare-type activities (as canvassed in our Chapter 2). As in the Mosaic Law case, the able-bodied poor are to be encouraged into these jobs in viable enterprises paying a living wage. Certainly, interpretive leaps have to be taken to relate some of the principles to the modern world. For instance, the family unit of items 8 and 9 in Table 3.2 has to be understood in modern terms. The OT extended family in no way serves as the model for today. Protecting the private capital of families (item 9) presupposes the simultaneous pursuit of all other items of the table, so that current inequalities in the distribution of capital would be reduced. Protection does not mean preservation of the status quo. How any of these principles might be translated into action in any specific context is a matter for debate, in which disagreement may exist between Christians.

The Law content investigated above unearthed ethical precepts intended to govern the social distribution of wealth and income in ancient Israel. Issues of distribution, equity and equality are reasserting themselves in contemporary social science and philosophy, including economics, sufficiently to have generated a comprehensive overview economics text (Champernowne and

Cowell, 1998). Partly, this is occurring because of the belated recognition that indicators of inequality have been increasing in at least the last few decades between, and in, most countries of the world. For example, Wolff (1998), Keister (2000), Marger (2002) and Schneider (2004) document recent increasing household wealth inequality in the United States. In Western countries, there is growing recognition that 'programs to assure a modicum of economic security for the poor and to guarantee equality of opportunity for all have faltered in recent years' (Arrow et al., 2000, ix). It was clear above that stringent regulations were laid down for a relatively egalitarian distribution of wealth and income between extended families in ancient Israel (although they were never followed closely). However, the OT Mosaic Law did not pursue just 'equality of opportunity'; it sought equality of outcome as well. This chapter is not the place for evaluating these two approaches to equality. Nevertheless, there is growing contemporary recognition that the equal opportunity approach on its own is insufficient; that it can lead to unforeseen inequitable outcomes (Phillips, 1999, 55–60), so that equality of outcomes is more relevant (e.g., Fleurbaey, 1995). It is also evident above that the OT normative indicators of equality were directed not just at economic quantities such as wealth and income. They also concerned issues of love and community because the economic measures of equality stemmed from these very phenomena. Surprisingly, these criteria also are being raised in current economics discussion of equality. For instance, Hausman (1998, 83; and also Hausman and McPherson, 1996, 138) justifies equality in part because 'inequalities . . . place barriers to friendship, community and love.' More comprehensive evidence than Hausman (1998, 79) cites shows current productivity benefits of equality (e.g., Ben-Ner et al., 1996). Nonetheless, Christians have long emphasized that equality is most effectively justified by the holistic approach characteristic of its system of thought, not by just focusing on narrowly conceived economic factors.

There is an overriding inference from Tables 3.1 and 3.2 that the equitable distribution of private financial capital (as distinct from human capital) is a prerequisite for optimal socio-economic development. Some recent economic thinking also trends in this direction (e.g., Todaro, 2000; Aghion et al., 1999). In one view perhaps contrary to prevailing economics' thinking (summarized in Champernowne and Cowell, 1998, 14), entrepreneurial effort at the micro level is regarded as being stifled by concentrated distributions of wealth (e.g., Blanchflower and Oswald, 1998; Hoff, 1998). At a macro level, Zucker (2001, 142–6) showed that for sixteen developed countries, no relationship existed between levels of inequality and national savings rates. Persson and Tabellini (1994) examined the relationship between income inequality and economic growth in a number of countries from the 1960s to the mid 80s, finding that inequality actually detracted from economic growth. An overview survey (Brandolini and Rossi, 1998) concluded that growth in productivity might actually be enhanced by institutions that encouraged equality. Solimano (1998b, 53) summarized the thrust of these types of studies as 'income inequality deters economic growth.' Similarly, an extensive empirical macro exercise concluded 'that income inequality has [a] significant negative effect on the growth rate' (Hung Mo, 2000, 312). To the extent that income inequality correlates with wealth inequality, these findings support the case here.

Reasons can be proposed why these relationships might hold. With greater equality, the rich may be less inclined to avoid taxation through capital flight or evasion. Less evasion and pressure for redistributive policy may allow either more tax to be collected or tax rates to be reduced, potentially helping to stimulate economic growth. Higher equality in wealth distribution implies more evenly dispersed educational opportunities important to increasing job take-up and economic growth. With greater equality, there may more acceptance of existing distribution levels with less political pressure for redistribution, producing greater social and political stability, and providing safe conditions for investment (Alesina, 1998). Contrary to a common view, higher equality might even lead to higher savings and investment rates, for the majority of the population would have more opportunity for investing. This might be compared with more unequal societies where the poor, the majority of the population, 'cannot borrow to finance even those investments that yield extraordinary returns' (Birdsall et al., 1998, 70), a notable phenomenon in less developed countries.

Although not accepted widely throughout economics, the propositions above conform to those held by some minority schools of economic thought, such as Post Keynesianism. Thus, Arestis (1992, 240, 241) proposes that economic policy should seek to 'reduce the inequalities that exist in a capitalist system,' that 'governments should also strive to promote a more equal distribution of market power and, thus, income and wealth.' Such ideas are consistent with the Judeo-Christian principles of Tables 3.1 and 3.2. These principles are held not only by the Protestant theologians and economists discussed above. They are promoted also by other orthodox traditions of Judeo-Christian belief, such as Catholic Social Thought, although this contention is not illustrated here in detail.

Catholic Social Thought has always depended more on Catholic church teaching (in the Roman tradition) and its magisterium than on direct Biblical interpretation and theology, emphasized by Protestants. However, a lengthy tradition of Papal Encyclicals, Bishops' Statements, and secondary comment by religious and lay Catholics has advocated similar socio-economic equity criteria for contemporary application to those revealed in this chapter. One instance is Williams who has long argued for a model of communitarian democratic capitalism. In (1997), he stresses the holistic interplay of social equality, efficiency, personal liberty and community criteria derived from the 1991 papal encyclical on socio-economic ethics, *Centesimus Annus*. The parallels in principle with Mosaic Law socio-economic organization are clear. They involve upholding a market economy, not as an idol, but including its regulation, a broadening of people's conception of self-interest, the advancement of the poor through voluntary acceptance of regulation, involving job creation, and the redistribution of wealth via taxation. Simons' (1995) review of Catholic Social Thought also points to its affiliation with the Mosaic Law ideal in their common emphasis on personal freedom, equality of personhood, and devotion to the wellbeing of others. He suggests that 'in recent and current Catholic social teaching, inequality has become *the* social question of the age' (1995, 96). Like other strands of Christian thought, of course, unanimity does not exist within Catholic Social Thought about the importance of greater equality in distribution. Thus, Charles (1998, 399) contends that 'the Christian vision of society is not egalitarian . . . that there should be different social classes, and differences of fortune between them, was accepted by the inspired writers of the Old and New Testaments.' No Biblical exegesis or theological reference other than Papal encyclicals is provided to support his contention, and it is not upheld by the analysis of this chapter.

In summary, the example illustrated in this chapter is how selected Biblical exegetes, and Protestant evangelical economists and theologians argue from one source of their Christian beliefs to principles for contemporary application governing the distribution of wealth and income. Within a Christian worldview, the focus has been on the Biblical Old Testament Law and its reinterpretation by Jesus as one fount of principles for achieving equitable economic distribution, and as one input source for socio-economist/Christians in their analytical work. There is a common emphasis in the distributional principles of the OT Law and their Jesus' reinterpretation, with their modern Protestant rendition, and Catholic Social Thought, although we have not considered all aspects of these matters here. Resting on criteria for achieving patterns of more equal distribution, the impracticability of considering distribution separately from the use of wealth and provision of jobs, and that wealth creation is not given priority over distribution, these emphases parallel issues beginning to reassert themselves in economics today.

Chapter Four

Christian Explanations for Unemployment

Previous chapters argued that the Judeo-Christian belief system contains normative intentions or principles for application to contemporary socio-economic life. This chapter (Beed and Beed, 2005a) shows how these principles can be used to construct theoretical explanations for the existence of socio-economic phenomena in modern industrialized economies. A particular example illustrating the process is developed here. Using the normative socio-economic intentional framework of the Judeo-Christian belief system outlined already, the chapter develops particular reasons why unemployment exists in a Western developed economy context. This explanation is compared with selected reasons canvassed in modern orthodox economics for particular types of unemployment. This first section of the chapter outlines its objectives, defends them within the context of social science, and explains the meaning of the term, 'Christian.' The second section proposes a Christian explanation for unemployment, such as occurred in most Western countries since the Second World War. This is approached by using the normative Christian framework for the organization of employment expounded in Chapter 2. The argument shows how unemployment can develop in relation to this system, and might conceivably have developed in Western economies after the Second World War. In the third section of this chapter, particular features of contemporary Western labor markets are outlined to show how they differ from the Christian scenario. Selected frictional and structural causes of unemployment as understood in conventional economics are interpreted in terms of the normative Christian framework outlined in the second section.

Bodies associated with the institutional Christian church have investigated unemployment periodically, a notable Catholic example being publications of conferences by the Pontifical Academy of Social Sciences (such as that of 1999). Less well known might be Protestant examples, like the UK CCBI

(1997). However, unanimity does not exist among Christian explanations for unemployment. The Christian starting point and the inferences drawn from it in this chapter might be dismissed as fanciful, therefore. However, a defense against possible dismissal of the Christian perspective here can be proposed. This is that economic theories, even between themselves, continue to contest which are the most adequate explanations for unemployment. No incontrovertible evidence exists confirming which of the competing economic theories of unemployment is the most accurate and comprehensive depiction of reality.

Economists specializing in unemployment concede this claim. To Junakar (2000, ix), 'we are still a long way from finding a general explanation for unemployment, and Snower and de la Dehesa (1997, xxii) point to the 'fragmentation of perspectives' about the causes of unemployment. A popular economics text complains in relation to two common explanations for European unemployment (structuralist and hysteresis) that 'the various structural factors seem to go in the wrong direction . . . [while] the hysteresis approach also rests on a flimsy foundation' (Gordon, 1993, 340). Jackman (1998, 39–40) noted that many of the conventional correlations between unemployment rates and particular economics' reasons 'are not very stable, and, perhaps worse, they appear to provide no explanation of the variation in countries' unemployment rates over time.' From a more critical perspective, Fleetwood (1999) suggested that tests of mainstream theories relating trade union behavior to unemployment do not satisfy adequate methodological criteria, and that in-use definitions of unemployment do not capture crucial qualities of labor utilization (2003). In general, 'there is not much consensus among economists about what is driving unemployment' (Bell, 2000, 7). Current labor economics textbooks, such as Smith (2003, 367, 377) are more likely to opt for 'eclectic' explanations for unemployment, in which unemployment is explained as a consequence of a range of institutional factors, where it is not always possible to distinguish clearly between those affecting aggregate demand and those affecting the supply side. In this respect, perhaps the situation has not changed much since Bean (1994) canvassed competing economic theories of unemployment. These types of comments could be multiplied. If the criticisms are valid, economic explanations for unemployment rest on less than determinate grounds. At the least, Christian rationalizations provide yet another perspective among the diversity of competing unemployment explanations.

The economics' literature on unemployment also complains that the link between unemployment theory and policy is tenuous. For Junakar (2000, ix), 'we are still struggling to find policies to tackle the problem of unemployment,' while policy makers supposedly 'have become increasingly disillusioned by unemployment theory' (Snower and de la Dehesa, 1997, xxii). Snower (1997, 15) criticizes the 'lamentably little attention' that has been given to the 'simple idea' that 'different theories of unemployment' produce 'different unemployment policies.' Another economics' view (from a Christian), is that we 'seem to have come to a point in the western world where none of the secular experts . . . really know what to do about unemployment' (Birnie, 1996, 26). An exposure of Christian reasons for unemployment contains within it specific policies for reducing unemployment, although these are not detailed here.

As we have implied in previous chapters, many divergent streams of Christianity exist. The decision here is to rely on a particular current in contemporary orthodox Christian thought familiar from previous chapters. This is a middle range in Protestant evangelical tradition (as assessed by Gay, 1991) that has the advantage of possessing its own economics interpretation (Tiemstra et al., 1990; Tiemstra, 1993, 1999), and that claims explicit empathy with Catholic Social Thought. This particular rendering has much in common with other Christian evangelical socio-economic analyses. The latter literature includes Storkey (1979, 1986), Hay (1989), Hoksbergen (1994a), Goudzwaard and de Lange (1995), and Beed and Beed (1996a). The assumption of common essence in economics interpretation between these sources is not justified here, but underpins the argument of this chapter, in which Tiemstra and Hay are taken as the focus. The rationale for analyzing unemployment is that work (paid and unpaid) 'has a central theological dimension within a Christian perspective' (Henley, 2001, 118). At a more general contextual level, the exercise is symptomatic that Christian belief and economics can conceptualize similar subject matters in contrasting ways (Britton and Sedgwick, 2003).

The mode of interpretation in this chapter is called for short 'Christian socio-economic analysis,' and is of a specifically Protestant persuasion. In common with much Christian writing, the terms, 'Judeo-Christian' and 'Christian' are used interchangeably. This is to emphasize the Jewish Old Testament basis on which the New Testament of Christianity rests, and the strong links stressed in the Christian thought above between the Old and New Testaments.

A CHRISTIAN EXPLANATION FOR UNEMPLOYMENT

Ostensibly, the two domains of Christianity and economics might seem to be concerned with incommensurable phenomena. Economics attempts to describe and explain economic reality. It ultimately grounds theory in empirical facts. A popular view of Christianity, by contrast, is that it grounds all in faith and uses stories, parables etc. to reveal God's will. In this view, a Christian approach to socio-economic problems is not generally descriptive and explanatory. Rather, it is prescriptive, advocating what is believed to be God's will. In the evangelical Christian perspective utilized here, this is seen to be a misconception of the methodology the Bible uses to expound its messages. When Biblical methodology is actually studied, it turns out that emphasis is on describing and explaining human behavior, as well as prescribing for it. Biblical thinking (at least as the sources here understand it) and economics pursue *comparable* projects. They both describe human behavior (personal and social), construct theories to explain it, and (for some economists, at least) advocate policies to change it.

In Protestant evangelical Christian thinking, the root cause of the ills in which humankind finds itself entangled (unemployment included) are differences between actual human behavior (personal and socio-economic), and the normative requirements to which God calls humankind, some of which were proposed in previous chapters. To the extent that it exists, Christian socio-economic analysis has to attend to the first descriptive part of this diagnostic process—it needs to describe actual human behavior. Otherwise, it has no way of knowing how existing behavior compares with the normative requirements in principle for human behavior such as those canvassed in earlier chapters. This is where attention to empirical detail comes in. For the second part of the analytical process, a reference point or datum is employed—God's intentions, principles or norms as outlined earlier. Christian socio-economic analysis encourages humankind toward these modes of behavior that do not necessarily conform to the status quo. In one sense, secular economics proceeds by a different route in its analyses. It strives to describe the status quo disconnected from Judeo-Christian norms (and sometimes from any norms in a positive economics framework), and to use this as a base from which to derive explanation and policy. Human behavior as it exists is taken as the datum and source for determining explanation. Given such disparate starting points, it is unsurprising that Christian and secular explanation, and policy proposals, may well diverge. Nevertheless, secular economics also uses reference points from which to construct its explanations—albeit totally different from the Christian. For example, if inflexible wage rates are a reason for unemployment, the datum is minimum wage rates; if the characteristics of secondary labor markets are a reason for unemployment, the characteristics of primary labor markets are the reference point. In principle, this is not different methodologically from the Christian socio-economic analytical process. An understanding of 'causation' exhibited in the two systems of thought is methodologically comparable, a matter explored in Chapters 10 and 13.

The personal, social and economic modes of behavior or reference points to which Judeo-Christian belief calls humankind stem from its entire belief framework. How that framework relates to socio-economic life has been explored in previous chapters and by other evangelical economists (e.g., Hay, 1989). A variety of approaches have been taken historically to investigate the relevance of the Christian belief system to socio-economic life. All have in common the attempt to derive normative socio-economic principles or themes contained in the system held to be applicable to all human societies. Human deviation from these principles is then taken to constitute explanation for socio-economic pathology. Historically, the task of deducing cross-cultural principles from Judeo-Christian belief has proven to be a formidable undertaking in which disagreement has arisen concerning the interpretation of this belief. Even where agreement has emerged in Christian thinking, a further source of potential disagreement stems from the application of any principle to the real world.

Previous chapters noted that two broad strategies have been taken in recent decades for deriving socio-economic principles or intentions from Judeo-Christian thought. The first is deduction from particular theological systems, such as Catholic Social Thought (e.g., Dorr, 1992), and the second is from direct Biblical exegesis (e.g., Wright, 1990). The second approach is the basis here, as derived from the two Christian sources in focus (Tiemstra and Hay). The starting point is to specify a selection of normative principles or norms from Tiemstra and Hay contained in the Judeo-Christian belief system that might be interpreted as relevant for inter-historical/cultural application to employment opportunity and organization. The comparability of the discussion following with Table 2.2 must be kept in mind.

How the principles cited below are deduced by the two sources from their Biblical exegesis is not discussed further here. That would be the subject of a separate investigation. However, it is important to note that the deductions made by the two authors in focus should be regarded as one of a number of possible illustrations of how Judeo-Christian principles might be derived, and how they might be relevant to the problem of contemporary Western-type unemployment. Certainly, each of the cited principles is explicitly regarded by the two authors under scrutiny as provisional, and additional principles can be resolved. Further, as noted above, each principle has to be made operational, in which disagreement between proponents of this approach can occur. Thus, differences could occur concerning the degree to which people existing in an unredeemed, fallen or sinful state, as Judeo-Christian belief puts it, are able to articulate even the principles that are deduced.

Hay initially interprets eight potentially relevant principles (1989, 72–77) from scripture, and Tiemstra et al., sixteen (1990, 109–110). Although the two sources do not express any principle identically, much commonality exists. Examples are that humans have 'a right and an obligation to work (Hay, 1989, 73), understood as the creation of wealth and its distribution, and that remunerated work capable of supporting family units should be available to all seeking it (Tiemstra et al., 1990, 109). An underlying purpose of their lists is to forestall disruption to family units, to maintain their socio-economic viability. Throughout their books, further principles can be deduced. For instance, Hay advocates that 'the legal and fiscal constitution of companies could be changed so that ownership and responsibility is shifted, in part if not completely, to the people who work in it', and he discusses business organizational forms that might encourage this aim. Hay also stresses 'the preservation of institutions such as marriage and family life' (Hay, 1989, 173, 174, 140). Thus, an inference for an ideal, first-best situation from Hay might be that workers as representative of family units should retain ownership and control of the financial capital that provides their paid work. Private financial capital in this context is to be protected in and by the family unit to preserve its stability and security. These deductions are comparable to Tiemstra et al.'s orientations (1990, 201, 202) of workers being encouraged 'to have a major role in decision making in their firms,' and having 'more opportunities for responsible stewardship of their labor' in the comparable types of enterprises advocated by Hay, such as producer cooperatives, 'commonwealth' foundation-owned firms. (Our own interpretations, relying on Biblical exegetes for the derivation of an analogous principle, including its basis from Genesis, are in Beed, 2005c.) These deductions are just one instance from a principle that can be derived from the two works in question, but that do not appear in their consolidated lists of principles mentioned at the beginning of this paragraph.

The principles expressed in the paragraph above have implications for the maintenance of employment within business firms. They imply that the labor force (as representatives of family units) would both retain control of employment decision making, and be united in its desire to maintain employment of that labor force. Being able to employ all workers on offer implies both a job guarantee (Hay, 1989, 174) and job security. It also implies the continual creation of new jobs as old ones are rendered obsolete by technological progress. Both requirements would be bolstered if working family members and units were encouraged to consider their own interests comparably with others (implied by Hay, 1989, 75, 76; and Tiemstra et al., 1990, 109, 110). The most effective framework within the firm for pursuit of this principle is seen above by the two sources to be democratic decision-making. Admittedly, family units and their individual members would possess other motivations in and for their work (for example, to gain personal satisfaction, to create products worthy of God's approval). Nothing is said in the two sources of encouraging competition between family units in work, or between family-based work units. This might be because no normative teaching is seen to exist in the Old or New Testaments encouraging this quality in relation to work (Volf 1991; Beed 2005b). Indeed, the discussion so far suggests that employment cooperation rather than competition within and between family unit representatives is to be the norm.

In the contemporary real world of Western industrial economies, few of the principles above are met. In the particular Judeo-Christian perspective under scrutiny here, lack of the principles is postulated as the cause of unemployment. How the causal influences operate in this explanatory schema or theory are described below. The explanation starts by noting that there is no requirement currently in the real world for family units or their representative members to retain ownership and control of the financial capital providing their remunerated work, and no mandate applies that remunerated work capable of supporting families be available to all who seek it. The real world is characterized often by the separation of ownership and control of corporate or financial capital, and also, that workers neither own nor control the financial capital with which they work in the enterprises where they do work. Labor managed firms (LMFs) are atypical. The unity of motivation and cohesion as per the principles above in controlling and maintaining employment levels is fractured. The three groups in the real world employment relation (owners of capital, controllers of capital, and workers) do not necessarily have cohesive or consonant interests. The equilibrium of interest in relation to employment implied by the principles above is abrogated, in so far as the principles thus far discussed would ideally operate as an integrated whole. For people having a relation to the employment function in the existing real world, different motivations from those implied in the principles above can operate. Asymmetries and principal-agent problems arise. Owners of capital might wish to maximize their returns without considering the employment implications of so doing. Controllers of capital might want to reduce costs of using capital and see reducing employment as a way of achieving this. Workers might strive to increase their wages without accounting for consequent employment effects, and so on. Possibilities and combinations are extensive and diverse, and their individual effects may compound each other. Their common net result may be to undermine the possibility that all who seek paid work can obtain it. In the ways described in this paragraph, unemployment can result. Where coterminous interests do not exist toward maintaining employment, it is unlikely that the competing interests of the different sets of actors will produce full employment by random effect.

The arguments above for a positive relation between the dearth of LMFs in advanced capitalist economies and the existence of unemployment parallel those made in secular contexts. For instance, Doucouliagos (1997, 152) contended that a major cause of unemployment arising from other than failures in effective demand in advanced capitalist countries is asymmetries in decision making power within firms. He reviewed economic arguments for and against LMFs, and concluded they possess net economic advantages over CMFs (capital managed firms), such as being able to achieve greater efficiency through heightened flexibility, worker motivation, etc., partly because they are typically smaller sized than CMFs. There is also empirical evidence that LMFs retain employment more than CMFs when effective demand declines (reviewed by Doucouliagos, 1997, 169). These arguments are consistent with empirical findings that control participation yields greater enterprise benefits where discriminated workforce groups (such as ethnic minorities and women) receive participatory opportunities (Perotin and Robinson, 2003).

Admittedly in the postwar West, governments espouse a commitment to full employment, but do not achieve it. No comparable commitment is expressed for the other principle discussed above—that workers as representative agents of families retain ownership and control of their jobs. It is plausible to suggest that this principle is totally ignored, either as a goal of public policy, or as something the private sector regards as desirable. As well as being thought irrelevant, it is possible that postwar economic trends have undermined the phenomenon of workers owning and controlling the financial capital or means of production of their paid work in the firms in which they work. That is, this principle might be decreasingly attained over time (as well as increasingly regarded as irrelevant). Remunerated employment in the post war period has probably become more concentrated in joint stock companies (characterized by separation of ownership and control) than in other organizational forms. Even where other business forms have grown, such as partnerships, an increasing proportion of workers probably has employee status, rather than part-owner status. The postwar growth of self-employment and small business might seem to counter this claim. However, the greater proportion of employment in small business (including self-employment) is not among owners, or even by family members, but by non-family employees.

This lack of common interest existing in the real world toward maintaining employment in the context of an holistic strategy for socio-economic life may be reflected, too, in the disregard of further principles espoused by the two Christian sources under scrutiny. Perhaps these principles also have become less characteristic of socio-economic behavior in the postwar period. For instance, work is held to require the stewardship of land, its non-human inhabitants and people. 'Stewardship' has the Judeo-Christian meaning of human responsibility in relation to God's creation (the natural environment and people) for the exercise of abilities God entrusts to people (Hay, 1989, 71). A contemporary Christian literature has developed to explain how this responsibility should be exercised in relation to particular domains of human life. Wilkinson et al. (1991) is an early example concerning the natural environment, a field that has since developed substantially. One of the themes of the Christian natural environmental literature is how stewardship is not being exercised appropriately nowadays. Whether it is being exercised more or less appropriately than earlier this century is moot.

In essence, the Judeo-Christian explanation for unemployment can be used to account for the increase in Western unemployment since the Second World War. The explanation stems from the supposition that the body of principles thus far outlined is being met decreasingly in the postwar period. Change in any empirical situation relating to a given principle does not necessarily explain unemployment growth; rather, the effects of empirical changes affecting combinations of principles are instrumental. Against such changes have to be pitted the effects of policies taken to alleviate unemployment. By and large, empirical data do not exist to test even the first of these propositions—that empirical changes *have* actually occurred in the postwar period affecting any given principle. Even so, consider how the effects might be played out. It might be reasonable to postulate that the distribution of financial capital has become less constrained by family ties (however defined) in all Western countries in the last fifty-five years. Increments of financial capital are unlikely to have siphoned to family-based conglomerations, much less to anything resembling family units embodying filial relations between members. In all likelihood, financial capital ownership has become less concentrated in family groupings and more concentrated in non-family assemblages (via joint stock companies), both national and extra-national, the latter reflecting tendencies to globalization. (Data do not exist to document the movement of financial capital to family versus non-family groupings.) This is not to suggest that non-family-based capital groupings *per se* produce unemployment. But, if family capital historically placed a higher emphasis on maintaining employment for family members, as implied by the Christian constraints, the transfer of financial capital to non-family groups in the postwar period could have weakened this orientation, as well as social cohesion.

Again, suppose the size of the ownership base of financial capital has declined in postwar years in particular countries, in the sense of a smaller population percentage owning a greater proportion of capital, as demonstrated for the US by Wolff (1995, 1998) and others. In this case, empirical changes in the real world imply that another principle espoused by the two Christian sources—that private financial capital be distributed more equally among family units, as per Hay (1989, 217) and Tiemstra et al. (1990, 97, 109, 156)—is being less attained. The narrowing of the ownership base suggests that capital owners attain this by seeking to maximize returns. Capital mobility increases, flowing to the highest bidder. Institutional constraints on capital flows decrease. Pressures for deregulation of the financial and banking system increase, and for reducing the progressivity of the income and capital gains taxation systems. Opportunities for high returns are appropriated more easily and less redistributed to lower wealth/income people as readily. The criterion of maximizing return is not necessarily that which maintains full employment. If the total proportion of capital becomes more concentrated in higher wealth groups, they may become less averse to risk taking. The exchange of assets and goods for resale rather than for employment-generating purposes grows. Investors look more to futures markets, for example. One claim about postwar Western capital markets is that, rather than job-creating investment, higher returns have been made in speculative paper investment or property resale. Inequality in the distribution of wealth fuels this phenomenon. In these scenarios, owners of financial capital are more inclined to make capital use decisions on other than employment effects' criteria.

The Judeo-Christian position on the distribution of income and wealth, or the mechanisms necessary to achieve distributional objectives, as the sources above see it, is not discussed here. This was examined for one subset of analogous sources of Judeo-Christian belief in Chapter 3. Recall these prevented or forestalled personal holdings of financial capital and income developing outside an equitable norm range (not involving strict numerical equality). The overriding principle was that 'inequalities in the conditions necessary to achieve the [necessary] standard of wellbeing be corrected to approximate equality' (Mott, 1982, 67). If inequitable tendencies developed in the Judeo-Christian framework because of unexpected occurrences (e.g., death of a breadwinner, or cost saving innovation), guaranteed measures were to be set in train to restore the balance. Where a disadvantaged person could perform paid work, the measures were instituted in a remunerated work or employment-generating context. Persons experiencing unanticipated misfortune (e.g., natural disaster) pushing them below the equitable norm were to be provided with the necessary increment, but mainly in the form of being given paid work. (A different set of redistributional requirements applied to the non-able-bodied poor.) A traditional Western concept of in-kind or money welfare handouts, or workfare schemes for the able-bodied poor is anathema to the Biblical job-based orientation of redistribution (Mason, 1996).

An explanation can be proposed as to why a more rather than a less equal distribution of income and capital leads to higher employment. The explanation is similar to that proposed for a possible positive correlation between greater equality and higher economic growth in the previous chapter. Opportunities for abnormal profit seeking would be more constrained with more rather less equal capital/income distribution. As noted above, super profits in the contemporary context may be less related to employment-generating activity than is the case of normal profit seeking. Capital use decisions in a more equal scenario may be forced to retain more proximate relationships with the actual state of employment-generating investment and thereby stimulate productivity. Even in purely secular terms, greater equality connotes less social pressure for redistributive policies, and greater sociopolitical stability that together enhance employment-related investment (Alesina, 1998, 301). Less pressure for redistributive fiscal policies could imply lower taxation levels thereby stimulating economic growth. Higher outcome equality might even lead to higher savings and investment rates (contrary to conventional wisdom), in so far as the majority of the population would not be precluded from investing. In more unequal societies the majority of the population (the poor) cannot even borrow to finance high-yield activities (Birdsall et al., 1998, 70)—a deficiency that microfinance agencies seek to counter (e.g., Versluysen, 1999). Simultaneously, greater equality suggests less need for the rich to escape taxation through capital flight or evasion. Finally, wealth equality indicates more evenly dispersed opportunities for education, vital for job take-up and economic growth, and perhaps less resort to illegal income-generating activity by those precluded from legal employment.

Only indirect empirical evidence bears on these propositions, and none of it is directly comparable to the Christian requirements for employment. As noted earlier, a series of studies examined the relationship between income inequality and economic growth in a variety of countries from the 1960s to the 80s. The main thrust of this literature was that income inequality inhibited economic growth. Bruno, Ravallion and Squire (1998, 140) stated that reducing inequality benefits the poor through a 'probably higher growth rate.' Although evidence for these propositions is not robust, no longer is the view widely held of a necessary trade-off between efficiency and equity (Stiglitz, 1998, 35).

This type of explanation might seem to run counter to the post 1982 reduction in US unemployment rates and increase in levels of wealth and earnings inequality. These phenomena are not necessarily inconsistent with the Christian explanation for unemployment. Rapid job growth is possible on criteria other than the Christian conditions, ranging from slave labor to exploitive 'sweat shops.' Recent US job growth has borne little resemblance to the Christian characteristics. For instance, the expansion of US post 1982 jobs has been associated with a decline in real wages among the unskilled (Blau, 1999, 13–14; Blank, 1997, 62–63), and with job growth in a 'third-rate,' 'bad job' part-time/casual sector (e.g., fast food selling). These phenomena have produced little job security or upskilling, but have yielded below poverty incomes, all contradicting several of the Christian principles mentioned above. Diminishing improvements in the quality of labor (as well as declining real wages and increasing inequality) have often been posed as a cause of the US decline in productivity growth rates since 1973. In the US, jobs have been marked by lower growth in capital productivity than that, experienced by Australia since the early 70s. The net result of these trends has been a US growth in real GDP per employee from 1973 to 1996, half that of Australia, despite the US having a 1996 unemployment rate 63 percent lower (Gregory and Sheehan, 1998, 296, 310).

In the US as well, it is questionable to what extent the unemployment rate continues to function as a measure of labor non-utilization. Unskilled (male) workers have deserted or never entered the workforce in droves (Murphy and Topel, 1997), surviving on temporary employment insurance, disability benefits, and crime, so that the US now has the highest incarceration rate in the Western world (Elikann, 1996, 5). All these phenomena are anathema to all the normative Christian principles above.

The exposition thus far of a Biblical Judeo-Christian explanation for the growth of unemployment in postwar Western economies has confined itself to phenomena with which economics is normally concerned. Ownership and use of financial capital, behavior of workers toward wages, and environmental effects of employment have been noted. But the Christian explanation proposed here suggests also a host of 'non-economic' factors as contributing to employment. In these matters, Judeo-Christian explanation diverges radically from conventional economics' explanations. For instance, a further principle that can be deduced from Hay and Tiemstra et al. is that mutual interrelationships exist between economic, social and religious considerations, already stated in Table 2.2. Other items in that table relate to secular concerns with institutional forms of employment regulation. Further comment is not made here on 'non-economic' factors. In the Judeo-Christian framework they are held to contribute importantly to the given level, organization and form of employment.

Overall, specific characteristics of the pattern of employment and production can be deduced from the Judeo-Christian principles discussed above. They bear little resemblance to production/employment features of the postwar West. For instance, localized, decentralized, self-managed labor (and commodity) markets are likely to be more pronounced from the Christian constraints. Maintaining employment for families implies lower labor turnover between firms and lower geographic labor mobility than occurs presently. The family-based affiliation and LMF characteristics of production suggest a lower maximum size for enterprises than exists currently. Geographic mobility of capital would also be lower than currently, because capital would not be seeking the highest return attainable (nor would it be achievable). Mason and Schaefer (1990) showed these same Christian-based qualities would extend also to the organization of the state, comparable to the picture of (secular) associative democracy painted by Hirst (1994). Greater equality would exist in levels of socio-economic development and of communal infrastructure provision than currently. The vision is a conglomeration of independent but collaborating worker owned managed enterprises (self-employment, small business, cooperatives, and other forms of employee-ownership and management). These depictions conform with the 'substantial tradition within Christian and particularly Catholic social teaching for a model of collective representation that works for social cohesion and the good of the whole' (Henley, 2001, 123).

Secular expressions of this ideal abound (e.g., Albert and Hahnel, 1991a and b). In the Christian case, a strong religious orientation in economic organization would be evident (for example, praying for production guidance would be the norm), but not connoting an organized institutional church basis or theocracy in so far as voluntary adherence is the rule. Little analogous to this depiction exists in the world currently (one UK worker co-operative instance is described by Sawtell, 2001). Few of the Biblical Judeo-Christian principles have been practiced historically with any degree of consistency, or on sufficient scale to bring the Christian pattern to fruition. Nevertheless, particular characteristics do exist on a secular basis in some Western firms, some of which were started by Christians (examples are described in Macariello, 1999, and Alford and Naughton, 2001). An example is Nucor Steel, the second largest steel maker in the United States, with a specific policy to maintain job security. Bluestone and Bluestone (1992, 148) reported other US companies that guaranteed employment security, and how they achieved it. As noted in previous chapters, perhaps the nearest production example to existing practice of the compendium of the Christian principles is the Mondragon conglomerate of workers cooperatives, instigated from a Christian religious context, but by today having lost this explicit orientation. Chapter 2 mentioned that a number of features of Mondragon do not conform with the required Christian principles, such as the existence of competition and gender discrimination between cooperative workers (Kasmir, 1996; Cheney, 1999). However, the Christian background was instrumental in generating Mondragon's continuing success, including its ability to generate internal sources of capital, and to compete successfully with conventional joint stock company multi-nationals. The experience of Mondragon suggests that Christian-type principles and pre-conditions are not utopian or unrealizable in a contemporary real world context, and do not depend on an unreal conception of human nature.

COMPARISON OF ORTHODOX ECONOMICS' AND CHRISTIAN REASONS FOR UNEMPLOYMENT

In this section, certain mainstream economics' reasons for unemployment are compared with the Christian explanation. Economics' reasons for unemployment can be examined at different levels of explanation. One common three-fold division is frictional, structural and cyclical unemployment, each having its distinct (if sometimes interrelated) causes. Frictional and structural reasons for unemployment are the focus here. The argument is that the Christian explanation for unemployment outlined above encompasses causal influences important in mainstream economics' explanations for frictional and structural unemployment, and that it is compatible with the current secular vogue of eclectic theory.

Frictional unemployment occurs when workers look for first jobs, switch jobs voluntarily, or are prevented from performing jobs on offer (say, because of seasonal conditions). Short-term voluntary or involuntary periods of unemployment result. The Christian unemployment explanation suggests that frictional unemployment possesses the importance it has in contemporary Western economies because few of the Christian pre-conditions are met.

For instance, social mechanisms do not exist to ensure that all the principles might be pursued. If such mechanisms existed, in say the forms advocated by Mason and Schaefer (1990) above, it is unlikely that first workers would need to spend the time they do looking for a first job. The importance of the imperfect information or job search component of frictional unemployment would be diminished. Part of the responsibility of the (local decentralized, democratically controlled) social administration would be to ensure that newly graduating potential workers were able to move into jobs. None of this need imply coercion. The process would be facilitated by the administrative agency encouraging entrepreneurial activities by people wanting to establish new LMF and other types of owner-controlled firms. Workers would be the decision-makers both in running existing enterprises and in developing new firms for new workers in cooperation with existing enterprises, including educational institutions. The job guarantee and the cooperation between work units would push in this direction. Indeed, cooperation between firms is vital to this process. As Layard et al. (1994, 66–67) point out, the main reason manual workers and young people suffer from high unemployment currently is because 'some firms are expanding and some are contracting.' Few modes of cooperation between firms to mitigate this process exist currently.

Frictional unemployment is sometimes thought to be a feature of dual labor markets, with higher job turnover rates, and higher movement in and out of the labor force by teenagers, women and colored people than by white adult males. The existence of dual labor markets is contentious, and competing reasons have been advanced for higher unemployment rates among teenagers etc. However, suppose 'bad' jobs exist in secondary labor markets, marked by low worker control of employment conditions (i.e. low trade union protection), unstable employment duration and tenure, low wages, and lack of promotion opportunities. These characteristics contradict the Christian preconditions for employment. In firms conforming to the latter conditions, all workers would be the decision-makers for employment terms. Workers would make those decisions on the basis of a more considered relation than currently between self-interest and altruism; job security and tenure would be emphasized, pay scales would be flatter than presently, and so on. Little incentive would exist for 'bad' jobs to be produced or maintained. It would become obvious to owners/controllers of firms that the simultaneous existence within a firm of primary and secondary labor markets impairs whole firm efficiency, as well as contradicting the equity criteria embodied in other of the Christian principles.

Thus, reasons for frictional unemployment would be lower than presently if the Christian conditions for employment organization were met. The inevitability and present levels of search and wait unemployment, and of dual labor markets, would be diminished. Some components of frictional unemployment are regarded as desirable currently because they siphon workers from low productivity to high productivity jobs and regions. These components are seen as desirable because (in theory) workers move from 'low-paying, low-productivity jobs to higher-paying, higher-productivity positions' (Jackson et al., 1998, 10:7). That this happens is only because of current structural and locational inequalities in pay and productivity. In the holistic compendium of the Christian principles, pay and productivity levels between jobs and locations would be more equal than presently. A need for efficiency wages to encourage employees to work harder and/or reduce labor turnover would be less pressing in so far as more compelling reasons exist in the Christian constraints for enhancing worker productivity. For instance, the separation between ownership and control in firms is well recognized currently as a depressor of labor productivity. Many studies show that firms with high levels of ownership and control by workers achieve the highest levels of productivity (e.g., Ben-Ner et al., 1996).

The Christian explanation can also be shown to encompass some causes of structural unemployment as economics perceives them. Structural unemployment occurs because changes in skills and locations of jobs respond slowly to changes in consumer demand and technology (although it is not always possible to distinguish frictional from structural unemployment). A mismatch occurs in that affected workers' skills are no longer relevant in time and place. Conventional advocacy favors these workers being retrained and/or relocated. For instance, one source of structural unemployment has been the deterioration of job opportunities in specific geographic locations, such as inner cities and rural areas. Market processes have not been able to rectify these job losses. Nor have public workfare or 'work for the dole' made up the leeway.

The absence in the real world of the Christian prerequisites for employment contributes to this type of structural unemployment. As noted above, existing enterprises and local public agencies (operating as regional organizations) would have the responsibility of maintaining full employment in a region—generating new enterprises and jobs along the lines of the advocated principles. A prerequisite for this process is to research new job opportunities and markets, and train workers for them. Insider-outsider theories of unemployment (also important to cyclical unemployment) would become less relevant, for the existence of 'insiders' (the employed) and 'outsiders' (the unemployed) would be curtailed. Research and training, and coordinated, cooperative decision making (rather than competitive decision making) would be oriented to preventing the types of structural unemployment that have occurred repeatedly in the real world. For instance, only such coordinated efforts could ameliorate effects of the 1970s' situation US car manufacturers found themselves in: That automated technology produced lower costs with fewer workers and/or that a rising market share of foreign cars reduced domestic labor demand in the industry. If lesser divisions of competitive economic interest existed between those having a relation to the employment function in a region, greater unanimity between owner-controllers of capital, as well as with the localized state, might eventuate. Abrupt plant closures and immediate worker layoffs, for example, would be lower than currently. In many respects, the necessary employment-maintaining/retraining steps resemble those practiced by the Mondragon conglomerate of workers' cooperatives (e.g., Mathews, 1999). As noted in Chapter 2, the result in Mondragon was an unemployment rate among the then 30,000 cooperators in the early nineties below 1 percent, compared with a region-wide unemployment rate over 20 percent (Morrison, 1991, 200; Whyte and Whyte, 1991, 155–156).

Certain additional phenomena in the contemporary Western world are posed as exacerbating structural (and frictional) unemployment, such as unemployment insurance, trade unions and minimum wages (e.g., Layard et al., 1994). These phenomena, therefore, can be classified as partial causes of structural unemployment. The Christian explanation for unemployment can subsume these factors as potential causes of unemployment. For instance, the argument for unemployment insurance as a cause of structural unemployment is that the higher the replacement ratio (unemployment benefits compared to actual wages), and the longer the duration of insurance benefits, the more inclined displaced workers are to remain unemployed (Layard et al., 1994, 75–77). Atkinson and Micklewright (1991, 1721) note that these 'findings are far from robust.' However, problems of moral hazard exist because society is not able to guarantee its members a continuing job; unemployment insurance is a fallback second best situation to job security.

Contrary to current real-world practice, a job guarantee and job security would exist in the Christian scenario. This means workers should be able to expect continuous full-time employment up to retirement age, even if not within the one firm. This guarantee is not inconsistent with workers deciding to become voluntarily unemployed as they look for another job. Within the firm, job security would not imply job immobility, for technological change occurs continually, doing away with particular jobs, which is why a simultaneous commitment is implied to job creation. These are neither far-fetched nor unrealizable, being objectives explicitly underlying the establishment and operation of the Mondragon cooperative complex (Whyte and Whyte, 1991, 274). In the existing Western world, few empirical studies exist of the effects of job security provisions on unemployment, compared to studies of effects of unemployment insurance, union strength, etc. on unemployment. Existing empirical evidence is mixed. Blank and Freeman's (1994) review of existing studies suggested no weight for a supposition of higher job security producing higher unemployment levels, echoed by Katz (1998, 21) that 'there appears to be little robust relationship between firing restrictions and overall national employment rates' (and by Jackman, 1998, 47).

The combined effect of the simultaneous practice of all the Christian principles discussed should ensure workers continuing jobs (by and large) because with these conditions most people would actually own their jobs. It would be expected that workers' resort to unemployment insurance (to tide over inadvertent job dislocation) would be less frequent than currently, and of shorter duration. It would be expected, too, that trade unions may play a different role in the Christian scenario than presently, in so far as separation between ownership and control of production would be low. Trade unions have been forced to exist to date because one set of people own most capital (typically), another conterminous set control it, and yet another (majority) set are told how to work with it—all of which contradicts the Christian principles.

Minimum wage legislation has also been presented as a cause of structural unemployment in contemporary Western society, especially among the unskilled and young (e.g., Minford, 1985). Empirical evidence for this proposition is less clear than for unemployment insurance. Indeed, 'in the last few years, the economic effects of minimum wages has been a very controversial topic' (Dawkins, 1997, 187). The contentious debate stimulated by the anomalous findings of Card and Krueger (1995, 2000) appears to be still unresolved. Using different methodologies, various empirical studies have questioned Card and Krueger's findings for the US, such as Neumark and Wascher (2000, 2002), Burkhauser et al. (2000), Neumark (2001), and Bazen and Marimoutou (2002). Nevertheless, a recent US text book summary of this debate (McConnell et al., 2003, 419) is that US minimum wages' effects have been overrated. Empirical data for the UK since the introduction of the minimum wage in 1999 is perhaps more clear-cut. Metcalf (2002, 575–576) summarized it as no evidence that the minimum wage had (yet) affected aggregate employment levels adversely, with the absence of consistent evidence for hours worked, even though particular less-skilled markets were affected, such as residential home care (Machin et al., 2003). Whether minimum wages do or do not reduce less-skilled and/or teenage employment (and on the job skilling, as per Neumark and Wascher, 2001) in particular existing labor markets as they are structured currently might not be greatly relevant to the differently structured Christian scenario. Here, the (ideal) worker owned and managed enterprise would set its own wage structure, (ideally) characterized by sufficient living wages. Each co-operator would receive an equitable share of the net income of the enterprise sufficient to allow her to participate fully in the socio-economic life of their community, as more detailed Christian discussion outside of the sources in focus here shows (Mason, 1987, 1996).

Mainstream economics today addresses a variety of factors affecting the magnitudes of unemployment. The factors relate to wage flexibility, such as efficiency wages, whether of the disciplinary Shapiro and Stiglitz (1984) type, or the gift-exchange Akerlof (1984) type, to hiring, training and firing costs, and to other transactions costs like job search. The factors also include employment insurance and duration dependency effects, trade union behavior, 'insider-outsider' phenomena, labor market segmentation and discrimination, internal labor markets, spatial mismatches, labor retraining, government regulation and/or as 'employer of last resort', path dependency and hysteresis, the effects of trade growth with developing countries, external shocks, and unpriced external costs of all these processes. All these theories contain employment policy implications, such as performance-based wage policies from efficiency wage theory. All the theories relate unemployment to aspects of existing structures of employment organization; for instance, how wages and their levels might be set. They do not proceed to the stage of showing how mechanisms inherent to the functioning of existing employment organization actually produce the phenomena of interest. Thus, if disciplinary efficiency wages are actually paid, mainstream theory concentrates on the employment effects of such wages, not that the ownership/control structures of firms preclude workers from determining their own wages. Existing mainstream explanations for unemployment do not address issues that the Judeo-Christian perspectives of this chapter see as fundamental to account for unemployment in Western (and developing) economies. An economist (Protestant) Christian expresses the thinking behind this judgement in more familiar language:

> The kind of theory about the operation of the labour market to which an economist subscribes will depend on the ideological preconceptions and value judgements which he or she brings to bear on his or her theorizing (Henley, 2001, 129).

The ideological preconceptions and value judgements of the Judeo-Christian perspective on both the labor market and employment organization are set out in section two of this chapter.

Only a selection of frictional and structural factors affecting unemployment has been discussed above. Others such as technological displacement of labor, involving the trend away from blue-collar, manual, unskilled jobs to white-collar, mental, differently skilled jobs, have not been canvassed. Nor have the impact of deregulation of markets, of opening up domestic markets to foreign competition, or of hysteresis been examined as reasons for structural and frictional unemployment. This is not only because of lack of space. It is also because economics' theories relating these phenomena to unemployment in Western countries have not produced determinate results. For instance, the contention that greater labor market flexibility produces lower unemployment (as is sometimes deduced from comparisons between US and Australia, or etc.) is still contested (e.g. Gregory et al.,1999). Again, the natural rate of unemployment (NAIRU) is affected by a host of institutional and historical factors specific to individual countries. Texts like Blanchard (1997, 354) summarize it that 'macroeconomists' understanding of exactly which factors determine the natural rate of unemployment is still very limited', in which there still exists 'considerable uncertainty about the exact list of factors'. This observation is sufficiently widespread to underline arguments for 'ditching' the NAIRU (Galbraith, 1997).

CONCLUSION

Selected contemporary Protestant interpretations of the Judeo-Christian thought system can be used to provide a partial theory explaining certain forms of unemployment in contemporary Western economies. This theory has been compared with a selection of mainstream economics' reasons for frictional and structural unemployment. The conclusion is that the absence of Judeo-Christian normative principles for employment organization causes some factors that economics adduces to explain frictional and structural unemployment. For instance, as noted, some economists have attributed structural unemployment to trade unions forcing wage increases in the post war West above market clearing equilibrium levels (itself a contentious empirical proposition). The Judeo-Christian conditions imply an entirely different role for trade unions from currently, so that no argument could be developed in this scenario that trade unions necessarily exacerbate unemployment. In the Judeo-Christian framework, trade unions' main task would be to ensure the Judeo-Christian employment principles were practiced.

In the absence of the normative Judeo-Christian preconditions for employment, both mainstream and heterodox economics attempt to formulate reasons for unemployment. Both might object to the idea of seeking a normative solution to a so-called scientific problem—the existence of unemployment. This chapter does not accept that unemployment *is* a scientific problem free of normative underpinnings. Moreover, secular economics might not be aware that the Judeo-Christian framework for explaining unemployment exists. Much less might economics be inclined to recognize the necessity of the Judeo-Christian constraints for employment, and may not accept they have anything to do with unemployment. In the Judeo-Christian view, the absence of the preconditions produces an extant real world characterized by dislocation and disequilibrium. Every economics' reason for frictional and structural unemployment discussed here is a reflection of social disorder—the extent to which real-world behavior departs from the Judeo-Christian requirements. An example is efficiency wages 'as a worker discipline device', producing equilibrium unemployment (Shapiro and Stiglitz 1984). To the extent that efficiency wages exist, they reflect an attempt to increase work effort from employees who, by and large, have little control over production decisions, and less stake in production ownership. These are chaotic social characteristics in the Judeo-Christian view under scrutiny here. From explanations such as efficiency wages, economics may seek to derive policies to overcome unemployment. In Judeo-Christian thinking, these are difficult to deduce from a reality embodying the high degree of unredeemed entropy characteristic of modern Western society.

Chapter Five

Socio-Economic Principles in Contemporary Christian and Islamic Thought

Previous chapters argued that a set of consistent socio-economic intentions or principles can be derived from Judeo-Christian thought, and that these apply to the contemporary world. This chapter (Beed and Beed, 2003a) shows that another major religious thought system of the world, Islam, claims a comparable set of such principles. The exposure of these principles in the two major religious belief systems of the world should alert both believers and non-believers. For instance, it is sometimes claimed that the religions of the world, far from fading away, will exercise increasing sway in presenting alternative personal and socio-economic principles to the status quo. Thus, Pope John Paul II was 'convinced that the various religions, now and in the future, will have a preeminent role . . . in building a society worthy of humanity' (CA, 1991, 82). This leader of the major Christian denomination extended his appeal to believers of diverse faiths, explicitly to all Christians, Jews, and 'Muslims who, like us, believe in the just and merciful God' (SRS, 1987, 107). The proposition of comparable socio-economic thought in these religious systems is demonstrated in this chapter through a comparison of some of the principles thus far exposed in Judeo-Christian belief with particular modern expositors of Islamic thought.

The comparison has policy implications for the contemporary socio-economic world. The representatives of the two religious systems examined here argue their systems can serve as bases for analyzing current socio-economic phenomena and for developing policy. Therefore, their contentions and any religious action associated with them, need to be analyzed in relation to secular thought. A potential area of investigation is how such claims measure up to those made by modes of thought not dependent on supernatural bases, making analogous claims to analyzing socio-economic phenomena, like conventional economics. Given that the two religious systems purport to provide personal and social guidance to humankind, another area of potential philosophical investigation is whether such claims relating to economic life require a religious basis.

Different practical reasons relating to economic matters suggest the exposure of socio-economic principles in Judeo-Christianity and Islam is important. Around fifty percent of world population professes allegiance to the two religions, which proportion is gradually increasing. The practical socio-economic-related influence of the two religions remains wide-ranging. Examples are the bearing Christian organizations have on welfare and health policy in Western countries (perhaps increasing with the trend to privatization of formerly government agencies), Christian international aid agencies, Islamic banks in Muslim countries and elsewhere, the Grameen Bank and its mimics, and the influence of Islamic organization in particular countries, such as the mandatory imposition of redistributive religious taxes in particular Muslim countries.

The comparison has philosophical implications for economics as well. For example, one inference relates to the distinction between positive and normative economics. The representatives examined here of both religious frameworks reject the conventional distinction between positive and normative economics for reasons outlined in section two of this chapter. Both systems cast their economic principles in normative terms on the grounds that even a description of what exists in the real world cannot be constructed except by using value-laden terms. Thus, contrary to claims by an author in the academic journal, *Economics and Philosophy*, the examined representatives of each religious system would not necessarily agree that an example of a 'nonethical true-or-false' claim is that 'minimum wage laws will tend to cause higher unemployment' (Weston, 1994, 4). 'Nonethical' (or 'ethical') is not defined by the author, Weston. He does use 'ethically neutral' as synonymous with 'value-free,' so perhaps it might be reasonable to infer that Weston takes 'nonethical' to mean statements devoid of terms embodying evaluation. As the quotation above is expressed by Weston, it is a blanket or ambit claim with no qualification. It is unlikely to be testable as such because the terms 'unemployment,' 'tend to' and 'minimum wage laws' have no absolute or value-free 'true-or-false' description. They are evaluative terms with no clear-cut boundaries. How each term is defined, and how the assertion might be assessed as true or false, depends on evaluations applied in contexts where the terms are identified and measured, and on value judgements employed in the testing procedure itself. On the first matter, for instance, unemployment in one temporal and geographical context is not necessarily that in another. As the empirical controversy over the effects of minimum wage laws demonstrates (initiated by Card and Krueger, 1995), it may be impossible to determine whether some version of Weston's claim does apply in any context. Nor does each religious thought system accept that normative economics is to be confined to propositions containing 'at least one assertion of what is ethically preferable' (Weston, 1994, 5). Normative economics, in their view, encompasses all practical possible economics relating to the real world on the grounds that it is impossible to attain a 'value-free or ethically neutral economics,' something explicitly conceded by Weston (1994, 1, 5).

The initial methodological issue here is how to compare principles with economic implication in Islam and Judeo-Christianity. An extensive and somewhat consistent secondary contemporary literature exists expounding Islam's economic principles and their applicability, although it is not unanimous. For instance, Kuran (1983, 1993a and b, 1995) is skeptical of the practical applicability of the norms of Islamic economics, contrary to its representatives examined here. Nevertheless, of all the systems of religious economics, Islamic economics has been claimed to be that 'best developed' (Oslington, 1999, 2905), and its output dwarfs that from Judeo-Christianity. Certainly, Islamic economics is now sufficiently coherent to have become a standard university subject in some Muslim countries (Chapra, 1993). A limited selection of the Islamic economics literature is used here as the Islamic base, rather than the primary sources of the Qur'an and the Sunnah (respectively, God's revelations to the Prophet Muhammad, and the record of Muhammad's sayings and actions). The assumption that Islamic economics, aided by Islamic tradition, has correctly interpreted these sources to derive principles applicable to contemporary society can be debated, but not here. For the purposes of this chapter, the assumption is accepted. The purview of modern Islamic economics in this chapter is limited to retain manageability in outlining its content. Selections from just two prolific and sympathetic economists writing on Islamic economics are used as sources: Chapra (1992, 1993, 1998, 1999), and Choudhury (1992, 1998).

Both the interpretations of Islam and Judeo-Christianity reflected in this chapter see their belief systems as overflowing with normative economic precepts. One of the currents in orthodox Judeo-Christianity examined in earlier chapters, for instance, proposes 'the almost embarrassing amount of economic guidance the people of Israel had' in the Old Testament (Tiemstra et al., 1990, 92). Nevertheless, the task of exposing economic principles is less straightforward for Judeo-Christianity than Islam. Partly, this is because Judeo-Christianity has diverged from its original unity into diverse streams, perhaps in greater degree than Islam. Historically, the various currents of Judeo-Christianity have often competed against each other, and their relations with secular thought have been checkered. Although the case has been argued in earlier chapters that a consistent set of economic principles also underlies Judeo-Christianity in its primary sources of the Jewish and Christian Bibles, disagreement still prevails in the contemporary secondary literature. For instance, the contributors on Christian thinking in Dean and Waterman (1999) exhibit diverse views, ranging from support for Neoclassical economics to its rejection as incompatible with Christianity. (Islamic economics trenchantly rejects Neoclassical economics.)

The chapter does not debate these contentions. Instead, it discusses economic principles current in one stream of orthodox Christianity. Again, just two proponents of this stream are examined here as representative of orthodox Christianity. First is a middle road in orthodox Protestant conservative or evangelical thought (according to Gay, 1991), the Christian Reformed tradition, that has its own academic economics' interpretation (Tiemstra et al., 1990; Tiemstra, 1993, 1999). This is the current above of orthodox Christianity that argues for a consistent set of economic principles in the Bible. Earlier antecedents of this current are Storkey (1979)—one of the co-authors of Tiemstra et al.—and its later authors are Hoksbergen (1994a), and Goudzwaard and de Lange (1995). This strain of Christian thought has much in common with other Protestant Christian-non-Reformed evangelical treatments of economic matters, such as Mott (1982), Kaiser (1983, 1994), Mason (1987, 1996), Hay (1989), Wright (1990, 1995), Sider (1997), and Hawtrey (1999). Hay (1989) is taken as the second illustrative example of this Christian tradition, a middle road (Gay, 1991) Anglican (Episcopalian) interpretation. All these sources collectively might be classed loosely as depicting an incipient form of 'Christian economics' (and is here so called). They certainly share the view that Judeo-Christian thought in its origins is saturated with economic implications; that 'the Bible writers deal with economic life on almost every page' (Tiemstra et al., 1990, 84). The Christian Reformed tradition also has explicit sympathy with Catholic Social Thought (CST) (Tiemstra, 1999, 87–88). CST, the official teaching of the Roman Catholic Church relating to socio-economic matters, is often held to date from a particular papal encyclical of 1891. The Christian economics sources derive similar economic principles to CST, but this is not demonstrated here.

The terms 'Christian' and 'Judeo-Christian' are used interchangeably in this chapter, but here they refer only to the Christian economics sources above. The identity of the terms reflects the integral interrelationship between the Old and New Testaments of the Bible in the thinking of Christian economics, although this position is not demonstrated here. No contemporary Jewish, purely Biblical (Torah)-based economics exists, although some examples occur relying on the written Torah and its later oral development (e.g., Tamari, 1987). Other Jewish writing related to Christian economics are Jewish social ethics (e.g., Novak, 1992), and direct Biblical exegesis (e.g., Levine, 1989; Sarna, 1991; Tigay, 1996). Both these latter Jewish sources display similarity in principles with economic relevance to the Christian economics sources above (but again, this claim is not demonstrated here).

Accepting the methodology above as legitimate allows comparison of economic principles in the selected representatives of Islamic and Judeo-Christian thought. The approach in section two is to outline progressively a selection of principles posed by the two Islamic economics authors. Each of these is compared in turn with any analogous economic principle revealed by the two 'Christian economics' authors cited above. Not all the economic principles exposed by each of the religious system representatives are discussed. In section two, it transpires that a number of principles with economic inference are common to both frameworks, at least as presented by the representatives dissected here. Section three discusses just two of the principles to permit fuller consideration. This chapter does not proceed to the stage of considering how the principles might be put into practice. That is a separate task, in which differences emerge among believers between favored policy instruments (and again, Islamic economics has developed a more coherent set of mechanisms than Judeo-Christianity). For both Islam and Judeo-Christianity, translating principles into action is the more difficult task than isolating principles *per se*.

The conclusion of the chapter offers a high degree of compatibility in normative economic principles within the examined representatives of Judeo-Christian and Islamic thought. (Interestingly, a similar case seems also to apply to political principles.) This finding does not overlook major theological and ethical differences between the two schemas, but these are not discussed here. *A priori,* the chapter's conclusion may not be surprising. Yet, it does not appear to have been made. For instance, Wilson's discussion of economic ethics in Jewish, Christian and Muslim belief (Wilson, 1997a) treats each system separately and not in terms of common economic themes, or systematic comparison. Theological claims have long existed that the two religions are first cousins in many respects. In this century, the Muslim Indian scholar, Syed Amir Ali, in his classic 1922 *Spirit of Islam*, contended that 'except for the conception of the sonship of Jesus there is no fundamental difference between Christianity and Islam' (cited in Guillaume, 1956, 160). Guillaume himself, in his *locus classicus,* also held 'that the Muslim doctrine of God in philosophical theology is not so far removed from the Christian system until the crucial question of the Trinity comes into question' (Guillaume, 1956, 199). These claims are exaggerated theologically, but to the extent they are true, it is not altogether unexpected that principles with economic implication may be similar in the two systems of thought.

NORMATIVE ECONOMIC PRINCIPLES IN CONTEMPORARY ISLAMIC AND JUDEO-CHRISTIAN THOUGHT

One feature of Islam is that its economic principles are held not to exist independently from the spiritual principles on which the Islamic religion is based; indeed, economic principles stem from the spiritual. The beliefs of Islam are non-dualistic (Choudhury, 1998, 56, 73) in the sense that they apply to both the material and spiritual domains of human existence. By the spiritual domain is meant God's unseen relations with people and vice versa. Within the material, it is not possible to separate God from the personal, social or the economic aspects of human life. Economic (and all) Islamic principles are based on a holistic and all-encompassing worldview or 'underlying philosophy' (Chapra, 1992, 4). This worldview is reflected in the *Shari'ah* (Islamic teachings) that is not of a materialist or naturalist orientation, but reflects the oneness of God (Choudhury, 1998, 60).

The worldview of Judeo-Christianity in relation to the interdependence of the spiritual and the material, as the Christian economics' sources above see it, is analogous to the Islamic. For the economic domain, Tiemstra et al. (1990, 66) express it that since 'the world in which we live comes from God . . . the full meaning of economic activity' has to be recognized 'before God, as well as our dependence on God's providence in the creation.' In this view, 'there is an intimate connection between right religion and proper economics' (Tiemstra et al., 1990, 93). Hay (1989, 309) puts it that the derivative socio-economic principles of Christianity stem from the authority of, and themes contained in, scripture. To a lesser degree, Christian historical tradition is also a source of these principles. Thus, the correct worship of the triune God, including adhering to principles He has laid down, cannot be divorced from correct economic understanding. Christian economics does not represent a return to the early twentieth century social gospel. This is because both personal and social salvation are equally important, that Jesus Christ is taken to seek both to redeem individual people and 'his Church, his chosen people' (Tiemstra et al., 1990, 68).

The qualities discussed above are summarized as principle 1 in Table 5.1. This table lists principles common to Islam and Judeo-Christianity with potential effects in the economic dimension of human life, derived from the sources used here. Each principle in Table 5.1 is abbreviated, and the list is selective. The abbreviation compresses the meaning of each principle that is capable of expansion. The selectivity means that many features relating to economic life contained in Islamic and Judeo-Christian thought are not specified. For instance, both systems believe people through work have an important role to play in pursuing God's plan for humankind. Both see humans as God's representatives on earth, viceregents (*khilafah)* in the case of Islam, made in the image of God for Judeo-Christianity. A difference in degree is apparent, however, by which each system believes that humankind is able to work with God. The Qur'an holds that people are 'by nature good and noble,' and capable of preserving their goodness and nobility in this task 'through the internal, self-regulating mechanism instilled in the inner consciousness of the individual himself' (Chapra, 1992, 202, 221). Judeo-Christianity, on the other hand, sees an inherent flaw in humans in their propensity to sinfulness, as being consciously prone to miss God's mark. Theology makes much of this difference in relation to 'original sin.' But the practical effects of the divergence in relation to socio-economic life can be overstressed. Both Islam and Judeo-Christianity believe people have made a mess of things on earth because they have not followed God or His principles. Acting independently from God's teachings produces only deformed patterns of human social behavior. Distorted social kinds do not possess sufficient coherency to enable economics and social science to extract principles either explaining or predicting this behavior with any precision.

Predominant among the goals of Islam (*maqasid al-Shari'ah*) and Judeo-Christianity are faith in God. This acts as the moral filter through which human relationships can be assessed and decisions made, enabling people to live in correct relationship with God and each other. The articulation of principles related to economic (and any other aspect of) life cannot be undertaken without God's spiritual moral filter or guidance. The moral code is held to 'have a Divine Origin' and 'be backed by belief in accountability before God' (Chapra, 1992, 216). According to Islam, this guidance includes beliefs, values and laws of behavior, that have been provided by God 'through a chain of Messengers, including Abraham, Moses, Jesus and Muhammad' (Chapra, 1993, 5–6). Judeo-Christianity would differ from Islam about the implied significance of these names, but not the general intention.

What are some of these values derived from the moral filter with the potential to affect economic relations? In Islam, relations between people under God should be guided by 'mutual sacrifice and cooperation to fulfil the basic needs of all.' This is because *khilafah* (people existing as God's viceregents) 'implies the fundamental unity and brotherhood of mankind.' Competition is to be encouraged only 'to the extent to which it is healthy, raises efficiency, and helps promote human wellbeing' (Chapra, 1992, 206–207). Again, the similarity of these precepts to Judeo-Christianity's is clear. People are accountable in their behavior to God. But, as well, people's relations with each other are to be guided by the Golden Rule. 'Do unto others as you would have them do unto you' is enshrined in both the Torah and the New Testament. No standing is accorded to unbridled self-interest, greed, acquisitiveness and selfishness. Expressions of Christian intentions by Hay (1989, 75, 76) are that 'every person has a right to share in God's provision' of humankind's 'basic needs of food, clothing and shelter.' Where this does not occur, 'the rich have an obligation to help the poor who cannot provide for themselves by work.' These values or ethical stances governing economic life are encapsulated as principle 2 in Table 5.1.

The view of the Islamic thinking above is that values and moral criteria underlie all economic actions. Such actions can only be described in relation to the values embodied in God's moral filter. This is because humans should submit to no other values than God's (Chapra, 1992, 206). Thus, in both describing human activity and in prescribing for it, value-neutrality is inconceivable. Numerous examples of this criterion apply in the economic sphere. Efficiency and equity, for instance, are to be defined in relation to the moral filter provided by God. Chapra (1993, 7) puts it that 'both "efficiency" and "equity" can neither be defined nor actualized without the injection of a moral dimension into economic pursuits.' He advocates that 'the value-neutrality inherent in Pareto optimality be abandoned' (Chapra, 1992, 246). Another example is that the moral dimension has to be injected into people's pursuit of self-interest, 'so that social interest is not jeopardized even when it is in conflict with self-interest.' Although this will not be achieved by moralizing or sermonizing to people, (Chapra, 1992, 252), all 'policies must be passed through the filter of Islamic values' (Chapra, 1993, 64).

Christian economics similarly does not believe that economic analysis or policy can or should be value-free (Tiemstra et al., 1990, 68–70); 'a pure positive economics, without reference to any value system, is simply not available' (Hay, 1989, 143). Since all aspects of life are to be assessed in relation to God, all economic principles are necessarily normative. They have to be related to the way God made people and intends them to live. Actual, observed human behavior does not constitute a basis for revealing these normative God-given principles or what an economic system might look like if the principles were actualized. Similar to the Islamic, this view has diverse ramifications. For instance, 'the economic health of a nation is not measured accurately by GNP' (Tiemstra et al., 1990, 69) because actual production patterns are likely to contain activity inimical to God's normative principles, such as environmental despoliation. An example from Hay (1989, 142) is his declared inadmissibility of applying cost-benefit analysis to road improvements that might reduce fatal accidents. In his view, monetary values cannot be put on human lives, and road improvements should be assessed by other quantitative and qualitative criteria. Principle 3 of Table 5.1 summarizes the contention of the value-laden nature of economic activity.

Correct modes of economic (and all other) behavior do not arise automatically. In Islamic thinking, people have to be reformed from within to achieve the *maqasid al-Shari'ah*; otherwise, 'nothing can succeed' (Chapra, 1992, 200). As the Qur'an (13:12) puts it, 'God will not change the condition of men until they change what is in themselves.' Likewise, in Judeo-Christianity, people have to be changed from within; in Christian thinking, by the indwelling of the Holy Spirit (Tiemstra et al., 1990, 68). Hay (1989, 15) expresses it that 'the presence and power of the indwelling Holy Spirit' enables 'the believer to deal with his sinful nature and to lead the new life of the kingdom.' However, both frameworks recognize mutual interaction between individual behavior and socio-economic institutions; people are affected by and affect the economic system. Accordingly, efforts have to be made to change both people and system simultaneously. Imposing a host of system controls on its own is unlikely to succeed. Hay (1989, 212) points to one instance of this deficiency, in the failure of state ownership in the former communist bloc to motivate individual moral incentive. A more effective strategy 'would be to change individual preferences' by motivating people 'morally and socially,' as well as instituting system changes (Chapra, 1992, 310). An appropriate balance would have to be found between individual and system in practice so that, for example, the individual will 'not find it possible to serve his self-interest except within the constraints of socio-economic justice' (Chapra, 1992, 252). However, without personal moral change, 'material development with justice is not possible' (Chapra, 1993, 7). For Hay (1989, 173), a revival of Christian social values is needed to change the market economy from its reliance 'on the values of Mammon' and its cornucopia of 'unjust features.' People's preference scales need to be changed to accord with given social priorities through the internalization of values provided by God. Only after resource claims have been passed through the moral filter, can the price filter mechanism take over. Principle 4 in Table 5.1 expresses the common observation of both religious systems that mutual interaction exists between individuals and socio-economic systems.

In Islam, the creation of wealth is part of the *maqasid*. Wealth is an important and indispensable means for realizing human wellbeing, but only a means. Moral criteria governing the mode of its creation and distribution are equally important (Chapra, 1992, 8). These claims have many dimensions. One is that manipulating the earth's resources to produce wealth is a task replete with awesome responsibility because the resources actually belong to God. Wealth does not belong absolutely to those who produce it. People are no more than mere trustees (*amin*), and will have to account to God for how resources have been used and distributed (Chapra, 1992, 207). Various implications flow from this belief. One is that resources are to be used for the common good, and not for the benefit of a few. Another is that wasteful production (and ostentatious consumption) (*israf*) are to be avoided, for wealth can become a form of idolatry (Choudhury, 1998, 111; 1992, 42).

The parallels with Judeo-Christian belief in this area are clear. As with Islam, 'wealth is a sign of God's blessing' but not as an end in itself. It is an effective sign of God's blessing 'only when it symbolizes dependence upon God' and is distributed equitably (Tiemstra et al., 1990, 95). People are not owners of wealth (or anything else), but 'stewards' of God's creation (Tiemstra et al., 1990, 66, 94) who 'do not hold absolute rights to the things' they own. Rather, these are held in trust for 'the rightful owner,' God. It follows that human 'purposes in pursuing economic activity must be those of the real owner of things, namely God.' Otherwise, the generation of wealth can become idolatrous. Christian economics regards this principle for economic life as the most important: 'Humans are stewards of God's good earth.' The earth means all aspects of it, including people themselves (Tiemstra et al., 1990, 93). For Hay (1989, 72), the resources of creation are to be used by humankind to provide for its existence, although they are not to be wasted or to destroy the natural order. Similar implications as for Islam flow from these positions. Belief in preservation and sustainability of the earth's physical resources has generated an extensive evangelical Christian environmental literature incorporating themes such as reduction of waste, sympathetic to Islamic economics (e.g., Wilkinson et al., 1991). Another shared implication is that 'while neoclassical economics operates with the concept of *scarcity* as its basic motif, Christian economics must substitute for scarcity the concept of *entrustedness'* (Tiemstra et al., 1990, 94). Principle 5 of Table 5.1 notes that each religious system advocates the creation and distribution of wealth as an important task God sets for humankind.

In both religious systems, it is believed people are meant to be able to express their stewardship and entrustedness in a productive and creative fashion. Therefore, work is to be available for all people (not necessarily equating to paid employment in Christian economics). Further, work is obligatory for people in so far as both systems believe people have been put on earth to exercise stewardship actively. These precepts infer that work should be of a participatory and communal nature, for work is intended to serve the common good, not just benefit those who perform it. Indeed, the aspect of 'social justice' of 'protecting the needy, the weak, the old, the young and the underprivileged . . . cannot be realized in the absence of productive work' (Choudhury, 1998, 110). Accordingly, it is 'the personal obligation of every person who is physically and mentally fit, to support himself and his family' and 'the collective obligation of the Muslim society to ensure proper training and optimal employment' (Chapra, 1993, 7).

For Christian economics, where people 'are unable to be productive for lack of work . . . biblical principles are not being followed' (Tiemstra et al., 1990, 109), for 'man has a right and an obligation to work' (Hay, 1989, 73). The only good work is that allowing people to be responsible stewards of the earth's resources, including people themselves. A close link exists between stewardship, the participatory, cooperative nature of work, and the returns issuing from it. This link 'gives purpose and direction to work' (Hay, 1989, 74). Thus, work should be of such a nature that people are able to use the creativity with which God endowed them, and at the same time, be oriented to preserving the physical resources of the earth; 'good work is not a "disutility",' but bad work is (Tiemstra, et al., 1990, 110). Work itself can become an idol if not done in cooperation with God. Protection against this happening is the need for regular rest from work, part of which should be spent in communion with God. Overall, work is meant to image back to God His creativity, because people are made in the image of the Creator (Tiemstra et al., 1990, 98). Principle 6 of Table 5.1 expresses the common belief of both religious systems that work is obligatory, should be available for all people, and be participatory.

In both Islam and Judeo-Christianity, wealth is such a potentially good thing that God wants all people to have a fair share of it. An equitable distribution of wealth and income is mandatory in both systems. Indeed for Islam, 'in the *shari'a* the guiding principle of the economy is to prefer distributive equity to maximization of economic efficiency *per se* . . .' (Choudhury, 1992, 41). This Islamic proposition has various dimensions. For instance, it requires that society ensures that the basic needs of the poor and disabled are met (Choudhury, 1998, 110). Chapra (1992, 209, 263) argues that the egalitarian goals of Islam stem from its all-pervading concept of brotherhood and justice (*adalah, a'dl*), and Choudhury (1998, 109) sees social justice as a 'unifying concept in Islamic political economy.' As the Prophet (Mohammed) put it, 'he is not a man of faith who eats his fill when his neighbour is hungry' (cited in Chapra, 1992, 210).

Christian economics expresses similar ideas. Wherever wealth is found in only the hands of a few, 'there biblical principles have been rejected.' Where 'many people are kept from ownership (wealth and means of production) . . . biblical principles are not being followed' (Tiemstra et al., 1990, 97, 109). Christian economics places emphasis on socio-economic principles contained in the Old Testament Law and on the Old Testament prophets who railed against the disregard of these principles. Thus, 'the Hebrew prophets often stress the injustice people have used to gain wealth, and they angrily excoriate the way the poor are enslaved and abused' (Tiemstra, et al., 1990, 96). Isaiah, for example, pronounces a curse on those who have joined house to house and field to field, undermining the equal sharing of land in its original distribution when Israel entered the promised land. In similar vein, Hay (1989, 217) stresses 'that the biblical criteria are addressed to the question of redressing inequality, especially poverty.' Neither Islam nor Judeo-Christianity advocate a flat arithmetical equality in the distribution of wealth and income (however that might be measured). Nevertheless, both promote the poorest having sufficient income and wealth (via the provision of work) to be able to participate fully in the social and economic life of the community. Item 7 of Table 5.1 expresses these common ideas as an equitable distribution of income and wealth being mandatory.

The principles of Table 5.1 are expressed in general terms. They parallel those explored in Chapters 2–4 of this book. From the Islamic and Judeo-Christian sources used for this chapter, it is possible to subdivide each principle of Table 5.1 more finely and to enumerate further principles, to yield further common beliefs with economic implication, as follows:

- The earth's resources belong to God and have been given in trust to people to use in stewardship with God.
- Protecting individual property rights (private property) is compatible with human trusteeship.
- God intends humankind to achieve material prosperity.
- Prosperity will be optimized only in collaboration with God.
- Resources are to be used for the common good and should not be wasted.
- The earth's resources are to be used consistently with environmental protection.
- Decentralized decision making through the market is preferable to other allocative systems.
- Work is integral to God's purposes for humankind.

Table 5.1. Selected Economic Principles Common to Islam and Judeo-Christianity

1. Economic principles are based on non-materialist/non-naturalist worldviews in which economic and spiritual principles are inseparably interrelated.
2. Economic interrelations are to be guided by God, emphasizing mutual sacrifice and cooperation.
3. Values underlie all economic description, and economic actions have value-laden effects.
4. Mutual interaction exists between individuals and socio-economic systems.
5. The creation and distribution of wealth is an important task God sets for humankind.
6. Employment is to be available for all people, is obligatory and should be participatory.
7. An equitable distribution of wealth and income is mandatory.

Sources: Chapra (1992, 1993, 1998); Choudhury (1992, 1998); Tiemstra (1993, 1999); Tiemstra et al. (1990); Hay (1989).

- Work should be participatory, and owned and controlled by those performing it.
- The value of work is assessed by the degree to which it encourages God's holistic program of spiritual and material requirements for humankind.
- Work should be balanced by times of rest.
- Self-interest can only be harnessed for the common good in accountability before God.
- A distinction exists between short-term and long-term self-interest because of Heaven, the Hereafter.
- People should lead modest lifestyles.
- Excessive money and possessions have a corrupting potential on people.
- A distinction can and should be drawn between human needs and wants.
- The non-able-bodied are to be supported in decent lifestyles.
- The state, also accountable to God, has an important supervisory role in the economy.
- Decentralized agencies should perform functions of the state as far as practicable.

This list could be continued. Indeed, Tiemstra et al. (1990, 92) claim that 'of enumerating biblical principles for economic activity there is no end.' Were such principles to be pursued explicitly as a holistic strategy, they would ameliorate many socio-economic problems existing in the world today, such as the negative effects of globalization. A joint preoccupation of Islam and Judeo-Christianity is the quest for justice on earth in cooperation with God. Both systems seek the eradication from human society of inequity, injustice, exploitation and repression (*zulm* in Islam). Realizing optimal human wellbeing (*falah)* and the good life (*hayat tayyibah)* depend on adhering to all the principles above. Both Islamic and Christian economics claim consistency in their economic principles, that each reinforces the other with mutual feedbacks, involving circular and cumulative causation. Both systems recognize that people's moral strength is undermined by deviation from the principles above, leading to socio-economic injustice. As the guide to economic activity, 'the general spirit of Islamic teachings is freedom of enterprise within the value-frame of Islam' (Chapra, 1992, 309). The Christian economics sources would see its mission similarly within the value frame of Judeo-Christianity.

ECONOMIC IMPLICATIONS OF TWO COMMON PRINCIPLES

In this section, just two of the principles in Table 5.1 are explored further to permit their fuller consideration. They are numbers 6 and 7, relating to work and wealth respectively. In both systems, an intimate connection exists between work and wealth. To Christian economics, for example, 'wealth is God's world entrusted to [human] stewardly use and care,' and work is what people 'do to use it and take care of it' (Tiemstra et al., 1990, 103).

Item 6 of Table 5.1 specifies that both Islam and Judeo-Christianity advocate that remunerated employment or work should be available for all able-bodied people, they have an obligation to work, and employment should be of a participatory nature. Islamic economics has a large body of precepts underlying labor and investment reform to achieve these ends. For investment, capital is to be used productively and for employment generation; it should not be hoarded, for instance, as happens commonly in less developed Muslim countries (Chapra, 1992, 304). For labor reform, wages and job security should enable an employee and his family reasonable standard of living sufficient to participate in the life of the community, principles identical with those of Christian economics (Tiemstra et al., 1990, 193, 194). Christian economics extends these ideas, explicitly rejecting the idea of living off the labor of others for those who can work. People should be 'economically free,' for only with this freedom can they 'be stewards of God's earth.' Since 'stewardship is in common with others,' work 'should serve and benefit others and be done in co-operation with others' (Tiemstra et al., 1990, 110), claiming this principle runs counter to 'the radical individualism of modern Western society.'

Rather than trying to tease out all economic implications of the employment-related principle, comment is confined to the participatory nature of work and the ways in which it might contribute to people becoming 'economically free.' Islamic economics advocates employment organization where workers have greater participation in decision making than in conventional joint stock companies or state-run enterprises. Worker participation in ownership and management is seen as an important component of *khilafah* (brotherhood) in a fully Muslim society. To Chapra (1992, 253), 'Islamic values require employers to consider employees as members of their own family.' This means 'that employees be treated with respect and compassion and that their wellbeing be ensured.' Christian economics similarly 'would expect a firm where the members shared a Christian commitment to exercise a greater concern to see that the needs of the families of all its members were taken care of' (Tiemstra et al., 1990, 194). Like Islam, Christian economics promotes industrial reform to encourage 'broad decision-making roles for all workers in the firm.' This is held to be 'a reflection of the biblical ideal of giving each family opportunity for decision making in the productive use of labor and a share of its society's other resources' (Tiemstra et al., 1990, 193).

These precepts about worker participation lead to advocacy of specific employment organizational forms. To Choudhury (1998, 110), 'an Islamic economy may have a significant profit-sharing and cooperative sector.' Chapra (1992, 254–255, 268–269; 1993, 67–8) favors ESOPs (Employee Stock Ownership Plans), profit-sharing schemes, and small and micro enterprises (family-owned and self-employment). Profit-sharing could accrue partly as bonuses and partly as ancillary services (training facilities, medical benefits, housing etc.). This type of participation is seen to harness individual self-interest to social interest at the enterprise level. Worker commitment could replace apathy, reduce industrial strife and increase productivity. ESOPs and profit-sharing also help reduce the concentration of wealth ownership. For Christian economics, Hay (1989, 173) advocates changing the 'legal and fiscal constitution of companies . . . so that ownership and responsibility is shifted, in part if not completely, to the people who work in it.' Like Islamic economics, this means ESOPs, cooperatives, and commonwealth or foundation-owned firms, like the UK Scott Bader chemical company. To Tiemstra et al., these are held to give workers 'more opportunities for responsible stewardship' than typical joint stock companies, and to provide workers with more influence over how their labor is used. Greater equity in internal personnel decisions, in pay rates and in availability of work is achieved within firms where 'workers have a greater role in management' (Tiemstra et al., 1990, 201–202). Involving workers more in decision making within the firm is seen as an effective way of increasing firm productivity. Both Islamic and Christian economics see more smaller firms rather than fewer large ones as the path to achieving these aims.

Profit-sharing (*mudarabah*), as in cooperatives and their like, has wider implications than just related to work organization in Islamic economics. Indeed, 'profit-sharing at all levels of the Islamic political economy is the principal alternative to interest-bearing transactions.' This is because 'the abolition of interest (*riba*) is a mandatory injunction of the *Qur'an* . . .' (Choudhury, 1998, 110), and of the Mosaic Law in the Old Testament. In relation to the latter, Hay (1989, 74) points out that the prohibition on usury (more accurately on interest) within the Israelite community 'meant that savings would be applied within the family enterprise, rather than lent for interest. There were no returns on resources without a direct exercise of stewardship responsibilities . . .' (Ballard, 1994, argues that the prohibition of interest is mandatory also in Christian thinking.) In Islamic thought, interest is believed to be part of a surplus that 'has no role to play in the actual cost of production' (Choudhury, 1992, 133). Indeed, cooperative profit-sharing and its measurement substitutes for the rate of interest in allocating and mobilizing financial resources. Although disagreement persists in Islamic economics about how interest might be defined in contemporary circumstances (a debate reviewed by e.g., Kuran, 1995; Wilson, 1997b), this injunction is one of the pillars of Islamic economics.

The dispersion of decision making in employment *per se* as in worker ownership/management is not seen in either Islamic or Christian economics as *the* means of achieving Table 5.1-type principles. For instance, the worker owned/managed firm can still produce harmful products or generate excessive pollution unless it seeks to operate within the umbrella of the Table 5.1 constraints. As Tiemstra et al. (1990, 202) put it, 'simply giving workers opportunities for responsible stewardship will not insure that they will always be responsible stewards.' Workers need to share the common goals and commitments of the Christian (or Islamic) holistic package.

Since Islam occurs predominantly in less developed countries, much of the orientation of Islamic economics in relation to employment is to increasing the ownership base of (virtually) landless peasants via land reform. This involves the abolition of latifundism, and the development of micro/small rural enterprises, in which Islamic banks could have a crucial role to play (Chapra, 1992, 327–333). Indeed, 'the importance of land reforms for creating the egalitarian and democratic climate that Islam visualizes cannot be overstated' (Chapra, 1992, 267). The concentration of land ownership by absentee landlords, and its perpetuation by moneylenders and the connivance of the state are anathema to realizing *maqasid* (the goals of Islam) (Chapra, 1992, 263–268). If the Islamic laws of inheritance had been followed in Muslim countries, landholdings would not have become concentrated. Similarly, if the Jewish Biblical laws governing landholding (Tigay, 1996; Levine, 1989; Sarna, 1991; Novak, 1992) had been followed throughout Judaism and into Christendom, a wide dispersion of land and capital ownership would have been fostered.

In both Islamic and Christian economics, items 6 and 7 of Table 5.1 are intimately related. Only if people are in paid employment will they have opportunity to exercise their obligations as responsible stewards of God's resources. This is because the 'close link between stewardship of resources, work and returns gives purpose and direction to work' (Hay, 1989, 74). Tiemstra et al. (1990, 234) express it that people need 'access to the goods and services necessary to live and fulfil their God-given roles in society,' they need 'opportunities to develop and use their labor resources and a share of the other resources of society so that can provide for themselves,' and 'opportunities to be responsible decision-making stewards of resources, both in production and in consumption.'

All the proposed work-related reforms above would contribute to a reduction of inequalities in wealth and income. Item 7 of Table 5.1 notes that both religious systems advocate an equitable distribution of wealth and income. Neither schema favors absolute distributional equality, irrespective of problems in defining equality. However, both extol the need to push toward a greater equality than has existed in any past or present society. To Islamic economics, the matter is so important that Chapra (1992, 263) declares the existing concentration of ownership of capital in Muslim countries the most serious obstacle to realizing the goals of Islam. For Christian economics, limitations have to be placed on existing concentrations 'of wealth, income, and economic power' (Tiemstra et al., 1990, 235).

'Proliferation of ownership and decentralization of decision-making' (Chapra, 1992, 263) are prerequisites for attaining *khilafah* (brotherhood). These ideas are compatible with those of Christian economics, that 'each person should have access to resources so that he can exercise his stewardship and provide for himself' (Hay, 1989, 217). In Islam, 'inequalities can be admitted . . . insofar as they are more or less in proportion to skill, initiative, effort and risk.' What is incompatible with Islam are 'extreme or highly skewed inequalities,' although Chapra (1992, 211, 339) also advocates policies to 'minimize inequalities of income and wealth.' Many reasons are advanced why the distribution of wealth and power should be made more equitable than now or at any time in history. Since resources belong to God and are only held in trust by people, no moral justification exists for highly concentrated patterns of income and wealth ownership. Such patterns are incompatible also with other aims of Islam, such as the need to encourage feelings of brotherhood *(khilafah)* among the members of society, and to attain specific characteristics of employment organization in a fully-committed Muslim society. Islamic thought closely relates reducing the concentration of wealth to attaining the reduction of concentration of political power. Socio-economic injustice occurs where 'resources become concentrated in a few hands, people do not fulfil their obligations towards others, the basic needs of all individuals in society are not fulfilled and there is misery alongside affluence' (Chapra, 1998, xii). In most Muslim countries, according to Chapra (1992, 252), 'the concentration of wealth and power . . . has restricted competition, generated widespread collusion, and created a climate conducive to the misery of the masses.' Christian economics would have little difficulty agreeing with Chapra (1993, 62) that socio-economic restructuring should address itself to:

> Reducing the existing concentration in the ownership of means of production as much as possible to complement the role of moral transformation in minimizing the influence of wealth and power in the allocation and distribution of resources.

Various means of achieving greater equality in the distribution of wealth and income are inherent to Islamic belief. These include the *zakat* or *zakah*, a voluntary but obligatory contribution from the well-off to the poor, acting as a specific form of wealth tax. The *zakat* (Choudhury, 1998, 110) is an integral part of Islamic worship, a requirement by God to ensure that the less well off are not deprived of basic needs, and a reminder to the rich that they are not the owner of the resources they have obtained—God is. To Chapra (1992, 272), the *zakat* 'is an absolutely binding religious obligation imposed by the Creator Himself,' and a prerequisite for ensuring that prayers are heard by God. *Zakat* is not to be identified with alms-giving or begging (proscribed by Islam), but a systematic endeavor to uplift the poor. Islamic inheritance laws also contribute to a more equitable distribution of wealth (outlined in Wilson, 1997a, 117–118). Inheritances proceed in a predetermined pattern, including one third for charitable objectives or for people not already in the pre-conditions. The remainder of estates are distributed on a fixed formula, the net effect of which is to ensure wide distribution among the deceased's descendants. The purpose of Islamic inheritance schemes is 'to bring about a broad-based distribution of the deceased person's wealth' (Chapra, 1992, 276). Christian economics takes a somewhat similar view of the necessary instruments to pursue greater equality. For instance, Hay (1989, 218) supports 'programmes that provide employment and access to resources' rather than pursuing 'equality in consumption by redistributive taxation and transfer payments, essential though these may be as a safety net.'

CONCLUSION

This chapter has argued that significant consistency exists in principles with economic implication between the religious belief systems of Islam and Judeo-Christianity, as far as their examined representatives here see it. The sources propose also that these principles are intended for contemporary application. Islamic economics summarizes itself in four principles: the unity of God, maximizing Islamic felicity, work and productivity, and distributive equity (e.g., Choudhury, 1992, 150). The sources of Judeo-Christianity here also appear to conform to their particular expressions of these principles (e.g. they are likely to express it as God-given felicity, and to define God in triune terms).

Economic principles thrown up by Islam and Judeo-Christianity resonate with the historico-institutionalist tradition in economics. Indeed, Choudhury (1992, 127) admits this, that 'Islamic economics can thus be considered a direct derivative of the general theory of humanistic institutional economics with assumptive extensions to other areas of economics with humanistic elements in them.' It is probably more accurate to say that humanistic institutional economics draws (some of) its origins from religious thought, in so far as the religious systems predate the economics by up to two millennia. Tiemstra (1993) explicitly accepts the compatible interrelation between Christian socio-economic thinking and institutionalism, as does Chapra (1999), while attempts to develop Catholic Social Thought into a more fully-fledged economics reflect similar thinking (e.g., Wilber, 1991; O'Boyle, 1998). Hay (1989), on the other hand, is only implicitly sympathetic to this view.

Despite the longevity of economic principles in Judeo-Christianity and Islam, no country claiming a Judeo-Christian or Islamic heritage has ever followed all the spiritual/economic principles contained in those belief systems. Chapra (1992, 9, 235) put it for today that 'the Islamic economic system does not prevail in any part of the Muslim world'; indeed, Islam is 'conspicuous by its absence, particularly in the political and the economic fields.' Unless there is a turnaround, Chapra believes so-called Islamic societies may near disintegrate. In the view of Chapra and Choudhury, it is not unrealistic to aim toward achieving this turnaround. Although difficult, it is nonetheless regarded as just and sane to design a socio-economic system embodying the principles of Islamic economics. This view is shared in relation to Judeo-Christian principles by the Christian economics sources here, and others of a similar Protestant persuasion, cited above, as well as by Catholic Social Thought. But both the Islamic and Judeo-Christian sources of this chapter impose many preconditions on this attainment. For Islamic economics, one of these is to ensure 'that the economic man does not get born, and, if born, does not survive' (Chapra, 1992, 221). These same sources are also skeptical that current practices within Islam and Judeo-Christianity themselves are sufficiently focused to achieve these ends. In their view, the risk is that the two systems today overstress simplistic, liturgical, institutional, other-worldly, emotional and nationalistic attachments to the faiths at the expense of their this-worldly personal, social and economic content. If this is the reality, it is ironic, because most of the contents of the Qur'an and Sunnah, and the Jewish and Christian Bibles are concerned with God's mutual and non-institutionalized relationships with people in the world, at both the personal and social level. These relationships are shown to be inseparable from relations between people themselves. If these holy books do aim to show God's path for humankind, it is unlikely God would ignore economic relations.

Chapter Six

A Christian Perspective on Economics

We have explored how the Judeo-Christian system (and Islam) contains numerous principles applicable to modern socio-economic life. Yet, a common Christian view (e.g., Meeks, 1995, 111) is that 'it has been difficult for modern Christian theology and ethics to relate to economics.' How is this discontinuity to be explained? Meeks evidently believes it occurs because it is 'against the scientific and cultural rules to invade the autonomous territory of the science of economics.' We now move to examine the second proposition of the book, that the Judeo-Christian system takes precedence over secular social science, a view some Christians resist. Christians, such as Meeks, exhibit a deferential quality to economics because of its 'stupendous accomplishments,' and 'the great gains in economy due to the creation of the modern science of economics' (Meeks, 1995, 111–112). Contrary to these beliefs, this (Beed and Beed, 1996a) and the next six chapters argue that for Christians, economic (and social science) theory does not possess an 'autonomous territory,' that calling economics a 'science' indicates little about the nature of the discipline, and that economics itself did not create any 'astounding rise in productivity' and 'living standards of millions of people'—and is certainly not doing so currently. Although we do not examine these last contentions closely, the 'astounding rise in productivity' in the Western world of the last few centuries created the secular discipline of economic theory. Chapters 2–4 argued against Meeks' further proposition that 'not one single technical economic problem of our time . . . can be solved by reference to Scripture' (Meeks, 1995, 112; and 1989, 3). They attempted to rebut Stackhouse's like claim (1987, 382) that it is not possible 'to derive a contemporary, normative economics exclusively from the pages of Scripture . . .'

In recent decades, exploration of the thinking underlying different conceptions of economic theory has flourished. The theoretical bases of Neoclassical, Marxist, Institutional, Austrian, Post Keynesian and other frameworks of economic thought have been investigated intensely. As well, inquiry into 'new' ways of analyzing socio-economic phenomena has accelerated, via critical realism, constructivism, and hermeneutics, and even via religious systems like Islam, as shown in Chapter 5. Probably at no other time in the history of economics as a professional discipline has so much attention been devoted to the philosophical and methodological underpinnings of the subject. Conspicuously lacking from the recent ferment in philosophical/methodological debate in economics (and in all social science), as far as the secular literature is concerned, has been acknowledgment of the relevance of Christian thinking.

Ostensibly, this omission might seem curious in Western countries where the majority of the population still describes itself formally as Christian. Yet, the disregard is not so surprising viewed in the context of the historical development of the social sciences that were mainly an outcome of Western post-Enlightenment non- and anti-Christian thought (Gay, 1975; Manicas, 1987; Gordon, 1991; Olson, 1993). One of the great struggles of Enlightenment intellectuals was to free thinking about natural processes and human behavior from what were seen as the shackles of the Christian church and its dogmatic theological interpretation. Church, as distinct from Christians, had a poor record of toleration of divergent theorizing about human action. It is little wonder that social inquiry tended away from dependence on explicitly Christian doctrine from the eighteenth century.

The metaphysical base on which post-Enlightenment exploration rested was mainly a non-Christian, naturalist and positivist conception of knowledge acquisition (Kolakowski, 1972). In its extremes, this exploration demonstrated justifiable frustration with religious dogma and with the controlling influence the institutional church sought to maintain on the pursuit of knowledge. Non-religious, non-positivist social investigation coexisted as a subdominant strand, making greater headway in the nineteenth century in, say, sociology than in economics. In the event, explicitly Christian philosophy and social analysis disappeared from the secular academic curricula, ending up as minor streams in theological colleges and the like. From about the middle of the twentieth century, the naturalist framework of social science began to erode, drawing on the earlier critique mounted against positivism in the physical sciences (summarized in, e.g., Chalmers, 1982, 1999a). The demise of positivism permitted pre-existing non-naturalist approaches in social science, such as hermeneutics and postmodernism, to gain stronger hold. However, Christian socio-economic analyses experienced no resurgence, probably because of the long-term trend to secularization (Gilbert, 1980), and continue to languish as minorities in some theological schools and Christian colleges.

Yet, the last forty years have seen an upswing of interest in Christian theology and philosophy with social import, and in social science with Christian religious import, although little of this is reflected in secular academic literature or curricula. This conforms to the resurgence of interest in non-naturalist social science (including realism, widely but wrongly regarded as a non-traditional form of naturalism, something discussed in Beed and Beed, 1997). Much contemporary Christian theology is interested in the economic implications of its analysis, straddling a diversity of theological perspectives, including Catholic, Evangelical, and Reformed. Some examples are Gutierrez, 1973; Taylor, 1975; Sider, 1977, 1980, 1997; Boerma, 1979; Hanks, 1983; Clouse, 1984; Wogaman, 1986; Stackhouse, 1987; Hobgood, 1991; Atherton, 1992; Davies, 1993; Gorringe, 1994; and Long, 2000. Simultaneously, there is growing Christian social science literature explicitly exploring the relevance of Christian belief, of which some economics' examples from the previous decade are Nevile, 1979; Storkey, 1979, 1986; Cramp, 1981; Griffiths, 1984; McKee, 1987, 1993; Beisner, 1988; Waterman, 1988; Hay, 1989; Tiemstra et al., 1990; Beed and Gill, 1990; Elliott, 1992; Scaperlanda, 1993; Smith, 1993; Tiemstra, 1993; Daly and Cobb, 1994; Hoksbergen, 1994a; and Lunn and Klay, 1994. In the last decade, this literature has increased markedly. Since the 1970s, North and colleagues at the US Institute for Christian Economics have propounded 'theonomics.' In keeping with all this interest, a US-based Association for Christian Economists has existed since 1982, together with a UK counterpart.

In terms of the latter literature, it could appear that economists who are Christians are endeavoring to formulate a Christian philosophical and methodological perspective in economics. It is tempting to think that this might be yet another paradigm, school of thought or disciplinary matrix being developed in economics. If this interpretation were valid, the Christian perspective would join the range of rival schools in contemporary economics, and compete in the market for acceptance of economic ideas. However, this interpretation is not valid because the economists (and theologians) cited above have no consensus about the relation of their Christian beliefs to economics, or vice versa (Smith, 1993 and Tiemstra, 1993 are surveys of the lack of consensus). This chapter presents a philosophical/methodological view of these interrelationships but its main concern is not to canvass the views of the economists and theologians cited above.

The chapter argues that, while a Christian perspective for analyzing economic issues can be formulated, it cannot serve as a disciplinary matrix potentially capable of competing with secular schools of economic thought on their own grounds. This is because Christian modes of thought differ in such fundamental ways from those underlying secular economic paradigms as to redefine the manner in which economic questions are apprehended. So discrepant is Christian thinking about economic affairs that it is incommensurable with secular analyses of the subject. Insofar as Christianity purports to explain human choice on the basis of its metaphysical framework, it provides an alternative and competing conceptualization to non-Christian explanations of human behavior, of which secular economics is one variant. We endeavor to show why this is so via analysis of three features of the Christian worldview; to show that this worldview is incompatible with that underlying secular economics, and that the two perspectives have divergent methodological implications.

Although there is some common ground between Christian views and those of secular economics, the argument contends that the differences are more fundamental (which is why they are emphasized here). In this way, the chapter argues against the idea of a Christian economic viewpoint, where economics is understood in its conventional meaning. Christian socio-economic analysis and theology is one way of conceptualizing reality, and secular economics/social science is a rival way. This line of argument touches common ground with Hoksbergen's (1994a, 135) contention that all secular schools of economics 'violate basic Christian beliefs at their very core.' It is in the tradition of Christian analysis such as McDonagh (1982), Kilpatrick (1983) and Bulkley (1993) who criticize the foundations of another social science, psychology, and of Clouser (1991), Pearcey and Thaxton (1994), and Johnson (1993, 1995) who deny the naturalistic basis of physical science.

The focus here is on macro philosophical and methodological differences between a Christian and a secular perspective on economic activity investigated via the metaphysical bases of these perspectives. The chapter does not proceed to the micro-level of contrasting the Christian view with characteristics of the various schools of secular economics. That task is feasible, but the chapter is not an intentional critique of any particular secular framework even though the dominant Neoclassical school receives most comment. No case is argued here that the Neoclassical approach to economics has more or less in common with the Christian approach than any other school of economics.

In this chapter, negative methodological implications are drawn out for the study of economic questions. They are negative insofar as they criticize the methodologies of secular economics but do not present an alternative methodology that might be utilized within secular economics. From the analysis of this chapter alone, no guide proceeds available to an economist who is a Christian for practicing a particular (Christian) methodology within what is conventionally thought of as economics. The analysis of just this chapter alone provides no sense to what a 'Christian economist' should do within economics. Economists who are Christians might still work within the various schools of secular economics, although they will probably be influenced by their Christian worldview in the type of work they undertake. But the investigation in this chapter precludes formulating a workable, self-contained, methodologically distinct Christian alternative within the traditional confines of economics (elastic as these might be). At most, it points to an alternative (Christian) philosophical and methodological basis for thinking about economic matters that has more in common with what is traditionally known as theology than economics. The practice of a distinct form of Christian socio-economic analysis was illustrated in Chapters 2–4, and is developed further in later chapters. It should be clear so far that the practice of a Christian socio-economic analysis has little theoretical base in common with secular forms of economics. Nevertheless, they do share, or at least should share, common ground in the analysis of empirical data.

The foci here are differences between Christian thinking and secular economics about how each views economic affairs. Therefore, the analysis does not proceed far into positive philosophical and methodological detail of the Christian view. Some of these elements were explored in Chapters 2–4, and further discussion is in Chapters 13 and 14. Suffice to say that the Christian alternative worldview to the secular (be it Neoclassical or whatever) encompasses the meta-methodological approach of realism (e.g., Trigg, 1989, 1993). In company with other Christians such as Polkinghorne (1991) and Johnson (1995), we term our methodological position Christian or theistic realism, and it is explicitly non-naturalistic. Realism is probably the most commonly held position in physical science today, although its appeal in social science is still muted. Its methodology is oriented to explanation rather than prediction, and realism and instrumentalism are widely held to be contradictory (e.g., Flew, 1984; Sayer, 1992; Lawson, 1994a).

THE CHRISTIAN WORLDVIEW AND ECONOMIC QUESTIONS

This section argues that Christian belief embodies a particular worldview, and the rest of the chapter contends that it has profound implications for the understanding of economic matters. The first contention is commonplace but the second will be shown to be controversial. The first holds that the basic characteristics of the Christian worldview are expounded in the Bible, in the historical teachings of the church (for example, in Catholic social teaching), and in Christian theology. Although there might be unanimous agreement among Christians that a Christian worldview exists, it is difficult to establish consensus about its content. Reviewing the two thousand-year-old debate here is not likely to resolve it. Nevertheless, so the argument can proceed, an attempt is made to distil aspects of the Christian worldview relevant to economic life involving the production and distribution of goods and services.

One possible approach to extracting the essence of Christian teaching relevant to this matter would be to summarize the Christian economic and theological material cited above. Christian perspectives on economic activity could be derived from these and other secondary sources. However, as there is no consensus among these writers, an alternative path is followed that summarizes earlier work, constructed with an academic theologian (Beed, 1990; Beed and Gill, 1990), derived directly from the primary source-book of Christian belief, the Bible. This approach seems more consistent with conventional academic methodology of relying on primary sources, even though it is subject to similar problems of interpretation. In that work, it was argued that the basic characteristics of Christian belief are expounded in the Bible via historical narrative, myth, legend, allegory, fable, parable, poem, proverb, and metaphor. Alternative exegeses of the Biblical text cannot be avoided, but the position taken here, argued from the Biblical text in the earlier work, is that a set of consistent themes and principles is developed and reiterated through the Old and New Testaments as constituting the foundations of Christian belief. Some themes relevant to economic life are listed below, although no Biblical references are cited here to avoid crowding the text (these are enumerated in the earlier work).

Among Biblical propositions taken from the above-cited work to be relevant to economic life are:

1. Human life has inseparable spiritual and material dimensions; the spiritual is pre-existent and the material can be understood only by reference to the spiritual.
2. God (in His trinitarian conception) has normative intentions for human spiritual and material life.
3. The norms include an active, interpersonal relationship between God and people.
4. The norms set the correct or true context for human behavior.
5. Personal behavior and social relationships can be understood only by reference to God's norms.
6. Often, human behavior does not conform to the norms; therefore, the behavior is without its correct foundation.
7. One of the effects at the personal and social level of not conforming to God's norms is that human understanding is blurred.
8. Given this blurring, people strive to understand personal and social behavior by developing modes of interpretation outside of God. These modes are misleading, and possess limited explanatory and predictive power.
9. Humankind is not in a position to help itself (to a great degree) because the subjects (people) are part of what is awry.
10. Diagnosis of human problems must come from outside the human situation, for without God's norms there is no correct understanding of sin.

11. The restoration of human behavior and relationships to their true meaning depends on people coming to live interactively with God, for which faith in God's Son, Jesus Christ, is a prerequisite norm.
12. This restoration can occur only if human independence is recognized as exhaustible, and if people are prepared to give up seeking exclusive faith in their own autonomous understanding and power.
13. The restoration of a person is an ongoing redemptive process by God of re-learning, healing, freeing, etc. from former habits of thought and behavior through the life of Christ within the person.

This list is not exhaustive. Further notions of similar generality could be added, and each item above could be subdivided more finely (Storkey, 1979, 136–139, presents an analogous Christian sociological perspective). The list depicts the authors' particular theological hermeneutics, and only brief comparison is made throughout the chapter with other conceptualizations of Christian belief. It is not possible to demonstrate in this chapter the theological derivation of all thirteen items and to show their unique Christian nature. For the case being presented, the complete list, or something similar, has to be assumed as datum. Subsequent discussion is focused on the relation of the items to contemporary economics, because, at first sight, they might appear to have little bearing on the subject.

Assuming that the above list of thirteen items (or something similar) depicts basic themes of Christian belief, their relevance to economic issues is now explored. Three items in the list (nos. 1, 2 and 8) are taken to show how their methodological applicability differs from that of secular economics in analyzing economic issues. These three items are selected because together they make a coherent and interconnected case. The argument could be made that the other ten items also differentiate Christian and secular thinking about economic issues.

HUMAN LIFE HAS INSEPARABLE SPIRITUAL AND MATERIAL DIMENSIONS

This item claims that human life has an inseparable spiritual and material dimension, in which the material component can be understood only by reference to the spiritual that is the fundamental aspect of human existence. God, the trinitarian, omnipotent creator, and sustainer of the universe, is spirit who seeks a personal relationship with each human being who, in some way, is made in the image of God (McGrath, 1997, 423–426). As Macquarrie put it, man is not intended to be an autonomous entity, but 'a being who is at once answerable for his being and empowered to fuller being, at once the subject of a demand and the recipient of grace' (1977, 213). God gives humans free will to seek this relationship which is intended to guide each person in their spiritual and material life, to be in this way 'a coworker with God in creation' (Macquarrie, 1977, 233). Everybody can opt to ignore this relationship, in which case they miss God's intentions for them, which is one way of conceptualizing the idea of sin. The material lives of believers who actively seek God's guidance are informed by God's designs for them which, nevertheless, can be frustrated by their own actions, by those of other people and by the spirit(s) of evil in the world (Macquarrie, 1977, 238).

From this understanding, the Christian explanation for human action differs from that of secular social science, including economics, and it has methodological consequences discussed below. In the Christian view, human action occurs in response to stimuli operating in the spiritual and in the material dimension. People are understood to respond to impulses received from the material world via their five senses and intellect. But as well, people are considered to possess the essential, separable, and unobservable attribute of spirit. This has the potential for a relationship with the unobservable spirit-entity, the trinitarian God, who is responsible for creating the total framework within which humans function. Other spirits may also exist within this framework, such as the embodiment of evil (the devil). In Christian belief, relationships between these spirits and people influence human action, whether people are conscious of it or not.

This conception of human make-up and action differs from common explanation in secular social science. In a popular secular view, human action occurs in response to tangible and intangible influences occurring in a materialist framework. 'Materialist' is taken to denote the self-existence of matter and energy in which matter/energy depends on nothing more fundamental; reality is identical with and/or relies on matter/energy. Humankind is part of the natural world, similar in physical make-up to other natural things, and not having any supernatural properties, such as non-physical minds. A materialist or naturalist conception of human action depends on that which is apprehended through sense-experience and the intellect, with emotion regarded as derivative from material substance. A separate spiritual dimension of human make-up is not recognized. The idea of a relationship between an unobservable attribute of the human being (spirit) and God (or devil) as affecting human action is not countenanced in, say, the Neoclassical or Marxist framework.

In the Christian view, to understand human behavioral motives, especially one's own, a relationship with the unseen, supernatural, spiritual, trinitarian entity of God is necessary input for attaining clarity. Certainly, God does not compel people to view human behavior from this perspective; humans have free choice about whether to adopt the Christian spiritual/material framework. In Christian belief, it is even possible to progress some distance in understanding God's design for humankind by functioning in an ostensibly materialist context. The second-century Christian theologian, Justin Martyr, explored this issue, with his contention that Christianity brought together the insights of both classical Greek philosophy and Judaism. In this Logos-Christology, Greek philosophy had partial access to truth, the 'logos' or the word, which came to its fullest revelation only in Jesus Christ (McGrath, 1997, 331).

Although the Judeo-Christian theory of human action dates back over three thousand years, it does have modern secular parallels with methodological implications. For example, the astronomer, Barrow (1991) argued that the world might have deep and unusual non-computable aspects to its make-up that may not be very apparent or amenable to conventional scientific investigation. In his view, the human brain and the way it thinks has evolved because it has been effective in making sense of observable reality. But, its evolution might not have depended on understanding less computable aspects of the world. Examples of these could be the processes of quantum mechanics (Davies, 1983), and more intangible concepts like the Gaia hypothesis (Lovelock, 1988), morphic resonance (Sheldrake, 1988, 1990) and Christian spiritual healing (McAll, 1985, 1989). Perhaps the reason the physical world looks so mathematical is that the mathematical aspects can be discerned more readily by the human brain, can be measured, and can even produce a deterministic or stochastic result. However, we may simply project on to the physical world the inner mathematical workings of our brains, and overlook phenomena that do not fit this framework.

Analogously, the fact that spiritual links between God and people cannot be observed does not mean they do not exist. But, since the Enlightenment, the spiritual dimension of human make-up has been downplayed, if not rejected as an idea. The thinking process favored by the Enlightenment repudiated abstract metaphysical ideas like 'spiritual,' and concentrated on ascertaining the nature of the material. Empiricism was favored, observing and measuring aspects of human behavior and the world. On both observational and measurement criteria, the idea of a spiritual dimension to human behavior performs poorly, and increasingly came to be discarded as superstition. As a separate discipline of study, economics began to take shape from the late Enlightenment, in company with other disciplines (psychology, sociology, political science) seeking to understand the nature of human behavior. They all had little time for empirically untestable ideas like 'spirit.' Attention came to be focused on observable phenomena, with the fledgling disciplines dividing up the range of measurable human behavior between them.

The metaphysical framework of Christianity implies that the methodologies of secular social science will have restricted ability to represent the nature of human behavior and relationships, insofar as they ignore the spiritual dimension of human life outlined above. Those methodologies may well be able to explicate corners of the whole web of these behaviors and interrelationships. For example, the rational choice theory of Neoclassical economics may be able to predict some aspects of human choice, Rational Emotive Therapy may be able to prescribe for some aspects of human dysfunction, and so on. But, in Christian thinking, these separate theories and their methodologies will not be able to synergize into an explanatory symbiosis of human behavior. They are not able to position, explain or prescribe for the entirety in an integrated, holistic manner within the context of a coherent, rational worldview (which Christianity believes itself capable of doing).

One illustration of this inability is that the hundreds of thousands of case studies, models, and theories of secular social science, propounded since the Enlightenment, have not coalesced into definitive explanatory or predictive science. This latter observation has been made many times by non-Christian and Christian social scientists (e.g. Diesing, 1972; Trigg, 1985). For instance, confined to economics, the complaint is that 'by the standards of accuracy applied to predictions in the natural sciences, economics make [*sic*] a poor showing' (Blaug, 1997, 695). Or, as a secular philosopher who has written extensively about economics complained, 'why is it that the vast majority of economists are indifferent to this failure of economics to generate the cumulative, practically useful predictions of the sort that other progressive [natural] sciences generally are capable of achieving?' (Rosenberg, 1987a, 217). The polar extremity of this type of thinking is 'the death of economics' (Ormerod, 1994). These claims are not debated in this chapter, but, to the extent that they are valid, they underline the nature of the Christian critique. Social science (economics, sociology, political science, psychology, and anthropology) is a heterogeneous enterprise in which many aspects of theory and practice are contested. It is possible that theorizing about human behavior is becoming increasingly contested and diffuse, despite (and/or because of) the avalanche of information about this behavior. A Christian view is that spiritual links between God and people, eschewed by social science, provide a missing key, although this would not persuade the secular critics above.

All the above serves as a first ground on which formulating a competing methodology for a 'Christian economics' (a Christian economic methodology) is incompatible with approaches in any school of contemporary economics. For instance, it is difficult to see how currently practiced economic methodologies such as instrumentalism could handle non-materialist input. On the basis of theoretical explanation, instrumentalism seeks to predict particular observable aspects of personal and social behavior. In its theories, there is no acceptance that a spiritual, unobservable relationship between God and people either exists or has any bearing on human decision making. The idea would probably be rejected (ridiculed?) by most economists and social scientists. They would probably believe their reasoning powers should function as independently as possible from such superstition. In secular economics, the observable aspects of human behavior with which it is concerned are data, and from these, efforts are made to formulate explanatory and predictive theories. Its data do not include unobservable phenomena that are supposed to exist in a non-materialist realm.

The problem affects also the divergent assumptions underlying the theories of secular economics and Christianity. Any theory has to stop asking 'why' at some point, otherwise an infinite regress occurs. Thus, economics does not usually ask why its given assumptions exist—that question might more commonly be regarded as the province of psychology or biology. So, if secular economics draws its limits within a materialist realm of human behavior (even though no consensus exists for the definition of 'materialist'), Christian theory seeks to progress further, pursuing the 'why' into the spiritual realm. Each approach can get different answers to the same questions. For instance, if Neoclassical economics requires the assumption that people usually behave self-interestedly, why do they? Is it a natural genetic propensity as sociobiology asserts, or is it a reflection of human alienation from God as Christians assert?

In sum, a Christian view of secular economic theories, of their assumptions, and of the methodologies used to test those theories (be it prediction or explanation) is that they are incomplete (a judgement with which secular theorists may concur). But the incompleteness in the Christian view is seen to come from a different source. In its belief, explanation and prediction of human behavior analyzed in materialist or naturalist terms will have only a low order of success because the matter/energy domain is merely part of the context affecting human decision making (and the subsidiary part to boot—although the above discussion has not addressed this issue).

GOD HAS NORMATIVE INTENTIONS FOR HUMAN SPIRITUAL AND MATERIAL LIFE

There are at least two methodological implications of this tenet relevant to economic activity. First, it reflects Christianity's view of what is important in economic life, and therefore what should be studied to understand given economic conditions. Second, it calls Christians to practice particular conducts in economic life, and therefore has policy implications.

The first implication is that Christianity's description or observation of what is important in economic life will have little contextual meaning without reference to God's norms. The idea that observation acquires meaning only when related to norms is not uniquely Christian. A commonly held secular belief is that observation is theory-laden—for example, how unemployment is construed depends on prior theoretical views of what constitutes employment. Here, the norms are definitions of employment. Only with prior norms constituting the basis of theoretical views is it possible for social science to decide what aspects of human behavior should be studied. For instance, the norm might be to define employment as paid work outside the home, but this need not be invariant, e.g., remain unchanging over time—the unpaid work of housewives could come to be regarded as 'employment' eventually. Thus, the 'facts' of personal and social behavior relevant to economic activity acquire meaning only with respect to norms. Values, philosophical presuppositions, ideologies, and so on, come into play all the time in establishing behavioral facts. Although secular economics has typically conflated 'value-free' with 'ethically neutral,' value judgements have a more encompassing definition than this, and they intrude inevitably into all research (Beed, 1992).

This approach is common in Christian thinking. For instance, in the Biblical view, the concept of 'work,' its identification in society, is assessed by its relation to God's norms (Preece, 1991, 1995). If work contributes to increasing inequality in wealth distribution, to environmental degradation, to alienation of one person from another and from God, it is not conforming to God's work norms. The matter is complicated further because different aspects of the same economic activity may contradict and conform to God's norms. Human behavior in all its aspects is likely to be a mixture of actions conforming to God's intentions and of activity contradicting them.

God's norms define the true or correct nature of human activity. That is, humans individually and therefore socially as the aggregate of individuals, have been designed by God to live and work with Him. This being the case, Christianity often has a different view from the secular about what constitutes the relevant set of behavioral facts explaining economic phenomena. For example, secular economics may focus on efficiency and productivity characteristics as affecting output. In contrast, Biblical understanding gives far more weight to spiritual and equity factors as affecting output (Beed and Gill, 1990). The Bible emphasizes 'stewardship, useful work, protection for the disadvantaged and the preservation of institutions such as marriage and family life' (Hay, 1989, 140) as of primary importance to economic life. The different metaphysical frameworks of secular economics and Christianity imply divergent methodological approaches; for instance, each framework has different objects of interest it wishes to study. Each framework proceeds from a different set of behavioral facts and theories regarded as being relevant to the question at hand. Between different paradigms in secular economics these conclusions are accepted widely (e.g., Wolff and Resnick, 1987). Thus, the Marxist paradigm studies social classes and social relations of production as of primary importance in affecting the given state of economic conditions, while the Neoclassical focuses on individual behavior, the act of choice in the market place.

This leads to a second methodological implication of this Biblical theme, concerning practice and policy in economic life. In Christian belief, God calls people to particular normative behaviors, as was argued in Chapters 2 and 3. Christianity is unashamedly normative in its calling for every aspect of life, including economic life. Here, the difference from, say, typical practice in Neoclassical economics is marked. Normative views of what people *ought* to do are usually eschewed in Neoclassical economics, which prefers instead to explain what *is,* i.e., that which exists. In contrast, Christianity holds that the what *is* in human relations can be seen only from a normative perspective (the theory-ladenness of observation above)—a view it shares with some secular perspectives in economics (e.g., the Marxist and Institutionalist). But, in addition, Christianity calls individuals to adopt particular modes of behavior—a view that sets it apart from most varieties of secular economics. In its view, the individual is not the best judge of her own actions, God is. Each person is designed to work in a cooperative interrelationship with God.

God's normative intentions for human economic life are embedded in the thirteen-item list above of Christian themes. For each person, and therefore for societies, the norms are intended to apply to every aspect of human behavior. In Christian belief, if all people sought consciously to practice these norms, each person and society would be on the path to an improving personal, social, and economic state. 'Improve' in Christian thinking means to encourage human behavior to conform increasingly to the Christian worldview. However, practice of the principles is extremely difficult. People are unable to pursue the norms in their own strength, but must rely on their relationship with God who enables them to make the necessary trade-offs integral to attaining the norms, or some compromise of the norms. People have to be guided by the life of Christ and the Holy Spirit dwelling within them. The paradox is of an inseparable interrelation between God's grace and human practice of the spiritual/practical norms.

As the spiritual and material domains of human existence cannot be disentangled in the Christian view, the norms guiding human spiritual life with God are of the utmost importance. Christianity is a supernatural belief system in which people are called to practice certain behavior toward the unseen entity of God (including Jesus Christ) who responds to them. Examples of these behaviors in the spiritual realm include acknowledging God as the creator and owner of the earth's resources, maintaining continual and explicit recognition of this belief, praying to God and waiting on His responses, seeking God's guidance, acknowledging Jesus as God's Son, accepting Jesus as the way to God, and loving and obeying God and Christ.

These normative principles of spiritual behavior are intended to guide people in their material life; for example, in their relationships with fellow humans and the natural world. A derivative and complementary set of norms is presented in the Bible to guide people in their interpersonal relations. For instance, believers are called to have their dealings with people influenced as much by altruism as by self-interest, to 'love your neighbour as yourself' (Mt. 22:39). However, to translate such norms into action requires that God shows believers how to do so in concrete situations (the difficult process of apprehending God's leading). Practice of the spiritual norms is a precondition for giving the material norms operational content. The methodological inference is that economic life is intended to be affected by normative God-guided human behavior in both spiritual and material domains.

HUMANKIND STRIVES FOR COHERENCE IN UNDERSTANDING PERSONAL AND SOCIAL BEHAVIOR THROUGH MODES OF INTERPRETATION OUTSIDE OF GOD

From the earliest recorded narratives in the Bible, probably put together at the beginning of the first millennium BC, humans are depicted as trying to explain and justify personal and social behavior without giving countenance to the intentions of the Hebrew God. Having derived these non-God rationalizations, humans seek to act upon them. A bold Biblically-based conjecture is that this process continues to the present day in most aspects of life by most people, including the analyses of secular social science (and in physical science, according to Johnson, 1995). This conjecture implies that the methodologies of social science and economics are likely to reject a role for God and any input from or about Him.

In social science, the process has perhaps been reflected in the veneration of the ideal of an absolutely objective scientific method. The weight of evidence of the last forty years from secular philosophers, sociologists, and historians of science (reviewed in Beed, 1991) suggests this idea to be a chimera. Yet, it is possible that most economists still believe in the desirability of adhering to some conception(s) of the method, such as falsification. In any case, input into economic analysis of such intangibles as unobservable/unmeasurable spiritual influences (including the Christian God's teachings and doings), and even of non-spiritual intangibles like value judgements, is eschewed.

The naturalist, non- and anti-Christian preoccupation in social science with so-called objective scientific method is a post-Enlightenment phenomenon, seeking to borrow what were perceived as techniques of natural science and thereby achieve its practical success. Naturalism thrust aside much older ways of thinking about personal and social behavior, of which Judeo-Christian thought had been the oldest Western variant. Contemporary economics, in company with most of the social sciences, often dates its beginnings from the late eighteenth century. Up to this time, in the words of a leading mainstream economist (Samuelson, 1980, 1), 'economic writing was frequently subservient to particular political or religious doctrines' (a statement omitted from Samuelson's later editions). Here, the freeing from a religious base is regarded as a positive step, and the assumption is that economics is no longer subservient to any philosophical/ideological doctrine(s)—both contestable claims, the latter of which has been subject to considerable scrutiny. Nevertheless, the ideal is clear: economics seeks to rely on logic and reasoning free from prior religious and philosophical standpoints. The intention of secular sociology is similar; as Milbank observes, 'its secret purpose is to ensure that religion is kept, conceptually, at the margins' (1990, 109). Only by viewing human activity through an objective lens, in much the same way as a physical scientist might view her specimen through a microscope, can uncontaminated data about human behavior be collected. These can then be analyzed using the idealized techniques of classical physical science.

A radically Biblical view does not accept this conceptualization. It contends that all theorizing in physical science, mathematics, and social science contains a religious viewpoint, that is, a belief in something as a nondependent divinity on which all else depends (Clouser, 1991; Pearcey and Thaxton, 1994). This might be Plato's forms, Leibniz's unseen eternal realm of mathematical entities, Russell's laws of logic, or Einstein's logical mathematical properties, etc. Disagreements between competing theories depend on differences in these religious/philosophical presuppositions. Christian theorizing is explicit about its divine basis, differing from the above theories in its belief that only God has the status of not depending on anything else.

The Christian position goes further than the secular critique of the last few decades of the conventional naturalistic methodological conceptualization. For a start, it ascribes a different role to reason in studying human behavior. God desires that reason, and every other human attribute, work in cooperation with Him, even though people have free will to do otherwise. One of the dominant themes of Biblical thought, is that human reason, judgement, wisdom, perception, and analysis trying to function as though they were autonomous from God is a thoroughly unreliable way to discern the truth about human behavior and relationships. Superficially, the Christian position is similar to the secular humanist critique of the nature of reason in modernist economics (as outlined in Beed, 1992). This claims that reason is not able to function uncontaminated by a range of subjective input, such as personal conviction. Like this critique, the Christian does not believe in the absolute power of reason.

Nevertheless, a long tradition in Christian theology asserts the importance of reason in the Christian faith. For example, the Middle Ages' theologian, Anselm of Canterbury (c 1033–1109) argued extensively that 'at its heart, the Christian gospel is rational, and can be shown to be rational' (McGrath, 1997, 43). Thomas Aquinas, Duns Scotus, and William of Ockham (Ockham's razor) were other scholastic medieval theologians who argued the rational justification of Christian belief. They recognized that human logic, the laws of valid inference and the forms of thought that go with it were gifts from God, intended to be used. However, in their view, reason is fallible, imperfect, and incomplete, like all human attributes. It is certainly not the sum total of the ways by which God intends people to acquire knowledge. Some contemporary humanists recognize the limitations of human reason, and accept that emotion and intuition are valid sources of human knowledge. Christianity takes this methodological criticism further. It claims that human sense experience, embodying reason, emotion, and intuition, does not encompass all the ways by which knowledge is obtained.

On the basis of the Biblical evidence and the historical experience of believers, Christians believe that God communicates knowledge in additional ways. These include God's responses to prayer, purposive acts by God (which may or may not be recognized by the human intellect), and through the normative principles God has established to guide human life (such as those in the earlier list of this chapter). These paths, collectively known as revelation, are not mutually exclusive and can be subdivided further. For example, response to prayer can be acts by God, but can also be information transmitted via the human intellect or intuition, or even by dreams and visions. These can be transmitted either directly to the person seeking God's guidance or through third parties. There are many ways by which God conveys knowledge to people, and they are not at all easy to discern. Nevertheless, to confine God's communication with humans merely to the intellectual attributes of the human mind does not conform to Biblical description nor to Christian experience.

One implication of this is that the Christian worldview provides an explanatory framework within which human experience may be interpreted. Martin Luther's 'theology of the cross,' and Augustine's 'theology of longing' in his *Confessions* are examples of this framework in theology, which is here related to socio-economic experience. Interpretation of that experience on its own, *per se*, is not capable of satisfactory resolution, despite the attempts of secular social science over the last few hundred years. Human reason requires a metaphysical context or worldview within which to function, and the claim is that Christian theology provides such a methodological framework.

In the Christian worldview, there is an alternative to people trying to depend on God in their reasoning functions, as in all else. This is to try and operate independently of God. God has given people this choice; human reason can try to work as though it were an autonomous mechanism. This is the methodological mode in which economics (and most thought and behavior) functions today. However, Christian belief holds that external influences will still enter into human reason that tries to work like this. These influences can be unrecognized directions from God, but they can also be forces not from God. From a Christian perspective, one danger with relying on humanistic attributes alone is that they readily become contaminated by sin. The New Testament contends that the world is locked into an ongoing struggle between God (good) and evil, that will only be resolved by God's future victory. As the apostle Paul put it, 'we are not contending against flesh and blood, but against the principalities, against the powers, against the world rulers of this present darkness, against the spiritual host of wickedness in the heavenly places' (Eph. 6:12). This continuing spiritual battle has manifest material effects in the socio-economic and natural world even though they are not comprehensible in these terms by the human intellect. Only by trying to function in partnership with God, in human reasoning, as elsewhere, can protection be had against forces of evil endemic in the world. The main inference is that where human reason seeks consciously to operate independently from God, it readily becomes susceptible to sin, or to missing God's mark.

Thus, Christianity ascribes a different methodological role from secular economics to human reason in seeking to understand the nature of human behavior. In Christian belief, human thought is designed to work sympathetically with God's overarching care for humankind, to function in conjunction with it, not to seek to operate independently of God, faith, and revelation. Roman Catholic theology, for example, 'has always sought a unity between faith and reason' (Fiorenza, 1991, 68). But, as Ratzinger (Pope Benedict XVI)(1987, 325) pointed out, Christian faith should not 'fall under the absolute power of enlightened reason and its methods.' This is not to downplay the importance of human reason, but neither is it to exaggerate its power, for like the rest of human attributes, the human intellect is fallible and imperfect, it is crippled by sin. Unlike the methodological approaches of secular economics, reason cannot serve as the final authority, nor is secular theory making the only or best way to truth.

CONCLUSION

One of the implications from the analysis of the three items above is that a Christian methodology for dealing with economic questions concerns itself with interrelationships between the different spheres of human life. With this emphasis, Christian methodology is drawn more to explanation than prediction. Given the variety of human behavioral response to spiritual and material stimuli postulated as possible in the Christian metaphysical framework (because of the uniqueness of people and their freedom of will), the bias to explanation is consolidated. Although there is an instrumentalist bent in much Neoclassical method, for example, neither Christian nor scientific realist method place great store on this methodology as an explicator of truth (reasons for this are discussed in Beed and Beed, 1997, and from a, secular realist perspective in Sayer, 1992). It is not appropriate to debate the relative merits of instrumentalism and realism here (Hausman, 1992, 162–169 and 285–288, provides an overview of the matter), but no claim can be made that a Christian methodology would make more accurate predictions than the instrumentalism of Neoclassical economics, any more than the realist method would. Neither Christian nor realist social science posits prediction as the major methodological goal. If Neoclassical economics, for example, is still enmeshed in an unconscious positivism that prizes prediction (as Beed, 1991 and Lawson, 1994a; 1997 contend), the Christian methodology mooted here is anti-, pre- and post-positivist.

Conventional forms of economic analysis have been transcended in recent years to endeavor to show the relevance of economics to a variety of human choice situations. For example, the narrowness of Neoclassical rational choice theory has been modified by the likes of Frank (e.g., 1988, 1994) and Thaler (e.g., 1991) in showing how its methods can be adapted to deal with the analysis of 'irrational choice' and of values, emotions, and norms. Clearly, there are tangents of interest between the Neoclassical and Christian methods. There are also overlaps between Christian methodology and the pattern-modelling of Institutionalist economics, the over-determining methods of Marxist economics, and the hermeneutics of the Austrian method. All these approaches take economic methodology beyond rational choice. There is common ground between secular economics and the Christian worldview, their philosophical presuppositions, values, and methodologies of studying personal and socio-economic behavior, although this is not the focus here.

Investigation of this common ground between Christian thinking on economic affairs and secular economics is a promising area. One aspect can be drawn from the contemporary disagreement between Christians who are economists in their regard for the Neoclassical model. The overriding view from Neoclassical economics of humans is that they seek to maximize their material and non-material needs. As Becker (1981, ix) put it, 'the economic approach . . . assumes that individuals maximize their utility from basic preferences that do not change rapidly over time.' This view has many strands in contemporary economics and it is debatable how far they accord with the Christian viewpoint. Becker (1981, 198) developed his strand to demonstrate that 'altruism dominates family behavior perhaps to the same extent as selfishness dominates market transactions.' Perhaps people do behave like this in advanced Western societies. But, if they do, it suggests that human behavior is removed from God's intentions. For God wants people to act in communion with Him—to follow certain spiritual principles—and He wants people to be at least as altruistic as they are selfish in all situations; in short, to serve God in all situations. From Becker's conclusions, the Christian and the secular economics conception of human motivation differ markedly. In the economics conception, human motivation is directed to maximizing personal satisfaction in the fulfillment of personal preferences. The Christian conception is that people should love God with all their hearts and minds, and their neighbors as themselves. However, human motivation can be defined more broadly in the Neoclassical framework. For instance, Lunn and Klay (1994, 156) point out that Christians who pursue God's will for their life as more important than their own will are maximizing utility. Self-interest can be defined to encompass more than selfishness. Frank's 'friendly amendment to the self-interest model,' his 'commitment model' (1988, 1994) takes this broader secular view of self-interest. An important question is how self-interest is usually viewed and taught in Neoclassical economics. Frank, Gilovich, and Regan (1993) suggested the possibility that selfishness and opportunism is the typical interpretation.

Given its metaphysical and worldview assumptions, Christian belief suggests a low degree of applicability and generality of secular socio-economic prediction and explanation. This is because the latter depend on a non-Christian view of humankind's purpose on earth. A paradox is apparent here. Social science and economics think they have liberated socio-economic understanding by freeing it from religious presuppositions. This is opposite from the Christian perspective which believes that personal and social knowledge is obscured when detached from God's framework. Secular social science tries to deduce principles of human motivation and to explain their workings independently of God's design for humankind. The Christian view is that people are intended to work with God, and that humans behave irrationally when they try to live independently of God. No clear system of explanation will emerge when people engage in irrational behavior. Secular social science ignores these propositions. Instead, it believes it can discover rational reasons for human socio-economic motivation separate from God.

From a Christian perspective, secular economics can be construed as working from an incomplete theoretical base of what is meant to motivate people. It is not surprising that its 'laws' or predictions of observed human behavior have only a low degree of empirical validity. Starting from an incomplete view of human purpose, it can deduce only partial explanation for human action. Human reason can function only within a broader metaphysical framework in which human behavior is viewed. If this framework is deficient, as the Christian conception implies about secular economics, human reason can end up with only fragmented explanation. In Biblical depiction, there is no suggestion that if truth is sought any area of human relationships, it can or should be analyzed independently of God's intentions. Since economics ignores the necessity of human relationships with God, it has no idea of the coherence of knowledge in God. Human alienation from God, which is another term for sin, obscures human understanding of the world.

A restricted view has been taken in this chapter of the ability of secular socio-economic analysis to ascertain the truth of human behavior and relationships. It has not been demonstrated that Christian analysis is or could be superior, although this has been an unstated assumption of the argument. Evidence for the superiority of Christian analysis must await actual use of Christian methodology in explaining socio-economic behavior and relationships. The historical record of the Christian church does not give much optimism to bolster the superiority claim. For instance, the Protestant evangelical individualistic reaction to the decadent Medieval church has led to no consensus on socio-economic matters. It should not appear that we have been developing a spiritual methodological individualism having no mechanism within it to develop consensus on Christian thinking. A materialistic, individualistic methodological hedonism has no part in our argument. Confusing these two might arise from the methodological approach of this chapter: to focus on negative methodological implications (methodological differences) between a Christian perspective and (an undifferentiated) secular economics.

This chapter has not examined the positive methodological aspects of the Christian operationalization. Some examples of its operation were given in Chapters 2–4. There are enough policy examples suggesting it is not merely an analytical toy. For instance, as Chapter 2 noted, the fifty-year-old cooperative movement centered around Mondragon in Spain was an exemplar in its instigation of integrated Christian thinking about economic and social processes, even though it suffers from specific deficiencies. In this case, private markets have been utilized in the interests of justice and caring. In devising such practical examples of Christian policy, individual Christians have used, and will continue to use, their reason and revelational input. This can be both inside the Christian church and in the wider community, in which the church can serve a vital role in sifting Christian thinking and unifying policy recommendations.

Chapter Seven

Christians and the Autonomy of Economics

Our earlier argument was that distinctly Christian-based perspectives can be developed toward economic matters and that these perspectives differ from those propounded by all schools of secular economics. The Christian viewpoints recognize the limited contribution secular economics (of any school) can make to describing and explaining reality, and providing policy prescription for the real world. However, the Christian positions do not accept that economic theory is more useful than the Christian-based perspectives for describing, explaining and prescribing for the real world, as long as the necessary empirical work is done to ascertain the reality of that world. The methodology of a Christian-based socio-economic analysis taking shape throughout this book—outlined in the concluding chapter—depends totally on relating the intentions inherent in Judeo-Christian thought to the complicated empirical reality of the real world. Data-based research is crucial to this process.

In the last few decades, economists who are Christians have been taking more seriously the relation between their two areas of commitment, and have been writing increasingly on the subject. This literature growth stems partly from the resurgence within economics of philosophical and methodological issues underlying the subject itself. Influential books, from McCloskey (1986) to Hands (2001b), and new academic journals, like the *Journal of Economic Methodology* and *Economics and Philosophy*, are both symptom and cause of the rekindled focus. As with the emerging philosophical and methodological interest in economics, great diversity characterizes the economist-Christian explorations. The spread ranges from those who see the two thought areas as compatible but independent, to those who see Christian thought as transforming economic understanding. Smith (1993, 166), for instance, identifies three views on the continuum of economist-Christians: disciplinary autonomy for economics; disciplinary interdependence between economics and Christian thought; and distinctively Christian economic analysis. As his labels imply, these perspectives range from economist-Christians who hold that 'scientific economic analysis is independent of any religious input' (disciplinary autonomy) to those who hold that 'special revelation has epistemological implications for the explanation of economic phenomena' (distinctively Christian economic analysis). This last view could reasonably be argued to be contradictory to the first. If economic knowledge is independent from religious input, this input has no implications for the description or analysis in which economics engages. Between the differing tendencies on the continuum of views, only limited engagement occurs. Representatives of the different positions might contribute to the one symposium, but they debate each other only marginally. For example, contributors in Brennan and Waterman (1994), and Dean and Waterman (1999) exhibit the divergent trends, but little argument occurs between the divergent viewpoints. One difference from this has occurred elsewhere. This was in pre-nineties' debates on the issue of capitalism versus socialism (surveyed, for example, in Gay, 1991). Nowadays, this controversy looks more like historical curiosity with the demise of communism, and no economist-Christian advocates complete state ownership of the means of production.

Here (Beed and Beed, 2003b), we evaluate two representative positions on the economist-Christian spectrum, as identified by Smith (1993), over the last decade or so. J. David Richardson is examined first, whom Smith identifies with the 'disciplinary interdependence' view. This position acknowledges 'the positivist view that economic analysis may serve as an input into biblically based ethical discussion,' but goes further in arguing that 'the Bible may also serve as an input into economic discourse' (Smith, 1993, 170). However, Smith suggests that 'in practice Christians who nominally adhere to the interdependence position easily lapse into the framework of disciplinary autonomy . . . .' The evaluation below of the major paper by Richardson on the relation between economics and Christian thought, argues that Richardson (1988) does portray a disciplinary autonomy approach more than interdependency, for he does not emphasize how Christian thought or the Bible might be an input into economics. An asymmetry characterizes his examination of economics in the relation between economics and Christian input.

The second representative examined here is an explicit advocate of the disciplinary autonomy approach, according to Smith (1993, 166). Anthony Waterman accepts the separation of economics from Christian belief as inevitable and desirable. Thus, he contends (Dean and Waterman, 1999, 4) that 'so far as any science can be — economics may in principle be regarded as "autonomous" with respect to theology,' a 'demarcation' that 'has become so much a part of methodological orthodoxy in economics' (Waterman, 2001, 58) to which Waterman subscribes. There is nothing about mainstream economics that troubles Waterman as a Christian (Webb, 2000, 11). According to Smith (1993, 167), this disciplinary autonomy view is the dominant position of 'contemporary secular and Christian economists.' This position does not advocate that economics should pay *no* attention to Christian belief. Rather, it holds that economics and Christian belief can proceed along their independent paths without each being too bothered by the other, that it is not possible to integrate economics and Christianity. This perspective is called here the separatist or autonomous view.

This chapter outlines and assesses selected work of the two prominent economist-Christians above. Like any evaluation, the critique is made within the confines of the particular perspectives on both economics and Christianity developed in earlier chapters. Rather than trying to explain at the beginning of this chapter what these might be, it is hoped they have been made explicit in earlier chapters and that they continue to stand out in this chapter. In terms of Smith's (1993, 171) classification, our perspectives are nearest to his 'distinctively Christian economic analysis' group, in which 'the Bible is cognitively significant for explaining economic phenomena.' In some ways, this approach represents an extension of the theological economics proposal by Oslington (2000). Smith associates this perspective with the Dutch neo-Calvinist tradition, but as an economics representative of this tradition pointed out (Tiemstra, 1999, 87–88), it also has affinities with Catholic Social Thought. The charge could be leveled, therefore, that the *a priori* standpoint utilized for the critique here predetermines the conclusions of the chapter. This is a valid observation on all analysis, and it applies to this chapter as much as to the economist-Christians surveyed.

The next section is an examination and appraisal of how Richardson sees his favored economics framework. The following section is a similar approach to how Richardson sees his chosen Biblical and theological system of interpretation. The intention is to establish where Richardson lies on the economist-Christian spectrum, and to critique it. In the last section of this chapter, Waterman is examined, relating to his views both on economics and Christianity.

Richardson has not written extensively on the issue, but his 1988 *Christian Scholar's Review* paper maintains considerable status and is still cited to support the separatist outlook (e.g., Elzinga, 1999). No published evaluation of this paper has been found, so this contribution is reviewed here, rather than less formal comment Richardson has published since. The paper was reprinted in 1988 in the *Journal of the UK Association of Christian Economists*, and in 1994 in the *Bulletin of the US Association of Christians Economists*, prefaced by informal comment by Richardson. An unreferenced conversation with Richardson was published in that Bulletin in 1998 in which his outlook on the matters appears to be similar to his earlier paper. Other economists of the autonomous outlook might have published more than Richardson on economics-Christian-related issues, such as Anthony Waterman (1994, 1999), Paul Heyne (1994, 1996, 1999), Kenneth Elzinga (1999) and Laurence Iannaccone (1992, 1993, 1998). Unanimity does not exist between all these economists in justifying the autonomous position, but Waterman is examined here as another representative of this viewpoint. The reason for examining Richardson first is that his Christian-related writing more pointedly justifies the contemporary separatist outlook than the Christian-related work of other separatist economists. For example, Waterman in his later work relies more on historical evidence to rationalize the parting of the ways between theology and economics in nineteenth century Britain, and Iannaccone is more concerned with applying microeconomic rational choice models to current church attendance and sect affiliation.

FROM INTERDEPENDENCE TO AUTONOMY: J. DAVID RICHARDSON ON ECONOMICS

This section outlines and criticizes the view of economics taken by Richardson in his 1988 paper, evaluating his case as he has presented it. The latter caveat is important, because this chapter does not attempt a comprehensive evaluation of contemporary economics *per se*. That task is beyond the province of this chapter, although some attempt is made to grapple with aspects of the topic in ensuing chapters. Evaluations of contemporary orthodox economics are, however, the subject of a recent, continuing, extensive and unresolved debate, to which reference is made. The argument of this section is that Richardson does not substantiate his case that orthodox economic theory provides the insights into real-world behavior or possess the robustness he suggests. It has a far weaker purchase on unraveling reality than he implies. The claimed advantages of new developments in orthodox economic theory to which Richardson points are not demonstrated by him, and have been claimed by critics to be dubious. If the interdependency position, as Smith describes it above, accords to economics, 'the positivist view that economic analysis may serve as an input into biblically based ethical discussion,' this precept has less validity if (orthodox) economic theory and analysis has a weak relation to reality. The section after this assesses the extent to which Richardson demonstrates how the Bible and Judeo-Christian thought can serve as in input to economic discourse.

According to Richardson (1988, 382), economics is 'the science of decision-making under scarcity,' and uses 'decision-making rules,' for example 'efficient rules' that reflect 'rationality.' This assertion is not demonstrated by

Richardson because none of the terms in these 'rules' is defined (such as 'rationality'), nor are specific examples given showing how the rules apply to real-life situations. Richardson needed to demonstrate his contention because a continuing debate has long occurred in economics and philosophy about the meaning of 'rationality' from which no consensus has emerged (some recent contributions are Hampton, 1994; Dennis, 1998, Schwartz, 1998). Nevertheless, by regarding 'rationality' and the 'rules' unproblematically, Richardson alleges economics to be 'relevant' and therefore presumably useful (1988, 384). An illustration of this modern relevance given by Richardson is held to be the theoretical discovery 'that ubiquitous perfectly competitive markets can satisfy economic desires efficiently and "Pareto optimally".' This 'theorem' is asserted by Richardson to be 'not at all obvious' (1988, 384). We take this to mean that the relevance of economic theory in the illustration is that it has revealed something about the real world that is not 'obvious.' This claimed theoretical discovery faces a number of intellectual barriers in the way of assessing it as relevant and useful. One is that 'ubiquitous perfectly competitive markets' do not characterize the overwhelming majority of markets in modern real-world economies. There is not a great deal in present reality against which to test predictions of the theorem. Thus, a judgement by an orthodox economist is that 'perfect competition is an utterly misleading concept' (Blaug, 2002, 27). There is also the question (again long debated in economics but never resolved) of the value of economic theorems that predict things about a reality that does not exist. Then there is the question that if preconditions (or axioms) for economic theorems do not exist in reality, of how the theorem can precisely predict things about this reality if it did exist. Although a voluminous and inconclusive literature exists post 1953 debating both issues, Richardson does not discuss them. (Some recent examples of this literature are Hausman, 1992; Kieta, 1992; Mayer, 1993; Boylan and O'Gorman, 1995; Lawson, 1997; Hands, 2001b). The practical relevance of the theoretical discovery mentioned by Richardson is assumed to be unproblematic. As the aforementioned cited literature implies, the insights into reality produced by such theorems, as distinct from the imaginary axiomatic scenario on which they rest, have long been questioned methodologically and philosophically. None of these considerations was canvassed by Richardson in terms of the critical literature existing up to 1988 (nor, indeed, up to 1994 in so far as Richardson does not appear to have revised his 1988 paper before it was reprinted in 1994).

Perhaps, then, an alternative interpretation is to be given to Richardson's assertion about the relevance of the economic theorem in question. Perhaps he means that it is effects of deviations from the theorem that are not obvious, that if perfectly competitive markets do not exist, then the theorem predicts that economic desires cannot be satisfied efficiently, and that this is 'not obvious.' But, again, Richardson does not persuade readers that these might be the case. For instance, he asserts (1988, 385) that if sellers and buyers enjoy concentrated market power (an abrogation of one of the preconditions for ubiquitous perfectly competitive markets), opportunities may be had 'to influence price or to coerce rivals or customers.' But people did not need the theorem above to persuade them that this could be the case. It was probably long obvious from the real-world experience of markets that if sellers or buyers possess concentrated market power, they are able to influence price, and coerce rivals or customers. The historical experience of markets probably convinced people of this behavior, not that a theorem was subsequently formulated that predicts this behavior. It was likely induction from history, not deduction from axioms, that persuaded people that their economic desires were not being satisfied efficiently when they were confronted with imperfectly competitive markets. Along the same lines, historical experience rather than theoretical debate probably persuaded people that 'markets are generally a desirable means of organizing economic activity' (Richardson, 1988, 384) compared with alternative socio-economic arrangements. The theorem of economics in question might have been just a *post hoc* formalistic representation of the historical common sense experience of people involved in buying and selling. Perhaps the theorem did not really add anything new to what was already known about market behavior in the real world.

Richardson (1988, 385–387) lists a collection of new topics to which economic theory has attended in the last few decades. These include theories relating to asymmetric information, to 'signalling' and 'reputation,' 'efficiency wages,' 'clubs,' public choice, 'bounded rationality,' 'rolling equilibria,' to marriage, divorce and the family. Richardson does not investigate whether insights into the real world offered by these developments represent intellectual gain over what was known about the phenomena in question prior to the theoretical developments listed. For example, one of Richardson's examples is 'recent developments in game theory and bargaining analysis' that 'have allowed economists to examine whether or not countervailing market power could maintain market benefits as well as the perfectly competitive absence of market power' (Richardson, 1988, 385). Countervailing power was written about widely in the 1950s (e.g., Galbraith, 1952). Richardson does not examine what new insights have been gained into real-world countervailing power situations by the more recent theoretical developments. Game theory use in industrial organization, for example, to which Richardson's reference can apply, has been criticized by the orthodox economist, Blaug. He (2002, 29) suggested that game theory has little to do with 'a positive descriptive account of interactive decisions,' and that it is impossible 'to think of a single novel observation that has come out of the "new" industrial organization infused by game theory that was not already part and parcel of the "old" industrial organization.' If Blaug is correct, the practical effects in policy making of recent theoretical developments about countervailing power using game theory are likely to have been marginal. Another of Richardson's examples relates to marriage, divorce and the family. Insights into these phenomena revealed by Becker, cited by Richardson as 'the foundation of this field,' were castigated by Blaug, a prominent economic methodologist. According to Blaug (1992,223, 224, 225, 227), Becker employed 'a cumbersome apparatus' (technical mathematics) to 'produce implications that are sometimes obvious, if not banal,' resembling 'the use of sledgehammer to crack a nut,' 'so generally formulated as to be compatible with almost any finding,' being 'left at the end of the argument, therefore, with almost empty conclusions that are presented as being more dramatic than they really are,' in which competing sociological or anthropological arguments were ignored. Feminist economists have maintained a separate critique of Becker's analysis. For instance, Bergmann (1995, 142–3) suggested that 'a close look at Becker's analysis of the family reveals its unreality and inapplicability to any real problems that people in or out of families have.' A less severe judgment is that 'the conclusions of each approach [Becker's and feminist economics] are therefore often at odds with each other, and continue to be so in spite of empirical assessment of the theories' (Dow, 2002, 24). Whether the criticisms above are valid or not, they need to be assessed before it can be concluded that the new topics to which economic theory is being applied represent gains in knowledge. They also highlight a more general problem noted by Dow (2002, 36), that 'it is extraordinarily rare for empirical evidence [in economics] to settle a theoretical dispute.'

In none of the theoretical examples cited by Richardson does he show how the 'new' analysis or theoretical development represented intellectual progress over what was already known about the topic in question, whether in economics or elsewhere. The meaning of 'intellectual progress' is not considered. Merely being 'new' or 'recent' seems to be implicitly sufficient for Richardson to declare it progress (with one caveat discussed below). That 'new is better' pervades much modern life, including intellectual pursuit. Analogously, that post-Enlightenment materialism and naturalism could construct explanations of real-world phenomena without the Christian God has been widely represented as intellectual progress by non-believers in the last three centuries. Just because modern economists now analyze 'non-material, non-measurable goods' like loyalty or altruism (Richardson, 1988, 389) does not necessarily mean they have added anything to what was known already about those phenomena, or what is known by other social sciences that have ignored modern economics on the issues. Some examples are explored here in chapter 12.

A critical stream both in and outside economics considers the recent theoretical developments in orthodox economics to constitute trivial intellectual progress in the explanation of real-world phenomena. As with the other critical literature above, this literature is also voluminous, but none of its pre 1988 contributions (except McCloskey, 1986), or those since, is mentioned by Richardson, such as Leontief (1971). A few of its more recent authors are Rosenberg (1992), Green and Shapiro (1994), Heilbroner and Milberg (1995), Perelman (1996), Middleton (1998), Keen (2001), and Fullbrook (2004). The same doubts have percolated into the mass media and into more popular literature, both by economists and non-economists, like Paul Ormerod (1994), Martin Anderson (1996), and John Ralston Saul (1997). A non-economist, Hugh Stretton (1999), has even gone to the length of writing a large alternative text book for undergraduate economics students. The continuing vitality of minority schools of non-orthodox economic thought—Post Keynesians, Institutionalists, Social Economists, Austrians and Radical Political Economists—and of newer streams, such as feminist and critical realist economists, and the PAE movement, is philosophical and methodological witness to dissatisfaction with the orthodox status quo.

Our discussion is not likely to resolve the dispute between economic orthodoxy and heterodoxy about the intellectual gains of modern orthodox economics. Nonetheless, the critics and non-orthodox economists are unrelenting in their attack on the orthodox mainstream Neoclassical perspective in the face of its new theoretical preoccupations. Their judgements apply not only to the knowledge increment revealed in and by the theories of orthodox economics themselves viewing them as self-contained systems. They apply also to what the new theories show about the real world, in so far as the theories are usually constructed on the basis of unreal or problematic assumptions and axioms. As is so often the practice by orthodox economists, little of the earlier literature critical of the so-called intellectual gains of modern economics is cited by Richardson. He does make an unwitting gesture (1988, 388) to the triviality issue, with his example that the 'new' economic theories differ from the 'old' by admitting 'that current information may only be partial and that learning takes place over time.' These considerations have been recognized for aeons by other social sciences, like sociology and psychology, and do not constitute new discovery, despite being dressed up by economics in the clothing of formalistic modelling.

One of the supposed gains demonstrated by modern economics is its greater reliance than in the past on complicated mathematical and statistical technique. It can be agreed with Richardson (1988, 384, 389) that 'economics is . . . the most mathematical of the social sciences' so much so 'that the technical skills necessary' to grapple with the 'new' economic theories 'are intimidating.' However, if the above critics are correct that the new economic theories reveal little new about reality, the question arises why so much adulation should be given to the mathematical underpinning of the theories. One of the criticisms of modern orthodox economics is that it has elevated mathematical form over, and out of all proportion to, real-world substance or content, exhibiting the disease of formalism (e.g., Beed and Kane, 1991; Montgomery, 1994; Blaug, 2002). As Blaug commented (1992, 167), 'theories that are truly rigorous are rarely practically relevant, and theories that are eminently relevant are rarely analytically rigorous.' If modern economic theory *is* decreasingly revealing insights into the real world, it might not be surprising that its practitioners are resorting increasingly to more complicated and abstruse technical (mathematical) paraphernalia. This would represent a anxious attempt to try and demonstrate the scientific credentials of economics and the relevance of economics to reality. Its critics believe they are not succeeding, that orthodox economic theory is on a self-defeating and unproductive path.

Admittedly, Richardson does perceive there are problems with orthodox economics today (the caveat mentioned above). Unlike critics above, Richardson does not think these problems are sufficiently strong to vitiate current trends in orthodox academic economics. After he has presented his discussion of ('more relevant') developments in modern economic theory, Richardson mentions problems that worry him. They are all related to the issues discussed above. One (1988, 390) is that the 'most brilliant scholars' are fixated with 'the latest ideas'. As discussed above, 'progress in the profession' is measured by new developments *per se*. Second, Richardson (1988, 390) is 'concerned that axiomatic reasoning and deductive logic are overrunning observational reasoning and inductive logic.' Stylized facts are replacing historical investigation. But, unlike the critics of modern economics, Richardson is not prepared to concede the possibility that economics has reached the stage of diminishing returns because of these developments.

Richardson (1988, 381) correctly observes that the 'core' of economics 'rests importantly on philosophy, law, history, and other social sciences.' Yet, academic students of economics are decreasingly, and minimally nowadays, required to study these disciplines. Instead, these have been replaced by the requirement to master increasingly complicated mathematical technique that is then applied to philosophy, law etc. Richardson might see this as due to economics' 'commendable scientific ambition,' for 'economics is . . . the most "scientific" of the social sciences, if by this is meant reliance on axiomatic reasoning, deduction, prediction, measurement, and hypothesis testing' (1988, 383). 'Historical investigation' in economics has been relegated, and is fading. The problem is that this approach carries with it a 'dubious scientific pretension.' Applying scientific methods to imaginary axioms, or to socio-economic data that do not encompass natural kinds (Wilkerson, 1995), or stable social kinds does not produce enduring conclusions explaining or predicting real-world behavior, matters explored in ensuing chapters. Nevertheless, 'among social sciences' economics has become 'the most arrogant, combative, and imperialistic' (Richardson, 1988, 383). Most orthodox academic economists, either do not see these problems or, like Richardson, do not acknowledge them as sufficiently severe to undermine the direction of their subject.

In summary, Richardson's view in outlining new theoretical developments in modern economics is commendatory. But he seems to be arguing something different from the first plank of an interdependency position, that economic analysis may serve as an input into Biblically based ethical discussion. In the first two-thirds of his paper discussed above, Richardson does not deal with this topic but rather with purely secular economics-related issues. This section two of his paper (pp. 382–390) is mainly an exposition and defense of the old and new in orthodox economics. In the section, Richardson does not explore how economic analysis might serve as an input into Biblically based ethical discussion. He seems to be implying more the autonomous position, that modern orthodox economics has every legitimacy to function as a separate scientific discipline, a conclusion questioned by most of the critics above even on purely secular grounds.

FROM INTERDEPENDENCE TO AUTONOMY: RICHARDSON ON ECONOMIC IMPLICATIONS OF CHRISTIAN THOUGHT

This section describes and evaluates the view Richardson (1988) takes of Judeo-Christianity, both in its sources and subsequent intellectual (as distinct from institutional) development. This consideration is necessary to ascertain the degree to which Richardson explores the second plank of the interdependency position, that the Bible and Christian beliefs may also serve as inputs to economic discourse. One aspect of this is to assess the degree to which Biblically based ethical discussion itself contains economic analysis. If ethical discussion in the Bible (or theology) already contains economic investigation, the issue of economic analysis constituting an additional input might not be so compelling.

In their consideration of the interrelationships between economics and Christianity, separatists invariably orientate more of their discussion to economics than to Christianity. This pattern is followed by Richardson who devotes the first eight plus pages of his (1988) paper to economics (pp. 382–390), discussed above, and his following five plus to how Christians should respond to modern economics. There is little discussion whether AD Christianity itself or the sources of Christian belief have anything to say about economic issues. This orientation and proportion in Richardson's paper, typical of the separatist approach, probably reflects the greater importance the separatists attach to the analytical nature of economics than to Judeo-Christian thought for revealing and prescribing for real-world socio-economic matters.

Christianity, nevertheless, is conceded by Richardson (1988, 390) to have a 'scholarly tradition in economics' before economics was ever conceived as a separate discipline from moral philosophy in the late eighteenth century. From where Christianity's interest in economic matters is held to stem is not discussed by Richardson, except that it goes back 'to before St. Thomas Aquinas,' (1988, 390) prior to the thirteenth century. After Aquinas is mentioned, an alphabetical list of twentieth century economist Christians receives most attention. What this approach omits is discussion of economic issues in the sources of Christian belief itself, the Judeo-Christian Bible, and in any Christian theological system (as distinct from church practice) from around 70 AD up to the present (despite some citations to other writers who have discussed the latter issue). This is a large omission, not permitting a reader to gain any sense of how the omitted sources might have attached importance to economic matters or to have discussed them. Nor does Richardson's alphabetical list of twentieth century economist Christians allow a reader to gain any sense of how any of its constituents regard the interrelation between economics and Christianity. They are all grouped together. Thus, Tony Cramp, a (now retired) Cambridge (UK) economist who maintains the pre-eminence of Christianity over orthodox economics for understanding reality, is listed with Anthony Waterman, a North American economist/ordained priest of separatist orientation. Many similar examples occur in the list.

In the first section of this chapter, it was argued that Richardson presented an assessment of developments in modern economic theory without examining their relevance to the real world. Richardson makes a similar type of broad evaluation of the work of the economist Christians in his list. No analysis is presented of the work of any individual or group of twentieth century economist Christians named in the list. Richardson (1988, 391) states that he is 'not eager or prepared to make detailed evaluations of the ratio of scholarship to commentary' in the reference list names (perhaps this is not wanting to offend fellow Christians). On what criterion Richardson distinguishes 'scholarship' from 'commentary' is not explained. Nevertheless, on the basis of this unstated criterion, Richardson judges 'recent work by Christian economists' as being 'on average too rich in commentary and too lean in scholarship, too preoccupied with methodology . . . too shallow, too rhetorical, too taxonomic, too dusty, musty, and fusty by comparison to that which modern economists were really doing' (1988, 391). ('Praiseworthy exceptions' to his 'general discontent' are mooted, again unnamed, although it might be inferred that Hay, 1989 is one exception.) These judgements are repeated in that 'much Christian commentary on economics [is] long on ideology and short on integrity, full of unsupported assertion, unsubstantiated allegation, and unrepresentative anecdote' (1988, 395).

If recent work by unspecified economist Christians fits into the categories above, so does Richardson's verdict. No empirical evidence is provided to back it up, even had an evaluative criterion been provided. No example of 'recent work by Christian economists" is analyzed by Richardson to support his assertions. This appears to be a doubtful way of doing and judging scholarship, whether one agrees with the scholarship or not (and particularly ironic coming from someone calling for greater integrity in scholarship). Richardson's judgements are unwarranted, given his lack of examination of any instance of the work of the eighteen Christian economists of his alphabetical list in their thirty cited books and papers ranging from 1926 to 1989. Nonetheless, the (unstated) evaluative criterion on which Richardson bases his assessment can be deduced. It is the degree to which the Christian economics scholarship meets the characteristics of modern orthodox economics, described in the first section of this chapter. Recall that these were its reliance on 'axiomatic reasoning, deduction, prediction, measurement, and hypothesis testing,' all involving complicated mathematical and statistical technique, the 'intimidating' technical skills of modern economics (1988, 383, 389), that separates it from much other social science. Richardson spends the rest of his paper advocating that 'believing economists . . . master the economics of' the topics of modern economic theory outlined in the first section of this chapter. When Richardson extols Christian economists 'to do the very best economics they can' (1988, 392), he means utilizing the mechanisms of modern orthodox economic theory, and perhaps to 'master rigorous Marxian economics thoroughly' (1988, 384).

The previous section of this chapter argued that a critical stream both in and outside economics disagrees with the validity and usefulness of the mechanisms of modern economic analysis. Shorn of its technical mathematical paraphernalia, the critics hold that the real-world content and relevance of modern economic theory is minimal. At least half, if not more, of Richardson's alphabetical list of eighteen economist Christians can be identified as belonging to schools of economic thought critical of the prevailing orthodoxy in academic economics. Economists taking the critical line (Christian or otherwise) are more likely to pursue their economic investigation with greater reliance on inductive verbal reasoning and historical investigation, using insights provided by the other social sciences, by philosophy and law, than by employing the techniques underlying modern economic theory. The critical economists are also interested in the philosophical and methodological bases of their own modes of analysis, and of their orthodox competitors. Needless to say, this type of economics' work undertaken by most Institutionalists, and majorities of Post Keynesians, Austrians, Marxist, other heterodox economists, and economic historians, is rarely cited or held in high regard by orthodox Neoclassical practitioners. Richardson apparently takes this latter view in his criticism of the economist Christian critics as being 'too preoccupied with methodology' (1988, 391). The critics are interested in methodology because they believe the methodologies used by the orthodoxy are defective and therefore reveal little new about the world. Ignoring the methodological and philosophical critique of orthodox economics, Richardson wishes 'that more believers were committed to being numbered among the apostles of modern economics' (1988, 392). But he does not examine why they are not in terms of the contemporary critique of mainstream economics.

The critical economist Christians are not 'committed to being numbered among the apostles of modern economics' for a second reason. This is their belief that Judeo-Christianity is of comparable, if not greater, importance than economics, as the analytical means for unraveling reality. Heterodox economist Christians in Richardson's list (1988, 390–391), like Cramp, Daly, Goudzwaard, Graham et al., McKee, North, Storkey, and Wilber, in different degree, believe that Christianity contains tools of at least equal if not greater importance than orthodox economics for understanding material reality—economic, social and personal. Other Christian economists not in Richardson's alphabetical list, but cited by him, could be added, such as Mason. To these names could be appended non-economist social ethicists/theologians cited by Richardson, like Mott, Wogaman, and the US National Conference of Catholic Bishops. As noted above, these critics are more closely associated with Smith's 'distinctively Christian economic analysis' position These critics do not have uniform views about the matter, but they cannot be dismissed collectively as fundamentalists for the content of their case does not fit any of the usual definitions of fundamentalism.

This chapter is not the place to evaluate this second reason the economist Christian and social ethicist-critics propose for the elevation of Christianity to equal or greater importance than economics for understanding human behavior. However, their case needs to be reiterated briefly (from our earlier chapters) because Richardson makes no mention of it. In general, the Christian critics believe that the Judeo-Christian Bible provides the triune God's normative guide, and the only correct one, for humankind's interconnected spiritual and material life. The Bible is seen to provide a teleological assessment of this life applying to specific contexts. Principles inherent in this teleology are intended to apply to other temporal/spatial contexts for both explanatory and prescriptive purposes. Hermeneutical problems in elucidating the principles inherent in this Biblical guide for human personal and social life are substantial, as are those in relating the principles to diverse contexts (a helpful discussion for economists of both these issues is Williams, 1996). However, these endeavors and their praxis were meant to be a major project of Christianity AD. As noted in Chapter 1, no suggestion occurs in the Bible that where God's purposes for humanity are ignored, true explanations or prescriptions for human behavior can be formulated (even assuming a natural law framework). If this were the case, God's system could be put aside, and the Bible need have little relevance. The Bible's intentions do not accept that this approach will be fruitful, that sinful human behavior can be comprehended outside God's normative guidelines, and that stable solutions outside God can be devised for fallen humanity.

The experience of physical science and mathematics do not contradict the claims above. The notion that physical science and mathematics can be practiced independently of God's purposes (a debatable premise as the likes of Clouser, 1991, have shown), does not mean that social science can. The Bible does not try to explain the physical world, but it does try to explain human action, as does social science. In the Bible's view, human action can only be fathomed in relation to God's normative purposes for humanity. Human behavior is only to be understood in relation to God, that is inherently connected with relations between people. If economics is defined as the search 'for principles on which aspects of the economic system work' (Smith, 1993, 165), the pursuit of these independently from principles God has ordained, in a human system effectively or explicitly operating apart from God's normative principles, is likely to produce sparse results. Humans either function as closely as possible with God or they do not function coherently. To further complicate the search for non-God principles, the idea that objective falsificationist criteria can be applied as the measure of science in social science and economics is being increasingly questioned. A large literature has developed in social science over the last few decades underlining this claim, reviewed in Hands (2001b). Yet social science, including economics, clings doggedly to the belief that principles ex-God can be discovered that will explain how existing socio-economic systems work and enable predictions to be made on these bases from which policy can be derived. As Chapter 1 noted, the development of social science throughout its history has involved the steady repudiation of anything to do with the triune Christian God (unfortunately, sometimes for the reason that the institutional church repressed exploration of how Biblical teaching might apply to contemporary material life).

As we have seen in earlier chapters, various examples occur of the economist Christian critics deducing and utilizing Judeo-Christian socio-economic intentions related to modern life. An example in the Catholic tradition is the social economist, McKee (1987). His exercise was to 'project attitudes and thought that are systematically and authentically grounded in the Christian religion and way of life on the economy and on the science that studies it' (1987, xi). He situates this discussion in a context of Christian philosophical response to that underlying orthodox economics, and develops a selection of Christian principles relating to social and economic life relying on natural law and scriptural sources, and the teaching of the Catholic church. He examines specific questions in relation to these principles, such as the just wage, inflation, welfare economics and the role of government. McKee subjects economics to a philosophical and methodological critique on the basis of the Christian viewpoint he develops, and points to a social economics in which Christian intentions could be accommodated. In general, McKee's project is sympathetic to the approach taken in this book, even if all his conclusions are not identical with those here. Recent work continues this overall approach, such as Massaro (1998), who with a more specific focus, assesses the implications of Catholic Social Thought for welfare policy and reform in the US from the 1980s. Again, this approach is similar to McKee's and that taken here: Extract principles from the selected source of Christian belief, and then take a particular policy issue and relate those principles to that issue. In Massaro's case, the issue is the history of the welfare reform policy, and secular responses to it are assessed, including those that philosophically might be made to its underlying framework.

The development of Biblical principles, or derivative social principles (Hay, 1989), relevant to socio-economic life is germane not only to potential policy making. As shown in Chapter 4, the principles can also provide a framework for explanatory analysis. Explanation for contemporary socio-economic phenomena can be cast in terms of observable empirical deviation from the principles. Even the mere description of aspects of human behavior would be influenced by the specifications of the principles. If it was agreed, say, that a Biblical principle is that all willing adults should be provided with socially-useful remunerated employment sufficient to enjoy a minimum socially-defined standard of living, the description of unemployment would be moulded by that norm. (All the terms in this principle require more precise definition). Unemployment would be defined or described empirically by the extent to which existing patterns of remunerated work deviated from the principle. Explanations for unemployment would revolve around discovering why existing patterns of work did deviate from meeting the principle's specifications (and here, plenty of scope exists for empirical methods in socio-economic investigation). The description and explanation of unemployment, like the other entities with which economics deals, are not value-free technical derivations or means expositions unrelated to given ends or values. Even prices reflect underlying values. The three stages of social science—description, explanation and policy prescription—would be guided by the normative requirements in principle God has ordained for humanity. This is as much the practice of social science as any alternative conception of the term.

THE AUTONOMOUS VIEWS OF ANTHONY WATERMAN

Anthony Waterman is the second economist-Christian representative of the separatist-autonomist school considered here. Waterman is probably best known as an historian of orthodox economics, in which his emphasis has been on the influence of English religious thought in the development of economics, and vice versa (e.g., Waterman, 1991). In his subsequent writing, Waterman makes much of this process to explain why modern orthodox economics is in the autonomous position it is (a position he favors). For instance, in (1999, 51–67, and 2001, 41–63), Waterman charts the history of the development of economics in England in relation to thought in the Protestant (Anglican) Episcopal Church of England. He points out that religious and economic thinking were intertwined for most of the eighteenth century, that economic study was then regarded as 'a branch of Christian moral science.' The reason for their parting of the ways, according to Waterman, was that the problem of scarcity became 'recognized scientifically' only for the first time in the work of Malthus (a clergyman); 'ineluctable laws of nature produce poverty and inequality . . . *Why then does God create a world in which most human beings must live in "misery" or "vice"?*' (Waterman, 1999, 56–57; original emphasis).

This problem created a great intellectual flurry in the nineteenth century in which none of the protagonists (Whately, Sumner, Copleston) studied the Old Testament where the problem and its reported God-planned resolution were proposed (examined, for instance, by Gordon, 1989; and Wright, 1990). The idea of scarcity was enshrined after the Fall in Genesis, and runs as a continuing theme throughout the Pentateuch. Scarcity was not a new discovery in the eighteenth century, but how it was to be dealt with differed in the Biblical texts from that of Malthus and his successors. Whately etc. offered little examination of Biblical texts, and presented no systemic analysis of them. Therefore, they did not present principles, intentions or themes relevant to grappling with the socio-economic issues of their day. Further, these mid-nineteenth century Christians had no conception of issues relating to science that were to redefine thinking about the subject from the mid twentieth century, examined in later chapters here. The contributions of these thinkers to modern understandings of the relation between Biblical thought/theology and economics/science can carry little weight. According to McDonald (1993), Olson (1993) and Avis (1995), the solution to scarcity and human socio-economic problems in the nineteenth century was sought not via Biblical principle, but in 'science' that was assuming increasing sway as the guide to socio-economic understanding. Simultaneously, an 'aggressively secular character' marked social-scientific thought from the early seventeenth century, (Olson, 1993, 11), and later important social theorists were often stridently anti-Christian (Avis, 1995, *passim*). This occurred even though less prominent Christian social scientists had significant but waning influence (e.g., in the U. S., as documented for sociology by Vidich and Lyman, 1985, and Ross, 1991, and for economics by Nelson, 1991 and 2001).

Rather than mentioning all the autonomous nineteenth and early twentieth century advocates of separation cited by Waterman (1999), we mention just one of Waterman's examples, a twentieth century representative, William Temple. Unlike his contemporary, R. H. Tawney, who believed in 1913 (p. 72) that 'there is no such thing as a science of economics,' Temple (1942, 72) acquiesced to the autonomous 'technical' nature of relations between cause and effect in the political and economic areas. This type of belief continued to hold sway among Christians. Waterman concludes by highlighting the two most prominent economists of the mid twentieth century discussing Christianity, Denys Munby and Frank Knight, who continued the justification for the autonomous technical and scientific nature of economics from theology. Two problems with Temple, Munby and Knight are that they used such terms as 'scientific' and 'technical' uncritically, and they made no assessment whether socio-economic principles intended for contemporary application might derive from primary sources of Christian belief itself. Munby, for instance, in his 1956 book did not derive socio-economic principles directly from the Bible. His first chapter on the basics of the Christian faith is substantiated by generous reference to the Bible, but his next chapter on Christian ethics contains no systematic analysis of how the ethical values are derived from the Biblical text overall, as distinct from *ad hoc* citations (five to the Gospels and eight to Paul). In Munby's second chapter also, his further authorities are Church fathers (especially Augustine) and other secondary Christian thinkers, but there is no systemic treatment of them either. Temple (1942) made no reference to the Bible or to any secondary sources.

Proponents of the traditional autonomous view, including Waterman, make much use of the term 'science,' but do not discuss the various understandings of science current nowadays. These interpretations of science will be examined in the next chapter here. The views of the autonomous proponents appear to rest on a constellation of unstated assumptions such as:

- The meaning of science is unproblematic.
- Scientific knowledge, including logic and mathematics, is the only objective and valid source of knowledge.
- Metaphysical claims, normative statements, and value judgements cannot be objective knowledge.
- Empirical data, based on sense experience, is the only source of objective and valid knowledge, except for logic and mathematics.
- Objective knowledge can only be obtained by the methods of the natural sciences, using logic and mathematics.
- Technical or scientific analysis does not contain value judgements.
- The methods of obtaining objective (scientific) knowledge are similar for the investigation of natural and social phenomena.
- Orthodox economics is a science.
- The distinction between positive (value-free) and normative (value-affected) economics can be sustained.
- The distinction can be sustained between the technical means of orthodox economic analysis and non-technical ends to which the analysis might be applied.
- Brute autonomous value-free economic 'facts' are the empirical data source for economics.
- Economics and social science have demonstrated intellectual progress.
- The meaning of intellectual progress in economics and social science is unambiguous.
- Economics and social science have discovered principles and theories that can be, and have been, applied to human improvement.
- The meaning of human improvement is clear-cut.

All the above claims are now contested and do not reflect debate on the reassessment of the meaning of science and economics from the 1960s, for which a voluminous literature exists (a recent helpful summary for science is Chalmers, 1999a, and for economics, Hands, 2001b). Little of the content of this debate is reviewed by Waterman (1987, 1988, 1999, 2001). The assumptions above in relation to economics also ignore the even longer standing critique from the diverse currents of heterodox economics (including Keynes) that are not discussed by Waterman either. One orthodox economist's summary of the re-evaluation on the scientific standing of economics from the 1960s is that economic knowledge is no longer well-defined, that 'the concept of "knowledge" in general and "scientific knowledge" in particular has been seriously challenged (many would say radically undermined) during the last few decades' (Hands, 2000, 450). Historians and philosophers of science from Kuhn through Rescher to Laudan, sociologists of science like Woolgar and Collins, economists such as McCloskey, Blaug, and Caldwell, philosophers like Trigg, and countless others, have all contributed to the demise of the traditional view of science, social science and economics. The influence of secular philosophies of post-positivism, postmodernism, realism, rhetoric, and neopragmatism continue to chip away at the traditional view of 'economic science.' To this type of critic, 'the necessarily neutral, "value-free" character of economic analysis' that has 'passed into the orthodox mainstream of modern economics' (Waterman, 1999, 63) is both an oxymoron and evidence of the erroneous thinking of modern economics. The separatist-autonomous economist-Christians, including Waterman, give little attention to the continuing debate about science and economics. They certainly do not consider how it might affect their views of economics or Christianity.

The nearest Waterman (1999) comes to contemplating these views is by basing an argument for the separation of economics and Christianity on Kolakowski (1982). For a Christian to found such an argument on a treatise so unsympathetic to Christian belief is unusual. This is especially so because Kolakowski barely mentions any theological system, or the primary source of Christian belief, the Bible, has no analysis of it, and instead presents his own speculations, occasionally mentioning secondary Christian and non-Christian sources. Kolakowski's and Waterman's claims are that religion and science are involved with incommensurable languages. Religion is supposed to supply 'values,' and science (of which economics is assumed to one variety) to supply value-free 'facts.' This argument depends partly on the distinction between 'fact' and 'value' that has long been rejected by post-positivist critics (e.g., Trigg, 1985; Wilber and Hoksbergen, 1984, 1986; Beed, 1992; Putnam, 2002). Neither do some of the critics think that much mileage is to be had by calling economics a 'science' (e.g., Steedman, 1999, 167, specifically in relation to Waterman), of which more is said in the next chapter.

Waterman's argument also betrays a deeper worry to Christians in his reliance on Kolakowski's treatment of religion, even if one agreed with the Wittgensteinian 'language game' base on which it rests. Kolakowski does not care to define religion (1982, 9–10). 'Religion' is often taken to mean a system of faith and worship, involving human recognition of a superhuman controlling power, especially a personal God entitled to obedience, including the effects of this on human conduct. This definition contains multifarious dimensions, including ideas of a worldview, normative guidelines for human behavior, and an associated institution or church. Kolakowski restricts his vision of religion to the last part of this constellation, to the 'socially established worship of the eternal reality' (1982, 12–13). With this description, it is not difficult to leap to the conclusion that the 'language of the Sacred' is concerned with trying to make the 'natural environment' intelligible, rather than 'reacting' to it (Kolakowski, 1982, 180). Many Christians, however, would not agree with Kolakowski that the 'language of the Sacred' and the 'actual language of secular life' serve different purposes. Christians are unlikely to accept that secular language is sufficient to enable 'communication in the realm of specifically human relationships.' Earlier chapters here, for example, argued that the Bible is saturated with descriptions of how its worldview and normative guidelines for human behavior affect human action. That is, these precepts relate to what Kolakowski understands as the 'moral and "intentional" characteristics' (Kolakowski, 1982, 180) of the human world as it existed. Kolakowski and Waterman seem to be assuming what they want to prove, that religion and science (read economics) are 'incompatible and non-intersecting' language-games (Waterman, 1999, 67).

The separate-autonomous view also seems to imply a constellation of contestable assumptions about the meaning and relevance of Christian belief vis-a-vis non-Christian or secular beliefs that cannot be debated in this chapter. Contrary to the argument of previous chapters, the assumptions appear to include that:

- A separate domain of human behavior—'the economic'—can be excised from the entirety of behavior, and analyzed as a separate secular entity to yield valid conclusions about that domain.
- The analysis of an economic domain of human behavior solely in terms of a materialistic/naturalistic framework (denying the influence of the supernatural spiritual world view of Biblical Christianity) yields valid conclusions about that domain.
- The analysis of an economic domain of human behavior independently from the normative intentions God and Jesus Christ have for human life yields valid conclusions about that domain.
- Economics and social science provide superior explanations and prescriptions for human personal and/or social behavior to those provided by Judeo-Christianity.
- 'Superior' can be measured by objective scientific criteria.

None of these assumptions is discussed by the separate-autonomous protagonists. If Christians were to accept none of the assumptions, an opposite scenario could be constructed about the significance of economics to Christians. This could include claims that orthodox economics:

- Does not contain self-contained hypotheses capable of explaining or predicting any aspect of human behavior, except as imprecise qualitative generalization.

- Can serve as no more than one input into a broader, 'common sense' secular view (Coates, 1996) seeking to explain human behavior.
- Casts little light on what additional influences beyond those defined as economic might be, and detracts from investigating them (despite the efforts of 'economics imperialism').
- Has limited relevance to the formation of public policy.
- Is not to be accorded preeminent intellectual importance because it rejects input from the supernatural triune Christian God into the explanatory matrix of human behavior.

Again, the nearest Waterman gets to considering these qualities above is his reliance on Knight's claim that Christianity has no social implications. To Waterman's knowledge (1999, 65), Knight's assertion has never been answered. Frank Knight was a prominent mid-twentieth century non-Christian US academic neo-orthodox economist who had a lifelong interest in, and frequent antagonism to, Christianity. Knight's entire corpus of work relating to religion demonstrates no theological or Biblical analysis, but consists of *ex cathedra* statements about how he saw Christianity, invariably with no reference to anybody else's writings. Knight believed that the 'Christian gospel of love' was 'directed at *personal relations*' while the central problem of economics, social science, and society was '*social relations*' (Emmett, 1999, 107–108; original emphasis). A large volume of Christian-based work both before and since Knight—some of it reviewed in earlier chapters here—has tried to show that Judeo-Christianity relates to both personal and social relations. For instance, Knight's position is today not accepted by a range of contemporary economist-Christians who hold divergent views between them on a range of political and economic matters. Despite their other differences, they all agree that Christianity has social implications, from Tiemstra et al. (1990), through Wilson (1997a) to Stapleford (2000). On the theological side, an abundance of writing has endeavored to demonstrate the social relevance of Biblical Christian ethics (four recent examples are Stackhouse, 1997b; Alford and Naughton, 2001; Hauerwas, 2001; and Carter, 2001). A widely-used, middle-road, Protestant evangelical theological text (Erickson, 1998) even devotes an entire chapter to social structures of sin, a standard concept in Catholic Social Thought. The problem is that Waterman (like Knight) cites and examines none of this, but bases his argument wholly on Knight, evidently believing Knight's claims to be unassailable. Waterman might not think any of the Christian writing endeavoring to show that Judeo-Christianity relates to both personal and social relations 'answers' Knight. But at least, Waterman should acknowledge the existence of this type of Christian thought, and explain why it does not 'answer' the non-Christian, Knight, on whom Waterman relies to carry his argument.

CONCLUSION

The views of the economist-Christians, J. David Richardson and Anthony Waterman are often interpreted differently from the analysis here. They are understood by orthodox economist-Christians to mean that economist-Christians should excel where possible in the mainstream, fulfilling career and research roles within the traditions, opportunities and constraints of existing university and government institutions. This can be interpreted as encouraging economist-Christians away from possible isolationist tendencies. Since orthodox economics is 'science', theologians and church people should be wary about making pronouncements on economic policy from a position of ignorance of economic science. In the orthodox view of Waterman (Webb, 2000, 14), economics is a 'word like physics, i.e., it's a study of something, like mechanics . . . ,' presumably with affinities to physical science. A contradictory dichotomy is assumed to exist between orthodox economist-Christians who are trying to scientifically describe and make sense of the fallen and sinful world as it is, and heterodox economist-Christians committed to a distinctively ('non-scientific') Christian socio-economic analysis (unacceptable to mainstream publication). Heterodox economist-Christians and their fellow travelers in social theologians are presumed not to be able to achieve the required (scientific) purchase on reality. If these critics question the claims of the orthodox economist-Christians, they are liable to be accused of having deficient knowledge of contemporary orthodox economics. This chapter (and book) questions all these judgements, given that the views of Richardson and Waterman have not been critically evaluated.

From the perspectives taken in this and earlier chapters about Christianity and economics, there are more fundamental reasons below than espoused by Richardson and Waterman for rejecting the notion of economics as a separate autonomous discipline (further explored in Beed, 2005d). If secular autonomous economics and social science had been able to produce unassailable theories about human behavior, and apply them to 'improving' society, this would be a reason for Christians to pursue these disciplines independently of their Christian beliefs. In contradistinction to the arguments of this book, the disciplines would then pose a dramatic challenge to the validity of Christian belief. However, in our view, social science has not produced the goods. Never has there been more information about human behavior, but never has it been more contested. Far from developing into an integrated science of human behavior over the last few hundred years, the separate social sciences relate little to each other, and each is rent by competing schools of thought (Rule, 1997). One judgement from a heterodox economist on contemporary sociology, for instance, is that its 'central theoretical project' is 'in virtual chaos' (Hodgson, 2002, 129).

The attraction of science to the separatist advocates is understandable. Physical science has long been seen as a way of explaining, controlling and changing the world. Yet, there is little evidence that the social sciences, including economics, are achieving these ends. For economics, at the time of Richardson's paper (1988), one observation consistent with (but not proving) this contention about explanation was that 'the state of economic knowledge [i.e., theory] has not greatly improved since 1943' (Epstein, 1987, 207). More recent and skeptical judgements are Anderson's (1996, 119) that 'perhaps 80 or 90 percent of the economics you need to know to make decent economic policy in the twentieth century was figured out and written down in the eighteenth and nineteenth centuries', and Nelson's (2001, 330), that 'the emperor of high economic theory has no clothes.'

A Christian explanation for this situation is that secular social science theory, including economics, is pursuing an unproductive mission. God made people for relationship with Him, not for them to pursue independent decision making, including analyzing human behavior as though it existed autonomously from God and His Biblical teaching, or as though stable second best solutions existed to accommodate sinful human behavior. Certainly, God has given people the free choice to think and act in this way. But from a Biblical perspective, it is an irrational way of behaving. Explanation or prediction of irrational human behavior that ignores or rejects God is not likely to produce coherent results. This is because the possibility and realization for each person of deviating from God's intentions and guidelines are enormous, the crippling nature of sin is endemic. Sin's rampant effects produce secular explanations for human behavior only at a level of trivial simplicity—which is more or less where social science theory, including economics, have been since its inception around three hundred years ago (despite its current mathematical veneer).

In contradistinction to the separate-autonomous view of economics and social science, the alternative interpretation here is that derivative social principles, themes or paradigms can be derived from the Christian Bible intended by the triune God to be applicable to contemporary personal behavior and socio-economic organization (and to all humanity for the last three thousand years or so). Contrary to objections raised by some economist Christian critics (e.g., Waterman, 1988, 208; Smith, 1993, 175; Wilson, 1997a, *passim*) these principles could be sufficiently refined to relate to contemporary socio-economic life, and Chapters 2–4 here tried to demonstrate just this. Catholic Social Thought has made most progress in this direction, but as this has occurred only in the last hundred years or so, it is insufficiently developed to capture the attention of Christians (compounded by anti-Catholic sentiment among some Protestant Christians). In the main, socio-economic principles, themes and paradigms from the Bible have been disregarded by human society in all history both by Christians and non-Christians. Therefore, they still appear as ill-formed and rudimentary. Nevertheless, attempts to discover socio-economic organizational principles outside of the triune God's framework are not proving successful, and have not produced anything enduring beyond common sense. All these are not fundamentalist arguments because they do not accord with specifications of fundamentalism, and the contentions are propounded also by diverse currents of Christian thought. Nevertheless, the arguments do question the autonomous claims of academic economic and social science theory.

Chapter Eight

Science and Contemporary Economics

The previous chapter argued against the view that economics, or indeed any social science, has an intellectual autonomy enabling its theories to stand apart from the normative requirements the triune God encourages for human life. In part, the 'autonomous' viewpoint developed historically because of the growing separation of scientific activity from Christian belief, a process examined in Chapter 13. Economics and the social sciences are the product of intellectual activity over the last three hundred years or so in which physical and natural science made tremendous discoveries. It was anticipated by fledgling social investigators of the eighteenth century that perhaps comparable discoveries could also be made about human behavior and action by the application of scientific methods. Increasingly, this exploration was pursued outside of a Christian framework that was seen as inimical to the process of the free pursuit of human knowledge. Unfortunately, part of this critique is valid, in so far as the institutional church periodically throughout Christian history has inhibited the free discovery of the human intellect. Science, unencumbered by religious constraints, has been seen in the last few centuries as the path to human emancipation. One problem with this depiction, however, is that the meaning of science never was clear-cut, and is becoming less so. The first half of this chapter is devoted to the recent changing meaning of science, and the second half to the way in which this changed meaning has impacted on social science and especially economics (Beed, 1991, 2005a). The following four chapters (9–12) show that the scientific claims of economic and social science theory to explain reality are sufficiently flawed to alert Christians to the need to analyze how the Christian framework itself can explain and prescribe for that reality, as per Chapters 2–4.

If we take just the 1950s to the present, there has been extensive debate within the philosophy of science over the meaning and content of scientific activity. Indeed, from the 1960s, previous ideas of what constituted science had been overturned (Suppe, 1974, 1977). This debate has had profound implications not only for the physical sciences but also for the social sciences, including economics. In so far as the social sciences have long regarded the physical sciences as their methodological models, the overthrow of traditional ideas about physical science has left the social sciences in some methodological and philosophical disarray.

The traditional idea of the content of physical science was well summarized in a widely used philosophy of science text in the 1980s (still enjoying widespread use in its 3rd 1999 edition):

> Scientific knowledge is proven knowledge. Scientific theories are derived in some rigorous way from the facts of experience acquired by observation and experiment. . . . Personal opinion or preferences and speculative imaginings have no place in science . . . Scientific knowledge is reliable knowledge because it is objectively proven knowledge (Chalmers, 1982, 1).

This view of science, sometimes called the Legend, held wide sway in the world in the nineteenth and twentieth centuries. But since the 1960s, a growing challenge has been mounted against it in the physical sciences. Antecedents of the challenge are found extending far back into history but gathered coherent shape only in the early decades of the twentieth century. From the late 1950s, however, the challenge to traditional idea of science took a decisive turn, and since the 1960s fewer thinkers on science accept the common view. The effects of this challenge are gradually filtering into the social sciences, including economics.

This chapter reviews the background to the traditional, or common view of science, and establishes its common elements. Then it moves on to the challenge that has been posed to the common view since the 1960s, focusing more on writings in that period than today. We then turn to consider the impact the challenge to the received view of physical science has had on the social sciences. Specifically, we examine three examples affecting economics from the 1980s, all of which reflect the methodological dilemmas posed for assessing progress in economic 'science.' The first example investigates the methodological writings of the eminent historian of economics, Mark Blaug; the second looks at the debate over the scientific claims of general equilibrium analysis; and the third example is the argument over the status of econometrics.

BACKGROUND TO THE TRADITIONAL VIEW OF SCIENCE

This section traces the origin of the traditional view of science that has steadily been rejected within the philosophy of science, and in the history and sociology of science. The common or received view, exemplified in the quote above from Chalmers, is a summation of particular ways of looking at the world. These ways can be summarized as the philosophy of positivism, aspects of which date back as far as Roger Bacon in the thirteenth century (Kolakowski, 1972). Bacon strove to encourage scientific experiment and to eliminate Aristotelian metaphysics from human knowledge, which Bacon asserted was to be assessed by the usefulness of its application. Through William of Ockham, de Mirecourt, d'Autrecourt, and Buridan, the face of positivism slowly took shape over four centuries until Galileo, in the seventeenth century, emerged as the founder of an explicitly positivist conception of science concerned with making quantitative descriptions of measurable phenomena. Building further on Mersenne, Gassendi, Descartes, and Leibniz, the next watershed of positivism is David Hume in the eighteenth century. Hume aimed to apply scientific reasoning to the study of human behavior, so that 'the empirical findings of psychology, epistemology, logic, conceptual analysis, ethics, aesthetics, social philosophy and politics would be unified together in one great empirical science of human nature' (Walsh, 1985, 276).

The Enlightenment of the eighteenth century encouraged the growth of positivist thinking (see, e.g., Gay, 1975), and contributed directly to its triumph in the post-Enlightenment era. Here, Auguste Comte was its chief developer, responsible for popularizing the term 'positivism.' Comte expounded the virtues of scientific knowledge acquired though the collection of facts and the formulation of descriptive laws. This was to be the common scientific method of all disciplines (except mathematics, which was purely logic). Human subjectivity, it was believed, could be eliminated by this process.

By the mid-nineteenth century, positivism was triumphant as a theory for obtaining human knowledge. Its influence affected most areas of study, including medicine (Claude Bernard), biology (Charles Darwin), ethics (John Stuart Mill), and sociology (Herbert Spencer). Says Kolakowski, 'positivism dominated the spirit of the age' (1972, 122). It was widely believed that 'truth, in the shape of objective facts about the world, must surely speak directly to unbiased observers, and give access to reality itself' (Richards, 1987, 201).

Given this dominance, it is not surprising that positivism continued to exert a strong influence into the twentieth century. One of this century's early proponents was the physicist Ernst Mach, who was, according to Walsh (1985, 474), 'widely regarded as the father of logical positivism'; Mach contended that scientific theories are only those that can be verified by empirical data. As a center for the development of positivist ideas, the Vienna Circle took shape in the early decades of the century under the leadership of physicist, Moritz Schlick. But by the mid-1930s, with the threat of nazism, the members of the circle dispersed to Great Britain and the United States, where logical positivism was subsumed into the broader character of international logical empiricism. Nevertheless, positivist theorists continued to be active, such as Rudolph Carnap, Ludwig Wittgenstein (who appeared to repudiate positivism before his death in 1951), Otto Neurath, Percy Bridgman, and Hans Reichenbach. Others sharing some features of a positivist outlook in the British school of analytic philosophy were G. E. Moore, Bertrand Russell, and Alfred Whitehead. Karl Popper was originally a participant in the Vienna Circle but broke away in the early 1930s. Carnap continued to write until the 1960s, although he did not maintain positivism, but Carl Hempel long pursued a logical positivist position, as did the best-known recent English positivist philosopher, Alfred Ayer. Given such an array of intellectual giants, it is not surprising that positivism maintained strong influence on the physical and social sciences in the twentieth century.

Positivist ideas have never formed a distinct, coherent whole; there never has been a clearly defined 'school of positivism.' Rather, positivism reflected individual views about how human knowledge can be acquired. This worldview built up and changed gradually over the seven centuries of its development. In its early stages (a time when the word 'positivism' is an inappropriate description), divine inspiration was accepted as a valid source of human knowledge. But since the eighteenth century, positivism rejected the validity, as knowledge, of metaphysics, and supernatural or 'unprovable' statements (i.e., statements about empirically unknowable phenomena).

Thus, says Kolakowski, positivism:

> Stands for a certain philosophical attitude to human knowledge . . . [It] is a normative attitude . . . a collection of prohibitions concerning human knowledge, intended to confine the name 'knowledge' or 'science' to the results of those operations that are observable in the evolution of the modem sciences of nature (1972, 10, 181).

Extracting the main tenets of positivism is a difficult task. The approach here is to rely on a number of thinkers conversant with the history of philosophy who, in the 1960s and 1970s when discussion of positivism was more prevalent than currently, identified the main elements of positivism. The following list captures their main characteristics of positivism. However, the authors from whom the list was generated (Abbagnano, 1967; Ayer, 1959b; Giedymin, 1975; Halfpenny, 1982; Kaplan, 1968; Kolakowski, 1972; Passmore, 1967; von Wright, 1971) do not agree on all the major features of positivism, or on which philosophers of the past might be called positivist.

1. Scientific knowledge (including logic and mathematics) is the only valid knowledge.
2. Metaphysical claims, normative statements, value judgments, and opinions are not valid knowledge.

3. Human sense experience (empirical data) is the only source of valid knowledge (except for logic and mathematics).
4. Valid knowledge can only be obtained by the methods of the natural sciences, especially physics, utilizing logic and mathematics.
5. Generalizations, principles, and theories in science can only be derived from empirical data (= induction) (except for theories in logic and mathematics).
6. Generalizations, principles and theories in science must be verifiable from empirical data (except for theories in logic and mathematics).
7. Generalizations, principles and theories should be expressible in mathematical logical form.
8. Normative views, value judgments, convictions, beliefs, and opinions should not enter into empirical data collection, theory formulation, or verification.
9. The methods of obtaining valid scientific knowledge are the same for all fields of experience (= unity of the scientific method).

Thus, positivism prescribed specific rules and evaluative norms for deriving valid knowledge. These rules were thought to characterize physical science, especially physics, which was the methodological ideal for all rational debate. The development of any field of human knowledge (such as social science) was to be measured against this ideal. Aside from logic and mathematics, which are constructions of the human mind, sense data, or what can actually be experienced and measured in the real world, was the only valid source of knowledge. Metaphysical and religious speculations or reflections on human life were ruled out as invalid or non-sense, since they could not be made amenable to controlled experiment.

By the beginning of the twentieth century, positivism had become the modem scientific worldview. It had succeeded in detaching science from religion by making science depend solely on sense data from the physical world, and thereby science pushed values aside. 'Hitherto,' writes Richards (1987, 178), 'facts and values had been essentially fused together as two aspects of one reality, in the Christian context at least, with values (which were transcendental) as definitely the dominant partner . . . Non factual propositions, such as those of religion,' were now disregarded as meaningless, 'while science rested on supposedly verifiable facts.'

ANTI-POSITIVISM

A range of responses developed to the positivist conception of science from the 1950s that fall broadly under the term 'anti-positivist' or 'post-positivist.'

As will become clear, the spectrum of anti-positivist responses to positivism is wide, and it is probably even more difficult to classify these responses than it is to classify positivism itself.

Some anti-positivist ideas about human knowledge have had a far longer history than positivist ideas. For example, a very early worldview that we may see as anti-positivist is religious thinking based on concepts of supernatural influence; thus, Biblical thought about the world poses a dominant metaphysical element as a sympathetic complement to the power of empiricism and human reason. Anti-positivist beliefs also include the philosophical tradition of non-religious idealism, the belief in mind as the fundamental substance, rather than matter. Immanuel Kant argued along these lines to suggest that human reason cannot discover all the secrets of the world. He believed that the human mind is structured so that it can only classify and synthesize sense data.

If we move to the late nineteenth and early twentieth centuries when positivism came to dominate scientific thought, anti-positivism continued in muted form. The German historian, Droysen emphasized the difference between explanation and understanding that was to have a great influence on the social sciences. These ideas were developed by Simmel, who discussed the importance of empathy in historical understanding (von Wright, 1971, 6). Within philosophy, idealism staggered under the onslaught of the positivist trends; the idea that mind or spirit was something different from matter paled. However, the Italian idealist, Croce remained undaunted and related his philosophy of spirit to a variety of areas, including economics. In France, Brunschvicg declared the inadequacy of the empiricist basis of positivism 'in the light of the brilliant inventiveness and spontaneous creativity of the intelligent scientist' (Walsh, 1985, 467). Collingwood in Britain and Blanshard in the United States were affected early in their lives by idealism, but later changed their ground. Neo-Kantian idealism persisted in Germany through the Baden school led by Windelband and Rickert, while Dilthey discussed the difference between explanation and understanding in the physical and human sciences.

Among those who did not think of themselves as idealists in philosophy, Henri Bergson in France struggled against the growing hold of positivism and scientism (and idealism). Edmund Husserl in Germany pursued his critique of positivism, relativism, and psychologism, while developing the new philosophy of phenomenology, the analysis of human consciousness.

ANTI-POSITIVISM AND THE PHYSICAL SCIENCES

As the twentieth century proceeded, the influence of non-positivist philosophy grew, and the logical positivists lamented their diminishing authority within philosophy. Ayer, for example, complained that since the Second World War, 'the prevailing tendency in England has been to replace this uncompromising positivism with its blanket rejection of metaphysics, its respect for scientific method.' He pointed to the enormous national divisions in world philosophy by the mid-1950s, noting that 'they do not occur to anything like the same extent in other branches of learning' (Ayer, 1959b, 8, 9).

Walsh (1985, 508) suggests that:

> Philosophical analysis . . . ended with logical positivism and with the widespread repudiation of analysis as the proper method of philosophy. In the 1950s, the new generation of young philosophers turned . . . towards the conception of philosophy as an activity which strives to describe and elucidate through language, difficult and basic questions relating to reality.

Linguistic philosophy—the exploration of the logical grammar of expressions—developed, metaphysical philosophy was rehabilitated, and phenomenology and existentialism continued. All of these contained anti-positivist tendencies, even though their main disagreements were not with positivism (nor were their main interests with science). Other strands of modern philosophy that had a more explicit anti-positivist, orientation included Popper's critical rationalism, Bachelard's naturalism, critical theory or the Frankfurt school associated with Marcuse and Habermas, and the scientific realism of Harre, Hesse, and Bhaskar. Although it might be thought that positivism in science received its body blows from Kuhn, Lakatos, and Feyerabend from the 1960s, the tradition of philosophical anti-positivist thinking about science clearly is much older than that. For this reason, the term, 'anti-positivism' is more accurate historically than 'post-positivism,' but the latter is the more common.

From the 1930s, Popper and Bachelard published alternative accounts of scientific reasoning and activity from the positivists. In his 1934 *Logic of Scientific Discovery*, Karl Popper criticized the positivist tenet of inductive inference and claimed that it was not an essential feature of science. He proposed the principle of falsification in contrast to the positivist principle of verification, and was prepared to admit the value of metaphysical knowledge. Bachelard, in his 1934 *The New Scientific Spirit*, suggested that science does not progress by following the positivist method, but rather jumps from one rupture or mutation in human thought to another, and is, to some extent, as unpredictable as a biological mutation. Bachelard specifically criticized positivism as an attempt to impose on science an idealized ideology that does not conform to the actual practice of science. Unlike Popper, however, Bachelard was not concerned with distinguishing between science and non-science.

These writers, however, had little impact on scientific thought in English-speaking cultures because they were not translated into English until long after their original publications (Popper's *Logic of Scientific Discovery* in 1959, Bachelard's *The New Scientific Spirit* in 1984). In the English-speaking world, Popper's influence has eclipsed that of Bachelard. But although Popper credited himself with having destroyed logical positivism, not everybody regarded Popper as so far from positivism itself. The logical positivists themselves were not eager to distance themselves too far from Popper (for example, Ayer 1959b, 6: 'the affinities between him and the positivists whom he criticized appear more striking than the divergences'). It has not been uncommon to find Popper labeled as a positivist or neo-positivist (e.g., Kolakowski, 1972; Halfpenny, 1982). (There are a number of reasons for this identification, including Popper's resurrection from the nineteenth-century positivist, Claude Bernard, of the falsification principle that theories can be falsified by empirical facts, Popper's aspiration for an ahistorical methodological criterion for science, and so on.)

These anti-positivist views that science could not attain certainty by following the positivist tenets were encouraged by developments in physics and mathematics in the early twentieth century. The quotations below are confined to those who wrote about the issues nearer to the overturn of the Legend about science than to those writing about them today. Thus, in physics, the discovery of fundamental properties of matter, 'such as the seemingly endless series of elementary "particles" or the so-called waves of probability, seemed unreal, while others, such as the relativity of time and space, seemed bizarre and unnatural" (Richards, 1987, 74). Positivism's confident belief that science would reveal the certainties of the world appeared to be undermined in science itself. Heisenberg's uncertainty principle (1929), implying 'that the law of universal causality had been overthrown' (Powers, 1982, 140), demonstrated the irony that even in physics, the archetype of positivist science, events cannot be precisely predicted.

The theory of relativity and the quantum theory, according to Davies (1983, vii), 'seemed to turn commonsense on its head and find closer accord with mysticism than materialism.' In studying the work of the new physicists, scientists were surprised to find that the likes of Einstein, Bohr, Schrodinger, and Dirac were poetic and religious men 'who imagined such unfamiliar immensities as to make . . . the "paranormal" almost pedestrian by comparison' (Pedlar, 1981, 11). The new physics left the nineteenth-century mechanical models of the universe behind and began to see 'the mind as playing an integral role in all physical events' (Morowitz, 1982, 34). The new physics can be contrasted with twentieth-century developments in biology (and perhaps economics) that 'have been moving relentlessly towards the hard-core materialism that characterized nineteenth-century physics' (Morowitz, 1982, 34). Instead, 'the new physics has given "the observer" a central role in the nature of physical reality,' (Davies, 1983, 8); quantum theory, writes Bohm (1980, 134), drops 'the notion of analysis of the world into relatively autonomous parts, separately existent but in interaction. Rather, the primary emphasis is now on undivided wholeness, in which the observing instrument is not separable from what is observed.' Holism rather than reductionism is its path, and the links between modem physics and religious philosophy became the subject of a flourishing popular and academic literature (e.g., Zukav, 1979; Capra, 1983; Restivo, 1985; Schindler, 1986). Finality of understanding was proving elusive in physics, and was casting doubt on 'the traditional Western dichotomy between the objective and subjective' (Richards, 1987, 75). Each newly discovered element of objective reality proved to be elusive. As Heisenberg put it, 'the common division of the world into subject and object, inner world and outer world, body and soul, is no longer adequate' (1958, 24). Such developments in theoretical physics in the 1920s and 1930s focused on the positivist idea that pure objective empirical data are actually available as a source of verification for theories, and asserted that there is more to reality than positivism conceived.

In so far as positivism placed great store on expressing scientific theories in mathematical logical form, developments in theoretical mathematics up to the 1930s also undermined the possibilities of attaining this positivist goal. By 1930, wrote the well-known mathematician, Kline (1980, 257):

> Four separate, distinct, and more or less conflicting approaches to mathematics had been expounded [logicism, intuitionism, formalism, and set theory], and the proponents of the several views were, it is no exaggeration to say, at war with each other. No longer could one say that a theorem of mathematics was correctly proven. By 1930 one had to add by whose standards it was deemed correct.

According to Kline, this loss of certainty and truth in mathematics persisted. Godel's incompleteness theorem (1931) 'that no set of logical relations can be established that does not also imply the existence of still other relations with which the set itself cannot cope' (Richards, 1987, 74, 75), 'produced a debacle' (Kline, 1980, 6). This was followed by a succession of theorems undermining the certainty of mathematics. The Lowenheim-Skolem theorems from 1920–33 showed that 'mathematical reality cannot be unambiguously incorporated in axiomatic systems . . . because each axiomatic system contains undefined terms,' while Church's theorem (1936) 'states that it is impossible to decide *in advance* whether a proposition is provable or disprovable' (Kline, 1980, 271–272, 267; original emphasis). With Godel's later work and Cohen's independence proofs (1963), 'mathematics reached a plight as disturbing as at the creation of non-Euclidean geometry' (Kline, 1980, 269).

The net result of these developments, according to Kline, was that 'the present state of mathematics is anomalous and deplorable. The light of truth no longer illuminates the road to follow . . . The loss of truth [is] . . . a tragedy of the first magnitude [in which] the concept of a universally accepted, infallible body of reasoning . . . is a grand illusion . . . The Age of Reason is gone.' Any thought that mathematics has 'absolute certainty or validity of its results, could no longer be claimed' and 'this turn of events is not far short of an intellectual disaster' (Kline, 1980, 275, 278, 6, 7, 263, 325). Evidently, twentieth century developments in physics and mathematics undermined the paths to discovering scientific knowledge through the rules positivism had formulated largely on the basis of pre-twentieth century thinking in physics and mathematics.

From the late 1950s, the anti-positivist philosophical tradition in the English-speaking scientific world gathered momentum. This development has been documented extensively (e.g., in physical science, Suppe, 1974, 1977; in social science, Bernstein, 1978; in economics, from Caldwell, 1982 to Hands, 2001b). Many of the positivist tenets were singled out for criticism. Hanson (1958) emphasized the normatively based nature of 'facts,' that our prior views influence what we see, that observation is theory-laden, and that neutral observation languages do not exist. Toulmin (1953, 1961) argued for a more relativistic and conditional conception of science than the positivist one. He contended that scientific theories are neither true nor false but are merely ways of looking at phenomena. The intellectual framework within the scientific community at any given time (*weltanschauung*) determines the standards of usefulness for judging a theory. Scientific theories are formulated in relation to the given criteria or *weltanschauung*, and the question is whether the criteria have any ahistorical validity independently of being so formulated.

Toulmin's ideas relate closely to Kuhn's (1962), that the actual historical practices of science bear little resemblance to the positivist ideals. On the contrary, each area of science is dominated by a paradigm that declares what is to be counted as science. Within the paradigm, positivist criteria for science may or may not exist, but the criteria that do exist have been formulated by the scientific community itself. Each new candidate applying for permission to practice in the paradigm has to subscribe to its particular rules. The paradigm is usually taken for granted, and within it, the scientist works away at 'normal science'—the process of 'mopping up . . . an attempt to force nature into the preformed and relatively inflexible box that the paradigm supplies' (Kuhn, 1977, 24). Periodically, paradigms supplant one another as each paradigm confronts unsolvable anomalies. In these periods of 'revolutionary science,' the old and the new paradigm struggle with one another until the new is victorious.

Insofar as positivism was about prescribing rules for individual scientific theories, Lakatos (Lakatos and Musgrave, 1970) can be regarded as contributing also to the anti-positivist push. Lakatos extended Popper's ideas to his own 'sophisticated methodological falsificationism,' which claimed that the appropriate vehicle for falsification is not the individual scientific theory but the methodological scientific research program (MSRP) of which it is a part. Falsification occurs when one MSRP is replaced by another that explains everything the first did but also additional phenomena not explained by the first. Here a progressive problem shift has occurred, and Lakatos claims this is the way science typically grows.

Finally, Feyerabend (1975), the most anarchistic of the anti-positivist philosophers of science, rejected completely that science proceeds by any methodological rules whatsoever. Feyerabend criticized Lakatos' view because it was unclear how to determine when one MSRP is superior to another, since there are no clear criteria for rejecting an MSRP; Lakatos' methodology was a 'verbal ornament.' Rather, when the history of science is studied, we see that scientists make concrete achievements through relying on intuition, guessing, imagination, hunches, lucky accidents, bluffs, propaganda, myth, metaphysics, induction and falsification; 'everywhere,' says Feyerabend, 'science is enriched by unscientific methods and unscientific results' (1975, 305).

The concerns of this selection of early anti-positivist philosophers and historians of science are very wide. Clearly, there was no common agreement to their critique of positivism. Each of the protagonists rejected different points of the positivism list above. As Suppe put it:

> Different philosophers find different criticisms more telling than others . . . The vast majority of working philosophers of science seem to fall on that portion of the spectrum which holds the Received View [positivism] fundamentally inadequate and untenable, but with considerable disagreement why it is untenable (1974, 115, 116).

A similar point applies to the alternatives to positivism that the philosophers and historians of physical science sought to construct in its place. Suppe could write in 1974 that 'none of the alternative analyses of scientific knowledge which have been suggested enjoy widespread acceptance. For more than fifty years philosophy of science has been engaged in a search for philosophic understanding of scientific theories; today it is still searching' (1974, 4). Exactly the same situation prevails nowadays.

Thus, agreement among anti-positivist philosophers of science was mainly of a negative kind—the things about positivism with which they disagreed. From this negative agreement, it is possible to construct a list of points summarizing the widest anti-positivist position; this list can be compared with the earlier positivism list. Broadly, the total effect is the opposite of the positivism list. However, as with the positivism list, it is important to note that no one anti-positivist philosopher of science would accept all the points:

1. The distinction between positive and normative science is untenable.
2. Value judgments play an integral role in all stages of scientific research.
3. No one 'correct' scientific method exists.
4. No universally agreed basis to evaluate scientific theories exists.
5. Prediction, explanation, internal consistency, economy in assumptions, etc., may all be valued in scientific theories, but none of these qualities is decisive for theory selection.
6. Scientific activity can rest on a metaphysical basis. For example, the empirical validity of all assumptions underlying a scientific theory may not be testable; some may be metaphysical assertions.
7. In their practice of science, scientists do not follow prescribed methodologies.
8. Scientists rely on convictions, beliefs, faith, rhetoric, and persuasion as well as on mathematical and statistical analysis.
9. In the social sciences, few laws or causal explanations have been discovered that hold in all times and places.
10. In the social sciences, verbal analysis is not necessarily inferior to mathematical and statistical analysis.

The whole tenor of these ten points was to undermine the objective, truth-laden, determinate, hard, value-free, positivist, complete, well-grounded, and fixed nature of scientific discovery that promulgates the attitude that science is *the* way to *the* Truth. In anti-positivism, instead, the findings of science become soft, subjective, problematic, fuzzy, probabilistic, partial, value-laden, uncertain, time- and place-specific, and perhaps even culturally specific. Scientific truth is conditional and rests on a normative metaphysical basis. This is a more relativist view of science compared with the positivist absolutist view. In the relativist view, scientific discoveries stand a high chance of being overturned in the future. This is, however, the most extreme stance that might be taken in anti-positivist or post-positivist philosophy of science, say, by a philosopher who accepted all ten points of our second list. Typically, this is not the case.

From the 1960s, the above ideas were canvassed extensively among philosophers of natural science. Debate occurred among anti-positivist philosophers of science about each point on the list above. For instance, in the 1970s and 1980s, although most agreed 'that there are no permanent universally accepted basic standards of scientific rationality' (Doppelt, 1988), some, such as Lakatos (1978), Laudan (1977, 1984), and Shapere (1984) sought to develop less relativistic approaches than others like Doppelt.

Similarly, the realists (e.g., Harre, Hesse, Bhaskar, etc.) feared that the 'irrational' accounts of science within anti-positivism obscured what are the rational elements of science. For instance, Harre (1986, vii) sought 'to repair the ramparts of scientific realism recently broached by new attacks from philosophers and by assault from an unexpected quarter, the sociology of science.' Not that the realist approach represented a retreat to positivism (although some of its critics saw it this way): positivist elements were still rejected. Thus, Harre attacked logical essentialism, 'the giving of primacy to logical structures as the inner essence of discourse,' claiming it had 'a disastrous effect in philosophy of science'; 'Logic does have a place in the creation of scientific discourse, but not at its core . . . logic is a socially motivated addition, a rhetorical contribution to persuasive power' (1986, 4, 5). The 'objective' and the 'rational' were not given pride of place in this realist view. Nevertheless, in the realist view, that may be the dominant contemporary view in philosophy of science, metaphysics is accorded a respectable standing. For example, to Aronson (1984, 199), 'metaphysics plays a predominant role in theory' referring to entities, 'some of which are impossible to observe.' Further discussion on the realist position is in Trigg (1989, 1993), its relation to secular economics is in Lawson (1997) and Hands (2001b, 320–334), and its relation to economics and Christian belief in Beed and Beed (1997).

The earlier challenges to positivism by the likes of Kuhn and Feyerabend also gave more weight to studying the actual practices of scientists. The sociology and anthropology of science became an active field of study, firmly anti-positivist in its orientation but coexisting uneasily with the study of the philosophy of science (e.g., Shapin, 1982).

The extensive literature in the sociology of science is mainly a post-1970s development, encouraged by some agreements with anti-positivist philosophy of science. These were the thesis of the theory-ladenness of observation and the thesis of the underdetermination of scientific theories by empirical data. It was realized that social factors might fill the gaps in scientific work implied by these two theses. In any event, sociology of science began to subject natural and physical scientific knowledge to the same kind of sociological analysis that had long been directed to, say, religious and political thought. However, studies in the sociology of science soon began to threaten the philosophy of science. In investigating the actual practices of scientists, sociology of science examined the non-technical, non-logical, and non-rational aspects of scientific work, elements that it believed had been ignored by philosophy of science. As such, sociology of science can be viewed as an alternative conceptualization of scientific activity to philosophy of science, and a challenging one to it.

As with post-positivist philosophy of science, no one research program has come to dominate the sociology of science. Ethnomethodological studies of scientific practice (e.g., Woolgar, 1988) emerged with ethnographic approaches (e.g., Latour and Woolgar, 1979; Knorr-Cetina, 1981), with discourse analysis of the talk and writing of scientists (e.g., Mulkay, 1988), with studies in the relativist program (e.g., Collins, 1985), and in the 'strong and 'weak' perspectives in the sociology of knowledge (e.g., Bloor, 1981, 1991; Barnes, 1983; Chubin and Restivo, 1983). These streams developed but with continuing disagreement within and between them, although they do share some common ground. One earlier area of agreement was the contention that scientific belief cannot be explained purely by technical-logical-rational considerations such as traditional philosophy of science held. In the view of sociology of science, as expressed by Knorr-Cetina and Mulkay (1983, 13), 'the contextually contingent logic of technical inquiry' inevitably incorporates a large measure of social factors. All streams continued to emphasize the need to study the actual practices of science and still share a 'rejection of theorizing which is detached from close empirical study of the complexities of social action.'

The results of its empirical studies demonstrated that scientific knowledge was not necessarily 'true' belief but rather whatever is socially and culturally conditioned is to be regarded as knowledge. The findings point to the relativistic nature of scientific knowledge, a conclusion disputed by scientific realists such as Bhaskar and Trigg. Like philosophy of science, the influence of sociology of science has extended steadily into the social sciences, including economics (a review of this penetration and its effects is Hands, 2001b, 172–212).

ANTI-POSITIVISM AND THE SOCIAL SCIENCES

Although it became a commonplace observation in philosophy of science by the 1970s that 'the positivistic analysis of scientific knowledge . . . has been rejected, or at least is highly suspect' (Suppe, 1974, 4), this contention was more slowly accepted in social science, especially economics. In part, this might have been because the philosophical critique of positivism had a longer history in the physical sciences. The social sciences often grew from the physical sciences in the eighteenth century and are regarded as having their scientific (i.e., positivistic) beginnings after that time. From that time, the social sciences looked to the physical sciences such as physics, astronomy, and mathematics as their models so that the spillover of the anti-positivistic critique in the physical sciences has lagged behind that in the social sciences.

Until the physical science critique of positivism gathered sway from the 1960s, earlier independently evolving critiques of positivism carried little weight within mainstream social science. For instance, the Austrian school's criticism of the positivist orientation of economics from the 1930s appeared to make little impact on the subsequent development of the subject, and was largely ignored until the 1960s. However, once the anti-positivist critique in physical science gathered momentum from the 1960s, its impact could not be ascribed merely to 'ideological' differences, as was the tendency in the earlier social science debate. Here were the 'hard' physical sciences being assailed by an anti-positivist deluge from which they were not to recover.

Sociology provides a clear example of the impact of the post-1960s anti-positivist physical science debate on a social science. Many introductory sociology textbooks from the 1980s presented a brief version of the recent physical science debate (Kuhn, etc.). Usually, unlike Suppe's verdict above about the physical sciences, the battle was perceived as continuing; no victor was recognized. However, sociology texts were and still are unlike economic texts that proceed as though disputes over the philosophical basis of their subject matter did not exist. Most sociology texts list the alternative philosophical approaches that can be taken toward the subject, such as structuralism, functionalism, conflict theory, Marxism and neo-Marxism, symbolic interactionism, phenomenology and ethnomethodology (e.g., Spencer, 1985; Haralambos and Holborn, 1991; Knapp, 1994; Giddens with Birdsall (2001). The author usually makes her position clear, and deals with the subject along her chosen lines.

At the more advanced level of analysis in sociology and social theory, reflected in journal articles and specialist books, positivism has been subject to a steady, critical barrage since the 1960s. From Peter Winch's path-breaking analysis of social science in 1958, through Richard Bernstein's 1978 seminal critique of social and political theory, to overviews such as Peter Halfpenny's *Positivism and Sociology* (1982) and Roger Trigg's *Understanding Social Science* (1985), a fair summary by the late 1980s was that 'attacking positivism in the social sciences has by now become old hat' (Davenport, 1987). Indeed, the anti-positivist stance in social science is now so well developed that specific strains of anti-positivist thought have evolved their own methodologies. For example, the realist strain was well exemplified in Andrew Sayer's *Method in Social Science* (1992), and has gathered ground even in economics, but yet with minor impact.

Notwithstanding the greater uncertainty nowadays about how to define or identify science, and how to demarcate it from 'non-science,' the social sciences remain determined to label their project 'science.' But no social science has resolved an unambiguous definition for the term. Therefore, 'science' tends to be defined differently between the various social sciences, between competing schools of thought in each social science, and even differently at times by the one social scientist. Thus, mainstream sociologists use a different definition of their 'science' from mainstream Neoclassical economics' definitions, examined in the next section of this chapter. Giddens with Birdsall (2001, 640) define the science of sociology as 'the use of systematic methods of investigation, the analysis of data, theoretical thinking, and the logical assessment of arguments, to develop a body of knowledge about a particular subject matter.' Nothing about falsification lurks here, but defined in this manner, science could include 'systematic methods of investigation' and 'theoretical thinking' applied to the study of literature, art, music and history—we could have literature science with its subdivisions of poetry-science etc., art and music science, rubbing shoulders with sociological science and economic science. Giddens might have rejected this prospect, for in his first and second editions (1989, 21; 1993, 20) he phrased the issue: 'When we ask, "Is sociology a science?," we mean two things: "Can the discipline be closely modelled on the procedures of natural science?" and "Can sociology hope to achieve the same kind of precise, well-founded knowledge that natural scientists have developed in respect of the physical world?"' Although he answered both questions negatively, this does not stop him from calling sociology a science, as per the first quote above.

If, 'according to its founders, sociology is a science,' as Giddens with Birdsall assert (2001, 660), this science 'shouldn't be seen as directly like a natural science' (2001, 640). This is because social life cannot even be described, let alone explained, 'unless we first grasp the concepts that people apply to their behaviour' (2001, 640). Apparently, the science of sociology is far away from procedures used to describe the phenomena of natural science whose objects of interest presumably do not self-reflectively ascribe concepts or meanings to their behavior. The behavior of an electron is taken as given, and the observer ascribes concepts to it. It makes no sense to ask the electron what concepts it thinks it is pursuing, even though the behavior of the observer may affect the behavior of the electron.

That philosophy or any other discipline and thinker on science has been unable to develop a watertight definition of science, of rules for its practice, or of its methods, since the demise of the received positivist view, opened the floodgates for the influence of post-positivist thought in social science. This influence did not occur in orthodox economics. It maintains the practice of many of elements of positivism, while eschewing the term 'positivism' itself. Mainstream economics never has been philosophically or methodologically self-reflective, so that continuing use of positivist precepts was business as usual. It is not exaggerating to claim that all nine positivist precepts of our list above are still vigorously pursued in the teaching and practice of orthodox Neoclassical economics. How this type of thinking works out in the practice of orthodox economics and how tenable it is, are the concerns of the remainder of this and following chapters.

Economics has remained more impervious to the anti-positivist critique than sociology. Although Friedman's highly influential (1953) advocated positive economics, he seemed unaware of its connection with the philosophy of positivism. The subsequent large response to his position (much before the physical science critique of positivism escalated in the 1960s) was also mainly not cast in the context of the positivist-anti-positivist dichotomy. Indeed, most of its participants did not emphasize this wider context in which the debate can be situated. Positive economics, positivism, and positive science therefore weathered the debate within economics more unscathed, and still constitute an important position in mainstream economics. Only in 1982 did the first substantive overview of the positivist/anti-positivist debate in physical science, and its relation to economics, appear in a form specifically aimed at the economics profession (Caldwell, 1982). This claim does not overlook McClelland (1975) that was oriented mainly to economic history nor Latsis (1976), mainly concerned with Kuhn's and Lakatos' views.

The history of the demise of the received positivist view of science, its supplanting by forms of post-positivism, and the effects this might have had or have on economics are still mostly ignored in the mainstream economics tradition. For instance, a major text like Ekelund and Herbert, *A History of Economic Theory and Method* in its fourth edition in 1997, contained no mention of the issue. Similarly, there has been little attempt within the mainstream tradition to explore the practical implications of post-positivism. These processes stand in marked contrast to other areas of social science. Nevertheless, from the 1960s, more articles began to appear in established non-economics journals than before discussing the issues, subsumed under the philosophy and methodology of economics. For example, such articles perhaps appeared more often in journals like *Philosophy of Science* (e.g., Hands, 1984a, Rosenberg, 1984); *British Journal for the Philosophy of Science* (e.g., Glass and Johnson, 1988); and *Philosophy of the Social Sciences* (e.g., Hands, 1984b; Caldwell, 1984; Hausman, 1985). More papers on the issue have appeared also in non-mainstream economics journals, such as the Institutionalists' *Journal of Economic Issues*. Little sign of this tendency yet occurs in mainstream economics journals. Mention could also be made of a claimed revival of interest in Austrian economics (e.g., Caldwell, 1982; Wiseman, 1983). The minority Austrian school has always had an anti-positivist bias, but again, the focus is on orthodox economics here.

Included in the influence of anti-positivist thought in economics is the development of Post Keynesian economics, although this had other roots as well. The editorial statement in the first (1978) issue of the *Journal of Post Keynesian Economics*, setting out its philosophical aims, objects to the separation of facts and values and contests 'the illusion that economics is a "positive science" without ideology—which itself is an ideological illusion' (1978, 6). Of course, such criticisms were stock-in-trade of the minority schools of economics of Institutionalists and Marxists, but the focus of discussion here is how the 'new' criticism affected orthodox Neoclassical economics.

Many more books are also being published exploring the influence of anti- and post-positivist thought in economics. After Caldwell (1982), the example that had, and continues to have, most impact was probably McCloskey (1986), who still promotes like views (e.g., 1996). Strongly influenced by the contemporary anti-positivist philosopher, Richard Rorty (1979), McCloskey (1986) argued that although the official rhetoric of mainstream economics was positivism, or modernism as she termed it, economists did not, and could not, practice what they preached. Modernism was obsolete in philosophy, claimed McCloskey, because it was impossible to practice. Through examining the writings of eminent orthodox economists such as Samuelson, Becker, Solow, Muth, and Fogel, McCloskey argued that none of them in fact followed modernism. Instead, they relied on metaphors, analogies, appeals to authority, persuasion, and a dash of modernism, the sum of all of which McCloskey termed 'rhetoric'—how people try to persuade one another. All sciences were alleged to rely on rhetoric, which is the proper and adequate mode for intellectual discourse (Nelson, Megill, and McCloskey, 1987).

Other influences of anti-positivist thought are suggested in the 1985 instigation of the journal, *Economics and Philosophy*, which noted in its first editorial that 'the final collapse of logical positivism' from the 1960s produced many intellectual casualties. These included 'the rigid distinction between facts and values, the sharp contrast between "theory" and "observation," and naive verificationist and falsificationist views of theory choice.' Indeed, 'the gulf between the methods economists actually employ and the potted positivism they preach in their textbooks is scandalous' (Editors' Introduction, 1985, 1, 3). Similarly, the *Journal of Economic Methodology* started as an informal network of critical economists in 1989, and established its refereed journal in 1994.

However, judging by recent articles in these two journals, and with changes in their editorships, they have developed a more mainstream image. They now appear to publish fewer articles critical of orthodox economics in which implicit positivist tendencies are still reflected, and more by orthodox economists exploring philosophical and methodological aspects of their present and past approaches. Be that as it may, the influence of articles in these journals, and of books associated with their interests, on the practices of mainstream economists, seems to be minimal. For example, they are rarely cited by the mainstream, and courses teaching the philosophy/methodology of economics or even the history of economics are not common (e.g., Blaug, 2001). In all probability, the philosophy and methodology of economics is still held in low esteem by most orthodox economists, particularly as it is a hotbed of internal controversy from which no signs of emerging consensus are apparent. This lack of consensus is probably welcomed by most philosopher/methodologist economists, because it gives them things to debate with each other *ad infinitum*. Thus, Hands (2001a, 49; original emphasis) praised the failure of the area to '*find a few clearly specified methodological rules for the proper conduct of economic science*', rules, that 'if followed, would guarantee that the resulting economic theory constituted legitimate scientific knowledge.' Whether economics need follow any particular rules to be regarded as 'science,' whether its theories can be regarded as 'legitimate scientific knowledge,' and therefore, whether economics makes intellectual progress, are still very much up in the air. Some philosophers of social science, for example, regard economics as only a '*semi-science*' (e.g., Bunge, 1998, 152; original emphasis).

IN WHAT SENSE IS ECONOMICS REGARDED AS SCIENCE?

The determination with which mainstream Neoclassical economists call their subject 'science' might seem like a rhetorical embellishment. Yet, the assertion is far more significant. Orthodox economists believe they have discovered, and are continuing to discover fundamental tendencies in human behavior and society. The status accorded to their subject matter depends on this avowal, and it is necessary to enculturate new students of economics into the belief that what they are learning is science. The claims of economics to be a science have a long history. For instance, Mirowski (1984) argued that Neoclassical price theory began in the late nineteenth century as a direct imitation of mid-nineteenth century energy physics; 'the adoption of the "energetics" metaphor and framework of mid-nineteenth century physics is the birthmark of neo-classical economics' (1984, 365). In Mirowski's view, 'the Marginalists appropriated the mathematical formalisms of mid-nineteenth century energy physics . . . made them their own by changing the labels on the variables, and then trumpeted the triumph of a truly "scientific economics"' (1989, 9). Neoclassical price theory's scientific status owed a great deal to the legitimacy of the mathematical structure of nineteenth-century energy physics.

The scientific claims of economics have been scrutinized periodically. For example, in 1932, Robbins investigated the issue and concluded that economics was a science in the sense that it sought to establish regularities in empirical data. Nevertheless, Robbins could not be labeled a positivist for he did not subscribe to a number of the tenets of positivism specified in our list of positivist characteristics. Thus, Robbins argued that the 'laws' of economics were time- and place-specific, and he was particularly critical of the efforts of quantitative economics to formulate 'concrete' economic laws. Various economists returned to the issue since Robbins. For instance, in the 1950s and 1960s, Machlup rejected positivism's approach to defining science. He pointed out that there existed no method-oriented definition of science under which all parts of physics, chemistry, biology, geology, and other generally recognized natural sciences could qualify as 'sciences' (Machlup, 1978, 336).

Many of the notable contributions in economics about its relation to science occurred before the anti-positivist critique of physical science began to bite from the early 1960s. We have seen that one of the effects of the anti-positivist groundswell since the 1960s has been increasing recognition of the difficulty, if not impossibility, of demarcating science from non-science. Whereas positivism defined science as the pursuit of knowledge via its tenets, anti-positivism did no such thing. Indeed, there was and is no agreement within anti-positivism about what science is. Views range from Feyerabend's, that science is no more rational than voodoo, that 'the separation between science and non-science . . . dissolves into thin air' (1975, 48) to Chalmers' that 'there is no general account of science and scientific method to be had that applies to all sciences at all historical stages in their development' (1999a, 247).

Mainstream economics is conspicuous among the social sciences for ignoring the impact of such views on its practices (the small number of orthodox economist philosopher/methodologists aside). For example, we saw in Chapter 7 that the two separatist economist Christians examined there (both orthodox economists) disregarded them. The aim of this section is to suggest that contemporary economics has generally failed to embrace the critique of the positivist conception of science. Thus, in so far as it can be seen as a science utilizing positivist precepts, it is in error. Further, it will be argued that even where some familiarity with this debate has been shown, the response to it within mainstream economics practice has been unclear. This difficulty will be illustrated later by three examples from recent contemporary economics.

Commonly, students are introduced to economics as science, a view reflected strongly in undergraduate textbooks promoting the dominant orthodox Neoclassical perspective. No apology need be made here for focusing on popular undergraduate textbooks. They reflect prevailing orthodox opinion in subject areas, and in economics are indispensable tools for convincing students about the scientific qualities of economics. Thus, the fourteenth edition of Samuelson's millions-selling text (1992, xiii, xv) opens by explaining that although 'economics is not an exact science,' it 'has developed as a science over more than 200 years,' and is therefore 'a dynamic science.' No definition of science emerges in Samuelson; instead, elements of its meaning are implied by degree. These include an emphasis on close attention to observation of 'history and facts,' to systematic reasoning in deducing 'logically certain predictions' from 'a set of assumptions' (1992, 4). In earlier editions, such as the eleventh of 1980 at page 8, the reader was told that 'great advances have resulted from mathematical scientific methods' in the human sciences, although no examples were cited, but this statement does not occur in the 1992 edition. Clearly, Samuelson has in mind the model of physical science to justify the value and validity of economics.

In fairness to Samuelson, he has also long accepted some anti-positivist views about science. For instance, he is very aware of the normative basis of observing and interpreting facts: 'the same facts may tell different stories to scientific observers who wear different theoretical spectacles' (1992, 7). To back up these claims, Samuelson reproduces the famous bird/antelope drawings from Hanson, one of the early anti-positivist philosophers of science. Nonetheless, and in seeming contradiction, contends Samuelson (1992, 9), we have to be careful to distinguish between factual statements, including behavior (positive economics), and value judgements (normative economics), as though value judgements do not enter into the designation of facts and explanation of behavior. And are theories in science superseded by new ones that fit the facts better? No, declares Samuelson, approvingly quoting the Nobel Physicist, Max Planck: 'a new scientific truth does not triumph by convincing its opponents and making them see the light, but rather because its opponents eventually die . . . '(1992, 7).

A stricter positivist view does not concede as much as Samuelson. For example, Lipsey and Chrystal's (1995, 29) widely used orthodox undergraduate text (in its eighth edition) was much more specific that positive economics consists of following 'the scientific method . . . an impersonal set of criteria' by which issues are related to empirical evidence. Lipsey and Chrystal make no admission of the normatively or value judgement impregnated nature of facts; on the contrary, facts or positive statements can be derived without reference to 'our philosophical, cultural and religious positions' (1995, 26). Unlike Samuelson, they appear to believe that 'the idea of an objective, fact-guided science of human behavior' (1995, 28) is achievable, without recognizing the contentious nature of this claim. Versions of Lipsey's textbook originated in 1963 and up to recent editions (including the 1995 version cited here), little concession is made to the claims of post-positivist views of science. Aside from mentioning logical positivism, none gives any clue of the nature of the debate about the demise of the received view of science, or how this might have affected economics.

Many other orthodox introductory economics textbooks are even more terse and categorical than Samuelson and Lipsey in alleging the scientific credentials of economics. Begg et al. (1994, 11) asserted the scientific status of positive economics that 'deals with objective or scientific explanations of the working of the economy,' as though 'objective' and 'scientific explanation' were unproblematic terms, and that economics was replete with them. Similarly, Jackson et al. (1998, 1: 7) claimed that positive economics 'deals with facts (and theories about these facts) and avoids value judgements. Positive economics then attempts to set out scientific statements (models or theories) about economic behavior.' Again, the assumptions are that facts avoid value judgements, and that scientific statements are unproblematic. No discussion occurs in either book of the post-positivist critique that has been levelled at these contentions. They are promoted to students as truth.

Why should orthodox Neoclassical economists be so concerned to present economics as science? Partly, the answer lies in the authority and respect that has been historically accorded to physical science. This idea gained strength progressively with the growth of positivism from the Enlightenment of the eighteenth century as the physical sciences produced all manner of amazing discoveries and technological innovations. Inevitably, the idea gathered sway that the techniques and methods of the physical sciences could yield analogous useful discoveries in the study of human behavior. The physical sciences, especially physics and mechanics, had around a 300 year start on the social sciences in their application of mathematical reasoning, which was then (and often still is) regarded as the epitome of scientific activity. But the human sciences caught on quickly, fanned by the emergence of positivism that regarded science as the only *true* knowledge. In relation to economics specifically, writes Mirowski (1987, 92), 'the physics metaphor implies that economics is a *science* and deserves all the legitimacy that is granted to physics itself.'

The dilemmas post-positivism has posed for the scientific claims of orthodox economics are discussed below via the three examples of (1) the methodological writings of Mark Blaug; (2) the debate about the scientific claims of general equilibrium analysis; and (3) the argument over the scientific status of econometrics.

Mark Blaug is the prominent mainstream author of three masterly surveys of the development of economics (1980b, 1992, 1997). He provided an excellent overview of the tumult of the previous thirty years that marked debate about the meaning of science (1980a). Blaug was one of the first to introduce economists to this issue, and he shows clearly that since the 1960s, debate about 'the philosophy of science has been in something of a turmoil.' The 'received view' — positivism — has been 'largely destroyed . . . without, however, putting any generally accepted alternative conception in its place' (Blaug, 1992, 3). Given this assessment, how does Blaug deal with the question of whether economics can still be thought of as a science?

Blaug is another who is most concerned that economics should be viewed as science. 'Economists have always regarded the core of their subject as "science," in the modem sense of the word,' he contends (1997, 689), as though there were a consensus on 'the modem sense of the word.' 'Economists do agree,' he asserts, 'that economics is a science' (1997, 698). Yet there has long been an underlying current in his writing that the authority and respect accorded to science and economics is in decline. Partly, this is because the certainty of scientific (including economic) knowledge is decreasingly accepted, a process he documents clearly. According to Blaug in the preface to the first (1980a) edition of his *The Methodology of Economics*, economists themselves were being infected with the disease: 'after many years of complacency about the scientific status of their subject, more and more economists are beginning to ask themselves deeper questions about what they am doing. At any rate, there are growing numbers who suspect that all is not well in the house that economics has built' (1980a, xiii). By his second 1992 edition, Blaug's assessment of the current 'scientific' state of economics was still unflattering. This judgement can be contrasted with the confidence reflected in the cited introductory economics textbooks above in the scientific abilities of positive economics.

Blaug's suggested way out of this problem is for economists to practice science more rigorously. But the difficulty with this approach is that post-positivist ideas of science have undermined *how* science should be practiced. Positivist conceptions of science have been subverted, but no generally accepted alternatives have been put in their place. Blaug tries to substantiate the claim that economists can still practice science, but not in a way that would find general acceptance within post-positivism. To Blaug, the goal of science is 'to produce accurate and interesting predictions that were, in principle at least, capable of being empirically falsified . . . theories are "scientific" if they are falsifiable, at least, in principle, and not, otherwise' (1997, 689).

This criterion for science has its legacy in positivism. For example, the nineteenth-century positivist medical researcher and philosopher Claude Bernard advocated 'counter-proof' that 'no scientific hypothesis can be regarded as established so long as the scientist knows only the facts that confirm it and has not undertaken to discover facts that disprove it' (Kolakowski, 1972, 93). Even at the time, however, falsificationism was not immune from criticism. For instance, the conventionalist physicist and historian of science Pierre Duhem pointed to its theoretical problems.

Falsificationism requires that theories generate testable predictions. In the later 1920s, the logical positivists of the Vienna Circle began to replace their idea of verification—to describe 'observational evidence . . . which, if actually obtained, would conclusively establish the truth of the sentence'

(Hempel, 1959, 110) with the idea of testability—a sentence has meaning only if it is possible to test it against sense data. Although the father of logical positivism, Ernst Mach, had earlier promoted the testing of scientific hypotheses, the later logical positivists never agreed among themselves on the necessary and sufficient conditions for testability.

From 1934, in the non-English-speaking European world of philosophy of science, the ideas of testing hypotheses and falsificationism became associated closely with Karl Popper. The logical positivists disagreed with Popper's formulation (how do you falsify the statement 'there are abominable snowmen?' [Ayer, 1959b, 14]). Nevertheless, Popper's idea that hypotheses could be falsified by disconfirming evidence carried overtones of the positivist certainty of formulating ahistorical criteria for scientific progress. As we have seen, this idea has led some commentators to classify Popper as a neopositivist, a label Popper rejected. A fairer evaluation might be to see Popper as trying to save some objective criterion for defining science, even though he rejected most other 'objectivist' aspects of positivist philosophy. Anti-positivism was not drawn to objective or ahistorical definitions of science and therefore parted company with Popper.

Blaug's attempt to resurrect a 'positivist-Popperian' criterion as the demarcation of science does not save him from the problem into which he is led. Blaug concedes the anti-positivist philosophy of science view that progress in science has neither depended on nor been characterized by falsificationism. Yet, he proposes to make it the criterion for scientific activity in economics (Hands, 1984b). The paradox deepens, for Blaug constructs a trenchant case against falsificationism but ends up positing it as the mark of scientific economics. Indeed, to Blaug, the economics profession's failure to practice falsificationism is 'the central weakness of modem economics . . . the reluctance to produce the theories that yield unambiguously refutable implications, followed by a general unwillingness to confront those implications with the facts' (1992, 238).

In economics, the idea that economic theories should be tested by comparing their predictions with the real world may go back over a hundred years (Blaug, 1997, 690–691). However, the idea received its greatest recent fillip in economics from Milton Friedman (1953), to whom prediction is the only test for economic theory: 'the only relevant test of the validity of a hypothesis is comparison of its predictions with experience' where theory is 'a body of substantive hypotheses' (1953, 8–9). Falsificationism would express the specification somewhat differently from this: a hypothesis can never be validated, merely not disproved; there is no logic of proof, only a logic of disproof. But falsificationism does require the testing of predictions.

The virtues of falsificationism and prediction testing in economics are still commonly advocated. For example, they are often recommended in the first chapters of undergraduate textbooks; thus, Lipsey and Chrystal (1995, 33) declare that 'a theory is tested by confronting its predictions with evidence.' It is worth considering why post-positivist philosophy of science does not regard the approach as the sole or even the main criterion for science. According to point five in the anti-positivist list presented earlier, prediction is but one element to be valued in scientific theories. The post-positivist reasons why prediction is not elevated above, say, retrodiction, internal consistency, economy of assumptions, simplicity, beauty, completeness, elegance, or generality of explanation are the allegedly insuperable methodological and philosophical difficulties in deciding how to compare predictions with real-world data.

The post-positivist objections to prediction testing as the criterion for science, including economics, are:

1. Tests of the predictive implications of the assumptions of a theory or of its auxiliary hypotheses cannot be distinguished unambiguously from tests of the assumptions or auxiliary hypotheses themselves (the Duhem-Quine thesis).
2. Therefore, tests of the empirical validity of assumptions may be helpful in assessing the value of a theory; but, some assumptions may not be testable, they may be metaphysical assertions (e.g., in economics, about human nature).
3. Theory resting on counterfactual assumptions cannot yield meaningful predictions.
4. Since all the connecting logical/causal links in a theory can never be specified exactly (especially in the social sciences), tests of predictions cannot distinguish causation from correlation.
5. Value judgments cannot be excised from observations of fact; observation is theory-laden.
6. Value judgments cannot be excised from testing procedures. There may be wide agreement on some aspects of normative methodology (e.g., about levels of probability for accepting and rejecting hypotheses) but there is no agreement on others (e.g., on specifying variables to include in testable theories).
7. Real-world data against which predictions are tested may be unreliable, unattainable, or inappropriate (e.g., in economics, many models give a poor fit to data).
8. Given all the above problems, we cannot judge objectively and impartially the predictive claims of any one theory, let alone between competing theories.
9. Therefore, we should look at the other features of any scientific theory as an aid in assessing its worth—its internal logic, simplicity, comprehen-

siveness, and so on. Scientists differ among each other in their normative perceptions about the worth of each of these features.

10. Notwithstanding any of the above, we can never say that a theory is proved; its best status is a lack of disproof.
11. Some theories yield no testable predictions: they are more related to puzzle solving or pattern explication.

We are not here debating the validity of any of these points. A large literature developed and persists about each one. For example, an early discussion of the first point in the list above is Harding (1976), and specifically economics treatments are Cross (1982), and Sawyer et al. (1997). But no one point on the list has been decisively put to rest either way. (Hands, 2001b, 88–93, 276–286, reviews many of the problems associated with the practice of falsification in economics). Of course, post-positivist thought about science might not be worried by the lack of agreement. It might be more worried if consensus had been reached. For one position in post-positivist philosophy of science is that normative, subjective disagreement depending on people's different value judgments, metaphysical beliefs, and so on is a hallmark and prerequisite for scientific activity.

Mark Blaug has an excellent perception of all these issues in his 1992 and 1997 books, where he notes:

> There is no demonstrative logic of justification . . . no formal algorithm, no mechanical procedure of verification, falsification, confirmation, corroboration, or call it what you will. . . . what we cannot do is to pretend that there is on deposit somewhere a perfectly objective method . . . that will positively compel agreement on what are or are not acceptable scientific theories (1992, 26).

In relation to economics specifically, Blaug declares that 'economists (and for that matter all social scientists) cannot agree on definite empirical criteria for falsifying a hypothesis,' that 'conclusive once-and-for all testing or strict refutability of theorems is out of the question in economics because all its predictions are probabilistic ones' (1997, 6, 695). Yet, despite these qualifications, Blaug posits prediction testing and falsificationism as the main measure of scientific activity in economics.

Blaug appears to hold an ambiguous position here because elsewhere in the same books he seems to believe that this approach may not get economists very far. For instance, he writes, 'in many areas of economics, different econometric studies reach conflicting conclusions, and, given the available data, there are frequently no effective methods for deciding which conclusion is correct' (1992, 245). Echoing Samuelson, Blaug places no great store in the quantitative nature of predictions anyway: 'we must begin by disenchanting ourselves of the idea that economic predictions must be quantitative in character to qualify as scientific predictions. Clearly, the predictions of most economic models are qualitative rather than quantitative in nature' (1997, 694). Thus, if prediction testing is about trying to establish general laws or causal explanations describing human behavior, rather than just producing thousands of case studies, theories, and models that add up to no overall view, Blaug again thinks that economics performs poorly, for 'by the standards of accuracy applied to predictions in the natural sciences economics makes a poor showing' (1997, 695). Blaug blames these deficiencies on economists for not practicing prediction testing and falsificationism. Yet at the same time, he recognizes that this methodology is bedeviled by normative problems. Blaug may not see his dilemma: a methodology that rests so heavily on intersubjective factors will not produce universally accepted results. Perhaps this is why many economists do not practice falsificationism; the prediction-testing methodology that underpins it is just too imperfect. So seriously are the above problems viewed by some critics that they question the value of Popperian falsificationism per se. For instance, Hausman (1988, 83) doubted 'that an enterprise that functioned according to Popper's methodology could exist. It would be a poor tool for acquiring knowledge and of no use in practice.' All the objections above to falsification do not prevent Blaug (1992, 244) from claiming, however, that 'for the most part, the battle for falsificationism has been won in modern economics . . .'

A second example can be cited from recent economics of dispute about science proceeding from an anti-positivist basis. This is the debate about the scientific status of General Equilibrium Analysis (GEA), the underlying theory of which ranked highly in intellectual prestige in economics for decades. A landmark in this debate was E. Roy Weintraub's (1985, 1987) case that GEA conformed to certain post-positivist ideas of science: specifically, that it represented a progressive theoretical and empirical research program in Lakatosian terms. Weintraub constructed a case that GEA conformed to Lakatos' definition of a progressive research program and therefore is science. Incidentally, note that neither the anti-positivist philosopher Lakatos nor the mainstream economist Weintraub accepted that theory prediction testing and falsificationism was the key to science. GEA had been criticized that its theories did not yield testable predictions (e.g., Coddington, 1975), that 'the empirical content of GE theory is nil' (Blaug, 1992). By casting GEA as scientific activity in a Lakatosian framework, Weintraub sidestepped this criticism, although Blaug (1992, 168) claimed that Weintraub's assignation of GE theory as the core of the Neoclassical scientific research program did not accord with the history of the development of Neoclassical economics.

As might be expected, Weintraub's case was challenged by others working in a post-positivist thought on science framework. For instance, the philosopher Alexander Rosenberg, who has written extensively on the philosophical bases of economics, did not believe that Lakatos' formulation represented an adequate conceptualization of science. Like Feyerabend and others, Rosenberg (1986) argued that Lakatos' schema was too imprecise to demarcate science from non-science. Lakatos' ideas of 'empirical content . . . novel fact,' and 'corroboration' were notoriously devoid of precise meaning so that 'philosophers have given up trying to make sense of them in a way that will shed light on the problem of demarcation.' So vague was Lakatos' system in Rosenberg's view that 'such paradigmatically non-scientific disciplines as literary theory, painting or music' could qualify as science. All this rendered economics' 'fixation with Lakatos philosophically dated' (Rosenberg, 1986, 136, 135). From a different tack, the anti-positivist economist Mayo Toruno (1988), reviewing the history of GE theory, argued that it was not a progressive but a degenerating scientific research program in Lakatosian terms, and therefore did not qualify as science. In retrospect, the judgements of Rosenberg and Toruno about GE theory were probably correct, and even Blaug now (2001, 169) regards GE theory as 'a journey down a blind alley'—largely on the basis of the analysis of Ingrao and Israel (1991).

A third instance of the continuing influence of post-positivist ideas about science on mainstream economics can be found in econometrics. The view was canvassed from the 1970s that econometrics was producing little in the way of enduring conclusions. In presidential addresses to learned societies, claims were made that 'running regressions between time series is only likely to deceive' (Phelps Brown, 1972, 6), that 'the predictive power of econometrics is rather low,' that 'econometric models are not, as a rule, sharp instruments for discriminating between hypotheses' (Worswick, 1972, 80), and that 'in no other field of empirical inquiry has so massive and sophisticated a statistical machinery been used with such indifferent results' (Leontief, 1971, 3). In studied understatement, Hicks (1980, xii) declared that 'econometrics is now in some disarray.' The views were casting doubt on the idea of econometrics producing objective, fixed, unchangeable, determinate, unchallengeable conclusions about the economy in the way the physical sciences might for the physical world.

This line of post-positivist criticism of econometrics continues within mainstream economics to the present time. What is perhaps more noticeable since the 1970s is a tendency by some eminent practicing econometricians to admit their explicit persuasion to some of the tenets of anti-positivist philosophy of science. Probably, the outstanding example is Leamer, who ridicules the idea that econometrics can lead to an objective, positive science of economics because, in his view, statistical inference depends on human opinion, judgment, and conviction: 'economists have inherited from the physical sciences the myth that scientific inference is objective, and free of personal prejudice. This is utter nonsense . . . the false idol of objectivity has done great damage to economic science' (Leamer, 1983, 36). Leamer's main complaint was that the typical mode of econometric work constitutes 'specification searches'; that is, selecting the set of estimated models that yields 'the most congenial results.' According to him, this approach invalidated the classical theory of inference; 'these searches have no foundation in any clearly articulated theory of inference.' The result is that 'some statisticians feel that there is no content at all to the data analyses in economics and other non-experimental sciences' (Leamer, 1985a, 298).

As a practicing econometrician, Leamer did not go as far as this conclusion. He was at pains to suggest an alternative operational statistical methodology (Bayesian theory) to overcome the problem. However, Leamer contended that few econometricians followed this line and therefore most econometric results had a high degree of fragility (Leamer, 1985b). Leamer might have been the most eminent econometrician calling attention to the value judgment-based nature of all econometric work, but he was not alone. Others who disagreed with his proposed solutions agreed with much of his critique (e.g., Hendry, 1980; McAleer, Pagan, and Volker, 1985; Walters, 1986; Blaug, 1988). The upshot has been increasing recognition that '"subjectivism" in econometrics is here to stay' (Denton, 1988, 181). As will be indicated in Chapter 11, these conclusions are still held by many.

CONCLUSION

The three cases discussed above (the argument over prediction testing and falsificationism; the argument over whether GE theory is science; and the debate over econometrics) show the current indeterminacy about the scientific claims of economics, and the difficulties in trying to assess progress in economics. Analogous debate is occurring in other sciences: for example, is Darwin's theory of evolution science, does it yield testable predictions? Is sociobiology science? And so on. We have seen that one view in post-positivist philosophy of science is that science has no distinctive characteristics; it cannot be demarcated from non-science. Even in the 1980s, Rosenberg (1986, 129) contended that 'economists are still trying to establish their discipline's scientific credentials while philosophers some time ago gave up the hope of formulating such credentials.' The extreme representative of this view in the philosophy of science was Feyerabend, even whose book titles conveyed his beliefs about the matter—*Against Method* (1975); *Farewell to Reason* (1987). Possibly there are no followers of this extremity in economics, although some economists may be moving in this direction. For instance, part of McCloskey's (1986) message was that contemporary economics is awash in a sea of metaphors, some of which are inappropriate to its subject matter (e.g., the metaphor of nineteenth-century physics' mathematics, which decreasingly describes both the real world and contemporary thought in physics). McCloskey is just as happy to employ alternative metaphors in economics, such as those involved in writing literary criticism or poetry. Needless to say, her ideas would lead economics far away from the mode in which it currently works.

Of course, it is not necessary to proceed as far as this to practice science and economics in an anti-positivist mode. There is some practice in minority school of economics, for example, of an alternative to attempts at formal falsification, and the like. This is colligation or pattern modelling and story telling, explained to the wider audience of academic economics by Wilber and Harrison (1978), and Wilber (1999). More familiar, perhaps, in economic history and applied economics, colligation makes extensive use of the tenets of anti-positivist philosophy of science, such as the explicit inclusion of value judgments in its explanations, a disinclination to emphasize prediction, the search for low-level generalization in the context of the researcher's worldview, and the attempt to integrate all these into a coherent narrative. All this is not vastly dissimilar from the orthodox economist, Solow's prescription for 'the true functions of analytical economics': 'to organize our necessarily incomplete perceptions about the economy, to see connections that the untutored eye would miss, to tell plausible-sometimes even convincing causal stories with the help of a few central principles, and to make rough quantitative judgments about the consequences of economic policy and other exogenous events.' Solow complained that 'modem economics has an ambition and style rather different from those I have been advocating' in that 'the best and brightest in the profession proceed as if economics is the physics of society' (Solow, 1985, 329, 330). One message of post-positivist ideas about science is that classical physics can no longer serve as the model for all scientific endeavor.

We can see why some scientists have worried by these approaches, for they do not lead to determinate, 'objective' answers. But practitioners of anti-positivist science and economics would reply that science has always been in this situation, and that it is about time we recognized scientific activity for what it is. Nor would they be worried that this recognition will diminish the practical utility of science. Decisions can still be made. Some decisions will produce desired results (sending rockets into space), some will not (rockets blow up occasionally), and some will produce totally unanticipated results like the greenhouse effect. All this shows the indeterminate, uncertain state and basis of scientific knowledge. Economics is no different from other sciences in these respects.

One of the difficulties with these anti-positivist views is that they offer no way to assess how 'progress' might be gauged in science. If science is no more than what scientists do, there are no objective, external yardsticks against which its development may be assessed. In this way, science becomes no different from writing poetry or literary criticism. One difference might be that science has long been seen as a way of controlling and changing the world. Many scientific theories are acted on in the world for they do produce their predicted effects; for instance, theories of the predicted strengths of materials are sufficiently reliable to base all manner of construction decisions on them. The practical value of the constructions depends totally on the validity of the scientific theories underlying them. Many theories in the physical sciences appear to be used with consistent success in this fashion.

Alas, the human sciences are not in such a happy position: whether in psychology, sociology, or economics, it is difficult to point to many theories whose universal truth has been established or that have been used enduringly for practical policy purposes. The history of the human sciences is replete with theories whose success in explaining, controlling, or changing the world has turned out in the long run to be minimal. It is such considerations that have led some anti-positivist theorists such as philosopher Richard Rorty, to speak of the failure of the human sciences. However, this is merely rediscovering the wheel, for the same conclusion has been drawn many times in the past. An example is the historian of economic thought, Alexander Gray, who claimed that 'economic science, if it be a science, differs from other sciences, in this, that there is no inevitable advance from less to greater certainty; there is no ruthless tracking down of truth which, once unbared, shall be truth to all times to the complete confusion of contrary doctrine' (1931, 2–3).

Gray, of course, was thinking of the idea of science of his age. There seems no doubt that in terms of today's post-positivist ideas, economics can qualify as a science. But so elastic are those ideas that probably much human endeavor can be classified as science. Whether anything is added to the substance of economics as distinct from its claimed status by calling it 'science' is moot. Nevertheless, mainstream economics is fiercely determined to call its economics 'science.' Lipsey and Chrystal (1995, 26) contend that 'the claim that economics is scientific stands or falls on the ability of economists to understand and predict events in the real world by stating theories, subjecting the theories to the test of real-world observations, and improving the theories in the light of what has been learned.' What Lipsey and Chrystal do not discuss is that there are many ways of understanding events, and that comparing predictions with real-world behavior does not seem to have been spectacularly successful in economics because of problems with falsification mentioned above.

Another way of putting this is to say that the question of whether or not economics is a science, or makes progress, is indeterminate because of a widespread uncertainty about what science is. Economist, Hands (2001b, 358) poses the question, 'how can (or can) science be epistemically privileged, given that it is underdetermined, theory-laden, socially conditioned, and practiced by individuals who appear to systematically violate all of the rules that philosophers of science have laid down as guidelines for the proper conduct of scientific inquiry?' Philosopher of science, Okasha (2002, 16, 17) suggests that 'the assumption that science has an "essential nature" is questionable', and that 'a simple criterion for demarcating science from pseudo-science is unlikely to be found.' These conclusions will not satisfy the purists for whom the Cartesian positivist image of science prevalent until the 1960s is still the only definition of science. Post-positivist theorists would retort that this view merely underlines their message—science is not a static phenomenon whose practice conforms to idealized precepts established in the eighteenth century. Notwithstanding this changed thinking about science, the next chapter examines how orthodox economics among the social sciences continues to aspire to just such precepts.

Chapter Nine

Naturalism and Contemporary Economics

This chapter examines the influence of naturalism and its foil, non-naturalism, in contemporary economics (Beed and Beed, 1996b). This discussion is closely tied to ideas of science discussed in the last chapter. Naturalism in social science is usually taken to mean that the description and explanation of socio-economic behavior can most adequately be pursued using the methods of the natural sciences. As Kincaid (1996, xv) puts it, 'we can and ought to study [those] social structures with the methods of the natural sciences, broadly construed . . . naturalism is thus the belief that social phenomena are part of the natural world and accordingly amenable to the methods of the natural sciences.' In the broadest sense of the term, naturalism nowadays means 'that whatever exists or happens in the world is susceptible to explanation by natural scientific methods; it denies that there is or could be anything which lies in principle beyond the scope of scientific explanation' (Callebaut, 1993, xv). As we saw in the previous chapter, sociologist Giddens might not seem to be sympathetic to naturalism in sociology in the sense used by Kincaid and Callebaut, but he still calls sociology science.

Here we show how orthodox economics tries to practice elements of naturalism, and how members of minority heterodox schools of schools eschew its practice by adopting less naturalistic methods, even though they might pay lip-service to following naturalism. We explore how naturalistic and non-naturalistic frameworks of thinking about economics differ at the fundamental levels of their philosophical presuppositions, the manner in which their theories are formulated and appraised, and the ways in which they relate to other social sciences. 'Naturalistic' and 'non-naturalistic' are familiar terms in the philosophy of social science, encompassing divergent ways of depicting and explaining human behavior and relationships. Although little used explicitly in economics, the terms provide an organizing schema within which to view disagreements between rival ways of 'doing' contemporary economics. Constructing the argument in this way also allows it to be situated in the context of the few hundred-year-old debate between naturalism and non-naturalism in the broader field of the social sciences (economics, sociology, anthropology, psychology, and political science).

Initially, terms are defined, followed by a description and history of the two main philosophical positions in social science, naturalism and non-naturalism, related particularly to economics. Then, bold conjectures are proffered of how naturalistic and non-naturalistic social sciences, including economics, differ from each other in philosophy and methodology. Three of the conjectures are considered more closely to illustrate the differences in economics. First is the nature of theories in economics, using Becker's (1976) economic theory of human behavior as the example (one that continues to attract wide following in orthodox economics). Second is the existence of causal laws in economics, and third, the degree of openness/closedness of the systems with which economics deals. Since naturalistic positions are dominant currently in these three areas in orthodox economics (and therefore are more familiar), each is evaluated from a non-naturalistic perspective to emphasize the disparities between the two philosophical positions.

NATURALISM

Naturalism is a metaphysical proposition about how to discover social knowledge (Trigg, 1989; 1993), for the proposition that social knowledge is to be discovered by scientific means is not amenable to falsification. The philosophical problem with naturalism is that naturalists still need to appeal to 'some body of *a priori* truths' (Rosenberg, 2000, 154) to justify their methods of reasoning. But they reject appealing to a 'first philosophy' or epistemology underlying science. Yet, appealing just to methodologies practiced in science or social science is no more than circular reasoning. The operational problem with naturalism is that there is no agreement nowadays about what correct natural scientific methods are, and even less agreement about how they might or should be applied in social science. Given this hiatus, it is unsurprising that many of the old positivist tenets for 'natural scientific methods' persist, especially in mainstream economics. One tactic naturalist philosophers of social science employ to try and overcome this problem is to focus on 'what social scientists actually do' instead of '*a priori* armchair theorizing' (Kincaid, 1996, xv). This does not save them from the philosophical impasse or regress above into which they are led. As well, the task then becomes one of trying to interpret the practices of social scientists in terms of the philosophy of naturalism. Chapter 10 will provide some evidence that this project is not clarifying the results of social science, while Chapters 11 and 12 argue that orthodox economics that tries to embody naturalistic approaches does not turn out to be a reliable vehicle for understanding reality. Chapter 13 shows that naturalism is not compatible with the Christian approach to socio-economic analysis raised in Chapters 2–4, for which some general methodological principles are posited in the concluding Chapter 14.

All the social sciences, including economics, now have this 'new' banner of naturalism instead of positivism by which to justify their practices (not that orthodox economics thinks it needs a banner, and it certainly does not talk about it). The term 'naturalism' has been appropriated from physical science, although not in any explicit way by (the majority of non-philosophically reflective) Neoclassical economists, and not only by them. On this latter point, and to complicate matters, the word 'naturalism' has also been purloined by a variety of social scientists who oppose the Neoclassical economics project, such as critical realists like Bhaskar and Lawson, and even by particular sociologists to justify their projects, such as by Bloor (1991), protagonist of the Strong Programme in the sociology of knowledge.

Naturalistic is not just a new terminology but is a common, long-used, and generic term in the philosophy of the social sciences depicting the model of explanation for human behavior drawn from approaches in the physical sciences. It is associated usually with formalistic modelling and with empirical research in which hypotheses are tested formally via quantitative data (e.g., Lessnof, 1974; Bohman, 1991; Clark, 1992; Rosenberg, 1995). In its explanations, emphasis is placed on the scientific representation of human behavior and relationships, at least as the term 'scientific' was understood up to about 40 years ago before the term started to break up. In direct opposition, non-naturalism contests the relevance of traditional natural science models, positing an alternative emphasis on understanding and interpreting human action, its meanings and intentions. In these interpretations, the roles of values, judgment, and individual insight are emphasized (e.g., Rabinow and Sullivan, 1979; 1987).

The dichotomy between naturalism and non-naturalism is sometimes considered no longer adequate to represent the diversity of philosophical positions in the social sciences today (e.g., Redner, 1993). One complication confronting the bifurcation has been the emerging strength in the last twenty-five years of the philosophical position in the social sciences of transcendental and critical realism (e.g., Bhaskar, 1989). This position construes itself as a 'new critical naturalism' that has resolved the dispute between conventional naturalism and non-naturalism (Bhaskar, 1994, 313). Realism has explicit advocates in economics (e.g., Hausman, 1992; Maki, 1993; Lawson, 1994a, 1997; Hoover, 1994). The implications of the resolution claim are considered below, where it will be argued that the traditional dual schemata is a useful first approximational heuristic for clarifying fundamental divergences between contemporary positions in economics, even though it has been little used in recent methodological debate in the area. It is still particularly relevant in economics because the dominant Neoclassical approach is one of traditional naturalism

Not all social scientists are convinced that critical realism has solved the dispute. One sociological theory text, for instance, adopts a wait-and-see position; noting the demise of positivism, Knapp (1994, 420) suggests that what this means for realism 'remains to be seen.' This hesitancy in accepting realism as a methodology in sociology probably depends on waiting to see if it generates distinct or unique results. As a prominent realist sociologist noted, 'the metatheoretical attachments of a particular theory will often, indeed turn out to be irrelevant to its explanatory power and the interest of its conclusions' (Outhwaite, 1987, 117). Perhaps the standard sociology textbooks are in this position for, in general, they make virtually no mention of realism (Haralambos and Holborn, 1991 excepted) that can be compared to the generous space they devote to critical theory, of similar age to critical realism.

Like all contenders for philosophical pre-eminence, realism has been criticized on a number of grounds in both the philosophy of science and social science. In the physical sciences, Fine (1991), for example, developing earlier critiques of Laudan (1981) and Putnam (1981), described it as 'a metaphysical doctrine that finds neither support nor refutation in scientific theories or investigations,' while advocates of its merits argue the contrary (e.g., Devitt, 1991). In the social sciences, from Stockman (1983) through Isaac (1990) and Fay (1990) to Fuller (1993), the limitations of critical realism have been explored. For example, on realism's claim of 'the ontological independence of the objects of experience from the objects of which they are the experiences' (Bhaskar, 1978, 311), Holmwood and Stewart (1991, 18–25) argue that this construal does not allow rival theories to be compared other than on the basis of their theoretical categories. It is possible for ontological realists and nonnaturalists to share some common ground—for example, a belief in epistemological relativism (Bhaskar 1994, 549), which makes it difficult to separate the positions at times. However, this commonality is not necessary; one could be an ontological realist but not an epistemological relativist. As Haack (1987, 284) noted, 'because "Realism" has so many, largely independent, senses it is seldom illuminating, and often misleading, to classify a philosopher either as Realist or as Anti-Realist,' which contention she illustrated in the work of Popper, Peirce, and Tarski. In addition, it is a moot point how much traditional 'naturalism' is left in critical realism, even in terms of the definition of naturalism given by critical realists themselves (e.g., as in Bhaskar, 1986, 118). While the debate continues, exploration in the philosophy of social science of the relevance of traditional non-naturalistic perspectives persists (e.g., Bohman, 1991; Hilley, Bohman, and Shusterman, 1992). This discussion is not intended to evaluate realism, but only to suggest that a variety of philosophical positions continue to exist in the social sciences, that no one position is approaching hegemony in the field, and that the traditional naturalism/non-naturalism dichotomy is still a helpful way to view disagreement in the social sciences. Realism need not be interpreted as a form of naturalism (Trigg, 1989; Beed and Beed, 1997), and is here construed in opposition to it.

In recent philosophical/methodological debate in economics, attention has been directed to realism (e.g., Backhouse, 1992) and honing up its specifications, versus constructivism (e.g., Weintraub, 1992), a form of relativism in which multiple conceptual schemes and the role of concepts in cognition are emphasized; reality is obscured behind a veil of appearances (e.g., Sankey, 1993; Devitt, 1991; Hoksbergen, 1994b). It is significant that this economics debate has moved into assessing the rival claims of traditional forms of non-naturalism and non-traditional naturalism (realism). However, this should not obscure the reality that most orthodox economists' practice is still oriented more to traditional naturalism than to non-naturalism and realism. For this reason, before the economics' philosophical/methodological debate becomes more oriented to comparing traditional non-naturalism and non-traditional naturalism (realism), it seems helpful to re-emphasize the gross distinctions between traditional non-naturalism and naturalism in contemporary economics practice. While this has been done implicitly in varying degrees (e.g., McCloskey, 1986; 1994), it has not been pursued explicitly in the context of the long-standing dispute in the social sciences between traditional naturalism and non-naturalism. Indeed, contemporary economics of any complexion is barely aware of the term, 'naturalism.' Thus, both *The Handbook of Economic Methodology* (1998) and the comprehensive history of economics by Perlman and McCann (1998) have no treatment of 'naturalism,' 'naturalized epistemology,' or variants of these terms, nor such mentions in their indexes.

The complication of critical naturalism/realism aside, the basic dichotomy between traditional naturalistic and non-naturalistic modes of human enquiry continues to be canvassed widely in the philosophy of the social sciences where it has been in the forefront of debate for some decades (e.g., Ryan, 1970; Macdonald and Pettit, 1981; Flew, 1985; Trigg, 1985; Braybrooke, 1987; Wallerstein, 1991; Holmwood and Stewart, 1991; Sayer, 1992; Rosenberg, 1995). In a common view, it has been 'the most salient controversy in the philosophy of social science' (Braybrooke, 1987, 7) and 'the primal problem in the philosophy of the social sciences' (Bhaskar, 1989, 1). As well, the issue is still debated in many of the social sciences themselves, for example, in sociology, although not necessarily flagged by the term 'naturalism.' Thus, Knapp (1994) demonstrated a common practice in sociology when he devoted his Chapter 9 to examining the issues in terms of a synonymous dichotomy labeled as positivism and humanism.

Economics is quite unlike other social sciences in this respect. Neither standard introductory nor advanced texts on economic theory (e.g., Samuelson and Nordhaus, 1992; Lipsey and Chrystal, 1995; Varian, 1992; Binger and Hoffman, 1998) mention the issue, nor do most tertiary economics courses. Partly this is because economics is unique among the social sciences in being dominated by a naturalistic approach (Neoclassicism). In all likelihood, the socialization of most economists may lead them to believe that Neoclassical naturalism is all that exists as genuine economics (Lawson, 1994b). Nonetheless, some strands of non-naturalistic influence persist in minority schools of economics like Institutionalism and Austrianism, but these are typically relegated to insignificant importance in training economists (Klamer and Colander, 1990).

In recent years, Neoclassical economics has been subject to increasing methodological and philosophical criticism, while methodological debate within economics (initially by non-naturalist and realist economists) has accelerated. Critiques of Neoclassical economics in the few decades have drawn from philosophies of the physical sciences and mathematics (e.g., Mirowski, 1989), from theories of literary criticism and rhetoric (e.g., McCloskey, 1986), or rested on alternative Marxist frameworks of economics (e.g., Wolff and Resnick, 1987). There are strong links between these approaches and central issues in the philosophy of the social sciences. However, this chapter situates disagreements between Neoclassical and alternative ways of thinking about economics in the framework of the historical dispute between naturalism and non-naturalism in the social sciences.

The few hundred-year-old debate about which view of social science (naturalist or non-naturalist) is the more valid for understanding human behavior is nowhere near settled. In the philosophy of social science, the unresolved question still is, 'how far can we expect the explanation of what people say and do to conform to the model of explanation suggested by the natural sciences' (Macdonald and Pettit, 1981, 11). As discussed below, the differences between naturalism and non-naturalism 'rest on very fundamental issues in philosophy, claims about epistemology, metaphysics and ethics. Since these issues were first raised by Plato almost twenty-four hundred years ago, philosophers have not been able to settle them' (Rosenberg, 1995, 22)—even though Christians would contend they were raised in Judeo-Christian thought well before that. Whereas the argument has little touched orthodox academic economics that tries to follow a naturalistic path almost exclusively, in other disciplines the opposite choice has been made—for instance, 'with philosophers, naturalistic social science is quite out of fashion' (Braybrooke, 1987, 71). The irony is that naturalism has a dominant hold in philosophy, but most philosophers have little truck for naturalistic social science. In sociology, psychology, political science, and anthropology, non-naturalistic approaches are far stronger than in mainstream economics. For instance, in sociology, the approaches of phenomenology, ethnomethodology, conflict theory, symbolic interactionism, critical theory, hermeneutics, and feminism all have significant but different non-naturalistic tendencies. Divergent philosophical positions have been at the forefront of sociology since its inception. As noted in the last chapter, it is standard practice for undergraduate students to be introduced to these approaches in similar degree as to naturalistic empirical sociology.

NATURALISM IN SOCIAL SCIENCE

As a generic term, naturalism embodies philosophy and methodology associated with positivism, empiricism, materialism, behaviorism, reductionism, rationalism, quantification, objectivity, formalism, scientism, and modernism that came to dominate physical science by the nineteenth century and then extended their influence into social science (e.g., Bryant, 1985; Outhwaite, 1987; Manicas, 1987; Holmwood and Stewart, 1991; Beare and Slaughter, 1993; Rosenberg, 1995). Naturalism has both ontological and epistemological dimensions, and a naturalist social scientist would not necessarily have to accept both dimensions. For the purposes of this chapter, however, naturalism is treated as a generic and undifferentiated term. The distinction between the two dimensions of naturalism is pursued in Chapter 14.

Each of the 'isms' above can be thought of as a subset within the general family of naturalism. Identification of each of the positions in social science is not a straightforward matter, nor is each mutually exclusive. Moreover, any social scientist who held to one or more of them (even unknowingly) would not necessarily follow them all; for example, it is feasible to uphold empiricism but not to accept all the tenets of positivist methodology. The substance of all these claims cannot be reviewed here. Instead, brief comment is made on some of the 'isms' to clarify their relation to naturalistic social science.

Enough has been said about positivism in the previous chapter to expose its links with naturalism. Bhaskar (1994, 412) describes positivism as 'a more or less unqualified naturalism,' and Stich (1996, 195) ascribes both to the tradition of 'philosophical puritanism.' If naturalism in social science is the belief that social processes ought to be studied by the methods of the natural sciences, this is a tenet of positivism already listed in the last chapter. Thus, Wacquant (1994, 495) emphasizes one element of positivism as the belief that 'the procedures of natural science are directly applicable to the social world.' Mainstream Neoclassical economists use further specific tenets of positivism in their naturalistic endeavors. One such is empiricism (Flew, 1984, 104; Bhaskar, 1994, 193), in which valid knowledge depends on sense-experience and evidence that can be examined and preferably measured (quantification). In naturalistic social science, emphasis is on the analysis of empirical data by ever more complicated statistical techniques, so much so suggests Wacquant (1994, 498) that positivism still 'dominates the design and implementation of empirical social research.' Mathematical model building and formalist abstraction (formalism) are practiced also in naturalist social science to clarify logical argument and to seek empirically testable models. The indispensable partner to formalism and empiricism is rationalism (Abercrombie at al., 1988, 201; Hollis, 1994, 544–546), and the application of reason through rigorous logic by which an objective, value-free picture of the world can be revealed. This has been associated invariably with reductionism (Flew 1984, 300), the attempt to break social processes down into their elemental parts so that each can be examined in microscopic detail; its antonym is holism, viewing social processes as interconnected wholes.

Neoclassical economics, that came to dominate academic economics from the 1930s, is naturalistic in drawing on philosophical presuppositions of positivism, empiricism, formalism, rationalism and reductionism (e.g., Caldwell, 1982; Redman, 1991; Clark, 1992; Hausman, 1992). The Neoclassical approach to analyzing human social interaction is built on the individual entity (contra Marxism) who is assumed to act self-interestedly. This axiomatic framework lends itself to formalist mathematical theory specification so much so, suggests Gordon (1991, 379), that among the social sciences, 'only economics has constructed models that are claimed to have the kind of universality that is characteristic of the natural sciences.' Ideally, these should yield propositions that can be tested empirically via econometrics. However, mathematical economic modelling is sometimes criticized for insufficient relation to the real world (Leontief, 1982; Sayer, 1992; Blaug, 1992; Mayer, 1993). Nevertheless, an outstanding feature of Neoclassical economics is its application of differential calculus to the behavior of the individual firm, person, and household that are assumed to behave 'rationally'; that is, make choices in accord with given axioms. Another naturalistic and positivistic aspect of Neoclassicism is its attempt to maintain objectivity (Abercrombie at al., 1988, 170), known as 'positive economics' (Friedman, 1953) as distinct from 'normative,' value-laden economics. A further side to the objectivity required by formalism is the presentation of the subject in noncontextual terms, abstracted from historical or cultural settings. Reductionism is also a feature of Neoclassicism (Gordon, 1991, 300). This is reflected, for example, in the way individual behavior is explained by concentrating on changes in the constraints to which the individual is exposed while assuming the individual's preferences remain constant (e.g., Binger and Hoffman, 1998). Conceding that constraints and preferences both change over time would take the analysis along holistic paths. In this sense, the reductionism of 'modern formalist economics focuses on the specific questions, paying little attention to general questions about how the specifies interact' (Landreth and Colander, 1990, 337). The philosophical presuppositions and approach of Neoclassicism have also been classed as modernism (McCloskey, 1986, 7), a term similar to the definition of positivism above, the specific influence of which on Neoclassical economics is discussed by Gordon (1991), Hausman (1992), and Clark (1992). It is now an unproblematic conclusion that the natural science model 'played a key generative role' in the development of Neoclassical mathematical economics (Porter, 1994, 128), that helps explain the continuing hold of naturalism. To confine attention to the influence of naturalism in current mainstream academic economics to the issue of naturalized epistemology, as does Hands (2001b), is to lay aside all the above influences.

The naturalistic tendency in social science and economics is only a few hundred years old. It gathered sway from the Enlightenment of the late eighteenth century and swept aside older non-naturalistic ways of thinking about human behavior that date back at least two to three thousand years. The reasons for the supplanting of non-naturalism by naturalism in social science are not the main concern here. They relate to the attempt to mimic the supposed methodologies of the natural sciences in the hope that social science would replicate the discoveries of natural science (Gay, 1975). Advocates of naturalistic social science from the early nineteenth century, such as Comte, believed that the successful practical methods of physical science could be transposed with similar success to explaining, predicting, and controlling human behavior.

In borrowing its methodology from late eighteenth and nineteenth century physical science, naturalism contended that the main raw material of social science was empirically measurable social data. Human sense experience, or sense data, was held to be the only source of valid knowledge in social science. Metaphysical, theological, or philosophical speculations about human nature, behavior, and relationships were inadmissible as evidence. Whether this depiction was ever an accurate analogue to the actual methods practiced by natural scientists in the late eighteenth and nineteenth century is debatable.

For instance, many natural scientists of that time, e.g., Helmholtz, Faraday, and Maxwell, speculated greatly about metaphysics and theology as a basis for their empirical work (Harman, 1982). Nevertheless, the mythology developed that metaphysics and philosophy had no part in social science. There was a strong hope in naturalistic theory that the study of human behavior would be liberated from speculative and non-empirical influences. One effect of this was to disengage 'facts' from 'values' and normative suppositions, as though the two categories were logically separable.

A major thrust of naturalism and positivism in the social sciences has been in trying to discover causal social laws (Wacquant, 1994; Brown, 1984). Indeed, Boyd et al. (1991, 778) hold that a criterion for the definition of naturalism is 'the view that all phenomena are subject to natural laws.' Causality came to be interpreted in the naturalist view as a relationship between two or more entities where one necessarily produces the other. A regular succession of events happens—a constant conjunction of separate occurrences (Ryan, 1970). Causal physical laws, defined in this way, appeared to account for the extraordinary practical success of the natural sciences. Necessary relationships were discovered between natural entities, such as energy and heat, that produced practical artifacts of immense social value like electricity. By using the methods of physical science applied to social phenomena, it seemed possible to discover causal laws of human behavior and relationships. Ideally, each discovered law should then be subsumable under a covering law; that is, particular instances or expressions of a law should be containable in a broader, more encompassing law. Thus, economic laws—that people respond in certain ways to economic stimuli—should be rooted in psychological laws: that people respond in the ways the economic laws predict because human nature conforms to particular psychological laws. In turn, these psychological laws might be embedded in laws of physiology, which are encased in laws of chemistry and physics. Thus, the basic building blocks of human beings could be unraveled. The quest for causality is not confined to traditional naturalism. Contemporary realism also seeks causality but defined in a different manner from customary naturalism.

NON-NATURALISM IN SOCIAL SCIENCE

Non-naturalistic views about human behavior and relationships have a far longer recorded history than naturalistic views. Whereas the faint beginnings of naturalistic thought about human action might not be discernible until the eighteenth century, recorded non-naturalistic thinking goes back at least to Yahwist sources in the Old Testament, perhaps written at the beginning of the first millennium BC (Bright, 1972; Anderson, 1991). Examples of these are Genesis 2:4 to 3:24 which, as exegeted by von Rad (1972), reflect a number of non-naturalistic human behavioral characteristics such as their dependence on a metaphysical theological base, their identification in normative rather than objective terms, their holistic description, extensive use of figures of speech, and an emphasis on non-rational behaviors. Non-naturalistic tendencies were also apparent in the later Greek philosophies of Socrates, Plato, and Aristotle with their interest in metaphysical exploration (Walsh, 1985), and in idealism, the belief in spirit or mind as the basis of the material world. These non-naturalistic philosophical strains reinforced each other; as Gordon (1991, 381) notes, 'the influence of Greek philosophy on Western thought in the medieval period supported the idealist thrust of Christian theology.' In the eighteenth century, Immanuel Kant developed his strand of transcendental idealism, maintaining that material objects had no independent existence outside the mind. Perhaps more importantly for the subsequent development of non-naturalistic social science, Kant held that humans live simultaneously in two realms—a factual one of nature and a moral one of human action in which meaning and value were crucial. Following Kant, Hegel pursued a monistic idealism, preoccupied with the Eternal Spirit (Geist) and holistic interpretation. For later non-naturalistic social science, Hegel's investigations of the relations between ethics and social structure were crucial.

But the thrust of non-naturalistic thinking in philosophy and the humanities, and even in theology, was steadily weakened by the rise of scientific knowledge and ideology from the Enlightenment. Although representatives of the Counter-Enlightenment in the eighteenth century, like Vico and Hamann, kept non-naturalism alive in the humanities (Berlin, 1979), empiricist, materialist, and anti-theological doctrines were used increasingly as mutual reinforcement from the late eighteenth century by those, such as Hume, wanting to study society in more 'scientific' terms than hitherto. Idealism and romanticism continued to have popular impact into the nineteenth century through the likes of Goethe, Carlyle, Coleridge, Wordsworth, and Shelley, but they were mainly related to literary and religious thinking. So telling was the impact of post-Enlightenment ideas in science and philosophy that from early in the twentieth century, idealism diminished as an intellectual force. At most, it could evidence only momentary resurgence, as in its effect on British educational practice from about 1870 to 1920 (Gordon and White, 1979). The influence of philosophical realists like Moore and Russell grew, and new philosophical systems developed such as pragmatism, logical positivism, and linguistic philosophy. Simultaneously, particular aspects of idealistic philosophy were assailed, as in Hobhouse's *The Metaphysical Theory of the State* (1918).

By the nineteenth century, the dichotomy was clear between scientific naturalistic methods in the newly emerging social sciences and the interpretive approaches of the humanities. Whereas naturalistic methods gained strength in most of Europe and the United States, non-naturalism maintained a stronger hold in Germany, reflecting the influence of Kant and Hegel. Wilhelm Dilthey (1833–1911), for example, a neo-Kantian professor of philosophy in Berlin, focused on the moral meaning of human action, on human inner life, experience, and thought, distinguishing explanation from understanding (Dilthey, 1883), and in so doing strongly affected contemporary theological hermeneutics. Dilthey influenced Georg Simmel (1858–1918), who ranged across general, formal, and philosophical sociology, seeking to understand the meaning of such diverse things as the human face, adventure, love, handles, secrecy, smell, fashion, and chairs. Rather than trying to explain the phenomena in which they were interested and to subsume them under causal laws, Dilthey and Simmel interpreted phenomena like social structures 'in terms of roles, meanings, intentions and plots,' more as one interprets a play (Knapp, 1994, 150).

The embattled strain of academic non-naturalism struggled into the twentieth century. A diverse group of mainly European philosophers and historians kept the vision alive, such as Kierkegaard, Droysen, Crow, Brunschvicg, Collingwood, Bergson, Windelband, Rickert, and Husserl. It is no accident that debate over methodology in the social sciences (*Methodenstreit)* focused on Germany in the 1890s, and that renowned figures of Germanic social science, such as Weber and Schutz, practiced non-naturalistic sociology. Von Mises, founder of Austrian economics, was influenced by the same Germanic non-naturalistic tradition (Lachmann, 1990, 140) as were Hayek and Adolf Lowe. Since the late nineteenth century, the more diverse character of non-naturalistic than traditional naturalistic philosophy and methodology has given rise to a variety of approaches in social science and philosophy such as phenomenology, ethnomethodology, hermeneutics, existentialism, postmodernism, structuralism, and post-structuralism, relativisms like constructivism (Sankey, 1993), and the varieties of realism, of which one author has identified seven (Haack, 1987).

It is not possible to summarize here all these non-naturalistic approaches to social science. Some have been reflected in minority schools in economics, such as hermeneutics and postmodernism in the Austrian school, and an example is considered below of the relevance of hermeneutics. Hermeneutics is sometimes defined loosely as 'the many strands of "interpretive" philosophy which share common ground . . . in their opposition to positivist-oriented philosophies' (Lavoie, 1990, 2). It is commonly thought of as the theory and method of interpretation of human action in which *verstehen* (understanding) is the starting point for social enquiry, which viewpoint is also embodied in critical realism. Indeed, to Bhaskar (1994, 470), 'the hermeneutical paradigm is . . . consistent with a realist metatheory of science.'

Hermeneutics was originally a form of philological exploration of theological texts in which the interpretation of meaning was sought (Gerrard, 1993). One thread of the critique of the growing domination of social science by positivism in the nineteenth century emphasized the role of interpretive meaning (e.g., by Dilthey in his 1900 paper, 'The Rise of Hermeneutics'), when the theological term 'hermeneutics' was appropriated to define this strand. In its view, the positivist project of creating a natural science of social phenomena gave insufficient emphasis to the interpretation of human intention and desire—phenomena that did not occur in relation to the objects of natural science. Critics in the German intellectual tradition, such as Hegel, Marx, Dilthey, Husserl, Weber, Heidegger, Mannheim, and Schutz, contended that the inclusion of human beliefs in the study of human behavior undermined the application of naturalistic methods (Bauman, 1978).

The complications hermeneutics places in the way of theorizing about human behavior can be illustrated as follows. Human action is guided by intention or belief, which often may be unexpressed by the actor(s). The only or main expression of the intention will be in the action itself. To read back from the action to the belief or desire is likely to be a very imperfect interpretive (hermeneutical) process. Elucidation of meaning is required at every point throughout this process. For instance, data have to be collected to describe the action, and the interpreter (researcher) makes value judgments about what is the relevant data. Probably, the theory of intention and motivation the interpreter wants to test will lead to the selection of particular data, that is, the 'facts' are theory-laden. At some stage of the interpretive (research) process, the interpreter has to make a leap into the mind(s) of the actor(s). He assumes or construes that his theory expresses the intentions by which the actors did act. Hermeneutics maintains that explaining human action unavoidably involves construals of meaning that may differ between researchers; that is, a Neoclassical approach involves a particular hermeneutic about human behavior, an Austrian approach, a different one, and so on.

Trying to unravel the unstated beliefs or intentions underlying the actions of humans who, to some degree, have free will is not something that plagues natural science. The sun has no choice about where it will rise or set, plants grow according to well-established botanical laws, and building construction proceeds according to known and unassailable laws of strengths of materials. Some of the natural sciences seem to have discovered reliable causal laws from which technologies for controlling nature have been constructed. A non-naturalistic complaint about naturalism in social science is that no well-established generalizations or laws have been discovered that connect human beliefs with action. Attempts to explain human action by desires, preferences, and beliefs have produced only generalizations that are riddled with exceptions (Rosenberg, 1995). Naturalistic social scientists are likely to reject this conclusion. For example, Neoclassical economists, believe that their theory of human behavior, predicated on assumed characteristics of humans such as self-interest, rationality, and maximizing tendencies, fits observed human action. Like every other difference between hermeneutics and naturalism in social science, this one is unresolved and has been marked by controversy for more than a hundred years.

Rather than trying to discover causal laws of human behavior, a consciously hermeneutical approach might strive to discern low-level regularities and connections in human action (as discussed in Wilber and Harrison, 1978). Human behavior is interpreted so that its meaning or significance can become intelligible. Regularities in this behavior may be discovered, but they are too weak to be used predictively. In one view, common sense and commonplace concepts, thousands of years old, inform this meaning; for example, that human action occurs because people desire particular ends, that these beliefs are affected by the environments in which people live, and so on. All these vague, trivial principles can be described as 'folk psychology' (Horgan and Woodward, 1993), a 'theory' that has produced little predictive improvement through its thousands of years of history. In folk psychology, the explanation of human action is to be found through people following rules, traditions, customs, and habits. Even though rules, etc., provide minimal explanation of causes, this is not the main interest of hermeneutical social science.

For such reasons, a hermeneutical approach is not likely to be sympathetic to the application of the methods of natural science to social science. It would maintain that application of naturalistic methods has not produced a comparable degree of agreement in explanation or precision in prediction for the behavior of people as exists for the objects of physical science. It is not only the relative disparity in the ages of natural versus social science, or the seemingly greater complexity of human versus non-human behavior that explains the greater predictive success of natural science. As well, it is that folk psychology long ago reached its maximum level of predictive power. The application of methods of natural science to social phenomena is a well-intentioned but misguided response to this impasse. Significantly greater predictive or causal power is not being discovered by applying ever more sophisticated mathematical and statistical methods to social data because, in truth, no 'science' of human behavior exists waiting to be discovered. The explanations or causal 'laws' about the real world that social science and economics have come up with in the last hundred years are permanently contested, riddled with exceptions, and only trivial extensions of folk psychology.

This discussion of the relevance of an interpretive approach in social science is only one illustration of the application of hermeneutical thinking. The example of the relation of intentionality and folk psychology to social science theory draws from Rosenberg (1980, 1992, 1995), who, as a self-confessed naturalistic philosopher (1990) adhering to an empiricist basis of knowledge, eschews a hermeneutical approach as the way forward for social science (1992, 15, 19). Nevertheless, it appears that hermeneutics possesses a strength (and weakness) in its flexibility to encompass even the views of those who disagree with it!

While it is possible to suggest how a hermeneutical viewpoint relates to social science, there is no claim that it can be assessed in any determinate sense as being nearer to truth than naturalistic viewpoints. The determination of truth does not seem to be at all settled in the philosophy and sociology of science. Nevertheless, contemporary academic economics has made a majority choice that naturalistic philosophy/methodology reveals truth more clearly than non-naturalistic. Academic economics is nearly monopolized by Neoclassical naturalism, while non-naturalistic alternatives are downplayed.

THE REFLECTION OF NON-NATURALISM AND NATURALISM IN CONTEMPORARY ECONOMICS

Table 9.1 following lists 36 polarities between non-naturalistic and naturalistic approaches in economics today. Only the widest range of difference between the two views is itemized. Each economist lies on a continuum between each polarity, so that each is a different mixture from the other, on at least 36 counts, which contributes to the given level of disagreement within economics. This chapter is written from a non-naturalistic viewpoint and contains biases inherent in that approach. Non-naturalistic social scientists admit unashamedly that their analyses are 'contaminated' inevitably by value judgments and philosophical predilections as part of the normal procedure of scientific research. The 36 criteria that divide non-naturalistic and naturalistic economists are derived therefore from our interpretive assessment of the history and philosophy of economics. Other non-naturalistic social scientists could read the evidence differently and present different criteria to separate the two approaches. For example, Mirowski (1994, 11) presents an alternative conceptualization of the distinction between the natural and the social. There is no absolute correctness to the particular classifications of Table 9.1. The approach is more one of reporting interpretations recognized as controversial than with trying to persuade readers of their correctness.

In making bold conjectures about non-naturalistic and naturalistic economics, it is not possible to discuss each of the 36 differences in Table 9.1. Instead, three polarities are singled out: items 1, 4, and 6. Item 1 on the non-naturalistic side alleges that many economic theories, such as Becker's economic theory of human behavior and the rational expectations hypothesis, are not theories in the natural science sense of the word. The reasons for this claim are considered by taking the example of Becker's theory (1976), for which one assessment is that 'it is not only not an economic theory, but not even a theory at all' (Rosenberg 1980, 87). There are three reasons for this evaluation, all of which relate to the non-naturalistic claim of the inapplicability of naturalistic methods of physical science to social science. First is Rosenberg's view that cognitive psychology suggests that people do not behave in the ways the theory postulates: 'people do not literally, consciously, make decisions about actions by the employment of principles which parallel or reflect his [Becker's] formalism' (1980, 84). That is, the causal sequence of actions by which people make decisions in the domains to which Becker claims his theory applies does not follow the postulated theoretical causal mechanisms. Certainly, there is no unanimity within cognitive psychology about what are the causal mechanisms people do follow. A variety of competing theories seeks to explain human behavior in terms of beliefs and desires, unconscious and subconscious forces, existing and past institutions, traditions, and roles (Rosenberg, 1995, 47, 53), including folk psychology. However, among these theories there is no agreement that people maximize anything or that they possess preferences that remain stable over time, both crucial planks of Becker's theory.

This alleged disconformity between the actual causal mechanisms by which people act and the theories of Neoclassical economics (of which Becker's is a leading example) long ago produced the 'as if' defense of Neoclassical theory. In Friedman's 1953 instrumentalist defense, for example, a sufficient warrant for the validity of theory was whether its predictions conformed with empirical reality. If this occurred, we were entitled to believe that the agents of the theory acted 'as if' the causal mechanisms applied. This defense is not regarded as adequate by non-naturalism and by realism. In the latter view (e.g., Sayer, 1992), causal theories are required to specify the actual mechanisms corresponding to real-world behavior; the 'as if' correspondence is insufficient warrant for the scientific validity of causal theory. Nevertheless, the 'as if' criterion continues to loom large as a defense of Neoclassical theory. For instance, in the theory of the firm, its constructs are only logical tools, 'they are not meant to be descriptions of *how* firms reach their decisions . . . the methods used to derive these predictions have no necessary connection with the thought process by which firms actually reach their decisions' (Lipsey and Chrystal, 1995, 319). Becker's economic theory of human behavior explicitly takes the same path (1976, 7).

A second non-naturalistic reason for questioning the naturalistic scientific basis of Neoclassical economic theory, and specifically Becker's, is that scientific theories ideally require independent specification of the variables that constitute their composition. For example, in Newton's force law, F = ma, independent means of specifying 'F' (force), 'm' (mass) and 'a' (acceleration) exist; thus, Hooke's spring law provides the explanation for 'm.' However, variables such 'preferences,' 'utility,' 'tastes,' 'beliefs,' 'desires,' and 'environment' in Becker's theory do not possess this quality. They are dialectical and multidimensional terms for which independent specification is not possible. Moreover, neither economics, psychology, cognitive or neuroscience has theories to explain the given state of preferences, for example, nor why they may change over time or vary between people at one time. The terms are those of folk psychology, capable neither of falsification nor of application. Theories based on them have the 'predictive accuracy of common sense' (Rosenberg, 1992, 134). Stich (1983, 209) argued that 'folk psychology and serious science are ill suited to one another.' Even so, economics and the social sciences 'are up to their ears' in folk psychology, so much so that 'if all talk of beliefs, desires, expectations, preferences . . . and the like were banished from the social sciences, those disciplines as we know them today would disappear' (1983, 213). Although Stich (1996, 29) has not been able to provide a superior crucial ingredient for science, he is now less inclined to regard folk psychology as a 'seriously mistaken theory.'

The two reasons above lead to a third for questioning the naturalistic scientific basis of Becker's theory. This claims it is a circular construct in which human behavior is observed and preferences are cited to explain the behavior. However, when explanation is sought to explain the preferences, all that can be offered by the theory is the behavior itself. That is, 'the crucial explanatory variables are characterized and individuated by the very events whose occurrence they are cited to explain' (Rosenberg, 1980, 74). An analogy with a physical science law may clarify this point. The ideal gas law relates the volume, pressure, and temperature of gases. Measuring temperatures in experiments testing the gas law requires the use of thermometers. It is important that thermometers do not depend for their operation on the ideal gas law or manifest as its outcome, for if they did, they would not provide independent specification of one of the variables in the law (Rosenberg, 1992, 125). Yet, in Becker's theory, measuring preferences of people in, say, marriage choices, can only be captured by the outcomes of the choices themselves.

A second disagreement between non-naturalistic and naturalistic approaches to economics is item 6 of Table 9.1. This cites the non-naturalistic claim that few causal economic laws exist or have been discovered in contrast to the naturalistic counterclaim. In this context, causal means a relationship between two entities where one necessarily produces the other or has a specified probability of so doing. The statement of the relationship is the law (e.g., Ryan, 1970, 11; Fay and Moon, 1977, 217; Skyrms, 1980, 5). This definition of causality is used because it accords most closely with the traditional naturalistic conception. It does not conform with the realist view in which causality is not confined to constant conjunctions. In this view, causal laws are separate from actual events, and powers are not to be confused with their exercise, for causal claims relate to the necessary powers of objects (e.g., Sayer, 1992). So, while causal powers can exist when A leads to B, they can exist also when A does not. The relation between A and B is contingent on other conditions that may not be known. The matter of causal laws in social science in this realist sense is canvassed in the following chapter.

Non-naturalistic economists believe some forms of economic laws exist. For instance, most might agree that an increase in the price of a good stands a high (but unspecified) probability of causing a reduction in the quantity of the good demanded. (Whether this can count as a causal law in the realist sense of the term is considered in the next chapter.) The disagreement is whether many such economic laws exist describing relationships between entities in the real world. This is a different issue from whether necessary relationships or laws exist in theoretical models—they obviously do.

The existence of real-world economic laws might be assessed in a number of ways. A first could be to actually identify these laws. This might be done by searching the writings of economists to uncover them. For example, Brown (1984) dissected the work of a string of economists from the sixteenth century to the nineteenth century looking for laws. But he found none, concluding that there are no 'scientific laws of society as there are scientific laws of nature' (1984, 262). Certainly, early economists, such as Von Thunen (1826), set up axiomatic systems from which theoretical economic laws were deduced. But, to retain his mathematical formulations, Von Thunen was not able to relax his assumptions, like that of perfect rationality by his farmers. Because of such axiomatic constraints, it can still be debated whether Von Thunen's theoretical economic laws are more helpful than non-naturalistic qualitative and verbal interpretation for explaining actual agricultural location patterns (e.g., Dicken and Lloyd, 1990, 61–67).

A second way of identifying the existence of real-world laws might be to consider their logical or empirical validity by those who have specified them. For instance, Popper (1961) listed nine socioeconomic laws that he believed were 'analogous to the laws or hypotheses of the natural sciences' (1961, 62). However, Popper merely asserted the existence of these laws and assumed nothing 'about the strength of the available evidence in favour' of them (1961, 63). One of Popper's candidates was 'you cannot introduce agricultural tariffs and at the same time reduce the cost of living' (1961, 62). Flew (1985, 101) and Trigg (1985, 182) pointed out that there is nothing logically inexorable about this 'law,' that a government could compensate for introducing tariffs by reducing the prices of other goods.

Table 9.1. Polarities between Non-naturalistic and Naturalistic Economics

Non-naturalistic	*Naturalistic*
Theory Formulation	
1. Many economic theories (e.g., Becker's economic theory of human behavior, the rational expectations hypothesis) are not theories in the natural science sense.	1. Economic theories are comparable with natural science theories.
2. Relations between human behavioral, including economic, variables are culturally, historically, and spatially contingent. They are context specific.	2. Relations between economic variables are acultural, ahistorical, and aspatial. They are context universal.
3. Cultural, historical, sociological, and political influences are included in explanations. Holistic/organic explanation is sought.	3. Cultural, etc., influences are excluded. They impair formalistic modelling. Reductionist/atomistic explanation is sought.
4. Open social systems are assumed.	4. Closed social systems are assumed.
5. Its theoretical aim is qualitative understanding, intelligibility, and explanation, not quantitative prediction.	5. Its theoretical aim is quantitative explanation and prediction.
6. Few causal economic laws exist in the real world or have been discovered. Human behavioral causality is problematic.	6. Causal economic laws exist and can be discovered. Causality is replicable.
7. Causal explanation requires the qualitative analysis of mechanisms.	7. Causal explanation requires quantitative analysis of mechanisms.
8. Causal explanation need not involve quantifiable knowledge or mathematical expression. Mathematical expression can be an aid at times.	8. Causal explanation is best expressed mathematically.
9. The role of rhetoric, metaphor, analogy, and other figures of speech is accepted explicitly.	9. The role of rhetoric, etc., is ignored or rejected. It is not 'scientific'.
Theory Appraisal	
10. Formal tests of theory validity are not emphasized. Storytelling, colligation, pattern-modelling are used (statistical data is one input).	10. Formal tests of theory validity are crucial, e.g. mathematical modelling is assessed by logical deduction; econometric testing by falsificationism and instrumentalism.
11. Methods of natural language (verbal expression) are paramount.	11. Methods of natural science analyses are paramount.
12. Methods/techniques are not a major concern.	12. Methods/techniques are a major concern. Continual search is made for improved techniques.

Table 9.1. *(continued)*

Non-naturalistic	*Naturalistic*
Theory Appraisal	
13. Brute facts do not exist. Theory ladenness of observation undermines formal efforts to test theory empirically. Reality does not necessarily equal appearance.	13. Brute facts exist. Theory ladenness of observation does not vitiate formal, empirical tests of theory.
14. Verbal and econometric analysis are on a par for causal explanation.	14. Econometric analysis is more reliable than verbal analysis for explanation and prediction.
15. Econometrics has not proven to be a necessary and sufficient vehicle for assessing the empirical claims of competing theories.	15. More sophisticated econometric theory/technique will overcome this problem.
16. Small samples/case studies help unravel explanation.	16. Case studies must be replicated; large samples are essential for developing theory.
17. No unambiguous methods of theory appraisal exist. Increasingly sophisticated mathematical technique is not leading to more certain methods of theory appraisal (or more empirically certain theories).	17. Unambiguous, objective methods of theory appraisal can be discovered by better mathematical/statistical techniques.
18. No means of decisively falsifying economic theories exist.	18. Theories can be falsified and discarded from the body of economic knowledge.
19. 'Falsified' theories are not discarded readily from the body of economic knowledge.	19. Falsified theories are discarded from the body of economic knowledge.
20. Progress in social science, including economics, cannot be assessed clearly. There is no cumulative development of economic theory and knowledge.	20. Progress in economics can be assessed. Economic theory and knowledge develops cumulatively.
21. The given state of accepted economic theory/knowledge is socially conditioned.	21. The given state of true economic theory/knowledge is scientifically determined.
Philosophical Presuppositions	
22. No unambiguous definition of 'science' or 'scientific method' exists.	22. 'Science' and 'scientific method' can be defined unproblematically.
23. Value judgments in analysis are unavoidable.	23. Value judgments can/should be excised from analysis.
24. No uniform agreement exists about the substance of human nature.	24. More uniform agreement is assumed about human nature (e.g., neoclassical image).

(continued)

Table 9.1. *(continued)*

Non-naturalistic	*Naturalistic*
	Philosophical Presupposition
25. Competing theories/paradigms/ viewpoints are normal. No one is best approximation to truth. Each studies different aspects of reality/ truth.	25. One theory/paradigm—perhaps the neoclassical—is the best approximation to truth.
26. The decision to work in this mode is based on metaphysical and scientific considerations.	26. The decision to work in this mode is based on scientific considerations ('it is more scientific').
27. A clear separation cannot always be made between metaphysical and scientific considerations.	27. A clear separation can usually be made between metaphysical and scientific considerations.
28. Metaphysical beliefs, including held values, influence hard cores and methodology.	28. Metaphysical influences should be excised.
29. 'Non-scientific' thinking cannot necessarily be judged as irrational.	29. Non-scientific thinking is usually irrational.
30. It has elements in common with scientific realism and with other forms of realism. It is not necessarily identical with relativism or constructivism.	30. Its philosophical position(s) is not consciously articulated.
	Policy Relevance
31. Tenuous links exist between economic theory and policy formulation. Policy formulation requires more holistic inputs and links than just the economic.	31. Stronger links exist between economic theory and policy formulation.
	Social Science Links
32. Economic thinking is but one way of conceptualizing social reality.	32. The rigor and universal applicability of economic theory justifies 'economic imperialism.'
	Who Is More Likely to Follow the Approach?
33. Institutionalists, behavioralists, most Marxists, Post Keynesians, Austrians, and social economists, most economic methodologists, most economic historians and geographers.	33. Neoclassical economists, a minority of Marxists, and Post Keynesians
34. More able to communicate with historians, sociologists, anthropologists, and philosophers.	34. More able to communicate with mathematicians, statisticians, and engineers.

Table 9.1. *(continued)*

Non-naturalistic	*Naturalistic*
Typical Journals	
35. *Journal of Economics Issues, Review of Social Economy, Journal of Socio-Economics.*	35. *American Economic Review, Journal of Political Economy, Review of Economics and Statistics.*
What Is the Situtation in Other Social Sciences?	
36. Most sociologists, anthropologists, political scientists, a smaller majority of psychologists.	36. Some psychologists, fewer sociologists, anthropologists, and political scientists.

Berelson and Steiner (1964) presented an encyclopedic compendium of purported laws in the behavioral sciences including 'the behavioral parts of economics' (1964, 11). They listed hundreds of 'propositions, generalizations, laws or principles' explaining and predicting 'the actions, thoughts, and feelings of human beings' (1964, 5, 3). However, many of their laws are more like simple common sense or folk psychology, as with 'job changes occur more frequently in the less skilled occupations than in the highly skilled ones' (1964, 407). Like the second criticism of item 1 above, none of the terms in their laws was either defined or provided with independent specification; therefore, many were vague and imprecise, such as 'social change is more likely to occur in heterogeneous societies than in homogeneous ones' (1964, 615)—the meaning of 'heterogeneous' and 'homogeneous' are left hanging in the air. Bunge's list (1998, 121) fares little better on this score with examples like 'capitalism is expansionary.' As Sayer (1992, 103) points out, 'the value of [such] generalizations depends upon the qualitative nature of the objects to which they refer.'

Today, opinion differs about whether economics has become more or less interested since the 1960s in trying to discover and test causal economic laws empirically. One view is that economists show little interest nowadays (Blaug, 1992). If this were true, it could reflect the lack of earlier payoff in isolating empirical laws and the practical difficulties of actually testing economic hypotheses and deciding which had the status of laws. Because of such problems, a prominent economics dictionary (Zamagni, 1987, 54) claimed that 'no scientific law, in the natural scientific sense' has been established in economics; indeed, 'the list of generally accepted economic laws seems to be shrinking.' However, it could be proposed that economics has become more interested in looking for real-world laws. Presumably, some of econometrics imagines itself to be striving to discover invariant relationships between economic variables.

If even part of econometrics is directed to this end, law seeking flourishes. Whether many universal, determinate, invariant, probabilistic, causal, ahistorical, acultural, and aspatial relationships have been discovered is doubtful. But it may be reasonable to suggest that econometrics thinks it has the capacity to do so. To discover that some economic relationship held in a particular country for a given time period, but not in other countries or times, might not warrant the explosive increase in econometric work in the last thirty years and its present hegemony with formalistic modelling in Neoclassical economics.

In the belief of traditional non-naturalism, relationships between economic variables in the real world do not have the nature of universal deterministic or probabilistic laws. Rather, they are rough, crude, and approximate generalizations and tendencies, bedeviled by exceptions, and not precise enough for useful policy prediction. Where they do exist, relationships have restricted scope, applying in specific historical, cultural, institutional, and spatial circumstances, which view has long been propounded in economics although not only by those who would think of themselves as non-naturalists (e.g., Robbins, 1932; Hutchison, 1981). This is also a common view in social science outside economics (e.g., Bunge, 1998).

A stronger non-naturalistic stance would deny that economic laws can exist. Its contention would be that economic laws are not produced or affected only by economic causes. Human behavior in the economic domain is affected by influences applying in other human behavioral domains—in the psychological and sociological, for example. But, as well, it is affected by influences operating in non-human behavioral domains like chemistry, physics, biology, etc. Trying to isolate the separate effects of all these influences affecting economic behavior is well-nigh impossible. Of course, the laws of physics are affected by other domains of natural science, but they, at least, seem to hold with greater reliability than economic laws.

That economic laws cannot stand on their own, in this view, is a reflection of the non-naturalistic position that there are no laws connecting human action with desires and beliefs. In this position, 'causal relations between mind and matter are singular and irregular . . . they reflect logical or conceptual relations between the intentional content of the mind, the statements describing what we believe and want, and descriptions of action' (Rosenberg, 1995, 216). However, neither economics, psychology, sociology, cognitive or neuroscience has universally accepted theories to describe these conceptual links (an analogous argument against the existence of social laws is made also by Searle, 1984). That is, why people do the things they do is unclear, and the nature of human causation is problematic (Ryan 1970, 110).

This objection emphasizes the lack of knowledge of the underlying mechanisms connecting events that ostensibly are causally related. However, lack of knowledge of mechanism is a matter of degree, for the specification of causal mechanism always presupposes a more fundamental underlying mechanism, ad infinitum. For instance, in Von Thunen's model, the economic rationality of farmers produces certain causally related location patterns. But what is the underlying mechanism explaining the rationality of the farmers? Von Thunen's economic laws presuppose psychological laws that relate states of mind to economic behavior, laws non-naturalists deny exist. Uncovering the ultimate mechanism responsible for a first-stated law is a process of infinite regress. This observation applies to any law in natural or social science. It is not a particular disadvantage of social or economic laws. Similar considerations apply to *ceteris paribus* restrictions that constrain all laws (Cartwright, 1983; Kincaid, 1990, 70).

Rather, the non-naturalistic complaint about economic (and social) laws is that they frequently appear to get the mechanism wrong—they describe the actual causal process incorrectly. This charge is made even though the axiomatic bases of ostensibly causal theories may be consistent with observed behavior, for many alternative axiomatic bases may be so constructed. This is part of the criticism, discussed above, of Becker's economic theory of human behavior. In so far as economics and social science do get the causal mechanisms wrong, they will not be able to produce reliable laws. Non-naturalists contend that this is, indeed, the situation in social science. The issue of explanatory laws in economics and social science is very much alive today. Recent influential claims have been made by naturalist social science thinkers outside economics (e.g., Kincaid, 1996) that the case for causal (realist) laws in social science is promising. The next chapter looks more closely at these claims from a purely secular viewpoint, while Chapter 13 responds to them from a Christian perspective.

The last issue to be considered in this chapter is item 4 of Table 9.1. Non-naturalists assume that socio-economic systems, the frameworks for their analysis, are open. Naturalists, on the other hand, treat systems as if they were closed. An open system is 'where no constant conjunction or regular sequence of events' holds (Bhaskar, 1978, 14). Influences within the system do not have a stable relationship with each other, and the system is not isolated from external influences.

This point is related to the preceding discussion of item 6. In an open socioeconomic system, the behavior of people constituting the system depends not only on economic and social influences, but on physical, chemical, environmental, and physiological forces. Given this definition, all socioeconomic systems are open. Causation is intractably difficult to uncover because open systems 'do not cover all the forces or causes effective in their domain' (Kincaid, 1990, 60). From this basis, as discussed under item 6 above, social and economic laws cannot be discovered because all the influences on human behavior cannot be separated.

In principle, of course, no physical, chemical, environmental, or socio-economic system is closed. Physical systems are subject to chemical influences and so on. However, like item 6 discussed above, the non-naturalistic criticism is that in the social sciences the failure to discover many social or economic causal laws is because all possible causes cannot be accounted for. Allegedly, this differs from physical, chemical, etc., systems that, even though they are subject to causal factors from other systems, are more closed than socio-economic systems and can draw on experimental closed systems. On this basis, analyzing physical, etc., systems as if they were closed can produce reliable causal laws at times. But this approach does not seem to work for socio-economic systems. Their openness means that their constituents can be interpreted in a greater variety of ways.

An example from economics of the openness/closedness issue illustrates the problem. Lawson (1989), a realist, analyzed the 1920s–40s arguments involving Keynes, Tinbergen, Haavelmo, and Vining on the scientific basis of econometrics. Lawson contended that the two conditions for closure (the intrinsic and the extrinsic) were (and are) not met in econometrics. In his view, Haavelmo did not rebut Keynes' criticism that economic systems are not susceptible to closed analysis; Haavelmo provided 'no grounds for supposing the extrinsic condition for closure' can be satisfied. The extrinsic condition is that each effect has the same cause(s). However, in the absence of well-defied or reliable laws in the social sciences, it 'almost always appears to be possible to conceive of further causal factors capable of impinging on the event in question' (Lawson, 1989, 243). Non-naturalists and realists hold that social science is only partially explanatory rather than reliably predictive, because it is not possible to consider explicitly all possible causes of socio-economic phenomena; 'it is unlikely to be practically possible to discover the extent to which the intrinsic and extrinsic conditions for system closure are not satisfied' (Sayer, 1992, 131). In the non-naturalist and realist interpretation, econometrics is forced to assume closed social systems, these do not exist, and therefore 'econometrics is a notoriously uncertain science, with a spotty record for predictive success' (Cartwright, 1989, 158).

CONCLUSION

Naturalistic tendencies have a strong influence in contemporary orthodox economics. The emphasis on abstract, mathematical model building, on formalistic representations of human choice and interaction, and quantitative measurement of empirical data via sophisticated statistical technique represents the appropriation of methods from the natural sciences. These methods reflect beliefs that the human science of economics should be oriented to the methods of physical science.

A particular metaphilosophical view of what constitutes scientific activity underlies the naturalistic domination of economics. This includes the proposition that valid knowledge of socio-economic behavior is discoverable only by naturalistic methods, so that in teaching economics, for example, major effort is devoted to techniques and formal analytical modelling. Conversely, little attention is given to metaphysical, philosophical, and theological speculation that are not regarded as sources of scientific knowledge. Formalistic modelling requires that assumptions or axioms be made about human behavior. However, empirical disconformity of those assumptions from real-world behavior does little to shake the theoretical edifice of orthodox economics (Hausman, 1992; Bunge, 1998). There is a belief also that the highest stage of refinement in causal explanation of socio-economic phenomena is to be found in its expression as a mathematical model. Less formal explanation is not 'scientific' in this view. Ideally, formal models should be testable via empirical data, but critics maintain this process is being followed decreasingly in academic economics (e.g., Morgan, 1988). This criticism can extend to the claim that formal models (e.g., game theory) are increasingly studied for their own mathematical sophistication, not because they are subsequently related to or derived from empirical data (e.g., Abu Turab Rizvi, 1994).

The contemporary domination of economics by naturalistic methods parallels the positivist domination of the physical sciences to the mid-1950s. However, in physical science, and particularly in social sciences other than economics, the hold of positivism and some of its associated naturalistic features has weakened steadily (e.g., Suppe, 1977; Bryant, 1985). In orthodox economics their hold seems to be steady, if not growing. This hold leads to the downplay in teaching academic economics of input concerned with the metaphysical and philosophical bases of the subject, with exploring why these philosophical bases have changed over time, with investigating alternative conceptions of economics, with the historical development of economics and its relation to other social sciences, and with analysis conducted in a natural language. Few of these are held in high value and therefore 'cannot be fitted into the curricula.'

The counter non-naturalistic view holds that traditional naturalistic methods are inappropriate as the dominant methodology for social science. In its view, social science can aspire only to qualitative understanding and explanation, not prediction, 'for social life has to do with meanings, and meanings can only be understood, not measured' (Kanth, 1991, 42). In this approach, the methods of natural language (verbal expression) assume more importance than quantification. The 'mad rush to measure' (Katzner, 1991) arose out of the conflation of objectivity with quantitative analysis, which is a mythical identity. As well, non-naturalists are skeptical that mathematics has added more than formal elegance to economics. They contend that the emphasis on mathematics is one of form rather than substance (e.g., Beed and Kane, 1991; Montgomery, 1994), a variant of the philosophical stance of conventionalism in which theories are regarded as neither true nor false. In the non-naturalistic view, many of the formal theorems of naturalistic economics are tautologies—they are logical rather than empirical truths.

Non-naturalistic economics as practiced by Institutionalists, most behavioralists and Austrians, and smaller majorities of Marxists and Post Keynesians is a great deal fuzzier, softer, messier, and wordier than the formalistic naturalism of Neoclassical economics. What is lost in abstract elegance, however, may be made up in real-world relevance and policy orientation through the use of a more holistic analysis. Two helpful Christian-influenced examples exemplifying this claim are Daly and Cobb (1994), and Hobgood (1991).

Chapter Ten

Causal Explanation and Laws in Naturalistic Social Science

The previous chapter suggested that one of the long time hopes of naturalistic economics and social science has been to discover well-confirmed causal explanations or theories for the phenomena in their purview. These explanations might then constitute laws that could be applied in various socio-economic contexts, in much the same way as laws in natural science apply. If this were achievable, social science might then have greater practical value in so far as its causal explanations or laws could be useful for policy purposes. The social sciences could then truly be called 'science' and be accorded the intellectual respectability that natural science attracts. This chapter (Beed and Beed, 2000a) examines recently expressed hopes and claims that naturalistic social science, especially economics, is well on the way to discovering laws. Contrary to those claims, the conclusion here is that naturalistic social science is as far as ever from discovering laws for human social behavior (as well as for personal behavior). Chapter 13 returns to this theme by showing that from a Christian perspective this failure is to be expected.

Harold Kincaid (1996) and Lee McIntyre (1996) are important contributions to the debate supporting the long-sought aim of discovering laws in the social sciences. This chapter argues against Kincaid's and McIntyre's cases that social science laws exist, as they define them. The prevailing reflection on social science, with a long pedigree (e.g., Cohen, Hayek, Popper), is that no laws govern social phenomena (e.g., MacIntyre, 1981; Little, 1993). In this account, regularities in social science data are phenomenal, weak and unreliable. Against this outlook, Kincaid and McIntyre (re)propose the potential and actual existence of social science laws. Although lamenting 'the failure of social scientists to produce unequivocal laws,' McIntyre (1996, ix) is optimistic 'about the prospects for nomological explanation in the social sciences.' This view is supported by Kincaid (1996) who regards social science generally, and economics specifically, as capable of achieving laws. Indeed, the aim of social science is to produce laws, for 'a real social science would provide us with laws, predictions, and understanding of large-scale social structure' (Kincaid, 1996, 6), useful for practical policy making.

In this introduction, the ways in which Kincaid and McIntyre define laws in social science are surveyed. In subsequent sections, four long-standing and familiar problems, discussed in different degree by Kincaid and McIntyre, are reviewed. The focus is how Kincaid and McIntyre attempt to overcome them. The assessment is made within the realist framework broadly adopted by Kincaid and McIntyre. The first section of the chapter, the identification and behavior of social kinds, outlines the first problem—the difficulty presented by the nature of the entities with which social science deals. The second section of the chapter, causal explanation and mechanisms, discusses the problem of exposing causal mechanisms in social science, while section three examines domain restrictions and mechanisms, including problems posed by *ceteris paribus* restrictions. In the fourth section, openness and mechanisms, the remaining problem is considered—the openness of social systems. The penultimate section of the chapter criticizes the claim made by Kincaid that in the 'test case' of economics, laws do exist. The chapter appraises Kincaid's and McIntyre's critique of the four barriers to producing social science laws as these two authors understand them. The conclusion here is that despite their comprehensive overviews of problems confronting laws in social science, little progress has been made to overcome the four issues examined here. Kincaid's and McIntyre's treatments do not provide new directions for social science to develop laws (at least, as they present them); for example, laws suitable for public policy determination continue to remain practically elusive.

Much debate has occurred in physical and social science about how 'law' might be defined (e.g., Carroll, 1994). As noted in Chapter 9, a law has been described as a necessary relationship between phenomena, an invariable sequence between at least two situations subject to the same conditions (e.g., Cartwright, 1997, 65). The meaning of each of the words in this description could be debated (e.g., what does 'necessary' mean?), but this is not pursued here. Suffice to say that no more precise uniformly-agreed definition of 'law' exists in social science, and therefore, neither does a generally accepted classification of 'laws.' This open-endedness persists in Kincaid's and McIntyre's treatments. McIntyre (1996, 2), for instance, noted that 'a whole constellation of possible criteria' exists for nomologicality, and he did not try to establish the combination that defined a natural or a social science law. It can be agreed that 'the final arbiter of what counts as a law is the extent to which the purported law lives up to the standards for nomologicality derived from good scientific practice' (McIntyre 1996, 94), but McIntyre made no suggestions about what these standards might be. Interpreting 'law' like this is indeterminate: what counts as a law depends on unstated standards. Leaving the matter up in the air makes it difficult to read McIntyre. Thus, he repeatedly uses the term 'law' in relation to natural and social science without being clear on which aspect(s) of the constellation criteria he is focusing.

Laws have been identified elsewhere with regularities in data (e.g., Hausman, 1992, 292; Little, 1993, 183, 186; Cartwright, 1995, 276; 1997, 65), but this identity does not conform to realist ideas (for well-canvassed reasons) that constitute the framework in which Kincaid's and McIntyre's cases are constructed. The most precision Kincaid attaches to the definition of 'law' is that the term is used interchangeably with 'successful causal explanations' or 'well-confirmed causal explanations' (1996, 10, 58). Kincaid derives this central feature of 'law' from naturalistic physical science, that 'at its best gives us well-confirmed accounts of particular causal processes' (1996, 55). The following sections of this chapter argue that the (naturalistic) social science examples provided by Kincaid do not illustrate unequivocally the qualities of 'successful' and 'well-confirmed' causal explanations, or how they might be used for policy purposes. This is because the examples do not overcome four long-observed problems in formulating social science explanation. Whether natural science is more 'successful' than social science in constructing causal explanations is not the focus here. Rather, this chapter emphasizes ways in which 'successful' and 'well confirmed' causal explanations in social science are assessed by Kincaid and McIntyre.

THE IDENTIFICATION AND BEHAVIOR OF SOCIAL KINDS

One difficulty for causal explanation in social science, not pursued by Kincaid and McIntyre, stems from problems in identifying the human behavioral entities on which these disciplines focus. This limitation relates to the probable absence of natural kinds in social science. In realist terminology, a natural kind is an entity possessing a 'real essence, understood as a property or set of properties both necessary and sufficient for membership of the kind.' Given that natural kinds have intrinsic properties, 'causal powers lie ultimately in the intrinsic properties of things' (Wilkerson, 1995, 30, 32). In realist thought, natural kinds share 'a common causal structure' (Little, 1993, 190). The (realist) task of science is to identify these intrinsic properties and their causal powers; as Wilkerson (1995, 62) puts it, 'scientific generalization consists in the articulation of *de re* necessary truths about the causal powers of things.' Causal explanations (laws) derive from the properties of natural kinds; 'it makes no sense to speak of a natural kind, e.g., being an electron, independently of the laws which govern its behavior' (Bigelow et al., 1992, 380). Thus, natural kinds are the objects of interest to physics and chemistry. These objects aim to capture the real essences of natural kinds of things. The essences are not necessarily all physical or observable, but nevertheless are postulated to be part of natural reality (at least, by realists).

The objects of interest to social science probably do not possess these qualities. For instance, some of the entities of economics may exist only by definition or custom; they might be viewed as conventions of language not reflecting underlying natural distinctions. Money, for example, is defined by what people customarily agree to regard as exchangeable stores of value, and it has differed historically and culturally; 'no very definite constraints' apply to its 'properties and behavior . . . [which are] governed by so many different legal, political and moral conventions' (Wilkerson, 1995, 31). This description applies even though money exists as a necessary characteristic of a market economy, as a unit of account. Another example from economics is utility. Broome (1991, 3) pointed out that no invariant definition of utility has been employed in the history of economics' practice; indeed, 'the term "utility" has become so ambiguous as to cause immense confusion.' Although 'utility' has been used widely in economics for some years as an indicator 'for ranking options in accord with one's preferences' (Alchian and Allen, 1972, 25), it remains unclear what is the attribute(s) people are supposed to be ranking. Nothing of a natural kind, as defined by the realists above, has yet been identified. Another way of expressing these problems is that uniform agreement on the meaning of economic ideas is difficult to achieve. This is because 'we cannot "see" many economic concepts in the same sense as we can see a polyhedron,' there is a 'lack of agreement on the basic concepts that economics should be seeking to explain' (Backhouse, 1997, 206–207). Such objects of interest to social science as 'beliefs,' 'desires,' 'intentions,' 'wants,' 'meanings,' 'motives,' 'purposes,' 'class,' 'clan,' 'alienation,' and 'anonymity' do not fit realist definitions above of natural kinds. Causal explanations in some degree can be constructed for such indeterminate and imprecise entities or social kinds relating to human social behavior. But such explanations are unlikely to constitute or to generate physically necessary or invariant laws, allegedly characterizing some laws of nature.

McIntyre (1996, 22) notes reasonably that 'we cannot treat a subject matter [or social science entity] as if it marks off a natural kind in the world, and we come upon it fully formed.' That is, the level of description of subject matter affects the explanation provided for it, and the discovery of natural kinds. However, McIntyre assumes that social science actually uses natural kinds, although no examples are given (1996, 27). But suppose instead, as in the realist frame above, that any descriptive level used by conventionally understood social science to date has encompassed only non-natural, social kinds. The likelihood is that causal explanations will not be able to expose a unique and simple underlying reality (Ellis, 1996). Even those physical sciences removed from natural kinds, like meteorology, depend for the scientific validity of their objects on other sciences, like physics, that are concerned with natural kinds. No comparable hierarchical-descriptive dependence exists between social sciences, or between the social and the physical sciences. Therefore, causal explanation in social science may remain at the inexact and imprecise. Explanation will not be able to reveal the causal powers of the objects described by social science because those objects have no intrinsic properties or real essences.

In this sense, a difference in kind rather than just a difference in degree might exist between the objects of social science and those of physical science (which is not to suggest that all the objects of physical science are natural kinds, however defined). Contra McIntyre, there may well be fundamental differences in kind between the objects of interest to social and natural science. Unlike the propositions demolished by McIntyre (1996, 17–34), it is not that differing levels of complexity between social and physical science systems create insuperable problems to formulating social science kinds and laws. Nor is the problem that social science has been using the 'wrong' natural kinds to describe the phenomena in which it has been interested. It is that social science historically has remained with describing non-natural social kinds (at least in the sense used by the realists above), while physical science historically has been trying to push towards revealing natural kinds. Social science, as it has been practiced to date, seems to want only (or is only able) to describe non-natural social kinds. Natural kinds, to the extent they exist, appear to have been left to physical science to unearth.

One qualification to the above, consistent with McIntyre's claim, is that natural kinds on any definition have emerged only in the process of the historical development of natural science. Redescription, redefinition and new discovery have been necessary to reveal natural kinds. The level of description of phenomena changes over time in both natural and social science, given that 'many different ways of describing the same reality' exist (McIntyre, 1996, 150). Perhaps the process has yet to reach a sufficiently honed level in social science to expose natural kinds. On the other hand, the nearly three centuries of social sciences' history do not generate optimism for such an outcome. There is little evidence that economics, for example, is making progress historically to isolate natural kinds relevant to its interests, something explored further in the next chapter.

One aspect of the kind problem in social science has been discussed extensively, namely, that the substance of most socio-economic variables is highly context dependent. Social kinds vary according to situation (Sayer,

1992, 127). They mean different things in different times and places. Such an entity derives its meaning from other entities on which it depends, as with the money example above on custom, or with utility on whatever determines preferences. Although Kincaid (1996, 62, 209) deals with aspects of this problem, it is not explored by McIntyre. However, as is so common in Kincaid, he counters this problem by analogy from physical science. Kincaid adopts this strategy because he is concerned to demonstrate that naturalistic criteria can produce both 'successful' physical and social science explanation or laws. Causal explanation in physical science is also contextual. The causative tendencies of some physical science natural kinds are specific to context (for example, the gas laws do not apply when gases become fluids). In these known contexts, the kinds in question (possessing unambiguous definition) behave with stable causative properties. Kincaid does not exemplify this problem for naturalistic social science. The questions are, what is the nature of its social kinds, do these kinds exhibit stable behavioral tendencies even in one context, and how might this be investigated?

These problems can be illustrated from Kincaid's main example (1996, 70–80) of naturalistic social science application outside economics. This is Paige (1975), which might seem to be a little-known, old, and therefore unusual work on which Kincaid places so much weight. Paige was a massive empirical exercise, but his methods did not address or resolve context-kind problems. Kincaid does not explore these problems in relation to Paige. First, Paige's social kind terms were defined on grounds that could relate only to his study itself. For example, in four basic hypotheses tested, Paige (1975, 70–71) used such social kind terms as 'cultivators,' 'dependent on land,' 'income,' 'capital' and 'revolt.' 'Revolt' was defined by Paige as a land invasion by cultivators. This definition of 'revolt' does not encompass all conventional uses of the term—the meaning of 'revolt' in Paige does not accord with uses of the term elsewhere. This social kind, 'revolt,' has a spatial, cultural and temporal relevance restricted to the Paige study. It is not possible to use Paige's results to derive causal explanations for revolts defined differently in, and relating to, other studies and contexts.

Second, the social kind, 'revolt' in Paige did not have an unambiguous definition. The identification of the magnitude of revolts over time (1948–70) in 70 countries was culled by Paige and his team (1975, 89) from the *New York Times* and the London *Times* indexes (themselves derived from local press reports), and for shorter periods within this time frame from other regional press summaries. It is unlikely that strict uniformity of meaning or occurrence of revolt existed between these multifarious sources, either at any one time, or over time. For instance, the determination whether a 'revolt' was a 'cultivators' revolt depended on whether the press report of the event mentioned other occupational groups than 'cultivators' in the 'revolt.' If, say, miners were mentioned in the revolt, 'the event is not agrarian' (Paige, 1975, 388). Surely, how the social kind, invasion of land by cultivators or 'revolt,' was reported in the media of 70 countries over a 12 year period would depend on a multitude of influences. These could include the political bias of the reporter and of the newspaper's management, the influence of prevailing political opinion, the power of the government and of other political forces, etc. 'Revolt' is but one example, for Paige's whole exercise was replete with ambiguous definitions, non-definition of terms, and arbitrary coding modes, all affecting the social kinds identified. Tendencies to divergent definition of kinds between studies do exist in natural science (D'Amico, 1995). For example, various studies in evolutionary biology define 'fitness' differently, because fitness 'clearly has no unique physical definition' (Kincaid, 1996, 60). However, one would expect that in any one hypothesis-test about 'fitness,' the term would be defined invariantly, that it had a stable definition in relation to the data being used to test the hypothesis. This differs from the definition of any number of variables in Paige (1975) where with 'revolt,' for instance, the definition was not derived from watertight parameters applying invariantly to each data set used.

Social kinds in the Paige exercise possessed indeterminate boundaries. Uncertainty in the behavior of the social kinds was compounded by unsubstantiated assumptions characterizing a number of Paige's background (not tested) hypotheses; for example, 'it is apparent that the upper class of the corporate plantation . . . is dependent on industrial capital,' as distinguished from commercial capital (Paige, 1975, 13). This assumption might have represented reality, but it was not demonstrated empirically, and some relations between social kinds in the statement (e.g., 'dependent on industrial capital') were not defined. It can be agreed that 'contextual factors . . . are no inherent obstacle to confirmation and explanation' (Kincaid, 1996, 209). The problems in Paige highlighted here are empirical, not inherent. Applying elaborate statistical technique (in Paige's case, correlation tests and path analysis) to (tested) hypotheses containing vague rubbery social kinds, concepts and data, does not engender confidence in results (for example, that his social kinds behaved in specific contexts with stable causative properties).

Although Kincaid does not explore the issue in naturalistic social science, the meaning ascribed to social kinds or qualitative language conventions is not determinate. For instance, the content of the term 'child abuse' has changed dramatically over time (Hacking, 1988). As noted above, the term 'utility' has not been used consistently throughout the history of economics. Similar problems have long been observed in social science. An early example occurs in Durkheim's analysis of causes of suicide. According to Dawson

(1967, 75–76), 'Durkheim did not provide specific enough theoretical and operational definitions for his fundamental forces to make it possible to establish any adequate systematic criteria for deciding when one force is acting and when it is not.' In realist parlance, Durkheim's 'fundamental forces' could not expose natural kinds. The same qualification applies to many of the variables (e.g., income, cost, utility, preferences) with which economics deals today. None of this is to assert that these problems represent an 'inherent' obstacle to social science. But, its social kind variables, from 'farmers' to 'feudalism' to 'capitalism' have consistently denied absolute definitional precision and empirical identification. Nor have these social kinds generated enduring, uniformly-accepted causal explanations useful for practical policy making (beyond those that might be derived from common sense). On the contrary, competing explanations seem to the norm. Whether this matter affects physical science similarly is not at issue here.

From the above discussion, the following summary might be made: in relation to the social sciences, 'there are no social kinds: types of social entities that share a common causal constitution giving rise to strong regularities' (Little, 1993, 183). With economics, for example, this is partly because 'the things that it is supposed to be dealing with are not there' (Nelson, 1990, 130). These might seem extreme statements, but they are pointing to the absence of natural kinds in social science, not that there is no reality to socio-economic phenomena, or that social kinds do not exist. Labeling the social kinds of social science as 'ideal types' or 'idealizations' does not enhance confidence in either their definition or how the kinds are supposed to behave in the real world (Sayer, 1992, 237–238). The indeterminate substance of the kinds with which social science is concerned reduces their practical policy relevance. Only in specifically restricted time periods and geographic locations, is it likely that social kinds have sufficient behavioral stability on which to base policy decisions. More typically, social kinds have uncertain applicability to practical policy. For example, consider the relevance of elasticities of road traffic demand to the potential design of US highway tolls. Gifford and Tolkington (1996, 56) cited estimates from sixteen existing toll facilities from -0.03 to -0.31, a variation of over one thousand percent. Highway agencies considering toll facilities would gain little guide to policy from such a disparity.

In some areas of physical science, 'at its best,' kinds have been discovered with sufficient temporal behavioral stability on which to base policy decisions, like building bridges and aircraft that serve their intended purposes for (usually) predictable time periods. But in social science to date, prediction derived from empirically-based or analytical causal explanations (laws), all of which embody qualitative, context-dependent, non-parametric variables (e.g., for economics: expectations, tastes, preferences, self-interest, altruism, rationality, demand, supply, income, cost) has a more limited temporal and conceptual relational correspondence to the real world. Its social kinds so far seem typically to be more context dependent than the natural kinds sought by physical science as constituting the bases of natural systems. (The effect of context on causal explanation is picked up again below). Perhaps problems of context are not 'inherent' to the nature of social kinds, and will be overcome in the future. Nevertheless, McIntyre does not discuss social kind issues, and Kincaid does not dissect the range of problems involved in identifying and measuring social kinds, or how they can be accommodated for policy purposes.

CAUSAL EXPLANATION AND MECHANISMS

Two related problems confronting the existence of causal laws in social science are discussed in the sections below, raised in different degree by Kincaid and McIntyre—domain restrictions, and the openness of social systems. Both issues relate to the presence of mechanisms in social science. This section briefly discusses the nature of mechanisms, and then outlines how Kincaid deals with them (McIntyre does not discuss them). Exploration of mechanisms—the nature of the variables themselves and of the processes that produce the necessary relationships—is regarded usually as crucial to realist causal explanation in social science. Realists hold that the aim of socio-economic investigation is to establish the essential nature of phenomena that gives them causal power. Mechanisms are 'the power or ability of various factors to produce characteristic effects' (Woodward, 1995, 31); they are 'causal powers' (and liabilities) or 'ways of acting of objects by reference to their structure and composition' (Sayer, 1992, 104, 131). Mechanisms and laws are connected intimately. Indeed, a common realist view is that laws describe the 'capacities, powers, tendencies, dispositions or propensities' of entities (Chalmers, 1999b). The mechanisms themselves are equated with causal explanations and laws.

Kincaid (or McIntyre) does not provide explicit examples of causal mechanisms operating in naturalistic social science, except for the Paige cases, and one other (relating to economics) discussed below. According to Kincaid (1996, 79), Paige's hypotheses were 'the mechanisms tying class relations to political behavior.' However, Paige's hypotheses were of ambiguous meaning and did not clarify the causal processes involved. For instance, hypothesis 'A' (1975, 70) was that 'a combination of both noncultivators and cultivators dependent on land as their principal source of income leads to agrarian revolt.' (The sources of income for noncultivators were 'land' and 'capital,' and for cultivators, 'land' and 'wages.'). The content of hypothesis 'A' has limitations relating to its definition of social kinds, discussed above, and to the absence of specification of a time frame in which revolt was to occur. Further, no data were provided by Paige for testing the hypothesis in which it was shown that noncultivators and cultivators *were* dependent on land as their principal source of income. In part, this was due to the absence of definitions of the key social kinds, 'capital' etc., and of 'dependent on.' Rather, for the data used to test the hypothesis, these conditions were assumed to exist in some unspecified form. Seemingly inconsistent with his hypothesis, Paige (1975, 10) was ambivalent about noncultivators' income sources. For example, 'as market penetration and industrialization increase, the agricultural upper classes come to depend less and less on income from land ownership.' Similar qualifications applied to cultivators' income sources. In hypothesis 'A,' 'dependent on land' meant self-subsistence farming. Haciendas were supposed to depict the archetype of serf-peasant cultivators depending on income from land, 'paid with the usufruct rights to small subsistence plots' (Paige, 1975, 5, 337). Yet for the only case studies of commercial (coastal) haciendas collected by Paige (in Peru), 'more than half of the total number of man-hours required annually are contributed by the resident [wage] laborers'—that is, not by resident cultivators (1975, 149). How the wage receipts of these wage laborers compared with other income they earned is unreported; it might be reasonable to assume that these 'cultivators' were not dependent on 'land' as distinct from 'wages' as their principal source of income. For the less commercialized (sierra) haciendas, cultivators' incomes appeared to be a mixture of self-subsistence farming, wages and cash crop income (Paige, 1975, 161–185). It is simply unknown from Paige's data if hacienda cultivators derived more than half of their incomes from their usufruct lands, as hypothesis 'A' assumed. In all likelihood, hacienda cultivators were much more dependent on subsistence usufruct plots in past times. With the absence of a definition of 'dependent on,' and of empirical data to the contrary, a test of hypothesis 'A' could equally well be testing the proposition that 'a combination of both noncultivators dependent on some combination of land and capital as their principal source of income, and of cultivators dependent on some combination of self-subsistence, wages, and cash crop income as their principal source of income leads to agrarian revolt.' Such a statement of a causal hypothesis (or mechanism) is near meaningless. A similar vagueness pervades all Paige's hypotheses. For example, hypothesis 1 (Paige, 1975, 18) proposes that 'a noncultivating class drawing its income from land tends to be economically weak and must rely on political restrictions on land ownership.' As mentioned above, no empirical data was provided to ascertain if such a 'noncultivating class drawing its income from land' (in contrast to 'capital') existed, that it was 'economically weak' (which was not defined), or that it relied on 'political restrictions on land ownership' (also undefined).

As noted, Kincaid labels Paige's hypotheses as the mechanisms under scrutiny. Yet, hypothesis 'A' above (Paige, 1975, 70) did not clarify the mechanisms supposedly causing it. Perhaps the first sentence of hypothesis 'A' was to be read in conjunction with the sentences following it making up the 'set of hypotheses' or 'joint' hypothesis 'A.' None of these specified causation either. The next sentence in Paige's set of hypotheses 'A' pointed out that 'this combination of income sources is typical of commercial haciendas and closely related systems.' This is a qualification of the first sentence, and does not qualify as a separate hypothesis. The rest of the set of hypotheses 'A' explains what an agrarian revolt was directed at, and the typical tactic it employed (these are not hypotheses but definitions of 'revolt'). The last sentence of (joint) hypotheses 'A' points to the political situation in which revolt is most likely to occur. None of these sentences explain why the first statement in hypotheses 'A' should necessarily occur. No causal mechanism is revealed in the set of hypotheses 'A.' These same qualifications apply to all of Paige's hypotheses (Paige, 1975, 18, 21, 23, 26, 30, 34, 70–71). It *is* possible to derive causation from Paige's discussion of aspects of these hypotheses elsewhere in his book, but, as noted above, the explanatory mechanisms lack definitional clarity in their basic social kind terms.

These problems with Page's mechanisms are symptomatic of the difficulty social science faces. Because it is dealing with non-natural social kinds, causal explanation in social science, both empirical and analytical (e.g., as in the formalistic abstractions of Neoclassical economic theory), cannot have comparable status with some physical science explanation. It is not able to produce essentialist models of reality, which does not necessarily mean the practice of essentialism that can differ from realism (Sayer, 1992, 162–165). Economic explanation, for instance, is not able to describe precisely any process of the kind that must occur in any real market economy. This applies whether causal exploration in economics is conducted in quantitative or qualitative terms—quantitative expression is not the *sine qua non* of causation. Indeed, quantitative expression may obscure causation if it searches mainly for regularities, as with econometrics. Further problems in ascertaining causal mechanisms in social science are continued below.

DOMAIN RESTRICTIONS AND MECHANISMS

Whatever kind the entities in any system, the functioning of mechanisms is obscured by background and *ceteris paribus* conditions—sometimes called a causal field (Mackie, 1974, 35). Every law is limited contextually, even the most fundamental laws of physics, like the law of gravitation (Cartwright, 1983, 57–58). All causal laws are *ceteris paribus* laws. Alfred Marshall recognized this for economics as far back as 1890 (1920, 36), which for decades has been a commonly held view for social phenomena generally (Kincaid, 1996, 63–70; Bunge, 1996, 28).

No argument need be made with Kincaid's observation (1996, 83) that 'causal generalizations are bound to be exception prone and to hold only for restricted domains.' But one unresolved issue for social science to date is isolation of specific restrictions applying to the domains with which these disciplines concern themselves. To gauge these, the full range of *ceteris paribus* assumptions and the effects of exception-producing influences would have to be known in the given causal explanatory context. This is another way of saying that prior causal explanations for the *ceteris paribus* restrictions underlie the causal explanation under scrutiny—mechanisms rest on other mechanisms. How these limitations apply in any specific world context with which economics, for instance, has been concerned is not known with any precision. Sawyer et al. (1997), for example, outlined four contemporary economic hypotheses dependent on background conditions whose informational content is not known accurately. They showed how this hiatus undermines attempts to test these hypotheses empirically. This is another *a priori* reason for causal social laws having limited explanatory and predictive policy making value.

It *is* possible to devise methods mitigating the confounding effect of *ceteris paribus* clauses in social science. Thus, Kincaid (1996, 67–69) lists nine widely-used testing practices 'that lend credence to *ceteris paribus* laws.' They lend credence, but do not overcome the problems discussed above. For example, Kincaid's practice (6) aims to show that *ceteris paribus* laws can be sturdy. 'Sturdy,' a term borrowed from the econometrician, Leamer (1983), means that 'we can add in possible counteracting influences and show that the law still holds . . . ' (Kincaid, 1996, 69). Yet, Leamer (1983, 38) pointed out also that this process is impossible to bring to a determinate conclusion, that 'the defect of this style is that the coverage of assumptions is infinitesimal, in fact a zero volume set in the space of assumptions.' Evidently, Leamer (in Hendry et al., 1990, 187) thinks the problem is not being resolved, for 'conclusions from data are very fragile . . . people with different private beliefs make different inferences from the same data set.' This chapter is not the place to evaluate econometric methodology, but 'sturdy' does not have unambiguous agreement among econometricians. It is also not a uniformly accepted conclusion that econometrics actually tests causal laws empirically. A fairly standard view among economic methodologists, for instance, is that 'econometric work does not "test" fundamental economic theory in a way that would satisfy most philosophers of science or in the way suggested by the standard rhetoric of econometric testing' (Hands, 1993, 144), while econometrics itself is the subject of recent fundamental criticism e.g. Lawson, 1997. There is not space here to discuss the theoretical content of Kincaid's nine testing practices further, none of which he exemplifies for a social science law. For instance, Paige (1975) endeavored to account for some complicating factors in his analysis, but none of Paige's adjustments are related by Kincaid (1996, 78–79) to any of the nine testing practices (or vice versa).

Kincaid's claim above about the 'exception prone' and 'restricted domains' applicability of causal generalization requires clarification. The exercise of causal powers *is* contingent on the causal field. Whether a postulated causal relationship holds in a different field depends on the given background conditions. But, logically, mechanisms are independent of the conditions that allow their articulation. In this sense, ascertaining *ceteris paribus* conditions is unnecessary for explaining the nature of mechanisms. This is because 'it is in principle impossible to specify all the conditions that the CP [*ceteris paribus*] clause may be required to cover' (Bhaskar, 1978, 96). Hausman (1992, 138) put it that scientists 'do not know exactly what property a *ceteris paribus* clause picks out.' Thus, the role of *ceteris paribus* conditions affecting socio-economic phenomena cannot be explained by treating them as additional variables in a structural model (Woodward, 1995, 43). This is an additional reason helping to undermine the 'sturdy' testing practice above aiming to establish the nature of *ceteris paribus* clauses. The fact that *ceteris paribus* restrictions exist makes it more difficult to see how mechanisms work. They are a reminder that all phenomena occur within systems that are not closed, even though analytical models might try to conceive otherwise. *Ceteris paribus* conditions compound the problem above that in causal explanation, the mechanism need not be dominant, or even realized.

OPENNESS AND MECHANISMS

A related difficulty (raised in Chapter 9) obscuring the identification of explanatory mechanisms is that the phenomena in which social science is interested occur within systems that typically are open; that is, are subject to disturbing exogenous influences. No system embracing human or natural phenomena is closed. Like complexity, the degree of openness is neither measurable for any one system, nor comparable between systems dealing with different domains. Arguing from analogy with physical systems, therefore, as per Kincaid or McIntyre, does not clarify the identification of explanatory mechanisms in social science. All it says is that openness is a problem for causal explanation in both physical *and* social systems. Closed experimental systems can be helpful for reducing the effect of *ceteris paribus* restrictions for both human and physical systems. But their construction presents an additional problem for social science, the uncertainty whether human behavior in experimental situations necessarily conforms with that in everyday life. Evidence for economics suggests it does not (e.g., O'Brien, 1998, 27–28).

McIntyre (1996, 36) draws a distinction between systems that are 'pragmatically open' versus those 'fundamentally open.' Pragmatic openness means the outside factors influencing the system have yet to be discovered and their relevance assessed. For human systems, this derives from the complexity of factors affecting human behavior. Fundamental openness means the system is thought to be affected by unspecified outside influences whose relevance cannot be assessed. In this case, the system may be insulated always from at least some unknown exogenous variables. It might prove impossible ever to isolate these variables.

However, a system believed at one time to be fundamentally open may turn out eventually only to be pragmatically open. An argument can be constructed within a materialistic or naturalistic worldview (McIntyre 1996, 36–45) casting doubt on the alleged permanent existence of fundamentally open human systems, as proposed by Popper, Taylor or Hayek. This argument revolves around the possibilities that human behavior is merely complex rather than open, and that openness *per se* does not necessarily preclude the discovery of laws. The first part of this argument requires accepting a naturalistic framework; it has less force if a non-naturalistic worldview (e.g., Christian) is accepted as influencing human behavior, something we explore more fully in Chapter 13. In the latter case, barriers standing in the way are fundamental, deriving from inherent qualities in humans that defy naturalistic causal explanation. Contra McIntyre (1996, 171), this presents 'a difference in the subject matter of natural and social science that would necessitate an essential difference in the methodology of explanation.' The second part of McIntyre's argument depends on what is meant by 'laws,' which elements of the constellation of nomological criteria are in question—for example, if it be regularity, whether this actually occurs in (open) human systems. McIntyre (1996, 44) held that if 'change occurs in a regular way, it is in principle possible for there to be laws describing it.' But regularity can be assessed only by looking at the specific human system in question, and no examples are provided by McIntyre. What if change in human systems does not occur in a regular way, even though there may be some event regularities in human behavioral systems? The constant flux in socio-economic systems is a common observation. Against McIntyre (1996, 52), it does not necessarily follow that the absence of regularity means 'we would not be able to understand them [human affairs] at all.' Perhaps each instance of human social behavior derives from a variable mix of unique non-regularity and shared regularity qualities (some of which are explainable) that cannot be transferred to explain other instances.

A related factor undermining the identification of mechanisms in (open) human behavioral systems is that people's behavior is prone to be characterized by multiple realizations. Kincaid (1996, 59–60) deals with the problem of multiple realization in social science by focusing on Searle's argument of the disassociation of social categories from physical realizations, and is able to criticize it on this basis. The difficulty of multiple realization is more encompassing than this, as D'Amico (1997) showed. In response to the same stimulus, ways of acting can vary between different people at the one time, while over time, responses for any one person or group may differ in the one context, as well as between contexts (like in the experimental versus normal daily life situation noted above). At any time, a potential range of responses between people can be generated by a stimulus. Causal powers in relation to people are varied, perhaps 'considerably more diverse and changeable (even volatile) than those of non-human objects' (Sayer, 1992, 234). Some of the entities with which natural science is concerned, e.g., antibodies in biology, can be characterized also by multiple physical realizations to a stimulus. But, in general, multiple realization of responses to stimuli may not characterize natural kinds to the same degree as non-natural kinds, either between kinds or in range of response. Even if the idea of natural kind is not accepted, 'multiple realization for social categories is indeterminate and open-ended in a way which is only a feature of social categories' (D'Amico, 1997, 318). This is an extreme statement, for it is possible that some physical science (non-natural) kinds too might fit this claim.

To the extent that natural kinds exist, it is known how they will behave; their responses can 'be predicted on the basis of the laws that govern the behavior of such entities' (Little, 1993, 190). But a variety of causal powers is inherent in each social kind. Any social kind may exhibit different spatial and temporal ways of acting. This probability of multiple realization 'is likely to undermine all but the roughest and least ambitious explanatory remarks' about the entities of social science (Wilkerson, 1995, 85–86). If socio-economic systems *are* more (fundamentally) open than the (pragmatic) openness of physical systems, and if human behavior is prone to a greater incidence and variety of multiple realization than the behavior of non-human entities, identifying mechanisms will be more problematic in the socio-economic. However, the comparison with physical systems is unnecessary. There is little evidence that (traditionally-understood) social science is succeeding in overcoming the potential for multiple realization in describing the mechanisms with which it has been concerned.

The identification of mechanisms in human systems, therefore, is complicated by a combination of non-natural social kind variables, background and *ceteris paribus* restrictions, openness, and the effects of human behavioral variables that both separately and interactively are capable of multiple realizations. The first and last considerations consolidate the likelihood not only that mechanisms in socio-economic explanation will not be revealed clearly, but perhaps less clearly than in some non-human or physical systems. Therefore, ascertaining the causal powers and liabilities of the objects of interest to social science, and of developing causal explanation is likely *a priori* to be difficult; again, perhaps more so than for some non-human and physical entities. Neither Kincaid nor McIntyre put these possibilities to the fore. The factors above consolidate the tendency to domain-restricted explanation, and inhibit the likelihood of policy relevance; for example, of providing accurate prediction of human behavior.

The discussion thus far has emphasized *a priori* conceptual qualities of the objects of interest to social science. Contrary to the view proposed here, such qualities are held sometimes not to detract from the search for causal laws. For example, to Kincaid (1996, 12, 96), mechanisms in causation need not be identified; 'causal explanation need not be solely or primarily about *mechanisms* . . . [it] can frequently proceed without citing underlying mechanisms.' Backhouse (1997, 113) supports this view by citing Kincaid's example of natural selection providing convincing causal explanation without explaining the precise mechanism through which it takes place. One reason why theistic realists (e.g., Johnson, 1993; Behe, 1996; Ankerberg and Weldon, 1998) are skeptical about some claims of contemporary Darwinian theory is that they do not find the causal mechanisms justifying some of its conclusions convincing. In any case, Kincaid's view does not fit comfortably with Backhouse's claim (1997, 78) that 'the major issue in economics is the reality of the causal mechanisms postulated by economists.' Nor does Kincaid actually follow his own admonition, for he continually justifies the applied social science examples he cites by emphasizing how they specify reasonable mechanisms (e.g., 1996, 79, re Paige).

Most social science realists *are* concerned to uncover causal mechanisms operating at the social level. Kincaid's belief above might stem from the aggregative level with which he identifies mechanism, namely, with the 'microlevel'—the individualistic contra the social level. Possibly, this emphasis derives from Kincaid's interest to criticize methodological individualism, with which more realists would concur. But, on the basis of his disagreements with the *a priori* arguments here, Kincaid (1996, 92) maintains the existence of causal laws in naturalistic social science. According to him, such laws specify kinds, hold for extensive domains, are resilient, and are grounded on reasonable mechanisms. The next section considers the main law by which Kincaid defends this position.

AN EXAMPLE OF A SOCIAL SCIENCE LAW

Kincaid presents economics as a test case of a naturalistic social science that has produced laws. Kincaid's (1996, 232–241) main example of laws in economics are the laws of demand and supply, meaning for a particular good or service that 'increases in price decrease demand and increase supply; increases in demand and decreases in supply raise price.' Like all laws, these laws apply *ceteris paribus*, taken to mean that the prices of other goods, and of people's tastes and incomes etc. remain constant. Much applied work in economics confirms the existence of the laws of demand and supply. The question arises, however, about the explanatory content of such laws, given that Kincaid defines laws in naturalistic social science as successful causal explanations. The causal mechanism that relates price to quantity demanded becomes an important question. The only answer Kincaid (1996, 236) provides for this question is that in the aggregate prices are 'exogenous causal factors determining the quantity demanded.' But given the definition of price, this is to be expected; it is a logical necessity dependent on the definition. Price is an arithmetical ratio between a sum of money and a given quantity of a good. A sum of money is exchanged for a quantity of the good. This causal mathematical relationship applies both at an individual and aggregate level. It is an irresistible conclusion from this definition that price will be related to quantity, because price is defined by quantity demanded. It is also an irrefutable deduction, *ceteris paribus*, that higher price means less quantity of the good will be demanded. The law of demand (and supply) is definitional or tautologous, an analytical law or law of reason that *can* be regarded as a causal phenomenological law, but not a very interesting one. To say no more than that in the aggregate price determines demand is not to say much. Kincaid (1996, 241) takes 'supply-and-demand explanations' to be a strong example of 'real causes' or 'causal generalization' in economics. An alternative judgement is that such explanations are only as revealing as informal common sense reasoning.

The laws of supply and demand have been known for hundreds of years but empirical work confirming their validity extends from the late nineteenth century (Morgan 1990, 133–189). Kincaid (1996, 235–236) reviews some of the twentieth century econometric work that confirms the law of demand's content. Thus, for the law of demand, changes in incomes, tastes etc. do not have as much effect on changing demand as price changes do. This is not altogether unsurprising given the pleonastic nature of the law of demand. Nevertheless, it is possible to conceive of real life situations where tastes, or some other *ceteris paribus* condition(s) have counteracted the law's operation. Much empirical work has been done for particular goods to assess the degree to which demand for a good depends on the price of substitutes and of complementary goods (e.g., video cassettes for VCRs), on changes in preferences (e.g., fads), and on levels of and changes in income and wealth. However, without auxiliary generalizations or hypotheses about the strength of different causal factors, it has proved difficult to predict even the direction of change in demand as price changes, much less its quantitative magnitude. Accordingly, the question arises whether the explanatory content of the laws has become clearer over the last hundred years and/or whether the laws have been characterized by increasing predictive success.

Kincaid (1996, 242) holds that the laws of supply and demand have shown 'a history of increased predictive success' over time, but it is not clear what this means. Thus, Kincaid concedes that the 'precise meaning' of predictive success 'is not at all obvious,' that 'increasing predictive success seems neither necessary nor sufficient for good science,' and that the laws of supply and demand still retain their age-old 'generic' (qualitative rather than quantitative) nature. The (generic) law of demand postulates no more nowadays than in the past: a negative relationship between changes in price and demand for a good at the aggregate level, *ceteris paribus*. If this relationship is as confidently explained via the law now as it was in the past, there has been no increased explanatory or predictive success. If the law of demand (and supply) is 'basically the right account of reality,' it 'will find improvement hard to come by' (Kincaid, 1996, 242). Indubitably, this is the case, for the laws of demand and supply are analytical propositions, *ceteris paribus*.

The claim that 'the economic theory of supply and demand . . . has improved strikingly since the eighteenth century' (McCloskey, 1994, 231) is widespread. McCloskey, for example, alleged this improvement by its mathematical formulation, its generation of spin-off concepts such as consumer and producer surplus, and of theoretical offshoots like welfare economics and rational expectations. McCloskey (1994, 231) calls these developments 'a progressive research program,' but this judgement can be questioned. Thus, Hutchison (1992, 36), asserting the demise of welfare economics, castigated its 'far-fetched' level of abstraction, 'with any significant real-world relevance as far away as ever.' Perhaps something similar is happening to rational expectations. As far as the mathematical formulation of the law of demand (and supply) is concerned, Kincaid himself provides an unwitting example of the sterility of this mode of expression. Kincaid (1996, 233–234) presents the law of demand in four mathematical equations where all the individual terms in the equations are not defined (e.g., expenditure elasticity). This is the only occasion in his book where mathematical equations are used. There is no analysis of the relation of the terms in the equations to any of the subsequent empirical work cited. The equations are discussed separately, look 'scientific,' and typify the penchant for academic economics to express common sense ideas in a language few can understand (Beed and Kane, 1991). None of the mathematical equations is necessary for the development of the verbal argument in which Kincaid's whole book is couched.

Because the supply and demand laws are used so much in economics, Kincaid thinks this is an indication of their strength. He cites six examples (1996, 246) of economics' supply and demand law application. More commonly, the exercises Kincaid cites come under the heading of rational choice theory. This chapter is not the place to assess rational choice theory, but there is an extensive literature casting doubt on its innovative and revelatory value (e.g., Green and Shapiro, 1994; Hauptmann, 1996; Beed and Beed, 1999). Further assessment of it is made in Chapter 12. An alternative judgement from Kincaid's is that the widespread use of rational choice theory reflects the weakness of orthodox economics, epitomized by Rosenberg's claim (1992, 134) that rational choice theory has only the 'predictive accuracy of common sense.' Blaug's comments (1992, 225) on a leading economics' rational choice study are apposite, that it produced 'almost empty conclusions that are presented as being more dramatic than they really are.' Rational choice's critics point to its simplistic explanations and unexceptional predictions, often overstated or trivial, little different from 'populist' deduction for already known phenomena. In these views, common sense and folk psychology have a similar reliability to rational choice theory for explaining and predicting phenomena. A caricature of rational choice theory along these lines is Boulier and Goldfarb (1991).

One of Kincaid's six examples above of supply and demand laws' 'successful causal explanations' is Becker et al. (1991). Becker's is a theoretical paper suggesting how demand for illicit drugs may change if use of currently banned drugs was legalized. No empirical evidence on drug taking was cited to demonstrate this, rather inferences were drawn from empirical studies of tobacco and alcohol use, and gambling. Becker's paper suggests that its innovative value is to contradict the 'conventional wisdom' (for which no references were provided) that demand for illegal drugs would not rise with prices lowered by decriminalization. The reasoning in such conventional (unstated) studies is not made clear, for without changes in *ceteris paribus* restrictions, 'the law of the downward-sloping demand function' (Becker et al., 1991, 237) has to mean drug consumption would rise if price were lowered. The main emphasis in the Becker et al. paper is to discuss how and whether some of the taste attributes of the *ceteris paribus* conditions may change if drug price were lowered via legalization. For instance, if users' tastes are more affected by 'reinforcement' (addiction) than anything else, lowering drug prices may increase consumption markedly. This is not an innovative conclusion, has no policy implications (as noted explicitly by Becker et al., 1991, 241), and has long been canvassed in the health literature relating to illegal drug consumption. The conclusion might be new to economics, and represent a 'successful causal explanation' in that arena, but the (similar) reasoning underlying it had been discussed in the drug control literature. One of the striking features of this paper, in common with much rational choice reasoning, is the absence of any reference to the empirical literature outside economics dealing with substance abuse. For instance, a fairly standard view among medical behavioral scientists at the time was that 'supply and demand clearly influence the price of any given substance . . . but the net effect on drug consumption is not clear.' Connors and Tarbox (1985, 286, 297) reviewed studies estimating elasticity of demand for drugs, reporting, for example, that movement toward decriminalization of marijuana use in eleven US states from 1973 to 1980 'has not resulted in significant increases in marijuana use.'

Kincaid did not cite further economic laws or 'successful causal explanations' useful for policy making. A list of other traditional economic laws is not encouraging to his case. Gresham's law, Gossen's second law, Say's law, Engel's law, Okun's law, the law of diminishing marginal utility and even the law of diminishing returns have been little used in any policy making sense. None isolate natural kinds or uniformly-defined social kinds. Engel's and diminishing returns probably meet the latter criterion most adequately. Yet, diminishing returns was not an economics' discovery, but one from agricultural records, and neither law has great policy significance today. Economics from the mid-twentieth century has become more circumspect in calling its discoveries 'laws,' perhaps because it is realizing that 'successful causal explanations' useful for policy making are more sparse than formerly thought.

CONCLUSION

Arguing within a naturalistic worldview, as Kincaid and McIntyre do, conceptual approaches to causal explanation in social science may well conform with those in physical science But applying these approaches to the objects of interest to (traditionally-conceived) social science produce severely domain-restricted and policy-limited explanations. Whether the domains of social science are more or less restricted than those pertaining to natural science has not been explored here. Nor need it be asserted that relationships between the entities of social science are more complex than those in natural science. These may well be meaninglessly incomparable exercises. For example, measuring 'complexity' in any one system, let alone comparing it between social and natural systems, may be impossible. It has not been argued, but is an implied assumption of this chapter, that examining natural science does not contribute greatly to the understanding of socio-economic phenomena (Fay, 1984). Various alleged bases of divergence between social and natural science have long been proposed by non-naturalists, and even some naturalists (e.g., Little, 1993) hold to a disconformity.

One way of assessing the validity of social science laws is to look at stated examples of them. The proof of the pudding is in the eating. Advocates of causal socio-economic laws and generalizations cite explicit instances of their occurrence. Some examples are that 'agents always perform those actions with greatest expected desirability' (Papineau 1978, 81); 'as small-scale societies evolve in complexity, they develop greater concentrations of wealth, political authority becomes more concentrated' (Kincaid, 1990, 78); in a given context, 'a combination of both noncultivators and cultivators dependent on land as their principal source of income leads to an agrarian revolt' (Paige, 1975, 70); in a given context (after Paige), 'dependence on land versus capital for income determines the economic strength of non-cultivating classes' (Kincaid, 1996, 72); 'in all capitalist societies the likelihood of getting out of unemployment falls as the unemployment rate increases' (Bunge, 1996, 28). The vagueness and self-evidential nature of these 'laws' or generalizations is striking. None specify uniformly-accepted definitions of social kinds, much less of natural kinds. They resemble propositions of folk psychology capable neither of application or policy relevance. None convey greater understanding of social (or individual) human behavior than Berelson and Steiner's (1964) compendium of like propositions. At the most, they are deductions that could be derived by applying common sense to analyze social phenomena occurring over time, yielding stable but imprecise empirical generalizations or stylized facts. This form of analysis is known more conventionally as the field of history—a discipline usually regarded as lying outside social science, although not by McIntyre (1996).

Yet, even McIntyre's exposition—'the first full-length defense of social scientific laws to appear in the last twenty years'—does not cite one example of a social science law. As he admits, 'we have yet to produce any unequivocal examples of social scientific laws' (McIntyre, 1996, 165, 189). All his analysis suggests is the possibility of nomological explanation. Much of the support for this argument derives from natural science. For example, most of McIntyre's discussion of the specifics of laws is from physical science; even in his Chapter 2 devoted to rejecting fundamental objections to social scientific laws, and in 3 criticizing practical objections to them. His Chapter 4 moves to a discussion of laws in evolutionary biology. McIntyre's reason for this is his assertion that if the complexity and openness of human systems preclude social science laws, any other field of inquiry 'that faces the same degree of complexity or openness . . . will be similarly impeded from the use of law-like explanation' (McIntyre, 1996, 76). The latter conclusion is held not to characterize evolutionary biology. McIntyre makes the heroic but undemonstrated assumption that it is possible to compare the degree of complexity and openness between (natural and social) systems dealing with different domains. More realistic is that these are features neither measurable nor comparable between different systems. In any case, McIntyre nowhere explains what actual social science laws might look like, despite his advocacy of redescription of data as the way forward (albeit without any social science specifics of what this might involve). Evidently, the empirical testability of the predictions of social science theories is not a key criterion for the development of laws. On the one hand, McIntyre (1996, 168) extols the need 'to employ a rigorous attitude toward testing' theories. Yet he claims simultaneously (pp. 174–175) that 'far too much confidence has been placed on testability as the arbiter for good scientific theories. For in social science, it is not so easy to come up with theories that are worth testing in the first place.'

As in physical science, identifying 'successful' and 'well-confirmed' causal mechanisms or laws in social science is a matter of value judgement. It is moot how far the application of comparable principles toward causal explanation in the natural and the social sciences has produced comparable results. If the objects of interest to social science differ qualitatively from those in natural science—as has been implied here—analogous results cannot be achieved. As Woodward (1995, 31) expressed it about social science, 'claims about capacities and mechanisms' are 'typically qualitative, exception ridden, and imprecise . . .' Thus, empirical attempts to establish social science laws continue to prove elusive. For example, econometrics' attempts to quantify the laws of economics (whatever these might be) have not produced explanations or equations lasting more than a few years duration; certainly nothing of a 'stable causes and fixed influences' nature that Cartwright (1989, 16) attributes to the purpose of econometrics. Indeed, Cartwright's econometrics' examples (1989, 56–57; 1991, 153) portray unstable temporal outcomes. As Duncan noted for social science decades ago (1975, 56), 'if all the model is good for is to describe a particular set of data . . . we might as well forego the effort of devising and estimating the model.' Nor does Kuezenkamp provide examples of econometric inference 'that are stable with respect to intended interventions' (2000, 259). Contrary to the hopeful expectations of Kincaid and McIntyre, economic and social science modelling still show few signs of being able to produce regularities, causal explanations or laws capable of effective policy manipulative and control application in the real world. For deriving causal explanation in social science, common sense analysis (Coates, 1996) and historical analysis of empirical data (McCullagh, 1998) may prove to be more fruitful. Even so, the kinds and causal fields of the socio-economic world may be too varied in temporal and spatial manifestation to expose necessary relationships between phenomena.

Chapter Eleven

The Status of Economics as a Naturalistic Social Science

It does not seem that economics is shaping up well as science if that means devising theory, finding that it predicts and explains empirical evidence well, and then is able to serve as a basis for practically useful policy. Economics' efforts to use positivistic and naturalistic methods do not seem to have led to much certainty or enduring discovery about real world processes. This chapter (Beed and Beed, 2000b) continues the evaluation of contemporary economics as a naturalistic social science, and makes an assessment of its standing as such. The second section of the chapter establishes criteria for naturalistic social science, at least as far as Kincaid (1996) identifies them. The rest of the chapter is an assessment via specific illustration of how economics today measures up to leading criteria of social science naturalism. Thus, the third section considers how and whether economics employs tests that facilitate choice between theories, and to what extent tests of even one theory yield resilient conclusions. In the fourth section, the innovative value of the predictive claims of economic theories supposedly utilizing naturalistic methods is assessed. The fifth section explores examples of policy implications from what commonly are taken to be naturalistic explications of economic theory. The conclusion is that economics is not able to practice or resolve contending issues by naturalistic means. The observations that testing does not produce choice between theories, that segments of economic theory do not offer innovative predictions, and that standard theory has little to offer policy formulation have been made before. But these claims have not been tied to the relevance of naturalism in social science and economics. Nor are the claims acknowledged in a number of recent philosophical assessments of social science and economics, in which the debate between naturalism and non-naturalism assumes importance, such as by Pettit (1993), Kincaid (1996), McIntyre (1996), and Rule (1997).

The difficulties for naturalistic social science in formulating successful causal explanations or laws were canvassed in the last chapter. Before that, the focus was on differences between naturalistic and less naturalistic approaches in contemporary economics. As we have noted, naturalism is a generic term encompassing philosophical and methodological norms often taken to apply in physical science. It is a common claim that the social sciences have sought historically to model their practice on natural science (e.g., Olson, 1993), and economics is viewed frequently as the social science relying most closely on scientific methods (e.g., Porter, 1994). We have argued that significant consequences are at stake for the standing of academic economics in the debate over the relevance of naturalism to economics. The social sciences, especially economics, desire to continue to be given the honorific prestige accorded to the natural sciences, as revealing the nature of reality. To substantiate this claim, it is important that economics be assessed by economists as conforming with the dominant naturalistic philosophy assumed to undergird the natural sciences.

We have seen that naturalism in social science has been under attack in recent decades (e.g., Fay, 1984; Bohman, 1991), and for social sciences other than economics, may be in retreat. This attack is in line with the rise of post-positivism in social science, and the development of numerous competing post-positivist tendencies in social science. Kincaid's (1996) defense of naturalism is the focus here, as in the last chapter, because his is the most profound and comprehensive analysis of recent times advocating the (re)application of naturalistic methods to social science. He uses economics as an illustrative and test case demonstrating that social science can and should practice naturalistic methods. This chapter shows that economics is not able to practice naturalistic methods to produce reliable, novel or policy-relevant conclusions.

This demonstration is separated in this chapter from describing characteristics of a Christian alternative non-naturalistic conception of social science and economics. That took incipient shape in the first few chapters, and comes to greater fruition in the concluding chapter. As already shown, non-naturalist and antipositivist approaches to social science have a long history, in which the model of the physical sciences was regarded as inappropriate to analyze social phenomena—which is not to denigrate the value of science *per se*. Non-naturalism has long contested the relevance of traditional (natural) scientific methods to human social behavior, at least as the term 'scientific' was understood to perhaps four decades ago. Among the thirty-five differences previously identified between naturalism and non-naturalism in economics were the latter's greater recognition of the importance of value judgements in socio-economic analysis, and its greater reliance on qualitative vis-a-vis quantitative data and analysis in which sharp boundaries cannot be drawn between variables. The definition of such variables (and their relationships) in economics suffers from imprecision and vagueness, bearing the marks of non-natural kinds or an impossibility of classification in mutually exclusive categories. A long-identified characteristic of naturalism is the search for well-established generalizations, laws or causal explanations for social phenomena, but the non-naturalistic response is that no such laws have been discovered for human social behavior, none connecting human beliefs with action, and certainly none of sufficient precision to be policy-useful. Greater predictive or causal power is not being discovered by applying increasingly complicated statistical technique to socio-economic data because no naturalistic science of human behavior exists waiting to be discovered. The reasons for this are examined from a Christian perspective in Chapter 13.

THE WEAK STANCE ON NATURALISM

No uniformity pervades the definition of naturalism in the physical or social sciences (e.g., King, 1994). Papineau (1993, 1) noted that 'there is little consensus on its meaning.' A generalized definition of naturalism is that only the natural world exists, that people are part of and dependent solely on a natural realm, and that the methods of investigation in the natural sciences are applicable to the human sciences. However, this denotation carries wide interpretation, and is insufficiently precise to apply to the classification of a subject discipline. Naturalism is not identical with positivism whose meaning and role in economics was discussed in Chapter 8, nor is naturalism necessarily the basis for realism (Beed and Beed, 1997). Suffice to note here that the relevance of naturalism and non-naturalism is still, and has long been, regarded as one of the major philosophical and methodological problems in social science (e.g., Bhaskar, 1989, 1). Rather than debating the 'correct' meaning of naturalism, if such exists, this chapter adopts Kincaid's (1996) specification of naturalistic social science that he applies to economics and other social sciences, as in Table 11.1 below. This list accords with the meaning of the term used elsewhere in social science (from Papineau, 1978, and Thomas, 1979, to McIntyre, 1996), although the detailed content and explicit relevance of naturalism in economics has not received specific attention (some investigation is in Jackson, 1995; and Lawson, 1997).

Together, the items signify a version of weak rather than strong naturalism in social science. So wide is the naturalistic list that it straddles almost the entire spectrum between weak naturalistic and traditional non-naturalistic positions. Almost, but not all, because even traditional non-naturalism baulks at

Table 11.1. Kincaid's (1996) Characteristics of Social Science Naturalism

1. 'Non-experimental evidence' is admissible (p. 230).
2. Observation is theory-laden (p. 230).
3. Background assumptions are important in the construction of theory (p. 230).
4. Methodology has a contingent nature (p. 230).
5. 'Rational, objective empirical' methods exist for choosing some theories over others (p. 230).
6. The crucial methods are 'fair tests, cross tests, and independent tests—of theories, assumptions, and methodological norms' (p. 230; and pp. 51–54).
7. 'Explanation comes from applying causal generalizations that specify some of the main variables and then factoring in causes unique to the case at hand' (p. 231).
8. For economics, 'important parts . . . are relatively well confirmed' (pp. 230; and 222).
9. Well-confirmed causal explanations constitute laws (pp. 10, 55, 58, 63, 91).
10. Laws can serve as a basis for policy formulation (p. 6).

Source: Kincaid (1996)

the assertions of say, a Christian realist non-naturalistic approach to analyzing socio-economic behavior (e.g., Beed and Beed, 1997). A stronger rendering of naturalism than in the table would encompass further propositions, particularly those emphasizing physical science. These could include claims that natural science constitutes the simplest comprehensive means for explaining human experience, and that Darwinian theory is central to naturalism.

Contra Kincaid, non-naturalistic social scientists would be skeptical that it is possible to attain 'a real social science [that] would provide us with laws, predictions, and understanding of large-scale social structure,' useful for policy making (Kincaid, 1996, 6). A majority of non-naturalistic economists, such as Institutionalists and Austrians, and even of Post Keynesians and Behavioralists, probably accept the relevance of non-experimental evidence, the theory-ladenness of observation, the importance of underlying assumptions, the conditional nature of methodology, and the mode of explanation described in Table 11.1. They are likely to be disinclined to use the term 'laws' in items 9 and 10. Admittedly, Kincaid (1996, 62) qualifies its meaning; for example, laws can be limited contextually. Nevertheless, the existence of laws is regarded widely as a leading criterion of naturalism (e.g., Boyd et al., 1991, 778). Even some economists, such as Blaug (1992, 138), who advocate the practice of economics according to what *they* see as norms of natural science, are skeptical about the existence of laws in economics, and whether they have policy relevance (Item 10 in Table 11.1). The issue of whether and what sort of laws exist in economics is not pursued here; we looked at the issue in chapter 10 (and see also Rappaport, 1998). Nor is there space to consider the relevance of all the items in Table 11.1 above to economics.

Economists of many persuasions may be skeptical that such clear-cut methods as implied in Table 11.1 can serve as a warrant for some theories over others, or enable choice between competing theories. Indeed, items 5 and 6 in the table are probably leading criteria there differentiating a naturalistic from a non-naturalistic viewpoint in all the social sciences. The focus here is how adequately these items are practiced in economics, and what they achieve (Item 9), particularly for public policy relevance (Item 10). Kincaid argues that economics measures up well in the application of the naturalistic criteria, and deservedly can be called a naturalistic social science. A contrary judgement from a self-professed naturalist is that 'the whole project [of economics] is riddled with confusion and incoherence' (Lawson, 1997, 14).

ASSESSING THE CLAIMS OF COMPETING THEORIES IN ECONOMICS

Item 5 of Table 11.1 (Kincaid, 1996, 230) postulates the existence of a 'rational, objective empirical warrant' for choosing some theories over others. This warrant is made up of 'fair,' 'cross' and 'independent' tests of 'theories, assumptions and methodological norms.' Unfortunately, Kincaid provides no illustration of how these tests have been applied or could be applied in economics (or any social science) to enable choice of 'some theories over others,' or between competing theories. Contra Kincaid is a long proposed view in economics (e.g., Tarascio and Caldwell, 1979) that 'there is no demonstrative logic of either confirmation or falsification, [that] no attempts to test theories can ever be conclusive' (Darnell and Evans, 1990, 37). Reasons for this judgement are not under consideration here, but its implication is that theory choice remains indeterminate. Consistent with this view, economics provides many examples demonstrating the impossibility of choosing between competing theories on an 'objective empirical warrant' basis.

Thus, the inability has long been apparent of econometric testing procedures to differentiate predictions of particular competing theories. This observation still applies today, as Chapter 14 suggests, despite the aspirations of contemporary econometricians. Delving back decades, both Sargent (1976), and McCallum (1979, 395) showed that 'it is literally impossible to distinguish between Keynesian and classical macroeconomic structures using *only* parameter estimates from a single policy regime.' The 'structures' were purportedly contradictory theories concerning the effects of monetary and fiscal policy on output, but the empirically generated predictions were indistinguishable. Similarly, Pesaran (1982) confirmed that a Keynesian explanation of unemployment provided at least as satisfactory an explanation for postwar US as New Classical theory. In these cases, standard econometric practice could not discriminate between competing theories with 'contradictory policy prescriptions' (Pesaran, 1982, 545)—they were observationally equivalent.

According to two methodological commentators on econometrics, even newer econometric techniques such as cointegration 'can contribute nothing to the task of distinguishing between theories' (Darnell and Evans, 1990, 143).

Aside from observational equivalence, other areas of economics show a persistent inability for a 'rational, objective empirical warrant' choice to be exercised between competing theories. Mayer (1993; 1995) surveyed the continuing dispute, showing little sign of resolution, between Keynesians, Monetarists and New Classical theorists about macroeconomic theory and policy implications. His conclusion about the Keynesian-Monetarist debate was that 'the new methodology and modern econometric technique have added virtually nothing useful' (Mayer, 1995, 89). This judgement resonates with Hendry's (Hendry et al., 1990, 186), 'that neither Monetarism nor Keynesianism has been refuted in any scientific sense from data evidence.' The problem affects other areas of economics. For example, Blinder (1991, 89, 90) thought that 'most economists' would 'agree that we know next to nothing about which of several dozen theories of wage-price stickiness are valid and which are not.' In his view, econometric modelling could not solve the problem, being too 'blunt,' even a 'useless, investigative tool.' Another example is efficient market theory that to Le Roy (1989, 1614) appeared to apply only marginally to financial markets; indeed, most of the 'nontrivial' implications of capital market efficiency theory were 'falsified.'

Among econometricians, it is recognized widely that econometrics has not been able 'to resolve economic dispute' between competing theories (Darnell and Evans, 1990, 51). The problems inherent in contention about econometric technique are epitomized by Spanos (1986, 660) that 'no economic theory was ever abandoned because it was rejected by some empirical econometric test,' a conclusion echoed by Hahn (1987) and Summers (1991). As well, we noted in Chapter 10 Hands' claim (1993, 144) that economic methodologists do not regard econometric testing procedures as satisfying philosophy of science requirements for theory testing.

The solution to these problems does not lie in seeking the philosopher's stone, the 'objective empirical warrant' to guide economic theory choice via econometrics, because no one incontestable econometric method exists (e.g., Pagan, 1987; Gerrard, 1995), and because econometricians practice their techniques disparately. On the second point, for instance, Kramer et al. (1985) showed that particular specification tests were used inconsistently between studies. They applied nine tests to eleven published econometric articles, concluding (1985, 122) that 'all empirical equations fail more tests than can be expected under correct specification.' Another example is the theory that speculative bubbles were part of the 1920s' German hyperinflation. This was punctured by Hamilton and Whiteman (1985) who argued that many of the statistical tests in previous studies were invalid. Again, tests of the theory of a negative relationship between money demand and interest rates were criticized by Cooley and Le Roy (1981) who pointed in earlier studies to 'selective reporting' of specification searches, to 'simultaneity problems,' and to 'prior beliefs' influencing results rather than 'sample information.' A notable example of econometric disagreement in reaching the 'objective empirical warrant' was Hendry and Ericsson (1991) versus Friedman and Schwartz (1982, 1991). The former reworked the latter's data in specific instances using different techniques, and arrived at opposite conclusions. Further examples of disagreement could be cited (e.g., Mayer, 1993, 142–145). In the last chapter, we saw that Leamer (Hendry et al., 1990, 187) suggested that econometric deduction from data is questionable because conclusions are affected by private beliefs. The problem of dissimilar application of econometric technique may not be diminishing with time. McCloskey and Ziliak (1996) surveyed the 182 1980s papers in the *American Economic Review* that used regression analysis, finding that 72 percent 'did *not* mention the work of other authors as a quantitative context for their own,' 59 percent 'used the word "significance" in ambiguous ways,' and 'only 4 percent considered the power of their tests.' McCloskey's later work has confirmed the persistence of that ambiguity.

A counter to these problems is to suggest that economics to date has not been undertaking the naturalistic fair, cross and independent tests of its theories, assumptions and methodological norms. But, from the examples above, it is clear that economists have long disagreed on what counts as a fair, cross or independent test, an issue revisited in Chapter 14. Even if all the technical disagreement between econometricians for testing theory could be resolved, the prize of 'objective empirical warrant' is still not attainable. Researchers have to make evaluative judgements about whether evidence confirms or disconfirms theory. There is no objective, value-free rule that can specify the 'correct' level of significance for testing an economic hypothesis (McCloskey, 1985; Beed, 1992; McCloskey and Ziliak, 1996). The originators of the theory of statistical inference recognized this clearly. Thus, in relation to Type 1 and 2 errors, Neyman (1950, 262) noted that 'which of these two errors is more important to avoid is a subjective matter.' McMullin (1983, 8–9) put it that 'the appraisal of theory is in important respects closer in structure to value-judgement' than to 'the rule-governed inference' of classical philosophy. For this and further technical reasons, the view is held widely that 'econometrics does not deliver truth' (Kuezenkamp, 2000, 259), an issue we return to in Chapter 14.

The examples above emphasize the problems of empirically testing predictions of economic theory. In the naturalistic Table 11.1 view (item 6), 'fair' etc. tests are held to be applicable to assumptions underlying theory, as well as to its theoretical predictions. This issue is not reviewed here, but nearly half a century of economics' debate casts doubt on the proposition. It is conceded widely, for example, that the maximization assumption of Neoclassical economic theory is an untestable metaphysical statement because preferences are not observable, and because introspection and surveys are unreliable (e.g., Boland, 1981; Caldwell, 1983).

Blaug (1992) exemplifies the dilemma inherent in all the above about the 'objective empirical warrant' for assessing the claims of economic theory. On the one hand, he suggests that 'empirical testing is so difficult and ambiguous that one cannot hope to find many examples of economic theories being decisively knocked down by repeated refutations' (Blaug, 1992, xii). Nevertheless, three pages later (p. xv) he asserts that 'actually it is perfectly easy' to think of economic propositions that have been decisively falsified by the evidence. He offers eight such examples, like the Phillips curve that was subject to 'wholesale rejection in the 1970s,' and claims that 'one could go on almost indefinitely expanding these examples.' If this were true, it appears to contradict Blaug's first quote above. The discrepancy between the two claims is not pursued here (and neither does Blaug do so). Nor is it possible here to assess the validity of Blaug's second quote for each of his eight examples. For instance, some economists disagree with him about the Phillips curve; they hold that a modified version holds up well empirically. Thus, Blinder (1987, 133) claimed that 'the Phillips curve, once modified to allow for supply shocks, . . . has been one of the best-behaved empirical regularities in macroeconomics.' In 1990, Gordon held that 'the econometric version, developed and refined in the late 1970s, has been validated in the 1980s' (quoted in Mayer, 1993, 99), while Summers (1991, 140) proposed that although the Phillips curve 'has gone through a number of interpretations . . . it has stood as a reality that any theory of the business cycle must confront.' One judgement about the disagreement on the Phillips curve, contradicting a naturalistic (and Blaug's) viewpoint, is that 'there does not seem to be any objective basis for determining which verdict is the appropriate one' (Heilbroner and Milberg, 1995, 56).

The unresolved issue is to what extent economic theories (and paradigms) are falsified, and whether this constitutes progress in building up a pool of non-falsified economic theories. Progress in economics is undoubtedly made in the sense of accumulating informational knowledge about the economy, and theorizing about it. But it is not necessarily clear what this adds up to. For instance, Hausman (1989) surveyed the history from the twelfth century explaining the existence of profits. But he provided no compelling reasons why this history showed that economists now are 'able to offer better explanations' of profits. It was unclear, for example, why now-dominant Neoclassical views are taken to be intellectually superior to their displaced Classical predecessors concerning the existence of profits. Certainly, the two approaches had different theoretical commitments and asked different if related questions about profits. An alternative reading of the history of profits from Hausman's is that the Neoclassicals explored issues with which the Classicals were not concerned. Each conclusion Hausman drew from seven criteria suggesting 'cumulative explanatory progress' in explaining the existence of profits could be challenged. For example, it is not incontrovertible that a uniform contemporary explanation for profits exists, that this has been integrated into systematizations such as intertemporal general equilibrium theory, and that the latter constitutes explanatory progress about the real world. Perhaps more is revealed about change than progress in economics by charting the historical development of particular subject areas. To take another area of economics, for example, Clower (1995, 317) declared that 'as a foundation for applied economics, Arrow-Debreu theory is empirically vacuous and conceptually incoherent.' Like this dominant form of mathematical economics, it can be doubted also whether the accumulation of historical reasoning about the existence of profits translates into theories useful for policy making. The assumptions that prevailing modes of analysis are more revealing of reality or more policy-useful than their predecessors are being questioned in many human sciences.

One possibility is that as economic theories are falsified, they are replaced by new theories no more enduring or policy-useful than their predecessors. Many economic theories could thus be falsified (and mistakes corrected), but this would not engender confidence that economic theory is increasingly capable of guiding real-world decision making. Indeed, if economic theory continues to be constructed typically on the basis of assumptions constraining its real-world applicability, and if theory testing can accommodate only some of the assumptions, this scenario might not be fanciful. Examples of these two processes occur in Fisher (1989), Summers (1991) and Mayer (1993, 60–65, 80–121, 127–129), who calls the second 'the principle of the strongest link.' Economic (and social science) theory probably has to rest on more *ceteris paribus* assumptions and auxiliary hypotheses than natural science theory because social phenomena are subject to more potentially disturbing influences than natural phenomena. The Duhem-Quine thesis complicates all scientific testing, including economics (Sawyer et al., 1997), but its additive effect in social science may be more undermining of temporally stable results than in natural science.

ASSESSING THE CLAIMS OF ANY ONE THEORY IN SOCIAL SCIENCE AND ECONOMICS

Kincaid (1996) extols particular social science case studies for meeting norms of good naturalistic science. There is an unstated implication that fair etc. tests were applied to their hypotheses (even though none of the cases was concerned with assessing claims of rival theories). However, in no case is it explained how the tests that were applied met Kincaid's criteria for fair, etc. tests—or what these criteria were in each case under scrutiny. Nor it is shown for each case that the particular tests employed were necessary or sufficient to test the hypotheses in question. Neither in any case are policy implications drawn out. Kincaid treats each case study as though the testing procedures that were employed and the predictive content of its hypotheses were unproblematic.

For example, as we saw in Chapter 10, great merit is attached by Kincaid to Paige (1975), presented as an exemplar of naturalistic methodology. Paige is analyzed mainly as an example of how *ceteris paribus* assumptions underlying theory can be handled. His data are held to 'support all of Paige's hypotheses' (Kincaid, 1996, 77). (Falsification is not accepted by Kincaid as a criterion for good science). Among his many predictions, Paige (1975, 70–71) postulated four about the relation between agrarian organization and political response. Each of these predictions had at least five sub-predictions, one of which was 'a combination of both noncultivators and cultivators dependent on land as their principal source of income leads to an agrarian revolt.'

Prior value judgement-filled issues have to be resolved before such hypotheses can be tested. For instance, a socio-economic/cultural context and time frame would need to be specified in which agrarian revolt was to occur, but these were not contained in the particular Paige sub-prediction above, nor specified by auxiliary hypotheses. Comment is made here about a different aspect of the Page argument already raised in the last chapter. There are at least six terms in the Paige sub-prediction above requiring definition, such as 'noncultivator,' 'dependent on land,' 'income,' and 'revolt.' Paige does not define any of these terms, and each of them is not a natural kind (Ellis, 1996). Membership of the classification 'noncultivator,' for instance, is fixed by human definition or convention, and is a term defined by degree or relationship, not by an essential property or structure of a 'noncultivator' class (Wilkerson, 1995). Sayer (1992, 127) put it that most socio-economic variables are qualitative in nature, whose substance varies according to context.

The natural kind difficulty in social science means specifically for economics, that even 'quantitative relationships embodied in structural equations often hold only for the population or particular background circumstances for which they are estimated' (Woodward, 1995, 31, 32). Undoubtedly, *ceteris paribus* assumptions also constrain natural science theories, but their conclusions appear to hold with greater reliability than those in social science; often sufficiently to base all manner of practical decisions on them, like constructing aircraft and bridges that serve their intended purposes.

If social scientists defined non-natural kind terms uniformly in formulating and testing different theories containing the same expressions, the non-natural kind status of social science entities would not be a problem for comparing results between studies. But, by theoretical choice, and by measurement constraint, invariably the terms are observed disparately between studies. Empirics sometimes mould the delimitation; whatever data exists in specific contexts determines how the term is defined. One result of using differently-defined non-natural-, nominal-, culturally generated-, dependent-, and real but superficial-kind terms for social science is to compound the imprecision of its qualitative conclusions that are difficult to compare between studies. Social science may well arrive at its conclusions via scientific methods; in Paige's case by correlation tests and path analysis. But, applying scientific methods to non-natural kinds does not overcome the problem of incomparability between studies.

There is little sign of the two problems above being rectified over time in economics (and other social science): that economics deals with non-natural kinds and therefore does not expose the real essence of things, and that these kinds are defined differently between studies. On the second point, some non-natural kind terms, such as income, output, price, commodity and money, may be acquiring more uniform definition with time; for example, in the national accounts of nation states. But others like cost, capital, utility, self-interest, efficiency, equity, expectations, rationality, preferences, marginal productivity, externality, wealth, class, and quality of life are not trending to theoretical consistency or uniform empirical definition. Some of the designations, like social dislocation costs, may not even be measurable in any uniformly agreed framework. Others, like unemployment, may be losing even the low degree of uniform definition they once had, given the changing nature of work. Even definitional clarifications of more 'concrete' terms like income are not accepted unproblematically within the economics profession. One criticism is that conventional definitions of income, cost and output do not capture either all the returns to inputs by factors of production, or all the effects of production (e.g., Daly and Cobb, 1994; Clark and Kavanagh, 1996). For instance, the contribution of the 'underground economy,' and of the unpaid services of housewives and other family members are probably undervalued enormously in standard measures of output and income (e.g., Ironmonger, 1989). Common-use definitions of standard (non-natural kind) economic terms are socially conditioned to some degree. A comparable tendency to the social conditioning of its basic categories does not characterize natural science to the same degree, especially in its long run development. Part of the initial emphasis in 'new' natural sciences like evolutionary biology is to identify natural kind terms (e.g. does 'fitness' meet criteria for a natural kind?), so that practitioners can agree on their focus.

The non-natural kinds of social science and economics do not dissolve these disciplines, but they do undermine practice of the Table 11.1 naturalistic methods. Keynes, for example, recognized that many of the key concepts of economics (and social science) were essentially vague notions that could not be reduced to quantitative measures, and therefore could not be theoretically tested in the naturalistic manner proposed by items 5 and 6 in Table 11.1 above (Coates, 1996, 81ff.). Coates argued that Keynes' solution to this dilemma was to formulate his (General) theory in natural language, using the concepts of ordinary discourse as far as possible. Although this mode of expression was criticized for being imprecise, Keynes defended it as embodying a wealth of tacit knowledge that could not be replicated as formal notation. Vagueness, as with non-natural kinds, is not the antithesis of knowledge, despite the contrary claims of analytic philosophy and post-structuralism. But vagueness does require social science and economics to be constructed in common sense, ordinary, everyday natural language, characterized by clear prose and argument. Such expression allows us to stay near mental constructs with which we retain immediate understanding, and is 'a weapon anyone can brandish' (Coates, 1996, 171). Highly specialized intellectual technique is not required. The case cannot be developed here, but common sense non-naturalistic economics (and social science) is compatible with realism, and does not have to imply relativism.

THE INNOVATIVE VALUE OF PREDICTIVE CLAIMS OF NATURALISTIC ECONOMIC THEORY

Kincaid advocates naturalism in social science because he believes that only a true understanding of social reality can derive from naturalistic methods, and that this understanding is a prerequisite to changing society 'for the better' (Kincaid, 1996, 4–5). For economics specifically, 'important parts' are held to be 'relatively well confirmed' (Kincaid, 1996, 4–5, 230). This optimism has been criticized for academic economics in many ways. One is that predictive claims of economic theory are not reliable enough for policy use, that predictions possess too large a margin of error for practical application in the real world (e.g., Meehan, 1982; Ormerod, 1994). This problem is not pursued here. Instead, a relatively neglected aspect of the critique is considered.

In the characterization of naturalism in Table 11.1, 'relatively well confirmed' theory implies explanatory and predictive accuracy, that naturalistic methods yield valid comprehension of human behavior. It carries the connotation that naturalistic methods lead to 'true understanding of social reality' whereas non-naturalistic methods lead to less true understanding. However, two examples are discussed below casting doubt on this presumption. They suggest that predictions from economic theory aspiring to meet naturalistic standards do not produce results different from those deduced by previously expressed non-naturalistic verbal reasoning. In the two cases, predictions from the economic theory did not lead to 'new' insights about human behavior or for policy formation. The two examples are of rational choice theory, a representation of naturalistic 'demand-and-supply explanations' in Kincaid's terms, that are held to be 'relatively well confirmed.' Neither example presents 'superior' predictions compared with prior common sense-based exposition. The examples suggest that predictions from rational choice theory, a, if not *the,* leading theory in Neoclassical economics, are neither as novel nor as unambiguous as their proponents proclaim.

Becker (1993) claimed that the rational choice model can produce innovative and unexpected predictions about human choice, that 'sometimes run sharply counter to received opinion.' As an example, 'contrary to common belief,' he asserted that 'economic analysis of family decisions shows that wealthier couples are *less* likely to divorce than poorer couples' (Becker, 1993, 396; original emphasis). This claim was made on the basis of Becker et al., 1977. Where the contrary 'common belief' was supposed to lie is unclear, for at the time Becker et al. made this claim, it had been common knowledge in family studies for at least twenty years that the rich divorce less than the poor (e.g., Kephart, 1955; Monahan, 1955; Udry, 1966; Nye and Berardo, 1973; Norton and Glick, 1976). Only prior to the 1940s was it believed widely that 'divorce was most prevelent [*sic*] among upper socioeconomic groups in American society' (Thompson, 1978, 70). The family studies' literature that theorized from the 1950s to the 70s about why the rich divorce less than the poor made no recourse to formalistic modelling. Instead, it formulated explanations in natural language terms: that extended familial support and/or desertion might be more common among poor people, or that poor women sought legal separation to formalize family maintenance payments, and so on. If these explanations are interpreted retrospectively to be examples of rational choice theory applied to family decisions, the theory looks merely like a rationalization and formalization of common sense. The observations here resonate with Blaug (1992, 223–226) on Becker's earlier (1976) application of the rational choice model to the family.

Another applied example of the rational choice model highlights the commonplace and everyday nature of its predictions, conforming with Rosenberg's claim (1992, 134) that the model has only the 'predictive accuracy of common sense.' This example indicates also that supposed innovative and unanticipated predictions of the model turn out to be public knowledge. Iannaccone (1992, 276) used the model to show 'that perfectly rational people can be drawn to decidedly unconventional groups.' These groups included religious cults and sects as well as nonreligious clubs. Iannaccone suggested that the above prediction 'sharply contrasts with the view, prevalent among psychiatrists, clinical psychologists, and the media, that conversion to deviant religious sects and cults is inherently pathological' (Iannaccone, 1992, 276). One reference (Robbins, 1988, 72–89) was cited to substantiate this supposedly prevalent notion. What the uninformed reader would not know is that the two disparate views above are those in a continuing two-decade battle between psychologists/psychiatrists/cult counsellors versus sociologists (of whom Robbins is a leading exponent) about why people join cults. In his own analysis, Robbins (1988, 17) acknowledged that he presented 'no exhaustive review' of the psychological/psychiatric position (unlike his treatment of the sociological position), but this did not stop Iannaccone from citing him as the source of the prevalent view among psychologists and other analysts.

The arguments between the two sides are more complex than depicted by Iannaccone, with each conceding aspects of the other's case. For example, the view that cults recruit 'perfectly rational people' has long been widespread in the psychological/cultic studies literature and is still proposed (recent examples are Hassan, 1990, 49–50; Langone, 1993, 6; Tobias and Lalich, 1994, 28; Singer, 1995, 107). As Tobias and Lalich (1994, 28) put it, 'people who join cults are *not* stupid, weird, crazy, or neurotic. Most cult members are of above-average intelligence, well-adjusted, adaptable, and perhaps a bit idealistic.' Pathological mind control is depicted in the cultic studies literature as explaining not conversion to cults, but the process of indoctrination in cults. This literature suggests that the process of commitment involves a psychological pattern of thought reform different from brainwashing. Even Robbins (1988, 74, 76, 77) admitted that 'the existence of manipulative, deceptive and coercive pressures in some movements has been widely acknowledged,' that 'the more sophisticated models' of thought reform 'are broadly applicable,' and that 'some broader models of "thought reform" . . . are indeed applicable to many cults.' These 'broader models of thought reform' can stem also from authoritarian structures and processes characterizing not only cults and sects, but church and other organizations generally. Cultures of secrecy, abuse and misuse of power can be 'broadly applicable' to all these organizations (Beed, 1998, 2001).

Iannaccone's explanations for the empirical evidence he reports may be consistent with the rational choice model, but this is not abundantly clear. For example, one of the pieces of evidence (Iannaccone, 1992, 283) is that the household incomes of church members—'whose norms generally mirror those of the prevailing culture'—are on average higher than sect members—who have 'deviant norms.' Iannaccone (1992, 283) does not explain how this observation accords with his model's predictions; indeed, 'the arguments needed to establish these [predictions] as formal consequences of the model are noted but not detailed.' Perhaps he takes the rational choice model to predict that sects limit the opportunities of their members to participate in outside activities, including employment, more than church members. If so, no disagreement need be made with this supposition which is common knowledge about sects. But it is not illuminating as a reason to explain the nature of sects and cults, or why people join and remain in them. Iannaccone (1992, 284) held that 'the church-sect distinction has heretofore lacked a theoretical foundation,' and he evidently believed his model provided this foundation. This claim is exaggerated for the church-sect distinction has had long theoretical exploration in theology, psychology and sociology (e.g., Wilson, 1990).

From the two cases above is a strong inference of the unwarranted claims and the unexceptional content of predictions of supposedly naturalistic rational choice models. Often, the claims are overstated, simplistic, trivial or banal, and little different from 'off-the-cuff' implications (a caricature drawing out these implications is Boulier and Goldfarb, 1991). Common sense reasoning and folk psychology have long predicted similar results, and alternative plausible explanations are available for the phenomena in their purview (e.g., Bruce, 1999, criticizes Iannaccone's work from this perspective). Depicting these modes of thinking as 'rational choice theory' expressed in mathematical formalism does not enhance the information content of the behavioral motivational processes involved. Moreover, it is debatable how far the predictions of rational choice theory can be called prediction. Invariably, the predictions are compared with already known empirical evidence. The 'predictions' look more like *post hoc* rationalizations or retrodiction.

Such limitations of the model's application may be well recognized in social sciences other than economics, sometimes regarded as under threat from 'economic imperialism.' In sociology, for example, postgraduate texts devote little space to rational choice theory. In his examination of theories of crime, for instance, Knapp (1994) devoted half a page to Neoclassical theories compared to sixteen and a half to alternative theories. If this is indicative of the impact of Neoclassical theory on sociology (which claim is echoed by Blaug, 1992, 228), it probably helps explain also why a search for the rational choice masthead journal, *Rationality and Society,* did not prove fruitful in any Victorian (Australia) university library. This limited intellectual impact harks back to the discussion above—it is doubtful whether the claims of competing theories in different social science disciplines trying to explain the same domain of human behavior are being resolved empirically by fair, cross and independent tests, as naturalism would imply. In Becker (1976), for example, competing sociological, anthropological or psychological explanations of family behavior received scant attention. Blaug (1992, 226) noted dryly that 'if these are the rules of the game, we simply cannot lose.' Naturalists might respond that sociologists, psychologists, and other social scientists have not been performing the 'right' tests. Any such response would be weakened by our discussion above showing disagreement among economists about what are 'right' tests. An analogous story could be told for other social sciences.

POLICY IMPLICATIONS FROM (NATURALISTIC?) ECONOMIC THEORY

Academic economics today is dominated by formalistic modelling and the application of statistical methods to empirical data. Ostensibly, this orientation looks scientific, the practices mimic those in the natural sciences, and they appear to conform to naturalistic precepts. The issue investigated in this section is whether this orientation of academic economics is consistent with the definition of naturalism in Table 11.1 above; also, whether the orientation yields conclusions useful for public policy formation. Initially, these questions are investigated via one book authored by a prominent academic economist with an impeccable curriculum vitae of international standing in the practice of economics as science.

John Quiggin (1996) presents an excellent evaluation of contemporary deregulation and privatization of a number of key industries in Australia. He claims (1996, ix) that 'the central message [of his book] is that economic analysis can be usefully applied to the task of assessing existing policies and suggesting improvements on those policies.' In his view, 'the problem with the current Australian policy debate [on deregulation and privatization] is not an excessive reliance on economics but the substitution of dogmatic precommitment for objective analysis.'

'Economic' and 'objective' analysis are not defined by Quiggin. Perhaps they are taken to be some form of reasoning different from common sense but characterized by economics. To substantiate his claim that 'economic analysis' can make the contribution he asserts above, Quiggin spends three chapters (4, 5 and 6) explaining aspects of economic theory. These are presented as a prerequisite to ten chapters evaluating the historical record of microeconomic reform in Australia. For instance, his Chapter 4 on welfare economics runs through standard theoretical topics: assumptions of welfare theory; Pareto improvements and optimality; efficiency rules, including elements like the Harberger triangle; efficiency and equity considerations; and revealed preference and problems of price indexes. Each topic is presented as a self contained theoretical whole, often developed by algebraic reasoning, with the qualification that 'a satisfactory analysis of welfare economics requires a level of analytical rigour' beyond that found in the book (1996, 35). Quiggin claims that an understanding of the theoretical issues of welfare economics (and the other two theoretical subjects he surveys) is necessary for evaluating microeconomic reform in Australia.

How valid is this claim? Not strongly, in terms of the conclusions Quiggin draws in his Chapter 4. For example, in the chapter, few of the theoretical terms are given empirical substance in the Australian situation. Little discussion occurs of how any of the theoretical topics relate to the Australian policy experience (this is rectified in later chapters only for a few of the theoretical constructs, such as Harberger welfare losses). Shorn of its abstract theoretical mathematical propositions, Chapter 4 is a compilation of what can only be described as common sense observations. For example, Quiggin (1996, 39–41) notes that different economists define efficiency differently (hardly surprising since efficiency is not a natural kind). He recounts (p. 41) a short verbal history showing that the sequencing of microeconomic reforms is important for policy outcomes. He observes, and is critical of, that 'many advocates of microeconomic reform focus solely on efficiency' at the expense of equity (p. 44). Pages 46–50 concern problems associated with the construction of price and output indexes. All these issues are capable of being discussed in a common sense verbal framework without the prejudgment that an understanding of welfare economics, based on higher level mathematics, is a prerequisite for evaluating microeconomic reform in Australia (or anywhere else).

In sum, Quiggin asserts but does not demonstrate in his Chapter 4 the practical value of welfare economic theory for evaluating microeconomic reform. Some of the constructs he examines do have a practical role to play, but they derive from the theory of statistics, such as price and other indexes, not from welfare economics. Typically, the theoretical constructs of welfare economics are not able to be given empirical substance which is one reason why they have little practical relevance (cost-benefit analysis notwithstanding). Another reason is noted by Quiggin himself (1996, 35), that even some economists reject the basic assumptions of welfare theory as applying to the real world. For example, Chapter 10 noted Hutchison's objection (1992, 36) to welfare economics—that it had dubious essence and no real-world relevance. Even Quiggin conceded (1996, 37) that the 'main assumptions . . . become progressively more problematic when they are applied to issues such as health, education, the environment and culture.' Kincaid's naturalism of Table 11.1 above requires the application and comparison of theoretical economic constructs to the real world, but on this score, Quiggin's welfare economics framework is of dubious relevance.

Aside from the qualifications above, Quiggin's book is a good example of non-naturalistic, common sense economics. It can be read and evaluated adequately by anyone who had never studied academic economic theory. The qualification to this statement is that if readers had not learned higher secondary school algebra in recent years, they would not be able to evaluate the mathematics in the book. However, neither the maths nor the presentation in mathematical form of the theory it underpins is necessary for the argument of the book. It could all have been presented in verbal form, as was Langmore's and Quiggin's previous excellent book (1994) on ways to create full employment in Australia.

The limitation of contemporary economic theory revealed in the above case of welfare economics is its inability to lend itself to the practice of the naturalistic criteria in Table 11.1—its failure to generate empirically testable predictions that can function as the 'objective empirical warrant.' Although welfare economic theory purportedly serves as a conceptual organizer of reality, it has limited empirical relevance in this instance as a vehicle for explicating public policy. This conclusion for understanding the rationale for, and effects of, recent deregulation and microeconomic reform in Australia might appear to contradict US findings. Winston's survey (1993, 1263) suggested that (US) microeconomists were 'able to develop a theoretical and empirical framework to explain regulation and its effects and to form predictions of deregulation's effects.' However, Winston did not discuss whether microeconomics ever had a satisfactory theory to explain why regulation was instituted in the US in the first place. The only theory he cited to explain regulation up to the 1960s, public interest theory, held that regulation was necessary to correct 'some form of market failure'; a theory, according to Winston, that had its 'high water mark' in 1887. That microeconomics still had such a weak theory as a rationale for regulation in the 1960s was unlikely to serve as an effective edifice capable of either explaining or predicting real-world behavior. If historical investigation of why regulation was instituted in nineteenth century US had served as the basis for the development of theory, instead of *a priori* theorizing, a more realistic microeconomic theory might have existed up to the 1960s. A theory more relevant to real life (perhaps even along Marxist lines) would have concerned monopoly practices and whether they encouraged higher prices. Even Winston (1993, 1266) conceded that the weakness of held theory up to the 1960s was 'its assumption that perfectly informed social welfare maximizers are either managing the regulation or running the regulated firms.' This theory was far removed from reality as an explanation for regulation. It is not surprising that Neoclassical economists since the 60s were able to demonstrate the lack of correspondence of this theory to the real world, given that the theory carried so many 'straw man' connotations. A critical, common sense-based analysis might have come to similar conclusions.

It is possible that other contemporary forms of orthodox economic theory are no more able than superseded theory to meet the naturalistic criteria of

Table 11.1, and therefore no more useful to serve as a public policy guide. If this is the case, it is not surprising that the *Economic Journal's* 1991 survey of the future of economics (Hey, 1992) contained no article of the past or present contribution of economics to the formation of public policy. This hiatus may not be changing. A more recent survey (Medema and Samuels, 1996) of how economists do economics contains no chapter on how economists (or anybody else) might use or have used economic theory for policy formulation. To one contributor, Lawson (1996, 170), prediction from economic theory is not the key to policy value for 'the successful prediction of economic events is not only unlikely, but also unnecessary and even unwanted' (he does not say by whom). Another contributor, Varian, asks what use is economic theory. He provides many reasons in principle why economic theory might be useful in policy formation (although does not clarify how this differs from common sense analysis), but no specific empirical example (anecdotes aside) of how economic theory has been so used. Or consider Little's (1995, 265) conclusions on the empirical role of simulation models in development economics:

> The most obvious approach to empirically evaluating a model is through direct evaluation of its predictions: compare the predictive results of the model with observed data. It is significant, however, that none of the dozen models contained in *Socially Relevant Policy Analysis* (Taylor, 1990) provides such post facto evaluation.

There is also a more impressionistic way of looking at the policy issue. The authors here (Beed and Beed) researched in particular applied socio-economic fields such as Australian urban transport policy, and recreation and family policy respectively. In our experience, in none of these fields has economic theory had more than marginal effect on policy analysis or outcomes. Urban transport policy in Australia, for instance, shows only incidental impact from economic theory, as distinct from statistical, mathematical, financial, and engineering analysis.

It is tempting to conclude that economists proclaiming the practical value of economic theory and models for public policy formation resemble the crowd adulating the emperor who had no clothes. Henderson (1986) offered an alternative explanation for the weak link between economic theory and policy, that policy makers did not understand the insights offered by economic theory, and instead relied on folk or 'do-it-yourself' economics. However, he discussed virtually none of the problems outlined here about relating economic theory to reality. Perhaps, contrary to Henderson, policy makers *are* more attuned to the difficulties than he perceives. Hansen's (1991) explanation for the tenuous links between economic theory and policy may be closer to reality: that the current theoretical content of economics, and therefore the training of graduate economists, does not emphasize public policy relevance, a conclusion echoed by Klamer and Colander (1990), and by Colander and Brenner (1992).

CONCLUSION

The emphasis in this chapter has been on ways by which economics' practice does not satisfy criteria for the definition of social science naturalism expounded by Kincaid (1996). Contrary to the norms of naturalism, economics does not, and is not able to, practice or resolve claims between theories by 'objective empirical warrant.' Economics uses multifarious testing techniques, most clearly revealed via econometric technique, but there are no unambiguous ways by which such tests in the practice of economics can be classified as 'fair,' 'cross,' and 'independent,' whether for tests of 'theories,' 'assumptions,' or 'methodological norms.' Tests of theories etc. in economics typically do not reveal unambiguous results, and therefore do not have strong relevance to public policy formulation. Economics is no different from other social sciences in this respect. Typically, a mix of naturalistic and non-naturalistic techniques are used in all social sciences to construct convincing argument. It is likely that whatever explanatory progress has been achieved in economics has not emanated from attempts to apply objective tests.

A separate study not undertaken here would be required to demonstrate ways by which alternative non-naturalistic common sense-based methods from those enshrined in Table 11.1 are used in economics. Many such methodological illustrations have been given for economics, from such as Wisman and Rozansky (1991) to Lawson (2003). All we conclude about this issue here is that academic economists from all schools of thought concede their use and value, although not under the designation 'non-naturalism.' Coates (1996) demonstrated Keynes' reliance on a common sense-based, non-naturalistic realism. McCloskey's (1986) story of the mode of orthodox economic analysis can be construed as recognizing the importance of non-naturalistic methods, but economists long before (and since) practiced and advocated non-naturalism (e.g., as in American Institutionalism). We close with a few such recognitions by economists since the 1970s that objective empirical warrants do not exist for economics (excluding Institutionalists and Austrians whose stock-in-trade non-naturalism is). Joskow (1975, 273) asserted that 'the important messages [in economics] are being carried by the informal theories, stories, and behavioral observations.' Even the work of Friedman, sometimes regarded as the archetype of Neoclassical naturalistic analysis, has been described via legal metaphor, as his trying to persuade like a criminal prosecutor piling up evidence to support his preferred theory; 'the marshalling of evidence to strengthen conviction is almost everything,' while 'proof, numerical or otherwise, is out of question when we are engaged in interpreting empirical reality' (Hirsch and de Marchi, 1990, 244). Solow's (1985, 329) contentions that the aim of economics should be 'to tell plausible . . . causal stories with the help of a few central principles,' and Friedman and Schwartz's (1991, 39) that 'there is no magic formula for wringing reasonable conjectures from refractory and inaccurate evidence' are consistent with recognition of the lack of objective empirical warrant. Such views are summarized by Summers (1991, 146), that 'good empirical evidence tells its story regardless of the precise way it is analyzed'. These approaches imply no dependence on all the naturalistic methods outlined in Table 11.1 above. This story is continued in the next chapter.

Chapter Twelve

Intellectual Progress and Academic Economics

If contemporary economics does not measure up to the supposed naturalistic standards of natural science that are held to be the most appropriate means for unraveling socio-economic reality, in what sense can it be said that economics produces reliable and useful conclusions, or achieves intellectual progress? This chapter (Beed and Beed, 2000c) considers the nature of intellectual progress and its relation to two aspects of mainstream academic economics. Some parameters of intellectual progress are canvassed to assess how the rational choice and game theory elements of mainstream economics in the recent past measure up to these interpretations. That orthodox economics has achieved progress in the long term is regarded usually as self-evident by the academic economics profession. For example, Backhouse (1985, 411, 412) claimed that 'mainstream economics has been reasonably progressive,' that it constitutes part of 'a progressive research programme.' Blaug similarly (1997, 3, 7) challenged 'anyone [to] seriously deny that in the matter of techniques and analytical constructs there has been progress in economics,' or that 'the workings of the economic system are better understood than ever before.' The purview of this chapter is a shorter time period for mainstream economics than embodied in these quotes, but the conclusions here are relevant to the longer term. Initially, the chapter overviews previous attempts to substantiate progress in economics. It concludes that they did not demonstrate (long-term) intellectual progress in the mainstream academic economics discipline.

The chapter offers a second conclusion, on the recent intellectual progress of economic theory, relating just to the rational choice and game theory elements of mainstream economics. It is incontestable that economics has made progress in the sense of acquiring a greater stock of information about certain aspects of human behavior. This could be called the 'we-know-more-about' criterion.

Progress in terms of this criterion is unremarkable, given growth in the number of academically trained economists, and this dimension of progress is not pursued here. Less certain is, whether this greater quantity of data has been, and is being, derived from or related to theories in economics. The accelerating collection of economic information is clear-cut. What is less clear is whether mainstream economic theories (illustrated here by rational choice and game theory) within the last decade or so are increasingly explaining or predicting this growing stock of observations. These elements of economic theory may increasingly just be redescribing already known information and explanations in terms of their own terminology and nomenclature rather than predicting new data that has yet to eventuate or be discovered. In this case, the explanations these theories provide would not necessarily enhance previously existing explanations, both within and outside of economics. Game theory, in particular, may illustrate mainly formal abstract constructions of untestable empirical relevance; such theories would not exhibit greater correspondence over time to real-world phenomena in so far as this was not being ascertained in the development of game theory. In this latter case, theoretical progress, as defined below, is not being achieved. In both cases (redescription and abstraction), the theories of economics examined would not be achieving empirical progress (also defined below), and would not be put to increasing real-world use in solving practical policy problems. The latter part of the chapter explores some of these propositions and concludes that the rational choice and game theory segments of academic economics are probably not showing theoretical or empirical progress, although a determinate answer is not clear-cut.

THE MEANING OF INTELLECTUAL PROGRESS IN SOCIAL SCIENCE AND ECONOMICS

The idea of intellectual progress in social science is not categorical and runs the risk of being defined loosely or not being defined at all. In economics, for example, Backhouse (1997, 4) noted that the concept of progress underlying the mathematization and econometrization of economics has 'remained largely unanalysed.' Various attempts have been made to tighten up this looseness and to apply criteria of progress to economics, although invariably relating them to the long-term historical development of the subject. Bliss's test (1986, 365) was the declining degree of entropy in the subject, but he did not demonstrate how this applied. The most Bliss did was to employ rhetorical flourishes like 'compare the theoretical power of economics at the end of the nineteenth century with its state fifty years earlier' (1986, 373). The reader is left waiting for the comparison, including an explanation of 'theoretical power.'

Hausman (1989, 364), as we noted in the previous chapter, concluded that 'cumulative explanatory progress' had been achieved over the long run for a particular subset of economic analysis (the existence of profits). But he was unable to demonstrate convincingly how this 'explanatory progress' had occurred. Partly, this was because no unchanging definition of profits was provided via which their existence might be theorized. Indeed, profits did not exist 'apart from an economic theory to define' them (1989, 366). Not surprisingly, therefore, 'the questions theorists have asked . . . have changed,' one reason being that 'the phenomena' (forms of profits) have changed with changing socio-economic structures (1989, 365).

The story Hausman told (1989, 365–376) of these changing questions about profits, from the ethical discussion of the Church Scholastics of the twelfth century, through the Classicals of the nineteenth century to the Neoclassicals of the twentieth century provides few grounds to justify conclusions of 'considerable explanatory progress' (1989, 376), or to confirm that 'better explanations' of profits have emerged (1989, 377). At most, the story underlines that the writers did indeed ask different questions from each other. A less charitable judgement that might be drawn from Hausman's account is that the theorizing, old and modern, has resembled hyperbolized common sense. Striking, too, is the imprecision attached to the categories concerned, such as uncertainty as to what constitutes 'capital.' All this is unsurprising as profits and capital are socially-constructed non-natural kinds.

More relevantly to this chapter, Hausman proposed seven criteria to justify his conclusion of 'cumulative explanatory progress' in economics' theoretical explanations of profits. For instance, criterion two was 'the discovery' (1989, 377) and 'recognition of relevant new facts' (1989, 378). But the examples cited by Hausman under this criterion seemed to stem more from everyday experience than from 'economic theorizing' (or its relations). Undoubtedly, progress occurred in the eighteenth century with the accumulation of written information about economic matters, including profits. But it is debatable whether the written information derived from theory than from the events of practical business life. It is more likely that the regular happenings in people's lives in their socio-economic contexts led them to realize that bond prices bore an inverse relation to the rate of interest, that it was costly to make loans, and that competitive markets encouraged equalizations in rates of return (Hausman, 1989, 378). These facts were not new discoveries by fledgling economics theorists of the eighteenth century, they were not predicted by theory, but became widely known from business practice. What *was* new was the theorists' writing about this common experience, but for the three of Hausman's examples mentioned above, it might not have been earth-shattering news to anyone. Unlike the physical sciences, social science theorists in the eighteenth and nineteenth centuries did not make new discoveries leading to new socio-economic concepts of practical enduring use, despite their continual claims to the contrary. Whatever new concepts these theorists 'discovered' were mainly products of their own theoretical constructions. Explanatory they might have been within those theoretical systems, but whether they added greatly to common sense or folk psychology explanation can still be debated. Each of Hausman's (1989) criteria supposedly justifying 'cumulative explanatory progress' in explaining profits is subject to similar equivocation (e.g., Hausman provided no reasons why superseded Classical theories of profits were intellectually inferior to Neoclassical theories).

A less formal approach to ascertaining long-run progress in economics was taken by Blaug (1994), who listed twelve innovations in economics, such as game theory and econometrics. He asked whether these constituted 'advances' in economics (1994, 116), by which he meant theoretical and/or empirical progress. Blaug's definition of theoretical progress was of the Lakatosian 'set of problem-solving techniques' type which, for Lakatos, was measured by its ability to lead to 'new unexpected predictions' (Lakatos, 1978, 179). Blaug (1994, 117) defined empirical progress as a more 'elusive' idea, involving 'a deeper grasp of the inner springs of economic behavior and hence of the operations of the economic system.' These definitions of both theoretical and empirical progress lack precision, and the first underlines long-observed problems in Lakatos' framework: that his notions of 'empirical content,' 'novel fact,' and 'corroboration' have uncertain applicability in social science and economics (e.g., Hands, 1993, 2001b). This chapter is not an analysis of Lakatos, but his ideas for demarcating science from non-science along the lines above have not retained strong influence in philosophy or physical and social science. Thus, Rosenberg early suggested (1986, 135) that economics' 'fixation with Lakatos [is] philosophically dated.' In any case, Blaug (1994) did not consider how Lakatos' criteria for theoretical progress related systemically to the twelve economics innovations.

With such an elastic meaning ascribed to empirical progress, it was not difficult for Blaug to make a case that the twelve innovations have given a 'deeper grasp of the inner springs of economic behavior.' Any new data collected about anything are likely to help us 'see farther' (1994, 117) than before. As discussed below, empirical progress can be defined differently from this. Blaug (1994, 119–121) examined each innovation on the basis of an undifferentiated mixture of his theoretical and empirical progress criteria and made a case of progress (albeit admitting to more theoretical than empirical, although novel predictions were not emphasized). What was not explored was how much of this progress stemmed from the greater stock of data about human behavior collected by the growing academic (and non-academic) economics industry, vis-à-vis that contributed by academic economic theory. Nor was the extent gauged of the progress as theoretical rigor unrelated to the real world. Nor was whether progress in any of the innovative areas (e.g., the theory and measurement of social inequalities) derived from disciplines outside economics. Even on Blaug's reading, progress in economics has been marred by dead ends, such as linear programming, in which 'expectations of a theoretical revolution around the theme of "linearities" have faded away without leaving much trace' (1994, 121).

Khalil (1995, 43) examined the question 'Has economics progressed?' by classifying 'the different existing historiographies of economic paradigms or research programs.' But he was unable to answer the question. What emerged from Khalil's analysis was that the different historiographers would have formulated different answers to the question, had they posed it. The criterion of progress of interest to Khalil was whether theoretical shifts 'entailed improvements, according to one criterion or another' (1995, 43–44). However, in examining the historiographies, Khalil focused only on their internal dynamic, on problems confronting each typology, and on which analysts might be included in each classification, than on whether their proponents demonstrated 'improvements' in economics. This is unsurprising, for defining 'improvements' in economics according to any criterion is not straightforward. Between proponents of the different historiographies, a common criterion is probably impossible to determine. Certainly, the different historiographers used different criteria of progress. Some assumed that economics tends 'to change toward the correct views' (Khalil, 1995, 49), a supposedly 'neutral' criterion of progress that for some proponents of a given (rectilinear) historiographical classification was equated with 'innovative analysis' (1995, 50), with superior technique (1995, 54), with being 'more successful' (1995, 56), or changing 'toward their favored paradigm' (1995, 57). The vagueness of these terms is striking. On the other hand, historiographers with a strong historicist bent maintained 'there are no neutral grounds upon which one could adjudicate among competing paradigms' (1995, 57). Despite Khalil's schema, he did not show for any of the historiographical types on any criterion that change has occurred in economics 'from lower, less desirable features to higher, more desirable ones' (1995, 76). In the context in which the terms were used by Khalil, 'progress,' 'success,' 'lower,' 'higher,' 'less desirable' and 'more desirable' had little empirical or objective content.

Backhouse (1997, 97–100) suggested (not in the order below) that intellectual progress could include dimensions of:

1. Closer approximation to the truth, improving the correspondence between theory and reality.
2. Improved explanatory power.

3. Increased practical, instrumental knowledge, enabling people to do things. Backhouse (1997, 99) claimed this 'pragmatist way of viewing progress has the merit of dispensing with the metaphysical problem of the relation between truth and reality.'
4. Increased agreement, consensus—not usually held in high regard.
5. Irreversible change—as per, Bliss above.

Relating any of these principles to economics is not a clear-cut task. They are no more than coarse macro guides for assessing intellectual progress and do not lend themselves easily to practical application. Nor are the principles mutually exclusive. Thus, it is possible to think of the first two criteria as interrelated. If a theory explains how something works, it might be reasonable to suppose that the theory points to truth and reality. But this is not a necessary connection, for many explanations throughout history have turned out eventually to be mistaken about reality. Reality and truth may be out there, but people may not be able to reach them easily because we are unable to assess the state of the world (reality) except through our beliefs.

The five macro criteria in the above list for assessing intellectual progress were honed more finely by Backhouse into those relating to theoretical and empirical progress. Theoretical progress can be defined (Backhouse, 1997, 100–103) to include greater generality and scope, precision, epistemic rigor, consistency, and simplicity in theoretical construction, as well as increased ability to predict novel facts. Some of these criteria concern the relevance of theories to real-world empirical data. For instance, increased scope means greater applicability to identifiable situations, and predicting novel facts requires that theory relate to data. Thus, theoretical progress is 'contingent on the relationship of economic theory to empirical evidence' (Backhouse, 1997, 131), that the aim of theory is to explain happenings in the real world. This view is echoed by other commentators, that 'even pure economic theory is framed for the purpose of throwing light on the actual workings of the economic system' (Blaug, 1997, 4). Such a view is often promoted by physical scientists, that theories need to be confronted with empirical evidence (e.g., Sokal and Bricmont, 1998, 182).

Empirical progress (Backhouse, 1997, 103–104) invokes connotations of an increasing 'number and quality of empirical generalizations,' of 'increased predictive success,' the 'successful prediction of novel facts,' and 'improved problem-solving ability.' These involve more than the 'we-know-more-about' criterion, but none of the criteria is open and shut. For instance, accurate prediction is sometimes taken to be the test of explanatory adequacy, that 'the test of explanatory power is the ability to predict successfully' (Backhouse, 1997, 99). This is a variant of the symmetry thesis between explanation and prediction held in economics by Blaug (1992, 1994), but not accepted by most realists (e.g., McCullagh 1998, 268). Prediction has long been a prized criterion for assessing progress in science, but much contention has ensued about its applicability in social science and economics (e.g., Lawson, 1997; Sayer, 1992). One problem is that trying to deduce causation or explanation from prediction is committing the philosophical fallacy of affirming the consequent, that prediction provides contingent grounds for expecting something to happen while explanation tells what makes things happen (Sayer, 1992, 134).

The prediction of novel facts features is a criterion by Backhouse above for both theoretical and empirical progress. As noted in relation to Blaug (1994), much contention has ensued about the meaning Lakatos ascribed to this criterion of progress. Hands (1991, 94–99), for instance, demonstrated that novel facts could be defined in five ways, although he had 'no idea what Lakatos "really meant" by novel facts.' Backhouse (1997, 114–115) suggested that novel facts could be defined in at least six ways, ranging from facts unknown when the theory was proposed either in general, or to the person(s) constructing the theory—to facts the theory was not designed to explain (heuristic novelty). However, it can never be certain that a fact was not known to a person constructing a theory, so that the strongest epistemic value attaches to theories that can predict facts unknown to anyone. In the discussion below, novel fact and prediction are used in this sense.

Backhouse (1997) did not investigate systematically how the above criteria for theoretical or empirical progress applied to the recent history of particular areas of economics. Applying any of the criteria can be a problematic exercise. Suppose the aim was to assess improvement (theoretical and empirical progress) in a segment of economics over time in terms of the correspondence between theory and reality (principle 1 in the list above), and improved explanation (principle 2). This might require theories to apply to a greater range of empirical situations, to provide explanations for as yet unexplained empirical phenomena, and/or to predict novel facts not yet known about reality. Improvement and progress might imply that new theory could explain both what was explained previously and new data as well. If we wanted to add in principle 3 in the list, we would require the segment to solve more and more real-world problems, as distinct from just describing them. Some areas of economics, such as rational choice theory, are sometimes thought to possess these necessary qualities and therefore count as progressive. The next section investigates how this generic family of economic theory, widely used in contemporary mainstream academic microeconomics, may fare on some of the above criteria for theoretical and empirical progress.

MAINSTREAM ECONOMIC THEORY AND ATTRIBUTES OF INTELLECTUAL PROGRESS

Examples from Rational Choice Theory

The issue in this section is the extent to which rational choice theory and its subset, game theory, provide explanations for real-world phenomena previously unexplained, are tending to greater empirical domain and prediction, and exhibit increased practical policy-solving ability. These qualities are just some of the parameters above of theoretical and empirical progress. Rational choice theory (RCT) is often presented both as the only theory in social science capable of straddling disciplinary boundaries, and as that theory within each discipline capable of explaining more and more aspects of human behavior. For example, Becker (1993, 403) held RCT as 'the most promising basis presently available for a unified approach to the analysis of the social world by scholars from different social sciences.' This contention is true insofar as RCT is being applied to a greater range of economic and non-economic empirical data. But what we examine here is whether this application is explaining more aspects of human behavior than were previously unexplained. Some economics examples of the application of RCT are discussed to explore whether it might mainly be redescribing already known conclusions in terms of the theoretical definitions contained in RCT. Perhaps it is not predicting novel facts (however defined), except in a heuristic sense. Redescription per se can be consistent with Backhouse-type definitions of intellectual progress (McIntyre, 1996), but it is investigated below whether the redescription in which RC theorists have been engaged has added to the explanation of the empirical phenomena in its purview.

For the purposes of this chapter, the definition of RCT is assumed to be known. We have explored the substance of RCT elsewhere (Beed and Beed, 1999), which meaning conforms to its more general embodiment in meta-economic principles underlying common practice in the academic economics discipline (Sawyer et al., 1998). Just as it is not possible to overview academic economics as a whole, neither is it possible to overview the use of RCT. Initially, just two examples of RCT use are considered below, from which some conclusions are drawn. Two cases prove nothing about the general state of RCT use; whether our conclusions apply more generally to the use of RCT can still be debated. Perhaps other examples of RCT could be suggested to support conclusions contrary to those in this chapter. Although we did look at a greater variety of RCT examples, that search did not invalidate our conclusions here. After discussing the two RCT examples below, an evaluation is made about some aspects of progress in the use of the game theory subset of RCT.

The two RCT examples are Bergstrom and Bagnoli (1993) and Bernheim (1994), both in the *Journal of Political Economy*. No specific criteria underlay the selection of the papers, but they were not randomly selected. The papers were chosen partly because they were interesting and clear. Another reason for selecting them was that they might be representative of the recent leading edge of RCT in academic economics. Indeed, the undemonstrated conjecture postulated here is that the two papers do reveal a pattern typical of RCT use in academic economics. This pattern is unraveled in the following discussion.

One aspect of the pattern is whether the RCT mathematical and verbal models in each paper add to what was known already about reasons for the phenomena under scrutiny. Bergstrom and Bagnoli (1993) developed a series of formal, mathematical expressions to explain the empirical phenomena that, in general, (1) men marry for the first time at an older age than women, (2) the age difference is diminishing over time, and (3) the age difference tends to be greater in 'traditional' than in 'modern' societies. A verbal explanation or model preceding the mathematical models was provided only for the first phenomenon, without supporting references. The verbal explanation was that, since male roles are more varied and specialized than females, 'information about an individual male's economic capabilities may be revealed only gradually after he has spent time in the work force.' For women, on the other hand, their anticipated tasks of childbearing, child care, and household labor may become clear 'once she has reached physical maturity, the passage of time [adding] little information about her capabilities for these tasks' (Bergstrom and Bagnoli, 1993, 186).

The demonstrations in Bergstrom and Bagnoli (1993), that the RCT mathematical models yielded predictions consistent with the three empirical phenomena above (e.g., that males who marry young tend to have lower earnings in later life), followed logically from assumptions underlying the models. That is, the mathematical deductions proceeded tautologously and unequivocally from the assumptions, within the chosen explanatory context of games of incomplete information. Assumptions included constant population size, equal numbers of males and females reach maturity every year, people marry in the first or second year of maturity, no divorce or remarriage occurs, members of each sex agree in their rankings of the opposite sex, the quality of each female is known to all persons when she reaches the first year of maturity but the quality of each male is known only to himself, the quality of each male is known to all persons when he reaches the second year of maturity, in the first year of maturity each male knows what his own quality will be in the second year of maturity, and so on. The ingenuity of the paper was in showing how the conclusions proceeded deductively from the assumptions (which formal mathematical demonstration occupied 85 percent of the text space).

The mathematical deductions themselves did not provide new explanations, insights, or novel predictions about the real world beyond those implicit in the verbal explanation preceding the exposition of the mathematical models (which was given only for the first empirical observation, that men are older than their wives). *A priori,* it is unlikely that the mathematical deductions might do so. The assumptions underlying these models were so removed from the real world that any novel predictions they might generate would relate only to a hypothetical world embodying the assumptions. Perhaps the authors were aware of this restriction because once the mathematical deductions started on the third page of the paper (p. 187), no reference was made further to empirical data (save, in the conclusion that discussed one disconformity between the models' predictions and the real world, namely, US men who first marry over thirty years of age earn less than those who marry in their mid-twenties). This relative lack of discussion between the models' predictions and the real world leads into the issue of interest here, whether the RCT model extended previously known explanations not canvassed in the paper for the three empirical phenomena.

Prior to 1993 (the date of the above paper), much literature existed in family studies, sociology, psychology, and anthropology, discussing why people married at the age they did. Indeed, so long-running had been the research that competing theories had developed to explain the phenomena (life-course theory, exchange theory, symbolic interaction theory), as well as more diverse explanations relating to feminism (Sussman and Steinmetz, 1987). These theories cannot be outlined here, but their explanatory variables duplicated and extended the personal and socio-historical variables in Bergstrom and Bagnoli's (1993) verbal explanation above. For example, life-course theory (e.g., Cooney and Hogan, 1991) was concerned with the effect of institutional arrangements on the timing of first marriage, such as education, labor force and military experience, and characteristics of family of origin, and contained predictions and observations similar to those of Bergstrom and Bagnoli. Numerous papers reported and theorized about differences in such characteristics between men and women (e.g., Michael and Tuma, 1985). Against the background of this debate, the self-contained verbal explanation (model) proposed by Bergstrom and Bagnoli above was incomplete and conveyed the impression that few others had discussed the issues. At the least, no interdisciplinary intellectual context was posited in which their explanation might be situated.

The second paper was Bernheim (1994) who developed an RCT explanation of conformity. Bernheim was aware that 'a large body of sociological, psychological, and anthropological research' had analyzed the causes of conformism, but he cited none of this (except to note that a portion of it was summarized in two economics references that were at least ten years old). Bernheim proceeded within the tradition of RCT exercises that typically fail adequately to acknowledge outside (contemporary) research; in this case, because 'theories developed within other social science disciplines are not easily adapted to the problems and modes of analysis that are familiar to economists.' Evidently, these other disciplines (and economics) lacked 'formal models of custom and conformity' (1994, 842). A major result of 75 percent of Bernheim's text space, including appendices (in a 36 1/2 page article), being devoted to the formal RCT mathematical model was the finding that 'when status is sufficiently important relative to intrinsic utility . . . many individuals will strive to conform to a single, homogeneous standard of behavior, despite heterogeneous underlying preferences' (Bernheim, 1994, 860). This finding had been common knowledge in psychology and sociology for decades (and probably part of lay common sense deduction and folk psychology for eons). For instance, it had been standard verbal explanation in social psychology in the 1980s and before (e.g., Donnerstein and Donnerstein, 1984; Moscovici, 1985) and continues to be repeated up-to the present (e.g., Taylor et al., 1997). The formal model emphasized by Bernheim added little to the verbal explanation of the phenomenon in his paper preceding the formal model. It also added little to the explanation provided outside economics for the phenomenon up to 1994. Nor did Bernheim's formalizing of the verbal explanation in his paper increase the precision or certainty with which the variables in the model might be observed in the real world. For instance, in the quote above, one of the key variables was 'status,' defined elsewhere in the paper as 'esteem' or 'popularity.' Because these terms are non-natural and socially constructed kinds, they have no invariant definition in the real world. Therefore, in the formal model, 'many interpretations of x [status] are consistent with the model . . . [it] might represent the fraction of an agent's time spent on some activity or the fraction of his budget spent on some good . . . [it] could also measure qualities such as the brightness of clothing' (Bernheim, 1994, 846).

The following conclusions are drawn from both papers:

1. The formal RCT (mathematical) models did not clarify explanation of real-world phenomena beyond the verbal models in the papers that the mathematical models endeavored to formalize.
2. Explicit links between the mathematical elements in the RCT models and their empirical real-world equivalents were not stated. Therefore, a reader is required to interpolate to establish the relevance of the algebraic variables in the model to the explanation and prediction of the empirical data with which the paper is concerned. A reader cannot be certain his or her interpolation conforms with the authors' intentions.
3. The formal RCT (mathematical) models did not yield novel predictions or 'novel facts' about real-world behavior. As noted above, 'novel facts' can

be defined in at least six ways. Strongest epistemic value attaches to the prediction of facts unknown when the theory was proposed. Neither of the papers met this criterion. The two cases here raise a possibility that such prediction of 'novel facts' might not have stemmed strongly from RCT generally.

4. Findings dealing with the topics of interest from outside their own research tradition in economics were virtually ignored. Studies in, say, sociology, psychology, anthropology, and even in non-orthodox schools of economics received little attention. Where research findings from other disciplines were reported, they were outdated. Accordingly, the RCT models were developed and presented as a self-contained intellectual category.
5. The verbal and formal (mathematical) models in the papers did not extend explanation of the empirical phenomena under scrutiny beyond what was already known about the phenomena at the time of the papers' construction.
6. The two example papers were not characterized by all elements of theoretical progress and did not yield empirical progress, in the sense used by Backhouse (1997) above.
7. The findings were marked by an unwarranted sense of discovery. This resonates with Blaug (1992, 225) on another RCT exercise, that the formal techniques produced 'almost empty conclusions that are presented as being more dramatic than they really are.' More generally, there is resonance also with the claim that RCT possesses mainly 'the predictive accuracy of common sense' (Rosenberg, 1992, 134). The intellectual acclamation accorded to RCT within academic economics appears to be an instance of the claim that 'judgements of the quality of theoretical ideas are highly context-dependent' (Rule, 1997, 97).

Examples From Game Theory

A flourishing subset of RCT is game theory (GT), 'rampant in economics' (Gibbons, 1997, 127), perhaps 'the premier fashionable tool of microtheorists' (Fisher, 1989, 113), and often claimed by its proponents as 'an opportunity to unify the social sciences' (Hargreaves Heap and Varoufakis, 1995, flyleaf). The GT literature reveals an overwhelming emphasis on formal, abstract, mathematical constructions dwarfing their empirical real-world application. This occurs from the level of undergraduate teaching to new journal and book contributions, and has characterized the field since its regrowth in economics from the early 1980s. For instance, in the book compilations of Shubik (1983), Rubinstein (1990), Gabszewicz et al. (1990), Friedman (1990), Fudenberg and Tirole (1991), Myerson (1991), Dutta et al. (1992), Aumann and Hart (1992), Norman and La Manna (1992), Eichberger (1993), Hargreaves Heap and Varoufakis (1995), and Hart and Neyman (1995), barely any pages examine how formal propositions relate to empirical real-world data. Rarely is any individual mathematical element given observational substance. Where empirical exploration is made outside experimental environments, it is invariably in descriptive verbal form without reference to the formal, abstract, mathematical elements that nearly monopolize each book. The mathematical constructions are neither mentioned nor necessary for any real-world empirical discussion that does occur in the books.

For example, consider a section entitled 'gender, class and functionalism' in Hargreaves Heap and Varoufakis' (1995) chapter on evolutionary games. This section follows twenty-six pages in the chapter devoted to the formal exposition of evolutionary games. Nearly one-third of the section consists of a one-page verbal summary box, from a book by another author on 'who gets the best jobs in West Virginia?' There is no discussion of information in the box, except for a statement that it constitutes an example that seems to fit the model exactly. In addition, some interesting verbal observations are made in the section (unrelated to the box) about the relation between class and gender/racial stratification. These would be acceptable to anyone familiar with and agreeable to natural language (verbal) ideas of strategic interaction and evolution. They do not depend on the lengthy formal presentation of evolutionary games preceding the section in the chapter. Accordingly, no reference is made in the section to any of the algebraic notations in the previous twenty-six pages of the chapter. The remaining 'empirical' discussion in the chapter is a qualitative treatment of how Hume and Marx on morality might be interpreted in evolutionary game terms. Overall, the technical apparatus of the bulk of the chapter is not decisive for the empirical illustrations canvassed in the section on 'gender, class and functionalism.' Journal contributions about game theory and economics (e.g., in *Games and Economic Behavior*) have as little relevance to real-world behavior as indicated in the examples above. Other commentators on the use of GT in economics have made similar observations (e.g., Peltzman, 1991). Blaug (1992, 240), for instance, noted that 'leading textbooks,' contain not so much as one 'definite empirical prediction' but rather a 'virtually endless conceptual proliferation of the fundamental notions of rational behavior.' Blaug was disturbed that empirically testable hypotheses are not generated by GT and that it has not 'produced a single "novel fact"' (Blaug, 1994, 128). Also alarming is that most game-theoretic constructions in economics are not even related to actual data about the real world, whether already existing or collected for the purpose of illustrating the game in question (experimental economics excepted).

Where the word 'empirical' is used in GT, it invariably means descriptive of an experimental situation (e.g., Camerer, 1997), not of human behavior outside experiments. The term 'applicable' in GT does not mean applicable to real-world historical data, but applicable to hypothetical data. For instance, Friedman's (1990) *Game Theory with Applications to Economics* has no instance of actual applications of GT to real historical data but is preoccupied with invented numerical and/or algebraic data, or the relation of game theories to abstract economic models. Similarly, Gibbons' (1997) paper, 'An Introduction to Applicable Game Theory,' does not include one example of an empirically applied real-world game, but instead concentrates on well-known hypothetical games (e.g., tournaments, the 'dating' game, the 'beer and quiche' signalling game). Occasionally, prominent game theorists sympathize with this criticism but do not change their commitment to non-experimental theorizing. Thus, Rubinstein (1995, 12) accepted that 'economic theory should deal with the real world,' but he lamented that 'the link between economic theory and practical problems . . . is tenuous at best'; indeed, 'economic theory has not delivered the goods,' it has not proved 'useful in achieving practical goals.' GT *has* achieved some policy relevance in the last few years with its contribution to the design of the auction system of the radio spectrum by the US Federal Communications Commission. But at least one game theorist (Gul, 1997) suggested that it was 'not easy to figure out what the cutting-edge theory was that went into the design of the auction.' In any case, this was not the most important contribution of GT to economics in Gul's view, at least as it was practiced by the likes of Nobel-prize winners, Harsanyi, Nash, and Selten. According to Gul (1997, 172), 'their greatest effect has been through their role as leading practitioners of a formal, rigorous and abstract approach.'

This paragraph moves from general criticisms of GT to one recent paper depicting its use in economics. Unlike the books cited above, this paper actually does attempt to relate particular game theory to real-world situations. Like the RCT cases discussed above, one paper does not prove anything. However, the conclusions here about the GT paper are consistent with the critique of RCT above. Young (1996) examined the process by which conventions emerge through the accumulation of precedent. The topic is introduced generally in two pages in which no reference is made to non-RCT or non-GT literature explaining conventions or norms. For instance, one philosophical reference is cited, Lewis (1969), and one sociological, Ullman-Margalit (1977), both heavily imbued with game-theoretic formulation (no substantive discussion occurs of their content). As in the two RCT papers above, no general context is established in which the relevance to convention formation of non-game theories in or outside economics is assessed. For instance, no reference is made to Turiel (1983), nor to any social psychology literature whose standard fare includes the formation of norms and conformity (e.g., Sears, Peplau, and Taylor, 1991).

The second section of Young's (1996) paper provides a simple GT exposition of the dilemma facing two coachmen in the middle of the eighteenth century approaching each other on the same road, while the third section, 'An Evolutionary Model of Convention Formation,' explains how the coachmen's decision making can be resolved in principle via evolutionary GT (using simple ordering arithmetic). To what extent is the decision-making matrix of the evolutionary GT framework in the third section necessary to explain the real historical situation of why particular road driving sides emerged in Europe? Some pointers are given in section four of the paper, 'Rules of the Road,' explaining the historical development of rules of the road in Europe. This section provides some interesting history accounting for the development, but mostly without directly linking the historical data to the GT terms in the preceding principle section (except in relation to the French Revolution as an example of punctuated equilibrium). The historical explanation for rules of the road in section four could stand on its own. The historical data in this section are not related to any of the arithmetic or algebraic terminology in the third section on the evolutionary GT model (nor to the three schematic diagrams introduced in section four itself, again, with the French Revolution excepted). The parallel with the Hargreaves Heap and Varoufakis example above is clear.

Three verbal principles are stated in the third GT model section of the Young paper that are helpful to understanding the history of rules of the road, but they do not derive from the evolutionary model. Rather, they are assumptions that underlie the model. The principles are that decision makers act on limited information, they are boundedly rational, and their behavior shows random variation. These are common sense principles underlying human behavior that most people would probably accept. In the real-world 'Rules of the Road' fourth section of Young's paper, the influence of these principles historically is apparent. It is possible to note the principles and their influence and to present the explanation in an alternative, non-formal, non-game theoretic mode without losing any real-world empirical detail, as in historical accounts (cited by Young) such as Kincaid (1986) and Lay (1992). Such qualitative predictions as the GT model presents in Young are not empirically innovative: for example, 'that even if we know the initial state of society, we cannot predict what the prevailing convention will be at each future date' (Young, 1996, 111), that 'most of the time most of the population will be using the same convention' (p. 111), or that 'the more countries who adopt the same convention, the more likely it is that the others will follow suit' (p. 113). These predictions may be theoretically innovative in terms of the model itself, but they provide no new predictions about human behavior, and the model itself provides no new explanations about actual behavior (for example, compared with those offered by social psychology).

The Young (1996) example suggests a lack of empirical progress in the application of game theory. In the example, game theory does provide explanations for observed phenomena, but not in the sense of different or more complete explanations than those that already existed (as in the historical references mentioned above). Nor does the model offer new predictions, or, more strictly, retrodictions, in relation to previously observed data. All that the paper does is redescribe existing information and explanation using GT terminology. Some qualitative predictions about rules of the road are made (amounting to little more than common sense), they are compared only with historical data, and they have been explained elsewhere. The last section of Young's paper provides another real-world example, relating to norms in distributive bargaining. Similar comments could be made about this illustration as for the rules of the road above.

We can see why some economics critics of rational choice and game theory have resorted to parody and caricature, purporting to explain sleeping, brushing teeth, and the behavior of fish (e.g., Boulier and Goldfarb, 1991). RCT and GT may be doing no more than producing simplistic, trivial, and commonplace theoretical and empirical conclusions about real-world behavior that have long been observed and theorized. Many of the conclusions from RCT and GT seem to be little more than common knowledge, in which the great (?) (mathematical) achievement of RCT and GT has been to formalize this knowledge. Small wonder that most of the emphasis in RCT and GT is on mathematical ingenuity.

Most of the GT references cited above before the Young example did not relate to real-world data. In these, GT is not exhibiting empirical progress or all the hallmarks of theoretical progress. Unrelated to existing empirical information, game theory may be marked by increasing precision, rigor, consistency, and simplicity within its mathematical formulations (regardless of how these qualities might be defined). But it is not characterized by increasing generality or scope, insofar as these relate to empirical situations. As noted above about the Backhouse-type view, theoretical progress requires theory increasingly to explain real-world behavior rather than hypothetical behavior (or even experimental behavior). Given this view of theoretical progress, a similar qualification about GT's theoretical progress could be directed to other aspects of economic theory. For example, Hahn (1984, 136), defended the Arrow-Debreu formulations on the grounds that they 'show what the world would have to look like if the claim [of the 'invisible hand' theorem] is to be true.' On this view, the Arrow-Debreu theorems do not predict or explain what is going on in the real world, except in the indirect sense of looking at the real world and comparing this with the theoretical formulation. Whether looking at the real world and discovering imperfections in the operation of the 'invisible hand' adds greatly to Adam Smith's observations is moot.

The criticism of the lack of empirical and theoretical progress of GT is separate from but related to internal problems in the theoretical construction of the games themselves. So extensive are these difficulties, according to Rivzi (1994, 1) that 'game theory has dissolved into a welter of special theories and subcases . . . and do not have the force of a general approach to economic problems.' In this case, too, increased generality and scope are not being achieved. Theoretical difficulties are widely conceded by game theorists themselves, but they do not, in their view, vitiate the potential value of game theory for understanding real-world behavior. Widely recognized problems include uncertain justification for the reliance on Nash equilibrium in game theory, the impossibility of defining all modes of rational behavior in unambiguous mathematical logical terms, the alleged lack of solution to games involving mixed strategies, and the alleged arbitrariness of solutions to repeated games (Rivzi, 1994, 6–24). As a subset of rational choice theory, game theoretical constructions can be made to predict A and non-A by changing elements such as the order of play, the number of players, or the discount rate used. System outcomes then become arbitrary, rather than being illustrations of distortions in application. Thus, whether formal GT models have enhanced what was already known about theoretical strategic interaction between economic agents continues to be contested. In Fisher's view (1989, 115), for example, 'years of intensive application of game theory' added little to what was already known about the theoretical manner in which oligopolists might react to each other, which opinion was challenged by Shapiro (1989). The criticisms of internal theoretical problems in GT are separate from whether it is increasing in general the elucidation of real-world behavior, despite instances of GT's empirical and policy relevance outside and inside experimental environments (e.g., McAfee and McMillan, 1997; Roth and Sotomayor, 1992).

RATIONAL CHOICE AND GAME THEORY USE OUTSIDE ACADEMIC ECONOMICS

If the above limitations of RCT (including GT) are valid, the theoretical family is unlikely to be greatly used for practical economic policy formulation. This possibility is part of a much older story not explored here. The relation of economic theory in general to practical problem solving has long been an issue fraught with contention. One line of thought has denied a close connection (e.g., Meehan, 1982), exemplified in Blaug's contention (1997, 2) that 'time and time again, economists have recommended diametrically opposed policies while appealing to the same theory for authority.' The problem might not just be a characteristic of contemporary economic theory, RCT or whatever. Nevertheless, an implication of the discussion in the section above is doubt that RCT and GT in general are demonstrating a practical policy problem solving nexus.

Rational choice theory, or the economic approach to human behavior, including its GT variant, has spread from economics to develop an important following in political science, less in sociology, and perhaps even less in other social sciences. Controversy persists in political science, for example, about the theoretical substance and empirical relevance of the approach (e.g., Hauptmann, 1996). Green and Shapiro (1994, x) attempted a comprehensive evaluation of the relevance of RCT to politics, posing the question 'what has been learned about politics' from its use. From looking at a large selection of RCT exercises, they 'gradually came to the view that exceedingly little has been learned'; rational choice theory has not made 'substantial empirical contributions to the study of politics' (p. 10). Needless to say, their conclusions have been challenged (e.g., Johnson, 1996).

Many of Green and Shapiro's observations parallel those made above about RCT in economics (and in sociology overall e.g., Sciulli, 1992; Archer and Tritter, 2000, and in the sociology of religion e.g., Bruce, 1999). For instance, RCT predictions about political behavior had conformed with empirical situations, but 'a good many of these claims might be compatible with arguments that have been made . . . in the past' (p. 10), although Green and Shapiro did not investigate this claim. This can be related to their contention that little attention had been given to showing that RCT explained 'more than do existing or rival theories' (p. 183), that rarely had an RC 'theoretical formulation' been gauged 'against that of alternative explanatory accounts' (p. 38), although again Green and Shapiro did not investigate the latter. Empirical conclusions of RCT exercises had often been 'banal: they do little more than restate existing knowledge in rational choice terminology' (p. 6), amounting to mere redescription of the processes by which previously known outcomes obtain. Green and Shapiro held that RCT had demonstrated few novel or counterintuitive empirical facts, that it consisted mainly of *post hoc* accounts of known data (p. 34), with emphasis directed to 'restating known facts in their preferred theoretical terms' (p. 183). In addition, Green and Shapiro (1994, 6) suggested that RC theorists have been preoccupied with devising formal (mathematical) models of political behavior than with examining their relevance to empirical situations; that its proponents 'seem to be most interested in theory elaboration' (p. x). They accepted 'that theoretical models of immense and increasing sophistication have been produced by practitioners of rational choice theory,' but, in their view, 'the case has yet to be made that these models have advanced our understanding of how politics works in the real world' (p. 6). In GT formulations of RCT in politics, for example, the focus had been on demonstrating formal theorems about what particular definitions of rationality might entail, while empirical relevance was downplayed.

The criticisms in the three subsections above undermine the likelihood that the family of RCT has been characterized by theoretical and empirical progress. For a discipline like economics that seeks to explain social choices, this undermining is increased. RCT does not explain the formation of socio-cultural structures that help mould individual choice; it does not explain the formation of individual preferences. As Rosenberg (1992, 119) put it, microeconomics 'has nothing to say about the causes of choice, owing to the exogenousness of preferences.' RCT may tell us 'how people cope with the choices available to them,' (Rule, 1997, 95), but the terms of individual response and choice are influenced by socio-historical constraints. An individual agent strategic calculation undoubtedly has to be made, but underlying this calculus is likely to be historical circumstances, tradition, norms, culture, and differing aspects of people's abilities. Kincaid (1996) criticized RCT because the methodological individualism on which it allegedly rests presupposes social influences on individual choice. Whether this criticism is decisive to RCT is uncertain, because some proponents of RCT (e.g., Satz and Ferejohn, 1994) claim it functions most appropriately as an explanation of social choices.

CONCLUSION

Theoretical progress is taken in the Backhouse-type view to include an increasing relation of theory to empirical data, as well as to characterize constructional characteristics of the theory itself (e.g., increasing simplicity, rigor). Given the doubts on the empirical relevance criterion explored above for rational choice and game theory (redescription rather than new explanation, and lack of application to real-world data), it is questionable whether these areas of economic theory are exhibiting this understanding of theoretical progress. Related observations have been made elsewhere. For instance, Backhouse (1997, 24) claimed that 'it is hard to defend [general equilibrium theory] against the charge that it has no empirical content,' adding dryly 'that similar charges have been made against game theory.' Whether such comments can apply to the entire contemporary project of mainstream economic theory has not been explored here. Defenders of the mainstream, such as Backhouse, do not go this far, suggesting that over the long term 'there would appear to have been significant theoretical progress' (1997, 206). Nevertheless, Backhouse admits that in becoming committed to 'theories based on individual agents making choices on the basis of their beliefs and preferences,' like RCT, economic theory has become difficult to test empirically (1997, 208). Indeed, it may be that the term 'economic theory' is redefining itself. 'Theory' is no longer seen as propositions purporting to describe, explain, or predict the real world. It is becoming schemata describing how the real world might look if people behaved in the way the theory suggested. Economic theories describing how people actually behave are less common.

If the theories of mainstream economics are increasingly taking this form (proposed by e.g., Beed and Kane, 1991; Lawson, 1997), they may not be providing a fertile ground for empirical progress on Backhouse-type lines. As outlined above, empirical progress denotes increase in the number and quality of empirical generalizations, in predictive success, particularly of novel facts, and in problem-solving facility. These are not the same things as intellectual innovation (cf. Deutsch et al., 1986). Nevertheless, it is possible to point to innovations in academic economics in the past, some of which have proven to be of practical application. National income accounting might be an example, where the innovations derived from the interplay of technique and theory. This might well have constituted empirical progress. Other areas of academic economics might also have achieved theoretical and empirical progress. For example, Leontief (1971) implied agricultural economics as characterized by progress, but he did not explore the issue. Backhouse (1997, 213–214) put financial and industrial economics into a similar category, but it is questionable how far some of the progress criteria apply (e.g., predictive success, especially of novel facts; problem solving), especially in industrial economics, which is now nearly monopolized by game theory. Financial economics is proving to be a fruitful ground for econometrics given the plethora of data. But its theories suffer from predictive limitations; for example, in their inability to deal with market failure, including the (quasi-legal) manipulation of financial markets by private operators that might well be as important as legitimate market transactions, as well as more outright corruption. No theories in financial economics predicted the recent Asian crisis, and none has provided satisfactory explanations of it—for instance, in accounting for the sources of crossmarket contagion. Nor are any of the examples in Boehm et al. (2002) able to point to empirical or theoretical progress in the sense specified by Backhouse (1997).

Our critique has been oriented mainly to the novelty of explanation of rational choice and game theories (they do not enhance already existing explanation), to whether they are providing increased real-world empirical application (not for game theory) and prediction previously unknown (they are not), and to whether they exhibit enhanced practical policy-solving ability (they do not). These conclusions are based on the examples we discuss. Another paper by one of us draws analogous conclusions in the application of rational choice theory to Biblical analysis (Beed, 2005f). Although mainstream academic microeconomics is almost totally dominated by rational choice and game theory, the magnitude of such research does not necessarily convey intellectual progress. Rule (1997, 200), for instance, was 'skeptical about the idea that the sheer extent of communication of theoretical ideas is indicative of greater enlightenment.' Mainstream academic economics currently prizes the magnitude and frequency of citation of its work as an indicator of intellectual achievement. This is an erroneous indicator of the quality of intellectual work (Beed and Beed, 1996c), and with this mistaken belief, orthodox economics is not necessarily achieving theoretical or empirical progress.

Chapter Thirteen

A Christian Response to Naturalistic Social Science

The five previous chapters argued that secular social science, illustrated mainly by current practice in mainstream orthodox academic economics, is so shot through with problems that it cannot adequately describe, explain or prescribe for human socio-economic behavior. The problems were outlined within the secular framework in which social science functions today. Although orthodox economics, for instance, lays claim to a naturalistic and scientific framework, the argument was that economics is not able to practice the framework it assumes or to show in its theorizing anything greatly revealing about the real world from trying to do so. This contributes to the general air of incoherence and irrelevance affecting the theory and application of economics. Economics asserts itself as 'science' but has exposed little in the way of enduring relationships between phenomena that might be used for practical policy purposes, such as have been revealed in physical science. Whatever academic economics has discovered seems to be little more informative than comparable discoveries in other social sciences, and many of these are long-known common sense folk psychology, but dressed up by mainstream economics in abstruse verbal or mathematical language. Early chapters had introduced a Christian response to the problems confronting social science, especially economics, before the specific problems affecting the discipline had been outlined in subsequent chapters. This chapter (Beed and Beed, 2004b) returns to the theme of a Christian response, and makes a specifically Christian rebuttal to one of the issues—the claims of social science to disclose reality by naturalistic means.

At the beginning of this book, we noted that the relation of Christian belief to social science is little investigated today. This is a curious hiatus because social science developed from the eighteenth to the early twentieth centuries partly in sympathetic relation to Christian belief. Increasingly, however, social science offered an alternative and even contradictory mode of explanation for human behavior from that provided by Christianity. In the last fifty years, attempts have been made to deal seriously with both revelatory texts and social science, a notable example being Leo Strauss who contrasted both to his own alternative of a revived classical political philosophy. Eric Voegelin is another case, accusing modern social science of gnosticism, from a Christian perspective (Emberley and Cooper, 1993). Other commentators have made Christian evaluations of figures in the history of social science (an example is Midgley's Thomist critique of Weber). More recent Christian assessments of aspects of social science are Lakeland (1990), Milbank (1990), Gill (1996) and Long (2000). Theology, however, has still comprehensively to address contemporary social science. As Milbank (1990, 3) put it, theologians have yet to be persuaded 'to acknowledge theoretical developments [in social science] which they have woefully ignored.' This chapter takes a different tack from the above Christian analyses in exploring how the orthodox Christian perspective outlined in early chapters might respond to naturalistic claims made for contemporary social science. One specific aspect of the Christian response is considered in each main section of this chapter: (i) the Christian rejoinder to the naturalistic/non-naturalistic dichotomy that characterizes contemporary social science, (ii) the role attributed to science and scientific methods in the Christian reply, and (iii) its relation to the normative stance that has often underlain social science historically. A more complete methodology of how the Christian perspective might analyze socio-economic phenomena is outlined in the next and concluding chapter.

To draw the argument closer to contemporary debate in social science and to provide a focus, the Christian response of this chapter is oriented to the important defense of naturalistic social science by Kincaid (1996), a name familiar from previous chapters. Two viewpoints are thus emphasized here—the Christian and Kincaid's naturalistic one—each an exemplar of particular paradigmatic positions concerning human social behavior (which is not to assume that other viewpoints do not exist). The demonstration here is of disparities between the Christian perspective toward socio-economic analysis developed in this book, and naturalistic social science as Kincaid conceives it. Taking a prominent social science text (Kincaid, 1996) and comparing it with Christian belief as it relates to socio-economic analysis seems an intellectually legitimate starting point from which to clarify elements of the difference as it exists today. Focusing on one influential book (Kincaid's) is likely to produce a clearer exposure of the distinctions than if the Christian response was made to a range of positions current in social science. This latter approach could become confusing, for any comparison between Christianity and social science would then have to take account of philosophical and methodological disagreement presently existing within social science itself.

Kincaid's viewpoint about how social science should proceed raises philosophical issues central to the Christian position advocated here. Overall, the Christian viewpoint is shown to differ diametrically from Kincaid's; for example, it denies the possibility of 'a science of society' as he conceives it. In so far as Kincaid represents an influential standpoint toward social science, especially as far as orthodox economics is concerned, this chapter implies a critique of his position from the Christian perspective of this book. Kincaid (1996, 2) intended to 'survey the general threats that confront any argument for a science of society.' As is standard practice in social science, he did not consider the threat posed by a Christian retort. We show what the Christian response aspires to philosophically, and why it does not seek Kincaid's aim (1996, 6) of 'a real social science [that] would provide us with laws, predictions, and understanding of large-scale social structure,' useful for practical policy making.

A CHRISTIAN RESPONSE TO NATURALISTIC SOCIAL SCIENCE

A philosophical view held by the Christian perspective developed in this book is that science and its practice rest on more fundamental metaphysical conceptions of the constitution of the world. This disputed proposition is examined in the next section. As previous chapters suggested, one common metaphysical conception of the world is naturalism, the belief that the natural world is all that exists. Humans are viewed as part of and dependent solely on the natural world, not different in kind from the rest of it; 'there is no sharp distinction between different kinds of organism reacting to their environment' (Trigg, 1993, 87). Naturalism is taken often to include the propositions that human minds have no existence apart from the brain, that supernatural beings or minds do not exist, and that scientific methods are the only valid means of discovering reality (e.g., Bhaskar, 1994, 373, 412; Trigg, 1993, 81, 88; 1998, 73). Some Christians define naturalism as the view that 'nature is a permanently closed system of material causes and effects that can never be influenced by anything outside of itself.' In this conception of naturalism, the reality of physical particles and impersonal laws, including those characterizing the human mind, are most reliably discoverable by scientific methods (Johnson, 1995, 38, 197).

Naturalism is not a uniformly defined philosophical position, and argument persists about its content. As Papineau (1993, 1) points out, 'there is little consensus on its meaning,' for it has characteristics relating both to the alleged nature of reality and to the means by which this reality might be ascertained. This distinction is sometimes classed as that between metaphysical or ontological naturalism, and methodological or epistemological naturalism. Table 13.1 below is an incomplete list of often identified ontological and epistemological features of naturalism, derived from Papineau, 1993; Wagner and Warner, 1993; French, Uehling and Wettstein, 1994; Drees, 1996; Kincaid, 1996; and Rosenberg, 1996. The list is non-exhaustive because further items could be added to unpack a consensus on naturalism, such as its relation to the theory-laden nature of observation (itself inherent to Christian belief). The sources cited above cover the range from agreement to disagreement with naturalism. Each item in the table is a quotation (or paraphrase) from one of the six sources that expresses, as far as possible, the consensus of them all. The table is a compromised compilation, for none of its sources accept all eight characteristics, although the first six items probably command greater agreement than the last two. Given the range of cover of the items, some could be interpreted as contradicting others, such as numbers 3 and 4 with 7 and 8. Potential contradictions are not pursued here.

There is not space here to demonstrate that Christian belief contradicts many items in the table. It has been argued (Alston, 1996) that item 6 does not conform to Christian doctrine, and that realism in social science does not depend on naturalism. Indeed, Christian belief, despite its supernatural basis, can appropriately be viewed as a form of realism (Trigg, 1998; Beed and Beed, 1997; McGrath, 2002 argue for the compatibility of theology with critical realism). However, Christian thought is not identified uniformly with realism, and, for instance, non-realist philosopher Christians exist (e.g., Rescher, Van Fraassen).

Table 13.1. Characteristics of Naturalism

1. 'The natural world is the whole of reality that we know of and interact with' (Drees, 1996, 12).
2. No 'supernatural or spiritual realm distinct from the natural world shows up *within* our natural world, not even in the mental life of humans' (Drees, 1996, 12; original emphasis).
3. 'The natural sciences (plus the logic and mathematics needed by them) constitute the simplest comprehensive theory that explains all, or most, of a person's experiences and/or observations' (Bealer, 1993, 163).
4. The sciences . . . are to be the guide to epistemology and metaphysics' = 'scientism—the central thesis of naturalism' (Rosenberg, 1996, 4, 10).
5. 'Darwinian theory is . . . the guide to philosophical theory'; 'the centrality of Darwinian theory to naturalism' (Rosenberg, 1996, 4, 22).
6. Naturalism is the basis for realism (Rosenberg, 1996, 5).
7. 'Epistemology is not to be treated as a propaedeutic to the acquisition of further knowledge' (Rosenberg, 1996, 4).
8. 'The description and explanation of phenomena may require concepts which do not belong to the vocabulary of fundamental physics' (Drees, 196, 16).

Sources: Papineau, 1993; Wagner and Warner, 1993; French, Uehling and Wettstein, 1994; Drees, 1996; Kincaid, 1996; Rosenberg, 1996.

More comprehensive Christian critiques of naturalism related to philosophy and physical science are Craig and Moreland (2000) and McGrath (2001).

The emphasis here is how naturalism relates to socio-economic phenomena. Consider items 1 and 2 in Table 13.1. The claim that the natural world is the whole of reality with which humans interact does not conform to basic tenets of Christian belief. Since Scripture is the core source of orthodox Christian belief, it can be quoted to substantiate this contention. Thus, the New Testament maintains that the supernatural spirit(s) of God, Jesus Christ and the Holy Spirit constitute part of the reality with which people can interact. These supernatural spirits are depicted as capable of influencing 'mental life' (item 2) within the natural world, if 'mental life' means activity within the human brain. Numerous New (and Old) Testament texts from the Bible can be cited to substantiate these contentions. For example, in the first two chapters of the first book of the New Testament, five cases are apparent (Mt. 1:20–21; 2:12; 2:13; 2:19–20; 2:22) where supernatural spirits (e.g., 'an angel of the Lord') 'interact[s] with' and 'show[s] up *within* . . . the mental life of humans.' These particular instances were of paramount importance to safeguarding Jesus' mission in the world. Analogous examples abound in the four New Testament gospels, and occur frequently in the later writings of the apostles (e.g., Acts 1:11; 2:4; Rev. 1:10ff.).

In the Christian perspective under scrutiny, people are taken to be part of the natural world, but different in kind from the rest of it. Although part of the natural world, humans are influenced also by an unobservable supernatural spirit-filled world, whether people are conscious of it or not. In this sense, people are part also of the supernatural world. God, in His trinitarian conception, is the main moving force in the supernatural world. However, other spirits also exist in this world, especially an influence of evil, sometimes called the devil. The Christian worldview holds that human action at the individual level, that can then aggregate into and impact on the social level, is influenced by these supernatural forces, as well as by natural factors. Spiritual influences impact on mental states. Many Biblical references can be cited (e.g., Jn. 14:16–17; 14:26; 15:5; 15:16; 16:13) to sustain this feature as constituting a foundational belief of Christianity that contradicts naturalism. On this and many other grounds, a common Christian perspective is that Christian belief is incompatible with naturalism (e.g., Feinberg, 2001, 90–91, 104–106). This incompatibility is highlighted in Rosenberg (2000, 153), for instance, that naturalistic science has no place for an omnipotent designer. If mental states also are regarded as part of the natural world, the Christian perspective is incompatible with physicalism, a close relation of naturalism, 'the thesis that all natural phenomena are . . . physical' (Papineau, 1993, 1).

One of the features of social science/naturalism is its commitment to descriptive and explanatory methods adapted from the natural sciences, otherwise known as methodological or epistemological naturalism (e.g., Rosenberg, 1995, 24). This aspect of naturalism is uppermost to Kincaid (1996, xv) who propounds that 'social phenomena are part of the natural world and accordingly amenable to the methods of the natural sciences.' The Christian worldview does not accept what might be some unstated presumptions in this statement. As noted above in its view, social phenomena are not *all* part of the natural world because God and other spiritual forces influence these phenomena. If 'the methods of the natural sciences' apply purely to 'the natural world,' the Christian outlook cannot accept that 'human society, as part of the natural world, can be understood by the general methods of the natural sciences' (Kincaid, 1996, 1). Only in part degree can human society be so understood. In so far as people are not able to know which part of any social phenomenon relates solely to the natural world, and which relates to the supernatural, social phenomena in their entirety are not 'amenable to the methods of the natural sciences.' Features making up the background normative worldview of Christianity are taken to influence human social behavior. This consideration is distinct from the secular non-naturalistic critique of naturalistic methods for describing and explaining human behavior (e.g., Fay, 1984; Benton and Craib, 2001).

Neither does Christian belief accept that humans individually are solely 'part of the natural order.' In part they are, but they are part also of the supernatural world. Humans are designed to function within the normative constraints of the God-given worldview, even though people have free will to do otherwise. Only a portion of individual and social human behavior, therefore, is 'amenable to scientific understanding' (Kincaid, 1996, 1), if 'scientific understanding' means a (naturalistic) understanding exercised outside the bounds of the assumed influences operating in the Christian worldview. In this worldview, there is no guarantee that scientific naturalistic explanation necessarily yields conclusions nearer to the explicatory truth of human action than the supernatural part. This is separate from the problem that the nature of 'scientific understanding,' applied to both physical and social science, has been recognized for the last forty years or so to be more problematic than thought previously (e.g., for physical science, Chalmers, 1999a; for social science, Flyvbjerg, 2001).

The Christian perspective, therefore, posits *a priori* conceptual arguments that naturalism in social science does not necessarily constitute 'our best chance at limning the true structure of reality' (Kincaid, 1996, 5). Conceptual arguments that naturalistic social science is impossible in principle are not accepted by Kincaid (1996, 3, 4). Perhaps he would not hold the Christian objections to constitute intellectual arguments. The assertion here is that they are within the confines of the Christian metaphysical worldview. Counter assertions can be made only within the confines of an alternate worldview, and for Kincaid, this is a naturalistic one. In part, Kincaid (1996, 4) rejects conceptual arguments against naturalistic social science because his standard of measurement or criterion for assessing social science is 'based on what we know about social scientific practice as it exists now and its likely permutations'. Whether naturalistic or non-naturalistic, this practice is predominantly non-Christian based. Christian-based arguments against a purely naturalistic science of social phenomena are ignored in contemporary social science literature. Kincaid (1996, 4) does not accept that naturalism, which he equates with 'the scientific world view,' would be so 'radically incomplete' as to suffer from the omission that 'naturalistic methods cannot explain society'; this would be 'a surprising conclusion.' The next section of this chapter argues that a Christian assessment does not find this conclusion surprising because it does not equate naturalism with science, and it does not accept science as the only path to truth.

As we saw in previous chapters, within the disciplines that collectively came to be labeled as social science from the late eighteenth century (McDonald, 1993; Olson, 1993), two well-known polarities emerged in the investigation of human behavior. The naturalistic polarity was exemplified by those such as Comte and Spencer seeking to apply methods from the physical sciences, and was epitomized in efforts to devise a positivistic analysis of human action. The non-naturalistic polarity was represented in the diverse tendencies of those who rejected this approach, such as Vico and Dilthey, but among whom little other unity existed. Probably, most social scientists have lain always, and continue to lie, on a continuum between these two polarities, and to practice varying degrees of mix between the two extremes. However, the relation of Christian belief to either view in social science has been little considered historically (even in the writings of early Christian social scientists who were more concerned with the practical application of Christian beliefs), and is less contemplated today, probably because Christianity is held to be irrelevant superstition by most social scientists.

One of the main thrusts of Kincaid (1996) is to reassert the supremacy of naturalistic socio-economic analysis. From about the 1960s, this form of analysis has been under attack, after having held sway from the nineteenth century. Non-naturalistic social science (e.g., constructivism, postmodernism) gathered influence with the demise of positivism, and in some areas, such as sociology, even threatens the continuing existence of naturalistic approaches. One example of non-naturalistic modes in sociology and economics is 'the interpretivist or hermeneutical tradition [which] denies that we can understand human behavior in terms of laws, causes, and predictions' (Kincaid, 1996, 8). If this is a hallmark of interpretive social analysis, it is surprising that Kincaid (1996, 13) admits that 'good interpretive social science is possible in practice.'

It is not clear whether Kincaid thinks that good non-naturalistic social science is as possible as its contrary naturalistic counterpart. If this *is* so, it undermines his case for the superiority of naturalism, and admits the relevance of non-naturalistic approaches, of which the Christian stance is one example.

Although Christian thought is constructed within a non-naturalistic framework, it *is* concerned with exploring causes of human behavior, as argued in Chapters 2–4. But, its explanation for human action is presented always in relation to the Judeo-Christian worldview (some Biblical examples are Lk. 1:1–23; 1:57–66; 5:18–26). This worldview engenders skepticism that laws or 'well-confirmed causal generalizations' (Kincaid, 1996, 58) derived purely from a naturalistic framework can have a conjunction of sufficiently wide domain applicability, precision and predictive accuracy to serve as a basis for policy decisions. Some of the reasons for this conclusion overlap the contemporary secular critique of social science prediction (e.g., Little, 1991, 1993) examined in earlier chapters, but specifically Christian reasons also exist. These are that since Christian belief holds the spiritual and material domains of human life to be inseparably interrelated, explanation and prediction of social human action based on the material domain alone can have only a low degree of empirical validity. This material/spiritual interconnection is not relevant in the same degree to the objects of interest to natural science (given the unique spiritual nature of humans in Christian belief) where explanation and prediction have higher empirical reliability.

In summary, the argument above contests Kincaid's view that the methodology of the natural sciences (methodological naturalism) is the sole key to understanding personal or social life. This is partly because Christian understanding does not accept key precepts of metaphysical or ontological naturalism, such as items 1 and 2 of 13.1. In this understanding, there is another part of reality beyond the natural world (a transcendent or supernatural domain) with which people interact, whether they are conscious of it or not. This interaction weakens the purchase with which natural science methods (understood as methodological naturalism) can ascertain the entire range of influences on personal and social life, for 'methodology is ultimately dependent upon ontology' (McGrath, 2002, 118). That is, the Christian viewpoint also challenges sole reliance on methodological naturalism. It would contest relevant items of Table 13.1, such as numbers 3 and 4, expressed by Kincaid above that 'human society, as part of the natural world, can be understood by the general methods of the natural sciences,' and that 'good social science must follow the standards of the natural sciences' (Kincaid, 1996, 1, 4). Only in part might these standards be relevant to explaining social phenomena. Table 13.2 summarizes differences thus far discussed between the Christian perspective for describing and explaining social phenomena, and Kincaid's (1996).

Table 13.2. Socio-economic Phenomena and Their Relation to Naturalism

Christian	*Kincaid*
1. Socio-economic phenomena derive from the natural and supernatural worlds, and are part of this reality.	1. Socio-economic phenomena are 'part of the natural world.'
2. These phenomena are only partly amenable to naturalistic (i.e., scientific) methods.	2. 'Amenable to the methods of the natural sciences'; 'can be understood by the general methods of the natural sciences.'
3. Scientific (naturalistic) methods only partly enable human behavior to be understood.	3. Scientific (naturalistic) methods enable humans, as part of the natural order, to be understood.
4. Postulates *a priori* arguments against understanding human behavior solely by naturalistic methods.	4. Rejects *a priori* arguments against understanding human behavior by naturalistic methods.
5. Current social science practice cannot be regarded as the assessment criterion for socio-economic analysis.	5. Current social science practice (and its likely permutations) is the assessment criterion.
6. Non-naturalistic, secular socio-economic analysis does not accept item 1 above.	6. Non-naturalistic e.g., interpretive, secular social science does not accept items 1–4 above.
7. Both non-naturalistic and naturalistic secular socio-economic analysis can help reveal reality.	7. 'Good interpretive social science is possible . . .'.

Source: Text above and Kincaid (1996)

CHRISTIAN BELIEF AND THE DEVELOPMENT OF PHYSICAL AND SOCIAL SCIENCE

This section suggests that even though the Christian response rebuts ontological, and a sole reliance on methodological, naturalism, it is compatible with science, but that science is not the only source of Christian knowledge about the social world. First, historical connections between Christian belief and the development of physical science are traversed briefly, then the case put that this differed from historical links between Christianity and the development of social science. After this, the basis of both physical and social science is discussed, and the argument made that non-naturalistic Christian belief rests on metaphysical principles conducive to physical science and socio-economic investigation. These latter arguments are contrasted with Kincaid's view of science. The main conclusions from this section overall are that science (physical and social) rests on a metaphysical base, and that philosophical and theological speculation can be independent sources of social (and personal) knowledge distinct from science. Further, the project of science (physical and social) involves the input of values and judgement. These conclusions flow from a Christian worldview, but they are not unique to it in all these matters.

Aside from the creation story of Genesis, little emphasis persists in the Bible on anything resembling physical science, such as description or explanation of natural phenomena. This is not surprising for the Bible is more interested in explaining, and providing norms of, human behavior in relation to the Hebrew God. Nevertheless, an underlying metaphysical tenet of Old Testament Biblical belief, predating recorded Greek philosophy, is that the natural and social worlds are discoverable and explicable. Ancient Greek and Islamic philosophers/scientists can be regarded as the originators of Western science, and the intertwining of Greek philosophy and Christian belief from the first century AD has been identified often by non-Christians as favorable to scientific advance (e.g., Davies, 1992; Singer, 1993). Indeed, a case has long been proposed (e.g., from at least Whitehead, 1926, through Foster, 1934, to Pearcey and Thaxton, 1994) that the Christian worldview was sympathetic to the development of modern Western science (i.e., post-Scientific Revolution); that Christian beliefs, as distinct from the establishment church, were a facilitator, or, at least provided an important encouraging background (e.g., Trigg, 1993, 232).

There is no contradiction between the observations that the Christian worldview is non-naturalistic, but that this worldview encouraged the pursuit of science. It is uncontroversial that the development of modern post-Scientific Revolution Western science depended on a philosophical framework, perhaps the intermixture of rediscovered Greek philosophy/science from the twelfth century, and Christian belief, encouraging investigation of the natural world. That Christian belief provided a significant impetus is accepted widely by non-Christians in different degree (e.g., Gay, 1975; Funkenstein, 1986). Although the contribution of Christianity should not be overstated, a standard Christian view is that 'the relationship between faith and science can best be described as an alliance' from the sixteenth to the nineteenth century (Pearcey and Thaxton, 1994, 19), that 'the case for the historical contribution of Christianity to the rise of science is convincing' (Barbour, 1990, 17). As Barbour points out (1997, 29), the importance of the Western religious tradition 'in moulding assumptions about nature that were congenial to the scientific enterprise' has been noted by many historians of science. Even the traditional interpretation of the inquisition of Galileo as a 'fundamental clash of values between science and religion' (Feldhay, 1995, 4) has been abandoned for over forty years. Galileo's trials are regarded now more as struggles between competing theological and philosophical systems within the Catholic church—between Jesuit and Dominican theology, between the revival of Aristotelianism (to counter Protestantism) and the newly emerging Copernican mechanistic worldview, etc. (Kearney, 1971, 148). From the late seventeenth century, the divided 'official' Christianity of the establishment church did not constitute a bulwark against the development of natural science. Only from the late nineteenth century did the Darwinian schism between official theology and science change this relationship. The extent to which this was (and is) a philosophical rather than a scientific cleavage is still debated (Addinall, 1991). In the first section of this chapter, our Christian perspective interpreted it as a metaphysical disjuncture, rejecting naturalism as a precondition for scientific investigation; 'there is nothing in the nature of science that requires legitimate empirical research to be based on dogmatic adherence to metaphysical naturalism' (Johnson, 1995, 190).

The development of *social* science from around the eighteenth century had a different genesis. Prior to this time, Christianity via the establishment church served as the official learned explicator and model for human behavior and relationships. Little formal toleration was extended even to Christians who did not support the authorized line, even though non-Christian thought existed about social issues (McDonald, 1993). That officially sanctioned explanations and social norms derived little from the Biblical text independently of its interpretation via Greek philosophy was ignored by the church hierarchy that zealously sought to preserve its privileged access to Biblical understanding, knowledge and power. The Scientific Revolution, the Reformation, the resulting Wars of Religion, the Enlightenment, and the Age of Revolutions brought this monopoly unstuck (e.g., Gay, 1975; Kearney, 1971; McGrath, 1997). The beliefs and practices of the Christian churches were wrongly conflated with Biblical teaching, the baby was thrown out with the bath water, and the prodigiously successful methods of the natural sciences were coveted as the best way to understand and control human action for good. Given centuries of religious conflict, it was not surprising that secular rationalists sought 'to extend the scientific method to all human problems as the common rationality capable of bringing unity to diversity' (Johnson, 1995, 200). One of the post-Enlightenment benefits to Christian belief was that Biblical scholarship was freed from the shackles of the established church. But one of the costs was that this scholarship became marginalized increasingly from an accelerating stream in non- and anti-Christian secular social thought (Avis, 1995).

Increasingly, the social sciences developed *alternative* explanations for human behavior and relationships from those depicted by Christian belief. As noted earlier, from the seventeenth century, an 'aggressively secular character' pervaded social-scientific thought (Olson, 1993, 11), and later prominent naturalistic and non-naturalistic social theorists often were harshly anti-Christian (Avis, 1995), although less prominent Christian social scientists had important but declining influence. Social science, first so called in the early nineteenth century, was helped take shape out of debate with Christianity. Some later nineteenth and early twentieth century social scientists were committed Christians trying to relate their beliefs to social action (e.g., their influence in economics is documented by Nelson, 1991 and Ross, 1991, and in American sociology by Vidich and Lyman, 1985), and for brief periods the social gospel movement made its mark (e.g., in US around 1870–1920). By the mid-twentieth century, however, non-Christian ideas had triumphed in social science whose Christian vestiges had become secularized. With the exception, at least until the 1960s, of minority non-naturalistic modes of analyzing human action (such as hermeneutics and other forms of postmodernism that are also mainly non- and anti-Christian), naturalistic approaches to analyzing human behavior triumphed by the latter part of the twentieth century, especially in orthodox economics. Despite the demise of positivism, the effects of this legacy persist. By the latter twentieth century, the study of Christian belief, and whatever relevance it might have to socio-economic phenomena, had become marginalized to theology. Between it and the rest of the social sciences little interaction still occurs (Milbank, 1990). To all intents and purposes, the social sciences today ignore Christian belief as pre-scientific superstition, so that Christian theology talks mainly to itself. These diametric changes occurred only in the last few hundred years, and are widely attributed to the success of the scientific (naturalistic) worldview.

As part of these processes over the last hundred years or so, the relevance of Christian belief has been considered decreasingly in both academic philosophy and social science. One reason for this is the supposed intellectual disconformity between the two categories. This chapter has argued that Christian socio-economic analysis can be viewed as compatible with rather than contradictory to scientific endeavor. As noted above, another reason for Christianity's academic demise stemmed from the legacy of dogmatic interpretation and control of learning exercised by the institutional Christian church for centuries up to the twentieth. This process never fitted comfortably with the freedom of belief and action promised to believers by Jesus in the Bible. In effect, the institutional church pulled the rug from under its own feet by denying that Biblical freedom in Christ to its followers, by undermining among believers their personal autonomy in and with God. Enlightenment thinkers had little toleration for the authoritarian control sought by the church, and increasingly rejected the institution *and* the Biblical basis of its beliefs. All was not lost for Christian belief in natural science, however, for it is possible that the metaphysical Christian beliefs of physical scientists from the seventeenth to the nineteenth centuries served as the basis for their scientific discoveries (e.g., Harman, 1982). Ideas of antithesis between science and Christian belief emerged only in the late nineteenth century, fanned by the hypotheses of non-Christian scientists, such as Darwin, the realistic status of whose hypotheses continues to be debated (e.g., Johnson, 1993; Behe, 1996). Even so, modern science has not succeeded in refuting revelation, as Strauss acknowledged.

Surveys suggest that social scientists today are less tolerant of religious belief than physical scientists (Stark et al., 1996), and that social scientists keep their religious convictions away from academic work more than natural scientists (Wuthnow, 1985, 198). This is not surprising given the thumbnail history above. It is gratifying that Kincaid (1996) wants to make social science emulate more the 'scientific' standards of physical science. Perhaps this will make social scientists more tolerant of Christian belief. An alternative view is proposed here, that naturalistic social science cannot become more 'scientific' because it depends on non-Christian views for the purposes of humankind. Historically, Christianity and science supported each other. Their last hundred-year's divorce has produced today's dominant version of science associated with anti-Christian naturalism. This is attempting to extend its metaphysical framework to explain diverse domains of human behavior. Nevertheless, applying this version of science to social phenomena is not producing increasing returns (e.g., theories are just as severely contested), and helps explain the growth of secular non-naturalistic postmodern analysis (also unsympathetic to Christian belief). In all likelihood, the anti-Christian bias of the social sciences will persist, in part because they are 'the *least scientific* disciplines' (Wuthnow, 1985, 197; original emphasis), in the sense that social sciences have lower levels of paradigmatic codification than natural sciences. The problem is that like religious belief systems, the social sciences are predicated on quasi-theological 'non-testable claims [that] puts them in direct competition with traditional religions' (Stark et al., 1996, 436). In what is commonly conceived as science today, these non-testable claims constitute the metaphysical framework of naturalism. However, in Christian belief, naturalistic attempts to explain social behavior have limited application because naturalism is not identical with science, and because both a naturalistic version of science and science itself have only partial relevance to explaining human behavior. The next section discusses the role of these worldviews and metaphysical frameworks in natural science, Christianity and social investigation.

WORLDVIEWS AND METAPHYSICAL FRAMEWORKS IN PHYSICAL AND SOCIAL SCIENCE

In the philosophies of physical and of social science (e.g., Bhaskar, 1989; McLoughlin, 1991; Trigg, 1989, 1993, 1998), and in the specific application of logic and rhetoric (e.g., Kahane, 1992), it is believed frequently that investigatory practice is pursued within the confines of conceptions of how the world works. These metaphysical conceptual frameworks or worldviews are intellectual schemas in which everything people believe is positioned consciously and unconsciously, and by which reality is interpreted. Thus, a standard logic and rhetoric text (Kahane, 1992, 12, 14) claimed that 'background beliefs play a crucial role in the evaluation of arguments,' and that worldviews 'influence how we deal with virtually every problem.' Worldviews are 'like lenses that cause us to view the world in a particular way or perhaps like filters through which we process all new ideas and information.' Proponents of this view hold that metaphysics, not physics, confronts the most fundamental questions of the universe (e.g., Benardete, 1989).

However, not all scientists or philosophers accept that the practice of science rests on a given worldview or metaphysical base, especially given the rise of naturalized epistemology (e.g., Churchland, 1987; Quine, 1992; Crick, 1994). Others take a middle position, 'that philosophy is continuous with empirical science' (Papineau, 1993, 1; Rosenberg, 1995, 217), 'that physics and metaphysics blend into a seamless whole' (Redhead, 1995, 87). Even some Christians underplay the reliance of science on metaphysical principles; for instance, to Drees (1996, 152, 11), 'a naturalist view of science does not need a great deal of metaphysics,' although he admits that his 'naturalism is a metaphysical position.'

In the first section of this chapter, the Christian schema classified naturalism as a metaphysical perspective about the nature of science. Given the specification of naturalism in Table 13.1, advocates of ontological and methodological dimensions of naturalism often equate it with science and the scientific worldview. Losee labels this position as normative naturalism that 'views science and philosophy of science as a seamless whole' (Losee, 2001, 241). Kincaid's philosophy of science, for instance, is metaphysical and methodological naturalism. The Christian response, encompassing realists and non-realists, is that this view (scientism) conflates naturalism with science, which is a false identity, and then elevates science as the best means of explaining human behavior (science imperialism). As the Christian non-realist, Rescher (1984, 213) put it, 'science is no longer a sector of the cognitive enterprise but an all-inclusive world-view' that does not celebrate but distorts science. Of course, non-Christians (who might think of themselves as ontological naturalists) also hold similar views; for example, Putnam (1990), that science does not exhaust the domain of facts, and that rationality is not identical with the scientific.

Argument between the two polar positions about science, of metaphysics first, or not all, has persisted for as long as anything like modern scientific investigation has occurred, and shows no signs of resolution. The metaphysical-priority view holds that science uses 'an extensive apparatus of concepts, principles, etc., that it is no part of the function of science to examine or establish' (Flew, 1984, 230). Realists hold that 'the "logic of science" cannot evade problems generated at the metaphysical level regarding necessity' (Sayer, 1992, 171). The priority of metaphysics is generally accepted by realists, such as Bhaskar (1994, 467) who alleged 'the incapacity of anti-metaphysical empiricisms to make sense of science.' Similarly, Trigg (1993, 11, 94) claimed that the physical sciences 'rest on metaphysical foundations which must be made explicit'; indeed, 'even materialists uphold a definite metaphysical position, which can only be supported or condemned on rational grounds that may not themselves be narrowly scientific.' Proponents of the metaphysical-priority view typically believe that 'science may lead to truth, but it does not have to be the only route,' unlike 'naturalists who are convinced that scientific method can be the only path to truth' (Trigg, 1993, 60, 102).

The Christian perspective of this book posits the priority of metaphysics underlying science and conforms to wide Christian agreement (e.g., Moreland, 1989; Clouser, 1991; Nash, 1992; Naugle, 2002). Its metaphysics is a particular worldview sympathetic to scientific undertaking, although not accepting that scientific methods *per se* are the sole road to human knowledge. On this view, both Christian belief and science need 'metaphysical presuppositions about the character of reality,' even if neither can 'provide a cast iron guarantee of their validity' (Trigg, 1993, 150). Many examples exist of Christian metaphysical assumptions that predate the Scientific Revolution and that are consistent with say, physics. Some of these are that reality is structured, orderly, determinate, regular, coherent, and not fundamentally chaotic. Again, nature is an object worthy of study, but is not a deity. Natural laws are taken to exist and can be discovered. The world is believed to have been created out of nothing for neither time nor space existed before creation. Many related Christian beliefs underlie science more generally, such as 'knowledge is possible,' 'the universe is intelligible,' 'the mind and senses inform us about reality', and that uniformity in nature sometimes 'justifies inferences from the past to the future' (Moreland, 1989, 45). On this basis, 'the explanatory laws and initial conditions of natural science can be embedded in a framework of theological explanation' (Wacome, 1997, 320).

The Christian worldview contains also a related set of metaphysical assumptions by which the reality of human action in the social world is to be understood. Indeed, the Bible itself 'is a worldview text proffering a comprehensive vision of and for life' (Walsh, 1996, 212). In relation to human social action, this worldview consists of an interwoven network of themes, such as that human life has inseparable spiritual and material dimensions, and that

God in His trinitarian conception has normative intentions for human spiritual and material life.

It is not exaggerating to say that the Bible, for example, is much more preoccupied with explaining, and providing norms of, human personal and social behavior in relation to the triune God than with discussing the nature of the physical world (or heaven). It is curious, therefore, that so much more discussion occurs today about the relation between Christian belief and physical science than between Christian belief and social science. The Bible calls Christians to view and interpret human behavior and relationships within the confines of its worldview; in effect, to investigate human action using the framework provided by its belief structure. It is this structure that provides the mechanism for scientific and for non-scientific investigation. This is not a version of foundationalism, however, for the translation from belief structure to action necessarily involves human interpretation. Nevertheless, in so far as no worldview can be proven to be objective truth, admitting the predominance of metaphysics weakens the ability of science to achieve truth. To committed naturalists, this is probably the most disturbing feature of the metaphysics-first view.

The naturalist, Kincaid, does not discuss philosophical/metaphysical principles underlying physical or social science; instead, 'scientific methods are the most powerful tools available for replacing superstition and prejudice with knowledge' (1996, xv). Here is no intimation that the use of 'scientific methods' or that an understanding of 'scientific rationality' depend on prior philosophical beliefs, or even that using 'scientific methods' requires values and judgement (let alone a social context). Instead, 'a science of society' (Kincaid, 1996, 1) is sought, but the philosophical bases of the methods to achieve it are not canvassed. This is perhaps an unexpected conclusion from Kincaid who has noted elsewhere (1990, 81) the absence of a 'simple property that separates science from nonscience . . . [for] . . . the science/nonscience distinction is a continuum.'

Those who do not emphasize the metaphysical framework on which natural and social science rest regard philosophical and theological speculation as of lesser importance than science for discovering reality. The revelational path, part of the Christian worldview, is eschewed completely. It is only by downgrading non-scientific paths to knowledge that claims like 'science constitutes our best chance at limning the true structure of reality' (Kincaid, 1996, 5) can be made. If it was acknowledged that the philosophical foundations of science (and every other belief structure) were primary, and that differences exist about their nature, it is the foundations themselves that affect limning reality. In Christian belief, knowledge about science is vital for understanding reality, 'but still more valuable is knowledge about the ultimate values and purposes behind the mechanisms of physics and biology' (Johnson, 1995, 13). Knowledge of value and purpose is inseparable from judgement and speculation. Such views resonate also with realist thought. For example, Trigg denies 'that science is its own justification,' and that 'all attempts to give science monopoly rights over human reason are bound to fail, since the reasons for doing so can never be adequately accounted for from within science.' In effect, Trigg questions the 'enormous metaphysical assumption that the reality to which science has access is the whole of reality' (1993, 209, 208, 60). To Rescher (1984, 214), 'science does not have exclusive rights to "knowledge"; its province is far narrower than that of inquiring reason in general.'

The Christian stance that physical and social science proceeds within a given worldview invites the contamination of scientific analysis by values and judgement. These are unavoidable in the project of science (McMullin, 1983), which contention Strauss, for example, long ago acknowledged (Gildin, 1989). However, contrary to Kincaid (1996, 44), the application of epistemic values (simplicity, objectivity etc.) in social science is problematic, and is the more 'interesting thesis' than the largely dated one 'that science presupposes *non-epistemic* values.' In economics, for example, the application of theory to policy turns invariably on epistemic, not non-epistemic values. The application of epistemic values in economics shows that in this discipline aspiring to be science, 'the prospects for a neutral, objective scientific enterprise' are indeed vitiated. In applying economic theory to the real world, it is rarely 'a perfectly objective, non-normative matter what the answer is' (Kincaid, 1996, 45). The Christian realist, McMullin (1983, 8–9) perceived this, as noted earlier, that 'the appraisal of theory is in important respects closer in structure to value-judgement' than to 'the rule-governed inference' of classical philosophy.

The relevance of worldviews, science and scientific methods is but one philosophical issue confronting the exploration of human behavior and relationships. Other issues pertaining to the Christian worldview, that cannot be explored here, also have implications for the analysis of human action. For example, one is the objects of interest to which scientific or other methods might be applied. Its continuing debate in social science is whether the individual or the social level is the more appropriate focus. Christian explanation of human behavior poses an intimate interrelationship between individual characteristics and social structure. Humans are regarded as acting on the basis of inherently unique and shared individualistic characteristics, including the state of their relationship with God. As well, they act on the basis of the influence of social wholes, such as those depicted in the Bible, like the family and tribe, the state—national and foreign, army, monarchy, the rich, the religious establishment, the slave system. Between (and within) the individualistic and social spheres of life, continuous mutual interaction occurs. To complicate matters, and to deny a naturalistic interpretation of human action, a third party is postulated to affect human action at both the individualistic and social (holistic) level. This is the unobservable trinitarian spirit-entity, God, who in Biblical belief is more than just responsible for creating the physical background within which human interaction occurs. Thus, Christian explanation of human behavior can be labeled neither pure holism nor individualism. Perhaps an appropriate label would be non-naturalistic interactionism.

In contrast, Kincaid (1996, xv) claims that social science analysis is best pursued at the level of social aggregates rather than the individual, that 'pressing social problems . . . are not simply the result of individual characteristics but result instead from larger social structures.' This view does not imply that social problems depend on the interplay of individual characteristics and social structures, or that individual characteristics have a role to play in the formation of social wholes. Indeed, social problems are held to result from social structures *instead* of individual characteristics. In the tradition of holism, the implication is that social structures have a life of their own, that they exist independently from the characteristics of their individual members.

THE NORMATIVE PURPOSE OF CHRISTIAN SOCIO-ECONOMIC ANALYSIS

Suppose it is accepted that social (and physical) science is embedded in a metaphysical framework. Can it be shown further than illustrated in Chapters 2–4 that the Christian belief system would make a difference to the way social (and personal) behavior was analyzed, and to any policy outcomes that might derive from it? This section discusses three aspects of Christian socio-economic analysis, and how it could differ in practice from naturalistic social science. A first aspect is to recapitulate the selection of principles from earlier chapters that Christians regard as being derived from their belief system, and intended to be applied to contemporary social (and personal) phenomena. A second aspect is to show that application of such Christian principles leads to specific social policy outcomes, and has been so used in the last few decades. A third aspect is to show that a line exists in practice between such a Christian socio-economic analysis, and non-Christian naturalistic social science. This latter intention is to show that a Christian perspective looks radically distinctive in how it views human behavior, and in its outcomes that might derive from this perception. From this third aspect, three generalizations are suggested about prospective Christian socio-economic analysis.

On the first aspect, Christianity's (mainly) non-naturalistic analysis of individual and social behavior has a normative intention. According to Christianity's worldview, the purpose of human life is to live in personal interrelationship with the trinitarian God as revealed, say, in the Bible, but not necessarily confined to this source. On the latter, secondary interpreters (theologians and the like) may be able to expose aspects of hitherto undiscerned implications from the primary source of Christian belief. Norms so revealed from these explorations are taken to be relevant to all humankind throughout subsequent history.

Exemplars for such norms or principles in the Bible, requiring further elaboration, are contained in Jesus' teachings, such as 'love your enemies and pray for those who persecute you' (Mt. 5:44); 'you cannot serve God and mammon' (Mt. 6:24); 'whoever would be great among you must be your servant' (Mt. 20:26); 'you shall love your neighbour as yourself' (Mt. 22:39); 'as you wish that men would do to you, do so to them' (Lk. 6:31); 'what is exalted among men is an abomination in the sight of God' (Lk. 16:15). These expressions represent parameters of the Christian worldview because their interpretation and application by a Christian believer implies potential variation between situations. The norms can be articulated only in specific contexts, and clearly involve some leeway and possible disagreement in interpretation between Christians. Another source of disagreement stems from Christian believers being at different levels of understanding of the Christian belief system. This is the empirical question of the extent to which different Christian believers include and take seriously each particular belief and its attendant practices. Nevertheless, human behavior is meant to be viewed and prescribed through the lens of Christian evaluation. There is no implication in the Christian worldview of a supposedly neutral, objective observation of human behavior; rather, behavioral 'facts' are theory/worldview-laden, and so is policy prescription from the 'facts.'

Examples of derivative social norms, intentions or principles presented in Chapters 2 and 3 were that distributional criteria should tend in the direction of greater equality of opportunity and outcome (and also Hicks, 2000; Forrester, 2001; Bauckham, 2003). Further examples are that market processes should be modified by regulatory constraint, and that systematic prevention of poverty should take precedence over *ad hoc* relief of poverty or welfare (e.g., Mason, 1996). Employment organization and the generation of employment opportunity are taken to be important in achieving these ends. Thus, workers could retain ownership and control of the financial capital that provides their paid work (Hay, 1989, 173). The poor could be assisted to economic independence by the better-off via jobs and loans, especially to self-owned/managed jobs. The able-bodied poor are expected to work to gain assistance; the disabled poor are not. In this type of thinking, poverty is to eliminated not just by voluntary charity, but formally and socially (Stapleford, 2002, 126–129), in which the extended family is to act as a protective economic base against its members' poverty. Moreover, the creation of wealth is not given preeminence over distribution; the two cannot be considered separately (Tiemstra et al., 1990). In the thinking of the orthodox Christian proponents of these intentions in Chapters 2 and 3, such socio-economic principles are not thought of as capable of independent application. They derive from religious values and should be promulgated in association with religious principles. The coterminous application of religious and socio-economic norms cannot be imposed in an authoritarian manner, but depends on their voluntary adoption by individual persons that if practiced sufficiently widely can then assume a social dimension. Unanimity does not exist among Christians in their derivation of such Christian social principles (Gay, 1991) or in how they might be applied. Moreover, some of the derivative social principles above parallel those long promoted by secular thinkers. However, the point at issue is to acknowledge that the listed principles stem directly from Christian interpretation in the minds of the Christians examined in Chapters 2–4. The sources from which they derive long predate secular thinking about the same topics. To what extent the principles have been appropriated historically by secular thinkers is a matter of debate

In relation to the second aspect, practical examples of contemporary socio-economic application of such Christian derivative social principles exist (some of which were mentioned in Chapters 2 and 3) both in their instigation and/or continuing emphases. These include:

- The extensive worker cooperative movement in Mondragon, Spain (e.g., Cheney, 1999).
- Direct financial assistance for economic projects benefiting poor people through international agencies such as Tear Fund (TEAR, 1997).
- Micro-credit extension to the poor through the likes of Opportunity International and Bridge Fund (Opportunity International, 1998).
- Sweat-equity/no interest loans through Habitat for Humanity that has built over one hundred and ten thousand homes internationally for low income people.
- Application of relationships auditing in schools, prisons and business by the UK Relationships Foundation/Jubilee Centre.

In addition, campaigns exist for the socio-economic application of Biblical principles, such as:

- The International Jubilee 2000 Debt proposals for canceling Third World debt (Jubilee 2000, 1998).
- The movement for instituting a Basic Income in the Republic of Ireland (Reynolds and Healy, 1995).
- Christian proposals for reforming US welfare policy (Carlson-Thies and Skillen, 1996; Massaro, 1998; Gushee, 1999).

These examples could be multiplied, including the long historical involvement of the Christian church in welfare and health care. Principles underlying such projects have often been secularized and replicated in non-Christian organizations, but this does not detract from the specifically Christian and Biblical inspiration for the cases cited above.

Thus, the Christian model of socio-economic analysis has practical policy implications. These implications differ from the naturalistic approach of Kincaid (1996). Like 'the Enlightenment thinkers who popularized naturalism,' Kincaid (1996, 4–5) thinks that only a naturalistic scientific understanding of how society works can tell us how 'to change it for the better.' It does not follow, however, that even if naturalistic science tells how the social world works, it necessarily shows how to improve it. For example, naturalistic social science may be able to do no more than expose generic relationships between social phenomena, as with say, laws of supply and demand in economics. The explicatory nature and quantitative predictive value of these laws has little practical policy application, despite their elaborate theoretical specification and empirical testing (e.g., Pollak and Wales, 1992). The explanatory truth contained in these laws is just as 'anemic' (Kincaid, 1996, 13) as individualistic reductionist explanations of social behavior; they are plausible (true in this case), but tautologous and uninteresting. In this instance, naturalistic economics is no more a producer of practically useful 'real knowledge about social processes' (Kincaid, 1996, 5) than alternative non-naturalistic modes of analysis, such as the pattern modelling of Institutionalist economics. In the wider field of secular social science, perhaps the 'well-confirmed generalizations about the causes of social phenomena' that Kincaid (1996, 6) thinks can only come from naturalistic science, might be found to come also from the humanities, such as history, that Kincaid contrasts explicitly with social science. If neither naturalistic or non-naturalistic social science (such as segments of history and sociology) has sufficient precision to enable useful policy decisions to be made on the basis of its analysis, alternative normative schemas offer themselves, of which the Christian perspective is one. This opens a Pandora's box, for disagreement then arises not only about the what 'is' in social phenomena, but what 'ought to be.' 'Change it for the better' becomes a more starkly value-laden, moral and ethical concept, the source for which need not derive from naturalistic science. The examples discussed in Chapters 2–4 of normative principles from Catholic Social Thought or from the Old Testament held by orthodox Christian advocates as relevant to contemporary socio-economic application did not depend on naturalistic science for their derivation. Instead, they stemmed from the metaphysical worldview of Biblical Christianity and particular interpretations of its source texts. Scientific means would be required to describe and monitor change in human behavior if the Biblical precepts were to be followed, but naturalistic science itself did not formulate the precepts.

Apropos the third aspect specified at the beginning of this section, three generalizations can be drawn about the content of a Christian-based social analysis and its difference from naturalistic social analysis, as far as orthodox Christians see it. First, as noted above, they believe it is possible to draw applicable policy implications from derivative social Biblical principles. This differs from secular approaches to social science, such as formalistic naturalistic modelling, that typically try to deduce policy from theory explaining how human behavioral variables are interrelated. For instance, in the case of existing patterns of wealth distribution, secular theory might be sought explaining what would happen if the existing distribution of wealth was changed (say, would it slow down economic growth?). However, no unassailable secular theories have yet been determined capable of explaining or predicting the effects of changing existing wealth distributions (e.g., Solimano, 1998a). Therefore, secular policy proposals stem more typically from the values' stance of policy proposers (e.g., politicians), reinforced by 'weak' contestable theory. Disagreement arises from different values' positions, from divergent theories, and from the most appropriate policy instruments to achieve the selected values. An orthodox Christian approach would not depend on assailable secular theories. In keeping with its adherence to Biblical principle, its policy advocacy would be for the distribution of wealth to be changed to accord more with Biblical guidelines (that is, toward a more equal distribution). Admittedly, no proven theory exists to assess what the effects of this might be, but this is no more damaging to the Christian than to secular approaches that have no reliable theories either. Rational argument employing scientific and non-scientific categories could be made to assess the advantages and disadvantages of Christian versus non-Christian policies. The idiosyncratic feature of the Christian perspective is that Biblical guidelines provide the values' stance and the theory.

A second generalization from the Christian approach described here is that exposing Biblical principles relevant to contemporary socio-economic phenomena provides a normative matrix beyond that of naturalistic social science to explain why observed social phenomena exist. For example, to explain the observed distribution of wealth at a secular level, a plethora of interrelated political and social factors can be proposed, operative over time. In the United States, for instance, grants of land from the state to private entrepreneurs in the nineteenth century, and consequent transport developments, were probably influential in generating high land value increments to the entrepreneurs allowing them to diversify into other wealth-producing activities. The Christian focus would then move beyond the secular explanation to more specifically normative concerns. It would ask how the influences moulding the social outcome differed from the mandatory forms of behavior required in the Bible to attain the distribution of wealth sought for humankind by God. The ways in which actual social behavior departed from that conducive to pursuing the Biblical guidelines would provide the focal explanatory framework. Here, the Christian question would be why the observed phenomenon (the distribution of wealth) came to differ from Biblical guidelines. A one-to-one transposition from the guidelines to the issue under analysis is difficult. Dispute can arise between Christians; for example, concerning the relevance of Biblical behavioral norms. Accepting potential disagreement between Christians in interpreting Biblical texts, deriving principles from them, and relating these principles to contemporary socio-economic life contradicts basic tenets of fundamentalism (Marty and Appleby, 1991).

A third generalization is that the characteristics of social phenomena to be investigated in the Christian approach would in part be influenced by the set of Biblical principles and matrix deemed relevant to its analysis. Data would need to be assembled about the characteristics of the phenomenon to be analyzed. If the phenomenon under scrutiny was the level of wellbeing in a population, a prior decision would have to be made to define 'wellbeing.' 'Wellbeing' is not a natural kind, but a socially conditioned category—the observation of 'wellbeing' is theory-laden. A Christian definition of 'wellbeing'(or 'unemployment'etc.) would not necessarily be identical with non-Christian definitions; for example, a Christian definition might want to include indicators of family life stability, and would want to assess the state of people's relationship with God (however defined) as part of 'wellbeing.' The description of social data is not objective, value-free, or unproblematic—unlike the characteristics ascribed to a naturalistic methodology for social data description (by Kincaid, 1996, for example, in his advocacy of the methodology of Paige, 1975, discussed in Chapter 10).

This process of investigation, interpretation and application of the norms contained in the Christian worldview require the dual use of people's reason and revelation from God. The revelational aspect derives from the preposterous concept of the life of God (in the form of the Holy Spirit) actually dwelling within the believer, guiding her decision making. The process of the simultaneous use of human reason and spiritual input from God can grow within the believer, following Christian guidelines. But there are many reasons why professing Christians make lifestyle decisions inimical to Biblical teaching. Personal decision-making can be frustrated by the actions of the believer herself, by other people, individually and socially, and by the actions of supernatural spirits unfriendly to God.

This manner of observing, explaining, and prescribing for human behavior differs wildly from a naturalistic conception. Most social science naturalists concede the theory-laden nature of observation, but here agreement with the

Christian worldview approach stops. An illustration of disagreement is the manner in which theory-laden data are used to explain and predict human behavior. For example, in economics, data might be collected to test predictions of naturalistic Neoclassical rational choice theory, the dominant matrix in contemporary microeconomics. This theory postulates human choice as founded on a restricted set of assumptions, such as persons having complete, consistent and stable preferences for goods and services. This contrasts with Christian explanation that depends on no such presuppositions (Beed and Beed, 1999). Chapter 12 noted that advocates of rational choice theory claim it explains a wide range of human choice situations, from marriage to drug-taking (e.g., Becker, 1993). If this is valid, limited opportunity exists for alternative explanations of human behavior, of which the Christian belief system is one. Some specific claims of rational choice theory were examined in Chapter 12, and their controversial nature noted (evidenced in the disagreement, for example, between Green and Shapiro, 1994, and Johnson, 1996).

Kincaid (1996, 245–246) contends that the fruitfulness of naturalistic Neoclassical rational choice theory—or, 'supply-and-demand analysis' as he calls it—is demonstrated because it 'turns up again and again as economists seek to explain new phenomena or more fully analyze standard ones.' The latter part of this observation is incontrovertible. However, the mere fact 'that the supply-and-demand argument strategy plays an important role in economic explanation' (Kincaid, 1996, 246) does not necessarily mean this 'economic explanation' reveals reality or truth. From the Chapter 12 critics of this form of economic explanation (e.g., Rosenberg, 1992; Blaug, 1992), all it means is that a uniform methodological mode is being applied to a variety of human choice situations. As we observed in Chapter 12, whether the 'supply-and-demand' mode explicates the choice situations more than alternative explanations found inside and outside economics is considered rarely by 'supply-and-demand' theorists.

Some advocates of rational choice theory (e.g., Satz and Ferejohn, 1994) argue that it applies more relevantly to social rather than to individual choice situations. Even Kincaid conceded that rational choice theory fails as an explicator of individual human choice, because the 'exogenous factors' underlying the theory 'all seem to be social. Rational choice theory seems to presuppose rather than eliminate social theory' (Kincaid, 1996, 158). This focus underlines the importance of examining the relevance of 'social theory' to demand and supply, but Kincaid does not pursue this investigation, and nor do most orthodox economists in their theoretical expositions. It is not appropriate here to consider what might be the social influences on demand and supply—their relation to 'social theory.' All we can conclude here is continuing disagreement about the relevance of 'supply-and-demand' explanations. Some minority schools within economics, like the Institutionalists, made up their minds long ago, and occasionally non-economists reveal a parallel judgement—that 'supply-and-demand' contributes little to explaining individual or social human choice outside a restricted domain (e.g., Knapp, 1994; Hauptmann, 1996).

Perhaps, then, the explanation of individual and social human choice is more of an open question. In Christian belief, human choice is explained by reference to its worldview. The uniqueness of each person and their freedom of will militate against explanation via a limited set of assumptions, as per Neoclassical rational choice theory. Since the influences within the Christian worldview affecting human choice are well nigh infinite, and since some derive from a supernatural domain that is only partially amenable to human comprehension, explanation is bound to be incomplete. Accordingly, Christian 'theory' makes no attempt to be predictive. Nevertheless, instances abound in contemporary Christian literature of efforts to explain human behavioral phenomena via derivations from the Christian worldview. For example, a contemporary Christian literature seeks to explain individual personal behavior compared with the efforts of psychology (e.g., Bulkley, 1993; Vitz, 1994). An analogous Christian literature explores particular aspects of sociology, like the nature of human work (e.g., Volf, 1991; Preece, 1995). Needless to say, none of these types of analyses is mentioned, let alone evaluated, in secular social science, and university libraries rarely hold the relevant books or journals. These are taken to belong to the 'separate' domain of theology. None of this is to imply that Christian ideas never get a mention in secular social science. For instance, Jeeves and Berry (1998, 203) point to the marginal citation of work relating personality theory in psychology to Christian belief in the *Annual Review of Psychology*. Christian belief in psychology may be in a better position than in the other social sciences for a variety of reasons. One of these might be that Christian belief is widely thought of as pertaining mainly to personal rather than social behavior. Stemming from this, a second more organizational reason is the existence of academic journals like the *Journal of Psychology and Theology*, given to discussing the interrelation between Christian belief and psychology.

CONCLUSION

Three issues have been examined in this chapter showing how a Christian perspective (at least as interpreted by a body of orthodox Christian thought) for analyzing socio-economic phenomena differs from a naturalistic viewpoint. The first issue examined in section two was how the Christian view relates to naturalism and non-naturalism. Differences between these two perspectives for examining human social behavior are still regarded as a primal problem in secular philosophy of social science. The Christian position was argued to be non-naturalistic in contrast to Kincaid's advocacy of naturalism in social science. There are common features between the Christian perspective and secular non-naturalistic social science like hermeneutics. The chapter did not discuss those features, but focused on unique aspects of the non-naturalistic Christian basis.

Classifying the Christian approach as non-naturalistic could imply a Christian response to naturalistic social science to object to the centrality of scientific norms in social investigation, in so far as naturalism is often identified with science. The third section argued this view is mistaken. The Christian view proposed here is a form of realism, but neither science nor reality is to be identified solely with or by naturalism. A Christian realist response proceeds within a given worldview and metaphysical framework in which science is regarded as an important source of knowledge about social phenomena, but not the complete source. The Christian worldview can encompass practice of the best norms of science as an aid to describing human behavior and relationships.

Finally, the normative intention of social science was considered. Historically, the social sciences have had long connection with endeavors to understand the condition of humankind in order to improve it. In the Christian conception, science *per se* is only one aid in this undertaking. For thousands of years longer than anything resembling modern science, the Judeo-Christian tradition has been trying to explain and improve the socio-economic world. The Christian perspective holds that the values and beliefs inherent in its worldview are more important than scientific methods *per se* for improving humankind's condition. Given the three issues canvassed here, if put into practice, the Christian response has the potential to affect social science analysis markedly. Except for some policy applications noted in this chapter, and in Chapters 2–4, the issue of policy is not explored further. This is because the emphasis of this book is on the philosophical and methodological implications of Christian socio-economic analysis, not on its practical policy implications. The aim is to float a methodology that Christians might practice to reach policy.

In summary, a Christian response is possible to the claims of naturalistic social science. In the Christian view, naturalistic social science explains only part of social (and individual) behavior, explanation for which has to be supplemented by non-naturalistic input, of which Christian beliefs (its worldview/metaphysical system) are one component. Christian socio-economic analysis presupposes a *different* approach to social investigation from the naturalistic one (at least as proposed by Kincaid, 1996). The Christian methodology would use scientific and non-scientific means, of which the latter include metaphysical Biblical principles and normative schemas, prayer, and revelation. None of this precludes Christians from employing scientific methods to collect and analyze human behavioral data. Nevertheless, no *a priori* reasons exist to suppose that secular social science of whatever variety can necessarily reveal socio-economic reality more validly than Christian socio-economic analysis. This is partly because, as McGrath (2002, 118–119, original emphasis; 2001, 17) points out, 'allegedly neutral, transcendent or "objective" disciplines—such as the social sciences—are no more than *narrated interpretations of reality* which possess no privileged status permitting them to judge or police others.' Indeed, 'one of the most influential myths of the modern period' is the belief that the social sciences 'offer a neutral and objective reading of reality, in which the ultimately spurious truth-claims' of theology may be 'deflated.' We can go further with Milbank (1990, 1) that this chapter (and book) has tried to show that 'the most important governing assumptions' of social and economic theory involve 'the modification or the rejection of orthodox Christian positions.'

Chapter Fourteen

The Methodology of Christian Socio-Economic Analysis

Economic theory is not a reliable path for ascertaining reality. Many instances have been given in earlier chapters of disagreement within economics relating to theoretical explanations, and to their empirical testing in so far as this is possible. An explanation has also been made about why this should not be surprising within the Christian worldview. Accordingly, there is no reason for Christians to hold mainstream economic theory in esteemed regard or to take the claims of economics to constitute 'science' as evidence of its certainty. Orthodox economic theory is no more than one secular input into the description and explanation of personal and social behavior. There is no way of demonstrating that the theories of mainstream economics accord more with reality in terms of explanation and prediction than competing secular social science theories purporting to explain the same phenomena. Such alternative theories can emanate both from minority heterodox schools of economics, and from social sciences outside economics, like sociology, social psychology, anthropology and political science. An example of lack of consensual agreement between mainstream and heterodox economists about appropriate modes for appraising economic theories is Moseley (1995). Even the prominent mainstream economist historian and methodologist, Blaug, who, as we have seen, has long advocated the practice of falsification as the test for scientific theories, is evidently not able to practice his advocated mode (for good reasons, we argued in Chapter 8). Blaug's (1990) *Economic Theories, True or False?* contains no example of a decisive falsification test for an economic theory. It is all very well to argue (as per Hoover 2000, 345) that it is the weight of evidence over time that determines the direction of the academic economics discipline, but if this weighting is no more than 'an informal, social process,' as Hoover puts it, the direction lays itself open to all manner of 'informal' influences, like the organizational stranglehold orthodoxy has had on the discipline for the last fifty years (other influences are explored in Beed and Beed, 1996c).

Just to reiterate the uncertainty of economic theory, two more instances are mentioned here of allegedly persisting unresolvable disputes in economics. Since nobody has resolved the disagreements, no attempt will be made to do so here. Cole et al. (1991, 240–252) argued that differences in non-testable, unfalsifiable metaphysical ideas about three alternative economic theories of value and their relation to socio-economic-political practice produced divergent economic policies in Chile between 1964–1989. These policies were encompassed by the social democrat government of Frei, the more radical of Allende, and the conservative of Pinochet. Cole et al. also suggested (1991, 253–275) that adherence to one of these theories was driving current international efforts of the IMF and the like, to restructure the economies of the less developed countries. This was in the face of criticism from the other two theories. The adage Cole et al. pose at the beginning of their book is that 'to learn one theory of economics is bad enough!' (1991, 12). In general, this is all most students of academic economics do learn. This becomes the criterion for practicing 'scientific' economics.

A second example is continuing academic disagreement over the effect of minimum wages on unemployment. Prior to Card and Krueger (1995), mainstream economic theory was that minimum wage legislation led to higher unemployment and less opportunity for low-income workers to increase job skills (e.g., Katz and Rosen, 1994). Card and Krueger's US empirical work suggested that minimum wages had no significant effects on employment levels, and, perversely, might even be associated with higher employment. Because the empirical work contradicted the predictions of orthodox theory, it generated great controversy in the academic literature that is not resolved to this day. One Nobel Laureate in economics (Buchanan) wrote in the *Wall Street Journal* that if minimum wages increased employment, this was 'equivalent to a denial that there is even a minimum scientific content in economics' (cited in Dawkins, 1997, 188). The *International and Labor Relations Review* (1995) ran a symposium on Card and Krueger's findings. Predictably, the responses lined up with the preexisting views of the participants (as per Buchanan). Some clung tenaciously to orthodox theory (e.g., Hamermesh, Welch) and were able to point to all manner of limitations in Card and Krueger's methodology. Others, such as Freeman and Osterman, who were already critical of aspects of orthodox theory, saw in Card and Krueger's work a partial vindication of their own views. Since 1995, opinion has vacillated in relation to the predictions of orthodox theory, and to the implications of subsequent empirical work about minimum wages and unemployment. A

1997 survey of the debate concluded that 'the jury is still out, although the pendulum seems to be swinging back in favour of those who believe that the minimum wage does reduce employment on the margin' (Seltzer, 1997, 212). This conclusion was challenged theoretically by those who contend the contrary (e.g., Prasch and Sheth, 1999). As we saw in Chapter 4, the unresolved debate has continued ever since.

Other examples of disagreement between economists, between economists and other social scientists, and the reasons for their disagreements, are reported increasingly. These range from such as Prychitko (1998), and Swartz and Bonello (1998), to Fullbrook (2003, 2004), by feminist and critical realist economists (e.g., Lawson, 2003), and in PAE publications (paecon.net). If the explanations and theories of economics manifest the degree of reported indeterminacy and disagreement, they cannot be used with any certainty for policy decision making. The argument has not been made in this book, but it could be shown that other fields of social science are rent by comparable theoretical disputation as is economics. One possible symptom of this disarray for economics is declining tertiary enrolments in economics worldwide, with the gap being made up by business and finance. If economics was the post-Second World War religion (as per Nelson, 2001), it may be losing its followers.

None of this is to deny that data collected by economists and social scientists continue to be used for socio-economic policy formulation, particularly in the short-term forecasting arena, but this data are not intrinsic to social science. They can just as well be collected and manipulated by statisticians/mathematicians (and often are), or even by theologically based social investigators.

Secular criticism of contemporary economics, echoed even by orthodox economists such as Friedman and Coase, is disputed by other orthodox economists. But the major defence by such as Kreps (1997) and Baumol (2000) is with the empirical content of modern economics, showing that it is more than abstract mathematical games. What these two defenders do not establish is whether the empirical content of today's economics, as it relates to the real world rather than just to experimental contexts, stems from theoretical deduction (as explanation and/or prediction) that either has long-term spatial stability or that can be made into stable long-term policy, or differs from deductions made by other social sciences. Nobody disputes the explosion in socio-economic information. Probably we do know more than Alfred Marshall. What is disputed is whether this information stems from economic theory that is adding up to a more coherent and/or true theoretical picture of socio-economic reality than existed previously.

An instance of the doubt about the role of contemporary economic theory can be illustrated in papers in the *International Journal of Forecasting* (*IJF*). One paper by four economists and an energy company representative (Engle et al., 1997) shows how their models can predict demand for particular hours of the day in a given period of the year for a given region. The variables in their models are days of the week, month, base load and temperature, and the models achieve high predictive success. No economic theory or economic data, as conventionally understood, are included. Another paper by two physicists (Darbellay and Slama, 2000) also achieves good success at predicting short-term demand for electricity with models different from Engle et al's., but still not including economic theory or conventionally defined economic variables. A study of further *IJF* papers suggests that neither economic theory nor economists are required for the prediction of energy demand. Indeed, one of the co-authors of the Engle et al. study, Clive Granger, co-winner with Engle of the 2003 Bank of Sweden Prize in Economic Sciences in Memory of Alfred Nobel (loosely, but incorrectly called the Nobel Prize in Economics) does not think of himself as an economist, but an econometrician, 'although some of my colleagues may consider me to be more of a statistician' (Granger, 2004, 96).

For those wanting to measure economics against the supposed standards of the natural sciences—something this book does not advocate—further questions present themselves. For example, how valid is the contention that 'it is difficult to identify any obvious successes (explanatorily powerful, revelatory, hypotheses) of mainstream academic economics, let alone find results that can be held up to the achievements of the sciences of nature' in the last fifty years (Lawson, 1997, 225)? Economic theorists are forced to take refuge in 'inexact laws' (e.g., Hausman, 1992), but these are little more revealing than common sense. As Hausman showed, empirical disconfirmations of such inexact laws do not lead to their abandonment. We saw in Chapter 10 that precisely formulated exceptionless generalizations or causal laws seem to be few and far between in economics. If these are explanations that are 'invariant over an extremely wide class of changes, there seem to be few if any plausible candidates for laws in economics or in the other social sciences' (Woodward, 1995, 26). Indeed, seeking causal explanations (or regularity laws) capable of long-term, or atemporal, acultural etc. application about non-natural social and economic kind entities is about as reliable as trying to ascertain temperatures from different thermometers filled with different liquids (Bohman, 1991, 51). Even orthodox economists echo such judgements, for example, that 'econometrics has failed to produce the quantitative laws that many economists, at one time, believed it would' (Backhouse, 1997, 136). Other economists, such as Birner (2002, 76) and Morgan (1990) also suggest that decisive tests of economic theories via econometrics have proved impossible to construct. In their view, work in this area was abandoned from the 1940s. A problem underlying all these comments, as we saw in earlier chapters, is that there is no common agreement nowadays about what science is or what are the correct methodological rules to pursue it. There is also the additional problem, not pursued in this book, of ascertaining the correct relation between theories and models, if it is just models of reality that can be constructed and tested (Morrison and Morgan, 1999).

Part of econometrician, Hoover's case (2002, 161) for the 'success of economics' is that 'robust' social regularities exist in the form of 'empirical generalizations,' the aim of econometrics being to characterize them. Such regularities are regarded as robust because they are 'imprecise.' Hoover does not specify what is the imprecision margin permissible for an empirical generalization or regularity 'law' to remain robust. Presumably, some margin of imprecision exists by which robustness dissipates. Nevertheless, being empirical generalizations, these regularity laws have the nature of inductive inferences from historical data, unlike much economic theory nowadays that connotes more the form of deductive inferences from axioms. To what extent economics has isolated empirical replicable generalizations deduced from economic theory remains an open question; replicable, in the sense of applicable to diverse temporal and spatial contexts. This raises the further question whether economic theory of the deductive form is necessary to ascertain social regularities. Perhaps, instead, the appropriate methodology to ascertain regularities is by looking for patterns in historical data. Perhaps theory can then be constructed from description of regularities. Hoover's sympathies might lie here for he places most weight for the success of economics on econometrics. To him, as for Granger, econometrics is mainly useful for forecasting, rather than for testing economic theories. We suggested above that it is also an open question as to how far economists, as distinct from statisticians/mathematicians, and even physicists, are required for this enterprise. Nevertheless, the application of econometrics to reveal regularities, and thereby to be useful for forecasting, is not unproblematic, despite its practical use in particular macro-economic areas. Granger (2004, 104) singles out an 'early success in econometrics' as the random walk model for prices from speculative markets in which the lack of forecastibility of returns is the regularity. Here an absence of something is a regularity, discovered 'without the use of an economic theory.' Although increasing interest among econometricians is in structural or causal models to investigate macro-economic time series behaviors, it is still the case as Zellner (2004, 39) points out, that it is difficult to formulate dependable models that explain and predict outcomes well.

Even if all the problems inherent to the matters above could be resolved determinately, the question persists whether economics and the other social sciences are making intellectual progress. The accumulation of economic and social science data, and the proliferations of theories cannot be doubted. But whether social science is achieving progress in any comparable sense with physical science—that its theories provide increasingly reliable explanations or predictions of and for social life, and that might have policy application—continues to be debated, even for given social, cultural and historical contexts. Part of the received view of physical science is that science is cumulative, building 'on the achievements of their predecessors, and the progress of science is a steady growth in our knowledge of the world' (Ladyman, 2002, 95). No social scientist or economist has been able to demonstrate that such criteria apply even to a micro-segment of their discipline, let alone to it as a whole. Theories and findings are contested between different schools of thought in the one social science, between different social sciences, and even from physical science itself. There is little evidence that this disputation is diminishing with time, but instead may be increasing with the exponential growth of socio-economic data. None of this is to infer that social science has produced no results of value either per se or in assisting policy decision making. Rather, the argument here suggests the possibility that despite the large undertaking of contemporary social science, the generation of results of value either per se or for policy decision making has been disproportionately small compared with the input of resources into the social science industry.

The dilemmas underlying the assessment of intellectual progress in social science, the role of economic theory and its relation to the real world, the role of econometrics in testing theory and in specifying regularity laws (as distinct from forecasting), and the role of economists in these undertakings are but symptoms of the contradiction economics and the social sciences find themselves in. In eschewing the supernatural spiritual dimension of reality, 'finding truth is not considered to be a plausible objective for an empirical analysis in most cases' (Granger, 2004, 97). Partly, this is because naturalist social scientists such as the majority of orthodox economists (but excluding Granger), are loath to concede fundamental conceptual differences between the behavior of natural and socio-economic systems. This is not only because they take the naturalism of natural science to be the clearest explication of reality. They believe also that this clearest understanding of social reality is a prerequisite to changing it 'for the better' (Kincaid, 1996, 4–5), something we have noted already. From its origins, social science has had a normative intention with its 'conviction that there is something terribly wrong with the social world as we now find it' (McIntyre, 1996, 5). Naturalist laws of human behavior have been pursued because their discovery might increase 'knowledge of how to improve human affairs.' In the Western world, naturalistic social science, and various forms of less naturalistic social science such as postmodernism—all non- and even anti-Christian—have sought to displace metaphysically non-naturalistic Christian belief in the last few centuries as the major guide to understanding and improving the human individual and social condition. This is an impossible and self-contradictory task according to the Christian viewpoint of this book.

THE CHRISTIAN WORLDVIEW AS AN ALTERNATIVE ORGANIZING FRAMEWORK

Yet, attempts to apply Christian belief systems to the analysis of socio-economic behavior seem to produce analogous disagreement among Christians as among secular social scientists. Disagreement in Christianity is a serious problem, but no more so than in economics and the other social sciences. The way through the dilemma of disagreement is not to throw in the towel, and move into secular social science as though it had a better grasp on socio-economic reality than Christianity. There is no compelling evidence that this is the case. The crucial question for the analysis of personal and socio-economic behavior is which starting point to take, the Christian, or the naturalistic and atheistic secular one. The argument of this book is that common definitions of economics, such as 'the discipline that studies the production, distribution, and consumption of material goods and services' are encompassed by the Judeo-Christian system of thought. If 'economics seeks to explain human behavior when making choices regarding the trade (or exchange) of material goods and services' (Gregg, 2001, 63), our Christian perspective is that such choices cannot be understood or made correctly without taking cognizance of the input of the requirements in principle to which the triune God is taken to call humans in all ages. Ascertaining both this cognizance and its relevance requires the mutual application of reason and prayer. Working within this Christian worldview, the next step in the analytical exercise is to employ the methodological tenets of Christian socio-economic analysis, such as those explored in Chapters 2–4, and pursued throughout this book.

The framework or Christian worldview expounded in this book is a conceptual scheme to which people consciously and unconsciously can relate their beliefs and by which they can interpret reality (Nash, 1992, 16). As discussed in the previous chapter, with a worldview, a person relates their own life to the general picture of the universe they possess. A worldview is a metaphysical system (Abraham, 1985, 104), akin to a noetic structure (Plantinga, 1983, 48–55), enabling people to make sense of reality. The idea of a worldview has links with, but is not identical with, Habermas' concept of a 'life world.' Each person, and even each Christian, probably possesses a specific worldview, sharing it in different degree with others. Epistemologically, we have argued that the Christian worldview underlying the arguments of this book can be described as a form of metaphysical realism (Trigg, 1993, 1998), sometimes called theistic realism (Johnson, 1995) or alethic realism (Alston, 1996). Like Christianity, realism cannot be shown incontrovertibly to depict what exists, for realism is a metaphysical theory about the status of reality.

It is inevitable that Christians, as everybody else, will read the Bible and anything via their particular worldview variant. Although a broad Christian worldview can be formulated, each Christian probably possesses a unique pair of glasses through which they view the world. This is preferable to Christians being forced to submit to a supposedly 'correct' doctrinal perspective formulated by institutional churches. The orthodox Christian perspective underlying this book claims to present an alternative framework and worldview from secular social science for describing, explaining and prescribing for socio-economic life. But it is not possible to 'prove' or demonstrate incontrovertibility that the Christian framework is 'superior' to those presented by the social sciences, however the term, 'superior' might be defined. Like all frameworks in social science, the Christian perspective rests on untestable metaphysical assumptions that constitute part of the Christian worldview.

Earlier chapters explained in principle how and why the Christian worldview can be construed as relevant to socio-economic application. The Christian worldview is shown as depicting reality in dualist form, in which mandates applicable to socio-economic life derive from the supernatural dimension of reality (the triune God). This is a highly unusual perspective to be presenting for socio-economic relevance, especially to the majority of social scientists who, by and large, ignore or reject the existence of supernatural reality. Indeed, this source of normative principles informing socio-economic life separates all schools of social scientific and economic thought from the Christian perspective. The chain of reasoning is that personal and socio-economic implications of Christian belief flow from spiritual to material reality. In this outlook, Christian belief cannot be separated from social science because Christianity has 'to provide its own account of the final causes at work in human history, on the basis of its own particular, and historically specific faith' (Milbank, 1990, 380). Nevertheless, it is also equally true that such a mode of reasoning articulates 'Christian difference in such a fashion as to make it strange' (Milbank, 1990, 381).

In postulating a duality between spirit and matter, Christian realism is not identical with scientific realism resting on a naturalistic base (e.g., Rosenberg, 1996) that characterizes much physical and social scientific activity. From a Christian perspective, neither physical science nor people have monopolistic access to truth. Science (physical or social) cannot provide an absolute ontology of what exists because its epistemology can reveal only (aspects of) the natural and social world. Even committed naturalist realists concede this, that 'the objective world in no way depends on thought' (Sankey, 2000, 224). People are not able to expose everything that exists, because humans only incompletely perceive aspects of the natural and social worlds. As well, naturalists deny the existence of supernatural reality. Chapter 9 suggested that a naturalist conception of reality is closely associated but not identical with a positivist framework. Nevertheless, 'positivism lives on in a naturalism that refuses to countenance specifically religious claims to truth, but restricts itself to what is within the province of science' (Trigg, 1998, 33).

With this claim, Christian belief presents a problem to both physical and social scientists. In positing a transcendent God, theism opens up 'an epistemological gap . . . between religious belief and its object. The metaphysical world of the theist becomes as problematic as the private world of introspection' (Trigg, 1998, 146). The private world of interrelationship between God and person is an important aspect of Christian practice because each individual person 'is an example of a bridge between the spiritual and the physical' (Trigg, 1998, 203). Throughout history, this individualistic path has proven invaluable for personal application of Christian belief, and for each individual believer, as we noted in Chapter 1, 'the inner illumination of the mind is strengthened' in the process (Milbank, 1990, 248). This individualistic path is highly valid to the person experiencing the spiritual reality. Efforts within the Christian tradition historically to demonstrate the reality of the spiritual world have relied greatly on the personal existential experience of believers. (Some of the major Christian contributors to this process throughout history are reviewed by Urban, 1995). The personal existential seems to be the mechanism people use for receiving input from spiritual reality and generating output back to it. No scientific theories of the brain can explain how the mechanism works in the communicative process. Most are not even interested in so doing; for example, naturalistic reductionist brain theories do not accept the existence of supernatural reality. The problem physical and social scientists have with this depiction is that the individual believer then has difficulty in confirming the inner existential reality to other people. Therefore, the personal existential is not a highly persuasive road to socio-economic application.

Other aspects of the Christian dualist realist belief system also have implications for social science, of which one instance can be noted. (Dualist here constitutes the inseparable relation between the spiritual and material realms of human life and reality.) Academic economics and social science recognize only the natural dimension of reality, and endeavor to construct self-contained explanation within this frame. The Christian response is that this project is incomplete, and will be unable to provide 'the essential categorical determinants for human social [or personal] existence' (Milbank, 1990, 64). Because they eschew the existence of spiritual reality, all varieties of secular philosophies and methodologies relating to socio-economic life can yield no more than indeterminate explanation. For example, secular realist methodologists will be able to reveal only limited material mechanisms explaining human behavior. It is a moot point whether realists in economics, for instance, have been able to uncover specific mechanisms affecting human behavior that were previously unknown. In part, this is because they 'can offer *no unique method*, no particular approach or technique' (Hands, 2001b, 327; original emphasis) that can uncover enduring causal structures that are taken to underlay the surface phenomena of social life.

The Christian worldview can explain this disconformity. The ontological reality of the material natural world does not translate unproblematically into an ontological material reality of the human socio-economic world. It is unable to do so because human behavior is affected by influences operating in material *and* transcendental reality. As a naturalist, Searle (1995, 191) can theorize only the material side of this problem, that 'the ontological subjectivity of the socially constructed reality requires an ontologically objective reality out of which it is constructed.' The other side of the coin is the Christian explanation of why objective material reality does not yield reliable material mechanisms explaining human behavior and relationships. Because of the naturalistic self-limitation, naturalistic realists lay themselves open to postmodern (de)constructionist, relativist and pragmatist criticism, pointing to the reliance of socio-economic analysis on contextual and literary constraints (e.g., McCloskey, 1994).

Christian realism repudiates also these forms of cultural relativism. Christian realism differs from interpretive social science (Rabinow and Sullivan, 1987) and from 'pragmatists and deconstructionists [who] agree that everything is a social construct' (Rorty, 1993, 100). 'Social construct' means something generated by humans in the material dimension, a self-contained naturalistic artifice. On this view, 'there is no extra-social standard to which we can appeal, nothing which can serve as a justification for social arrangements' (Trigg, 1998, 171). The Christian worldview appeals to an external justification, the triune God, and to the mandatory requirements He sets for material reality. God is the transcendent reality that undergirds human values and challenges human behavior. This explicitly contradicts a relativist conception for all aspects of human personal and socio-economic life.

Chapters 2 and 3 provided illustrations of how this is taken to work. The focus was to show how principles intended to inform socio-economic life derive from the transcendental reality of God. The specific case of revelation discussed there was the manner in which God's transcendental reality provided normative input for particular elements of material socio-economic organization. As those chapters argued, human reason has a crucial role to play in that process. In the Christian perspective developed in this book, human reason works compatibility with, and is reinforced by, revelatory means of receiving input from spiritual reality (and giving output back to it). The brain-mind-spirit matrix is taken to be the mechanism possessed by each person through which communication with transcendent reality is effected. Human response is reported in the Bible as being required to revelation at the group, social level as well as at the individual, personal level. The collective of individual human brain-mind-spirit is taken to be required to establish the meaning of specific revelation, and then relate/apply it in the particular material context confronting the group. This is the area of relevance to socio-economic activity.

Thus, indissoluble interrelationships are postulated in the Christian realist worldview to exist between the spiritual and the material spheres of reality. God is reported as establishing normative intentions in the Bible for human behavior in both domains. These mandates represent an intrinsic part of the mutual relationship between God and people. The two examples in Chapters 2 and 3 of the relevance of the mandates to socio-economic behavior were extracted from a greater range of normative principles set down by the triune God (a major part of spiritual reality). These are intended to guide human behavior in material reality. In the Bible, the transcendental God is portrayed frequently as seeking to influence socio-economic life. Often, the reality of the spiritual world to people is shown by the triune God or His agent instructing people to do something in relation to the socio-economic, or announcing something about to happen in this realm. This can involve God revealing what will happen in material reality if people follow the instruction, or if they do not. Virtually absent from the Bible are reports of purely numinous experiences *per se* from which no didactic implication or message for material life is conveyed to the people involved. Since the didactic is so important in God's revealing of spiritual reality to people, human response is invariably required by God. Human consciousness and reason, therefore, have the crucial role of interpreting for people the reality of the spiritual domain, and its relevance to the material world.

In this type of thinking, the 'religious' and the 'social' are not essentially separate concerns, if the 'religious' is shorthand for spiritual reality. In the examples of Chapters 2 and 3, spiritual and religious notions were constitutive of, and formed the basis of, the socio-economic measures striving for the wide availability of self-managed jobs for families and a relatively equal distribution of wealth and income. Another way of saying this is that the 'social' is 'an illusory *a priori* construct' (Milbank, 1990, 249). In Christian thinking, economic factors cannot be analyzed or economic policy derived as though they were entities autonomously existing from the normative requirements

God has for humankind. In the Old Testament and New Testament frameworks, human behavioral entities of interest to contemporary social science, such as the 'economic,' or the 'social' are seen not to exist self-containedly and independently from spiritual reality. Thus, 'the Bible's teaching about material possessions is inextricably intertwined with more "spiritual" matters' (Blomberg, 1999, 246). The idea underlying contemporary economics of regarding human personal or social behavior in its description or explanation as independent and separate from God's requirements has no precedent in Biblical thinking. As the Protestant economist, Hay (1993b, 139) expressed it, the dependence of human behavior on God's leading undercuts any claim of economics to 'intellectual autonomy in parallel with natural sciences.' The Christian church ignores this Biblical principle if it accepts 'economic analysis as an objective study of the economy, just as it has accepted the findings of the physical sciences' (Hay, 1993b, 134).

Like the project of this book, Milbank (1990, 1) attempted 'to disclose the possibility of a sceptical demolition of modern, secular social theory from a [Christian] perspective with which it is at variance.' His starting point was that 'the most important governing assumptions of such theory' involve 'the modification or the rejection of orthodox Christian positions.' Analogous to the Christian socio-economic perspective explored here, Milbank exposed 'the questionable idea of an autonomous secular realm' as inconsistent with Biblical Christianity, that 'the "autonomy" of secular reason involves as a condition of its very independence, the endorsement of a viewpoint which Christianity earlier presumed to call into question' (Milbank, 1990, 1, 37). Consistent with an implication of this book, Milbank identified conventional economics as a new object of worship, castigating 'the "neo-pagan" character of this clear-sighted vision of political economy and its outright celebration of what Christian theology rejected, namely the *libido dominandi*' [domination of man] (1990, 37). Milbank called for the recapture of the original intent of Christianity, to provide its own explanation of causes in human affairs, as a form of 'metanarrative realism' (1990, 251), replacing theology now mainly mediated by social science.

Our arguments can be regarded also as complementary to Long's (2000) advocacy of a 'residual tradition' in theology. Long defines this tradition as rejecting the fact-value distinction, in which 'theological descriptions' become 'as constitutive of the real as are economic ones.' In this tradition, the modern era is not taken 'as the benchmark against which theology must be measured' (Long, 2000, 177). Unlike Long's interpretation of this tradition, however, the arguments here have not devolved from a rationality inherent in Thomas Aquinas, but from modern orthodox Protestant and Catholic readings of the primary sources of Judeo-Christian belief. Nonetheless, the contemporary Papal Social Teachings examined here utilized a wider base of sources than this, as

Long demonstrates via the origins of Catholic social teaching and the work of Bernard Dempsey. In common with the three examples of the residual tradition examined by Long—Catholic Social Teaching, MacIntyre, and Milbank—the case here is 'at odds with contemporary economic arrangements', and calls for 'a reconstruction of the social order' (Long, 2000, 181). However, here, these deductions were made by investigating what are seen to be the original socio-economic intentions of Judeo-Christian thought.

The Christian methodology illustrated here for deriving intentions relevant to contemporary socio-economic organization is totally foreign to orthodox social science and economics. Even heterodox non-Christian economists may regard it as so strange as to not constitute economics. However, as suggested in Chapter 5, the approach is consistent with that taken by Islamic economics. In the Christian and Islamic frameworks, God's guidelines for economic arrangement are part of an holistic package stemming from the supernatural dimension of the respective belief systems. This domain constitutes part of the reality with which humankind is confronted. In this book, for example, a reasonably equal distribution of wealth and income was argued to apply from OT Law texts as constituting a God-given eternal norm for socio-economic organization (a view also held by many Islamic economists from their source materials). Numerous aspects of God's holistic personal/social system also have socio-economic application, and can be derived from the Christian Bible (and Muslim Qur'an and Sunnah), only some of which have been demonstrated in this book. For instance, wealth creation is not given priority above distribution. Judeo-Christianity and Islam posit ways of looking at economic matters that seem peculiar to secular economists.

Native English-speaking economists/Christians are divided on the issue of relating Christian belief to economics, and *vice versa*. In Chapter 7, we criticized two economists/Christian who advocate the autonomy of economics from Christian belief. However, we emphasize the contributions of contemporary economist/Christians committed to the exercise of relating Christian thought to economic life, and in positing the primacy of Christian belief to this enterprise. Some are associated with an orthodox Dutch or American Protestant evangelical viewpoint. Examples of these are Goudzwaard and de Lange (1995), Tiemstra et al. (1990), Tiemstra (1993) and Hoksbergen (1994a), affiliated with Reformed church thought, explicitly sympathetic to Catholic Social Thought (Tiemstra, 1999, 87–88). Others are within the British Anglican fold, like Hay (1989) and Cramp (1981, 1994). Others comfortable with this approach in varying degree are Mason (1987, 1996), Daly and Cobb (1994), and Hawtrey (1999). Pursuing this approach also are some within the Catholic tradition, like the American social economist, Arnold McKee (1987), the Institutionalists/social economists, Charles Wilber (1991, 1998) and Charles Clark (1992), the Personalist, Edward O'Boyle (1998), Helen Alford and Michael Naughton (2001), and Daniel Finn (1997). The compatibility of approach taken by these authors with social theologians such as Stephen Mott and Ronald Sider (1999), and Duncan Forrester (2001) is clear. With perhaps a lesser explicit degree of commitment to the primacy of Christian thought in the project of relating Christianity to economics are economists, Blank (1992), and Dow (1997, 1999). Except for Blank and Hawtrey, and the intermediate case of Hay, all the economists above are explicitly non-orthodox or heterodox economists. As well as being influenced by their 'normal' economics practices and Biblical interpretation, each of these economists is influenced by their favored theologians past and present. Despite broad agreement, unanimity is still developing in formulating a Christian methodology and relating it to the real world. The development of such a methodology, as pursued in this book, seeks to facilitate the specifics of how social science/Christians can relate their Christian beliefs to social science, including economics, and vice versa.

Although most of the economist/Christians cited above are heterodox, their secular non-orthodox colleagues are not necessarily more sympathetic to their efforts to relate Christian beliefs to economics than are orthodox economists. However, one of the reasons why heterodox economists/Christians may be more inclined than orthodox economists/Christians to relate their Christian beliefs to economics is that features of non-orthodox approaches to economics are embodied in Biblical and Christian thinking. For instance, precepts used in Post Keynesian-Institutionalist economics parallel Biblical exposition. Thus, Arestis et al. (1999, 528, 533) identify key features of Post Keynesian economics as 'a concern for history, uncertainty, distributional issues, and the importance of political and economic institutions in determining the level of activity in an economy,' and 'organicism and holism.' Post Keynesianism and Institutionalism, for example, have always stressed the importance of distributional issues. In, say, the minds of Post Keynesian exponents, Davidson and Davidson (1996, 69, 125), unequal distribution is unhealthy for employment in an industrialized economy that depends 'on mass production and domestic mass consumption for its prosperity.' Inequality contributes also to 'the erosion of the civic values of the community.' Only a wide dispersion of goods will encourage people to believe that the economic system is working for all, so that conflict can be mitigated. Earlier chapters showed that many of these concerns mooted above are intrinsic to Biblical Christianity. In so far as the heterodox economist/Christians who assert the primacy of Christian belief over economics, use such analytical precepts, they derive from their Christian beliefs as much as or more than their economics' beliefs.

THE METHODOLOGY OF CHRISTIAN SOCIO-ECONOMIC ANALYSIS

From the work of the heterodox economist/Christians above, and from the approach taken in this book, it is possible to clarify the methodology implied in Christian socio-economic analysis. 'Methodology' means the complex of notions, concepts, procedures, theories, and models of behavior used in any system of thought, as per Boudon (1994, 379–380). To engage in methodological analysis is to systematically evaluate and criticize such notions etc. This meaning of methodology is more encompassing than defined merely as 'a study of the relationship between theoretical concepts and warranted conclusions about the real world' (Blaug, 1992, xii), or as focusing on 'questions of theory confirmation or disconfirmation or empirical theory choice' (Hausman, 1992, 13). In the broader definition adopted here, methodology includes questions such as, 'what are the goals of economics?,' thus incorporating consideration of the objects of interest of the discipline, 'what is the role of social science in guiding conduct?,' as well as 'what methods are employed?' (Sent, 1999, 728, 729). A related perennial question of methodology is whether research can be, or should be, value-free. Methodology as the 'philosophical study of scientific method' (Honderich, 1995, 565), incorporates diverse and wide-ranging questions.

The conclusion is that Christian socio-economic analysis practiced by the above economist/Christians, and in this book, embodies a particular methodology that is capable of being codified. This finding is potentially significant because the Christian belief system is still the worldview (despite its variations) to which coheres the largest group of adherents internationally. Debate continues among Christians about the methodological relevance of their beliefs to contemporary socio-economic issues. The isolation of methodological precepts that are and could be used in contemporary Christian socio-economic analysis shows how Christianity relates to social science and economics more generally. A popular view of Christianity and economics is that they are both so heterogeneous that it is almost impossible to expose their essences. This book does not accept this conception. Suggesting that Christianity and economics are each so diverse within themselves as to preclude extracting their core content implies a view of such loose philosophical and methodological flexibility embodied in each system as to deny each a coherent structure.

We have argued that fundamental differences exist between the orthodox Christian perspectives on which this book are based, and secular social science systems of thought. One, for instance, is that many Christians probably believe with Catholic Social Thought that 'there can be *no genuine solution of the "social question" apart from the Gospel.*' Another, from the same source, may be the common Christian belief that only in the Bible can a context for the correct understanding of socio-economic questions and 'the proper moral perspective for judgement on them' be found (CA, 1991, 12; original emphasis). These are unique Christian perspectives. Again, Christian socio-economic analysis takes empirical facts and relates them to God's normative will. The secular economist takes empirical facts and endeavors to derive explanations from them. Ostensibly, the two domains appear to address radically different projects. However, each is endeavoring to construct an explanation for socio-economic behavior and to provide policy guidance. Christian socio-economic analysis is intended to be descriptive and explanatory, as well as prescriptive, all embodying what are believed to be values expressed in God's will.

The first step, therefore, in Christian socio-economic analysis is to ascertain just what God's will might be for particular socio-economic domains. Chapters 2–4 gave examples how these might be derived. Similarly, Catholic Social Thought has a long tradition of so doing. Once these have been deduced (the process of which may involve disagreement between Christians), subsequent methodological tenets can be pursued in relating these intentions to specific cultural-historical contexts. Following is a selection of these methodological features as they could be undertaken, some of which have been so done in particular instances by Christian socio-economic analysts (e.g., O'Boyle, 1998). Two core and, as yet in this book, undiscussed methodological characteristics are the focus, and each is assessed in terms of how Christian socio-economic analysis might use them. Just two characteristics are emphasized to allow a full treatment. Subsequently and more briefly, methodological implications of a number of the remaining Christian methodological features are suggested.

Table 14.1 below is a summary of major methodological characteristics of Christian socio-economic analysis as practiced by a selection of its advocates in recent decades, namely, the non-orthodox economist/Christians cited above (plus the intermediate case of Hay, 1989), and this book. The similarity of items in the table with characteristics of Institutionalist economics has been emphasized before (e.g., Tiemstra, 1993, Halteman, 1999). The actual derivation of each characteristic in the table from each source author is not spelled out here. In part, this is because the last sections of the last chapter of a book are not the appropriate place to do so, and also because each cited author has usually practiced each methodological tenet tacitly rather than overtly. All the discussion below does is to suggest how each methodological characteristic derives from specific base Christian source materials, such as the Bible and CST. Table 14.1 is not exhaustive because any listing has to be selective. The table focuses on key methodological characteristics discernible from the cited authors as a whole, even if each author does not follow them consistently. Each author underlying the table would not necessarily agree with all items, and each in their own work does not pursue each tenet in like manner. For instance, Hay (1989) and Tiemstra et al. (1990) have characteristic one at the beginning and as the basis for their books, while Daly and Cobb (1994) wait until their last chapter to pursue the matter. Nor does the common listing of Protestant evangelicals and Catholics as sources for Table 14.1 assume that Protestant evangelical theology and Catholic Social Thought are necessarily compatible on all issues. Hutter and Dieter (1998), for example, explore differences and similarities between the two streams of Christian thought on a number of ethical questions not discussed here.

Table 14.1. Methodological Characteristics of Christian Socio-economic Analysis

1. Establish transcultural Christian/Biblical intentions or principles for socio-economic life.
2. Relate these intentions to specific socio-economic contexts, as per 3–15 below.
3. Study organization and control of the socio-economic system, including institutions, rights of participants, power structure and distributional outcomes.
4. Emphasize role of technology and culture in socio-economic development.
5. Seek holistic/organicistic, cumulative circular causation of socio-economic change.
6. Investigate nature of socio-economic change as dynamic, evolutionary, unstable, and in disequilibria.
7. Welcome interconnection with other disciplines; interdisciplinary.
8. Emphasize role of socio-historico-cultural context; therefore encourage case studies.
9. Rely on empirical investigation rather than theoretical models; induction rather than deduction.
10. Explicit value premises underlie research and policy; values are not necessarily reflected in prices.
11. Investigate 'non-economic' factors e.g., uncertainty, belief, custom, habit, status emulation, conflict, coercion, work as a way of realizing social identity, reject hedonism and utilitarianism.
12. Study behavior of social wholes and individuals; individuals both form and are formed by their social environments.
13. Critically assess quality of socio-economic life; practical problem-solving nexus.
14. Non-predictive.
15. Conform with realism, not relativism or constructivism.

Sources: Wilber (1978; 1998); Cramp (1981, 1994); McKee (1987); Mason (1987, 1996); Hay (1989); Clark (1992); Goudzwaard and de Lange (1995), Tiemstra et al. (1990), Tiemstra (1993, 1999); Daly and Cobb (1994); Hoksbergen (1994); Beed and Beed (1996b, 1997); O'Boyle (1998).

HOLISM AND CIRCULAR CAUSATION IN CHRISTIAN SOCIO-ECONOMIC ANALYSIS

The two items from Table 14.1 under close inspection in this section are numbers five and six: the holistic or organicistic, cumulative circular causation of socio-economic change, and the content of this change as dynamic, evolutionary and unstable. The two items are regarded usually as part of holism, which approach is followed below. The principle of holism is a key methodological feature of Christian socio-economic analysis. Holism is both a key and methodological because it seeks to underpin all the critical activity the economist/Christians apply to their research, thereby consistent with the definition of methodology above. A discussion follows of common secular economics meaning of holism (e.g., as per Wilber, 1999) and then how features of this definition relate to Christian methodological principles in Table 14.1. Holism can have broader implications than featured here, as in Diesing (1971), Phillips (1976) and James (1984). Conversely, holism is delimited sometimes with a narrower focus, as in Kincaid (1996). However, holism in a secular economics sense (e.g. Kapp, 1976, 212, 213, 222) is often taken to involve 'a denial that economic processes . . . can be adequately understood and analyzed as closed, *i.e.* self-contained and self-sustaining systems isolated from a social and physical "environment" of which the economic system is a part . . .' This is because 'the economy is an open system in continuous dynamic interaction with a more comprehensive social and political as well as physical system.' This approach involves studying 'the reciprocal interaction of the parts with one another and with the "whole",' it is 'unacceptable to draw classificatory distinctions between so-called economic and non-economic factors and between economic and social processes'; indeed, 'there are no economic (or, for that matter, sociological) problems; there are only problems and they are all complex'. In this secular view of Kapp's, searching for a basic cause of existing socio-economic conditions is out of the question, given the reciprocal interdependence existing with the socio-economic system.

The methodological principle of circular (including cumulative) causation is central to holism. Circular causation means that a change in an endogenous factor causes change in others, and it normally has cumulative effects out of all proportion to the initial effect (Myrdal, 1978, 774). The holistic methodological principles of circular and cumulative causation are inseparably connected with and in the transformation or evolution of social processes, and with that change as being unstable and in disequilibrium (item 6 in Table 14.1). This is because causative influences (item 3 in Table 14.1) change the content of the socio-economic system and impart instability to social change itself (item 6). Accordingly, 'incessant change and flux are fundamental to open systems, where dynamic feedback processes ensure continual motion and reorganization' (O'Hara, 1993, 58). Variables change discontinuously, in which the methodological distinction between statics and dynamics is not useful for socio-economic analysis. Nevertheless, 'although unceasing change is envisioned, no necessary pattern exists' for 'no law or principle underlies either the growth of understanding or the development of an economy' (Miller, 1978, 17). Change, development, evolution, and adaptation are integral to the system, pointing to the 'impermanence of both the present set of economic arrangements and the adequacy of any current set of policy proposals' (Petr, 1984, 6). Disruption, disparities, and non-self-regulating characteristics of socio-economic systems are the normal situation, in which equilibrium and balance are transitory and provisional.

To Wilber and Harrison (1978, 71, 79, 80; original emphasis), holistic analysis 'focuses on the pattern of relations among parts and the whole.' Accordingly, 'social reality must be studied as a whole human system in its natural setting,' for 'an intelligible and relevant model of the economic *system* cannot be obtained by isolating the phenomenon of exchange from its interrelationship with the social whole.' Nevertheless, as O'Hara (1993, 54) points out, 'both unity and some limited degree of separateness of phenomena must be recognized,' for an entry point into social inquiry is required.

Hodgson (1993) prefers the term organicist to holist, although organicism can convey wider connotation than holism as identified here (e.g., Winslow, 1994). To Hodgson, 'organicism denies that individuals can be treated as elemental or immutable building blocks of analysis . . . Individuals both constitute and are constituted by society' (Hodgson, 1993, 110). In Table 14.1 above, these ideas are related more to item twelve concerning the interrelation between individuals and social phenomena. A broad reading of holism could well include this methodological principle, but item twelve of the table is not discussed in this section.

In summary, holism in the secular economics sense appears to imply at least the following methodological characteristics:

- Holist explanation requires investigation of mutual interconnections between social/economic/political factors operating in open socio-economic systems.
- No one factor is necessarily preeminent in explaining any given socio-economic phenomenon—everything causes everything else.
- Nevertheless, to comprehend the whole, investigation of separate parts may be required, for wholes cannot necessarily be explained without reference to the parts.

- The holistic concept of causation embodies circular properties—change in one part of the system causes change in another.
- Causation is also cumulative, generating feedbacks that can be amplified, lags that produce instability, and relationships that are non-linear.
- Accordingly, prediction of socio-economic behavior is not possible in the long-term.
- Socio-economic arrangements are characterized by indeterminism.
- The entire system is in continual change and flux marked by multiple conflict and contradiction.
- Holist explanation is non-reductionist, and concatenated rather than hierarchical, in which subject-matter moulds methods.

CHRISTIAN METHODOLOGICAL CONNECTIONS WITH HOLISM

Holism extends as far back as the Bible. The argument of this section is that the methodological framework embodied in the Bible's description of principles of socio-economic behavior, and its conception of causation, is holistic. Therefore, a Biblically-based Christian socio-economic methodology should employ an holistic perspective. Unfortunately, the history of the methodology of Christian investigation is not replete with examples of socio-economic analysis (although it should be), much less with holistic versions of them. This section does not explore the reasons for this hiatus. A separate study would be required to document and explain the neglect of such Christian socio-economic analysis, and associated lack of holistic versions of it. Nonetheless, some examples are presented below to substantiate the contention that holistic thinking is integral to Christian methodology: from the Bible itself, from CST, and from evangelical theology.

In both the Old and New Testaments of the Christian Bible, there is an holistic emphasis in both the depiction and explanation of human behavior. Consider the mode used in the Bible to describe and observe human socio-economic behavior, as distinct from explaining it. The holistic methodological framework is revealed by the absence of attempts to divide the description of human conduct into separate spheres of economic, social, religious, recreational, or family life—even though activity in each of these areas is presented in meticulous detail. The portrayal of human life flows rapidly between work, rest, sickness, religious observance, marriage, travel, pillage, child rearing, talking with God, listening to Jesus, buying, selling, and every conceivable detail of human action. For example, the second book the Old Testament, Exodus, setting the scene for the Israelites' escape from Egypt, starts by describing Pharaoh's political plotting to keep the Israelites in servitude, and ends by revealing how the Israelites responded to Pharaoh's machinations. The stories of people throughout the Bible show them doing a diverse and interrelated range of things. The mixture of activity, and the interaction of activities, are hallmarks of the human condition described in the Bible. This is not surprising because God and Jesus are concerned with the ordinary things of life, including the non-religious. A central part of their message is to show that They should be Lord of every facet of human existence. Since the triune God created the entire scope of human action, it is likely that a book teaching people how He intends them to behave would describe the whole spectrum of what people do, including their interactions between activities. Holistic methodological principles are paramount in this descriptive and prescriptive process.

Biblical *explanations* of human behavior (as distinct from description) maintain this holistic, interactive, interrelational methodology. The overriding and proximate cause presented in the Bible of any human socio-economic situation, such as poverty, unemployment, high prices and other socio-economic ills is human deviation from norms God establishes for socio-economic life. This religious core-belief acts as a guiding methodological and philosophical presupposition to theorizing (Clouser, 1991, 106). A concrete instance in the Bible illustrates this contention—the disparity between rich and poor in the settled Israel (examined in detail, for example, by the evangelical theologian, Wright, 1990; 1995). The existing state of affairs is represented in the Old Testament as deriving from people not following a multiplicity of the God-given normative principles affecting spiritual, political, economic and social life. A lack of correct behavior in the spiritual domain of life—that is, not following normative principles provided by God—causes people to engage in incorrect behavior in the economic domain. This behavior contributes to a distortion of spiritual life even more, and thereby deforms behavior in other aspects of human life. Human sinfulness (i.e., missing the mark of God's norms) rebounds from one domain of life to another—again, holistic methodological principles are used.

Consistent with an holistic methodology, no simple one-to-one relationship between cause and effect is presumed in this explanatory Biblical matrix. Therefore, explanatory links are not necessarily separably amenable to empirical discovery. For instance, take Biblical explanations for the disintegration of the states of Israel and Judah in the Old Testament. Again, these are cast invariably in terms of the people and rulers disregarding God's normative teaching. But there is no singling out of any one or few failures in Israel's and Judah's apostasy. The list is wide-ranging, including ignoring God *per se* and failing to seek His guidance, the practice of sexual immorality, lack of action to improve the wellbeing of the poor, worship of other gods, dishonest business practices, and so on. Each of these is subdivided still further. The major and minor prophets recount with minute detail the sins with which God charged the two nations. The explanation of the nations' demise is holistic and multidimensional, extending to virtually every aspect of daily life and the interrelation between them.

In sum, socio-economic behavior in its Biblical depiction and explanation is presented as an embodied whole in which each aspect of behavior is interrelated. There is no suggestion that any particular aspect of behavior, such as the economic, can be disentangled from the totality of human action, or that economic behavior can be explained as though it existed self-containedly as some separate category of human life. This mode of representation is foreign to the Bible's depiction of human action. Attributes like scarcity, preferences and choice are depicted in the Bible not only as causes, but simultaneously as effects of human social and personal activity. Human choice is affected by influences operating in all spheres of life, including the spiritual. The secular economist, O'Hara (1993, 53), expresses what could well characterize Biblical holism, that 'the dualities of thought-action, subjective-objective, and idealism-materialism are inconsistent with a holistic understanding of social processes and institutions.' The normative precepts the triune God intends for human behavior in the Bible, and the consequences of people following and not following God's norms (thereby producing human problems) are expressed as an embodied whole.

This framework for explanation is similar to secular ideas of circular and cumulative causation above, that 'there are no economic, sociological, or psychological problems, but just problems, and they are all mixed and composite . . . the only permissible demarcation is between relevant and irrelevant conditions' (Myrdal, 1978, 772). This conception is akin also to Wolff and Resnick's (1987, 20) holistic (Marxian) concept of overdetermination. Nonetheless, major differences exist between the Biblical version of holism and its secular expressions. For example, in the Biblical version, the underlying cause of the human social condition is the interplay between God (including the normative requirements He has set for humankind), and human free will. In the secular summary of holism above, no one factor is necessarily basic for explaining a socio-economic phenomenon. In the Biblical view, the triune God is explanatorily preeminent. Again, a Biblical view of social change is teleological in contrast to a typical secular view of change as non-teleological.

Catholic Social Thought (CST) also embodies an holistic methodology—an expected characteristic since CST depends on the Bible. This contention can be demonstrated from an encyclical of Pope John Paul II. In CA (1991), John Paul reviews an 1891 encyclical, *Rerum Novarum*. In both these documents, a mutually-supporting program of social and economic policies is advocated, in which each one is depicted as encouraging others. Reflecting an holistic orientation also, the rationale for each policy is argued to derive from its impact on a diverse range of aspects of personal and social life that interrelate with each other. For example, both state socialism and unfettered capitalism are proscribed not primarily for their economic implications, but because each is held to distort the essential bond between human freedom and truth. In so far as this unity is threatened, the requirement for social peace on a foundation of distributive justice is not achievable; the risk would be a society torn by harsh and inhumane conflict. A society so rent would not be capable of achieving effective stewardship of natural resources or optimal economic efficiency. What starts out as a theological proposition (human freedom depending on truth) is shown to end up having economic consequences—relational and holistic links are to the fore.

Again, in CST, the right to free association of people is advocated, such as trade unions. CST recognizes the potentially disadvantaged situation in which workers often find themselves. But free association is advocated primarily from the theological criterion that it is 'a natural right of the human being' (CA, 1991, 13). Theological reasoning is used to buttress a socio-economic proposal (trade unions) that feeds back to strengthen the theological proposition. Work also is seen as having mutually supportive and interdependent qualities, that 'more than ever, work is *work with others* and *work for others*' (CA 1991, 45; original emphasis). This form of interrelational and holistic thinking about social issues dates far back in CST, but just one further example is cited here from another encyclical of Pope John Paul II, *Sollicitudo Rei Socialis* (SRS, 1987). In discussing the concept of socio-economic development, SRS notes the interdependence between the nations of the world. However, 'when this interdependence is separated from its ethical requirements, it has *disastrous consequences* for the weakest' that under the influence of perverse mechanisms, 'triggers *negative effects* even in the rich countries' (SRS, 1987, 34; original emphasis). Again, reciprocal feedbacks are emphasized. Secondary Catholic comment maintains this recognition of the holistic nature of the primary papal sources of CST; for example, that social 'structures of sin are to be understood not merely in terms of a social analysis . . . but in theological terms' (Dorr, 1992, 330). All the preceding are examples of interrelational, mutual-type methodological thinking, for no one policy is advocated or social phenomenon analyzed without considering its repercussions on a range of human behavioral responses that also have the capacity to interact with each other. They are holistic too in that the church's evangelizing mission is interwoven with and part of its social mission.

This integral interrelation between the theological basis of CST and its socio-economic implications reflect circular causative thinking. In secondary

CST discussion, a reciprocal interdependency exists because 'the human construction of the world does not lie outside God's plan but is intimately involved with the dynamic of the Reign of God.' Socio-economic qualities of God's rule are that 'a preferential love' should be shown to the economically disadvantaged whose needs are 'given special attention in God's eyes,' that 'the resources of the earth are to be shared equitably by all,' that all property has a social mortgage in stewardship, and that 'work is a way that humans share in the activity of God' (Henroit et al., 1992, 22–24). God's normative teachings for human spiritual and material life are interwoven methodologically throughout the Bible and CST, holding together as an essential unity. This unity reflects and embodies an holistic conception of human behavior and society.

The methodological unity between the spiritual and material dimensions of human life is described explicitly as 'holistic' in evangelical Protestant theology (e.g., Spykman, 1992, 236–240). Nevertheless, evangelical theology (e.g., Spykman, 1992; Grudem, 1994; McGrath, 1997; Erickson, 1998), like theology in general, has not explored greatly the relation between Christian belief and socio-economic phenomena. Where evangelical exceptions to this statement occur (e.g. Birch, 1991; Yoder, 1994; Wright, 1995), it can be shown they employ an holistic methodological approach and reach holistic conclusions, even if, like CST, the term 'holistic' is not used. In one strain of evangelical thinking, discussed in Chapter 3, the principles underlying the intended organization of the Old Testament state of Israel are taken as paradigmatic for the life of all nations. Wright (1990, 1995, 1996), for example, has made a close study of the political, religious, economic and social design of Israel. In his view, an intrinsic mutual or holistic interrelationship existed between Israel's socio-economic organization and its religious basis. This was so because Israel's planned 'socio-economic equality facilitated religious equality, and *vice versa*, and that socio-economic unity facilitated religious exclusiveness, and *vice versa*, in such a way that neither would have been the same if the other had been different' (Wright, 1995, 164; original emphasis). Israel was to be holistic in its internal organization, but also to have a methodologically holistic purpose in the world. Israel was 'a vehicle both for God's revelation and for the redemption of humanity . . . a model of what a redeemed community would look like, living in obedience to God's will' (Wright, 1995, 165).

The discussion above reveals that the Bible, CST, and examples of evangelical theology that have discussed the relation between Biblical thought and socio-economic behavior, employ holistic methodological thinking. This applies to the relation between God and humankind, and to the relations between people themselves, including the links between personal and social action. Mutual interconnections are stressed between spiritual, social, economic and political factors operating in open socio-economic systems. This section has argued that Christian socio-economic analysis should employ an holistic methodology. In addition, Christian socio-economic analysis as per item 7 of Table 14.1 is intended to be methodologically interdisciplinary, in which its interconnections with other disciplines are sought. In Christian socio-economic analysis, however, not quite *every* factor is held to cause every other because the triune God is taken to be the prime moving force in the human system. Consistent with this version of concessional holism, the separate factors are sometimes treated individually—for example, the lack of religious observance in the Old Testament—but invariably the impact of each factor on others is presented—for example, the ways in which lack of religious observance spilt over to affect the poor unjustly. The relation is two way, because change in religious observance (one part of the system) is depicted not only as causing change in another, but feeding back to distort people's spiritual relations with God even more. Causation is cumulative, generating system disruption, contradiction, and disequilibrium—exemplified most starkly in the Old Testament in the destruction of Israel, and in the New Testament in the crucifixion of Jesus.

FURTHER METHODOLOGICAL FEATURES OF CHRISTIAN SOCIO-ECONOMIC ANALYSIS

This section draws out more briefly than the previous section implications of further methodological features of the Christian socio-economic analytical system of Table 14.1. Initially, two items from the table are discussed. First is item ten, that explicit value premises underlie Christian socio-economic research and policy. Examining this item conforms to the long-standing methodological interest in the degree to which social science is value-free. Second, item three in Table 14.1 is discussed, that Christian socio-economic analysis studies the organization and control of the economic system, including institutions, rights of participants, power structure and distributional outcomes. Reviewing this item is consistent with our initial definition of methodology as studying the objects of interest to specific systems of thought. This section concludes with briefer methodological comparisons between some remaining features of the Christian socio-economic analytical framework from Table 14.1.

Item ten in Table 14.1 points to Christian socio-economic research and policy as undergirded by explicit values. Explicit value premises have to guide its search for policy proposals which means that Christian socio-economic analysis produces a normative system of knowledge. All the heterodox economist/Christians reject the positive-normative distinction in economics, and Christian socio-economic policy is values-driven. Christian socio-economic analysis not only embodies particular values in its research and policy proposals, but seeks also to expose the values inherent in existing socio-economic arrangements. Its theory of value would be concerned not merely with the relative prices of commodities. It would be concerned also with the processes by which the values are reflected in socio-economic behavior, and therefore in institutions and social structures in which values are reflected.

The Biblical writers, holding people to be moral agents, were preoccupied with exposing the values reflected in actual human personal and socio-economic behavior, compared with the normative value system the triune God had established for this behavior. The Old Testament is saturated with such value-based themes. For instance, even in the first few chapters of the first book of the Old Testament, Genesis, values' issues predominate. They concern the description and then human despoliation of the 'good' physical and social environment God had created initially (the ethical basis of the physical environmental creation is examined in Beed and Beed, 1998). This first chapter of the Bible also examines God's preservation of free will for people, human exercise of this free will to usurp or ignore God's values, and the disastrous consequences flowing from such (personal and social) human action. In the New Testament, Jesus Christ maintained and extended the values God had provided to people 'in the beginning.' Values underlying forgiveness, serving God, genuine leadership, and love of neighbor, for example, are embodied in many of Jesus' statements. Other values integral to Christian thought, such as mercy, justice, faithfulness, wisdom, fortitude, and self-discipline, are encased and reiterated in the Old and New Testaments. In much Christian thinking, Biblical values act as a lens through which human behavior is meant to be viewed and for which prescription is sought.

The values embodied in such Biblical portrayal are sympathetic to humanist aims for human betterment and the common good, such as choosing whatever ensures the continuity of human life, the re-creation of community, the pursuit of non-invidious change, and the instrumental use of knowledge. For instance, invidious distinctions (those based on status, wealth, ownership etc.) contradict the equity basis of Old Testament Law, and Jesus' development of it in the New Testament (such as in Mt. 20:26). Although the institutional church historically has often practiced invidious distinction, it has no normative basis in Biblical thought.

Biblical values underlying the analyses of CST are sympathetic also to those expressed above. For instance, in SRS (1987), 'true development *cannot* consist in the simple accumulation of wealth and in the greater availability of goods and services, if this is gained at the expense of the development of the masses, and without due consideration for the social, cultural and spiritual dimensions of the human being.' True human priorities are upset where '*huge sums of money*, which could and should be used for increasing the development of peoples, are instead utilized for the enrichment of individuals or groups . . .' What SRS looks for is 'a different world, ruled by concern for the *common good* of all humanity,' by concern for the 'spiritual and human development of all instead of by the quest for individual profit . . .' (SRS, 1987, 21, 23, 24; original emphasis). These ideas embody values consistent with Christian socio-economic analysis and with humanist economic thought; in the latter, for example, with making the community work well for its inhabitants, in which 'productive participation, the realization of potential, the nurture and protection of the vulnerable and powerless is facilitated,' and 'polarization and isolation is thwarted' (Miller, 1995, 126). Christian socio-economic analysis seeks a social system in which cooperation rather than competition is the value guide (Beed, 2005b) and in which equitable inclusion and outcome are the value products rather than personal and social selfishness. In relation to item thirteen of Table 14.1 above, a critical stance to the assessment of the quality of socio-economic life is required.

Item three of Table 14.1 emphasizes the orientation of Christian socio-economic analysis to studying the organization and control of the economic system. The Biblical writers spent much space discussing these matters in the socio-economic systems of their times. Reflecting holistic thinking and the philosophical worldview underlying this thinking, the socio-economic system, in their view, could not be divorced from the spiritual 'system' (people's relations with the triune God, and vice versa) affecting human behavior, and from any other aspect of personal and social action. The Biblical authors deliberated over institutions such as the market, land tenure system, army, monarchy, ruling class or cast, priest system, and quasi-institutions like the rich and poor (including their subdivisions), and aliens. It is not exaggerating to say the Biblical writers were preoccupied with describing and explaining people's mutual relations with God and Jesus Christ, in a wide range of cultural and institutional settings, and how these affected personal and social behavior and vice versa. For instance, the Old Testament returns again and again to these themes. The Covenant and Mosaic Law, intended to provide the normative personal and social requirements for Israel's life, describe in meticulous detail the mandatory organizational features of the spiritual-socio-economic system, focusing on institutional arrangements necessary to achieve the sought ends, on the rights of those involved in this system, on the power structure inherent in it, and on the efficiency and distributional outcomes that should flow from it. That Israel did not follow the norms was the preoccupation of the Prophets who railed at Israel's failure, and foretold the destruction that followed. In the New Testament, Jesus Christ, the Son of

God, maintained the crucial importance of the Law's intentions. He interpreted and developed them in the new socio-cultural context in which the remnant of Israel found itself, as a Roman-occupied nation, one thousand years or so from the Covenant and Law's original formulation.

In terms of distributional outcomes in item three of Table 14.1, the Bible and CST portray the socio-economic systems of their times as marked by inequity and injustice. The latter's concern with this issue is reflected again in *Sollicitudo Rei Socialis* (SRS, 1987). One theme in SRS (1987, 20) is the 'serious problem of *unequal distribution* of the means of subsistence originally meant for everybody, and thus also an unequal distribution of the benefits deriving from them.' In his review of CST, Simons (1995) suggested that 'in recent and current Catholic social teaching, inequality has become *the* social question of the age.' Inequality in the distribution of socio-economic opportunities in contemporary society is emphasized also in evangelical thought. For example, the evangelical economist, Mason (1996) applied guidelines drawn from the Bible to analyze current American welfare policy. He argued that the Biblical materials lend confidence to 'government-mediated income redistribution' but not in the form presently existing in the United States. Rather, 'assistance to the poor should have as its chief goal establishing and maintaining economically and socially secure families' because the family is the surest setting in which faith in God can be moulded, in which a person finds an enduring sense of meaning, and in which effective service can be offered to the larger community (Mason, 1996, 154, 147, 166–167). The Bible, CST, and evangelical writers expose inequality, polarization and domination both as characteristics of socio-economic life, and as tendencies to be resisted—the Bible in past societies, CST and evangelicals in more recent history and the present.

This section concludes by briefly commenting on methodological implications of remaining items of Christian socio-economic analysis in Table 14.1. Item twelve in the table suggests that Christian socio-economic analysis studies both the behavior of social wholes and individuals, that individuals both form and are formed by their social environments. This is pertinent to the argument between methodological individualism and collectivism. Christian socio-economic analysis stands between methodological individualism and methodological collectivism (sometimes called methodological holism). According to Hodgson et al. (1994, 63–64), quoting Elster, methodological individualism is 'the doctrine that all social phenomena (their structure and their change) are in principle explicable only in terms of individuals—their properties, goals and beliefs'—a system often believed to underlie Neoclassical economics. Conversely, methodological holism holds that social science 'explains in terms of social entities—such as classes, institutions, and so on—and their characteristics' (Kincaid, 1996, 6).

Christian socio-economic analysis lies methodologically between these two conceptions of viewing social phenomena in emphasizing the interrelation between personal and social behavior. For instance, a common evangelical view of human behavior in the Old Testament is that the values individual people exercised in their decision making were 'seen in the context of a community identity' (Birch, 1991, 30). This theme runs through much evangelical analysis of contemporary ethical problems, of a focus 'on the community in the midst of which and according to the ideals of which personal character finds its reference point' (Grenz, 1998, 399). Nevertheless, the individual person is still paramount in this context, having been given the free will by God to exercise personal choice and decision making. The intrinsic relation between individual person and social context has always been to the fore in CST. These links are brought out in another encyclical by Pope John II, *Laborem Exercens* (LE, 1981), discussing the nature of human work. The individual nature of work (and its ethical value) is highlighted as the person being in 'the image of God,' as 'a subjective being . . . capable of deciding about himself, and with a tendency to self-realization.' 'Work is a good thing for man' because in work people share with God the activity of creation (LE, 1981, 26, 39, 95). However, work 'is the key to the social question' (LE, 1981, 17) for work constitutes the foundation of social organization, in family, workplace, trade union and society. In this analysis, both personal and social dimensions of work are emphasized. Harking back to the values issue above, '*the principle of the priority of labour* over capital is a postulate of the order of social morality' (LE, 1981, 64; original emphasis).

Item eight in Table 14.1 above suggests that in Christian socio-economic analysis the role of the socio-historico-cultural context relevant to the location of the analysis is emphasized. Methodologically, it is a question of applying God's immutable principles in specific times and places. This is the reason why case studies can be held in high regard even though the base of the analysis, as per items 1 and 2 of Table 14.1 is to uncover principles that might be applicable to other times and places. A similar but not identical methodological orientation pervades the Bible. At no time are principles there revealed as unrelated to an empirical situation. Further, the principles contained in the particular culture of a Biblical text are intended usually to be applied in other contexts as well. For instance, the Ten Commandments were proclaimed in the course of the Israelites' escape from Egypt, and were linked integrally to the covenant God had made with the Israelites. Nevertheless, the Commandments carried wider import than their mere application to the Israelites. Most contemporary Christian and Jewish thought, and even some non-Christian thought, still accept their validity. At other times in the Bible, principles are not necessarily stated explicitly, as in

Jesus' parables. Here, the exercise for readers of the text is to derive the principles from the given specific historico-cultural context. Story after story in the Bible—historical narratives, parables, allegories, myths, metaphors, proverbs, legends, poems, and fables—depicts empirical situations specific to a cultural setting. The challenge provided to people by God and Jesus is to interpret the text (or for the people at the time, the actual saying/event), and to determine its meaning in principle, the significance of which is invariably transcultural. To object that this process is thereby to represent Jesus' sayings, for example, as ahistorical and acultural is to miss the point of their eternal relevance. A recognition of the variability of culture through time and space in Biblical thought should not obscure the aim of Christian socio-economic analysis to seek principles of human behavior applicable to other cultures. Actual socio-cultural-temporal occurrences are the meat from which tenets, theories and doctrines are to be established from the Bible, and the different contexts in which they are to be applied (both of which raise the possibility of disagreement among Christian believers, to which the history of Christianity attests).

As item eleven in Table 14.1 suggests, Christian socio-economic analysis is interested in the role of 'non-economic' factors in causal explanations. These factors include beliefs, conflict, folkways, inherited mores, and aspects of work from which people derive satisfaction other than pecuniary reward. Many tendencies within Christianity uphold the importance of influences such as these in their methodological efforts to achieve explanation. For example, the importance of non-pecuniary influences in explaining the value of human work has been noted above for CST. In terms of human purpose, Christian socio-economic analysis is not concerned only with narrowly defined economic motives like the profit motive, or self-interest, however defined. The overriding purpose of human life in Christian thinking is to love and serve the triune God, neighbor, and self. The motives or intentions of human action are as important, if not more so, than their consequences. On these grounds, Christianity rejects methodological principles devolving on hedonism and utilitarianism (item 11 of Table 14.1).

Finally, the methodology of Christian socio-economic analysis is held here to expose the nature of reality. Christianity has been aligned historically with many secular schools of philosophical thought. In relation to item fifteen of Table 14.1 above, some Christians (e.g., McGrath, 2002; Trigg, 1998; Alston, 1996) have argued recently that Christian belief is consistent with philosophical realism. Elsewhere (Beed and Beed, 1997), we have shown that methodological application of this form of realism differs from the critical realism underlying Lawson's (1997) approach in economics, but that nonetheless Christian metaphysical realism can be used as a basis for socio-economic analysis.

CONCLUSION

From the basic sources of analysis depicted in this book (Biblical exegetes, Protestant evangelical theologians and economists, and Catholic Social Thought), and from the approaches of a cited selection of heterodox economist/Christians, many methodological features have been exposed underlying Christian socio-economic analysis. Considering the list of items in Table 14.1, these methodological principles include the objects of interest in the Christian frameworks of thought: their interest in the organization of the socio-economic system, in the rights of those participating in it, in the power structure that characterizes the system, and in the distributional effects produced by the system. The Christian analytical mode of thought has a methodological commitment to holism, and to exploring the mutual interaction between explanatory influences occurring in the different dimensions of human behavior, particularly as individuals are seen to both form and be formed by their social environments (although not exclusively so in the Christian perspective because the triune God is basic to this purpose).

Further characteristics underlie the analytical and policy orientations of the Christian viewpoint promoted throughout this book (and expressed in Table 14.1), such as improving the position of the socio-economically disadvantaged, and the preference to direct policy toward human betterment and the common good, as defined previously. Methodological concepts of change and process are hallmarks of the Christian analytical system, empathetic to the orientation for analyzing social change characterized by discontinuity, conflict and coercion. In the interdisciplinary view it has of human behavior, 'non-economic' factors like culture and custom are central to its explanatory methodology. Christian socio-economic analysis emphasizes the role of socio-historico-cultural context helping to mould beliefs (even though general principles are sought); therefore, empirical investigation in these contexts is to the fore, and great store is put on case studies. Biblical thought in its original formulation was intended to provide a critical assessment of the quality of socio-economic life, a legacy that has been carried on by CST and some strains of evangelical thought, that also in part have had a practical problem-solving nexus. Finally, the Christian analytical system of thought does not endeavor to be predictive, and a case can be made that it is methodologically committed to realism.

If social science and economics practiced even the secular methodological characteristics of Table 14.1—instead of being confined to minority schools in these disciplines—secular social science might be more inclined to examine a range of metaphysical claims and worldview frameworks more closely. At long last, Christianity's claims in the socio-economic arena might be acknowledged. A different sort of economics from the orthodox *status quo* would become apparent if this occurred. Christian socio-economic analysis would be more concerned with context-based, non-predictive explanation, more like empirical sociology as it occurs currently. There would be parallels in its approach with analogous advocacy made for secular social science by realists, such as Sayer. He (1992, 145, 190, 215; original emphasis) favors the promotion of 'theoretically-informed and informative *narratives* rather than formal analyses of apparently timeless mechanisms.' This would require social scientists moving from 'formal models to narrative in order to capture the openness, contingency, qualitative change and novelty that characterize social systems.' Here, the aim would be for social science to try and explain what happens by 'examining the nature of the objects possessing the relevant powers and liabilities and the mechanisms by which they work.' All these features are compatible with the content of Christian socio-analysis developed in this chapter and book. They are similar to the common sense reasoning explained by Coates (1996). Little's (1993, 189–190) secular explanation for causal links between low gross national product per capita and high infant mortality rates conforms with the common sense Christian methodology advocated in this book. Qualitative reasoning underlies the Christian methodology, not depending on 'high theory' or mathematical modelling in which all explanatory variables (social kinds) need to be defined rigorously. As such, it differs markedly from typical orthodox economics' reasoning. This form of analysis does not imply a slide into the relativism of constructivist interpretivism or postmodernism, but it does require a move from the mathematical formalism that characterizes orthodox economics today. The realist Christian perspective underlying this book offers such secular analysis deeper dimensions. The normative requirements of the triune God for humankind's interconnected spiritual and material life are available to guide socio-economic analysis, explanation and policy. Without the input of the triune God, secular approaches will continue without benefit of discovering natural socio-economic kinds, laws or successful causal explanations useful for policy making. Christian socio-economic analysis, therefore, has something additional, different and new to offer social science.

Bibliography

Abbagnano, N. "Positivism," in *The Encyclopedia of Philosophy*, edited by P. Edwards. New York: Macmillan, 1967:414–19.

Abercrombie, N., S. Hill, and B. Turner. *Dictionary of Sociology*. 2d ed. London: Penguin, 1988.

Abraham, W. *An Introduction to the Philosophy of Religion*. Englewood Cliffs, N.J.: Prentice Hall, 1985.

Abu Turab Rizvi, S. "Game Theory to the Rescue?" *Contributions to Political Economy* 13 (1994): 1–28.

Addinall, P. *Philosophy and Biblical Interpretation*. Cambridge: Cambridge University Press, 1991.

Aghion, P., E. Caroli, and C. Garcia-Penalosa. "Inequality and Economic Growth: The Perspective of the New Growth Theories." *Journal of Economic Literature* 37, no. 4 (1999): 1615–60.

Akerlof, G. "Gift Exchange and Efficiency Wage Theory–4 Views." *American Economic Review* 74, no. 1 (1984): 79–83.

Albert, M., and R. Hahnel. *The Political Economy of Participatory Economics*. Princeton, N.J.: Princeton University Press, 1991a.

———. *Looking Forward: Participatory Economics for the Twentieth First Century*. Boston, Mass.: South End Press, 1991b.

Albertz, R. *A History of Israelite Religion*. Vols. 1 & 2. London: SCM, 1994.

Alchian, A., and W. Allen. *University Economics*. 3d ed. Belmont, N.Y.: Wadsworth, 1972.

Alesina, A. "The Political Economy of Macroeconomic Stabilizations and Income Inequality," in *Income Distribution and High-quality Growth*, edited by V. Tanzi and K. Chu. Cambridge, Mass.: MIT, 1998:299–326.

Alford, H., C. Clark, S. Cortright, and M. Naughton. *Rediscovering Abundance*. Notre Dame, Ill.: University of Notre Dame Press, 2005.

Alford, H., and M. Naughton. *Managing As If Faith Mattered: Christian Social Principles in the Modern Organization*. Notre Dame, Ill.: University of Notre Dame Press, 2001.

Alston, W. *A Realist Theory of Truth*. Ithaca, N.Y.: ILR Press, 1996.

Anderson, G. *The Living World of the Old Testament*, 4th ed. Harlow, U.K.: Longman, 1991.

Anderson, J. "Taxation and Economic Justice," in *Toward and Just and Caring Society*, edited by D. Gushee. Grand Rapids, Mich.: Baker, 1999:261–304.

Anderson, M. *Imposters in the Temple*. 2d ed. New York: Simon & Schuster, 1996.

Ankerberg, J., and J. Weldon. *Darwin's Leap of Faith*. Eugene, Oreg.: Harvest, 1998.

Appelbaum, E., and R. Batt. *The New American Workplace*. Ithaca, N.Y.: ILR Press, 1994.

Archer, M., and J. Tritter, eds. *Rational Choice Theory: Resisting Colonization*. London: Routledge, 2000.

Arestis, P. *The Post-Keynesian Approach to Economics*. Aldershot: Edward Elgar, 1992.

Arestis, P., S. Dunn, and M. Sawyer. "Post Keynesian Economics and Its Critics." *Journal of Post Keynesian Economics* 21, no. 4 (1999): 527–49.

Aronson, J. *A Realist Philosophy of Science*. New York: St. Martin's, 1984.

Arrow, K., S. Bowles, and S. Durlauf, eds. *Meritocracy and Economic Inequality*. Princeton, N.J.: Princeton University Press, 2000.

Arum, R., and W. Muller, eds. *The Reemergence of Self-Employment*. Princeton, N.J.: Princeton University Press, 2004.

Ashley, T. *The Book of Numbers*. Grand Rapids, Mich.: Eerdmans, 1993.

Atherton, J. *Christianity and the Market*. London: SCM, 1992.

Atkinson, A. and J. Micklewright, J. "Unemployment Compensation and Labour Market Transitions: A Critical Review." *Journal of Economic Literature* 29, no. 4 (1991): 1679–727.

Aumann, R., and I. Hart. eds. *Handbook of Game Theory with Economic Applications*. Vols. 1 & 2. Amsterdam: North Holland, 1992.

Averill, L. *Religious Right, Religious Wrong*. New York: Pilgrim Press, 1989.

Avis, P. *Faith in the Fires of Criticism*. London: Darton, Longman & Todd, 1995.

Ayer, A. ed. *Logical Positivism*. New York: Free Press, 1959a.

———. "Editor's Introduction," in *Logical Positivism*, edited by A. Ayer. New York: Free Press, 1959b: 3–28.

Bachelard, G. *The New Scientific Spirit*. Boston: Beacon, [1934] 1984.

Backhouse, R. *A History of Modern Economic Analysis*. Oxford: Blackwell, 1985.

———. "Rejoinder: Why Methodology Matters." *Methodus* 4, no. 2 (1992): 58–62.

———. *Truth and Progress in Economic Knowledge*. Cheltenham: Edward Elgar, 1997.

Balkin, S. *Self-Employment for Low-Income People*. New York: Praeger, 1989.

———. "Entrepreneurial Activities of Homeless Men." *Journal of Sociology and Social Welfare* 19, no. 4 (1992): 129–50.

Ballard, B. "On the Sin of Usury: A Biblical Economic Ethic." *Christian Scholar's Review* 24, no. 2 (1994): 210–28.

Barbour, I. *Religion in an Age of Science*. San Francisco: Harper, 1990.

———. *Religion and Science*. New York: Harper Collins, 1997.

Barnes, B. "On the Conventional Character of Knowledge and Cognition," in *Science Observed: Perspectives on the Social Study of Science*, edited by K. Knorr-Cetina and M. Mulkay. London: Sage, 1983: 19–51.

Barr, J. *The Bible in the Modern World*. London: SCM, 1973.

———. *Fundamentalism*. London: SCM, 1977.

———. *Explorations in Theology 7: The Scope and Authority of the Bible*. London: SCM, 1980.

———. *Old and New in Interpretation*. 2d ed. London: SCM, 1982.

———. *Holy Scripture: Canon, Authority, Criticism*. Oxford: Clarendon, 1983.

———. *Beyond Fundamentalism*. Philadelphia, Pa.: Westminster (U.K. title: *Escaping from Fundamentalism*), 1984.

———. *The Concept of Biblical Theology: An Old Testament Perspective*. London: SCM, 1999.

———. *History and Ideology in the Old Testament*. Oxford: Oxford University Press, 2000.

Barrow, J. *Theories of Everything: The Quest for Ultimate Explanation*. Oxford: Oxford University Press, 1991.

Bartlett, W., J. Cable, S. Estrin, D. Jones, and S. Smith. "Labor-Managed Co-operatives and Private Firms in North Central Italy: An Empirical Comparison." *Industrial and Labor Relations Review* 46, no.1 (1992): 103–18.

Barton, J. *The Spirit and the Letter*. London: SPCK, 1997.

Bauckham, R. *The Bible in Politics*. London: SPCK, 1989.

———. *God and the Crisis of Freedom*. Louisville, Ky.: Westminster John Knox, 2003.

Baum, G. *The Priority of Labor: A Commentary on Laborem Exercens Encyclical Letter of Pope John Paul II*. New York: Paulist, 1982.

Baumol, W. "What Marshall Didn't Know: On the Twentieth Century's Contributions to Economics." *Quarterly Journal of Economics* 115, no.1 (2000): 1–44.

Bauman, Z. *Hermeneutics and Social Science*. London: Hutchinson, 1978.

Bazen, S., and V. Marimoutou. "Looking for a Needle in a Haystack? A Re-examination of the Time Series Relationship between Teenage Employment and Minimum Wages in the United States." *Oxford Bulletin of Economics and Statistics* 64 Supplement (2002): 699–725.

Bealer, G. "The Incoherence of Empiricism," in *Naturalism: A Critical Appraisal*, edited by S. Wagner and R. Warner. Notre Dame, Ill.: University of Notre Dame Press, 1993: 163–96.

Bean, C. "European Unemployment: A Survey." *Journal of Economic Literature* 32, no. 2 (1994): 573–619.

Beare, H., and R. Slaughter. *Education for the Twentieth-First Century*. London: Routledge, 1993.

Becker, G. *The Economic Approach to Human Behavior*. Chicago: University of Chicago Press, 1976.

———. *A Treatise on the Family*. Cambridge, Mass.: Harvard University Press, 1981.

———. "The Economic Approach to Human Behavior," in *Rational Choice*, edited by J. Elster. Oxford: Blackwell, 1986: 108–22.

———. "Nobel Lecture: The Economic Way of Looking at Behavior." *Journal of Political Economy* 101, no. 3 (1993): 385–409.

Becker, G., G. Grossman, and K. Murphy. "Rational Addiction and the Effect of Price on Consumption." *American Economic Review* 81, no. 2 (1991): 237–41.

Becker, G., E. Landes, and R. Michael. "An Economic Analysis of Marital Instability." *Journal of Political Economy* 85, no. 6 (1977): 1141–87.

Beed, C. *Cultures of Secrecy and Abuse: A Paradox for Churches*. Melbourne, 1998.

———. "Cultures of Secrecy, Abuse and Bullying: Paradoxes in Religious Organizations, Families and Social Networks," in *Bullying From Backyard to Boardroom*, edited by P. McCarthy, J. Rylance, R. Bennett, and H. Zimmermann. Leichardt, N.S.W.: Federation Press, 2001: 44–53.

Beed, C. "God's Economic Strategy: A Biblical Study." Collected Papers presented at Uniting Church Continuing Education for Ministry Seminar, Melbourne, 1990.

———. "Philosophy of Science and Contemporary Economics: An Overview." *Journal of Post Keynesian Economics* 13, no. 4 (1991): 459–94.

———. "Do Value Judgements Affect Testing Economic Theory?" *International Journal of Social Economics* 19, no. 2 (1992): 6–24.

———. "The Relationship between Christian Theology and Economics." Paper presented at 32d Conference of Economists, Canberra, September 2003a.

———. "The Relevance of Christian Fictive Domestic Economy." *Forum for Social Economics* 32, no. 2 (2003b): 23–39.

———. "The Dilemma of *Economic Theory and Christian Belief*." *Journal of the Association of Christian Economists (U.K.)* 33 (2004): 13–24.

———. "Naturalised Epistemology and Economics." *Cambridge Journal of Economics* 29, no. 1 (2005a): 99–117.

———. "Jesus and Competition." *Faith and Economics* 45 (2005b): 41–57.

———. "What is the Correct Relationship of Religion to Economics?" *Review of Social Economy* forthcoming (2005d).

———. "Egalitarianism and its Counter Arguments in Contemporary Christian Thought." Unpublished paper, Melbourne, 2005e.

———. "A Rational Choice Model of the Book of Revelation: Comment on Ian Smith." Unpublished paper, Melbourne, 2005f.

Beed, C., and C. Beed. "A Christian Perspective on Economics." *Journal of Economic Methodology* 3, no. 1 (1996a): 91–112.

———. "Polarities between Naturalism and Non-naturalism in Contemporary Economics: An Overview." *Journal of Economic Issues* 30, 4 (1996b): 1077–104.

———. "Measuring the Quality of Academic Journals: The Case of Economics." *Journal of Post Keynesian Economics* 18, no. 3 (1996c): 369–96.

———. "Realism and a Christian Perspective on Economics." *Review of Political Economy* 9, no. 3 (1997): 313–33.

———. "Peter Singer's Interpretation of Christian Biblical Environmental Ethics." *Worldviews Environment, Culture, Religion* 2, no. 1 (1998): 53–68.

———. "A Christian Perspective on Neoclassical Rational Choice Theory." *International Journal of Social Economics* 26, no. 4 (1999): 501–20.

———. "Is the Case for Social Science Laws Strengthening?" *Journal for the Theory of Social Behaviour* 30, no. 2 (2000a): 131–53.
———. "The Status of Economics as a Naturalistic Social Science." *Cambridge Journal of Economics* 24, no. 4 (2000b): 417–35.
———. "Intellectual Progress and Academic Economics." *Journal of Post Keynesian Economics* 22, no. 2 (2000c): 163–85.
———. "Work Ownership Implications of Recent Papal Social Thought." *Review of Social Economy* 60, no. 1 (2002a): 47–69.
———. "Judeo-Christian Principles for Employment Organization." *Journal of Socio-economics* 31, no. 5 (2002b): 457–68.
———. "Socio-economic Principles in Contemporary Islamic and Judeo-Christian Thought." *Journal of Interdisciplinary Economics* 14, no. 3 (2003a): 227–48.
———. "The Autonomy of Economics from Judeo-Christian Thought: A Critique." *International Journal of Social Economics* 30, no. 9 (2003b): 942–66.
———. "Distributional Implications of Contemporary Judeo-Christian Economics." *International Journal of Social Economics* 31, no. 10 (2004a): 903–22.
———. "An Evangelical Christian Response to Naturalistic Social Science." *Christian Scholar's Review* 34, no. 1 (2004b): 21–41.
———. "A Judeo-Christian Theory of Unemployment." *Journal of Interdisciplinary Economics* 16, no. 2 (2005a): 121–43.
———. "Jesus and Equity in Material Distribution." *Evangelical Quarterly* 77, no. 2 (2005b): 99–118.
———. "Applying Judeo-Christian Principles to Contemporary Economic Issues." *Journal of Markets and Morality* 8, no. 1 (2005c): 53–79.
Beed, C., and A. Gill. "Equity and God's Economic Programme: A Biblical Study." Collected Papers presented at Uniting Church Continuing Education for Ministry Seminar, Melbourne, 1990.
Beed, C., and O. Kane. "What Is the Critique of the Mathematization of Economics?" *Kyklos* 44, no. 4 (1991): 581–612.
Begg, D., S. Fischer, and R. Dornbusch. *Economics*. 4th ed. London: McGraw-Hill, 1994.
Behe, M. *Darwin's Black Box: The Biochemical Challenge to Evolution*. New York: Free Press, 1996.
Beisner, E. *Prosperity and Poverty*. Westchester: Crossway, 1988.
Bell, S., ed. *The Unemployment Crisis in Australia*. Cambridge: Cambridge University Press, 2000.
Benardete, J. *Metaphysics: The Logical Approach*. Oxford: Oxford University Press, 1989.
Ben-Ner, A., H. Tzu-Shian, and D. Jones. "The Productivity Effects of Employee Participation in Control and in Economic Returns: A Review of Empirical Evidence," in *Democracy and Efficiency in the Economic Enterprise*, edited by U. Pagano and R. Rowthorn. London: Routledge, 1996: 209–44.
Benton, T., and I. Craib. *Philosophy of Social Science: The philosophical Foundations of Social Thought*. New York: Palgrave, 2001.

Berelson, B., and G. Steiner. *Human Behavior: An Inventory of Scientific Findings*. New York: Harcourt, 1964.

Bergmann, B. "Becker's Theory of the Family: Preposterous Conclusions." *Feminist Economics* 1, no. 1 (1995): 141–50.

Bergstrom, T., and M. Bagnoli. "Courtship as a Waiting Game." *Journal of Political Economy* 101, no. 1 (1993): 185–202.

Berlin, I. *Against the Current*. London: Hogarth, 1979.

Bernard, C. *Introduction to the Study of Experimental Medicine*. New York: Dover, 1952.

Bernheim, B. "A Theory of Conformity." *Journal of Political Economy* 102, no. 5 (1994): 841–77.

Bernstein, R. *The Restructuring of Social and Political Theory*. Pittsburgh, Pa.: University of Pennsylvania Press, 1978.

Bhaskar, R. *A Realist Theory of Science*. 2d ed. Brighton: Harvester, 1978.

———. *Scientific Realism and Human Emancipation*. London: Verso, 1986.

———. *The Possibility of Naturalism*. 2d ed. New York: Harvester/Wheatsheaf, 1989.

———. "Empiricism," "Knowledge, Theory of," "Naturalism," "Philosophy of Social Science," and "Realism," in *The Blackwell Dictionary of Twentieth-Century Social Thought*, edited by W. Outhwaite and T. Bottomore. Oxford: Blackwell, 1994: 193–95, 311–14, 412–14, 469–71, 547–49.

Bigelow, J., B. Ellis, and C. Lierse. "The World As One of a Kind: Natural Necessity and Laws Of Nature." *British Journal for the Philosophy of Science* 43, no. 3 (1992): 371–88.

Binger, B., and E. Hoffman. *Microeconomics with Calculus*. 2d ed. Reading: Addison-Wesley, 1998.

Birch, B. *Let Justice Roll Down*. Louisville, Ky.: Westminster John Knox, 1991.

Birdsall, N., C. Pinckney, and R. Sabot, R. "Why Low Inequality Spurs Growth: Savings and Investment by the Poor." in *Social Inequality: Values, Growth and the State*, edited by A. Solimano. Ann Arbor, Mich.: University of Michigan Press, 1998: 68–81.

Birner, J. "A Conservative Approach to Progress in Economics," in *Is There Progress in Economics?*, edited by S. Boehm, C. Gehrke, H. Kurz, and R. Sturn. Cheltenham: Edward Elgar, 2002: 65–88.

Birnie, E. "Unemployment: A Christian Response." *Journal of the Association of Christian Economists (U.K.)* 21 (1996): 9–32.

Blanchard, O. *Macroeconomics*. Upper Saddle River, N.J.: Prentice Hall, 1997.

Blanchflower, D., and A. Oswald. "What Makes an Entrepreneur?" *Journal of Labour Economics* 16, no. 1 (1998): 26–60.

Blank, R. *Do Justice: Linking Christian Faith and Modern Economic Life*. Cleveland, Ohio: United Church Press, 1992.

———. *It Takes a Nation: A New Agenda for Fighting Poverty*. Princeton, N.J.: Princeton University Press, 1997.

———. "Distinguished Lecture on Economics in Government–Fighting Poverty: Lessons from Recent U.S. History." *Journal of Economic Perspectives* 14, no. 2 (2000): 3–19.

Blank, R., and Freeman, R. "Evaluating the Connection between Social Protection and Economic Flexibility," in *Social Protection Versus Economic Flexibility*, edited by R. Blank. Chicago: Chicago University Press, 1994: 21–41.

Blasi, J., and D. Kruse. *The New Owners*. New York: Harper, 1991.

Blau, J. *Illusions of Prosperity*. New York: Oxford University Press, 1999.

Blaug, M. *The Methodology of Economics*. Cambridge: Cambridge University Press, 1980a.

———. *A Methodological Appraisal of Marxian Economics*. Amsterdam: North Holland, 1980b.

———. *Economics Through the Looking Glass*. London: IEA, 1988.

———. *Economic Theories, True or False?* Aldershot, U.K.: Edward Elgar, 1990.

———. *The Methodology of Economics*. 2d ed. Cambridge: Cambridge University Press, 1992.

———. "Why I Am Not a Constructivist," in *New Directions in Economic Methodology*, edited by R. Backhouse. London: Routledge, 1994: 109–36.

———. *Economic Theory in Retrospect*. 5th ed. Cambridge: Cambridge University Press, 1997.

———. "No History of Ideas, Please, We're Economists." *Journal of Economic Perspectives* 15, no. 1 (2001): 145–64.

———. "Is There Really Progress in Economics?" in *Is There Progress in Economics?* edited by S. Boehm, C. Gehrke, H. Kurz, and R. Sturn. Cheltenham, U.K.: Edward Elgar, 2002: 21–41.

Blinder, A. "Keynes, Lucas, and Scientific Progress." *American Economic Review* 77, no. 2 (1987): 130–36.

———. "Why Are Prices Sticky? Preliminary Results from an Interview Study." *American Economic Review* 81, no. 2 (1991): 89–96.

Bliss, C. "Progress and Anti-progress in Economic Science," in *Foundations of Economics*, edited by M. Barazini and R. Scazzieri. Oxford: Blackwell, 1986: 363–76.

Blomberg, C. *The New American Commentary: Matthew*. Nashville, Tenn.: Broadman, 1992.

———. *Neither Poverty Nor Riches: A Biblical Theology of Material Possessions*. Leicester, U.K.: Apollos, 1999.

Bloor, D. "The Strengths of the Strong Programme." *Philosophy of the Social Sciences* 11, no. 2 (1981): 173–98.

———. *Knowledge and Social Imagery*. 2d ed. Chicago: University of Chicago Press, 1991.

Bluestone, B., and I. Bluestone. *Negotiating the Future*. New York: Basic Books, 1992.

Bock, D. *Luke: The NIV Application Commentary*. Grand Rapids, Mich.: Zondervan, 1996.

Boehm, S., C. Gehrke, H. Kurz, and R. Sturn, eds. *Is There Progress in Economics?* Cheltenham, U.K.: Edward Elgar, 2002.

Boerma, C. *Rich Man, Poor Man–And The Bible*. London: SCM, 1979.

Bohm, D. *Wholeness and the Implicate Order*. London: Routledge & Kegan Paul, 1980.

Bohman, J. *New Philosophy of Social Science*. Cambridge, Mass.: MIT, 1991.

Boland, L. "On the Futility of Criticizing the Neoclassical Maximization Hypothesis." *American Economic Review* 71, no. 5 (1981): 1031–36.

Bonin, J., D. Jones, and L. Putterman. "Theoretical and Empirical Studies of Producer Co-operatives: Will Ever the Twain Meet?" *Journal of Economic Literature* 31, no. 3 (1993): 1290–320.

Boudon, R. "Methodology," in *The Blackwell Dictionary of Twentieth-Century Social Thought*, edited by W. Outhwaite and T. Bottomore. Oxford: Blackwell, 1994: 379–81.

Boulier, B., and R. Goldfarb "Pisces Economicus: The Fish As Economic Man." *Economics and Philosophy* 7, no. 1 (1991): 83–6.

Bowles, S. and H. Gintis. *Recasting Egalitarianism*. London: Verso, 1998.

Boyd, R., P. Gasper, and J. Trout, eds. *The Philosophy of Science*. Cambridge, Mass.: MIT, 1991.

Boylan, T., and P. O'Gorman. *Beyond Rhetoric and Realism in Economics*. London: Routledge, 1995.

Brandolini, A., and N. Rossi. "Income Distribution and Growth in Industrial Countries," in *Income Distribution and High-quality Growth*, edited by V. Tanzi and K. Chu. Cambridge, Mass.: MIT, 1998: 69–105.

Bray, G. *Biblical Interpretation: Past and Present*. Downers Grove, Ill.: IVP, 1996.

Braybrooke, D. *Philosophy of Social Science*. Englewood Cliffs, N.J.: Prentice Hall, 1987.

Brennan, G., and A. Waterman, eds. *Economics and Religion: Are They Distinct?* Boston, Mass.: Kluwer, 1994.

Brett, P. *Love Your Neighbour*. London: Darton, Longman and Todd, 1992.

Bright, J. *A History of Israel*. 2d ed. London: SCM, 1972.

Britton, A., and P. Sedgwick. *Economic Theory and Christian Belief*. Bern: Peter Lang, 2003.

Broersma, L. *The Relation between Unemployment and Interest Rate*. Amsterdam: Thesis Publishers, 1992.

Broome, J. "Utility." *Economics and Philosophy* 7, no. 1 (1991): 1–12.

Brown, R. *The Nature of Social Laws: Machiavelli to Mill*. Cambridge: Cambridge University Press, 1984.

Bruce, S. *Choice and Religion: A Critique of Rational Choice Theory*. Oxford: Oxford University Press, 1999.

Bruner, F. *The Christbook, A Historical/Theological Commentary: Matthew 1–12*. Waco, Tex.: Word, 1987.

Bruno, M., M. Ravallion, and L. Squire. "Equity and Growth in Developing Countries," in *Income Distribution and High-quality Growth*, edited by V. Tanzi and K. Chu. Cambridge, Mass.: MIT, 1998: 117–46.

Bryant, C. *Positivism in Social Theory and Research*. London: Macmillan, 1985.

Budd, P. *The New Century Bible Commentary: Leviticus*. London: Marshall Pickering, 1996.

Bulkley, E. *Why Christians Can't Trust Psychology*. Eugene, Oreg: Harvest House, 1993.

Bunge, M. *Finding Philosophy In Social Science*. New Haven, Conn.: Yale University Press, 1996.

——. *Social Science Under Debate: A Philosophical Perspective.* Toronto: University of Toronto Press, 1998.

Burkhauser, R., K. Couch, and D. Wittenburg. "A Reassessment of the New Economics of the Minimum Wage Literature with Monthly Data from the Current Population Survey." *Journal of Labor Economics* 18, no. 4 (2000): 653–80.

Cairns, I. *Word and Presence: A Commentary on the Book of Deuteronomy.* Grand Rapids, Mich.: Eerdmans, 1992.

Caldwell, B. *Beyond Positivism: Economic Methodology in Twentieth Century.* London: Allen & Unwin, 1982.

——. "The Neoclassical Maximization Hypothesis: Comment." *American Economic Review* 73, no. 4 (1983): 824–27.

——. "Some Problems with Falsificationism in Economics." *Philosophy of the Social Sciences* 14, no. 4 (1984): 489–95.

Callebaut, W. *Taking the Naturalistic Turn.* Chicago: University of Chicago Press, 1993.

Camerer, C. "Progress in Behavioral Game Theory." *Journal of Economic Perspectives* 11, no. 4, (1997): 167–88.

Capra, F. *The Tao of Physics.* 2d ed. Boston: New Science Library, 1983.

Card, D., and A. Krueger. *Myth and Measurement: The New Economics of the Minimum Wage.* Princeton, N.J.: Princeton University Press, 1995.

——. "Minimum Wages and Employment: A Case Study of the Fast-food Industry in New Jersey and Pennsylvania: Reply." *American Economic Review* 90, no. 5 (2000): 1397–420.

Carlson-Thies, S., and J. Skillen, eds. *Welfare in America: Christian Perspectives on a Policy in Crisis.* Grand Rapids, Mich.: Eerdmans, 1996.

Carroll, J. *Laws of Nature.* Cambridge: Cambridge University Press, 1994.

Carter, C. *The Politics of the Cross.* Grand Rapids, Mich.: Brazos, 2001.

Cartwright, N. *How The Laws of Physics Lie.* Oxford: Clarendon, 1983.

——. *Nature's Capacities and Their Measurement.* Oxford: Clarendon, 1989.

——. "Replicability, Reproducibility, and Robustness: Comments on Harry Collins." *History of Political Economy* 23, no. 1 (1991): 143–55.

——. "Ceteris Paribus Laws and Socio-Economic Machines." *The Monist* 78, no. 3 (1995): 276–94.

——. "Where Do Laws Of Nature Come From?" *Dialectica.* 51, no. 1 (1997): 65–78.

Centesimus Annus (CA). *Encyclical Letter of the Supreme Pontiff John Paul II on The Hundredth Anniversary of Rerum Novarum.* Boston, Mass.: St. Paul, 1991.

Chalmers, A. *What Is This Thing Called Science?* 2d ed. St. Lucia, Qld.: University of Queensland Press, 1982.

——. *What Is This Thing Called Science?* 3d ed. St. Lucia, Qld.: University of Queensland Press, 1999a.

——. "Making Sense of Laws of Physics," in *Causation and Laws of Nature*, edited by H. Sankey. Dordrecht: Kluwer, 1999b: 3–16.

Champernowne, D., and F. Cowell. *Economic Inequality and Income Distribution.* Cambridge: Cambridge University Press, 1998.

Chapra, M. *Islam and the Economic Challenge.* Leicester and Herndon, U.K.: The Islamic Foundation and The International Institute of Islamic Thought, 1992.

——. *Islam and Economic Development*. Islamabad: International Institute of Islamic Thought and Islamic Research Institute, 1993.

——. "Foreword." in *Studies in Islamic Science and Polity*, by M. Choudhury. Houndmills, U.K.: Macmillan, 1998: xi–xv.

——. "Is it Necessary to Have Islamic Economics?" *Journal of Socio-Economics* 29, no. 1 (1999): 21–37.

Charles, R. *Christian Social Witness and Teaching*. Vols. 1 & 2. Leominster, U.K.: Gracewing, 1998.

Cheney, G. *Values at Work: Employee Participation Meets Market Pressure at Mondragon*. Ithaca, N.Y.: ILR Press, 1999.

Childs, B. *Exodus: A Commentary*. London: SCM, 1974.

Chirichigno, G. *Debt Slavery in Israel and the Ancient Near East*. Sheffield, U.K.: JSOT Press, 1993.

Chmielewski, P. "Co-operative Associations," in *The New Dictionary of Catholic Social Thought*, edited by J. Dwyer. Collegeville, Minn.: Liturgical Press, 1994: 235–37.

——. "Workers' Participation in the United States: Catholic Social Teaching and Democratic Theory." *Review of Social Economy* 55, no. 4 (1997): 487–508.

Choudhury, M. *The Principles of Islamic Political Economy*. New York: St. Martin's, 1992.

——. *Studies in Islamic Science and Polity*. Houndmills, U.K.: Macmillan, 1998.

Christensen, D. *Word Biblical Commentary Vol. 6A: Deuteronomy 1:1–21:9*. Revised. Nashville, Tenn.: Thomas Nelson, 2001.

Christensen, S., and D. Turner, eds. *Folk Psychology and the Philosophy of Mind*. Hillsdale, Mich.: Lawrence Erlbaum, 1993.

Chubin, D., and S. Restivo. "The 'Mooting' of Science Studies: Research Programmes and Science Policy," in *Science Observed: Perspectives on the Social Study of Science*, edited by K. Knorr-Cetina and M. Mulkay. London: Sage, 1983: 53–83.

Churchland, P. "Epistemology in The Age of Neuroscience." *Journal of Philosophy* 84, no. 10 (1987): 544–53.

Clark, C. *Economic Theory and Natural Philosophy*. Aldershot, U.K.: Edward Elgar, 1992.

——. *Economic Insights from the Catholic Social Thought Tradition*. New York: Forthcoming.

Clark, C., and C. Kavanagh. "Progress, Values and Economic Indicators," in *Progress, Values and Public Policy*, edited by B. Reynolds and S. Healy. Dublin: Conference of Religious in Ireland, 1996: 60–92.

Clements, R. *Exodus: The Cambridge Bible Commentary*. Cambridge: Cambridge University Press, 1972.

Clouse, R., ed. *Wealth and Poverty: Four Christian Views on Economics*. Downers Grove, Ill.: IVP, 1984.

Clouser, R. *The Myth of Religious Neutrality*. Notre Dame, Ill.: University of Notre Dame, 1991.

Clower, R. "Axiomatics in Economics." *Southern Economic Journal* 62, no. 2 (1995): 307–19.

Coates, J. *The Claims of Common Sense*. Cambridge: Cambridge University Press, 1996.

Coddington, A. "The Rationale of General Equilibrium." *Economic Inquiry* 13, no. 4 (1975): 539–58.

Colander, D., and R. Brenner, eds. *Educating Economists*. Ann Arbor, Mich.: University of Michigan, 1992.

Cole, A. *Exodus: An Introduction and Commentary*. London: Tyndale, 1973.

Cole, K., J. Cameron, and C. Edwards. *Why Economists Disagree*. 2d ed. London: Longman, 1991.

Coleman, J. "Catholic Integralism as a Fundamentalism," in *Fundamentalism in Comparative Perspective*. Edited by L. Kaplan. Amherst, Mass.: University of Massachusetts, 1992: 74–95.

Collins, H. *Changing Order: Replication and Induction in Scientific Practice*. London: Sage, 1985.

Connors, G., and A. Tarbox. "Macroenvironmental Factors As Determinants of Substance Use and Abuse," in *Determinants of Substance Abuse*, edited by M. Galizio and S. Maisto. New York: Plenum, 1985: 283–314.

Cooley, T., and S. Le Roy. "Identification and Estimation of Money Demand." *American Economic Review* 71, no. 5 (1981): 825–44.

Cooney, T., and D. Hogan. "Marriage in an Institutionalized Life Course: First Marriage among American Men in the Twentieth Century." *Journal of Marriage and the Family* 53, no. 1 (1991): 178–89.

Council of Churches for Britain and Ireland (CCBI). *Unemployment and the Future of Work*. London: CCBI, 1997.

Craig, W., and J. Moreland, eds. *Naturalism: A Critical Approach*. London: Routledge, 2000.

Craigie, P. *The Book of Deuteronomy*. Grand Rapids, Mich.: Eerdmans, 1976.

Cramp, A. *Economics in Christian Perspective*. Cambridge: Emmanuel College, 1981.

———. "Mappings of (Economic) Meaning: Here Be Monsters," in *Economics and Religion: Are They Distinct?*, edited by G. Brennan and A. Waterman. Boston, Mass.: Kluwer, 1994: 179–91.

Crick, F. *The Astonishing Hypothesis*. London: Simon & Schuster, 1994.

Cross, R. "The Duhem-Quine Thesis, Lakatos and the Appraisal of Theories in Macroeconomics." *Economic Journal* 92, no. 2 (1982): 320–40.

D'Amico, R. "Is Disease A Natural Kind?" *Journal of Medicine and Philosophy* 20, no. 4 (1995): 551–69.

———. "Impossible Laws." *Philosophy of the Social Sciences* 27, no. 3 (1997): 309–27.

Daly, H., and J. Cobb. *For the Common Good: Redirecting the Economy Toward Community, the Environment and a Sustainable Future*. 2d ed. Boston, Mass.: Beacon, 1994.

Darbellay, G., and M. Slama. "Forecasting the Short-term Demand for Electricity: Do Neural Networks Stand a Better Chance?" *International Journal of Forecasting* 16, no. 1 (2000): 71–83.

Darnell, A., and L. Evans. *The Limits of Econometrics*. Aldershot, U.K.: Edward Elgar, 1990.

Daube, D. *Studies in Biblical Law*. Cambridge: Cambridge University Press, 1947.

Davenport, E. "The New Politics of Knowledge: Rorty's Pragmatism and the Rhetoric of the Human Sciences." *Philosophy of the Social Sciences* 17, no. 3 (1987): 377–94.

Davidson, G., and P. Davidson. *Economics for a Civilized Society*. 2d (rev) ed. Houndmills, U.K.: Macmillan, 1996.

Davies, G. *Exodus*. London: SCM, 1983.

Davies, J., ed. *God and the Market Place*. London: IEA, 1993.

Davies, P. *God and the New Physics*. London: Dent, 1983.

———. *The Mind of God*. London: Simon & Schuster, 1992.

Davis, J., W. Hands, and U. Maki, eds. *The Handbook of Economic Methodology*. Cheltenham, U.K.: Edward Elgar, 1998.

Dawkins, P. "The Minimum Wages Debate and Policy Developments in Australia, the UK and the US: An Introductory Overview." *Australian Economic Review* 30, no. 2 (1997): 187–93.

Dawson, J. *The Social Meanings of Suicide*. Princeton, N.J.: Princeton University Press, 1967.

Dawson, S. "Start-Ups and Replication," in *Jobs and Economic Development*, edited by R. Giloth. Thousand Oaks, Calif.: Sage, 1998: 123–36.

Dean, J., and A. Waterman, eds. *Religion and Economics: Normative Social Theory*. Boston, Mass.: Kluwer, 1999.

Demarest, G. *The Communicator's Commentary: Leviticus*. Dallas, Tex.: Word, 1990.

Dennis, K., ed. *Rationality in Economics: Alternative Perspectives*. Boston, Mass.: Kluwer, 1998.

Denton, F. "The Significance of Significance: Rhetorical Aspects of Statistical Hypothesis Testing in Economics," in *The Consequences of Economic Rhetoric*, edited by A. Klamer, D. McCloskey, and R. Solow. Cambridge: Cambridge University Press, 1988: 163–83.

Deutsch, K., A. Markovits, and J. Platt, eds. *Advances in the Social Sciences 1900–1980*. Lanham, Md.: University Press of America, 1986.

Devitt, M. *Realism and Truth*. 2d ed. Oxford: Blackwell, 1991.

Dicken, P., and P. Lloyd. *Location in Space*. New York: Harper and Row, 1990.

Diesing, P. *Patterns of Discovery in the Social Sciences*. London: Routledge & Kegan Paul, 1971.

Dilthey, W. *Introduction to the Human Sciences*. Detroit, Mich.: Wayne State University Press, [1883]1988.

Donnerstein, M., and E. Donnerstein, eds. *Social Psychology*. Dubuque, Iowa: Brown, 1984.

Doppelt, G. "The Philosophical Requirements for an Adequate Conception of Scientific Rationality." *Philosophy of Science* 55, no. 1 (1988): 104–33.

Dorr, D. *Option for the Poor: One Hundred Years of Catholic Social Teaching*. Maryknoll, N.Y.: Orbis, 1992.

Doucouliagos, C. "Unemployment and Workers' Control." *Review of Political Economy* 9, no. 2 (1997): 151–79.

Dow, G. *Governing the Firm: Workers' Control in Theory and Practice*. Cambridge: Cambridge University Press, 2003.

Dow, S. "Economics and Religion," in *Capital Controversy, Post-Keynesian Economics and the History of Economics: Essays in Honour of Geoff Harcourt Vol. 1*, edited by P. Arestis, G. Palma, and M. Sawyer. London: Routledge, 1997: 466–73.

———. "Ethics, Economics and Knowledge," in *Religion and Economics: Normative Social Theory*, edited by J. Dean and A. Waterman. Boston, Mass.: Kluwer, 1999: 123–30.

———. *Economic Methodology: An Inquiry*. Oxford: Oxford University Press, 2002.

Drees, W. *Religion, Science and Naturalism*. Cambridge: Cambridge University Press, 1996.

Duncan, B. *The Church's Social Teaching: From Rerum Novarum to 1931*. North Blackburn, Vic.: Collins Dove, 1991.

Duncan, O. *Introduction to Structural Equation Models*. New York: Academic Press, 1975.

Durand, J-P., P. Stewart, and J. Castillo, eds. *Teamwork in the Automobile Industry: Radical Change or Passing Fashion?* Houndmills, U.K.: Macmillan, 1999.

Durham, J. *Word Biblical Commentary Vol. 3 Exodus*. Waco, Tex.: Word, 1987.

Dutta, B., D. Mookherjee, T. Parthasarathy, T. Raghavan, D. Ray, and S. Tijs, eds. *Game Theory and Economic Applications*. Berlin: Springer-Verlag, 1992.

Earle, J. *The Italian Co-operative Movement*. London: Allen & Unwin, 1986.

"Editors' Introduction." *Economics and Philosophy* 1, no. 1 (1985): 1–6.

Eichberger, J. *Game Theory for Economists*. San Diego, Calif.: Academic Press, 1993.

Ekelund, R., and R. Herbert. *A History of Economic Theory and Method*. 4th ed. New York: McGraw-Hill, 1997.

Elikann, P. *The Tough-on-Crime Myth*. New York: Plenum, 1996.

Elliott, J. "Oppression, Exploitation and Injustice in the Old Testament: The View from Liberation Theology." *International Journal of Social Economics* 19, no. 10–12 (1992): 15–52.

Ellis, B. "Natural Kinds and Natural Kinds Reasoning," in *Natural Kinds, Laws of Nature and Scientific Methodology*, edited by P. Riggs. Dordrecht: Kluwer, 1996: 11–28.

Elzinga, K. "Economics and Religion: Comment," in *Religion and Economics: Normative Social Theory*, edited by J. Dean and A. Waterman. Boston, Mass.: Kluwer, 1999: 131–39.

Emberley, P., and B. Cooper. *Faith and Political Philosophy: The Correspondence between Leo Strauss and Eric Voegelin 1934–1964*. Uni. Park, Pa.: Penn. State Uni. Press, 1993.

Emmett, R. "Frank Knight: Economics versus Religion," in *Economics and Religion: Are They Distinct?* edited by G. Brennan and A. Waterman. Boston: Kluwer, 1994: 103–20.

Engle, R., C. Granger, V. Ramanathan, F. Vahid-Aaraghi, and C. Bruce. "Short-run Forecasts of Electricity Loads and Peaks." *International Journal of Forecasting* 13, no. 2 (1997): 161–74.

Epstein, R. *A History of Econometrics. Contributions to Economic Analysis*, no. 165. Amsterdam: North Holland, 1987.

Erickson, M. *Christian Theology*. 2d ed. Grand Rapids, Mich.: Baker, 1998.

Fager, J. *Land Tenure and the Biblical Jubilee*. JSOT Supplement Series 155. Sheffield: JSOT Press, 1993.

Fay, B. "Naturalism As a Philosophy of Social Science." *Philosophy of the Social Sciences* 14, no. 4 (1984): 529–42.

———. "Critical Realism?" *Journal for the Theory of Social Behaviour* 20, no. 1 (1990): 33–41.

Fay, B., and J. Moon. "What Would an Adequate Philosophy of Social Science Look Like?" *Philosophy of the Social Sciences* 7, no. 3 (1977): 209–27.

Feinberg, J. *No One Like Him*. Wheaton, Ill.: Crossway, 2001.

Feldhay, R. *Galileo and the Church*. Cambridge: Cambridge University Press, 1995.

Feyerabend, P. *Against Method*. London: New Left Books, 1975.

———. *Farewell to Reason*. London: Verso, 1987.

Fine, A. "Is Scientific Realism Compatible with Quantum Physics?" in *Philosophy of Science*, edited by R. Boyd, P. Gasper and J. Trout. Cambridge, Mass.: MIT, 1991: 529–44.

Finn, D. *Just Trading: On the Ethics and Economics of International Trade*. Nashville, Tenn.: Abington Press, 1997.

Fiorenza, F. "Systematic Theology: Task and Methods," in *Systematic Theology: Roman Catholic Perspectives. Vol.1*, edited by F. Fiorenza and J. Galvin. Minneapolis, Minn.: Fortress, 1991: 1–87.

Fisher, F. "Games Economists Play: A Non-cooperative View." *Rand Journal of Economics* 20, no. 1 (1989): 113–24.

Fitzgerald, M. "Focus on Labor," in *Co-Creation and Capitalism: John Paul II's Laborem Exercens*, edited by J. Houck and O. Williams. Washington, D.C.: University Press of America, 1983: 254–80.

Fitzmyer, J. *The Anchor Bible: The Gospel According to Luke*. Vols. 1 & 2. New York: Doubleday, 1985.

Fleetwood, S. "The Inadequacy of Mainstream Theories of Trade Union Behavior." *Labour* 13, no. 2 (1999): 445–80.

———. "Conceptualizing Unemployment in a Period of Atypical Employment: A Critical Realist Approach," in *Applied Economics and the Critical Realist Critique*, edited by P. Downward. London: Routledge, 2003: 27–50.

Fleurbaey, M. "Equal Opportunity or Equal Social Outcome?" *Economics and Philosophy* 11, no. 1 (1995): 25–56.

Flew, A., ed. *A Dictionary of Philosophy*. 2d ed. London: Pan/Macmillan, 1984.

———. *Thinking about Social Thinking: The Philosophy of the Social Sciences*. Oxford: Blackwell, 1985.

Flyvbjerg, B. *Making Social Science Matter*. Cambridge: Cambridge University Press, 2001.

Forrester, D. *On Human Worth: A Christian Vindication of Equality*. London: SCM, 2001.

Foster, M. "The Christian Doctrine of Creation and the Rise of Modern Natural Science." *Mind* 43, no. 172 (1934): 446–68.

Francis, J. "Children and Childhood in the New Testament," in *The Family in Theological Perspective*, edited by S. Barton. Edinburgh: T. & T. Clark, 1996: 65–85.

Frank, R. *Passions Within Reason*. London: Norton, 1988.

———. *Microeconomics and Behavior*. 2d ed. New York: McGraw-Hill, 1994.

Frank, R., T. Gilovich, and D. Regan. "Does Studying Economics Inhibit Co-operation?" *Journal of Economic Perspectives* 7, no. 2 (1993): 159–71.

French, P., T. Uehling, and H. Wettstein, eds. *Philosophical Naturalism*. Notre Dame, Ill.: University of Notre Dame Press, 1994.

Friedman, J. *Game Theory with Applications to Economics*. 2d ed. New York: Oxford University Press, 1990.

Friedman, M. *Essays in Positive Economics*. Chicago: University of Chicago Press, 1953.

Friedman, M., and A. Schwartz. *Monetary Trends in the United States and the United Kingdom: Their Relations to Income, Prices, and Interest Rates, 1867–1975*. Chicago: University of Chicago Press, 1982.

———. "Alternative Approaches to Analyzing Economic Data." *American Economic Review* 81, no. 1 (1991): 39–49.

Fry, M. *Money, Interest, and Banking in Economic Development*. 2d ed. Baltimore, Md.: Johns Hopkins, 1995.

Fudenberg, D., and J. Tirole. *Game Theory*. Cambridge, Mass.: MIT, 1991.

Fullbrook, E., ed. *The Crisis in Economics*. London: Routledge, 2003.

———, ed. *A Guide to What's Wrong with Economics*. London: Anthem, 2004.

Fuller, S. *Philosophy of Science and Its Discontents*. 2d ed. New York: Guilford, 1993.

Funkenstein, A. *Theology and the Scientific Imagination from the Middle Ages to the Seventeenth Century*. Princeton, N.J.: Princeton University Press, 1986.

Gabszewicz, J., J. Richard, and L. Wolsey, eds. *Economic Decision-Making*. Amsterdam: North Holland, 1990.

Gaburro, G., and G. Cressotti. "The Social Teaching of the Church on Human Work." *International Journal of Social Economics* 25, no. 11/12 (1998): 1618–39.

Galbraith, J. *American Capitalism: The Concept of Countervailing Power*. Boston, Mass.: Houghton Mifflin, 1952.

Galbraith, J. "Time to Ditch the NAIRU." *Journal of Economic Perspectives* 11, no. 1 (1997): 93–108.

Gardner, R. *Matthew*. Scottdale, Pa.: Herald, 1991.

Gates, J. *The Ownership Solution*. London: Penguin, 1998.

———. *Democracy at Risk*. Cambridge, Mass.: Perseus, 2000.

Gay, C. *With Liberty and Justice for Whom?: The Recent Evangelical Debate over Capitalism*. Grand Rapids, Mich.: Eerdmans, 1991.

Gay, P. *The Enlightenment: An Interpretation. Vol. 1: The Rise of Modern Paganism*. New York: Knopf, 1975.

Gerrard, B. The Significance of Interpretation in Economics," in *Economics and Language*, edited by W. Henderson, T. Dudley-Evans, and R. Backhouse. London: Routledge, 1993: 51–63.

———. 1995 "The Scientific Basis of Economics: A Review of the Methodological Debates in Economics and Econometrics." *Scottish Journal of Political Economy* 42, no. 2 (1995): 221–35.

Gerstenberger, E. *Leviticus: A Commentary*. Louisville, Ky.: Westminster John Knox, 1996.

Gianaris, N. *Modern Capitalism: Privatization, Employee Ownership, and Industrial Democracy*. Westport, Conn.: Praeger, 1996.

Gibbons, R. "An Introduction to Applicable Game Theory." *Journal of Economic Perspectives* 11, no. 1 (1997): 127–49.

Giddens, A. *Sociology*. Cambridge, U.K. Polity, 1989.

———. *Sociology*. 2d ed. Cambridge, U.K.: Polity, 1993.

———. *Sociology*. 3rd ed. Cambridge, U.K.: Polity, 1997.

Giddens, A., with K. Birdsall. *Sociology*. 4th ed. Cambridge, U.K.: Polity, 2001.

Giedymin, J. "Antipositivism in Contemporary Philosophy of Social Science and Humanities." *British Journal for the Philosophy of Science* 26, no. 4 (1975): 275–301.

Gifford, J., and S. Tolklington. "Demand Elasticity Under Time-Varying Prices: Case Study of Day-Of-Week Varying Tolls on Golden Gate Bridge." *Transportation Research Record* no. 1558 (1996): 55–59.

Gilbert, A. *The Making of Post–Christian Britain*. London: Longman, 1980.

Gildin, H. *An Introduction to Political Philosophy: Ten Essays by Leo Strauss*. Detroit, Mich.: Wayne State University Press, 1989.

Gill, R., ed. *Theology and Sociology*. 2d ed. London: Cassell, 1996.

Giloth, R. "Jobs and Economic Development," in *Jobs and Economic Development*, edited by R. Giloth. Thousand Oaks, Calif.: Sage, 1998: 1–16.

Glass. J., and W. Johnson. "Metaphysics, MSRP and Economics." *British Journal for the Philosophy of Science* 39, no. 3 (1988): 313–29.

Goldingay, J. *Theological Diversity and the Authority of the Old Testament*. Carlisle, U.K.: Paternoster, 1995.

Gordon, B. *The Economic Problem in Biblical and Patristic Thought*. Leiden: Brill, 1989.

Gordon, P., and J. White. *Philosophers as Educational Reformers*. London: Routledge & Kegan Paul, 1979.

Gordon, R. *Macroeconomics*. 6th ed. New York: Harper Collins, 1993.

Gordon, S. *The History and Philosophy of Social Science*. London: Routledge, 1991.

Gorringe, T. *Capital and the Kingdom*. Maryknoll, N.Y./London: Orbis/SPCK, 1994.

Gottwald, N. *The Tribes of Yahweh*. London: SCM, 1979.

Goudzwaard, B., and H. de Lange. *Beyond Poverty and Affluence*. Grand Rapids, Mich.: Eerdmans, 1995.

Gowler, D. *What Are They Saying About the Parables?* New York: Paulist, 2000.

Graham, F., G. Monsma, C. Sinke, A. Storkey, and J. Tiemstra. *Reforming Economics: A Christian Perspective on Economic Theory and Practice*. Grand Rapids, Mich.: Calvin College, 1986.

Granger, C. "Critical Realism and Econometrics: An Econometrician's Viewpoint," in *Transforming Economics*, edited by P. Lewis. Abingdon, U.K.: Routledge, 2004: 96–106.

Gray, A. *The Development of Economic Doctrine*. London: Longman, 1931.

Green, D., and I. Shapiro. *Pathologies of Rational Choice Theory*. New Haven, Conn.: Yale University Press, 1994.

Green, J. *New International Commentary on the New Testament: The Gospel of Luke*. Grand Rapids, Mich.: Eerdmans, 1997.

Greenberg, M. *Ezekiel 1–20*. New York: Doubleday, 1983.

Gregg, S. *Economic Thinking for the Theologically Minded*. Lanham, Md.: University Press of America, 2001.

Gregory, R., and P. Sheehan. "Unemployment Trends in Australia and the US: The Natural Rate, Wage Flexibility and Path Dependence," in *Working for the Future*, edited by P. Sheehan and G. Tegart. Melbourne: Victoria University Press, 1998: 293–350.

Gregory, R., E. Klug, and Y. Martin. "Labour Market Deregulation, Relative Wages and the Social Security System," in *Reshaping the Labour Market*, edited by S. Richardson. Cambridge: Cambridge University Press, 1999: 200–22.

Grenz, S. "Christian Integrity in a Postmodern World (Theological Ethics)," in *New Dimensions in Evangelical Thought*, edited by D. Dockery. Downers Grove, Ill.: IVP, 1998: 394–410.

Griffiths, B. *The Creation of Wealth*. London: Hodder & Stoughton, 1984.

Grudem, W. *Systematic Theology*. Leicester, U.K.: IVP, 1994.

Gruenberg, G. "Papal Pronouncements on Labor Unions and Workplace Democracy." *International Journal of Social Economics* 25, no. 11/12 (1998): 1711–26.

Guillaume, A. *Islam*. Harmondsworth: Penguin, 1954.

Gul, F. "A Nobel Prize for Game Theorists: The Contributions of Harsanyi, Nash and Selten." *Journal of Economic Perspectives* 11, no. 3 (1997): 159–74.

Gundry, R. *Matthew: A Commentary on His Handbook for a Mixed Church Under Persecution*. 2d ed. Grand Rapids, Mich.: Eerdmans, 1994.

Gushee, D., ed. *Toward a Just and Caring Society*. Grand Rapids, Mich.: Baker, 1999.

Gutierrez, G. *A Theology of Liberation*. Maryknoll, N.Y.: Orbis, 1973.

Haack, S. "Realism." *Synthese* 73, no. 3 (1987): 275–99.

Hacking, I. "The Sociology of Knowledge about Child Abuse." *Nous* 22, no. 1 (1988): 53–63.

Hagner, D. *Word Biblical Commentary Matthew 1–13*. Dallas, Tex.: Word. 1993.

Hahn, F. *Equilibrium and Macroeconomics*. Oxford: Blackwell, 1984.

——. "Book Review of *The Rhetoric of Economics* by Donald N. McCloskey." *Journal of Economic Literature* 25, no. 1 (1987): 110–11.

Halfpenny, P. *Positivism and Sociology*. London: Allen & Unwin, 1982.

Haltmann, J. "The Market System, the Poor, and Economic Theory," in *Toward a Just and Caring Society*, edited by D. Gushee. Grand Rapids, Mich.: Baker, 1999: 72–111.

Hamilton, J. *Social Justice and Deuteronomy*. Atlanta, Ga.: Scholars, 1992.

Hamilton, J., and C. Whiteman. "The Observable Implications of Self-fulfilling Expectations." *Journal of Monetary Economics* 16, no. 4 (1985): 353–73.

Hampton, J. "The Failure of Expected-Utility Theory as a Theory of Reason." *Economics and Philosophy* 10, no. 2 (1994): 195–242.
Hands, D. "What Economics Is Not: An Economist's Response to Rosenberg." *Philosophy of Science* 51, no. 3 (1984a): 495–503.
———. "Blaug's Economic Methodology." *Philosophy of the Social Sciences* 14, no. 1 (1984b): 115–25.
———. "The Problem of Excess Content: Economics, Novelty and a Long Popperian Tale" and "Reply," in *Appraising Economic Theories*, edited by N. de Marchi and M. Blaug. Aldershot, U.K.: Edward Elgar, 1991: 58–75, 91–102.
———. *Testing, Rationality, and Progress*. Lanham, Md.: Rowman & Littlefield, 1993.
———. "Expert Knowledge, Ersatz Knowledge, and Economics." *Journal of Economic Methodology* 7, no. 3 (2000): 449–54.
———. "Economic Methodology is Dead–Long Live Economic Methodology." *Journal of Economic Methodology* 8, no. 1 (2001a): 49–63.
———. *Reflection Without Rules*. Cambridge: Cambridge University Press, 2001b.
Hanks, T. *God So Loved The Third World*. Maryknoll, N.Y.: Orbis, 1983.
Hansen, W. "Policy Research: A Withering Branch of Economics?" in *Policy Analysis and Economics*, edited by D. Weimer. Boston, Mass.: Kluwer, 1991: 187–204.
Hanson, N. *Patterns of Discovery*. Cambridge: Cambridge University Press, 1958.
Haralambos, M., and M. Holborn. *Sociology*. 3d ed. London: Collins, 1991.
Harding, S., ed. *Can Theories Be Refuted? Essays on the Duhem-Quine Thesis*. Dordrecht: Reidel, 1976.
Hare, D. *Matthew*. Louisville, Ky.: John Knox, 1993.
Hargreaves Heap, S., and Y. Varoufakis. *Game Theory: A Critical Introduction*. London: Routledge, 1995.
Harman, P. *Metaphysics and Natural Philosophy*. Brighton, U.K.: Harvester, 1982.
Harre, R. *Varieties of Realism: A Rationale for the Natural Sciences*. Oxford: Blackwell, 1986.
Harrington, D. *The Gospel of Matthew*. Collegeville, Minn.: Liturgical Press, 1991.
Harris, H. *Fundamentalism and Evangelicals*. Oxford: Clarendon, 1998.
Harrison, R. *The Wycliffe Exegetical Commentary: Numbers*. Chicago: Moody, 1990.
Hart, S., and A. Neyman, eds. *Game and Economic Theory*. Ann Arbor, Mich.: University of Michigan Press, 1995.
Hartley, J. *Word Biblical Commentary Vol. 4 Leviticus*. Dallas, Tex.: Word, 1992.
Haslett, D. *Capitalism With Morality*. Oxford: Clarendon, 1994.
Hassan, S. *Combatting Cult Mind Control*. Rochester, Minn.: Park Street, 1990.
Hauerwas, S. *The Hauerwas Reader*, edited by J. Berkman and M. Cartwright. Durham, N.C.: Duke University Press, 2001.
Hauptmann, E. *Putting Choice Before Democracy*. Albany, N.Y.: SUNY Press, 1996.
Hausman, D. "Is Falsification Unpractised or Unpracticable?" *Philosophy of the Social Sciences* 15, no. 3 (1985): 313–19.
———. "An Appraisal of Popperian Methodology," in *The Popperian Legacy in Economics*, edited by N. De Marchi. Cambridge: Cambridge University Press, 1988: 65–85.

———. "Explanatory Progress in Economics." *Social Research* 56, no. 2 (1989): 361–81.

———. *The Inexact and Separate Science of Economics*. Cambridge: Cambridge University Press, 1992.

———. "Problems with Supply-side Egalitarianism," in *Recasting Egalitarianism*, edited by S. Bowles and H. Gintis. London: Verso, 1998: 75–85.

Hausman, D., and M. McPherson. *Economic Analysis and Moral Philosophy*. Cambridge: Cambridge University Press, 1996.

Hawtrey, K. "Economics and Evangelicalism," in *Religion and Economics: Normative Social Theory*, edited by J. Dean and A. Waterman. Boston, Mass.: Kluwer, 1999: 99–112.

Hay, D. *Economics Today: A Christian Critique*. Leicester: Apollos, 1989.

———. "Evangelicalism and Economic Issues," in *Evangelical Anglicans*, edited by R. France and A. McGrath. London: SPCK, 1993a: 120–33.

———. "Economic Analysis and Ethics," in *The Blackwell Encyclopedia of Modern Christian Thought*, edited by A. McGrath. Oxford: Blackwell, 1993b: 134–40.

Heilbroner, R., and W. Milberg. *The Crisis of Vision in Modern Economic Thought*. Cambridge: Cambridge University Press, 1995.

Heisenberg, W. *The Physicist's Conception of Nature*. London: Hutchinson, 1958.

Heller, F., E. Pusic, G. Strauss, and B. Wilpert. *Organizational Participation: Myth and Reality*. Oxford: Oxford University Press, 1998.

Hempel, C. "The Empiricist Criterion of Meaning," in *Logical Positivism*, edited by A. Ayer. New York: Free Press, 1959: 108–29.

Henderson, D. *Innocence and Design: The Influence of Economic Ideas on Policy*. Oxford: Blackwell, 1986.

Hendry, D. "Econometrics-Alchemy or Science?" *Economica* 47, no. 188 (1980): 387–406.

Hendry, D., and H. Ericsson, "An Econometric Analysis of UK Money Demand in Friedman, M. and Schwartz, A., Monetary Trends in the United States and the United Kingdom." *American Economic Review* 81, no. 1 (1991): 8–38.

Hendry, D., E. Leamer, and D. Poirer. "The ET Dialogue: A Conversation In Econometric Methodology." *Econometric Theory* 6, no. 2 (1990): 171–261.

Henley, A. "Work and Unemployment," in *Christianity and the Culture of Economics*, edited by D. Hay and A. Krieider. Cardiff: University of Wales Press, 2001: 114–37.

Henroit, P., E. De Berri, M. Schultheis, and M. O'Connor. *Catholic Social Teaching: Our Best Kept Secret.* North Blackburn, Vic.: Collins Dove, 1992.

Hey, J., ed. *The Future of Economics*. Oxford: Blackwell, 1992.

Heyne, P. "Review of the Evidence," in *Economics and Religion: Are They Distinct?* edited by G. Brennan and A. Waterman. Boston, Mass.: Kluwer, 1994: 213–25.

———. "Theological Visions in Economics and Religion." *Forum for Social Economics* 25, no. 2 (1996): 1–7.

———. "If the Trumpet Does Not Sound a Clear Call," in *Religion and Economics: Normative Social Theory*, edited by J. Dean and A. Waterman. Boston, Mass.: Kluwer, 1999: 141–51.

Hicks, D. *Inequality and Christian Ethics*. Cambridge: Cambridge University Press, 2000.

Hicks, J. *Causality in Economics*. Canberra: ANU Press, 1980.

Hilley, D., J. Bohman, and R. Shusterman, eds. *The Interpretive Turn: Philosophy, Science and Culture*. New York: Cornell University Press, 1992.

Hindess, B. *Choice, Rationality and Social Theory*. London: Unwin Hyman, 1988.

Hirsch, A., and N. de Marchi. *Milton Friedman: Economics in Theory and Practice*. Brighton, U.K.: Harvester/Wheatsheaf, 1990.

Hirst, P. *Associative Democracy*. Cambridge, U.K.: Polity, 1994.

Hobgood, M. *Catholic Social Teaching and Economic Theory*. Philadelphia, Pa.: Temple University Press, 1991.

Hodgson, G. "Commentary," in *Institutional Economics: Theory, Method, Policy*, edited by M. Tool. Boston, Mass.: Kluwer, 1993: 108–18.

———. "Visions of Mainstream Economics: A Response to Richard Nelson and Jack Vromen." *Review of Social Economy* 60, no. 1 (2002): 125–33.

Hodgson, G., W. Samuels, and M. Tools, eds. *The Elgar Companion to Institutional Economics*. Aldershot, U.K.: Edward Elgar, 1994.

Hoff, K. "Market Failures and the Distribution of Wealth: A Perspective from the Economics of Information," in *Recasting Egalitarianism*, Edited by S. Bowles and H. Gintis. London: Verso, 1998: 332–57.

Hoksbergen, R. "Is There a Christian Economics?" *Christian Scholar's Review* 24, no. 2 (1994a): 126–42.

———. "Postmodernism and Institutionalism: Toward a Resolution of the Debate on Relativism." *Journal of Economic Issues* 28, no. 3, (1994b): 679–713.

Hollis, M. "Rationality and Reason," in *The Blackwell Dictionary of Twentieth-Century Social Thought*, edited by W. Outhwaite and T. Bottomore. Oxford: Blackwell, 1994: 544–6.

Holmwood, J., and A. Stewart. *Explanation and Social Theory*. London: Macmillan, 1991.

Holstrom, M. *Spain's New Social Economy*. Oxford: Berg, 1993.

Homer, S., and R. Sylla. *A History of Interest Rates*. New Brunswick, N.J.: Rutgers, 1991.

Honderich, T. "Methodology," in *The Oxford Companion to Philosophy*, Edited by T. Honderich. Oxford: Oxford University Press, 1995: 565.

Hoover, K. "Econometrics as Observation: The Lucas Critique and the Nature of Econometric Inference." *Journal of Economic Methodology*. 1, no. 1 (1994): 65–86.

———. "Book Review of Backhouse, R., *Truth and Progress in Economic Knowledge*, and *Explorations in Economic Methodology*." *Economics and Philosophy* 16, no. 2 (2000): 338–46.

Hoover, K. "Economics and Reality," in *Fact and Fiction in Economics*, edited by U. Maki. Cambridge: Cambridge University Press, 2002: 152–77.

Hoppe, L. *There Shall Be No Poor Among You: Poverty in the Bible*. Nashville: Abingdon, 2004.

Horgan, T., and J. Woodward. "Folk Psychology Is Here to Stay," in *Folk Psychology and the Philosophy of Mind*, edited by S. Christensen and C. Turner. Hillsdale, Mich.: Laurence Erlbaum, 1993: 144–68.

Houck, J., and O. Williams, eds. *Co-Creation and Capitalism: John Paul II's "Laborem Exercens"*. Washington, D.C.: University Press of America, 1983.

Hung Mo, P. "Income Inequality and Economic Growth." *Kyklos* 53, no. 3 (2000): 293–316.

Hurp, W., ed. *The World of Co-operative Enterprise 1998*. Oxford: Plunket Foundation, 1998.

Hutchison, T. *The Politics and Philosophy of Economics*. Oxford: Blackwell, 1981.

———. *Changing Aims in Economics*. Oxford: Blackwell, 1992.

Hutter, R., and T. Dieter, eds. *Ecumenical Ventures in Ethics*. Grand Rapids, Mich.: Eerdmans, 1998.

Hyatt, J. *Exodus*. Grand Rapids, Mich: Eerdmans, 1980.

Iannaccone, L. "Sacrifice and Stigma: Reducing Free-riding in Cults, Communes, and Other Collectives." *Journal of Political Economy* 100, no. 2 (1992): 271–91.

———. "Heirs to the Protestant Ethic? The Economics of American Fundamentalists," in *Fundamentalisms and the State*, edited by M. Marty and R. Appleby. Chicago: University of Chicago Press, 1993: 342–66.

———. "Introduction to the Economics of Religion." *Journal of Economic Literature* 36, no. 3 (1998): 1465–95.

Ingrao, B., and G. Israel. *The Invisible Hand*. Cambridge, Mass.: MIT, 1991.

Ironmonger, D., ed. *Households' Work*. Sydney: Allen & Unwin, 1989.

Isaac, J. "Realism and Reality: Some Realistic Reconsiderations." *Journal for the Theory of Social Behaviour* 20, no. 1 (1990): 1–31.

Jackman, R. "European Unemployment: Why Is It So High and What Should Be Done About It?" in *Unemployment and the Australian Labour Market*, edited by G. Debelle and J. Borland. Sydney: Reserve Bank of Australia, 1998: 342–66.

Jackson, J., R. McIver, C. McConnell, and S. Brue. *Economics*. 5th ed. Sydney: McGraw-Hill, 1998.

Jackson, W. "Naturalism in Economics." *Journal of Economic Issues* 29, no. 3 (1995): 761–80.

Jacob, B. *The Second Book of the Bible: Exodus*. Hokoben, N.J.: KTAV, 1992.

Jacobs-Malina, D. *The Images of Family in Jesus*. New York: Paulist, 1993.

James, S. *The Content of Social Explanation*. Cambridge: Cambridge University Press, 1984.

Jeeves, M., and R. Berry. *Science, Life and Christian Belief*. Leicester, U.K.: Apollos, 1998.

Johnson, J. "How Not to Criticize Rational Choice Theory: Pathologies of 'Common Sense'." *Philosophy of the Social Sciences* 26, no. 1 (1996): 77–91.

Johnson, P. *Darwin on Trial*. 2d ed. Downers Grove, Ill.: IVP, 1993.

———. *Reason in the Balance: The Case Against Naturalism in Science, Law and Education*. Downers Grove, Ill.: IVP, 1995.

Jones, A. *Capitalism and Christians*. North Blackburn, Vic.: Collins Dove, 1993.

Jones, D., and J. Svejnar. "Participation, Profit-Sharing, Worker Ownership and Efficiency in Italian Producer Co-operatives." *Economica* 55, no. 208 (1985): 449–65.

Jones, P. *Studying the Parables of Jesus*. Macon, Ga.: Smyth & Helwys, 1999.

Joskow, P. "Firm Decision-making Processes and Oligopoly Theory." *American Economic Review* 65, no. 2 (1975): 270–9.

Journal of Post Keynesian Economics Editors. "A Statement of Purposes." *Journal of Post Keynesian Economics* 1, no.1 (1978): 3–7.

Jubilee 2000 Coalition. *The Jubilee 2000 Organizer's Pack*. Melbourne, 1998.

Junakar, P., ed. *The Economics of Unemployment* Vol. 1–4. Cheltenham: Edward Elgar, 2000.

Just Jr., A. *Concordia Commentary Luke 1:1–9:50 and 9:51–24:53*. St. Louis, Miss.: Concordia, 1997.

Kahane, H. *Logic and Contemporary Rhetoric*. 6th ed. Belmont: Wadsworth, 1992.

Kaiser Jr. W. *Toward Old Testament Ethics*. Grand Rapids, Mich.: Zondervan, 1983.

———. "How Can Christians Derive Principles from the Specific Commands of the Law?" in *Readings in Christian Ethics. Vol. 1*, edited by R. Clark and R. Rakestraw. Grand Rapids, Mich.: Baker, 1994: 192–201.

Kaiser Jr., W., P. Davids, F. Bruce, and M. Brauch. *Hard Sayings of the Bible*. Downers Grove, Ill.: IVP, 1996.

Kammer, F. *Doing Faithjustice: An Introduction to Catholic Social Thought*. New York: Paulist, 1991.

Kanth, R. "Economic Theory and Realism: Outlines of a Reconstruction." *Methodus* 3, no. 2 (1991): 37–46.

Kaplan, A. "Positivism," in *International Encyclopedia of Social Sciences*. New York: Macmillan/Free Press, 1968: 389–95.

Kapp, K. "The Nature and Significance of Institutional Economics." *Kyklos* 29, no. 2 (1976): 209–32.

Kasmir, S. *The Myth of Mondragon*. New York: SUNY, 1996.

Katz, L. "Reflections on US Labour Market Performance," in *Unemployment and the Australian Labour Market*, edited by G. Debelle and J. Borland. Sydney: Reserve Bank of Australia, 1998: 8–33.

Katz, M., and H. Rosen. *Microeconomics*. 2d ed. Burr Ridge, Ill.: Irwin, 1994.

Katzner, D. "Our Mad Rush to Measure: How Did We Get into This Mess?" *Methodus* 3, no. 2 (1991): 18–26.

Kearney, H. *Science and Change 1500–1700*. London: Weidenfeld & Nicolson, 1971.

Keating, M., and B. Keating. "The Crossroads between John Paul II's Social Vision and Conservative Economic Thought." *International Journal of Social Economics*. 25, no. 11/12 (1998): 1790–802.

Keen, S. *Debunking Economics*. Sydney: Pluto, 2001.

Keener, C. *A Commentary on the Gospel of Matthew*. Grand Rapids, Mich.: Eerdmans, 1999.

Keister, L. *Wealth in America*. Cheltenham: Edward Elgar, 2000.

Kephart, W. "Occupational Level and Marital Disruption." *American Sociological Review* 20, no. 4 (1955): 456–65.

Keynes, J. *The General Theory of Employment, Interest and Money*. London: Macmillan, [1936] 1973.

Khalil, E. "Has Economics Progressed? Rectilinear, Historicist, Universalist, and Evolutionary Historiographies." *History of Political Economy* 27, no. 1 (1995): 43–87.

Kieta, L. *Science, Rationality, and Neoclassical Economics*. Newark, Del.: University of Delaware Press, 1992.

Kilpatrick, W. *Psychological Seduction: The Failure of Modern Psychology*. Nashville, Tenn.: Nelson, 1983.

Kincaid, H. "Defending Laws in the Social Sciences." *Philosophy of the Social Sciences* 20, no. 1 (1990): 56–83.

———. *Philosophical Foundations of the Social Sciences*. Cambridge: Cambridge University Press, 1996.

Kincaid, P. *The Rule of the Road*. New York: Greenwood, 1986.

King, J. "Can Propositions be Naturalistically Acceptable?" in *Philosophical Naturalism: Midwest Studies in Philosophy Vol. 19*, edited by P. French, T. Uehling, and H. Wettstein. Notre Dame, Ill.: University of Notre Dame Press, 1994: 53–75.

Kirkham, R. *Theories of Truth*. Cambridge: MIT, 1992.

Klamer, A., and D. Colander. *The Making of an Economist*. Boulder, Colo.: Westview, 1990.

Klamer, A., D. McCloskey, and R. Solow, eds. *The Consequences of Economic Rhetoric*. Cambridge: Cambridge University Press, 1988.

Kline, M. *Mathematics: The Loss of Certainty*. New York: Oxford University Press, 1980.

Knapp, P. *One World-Many Worlds: Contemporary Sociological Theory*. New York: Harper Collins, 1994.

Knorr-Cetina, K. *The Manufacture of Knowledge*. Oxford: Pergamon, 1981.

Knorr-Cetina, K., and M. Mulkay. "Emerging Principles in Social Studies of Sciences," in *Science Observed: Perspectives on the Social Study of Science*, edited by K. Knorr-Cetina and M. Mulkay. London: Sage, 1983: 1–17.

Kolakowski, L. *Positivist Philosophy: From Hume to the Vienna Circle*. Harmondsworth, U.K.: Penguin, 1972.

———. *Religion*. New York: Oxford University Press, 1982.

Kramer, W., H. Sonnberger, H. Maurer, and P. Havlik. "Diagnostic Checking in Practice." *Review of Economics and Statistics* 67, no. 1 (1985): 118–23.

Kreps, D. "Economics–The Current Position." *Daedalus* 126, no. 1 (1997): 59–85.

Kuezenkamp, H. *Probability, Econometrics and Truth*. Cambridge: Cambridge University Press, 2000.

Kuhn, T. *The Structure of Scientific Revolutions*. Chicago: University of Chicago Press, 1962.

———. *The Essential Tension*. Chicago: University of Chicago Press, 1977.

Kuran, T. "Behavioral Norms in the Islamic Doctrine of Economics: A Critique." *Journal of Economic Behavior and Organization* 4, no. 4 (1983): 353–79.

———. "Fundamentalisms and the Economy," in *Fundamentalisms and the State*, edited by M. Marty and R. Appleby. Chicago: University of Chicago Press, 1993a: 289–301.

———. "The Economic Impact of Islamic Fundamentalism," in *Fundamentalisms and the State*, edited by M. Marty and R. Appleby. Chicago: University of Chicago Press, 1993b: 302–41.

———. "Islamic Economics and the Islamic Subeconomy." *Journal of Economic Perspectives* 9, no. 4 (1995): 155–73.

Laborem Exercens (LE). *Encyclical Addressed by the Supreme Pontiff John Paul II to . . . on the Ninetieth Anniversary of Rerum Novarum*. Homebush, N.S.W.: St. Paul, 1981.

Lachmann, L. "Austrian Economics: A Hermeneutic Approach," in *Economics and Hermeneutics*, edited by D. Lavoie. London: Routledge, 1990: 134–46.

Ladyman, J. *Understanding Philosophy of Science*. London: Routledge, 2002.

Lakatos, I. *The Methodology of Scientific Research Programmes: Philosophical Papers*. Vols. I & 2. Cambridge: Cambridge University Press, 1978.

Lakatos, I., and A. Musgrave, eds. *Criticism and the Growth of Knowledge*. London: Cambridge University Press, 1970.

Lakeland, P. *Theology and Critical Theory*. Nashville, Tenn.: Abingdon, 1990.

Landreth, H., and D. Colander. *History of Economic Theory*. 2d ed. Boston, Mass.: Houghton Mifflin, 1990.

Langmore, J., and J. Quiggin. *Work For All*. Carlton, Vic.: Melbourne University Press, 1994.

Langone, M., ed. *Recovery from Cults*. New York: Norton, 1993.

Latour, B., and S. Woolgar. *Laboratory Life: The Social Construction of Scientific Facts*. Beverly Hills, Calif.: Sage, 1979.

Latsis, S., ed. *Method and Appraisal in Economics*. Cambridge: Cambridge University Press, 1976.

Laudan, L. *Progress and Its Problems*. Berkeley, Calif.: University of California Press, 1977.

——. "A Confutation of Convergent Realism." *Philosophy of Science* 48, no. 1 (1981): 19–48.

——. *Science and Values*. Berkeley, Calif.: University of California Press, 1984.

Lavoie, D., ed. *Economics and Hermeneutics*. London: Routledge, 1990.

Lawson, T. "Realism and Instrumentalism in the Development of Econometrics." *Oxford Economic Papers* 41, no. 1 (1989): 236–58.

——. "Why Are So Many Economists So Opposed to Methodology." *Journal of Economic Methodology* 1, no. 1 (1994a): 105–33.

——. "The Nature of Post Keynesianism and Its Links to Other Traditions." *Journal of Post Keynesian Economics* 16, no. 4 (1994b): 503–38.

——. "The Predictive Science of Economics?" in *Foundations of Research in Economics: How Do Economists Do Economics?*, edited by S. Medema and W. Samuels. Cheltenham, U.K.: Edward Elgar, 1996: 163–74.

——. *Economics and Reality*. London: Routledge, 1997.

——. *Reorienting Economics*. London: Routledge, 2003.

Lawson T., and H. Pesaran. eds. *Keynes' Economics: Methodological Issues.* For the *Cambridge Journal of Economics*. London: Routledge, 1989, c1985.

Lay, M. *Ways of the World*. New Brunswick, N.J.: Rutgers University Press, 1992.

Layard, R., S. Nickell, and R. Jackman. *The Unemployment Crisis*. Oxford: Oxford University Press, 1994.

Leamer, E. "Let's Take the Con out of Econometrics." *American Economic Review* 73, no. 3 (1983): 31–43.

——. "Self-Interpretation." *Economics and Philosophy* 1, no. 2 (1985a): 295–302.

——. "Sensitivity Analyses Would Help." *American Economic Review* 75, no. 3 (1985b): 308–13.

Leontief, W. "Theoretical Assumptions and Nonobserved Facts." *American Economic Review* 61, no. 1 (1971): 1–7.

——. "Academic Economics." *Science* 217, no. 4555 (1982): 104–7.

Le Roy, S. "Efficient Capital Markets and Martingales." *Journal of Economic Literature* 27, no. 4 (1989): 1583–621.

Lessnof, M. *The Structure of Social Science*. London: Allen & Unwin, 1974.

Levine, B. *The JPS Torah Commentary: Leviticus*. Philadelphia, Pa.: Jewish Publications Society, 1989.

Levine, D. *Reinventing the Workplace*. Washington: Brookings, 1995.

Lewis, D. *Convention: A Philosophical Study*. Cambridge: Harvard University Press, 1969.

Lipsey, R., and K. Chrystal. *An Introduction to Positive Economics*. 8th ed. Oxford: Oxford University Press, 1995.

Little, D. *Varieties of Social Explanation*. Boulder, Colo.: Westview, 1991.

——. "On The Scope and Limits of Generalizations in The Social Sciences." *Synthese* 97, no. 2 (1993): 183–207.

——., ed. *On the Reliability of Economic Models*. Boston, Mass.: Kluwer, 1995.

Logue, J., and J. Yates. "Worker Ownership American Style: Pluralism, Participation and Performance." *Economic and Industrial Democracy* 20, no. 2 (1999): 225–52.

Long, S. *Divine Economy: Theology and the Market*. London: Routledge, 2000.

Long, T. *Matthew*. Louisville, Ky.: Westminster John Knox, 1997.

Losee, J. *A Historical Introduction to the Philosophy of Science* 4th ed. Oxford: Oxford University Press, 2001.

Lovelock, J. *The Ages of Gaia*. Oxford: Oxford University Press, 1988.

Lunn, J., and R. Klay. "The Neoclassical Economic Model in a Postmodern World." *Christian Scholar's Review* 23, no. 2 (1994): 143–63.

Lutz, M. "The Mondragon Co-operative Enterprise System in Today's Global World," in *Self-Transformation of the Forgotten Four-Fifths*, edited by R. Dyck and M. Mulej. Dubuque, Iowa: Kendall/Hunt, 1998: 39–54.

Luz, U. *Matthew 1–7: A Commentary*. Minneapolis, Minn.: Augsburg Fortress, 1989.

McAfee, R., and J. McMillan. "Analyzing the Airwaves Auction." *Journal of Economic Perspectives* 10, no. 1 (1996): 159–75.

McAleer, M., A. Pagan, and P. Volker. "What Will Take the Con out of Econometrics?" *American Economic Review* 75, no. 3 (1985): 293–307.

McAll, K. *Healing the Family Tree*. London: Sheldon, 1985.

——. *Healing the Haunted*. London: Darley Anderson, 1989.

Macariello, J. "Business and Empowerment: Management Systems with a Heart for the Poor," in *Toward a Just and Caring Society*, edited by D. Gushee. Grand Rapids, Mich.: Baker, 1999: 427–72.

McCallum, B. "On the Observational Inequivalence of Classical and Keynesian Models." *Journal of Political Economy* 87, no. 2 (1979): 395–402.

McClelland, P. *Causal Explanation and Model Building in History, Economics and the New Economic History*. Ithaca, N.Y.: Cornell University Press, 1975.

McCloskey, D. "The Loss Function Has Been Mislaid: The Rhetoric of Significance Tests." *American Economic Review* 75, no. 2 (1985): 201–5.

——. *The Rhetoric of Economics*. Brighton, U.K.: Wheatsheaf, 1986.

——. *Knowledge and Persuasion in Economics*. Cambridge: Cambridge University Press, 1994.

——. *The Vices of Economists–The Virtues of the Bourgeoisie*. Amsterdam: Amsterdam University Press, 1996.

McCloskey, D., and S. Ziliak. "The Standard Error of Regressions." *Journal of Economic Literature* 34, no. 1 (1996): 97–114.

McConnell, C., S. Brue, and D. MacPherson. *Contemporary Labor Economics* 6th ed. Boston, Mass.: McGraw-Hill Irwin, 2003.

McConville, G. *Apollos Old Testament Commentary: Deuteronomy*. Leicester, U.K.: Apollos, 2002.

McCullagh, C. *The Truth of History*. London: Routledge, 1998.

McDonagh, J. *Christian Psychology*. New York: Crossroad, 1982.

Macdonald, G., and P. Pettit. *Semantics and Social Science*. London: Routledge, 1981.

McDonald, L. *The Early Origin of the Social Sciences*. Montreal: McGill-Queen's, 1993.

McGrath, A. *Evangelicalism and the Future of Christianity*. London: Hodder & Stoughton, 1994.

——. *Christian Theology: An Introduction*. 2d ed. Oxford: Blackwell, 1997.

——. *A Scientific Theology Vol.1: Nature*. Edinburgh: T.&T. Clark, 2001.

——. *A Scientific Theology Vol. 2: Reality*. Edinburgh: T.&T. Clark, 2002.

Machin, S., A. Manning, and L. Rahman. "Where the Minimum Wage Bites Hard: Introduction of Minimum Wages to a Low Wage Sector." *Journal of the European Economic Association* 1, no. 1 (2003): 154–80.

Machlup, F. *Methodology of Economics and Other Social Sciences*. New York: Academic Press, 1978.

McHugh, P., J. Cutcher-Gershenfeld, and M. Polzin. "Employee Stock Ownership Plans: Union Influence and Stakeholder Interests." *Economic and Industrial Democracy* 20, no. 4 (1999): 535–60.

MacIntyre, A. *After Virtue: A Study In Moral Theory*. London: Duckworth, 1981.

McIntyre, L. *Laws and Explanation in the Social Sciences: Defending a Science of Human Behavior*. Boulder, Colo.: Westview, 1996.

McKee, A. *Economics and the Christian Mind*. New York: Vantage Press, 1987.

——. "Christian Thought and Microeconomic Theory." *International Journal of Social Economics* 20, no. 2 (1993): 51–64.

McKenzie, J. "The Gospel According to Matthew," in *The Jerome Biblical Commentary*, edited by R. Brown, J. Fitzmyer, and R. Murphy. London: Chapman, 1986: 62–114.

Mackie, J. *The Cement of the Universe*. Oxford: Oxford University Press, 1974.

MacLeod, G. *From Mondragon to America: Experiments in Community Economic Development*. Sydney: University College of Cape Breton Press, 1997.

McLoughlin, Q. *Relativistic Naturalism*. New York: Praeger, 1991.

McMullin, E. "Values in Science," in *Philosophy of Science Association, Vol. 2. 1982*, edited by P. Asquith and T. Nickles. East Lansing, Mich.: Philosophy of Science Association, 1983: 3–28.

Macquarrie, J. *Principles of Christian Theology*. London: SCM, 1977.

Maki, U. "Two Philosophies of the Rhetoric of Economics," in *Economics and Language*, edited by W. Henderson, T. Dudley-Evans, and R. Backhouse. London: Routledge, 1993: 23–50.

Malina, B., and R. Rohrbaugh. *Social Science Commentary on the Synoptic Gospels*. Minneapolis, Minn.: Fortress, 1992.

Mally, E. "The Gospel According to Mark," in *The Jerome Biblical Commentary*, edited by R. Brown, J. Fitzmyer, and R. Murphy. London: Chapman, 1986: 21–61.

Manicas, P. *A History and Philosophy of the Social Sciences*. Oxford: Blackwell, 1987.

Mann, C. *The Anchor Bible: Mark*. Garden City, N.Y.: Doubleday, 1986.

Mann, T. *Deuteronomy*. Louisville, Ky.: Westminster John Knox, 1995.

Marger, M. *Social Inequality* 2d ed. Boston: McGraw-Hill, 2002.

Marshall, A. *Principles of Economics*. 8th ed. London: Macmillan, [1890] 1920.

Marty, M., and R. Appleby, eds. *Fundamentalisms Observed*. Chicago: University of Chicago Press, 1991.

———. *Fundamentalisms and the State*. Chicago: University of Chicago Press, 1993.

Mason, J. "Biblical Teaching and Assisting the Poor." *Transformation* 4, no. 2 (1987): 1–14.

———. "Centralization and Decentralization in Social Arrangements: Explorations into Biblical Social Ethics." *Journal of the Association of Christian Economists (U.K.)* 13 (1992): 3–47.

———. "Biblical Teaching and the Objectives of Welfare Policy in the United States," in *Welfare in America: Christian Perspectives on a Policy in Crisis*, edited by S. Carlson-Thies, and J. Skillen. Grand Rapids, Mich.: Eerdmans, 1996: 145–85.

Mason, J., and K. Schaefer. "The Bible, the State, and the Economy: A Framework for Analysis." *Christian Scholar's Review* 20, no. 1 (1990): 45–64.

Massaro, T. *Catholic Social Teaching and United States Welfare Reform*. Collegeville, Minn.: Liturgical Press, 1998.

Mathews, R. *Jobs of Our Own: Building a Stake-Holder Society*. Annandale, N.S.W.: Pluto/Comerford and Miller, 1999.

Mattioni, F., and D. Tranquilli. *Social Entrepreneurs: The Italian Case*. Rome: D'Anselmi Editore, 1998.

Maxwell, J. *The Communicator's Commentary: Deuteronomy*. Waco, Tex.: Word, 1987.

May, H., and B. Metzger, eds. *The New Oxford Annotated Bible with The Apocrypha. Revised Standard Version*. New York: Oxford University Press, 1977.

Mayer, T. *Truth Versus Precision in Economics*. Aldershot, U.K.: Edward Elgar, 1993.

———. *Doing Economic Research: Essays on the Applied Methodology of Economics*. Aldershot, U.K.: Edward Elgar, 1995.

Mayes, A. *Deuteronomy: New Century Biblical Commentary*. Grand Rapids, Mich.: Eerdmans, 1979.

Medema, S., and W. Samuels, eds. *Foundations of Research in Economics: How Do Economists Do Economics?* Cheltenham, U.K.: Edward Elgar, 1996.

Meehan, E. *Economics and Policymaking: The Tragic Illusion*. Westport, Conn.: Greenwood, 1982.

Meeks, D. *God the Economist*. Minneapolis, Minn.: Fortress, 1989.

———. "God's Oikonomia and the New World Economy," in *Christian Social Ethics in a Global Era*, by M. Stackhouse, P. Berger, D. McCann, and D. Meeks. Nashville, Tenn.: Abingdon, 1995: 111–26.

Merrill, E. *The New American Commentary Vol 4 Deuteronomy*. Dallas, Tex.: Broadman & Holman, 1994.

Metcalf, D. "The National Minimum Wage: Coverage, Impact and Future." *Oxford Bulletin of Economics and Statistics* 64 Supplement (2002): 565–82.

Michael, R., and N. Tuma. "Entry into Marriage and Parenthood by Young Men and Women: The Influence of Family Background." *Demography* 22, no. 4 (1985): 515–44.

Middleton, R. *Charlatans or Saviours?* Cheltenham, U.K.: Edward Elgar, 1998.

Midgley, E. *The Ideology of Max Weber: A Thomist Critique*. Aldershot, U.K.: Gower, 1983.

Milbank, J. *Theology and Social Theory*. Oxford: Blackwell, 1990.

Milgrom, J. *The JPS Torah Commentary: Numbers*. Philadelphia, Pa.: Jewish Publications Society, 1990.

Miller, D. *Principles of Social Justice*. Cambridge, Mass.: Harvard University Press, 1999.

Miller, E. 1978 'Institutional Economics: Philosophy, Methodology and Theory." *Social Science Journal* 15, no. 1 (1978): 13–25.

———. "The Instrumental Efficiency of Social Value Theory," in *Institutional Economics and the Theory of Social Value: Essays in Honor of Marc R. Tool*, edited by C. Clark. Boston, Mass.: Kluwer, 1995: 113–27.

Miller, R. *The Jesus Seminar and its Critics*. Santa Rosa, Calif.: Polebridge, 1999.

Mills, P., and J. Presley. *Islamic Finance: Theory and Practice*. Houndmills, U.K.: Macmillan, 1999.

Minford, P. *Unemployment, Causes and Cures*. 2d ed. Oxford: Blackwell, 1985.

Miranda, J. *Communism in the Bible*. London: SCM, 1982.

Mirowski, P. "Physics and the Marginalist Revolution." *Cambridge Journal of Economics* 8, no. 4 (1984): 361–79.

———. "Shall I Compare Thee to a Minkowski-Ricardo-Leontief-Metzler Matrix of the Mosak-Hicks Type?" *Economics and Philosophy* 3, no.1 (1987): 67–96.

———. *More Heat Than Light*. Cambridge: Cambridge University Press, 1989.

———. "Doing What Comes Naturally: Four Metanarratives on What Metaphors Are For," in *Natural Images in Economic Thought*, edited by P. Mirowski. Cambridge: Cambridge University Press, 1994: 3–19.

Monahan, T. "Divorce by Occupational Level." *Marriage and Family Living* 17 (1955): 322–24.

Mondragon Co-operative Corporation (MCC) 2005 Web site: www.mondragon.mcc.es

Montgomery, M. "Fully Inarticulate Model Economics: Or, Does Math Equal Macro?" *Journal of Post Keynesian Economics* 17, no. 1 (1994): 45–68.

Moreland, J. *Christianity and The Nature of Science*. Grand Rapids, Mich.: Baker, 1989.

Morgan, M. *The History of Econometric Ideas*. Cambridge: Cambridge University Press, 1990.

Morgan, T. "Theory Versus Empiricism in Academic Economics: Update and Comparison." *Journal of Economic Perspectives*. 2, no. 4 (1988): 159–64.

Morowitz, H. "Rediscovering the Mind," in *The Mind's I*, edited by D. Hofstadter and D. Dennett. New York: Basic Books, 1982: 34–42.

Morrison, M., and M. Morgan. "Models as Mediating Instruments," in *Models as Mediators: Perspectives on Natural and Social Science*, edited by M. Morgan and M. Morrison. Cambridge: Cambridge University Press, 1999: 10–37.

Morrison, R. *We Build the Road as We Travel*. Philadelphia, Pa.: New Society, 1991.

Moscovici, S. "Social Influence and Conformity," in *Handbook of Social Psychology* 3rd ed., edited by G. Lindzey and E. Aronson. New York: Random House, 1985: 347–412.

Moseley, F., ed. *Heterodox Economic Theories. True or False?* Aldershot, U.K.: Edward Elgar, 1995.

Mott, S. *Biblical Ethics and Social Change*. Oxford: Oxford University Press, 1982.

Mott, S., and R. Sider, "Economic Justice: A Biblical Paradigm," in *Toward a Just and Caring Society*, edited by D. Gushee. Grand Rapids, Mich.: Baker, 1999: 15–45.

Mueller, E., and A. Schwartz. "Why Local Economic Development and Employment Training Fail for Low-Income Communities," in *Jobs and Economic Development*, edited by R. Giloth. Thousand Oaks, Calif.: Sage, 1998: 42–63.

Mulkay, M. "Don Quixote's Double: A Self-Exemplifying Text," in *Knowledge and Reflexivity*, edited by S. Woolgar. London: Sage, 1988: 81–100.

Munby, D. *Christianity and Economic Problems*. London: Macmillan, 1956.

Murphy, K., and R. Topel. "Unemployment and Non-employment." *American Economic Review* 87, no. 2 (1997): 295–300.

Myerson, R. *Game Theory: Analysis of Conflict*. Cambridge: Harvard University Press, 1991.

Myrdal, G. "Institutional Economics." *Journal of Economic Issues* 12, no. 4 (1978): 771–83.

Nash, R. *Worldviews in Conflict*. Grand Rapids, Mich.: Zondervan, 1992.

Naughton, M. *The Good Stewards*. Lanham, Md.: University Press of America, 1992.

Naugle, D. *Worldview: The History of a Concept*. Grand Rapids, Mich.: Eerdmans, 2002.

National (US) Center for Employee Ownership (NCEO) 2001 Web site: www.nceo.org

Nelson, A. "Are Economic Kinds Natural?" *Minnesota Studies in Philosophy of Science* 14 (1990): 102–35.

Nelson, J., A. Megill, and D. McCloskey, eds. *The Rhetoric of the Human Sciences*. Madison, Wis.: University of Wisconsin Press, 1987.

Nelson, R. *Reaching for Heaven on Earth: The Theological Meaning of Economics*. Lanham, Md.: Rowman & Littlefield, 1991.

———. *Economics as Religion*. Uni. Park, Pa.: Penn. State Uni. Press, 2001.

Neumark, D. "The Employment Effects of Minimum Wages: Evidence from a Pre-specified Research Design." *Industrial Relations* 40, no. 1 (2001): 121–44.

Neumark, D., and W. Wascher. "Minimum Wages and Employment: A Case Study of the Fast-Food Industry in New Jersey and Pennsylvania: Comment." *American Economic Review* 90, no. 5 (2000): 1362–96.

Neumark, D., and W. Wascher. "Minimum Wages and Training Revisited." *Journal of Labor Economics* 19, no. 3 (2001): 563–95.

Neumark, D., and W. Wascher. "State-level Estimates of Minimum Wage Effects–New Evidence and Interpretations from Disequlibrium Methods." *Journal of Human Resources* 37, no. 1 (2002): 35–62.

Nevile, J. *The Root of All Evil*. Sydney: Australian Council of Churches, 1979.

Neyman, J. *First Course in Probability and Statistics*. New York: Henry Holt, 1950.

Norman, G., and M. La Manna, eds. *The New Industrial Economics*. Aldershot, U.K.: Edward Elgar, 1992.

North, R. *A Sociology of the Biblical Jubilee*. Rome: Pontifical Biblical Institute, 1954.

Norton, A., and P. Glick. "Marital Instability in America: Past, Present, Future." *Journal of Social Issues* 32, no. 1 (1976): 5–20.

Noth, M. *Leviticus*. London: SCM, 1965.

Novak, D. *Jewish Social Ethics*. New York: Oxford University Press, 1992.

Novak, M. *The Spirit of Democratic Capitalism*. New York: Simon & Schuster, 1982.

———. *The Catholic Ethic and the Spirit of Capitalism*. New York: Free Press, 1993.

Nye, I., and F. Berardo. *The Family: Its Structure and Interaction*. New York: Macmillan, 1973.

O'Boyle, E. *Personalist Economics*. Boston, Mass.: Kluwer, 1998.

O'Brien, D. "Four Detours." *Journal of Economic Methodology* 5, no. 1 (1998): 23–41.

O'Hara, P. "Methodological Principles of Institutional Political Economy: Holism, Evolution and Contradiction." *Methodus* 5, no. 1 (1993): 51–71.

Okasha, S. *Philosophy of Science: A Very Short Introduction*. Oxford: Oxford University Press, 2002.

O'Neill, W. "Private Property," in *The New Dictionary of Catholic Social Thought*, edited by J. Dwyer. Collegeville, Minn.: Liturgical Press, 1994: 785–90.

Olson, R. *The Emergence of the Social Sciences 1642–1792*. New York: Twayne, 1993.

Opportunity International. *Annual Report 1997*. Sydney, 1998.

Ormerod, P. *The Death of Economics*. London: Faber and Faber, 1994.

Oslington, P. "Islamic Economics," in *The Current State of Economic Science. Vol. 5*, edited by S. Dahiya. Rohtak: Jan Tinbergen Institute of Development Planning, 1999: 2905–12.

———. "A Theological Economics." *International Journal of Social Economics* 27, no. 1 (2000): 32–44.

———., ed. *Economics and Religion* 2 Vols. Cheltenham, U.K.: Edward Elgar, 2003.

Outhwaite, W. *New Philosophies of Social Science*. Houndmills, U.K.: Macmillan, 1987.

Pagan, A. "Three Econometric Methodologies: A Critical Appraisal." *Journal of Economic Surveys* 1, no. 1 (1987): 3–24.

Paige, J. *Agrarian Revolution*. New York: Free Press, 1975.

Papineau, D. *For Science In The Social Sciences*. London: Macmillan, 1978.

——. *Philosophical Naturalism*. Oxford: Blackwell, 1993.

Passmore, J. "Logical Positivism," in *The Encyclopedia of Philosophy*. New York: Macmillan, 1967: 52–7.

Patte, D. *The Gospel According to Matthew*. Philadelphia, Pa.: Fortress, 1987.

Pearcey, N., and C. Thaxton. *The Soul of Science: Christian Faith and Natural Philosophy*. Wheaton, Ill.: Crossway, 1994.

Peltzman S., "The Handbook of Industrial Organization" in *Journal of Political Economy* 99, no. 1 (1991): 201-217.

Pemberton, P., and D. Finn. *Toward a Christian Economic Ethic: Stewardship and Social Power*. Minneapolis, Minn.: Winston Press, 1985.

Perelman, M. *The End of Economics*. London: Routledge, 1996.

Perlman, M. and C. McCann, eds. *The Pillars of Economic Understanding: Ideas and Traditions*. Ann Arbor, Mich.: University of Michigan Press, 1998.

Perotin, V., and A. Robinson. "Equal Opportunities and Productive Efficiency in the Workplace," in *Industrial and Labour Market Policy and Performance*, edited by D. Coffey and C. Thornley. London: Routledge, 2003: 146–57.

Persson, T., and G. Tabellini, eds. Monetary and Fiscal Policy. Cambridge, Mass.: MIT Press, 1994.

Pesaran, M. "A Critique of the Proposed Tests of the Natural Rate-Rational Expectations Hypothesis." *Economic Journal* 92, no. 367 (1982): 529-554.

Pettit, P. *The Common Mind: An Essay on Psychology, Society, and Politics*. New York: Oxford University Press,1993.

Phelps Brown, E. "The Underdevelopment of Economics." *Economic Journal* 82, no. 1 (1972): 1–10.

Phillips, A. *Which Equalities Matter?* Cambridge, U.K.: Polity, 1999.

Phillips, D. *Holistic Thought in Social Science*. Stanford, Calif.: Stanford University Press, 1976.

Pixley, J. *Citizenship and Employment: Investigating Post-Industrial Options*. Cambridge: Cambridge University Press, 1993.

Plantinga, A. "Reason and Belief in God," in *Faith and Rationality*, edited by A. Plantinga and N. Wolterstorff. Notre Dame, Ill.: University of Notre Dame Press, 1983: 16–93.

Pleins, J. *The Social Visions of the Hebrew Bible*. Louisville, Ky.: Westminster John Knox, 2001.

Polkinghorne, J. *Reason and Reality: The Relationship between Science and Theology*. London: SPCK, 1991.

Pollak, R., and T. Wales. *Demand System Specification and Estimation*. New York: Oxford University Press, 1992.

Pontifical Academy of Social Sciences. *Towards Reducing Unemployment*. Proceedings of the Fifth Plenary Session of the Pontifical Academy of Social Sciences. Vatican City, March 1999.

Popper, K. *The Poverty of Historicism*. London: Routledge & Kegan Paul, 1961.

———. *The Logic of Scientific Discovery*. 6th imp. (rev.). London: Hutchinson, 1972.

Porter, T. "Rigor and Practicality: Rival Ideas of Quantification in Nineteenth-century Economics," in *Natural Images in Economic Thought*, edited by P. Mirowski. Cambridge: Cambridge University Press, 1994: 128–70.

Powers, J. *Philosophy and the New Physics*. London: Methuen, 1982.

Prasch, R., and F. Sheth. "The Economics and Ethics of Minimum Wage Legislation." *Review of Social Economy* 57, no. 4 (1999): 466–87.

Preece, G. "Biblical Distinctives for Work," in *Choices at the Coalface*, edited by G. Cooper. Sydney: Anglican Information Office, 1991: 1–14.

———. *Changing Work Values: A Christian Response*. Melbourne: Acorn, 1995.

Preston, R. "Book Review of Hay, D. (1989), *Economics Today: A Christian Critique*, Apollos, Leicester." *Journal of Theological Studies* 41, no. 2 (1990): 792–99.

———. *Religion and the Ambiguities of Capitalism*. London: SCM, 1991.

———. *Confusions in Christian Social Ethics*. London: SCM, 1994.

Prychitko, D., ed. *Why Economists Disagree*. New York: SUNY, 1998.

Putnam, H. *Reason, Truth and History*. Cambridge: Cambridge University Press, 1981.

———. *Realism with a Human Face*. Cambridge, Mass.: Harvard University Press, 1990.

———. *The Collapse of the Fact/Value Dichotomy*. Cambridge, Mass.: Harvard University Press, 2002.

Putnam, R. *Making Democracy Work: Civic Traditions in Modern Italy*. Princeton, N.J.: Princeton University Press, 1993.

Quiggin, J. *Great Expectations: Microeconomic Reform and Australia*. St. Leonards, N.S.W.: Allen & Unwin, 1996.

Quine, W. "Structure and Nature." *Journal of Philosophy* 89, no. 1 (1992): 5–9.

Rabinow, P., and W. Sullivan, eds. *Interpretive Social Science*. Berkeley, Calif.: University of California Press, 1979.

———. *Interpretive Social Science: A Second Look*. Berkeley, Calif.: University of California Press, 1987.

Rappaport, S. *Models and Reality in Economics*. Cheltenham, U.K.: Edward Elgar, 1998.

Ratzinger, J. (Pope Benedict XVI). *Principles of Catholic Theology: Building Stones for a Fundamental Theology*. San Francisco, Calif.: Ignatius, 1987.

Redhead, M. *From Physics to Metaphysics*. Cambridge: Cambridge University Press, 1995.

Redman, D. *Economics and the Philosophy of Science*. New York: Oxford University Press, 1991.

Redner, H. "Book Review of P. Livingston, *Literary Knowledge: Humanistic Inquiry and the Philosophy of Science*." *Philosophy of the Social Sciences* 23, no. 3 (1993): 388.

Reich, R. *The Work of Nations*. London: Simon & Schuster, 1991.

Rescher, N. *The Limits of Science*. Berkeley, Calif.: University of California, 1984.

Restivo, S. *The Social Relations of Physics, Mysticism and Mathematics*. Dordrecht: Reidel, 1985.

Reynolds, B., and S. Healy, eds. *An Adequate Income Guarantee for All*. Dublin: Justice Commission, 1995.

Rice, N. "Foreword: Jobs–The Real Goal." Pp xi-xiii in *Jobs and Economic Development*, edited by R. Giloth. Thousand Oaks, Calif.: Sage, 1998.

Richards, S. *Philosophy and Sociology of Science: An Introduction*. 2d ed. Oxford: Blackwell, 1987.

Richardson, D. "Frontiers in Economics and Christian Scholarship." *Christian Scholar's Review* 17, no. 4 (1988): 381–400.

Rifkin, J. *The End of Work*. New York: Putnam's Sons, 1995.

Ringe, S. *Westminster Bible Companion: Luke*. Louisville, Ky.: Westminster John Knox, 1995.

Rivzi, S. "Game Theory to the Rescue?" *Contributions to Political Economy* 13 (1994): 1–28.

Robbins, L. *An Essay on the Nature and Significance of Economic Science*. London: Macmillan, 1932.

——. *Cults, Converts and Charisma: The Sociology of New Religious Movements*. London: Sage, 1988.

Roels, S. "Evangelical Christians and Economic Democracy," in *On Moral Business*, edited by M. Stackhouse, D. McCann, S. Roels, with P. Williams. Grand Rapids, Mich.: Eerdmans, 1995: 561–71.

Rogerson, J. "The Family and Structures of Grace in the Old Testament," in *The Family in Theological Perspective*, edited by S. Barton. Edinburgh: T. & T. Clark, 1996: 25–42.

——. "The Old Testament and Christian Ethics," in *The Cambridge Companion to Christian Ethics*, edited by R. Gill. Cambridge: Cambridge University Press, 2001: 29–41.

Rooker, M. *The New American Commentary. Vol. 3A Leviticus*. Nashville, Tenn.: Broadman and Holman, 2000.

Rorty, R. *Philosophy and the Mirror of Nature*. Princeton, N.J.: Princeton University Press, 1979.

——. "Feminism, Ideology and Deconstruction: A Pragmatist View." *Hypatia* 8, no. 2 (1993): 96–103.

Rosenberg, A. *Sociobiology and the Preemption of Social Science*. Baltimore, Md.: Johns Hopkins, 1980.

——. "If Economics Isn't Science, What Is It?" *The Philosophical Forum* 14, no. 3–4 (1983): 296–314.

——. "What Rosenberg's Philosophy of Economics Is Not." *Philosophy of Science* 53, no. 1 (1984): 127–32.

——. "Lakatosian Consolations for Economists." *Economics and Philosophy* 2, no. 1 (1986): 127–39.

——. "Methodological Diversity in Economics." *Research in the History of Economic Thought and Methodology* 5 (1987a): 207–39.

——. "Weintraub's Aims." *Economics and Philosophy* 3, no. 2 (1987b): 143–44.

——. "Normative Naturalism and the Role of Philosophy." *Philosophy of Science* 57, no. 1 (1990): 34–43.

——. *Economics–Mathematical Politics or Science of Diminishing Returns?* Chicago: University of Chicago Press, 1992.

——. *Philosophy of Social Science*. 2d ed. Boulder, Colo.: Westview, 1995.

——. "A Field Guide to Recent Species of Naturalism." *British Journal for the Philosophy of Science* 47, no. 1 (1996): 1–29.

——. *Philosophy of Science: A Contemporary Introduction*. London: Routledge, 2000.

Ross, D. *Origins of American Social Science*. New York: Cambridge University Press, 1991.

Roth, A., and M. Sotomayor. "Two-Sided Matching," in *Handbook of Game Theory with Economic Applications*, Vol. 1., edited by R. Aumann and S. Hart. Amsterdam: North Holland, 1992: 485–541.

Rubinstein, A., ed. *Game Theory in Economics*. Aldershot, U.K.: Edward Elgar, 1990.

——. "John Nash: The Master of Economic Modelling." *Scandinavian Journal of Economics* 97, no. 1 (1995): 9–13.

Rule, J. *Theory and Progress in Social Science*. Cambridge: Cambridge University Press, 1997.

Ryan, A. *The Philosophy of the Social Sciences*. London: Macmillan, 1970.

Sakenfeld, K. *Numbers: Journeying with God*. Grand Rapids, Mich.: Eerdmans, 1995.

Samuelson, P. *Economics*. 11th ed. New York: McGraw-Hill, 1980.

Samuelson, P., and W. Nordhaus *Economics*. 14th ed. New York: McGraw-Hill, 1992.

Sankey, H. "Five Varieties of Cognitive Relativism." *Cogito* 7 (1993): 106–11.

——. "Methodological Pluralism, Normative Naturalism, and the Realist Aim of Science," in *After Popper, Kuhn and Feyerabend*, edited by R. Nola and H. Sankey. Dordrecht: Kluwer, 2000: 211–29.

Sargent, T. "The Observational Equivalence of Natural and Unnatural Rate Theories of Macroeconomics." *Journal of Political Economy* 84, no. 3 (1976): 631–40.

Sarna, N. *The JPS Torah Commentary: Exodus*. Philadelphia, Pa.: Jewish Publications Society, 1991.

Satz, D., and J. Ferejohn. "Rational Choice and Social Theory." *Journal of Philosophy* 91, no. 2 (1994): 71–87.

Saul, J. *The Unconscious Civilization*. Ringwood, Vic.: Penguin, 1997.

Sawtell, R. "Co-operatives: Regenerating Business in the Twentieth-first Century," in *Christianity and the Culture of Economics*, edited by D. Hay and A. Krieider. Cardiff: University of Wales Press, 2001: 53–75.

Sawyer, K., C. Beed, and H. Sankey. "Underdetermination in Economics: The Duhem-Quine Thesis." *Economics and Philosophy*. 13, no. 1 (1997): 1–23.

Sawyer, K., B. Ellis, C. Beed, and H. Sankey. "Meta-economic Principles." Paper presented at *American Philosophical Association Conference*, Los Angeles, March 1998.

Sayer, A. *Method in Social Science: A Realist Approach*. 2d ed. London: Routledge, 1992.

Scaperlanda, A. "Christian Values and Economic Ethics." *International Journal of Social Economics* 20, no.10 (1993): 4–12.

Schneider, J. *The Good of Affluence*. Grand Rapids, Mich.: Eerdmans, 2002.

Schneider, M. *The Distribution of Wealth*. Cheltenham, U.K.: Edward Elgar, 2004.

Schindler, D., ed. *Beyond Mechanism: The Universe in Recent Physics and Catholic Thought*. Lanham, Md.: University Press of America, 1986.

Schlossberg, H., V. Samuel, and R. Sider, eds. *Christianity and Economics in the Post-Cold War Era*. Grand Rapids, Mich.: Eerdmans, 1994.

Schmitt, R. *Truth: A Primer*. Boulder, Colo.: Westview, 1995.

Schwartz, H. *Rationality Gone Awry?* Westport, Conn.: Praeger, 1998.

Sciulli, D. "Weaknesses in Rational Choice Theory's Contribution to Comparative Research," in *Rational Choice Theory: Advocacy and Critique*, edited by J. Coleman and T. Fararo. Newbury Park, Calif.: Sage, 1992: 161–80.

Searle, J. *Minds, Brains and Science*. London: BBC, 1984.

———. *The Construction of Social Reality*. New York: Free Press, 1995.

Sears, D., L. Peplau, and S. Taylor. *Social Psychology*. 7th ed. Englewood Cliffs, N.J.: Prentice Hall, 1991.

Seltzer, A. "An Evaluation of the International Evidence on the Employment Effects of Minimum Wage Legislation." *Australian Economic Review* 30, no. 2 (1997): 208–14.

Senior, D. *Matthew*. Nashville, Tenn.: Abingdon, 1998.

Sent, E-M. "Methodology," in *Encyclopedia of Political Economy*. Vols. 1 & 2, edited by P. O'Hara. London: Routledge, 1999: 727–31.

Shapere, D. *Reason and the Search for Knowledge*. Dordrecht: Reidel, 1984.

Shapin, S. "History of Science and Its Sociological Reconstructions." *History of Science* 20, no. 3 (1982): 157–211.

Shapiro, C. "The Theory of Business Strategy." *RAND Journal of Economics* 20, no. 1 (1989): 125–37.

Shapiro, C., and J. Stiglitz, J. "Equilibrium Unemployment as a Worker Discipline Device." *American Economic Review* 72, no. 3 (1984): 433–44.

Sheldrake, R. *The Presence of the Past: Morphic Resonance and the Habits of Nature*. London: Collins, 1988.

———. *The Rebirth of Nature*. London: Century, 1990.

Shillington, V. "Engaging with the Parables," in *Jesus and His Parables*, edited by V. Shillington. Edinburgh: T. & T. Clark, 1997: 1–20.

Shubik, M. *Game Theory in the Social Sciences: Concepts and Solutions*. Cambridge, Mass.: MIT, 1983.

Sider, J. *Interpreting the Parables*. Grand Rapids, Mich.: Zondervan, 1995.

Sider, R. *Rich Christians in an Age of Hunger*. 1st ed. London: Hodder & Stoughton, 1977.

———. *Living More Simply*. London: Hodder & Stoughton, 1980.

———. *Rich Christian in an Age of Hunger*. 4th ed. Dallas, Tex.: Word, 1997.

Simons, R. *Competing Gospels: Public Theology and Economic Theory*. Alexandria, N.S.W.: Dwyer, 1995.

Singer, M., with J. Lalich. *Cults in Our Midst*. San Francisco, Calif.: Jossey-Bass, 1995.

Singer, P. *Practical Ethics*. 2d ed. Cambridge: Cambridge University Press, 1993.

Skyrms, B. *Causal Necessity*. New Haven, Conn.: Yale University Press, 1980.

Sloyan, G. *Interpretation Commentary: John*. Atlanta, Ga.: John Knox, 1988.

Smith, I. "God and Economics," in *God and Culture*, edited by D. Carson and J. Woodbridge. Grand Rapids, Mich.: Eerdmans, 1993: 162–79.

Smith, S. *Labour Economics* 2d ed. London: Routledge, 2003.

Snower, D. "Evaluating Unemployment Policies: What Do the Underlying Theories Tell Us?" in *Unemployment Policy* , edited by D. Snower and G. de la Dehesa. Cambridge: Cambridge University Press, 1997: 15–53.

Snower, D., and G. de la Dehesa, eds. *Unemployment Policy*. Cambridge: Cambridge University Press, 1997.

Soane, B. "Property," in *A New Dictionary of Christian Ethics*. 4th imp., edited by J. Macquarrie and J. Childress. London: SCM, 1993: 507–9.

Sokal, A., and J. Bricmont. *Intellectual Impostures*. London: Profile, 1998.

Solimano, A. "Alternative Theories of Distributive Justice and Social Inequality: Liberal, Socialist and Libertarian Perspectives," in *Social Inequality: Values, Growth and the State*, edited by A. Solimano. Ann Arbor, Mich.: University of Michigan Press, 1998a: 15–27.

———. "The End of Hard Choices? Revisiting the Relationship between Income Distribution and Growth," in *Social Inequality: Values, Growth and the State*, edited by A. Solimano. Ann Arbor, Mich.: University of Michigan Press, 1998b: 46–67.

Sollicitudo Rei Socialis (SRS). *Encyclical Letter of the Supreme Pontiff John Paul II to . . . for the Twentieth Anniversary of Populorum Progressio*. Homebush, N.S.W.: St. Paul, 1987.

Solow, R. "Economic History and Economics." *American Economic Review* 75, no. 2 (1985): 328–31.

Spanos, A. *Statistical Foundations of Econometric Modelling*. Cambridge: Cambridge University Press, 1986.

Sparkes, R. *The Ethical Investor*. London: Harper Collins, 1995.

Spencer, M. *Foundations of Modern Sociology.* 4th ed. Englewood Cliffs, N. J.: Prentice Hall, 1985.

Spykman, G. *Reformational Theology*. Grand Rapids, Mich.: Eerdmans, 1992.

Stackhouse, M. "What Then Shall We Do? On Using Scripture in Economic Ethics." *Interpretation* 41, no. 4 (1987): 382–97.

———. *Covenant and Commitments: Faith, Family and Economic Life*. Louisville, Ky.: Westminster John Knox, 1997a.

———. (ed.) *Christian Social Ethics in a Global Era*. Nashville, Tenn.: Abingdon, 1997b.

Stapleford, J. "Christian Ethics and the Teaching of Introductory Economics." *Journal of Markets and Morality* 3, no. 1 (2000): 67–87.

———. *Bulls, Bears and Golden Calves: Applying Christian Ethics in Economics*. Downers Grove, Ill.: InterVarsity, 2002.

Stark, R., L. Iannaccone, and R. Finke. "Religion, Science and Rationality." *American Economic Review* 86, no. 2 (1996): 433–37.

Steedman, I. "On Doing the Impossible," in *Religion and Economics: Normative Social Theory*, edited by J. Dean and A. Waterman. Boston: Kluwer, 1999: 165–73.

Stegemann, W. *The Gospel and the Poor*. Philadelphia, Pa.: Fortress, 1984.

Stein, R. *The New American Commentary Vol. 24 Luke*. Nashville, Tenn.: Broadman, 1992.

Stich, S. *From Folk Psychology to Cognitive Science*. Cambridge, Mass.: MIT, 1983.

——. *Deconstructing the Mind*. New York: Oxford University Press, 1996.

Stiglitz, J. "The Role of Government in the Contemporary World." In *Income Distribution and High-quality Growth*, edited by V. Tanzi and K. Chu. Cambridge: MIT, 1998: 21–53.

Stockman, N. *Antipositivist Theories of the Sciences*. Dordrecht: Reidel, 1983.

Storkey, A. *A Christian Social Perspective*. Leicester, U.K.: IVP, 1979.

——. *Transforming Economics*. London: SPCK, 1986.

Stove, D. *Popper and After: Four Modern Irrationalists*. Oxford: Pergamon, 1982.

Stretton, H. *Economics: A New Introduction*. Sydney: University of N.S.W. Press, 1999.

Stuhlmacher, P. *Reconciliation, Law, and Righteousness*. Philadelphia, Pa.: Fortress, 1986.

Summers, L. "The Scientific Illusion in Empirical Macroeconomics." *Scandinavian Journal of Economics* 93, no. 2 (1991): 129–48.

Suppe, F., ed. *The Structure of Scientific Theories*. Urbana, Ill.: University of Illinois Press, 1974.

——. *The Structure of Scientific Theories*. 2d ed. Urbana, Ill.: University of Illinois Press, 1977.

Sussman, M., and S. Steinmetz, eds. *Handbook of Marriage and the Family*. New York: Plenum, 1987.

Swartz, T., and F. Bonello. *Taking Sides: Clashing Views on Controversial Economic Issues*. 8th ed. Guilford, Conn.: Dushkin/McGraw-Hill, 1998.

Tamari, M. *With All Your Possessions: Jewish Ethics and Economic Life*. New York: Free Press, 1987.

Tarascio, V., and B. Caldwell. "Theory Choice in Economics: Philosophy and Practice." *Journal of Economic Issues* 13, no. 4 (1979): 983–1006.

Tawney, R. *Commonplace Book*. Cambridge: Cambridge University Press, [1913] 1972.

Taylor, J. *Enough Is Enough*. London: SCM, 1975.

Taylor, L. *Socially Relevant Policy Analysis: Structuralist Computable General Equilibrium Models for the Developing World*. Cambridge, Mass.: MIT, 1990.

Taylor, S., L. Peplau, and D. Sears. *Social Psychology*. 9th ed. Upper Saddle River, N.J.: Prentice Hall, 1997.

Tear Fund (TEAR). *Annual Report*. Melbourne, 1997.

Temple, W. *Christianity and Social Order*. London: Shepheard-Walwyn/SPCK, [1942] 1976.

Thaler, R. *Quasi Rational Economics*. New York: Sage, 1991.

Thomas, D. *Naturalism and Social Science*. Cambridge: Cambridge University Press, 1979.

Thompson, K. *The Divorce Profile: Differential Social Correlates in 1952 and 1972*. San Francisco, Calif.: R & E Research, 1978.

Tiemstra, J. "Christianity and Economics: A Review of the Recent Literature." *Christian Scholar's Review* 22, no. 3 (1993): 227–47.

——. "Every Square Inch: Kuperyian Social Theory and Economics," in *Religion and Economics: Normative Social Theory*, edited by J. Dean, and A. Waterman. Boston, Mass.: Kluwer, 1999: 85–98.

Tiemstra, J., F. Graham, G. Monsma, C. Sinke, and A. Storkey. *Reforming Economics: Calvinist Studies on Methods and Institutions*. Lewiston, Maine: Edwin Mellen 1990.

Tigay, J. *The JPS Torah Commentary: Deuteronomy*. Philadelphia, Pa.: Jewish Publications Society, 1996.

Tilghman, B. *An Introduction to the Philosophy of Religion*. Oxford: Blackwell, 1994.

Tobias, L., and J. Lalich. *Captive Hearts, Captive Minds*. St. Leonards, N.S.W.: Allen & Unwin, 1994.

Todaro, M. *Economic Development*. 7th ed. Reading, Miss.: Addison Wesley Longman, 2000.

Tondini, G. "Man and Work According to the Social Doctrine of the Church, Particularly in the Thought of John Paul II." *International Journal of Social Economics* 25, no. 11/12 (1998): 1640–57.

Toruno, M. "Appraisals and Rational Reconstructions of General Competitive Equilibrium Theory." *Journal of Economic Issues* 22, no. 1 (1988): 127–55.

Toulmin, S. *The Philosophy of Science*. London: Hutchinson, 1953.

———. *Foresight and Understanding*. London: Hutchinson, 1961.

Trigg, R. *Understanding Social Science*. Oxford: Blackwell, [1985] 2d ed., 2001.

———. *Reality at Risk*. 2d ed. New York: Harvester, 1989.

———. *Rationality and Science*. Oxford: Blackwell, 1993.

———. *Rationality and Religion*. Oxford: Blackwell, 1998.

———. *Ideas of Human Nature: An Historical Introduction*. 2d ed. Oxford: Blackwell, 1999.

———. *Philosophy Matters: An Introduction to Philosophy*. Oxford: Blackwell, 2002.

Turiel, E. *The Development of Social Knowledge: Morality and Convention*. Cambridge: Cambridge University Press, 1983.

Ullmann-Margalit, E. *The Emergence of Norms*. Oxford: Clarendon, 1977.

Urban, L. *A Short History of Christian Thought*. rev. ed. Oxford: Oxford University Press, 1995.

Urdy, R. "Marital Instability by Race, Sex, Education, and Occupation Using the 1960 Census Data." *American Journal of Sociology* 72, no. 2 (1966): 203–9.

Varian, H. *Microeconomic Analysis* 3rd ed. New York: Norton, 1992.

———. "What Use is Economic Theory?" in *Foundations of Research in Economics: How Do Economists Do Economics?*, edited by S. Medema and W. Samuels. Cheltenham, U.K.: Edward Elgar, 1996: 238–47.

Versluysen, E. *Defying the Odds: Banking for the Poor*. West Hartford, U.K.: Kumarian, 1999.

Vidich, A., and S. Lyman. *American Sociology: Worldly Rejections of Religion and Their Directions*. New Haven, Conn.: Yale University Press, 1985.

Vitz, P. *Psychology as Religion*. 2d ed. Grand Rapids, Mich.: Eerdmans, 1994.

Volf, M. *Work in the Spirit*. New York: Oxford University Press, 1991.

von Rad, G. *Deuteronomy*. London: SCM, 1966.

———. *Genesis*. rev. ed. London: SCM, 1972.

von Wright, G. *Explanation and Understanding*. London: Routledge & Kegan Paul, 1971.

Wacome, D. "Evolution, Foreknowledge and Creation." *Christian Scholar's Review* 26, no. 3 (1997): 306–21.

Wacquant, L. "Positivism," in *The Blackwell Dictionary of Twentieth-Century Social Thought*, edited by W. Outhwaite and T. Bottomore. Oxford: Blackwell, 1994: 495–98.

Wagner, S., and R. Warner, eds. *Naturalism: A Critical Appraisal*. Notre Dame, Ill.: University of Notre Dame Press, 1993.

Wallerstein, I. *Unthinking Social Science*. Cambridge, U.K.: Polity, 1991.

Walsh, B. "Reimaging Biblical Authority." *Christian Scholar's Review* 26, no. 2 (1996): 206–20.

Walsh, M. *A History of Philosophy*. London: Geoffrey Chapman, 1985.

Walters, A. "The Rise and Fall of Econometrics," in *The Unfinished Agenda*, edited by M. Anderson. London: IEA, 1986: 117–24.

Waterman, A. "Economists on the Relation Between Political Economy and Christian Theology: A Preliminary Survey." *International Journal of Social Economics* 14, no. 6 (1987): 46–68.

——. "Can Economic Policy Be 'Christian?'" *Review of Social Economy* 17, no. 2 (1988): 203–11.

——. *Revolution, Economics and Religion: Christian Political Economy 1798–1833*. Cambridge: Cambridge University Press, 1991.

——. "Whately, Senior, and the Methodology of Classical Economics," in *Economics and Religion: Are They Distinct?*, edited by G. Brennan and A. Waterman. Boston, Mass.: Kluwer, 1994: 41–60.

——. "Social Thinking in Established Protestant Churches," in *Religion and Economics: Normative Social Theory*, edited by J. Dean, and A. Waterman. Boston, Mass.: Kluwer, 1999: 51–67

——. "The Beginning of "Boundaries": The Sudden Separation of Economics from Christian Theology," in *Economics and Interdisciplinary Exchange* , edited by G. Erreygers. London: Routledge, 2001: 41–63.

Webb, B. "A Conversation with Anthony Waterman." *Faith and Economics* 36 (2000): 10–18.

Weinfeld, M. *Deuteronomy and the Deuteronomic School*. Oxford: Clarendon, 1972.

——. *Social Justice in Ancient Israel and in the Ancient Near East*. Jerusalem: Magnes, 1995.

Weintraub, R. *General Equilibrium Analysis: Studies in Appraisal*. Cambridge: Cambridge University Press, 1985.

——. "Rosenberg's 'Lakatosian Consolations for Economists'." *Economics and Philosophy* 3, no. 1 (1987): 139–42.

——. "Roger Backhouse's Straw Herring." *Methodus* 4, no. 2 (1992): 53–7.

Wells, P. *James Barr and The Bible*. Phillipsburg, N.J.: Presbyterian & Reformed, 1980.

Wenham, G. *The Book of Leviticus*. Grand Rapids, Mich.: Eerdmans, 1979.

Weston, S. "Toward a Better Understanding of the Positive/Normative Distinction in Economics." *Economics and Philosophy* 10, no. 1 (1994): 1–17.

Whitacre, R. *The IVP New Testament Commentary Series: John*. Downers Grove, Ill.: IVP, 1999.

Whitehead, A. *Science and the Modern World*. Cambridge: Cambridge University Press, 1926.

Whyte, W., and K. Whyte. *Making Mondragon: The Growth and Development of the Worker Co-operative Complex*. rev. ed. Ithaca, N.Y.: ILR Press, 1991.

Wilber, C. "Roman Catholic Social Thought and Economic Theory: An Agenda for the Future." *Review of Social Economy* 49, no. 4 (1991): 566–77.

———. "John Paul II, Catholic Social Thought and the Ethics of Consumption." *International Journal of Social Economics* 25, no. 11–12 (1998): 1595–607.

———. "Holistic Method." and "Storytelling and Pattern Models," in *Encyclopedia of Political Economy*, Vols. 1 & 2, edited by P. O'Hara. London: Routledge, 1999: 451–54, 1112–15.

Wilber, C., and R. Harrison. "The Methodological Basis of Institutional Economics: Pattern Model, Storytelling, and Holism." *Journal of Economic Issues* 12, no. 1 (1978): 61–89.

Wilber, C., and R. Hoksbergen. "Current Thinking on the Role of Value Judgements in Economic Science: A Survey." *Research in the History of Economic Thought and Methodology* 2 (1984): 179–94.

———. "Ethical Values and Economic Theory." *Religious Studies Review* 12, 3/4 (1986): 208–14.

Wilkerson, T. *Natural Kinds*. Aldershot, U.K.: Avebury, 1995.

Wilkinson, L., P. De Vos, C. De Witt, E. Dykema, and V. Ehlers. *Earthkeeping in the Nineties: Stewardship of Creation*. rev. ed. Grand Rapids, Mich.: Eerdmans, 1991.

Williams, O. "Catholic Social Teaching: A Moral Compass for the Next Millennium." *Review of Business* 19, 1 (1997): 15–21.

Williams, O., and J. Houck, eds. *The Making of an Economic Vision: John Paul II's "On Social Concern"*. Washington, D. C.: University Press of America, 1991.

Williams, P. "Hermeneutics for Economists: Issues in Interpretation." *Journal of the Association of Christian Economists (U.K.)* 22 (1996): 13–37.

Wilson, B. *The Social Dimensions of Sectarianism: Sects and New Religious Movements in Contemporary Society*. Oxford: Clarendon, 1990.

Wilson, R. *Economics, Ethics and Religion*. New York: New York University Press, 1997a.

———. "Comparative Religious Thought on Economic Behavior and Financial Transactions." *Journal of the Association of Christian Economists (U.K.)* 23 (1997b): 1–10.

Winch, P. *The Idea of a Social Science*. New York: Routledge & Kegan Paul, 1958.

Winslow, T. "Atomism and Organicism," in *The Elgar Companion to Institutional and Evolutionary Economics A-K*, edited by G. Hodgson, W. Samuels, and M. Tool. Aldershot, U.K.: Edward Elgar, 1994: 11–16.

Winston, C. "Economic Deregulation: Days of Reckoning for Microeconomists." *Journal of Economic Literature* 31, no. 3 (1993): 1263–89

Wiseman, J., ed. *Beyond Positive Economics*. Houndmills, U.K.: Macmillan, 1983.

Wisman, J. "Christianity, John Paul II and the Future of Work." *International Journal of Social Economics* 25, no. 11/12 (1998): 1658–71.

Wisman, J., and J. Rozansky. "The Methodology of Institutionalism Revisited." *Journal of Economic Issues* 25, no. 3 (1991): 709–37.

Wogaman, J. *Economics and Ethics: A Christian Enquiry*. London: SCM, 1986.

Wohlgemut, J. "Entrusted Money (Matt. 25: 14–28)," in *Jesus and His Parables*, edited by V. Shillington. Edinburgh: T. & T. Clark, 1997: 103–20.

Wolff, E. *Top Heavy: A Study of the Increasing Inequality of Wealth in America*. New York: Twentieth Century Fund, 1995.

———. "International Comparisons of Wealth Inequality." *Review of Income and Wealth* 42, no. 4 (1996): 433–51.

———. "Recent Trends in the Size Distribution of Household Wealth." *Journal of Economic Perspectives* 12, no. 3 (1998): 131–50.

Wolff, R., and S. Resnick. *Economics: Marxian Versus Neo-classical*. Baltimore, Md.: Johns Hopkins, 1987.

Woodward, J. "Causation and Explanation in Econometrics," in *On The Reliability Of Economic Models*, edited by D. Little. Boston, Mass.: Kluwer, 1995: 9–61.

Woolgar, S. "Reflexivity Is the Ethnographer of the Text," in *Knowledge and Reflexivity*, edited by S. Woolgar. London: Sage, 1988: 14–34.

Worswick, G. "Is Progress in Economic Science Possible." *Economic Journal* 82, no. 1 (1972): 73–86.

Wright, C. *God's People in God's Land*. Grand Rapids, Mich.: Eerdmans, 1990.

———. *Knowing Jesus Through the Old Testament*. London: Marshall Pickering, 1992.

———.*Walking in the Ways of the Lord*. Leicester, U.K.: Apollos, 1995.

———. *New International Biblical Commentary: Deuteronomy*. Peabody, N.J.: Hendrickson, 1996.

———. *Old Testament Ethics for the People of God*. Leicester, U.K.: Inter-Varsity Press, 2004.

Wuthnow, R. "Science and the Sacred," in *The Sacred in a Secular Age*, edited by P. Hammond. Berkeley, Calif.: University of California Press, 1985: 187–203.

Yoder, J. *The Politics of Jesus*. 2d ed. Carlisle, U.K.: Eerdmans/Paternoster, 1994.

Young, H. "The Economics of Convention." *Journal of Economic Perspectives* 10, no. 2 (1996): 105–22.

Zamagni, S. "Economic Laws," in *The New Palgrave: A Dictionary of Economics*, edited by J. Eatwell, M. Milgate, and P. Newman. London: Macmillan, 1987: 52–4.

Zellner, A. *Statistics, Econometrics and Forecasting*. Cambridge: Cambridge University Press, 2004.

Zukav, G. *The Dancing Wu-Li Masters*. Bungay, U.K.: Flamingo, 1979.

Zucker, R. *Democratic Distributive Justice*. Cambridge: Cambridge University Press, 2001.

Index

able-bodied, 38, 39, 40, 43, 55, 99, 128; poor, 91, 319. *See also* non-able-bodied
abstraction, 217, 254, 281. *See also* formalism
Alford, Helen, 23, 341
alienation, 41, 42, 144, 145, 153
altruism, 109, 147, 152, 160, 245
anti-positivism, 182–83; economics, 193, 204, 205, 207, 208; physical science, 183–91; social sciences, 191–96. *See also* non-naturalism; post-positivism; postmodernism
Antigonish movement, 52, 54. *See also* cooperatives
Appleby, R., 15
Arrow-Debreu theory, 267, 295
assets, 43, 47, 49–50, 55, 91, 104; distribution, 91. *See also* capital; wealth
assumptions, 17, 144, 248, 265–67, 288–89, 324; Judeo-Christian beliefs, 173. *See also* axioms; causal explanation; *ceteris paribus* restrictions; domain restrictions; metaphysical assumptions
Austrian economics, 134, 151, 161, 192, 194, 221
authentic human development, 29
autonomy of economics, 154–77
axiomatic reasoning, 162, 165
axioms, 158, 162, 186, 217, 227, 233, 332. *See also* assumptions; *ceteris paribus* restrictions; domain restrictions

Bachelard, G., 184–85
Backhouse, Roger, 214, 240, 252, 280, 285, 286, 287, 291, 295, 298, 299
Bagnoli, M., 288–89
Balkin, Steve, 50
Ballard, B., 31
Barr, James, 9–15, 17–19, 56, 62, 64, 68–70, 73, 84–90
Bauckham, Roger, 32
Becker, Gary, 224–26, 233, 271, 273
Beisner, E. Calvin, 70–71
belief. *See* Islamic belief; Judeo-Christian belief; secular belief
Bergstrom, T., 288–89
Bernheim, B., 289–90
Bhaskar, Roy, 184, 191, 212, 216, 221, 315
Bible, 8, 9, 166; explanations of human behavior, 348–49; foundations of Christian belief, 139–40; guide to Christian living, 31; inerrancy, 15, 17–19; intentions in the modern

world, 64; interpretation of, 9–14, 16, 21–22; research, 9; socio-economic principles, 320; translations, 82
Biblical exegesis-based principles for economic distribution, 56–94
Blank, Rebecca, 51
Blaug, Mark, 159–60, 162, 179, 199–201, 203–5, 262, 266, 280, 281, 283, 329
Blomberg, Craig, 59, 60

Cairns, I., 68
Caja Laboral credit union, 54
capital, 28; ownership, 48; ownership by workers, 41–42, 51. *See also* financial capital; human capital; social capital
capital managed firms (CMF), 101–2
capitalism, 43, 51, 94, 155, 231, 244, 350
case studies, 356
Catholic Church, 9, 15, 26, 168
Catholic encyclicals. *See* encyclicals
Catholic Social Thought (CST), 21, 93–94, 118, 156, 176; embodies an holistic methodology, 349–52; non-Church, 44, 45; organization of employment, 26–31, 40, 55; property, 34, 38; socio-economic domains, 343; welfare policy and reform, 168; worker ownership, 47
Catholics, 16
causal explanation, 48, 108, 219, 223, 225–26, 233, 245–47; circular, 345–47; in naturalistic social science, 237–58; mechanisms, 245–47, 252, 253; non-economic factors, 357. *See also ceteris paribus* restrictions; domain restrictions; mechanism; prediction
causal generalization, 249
causative thinking, 350
Center for Employment Training, 50–51
ceteris paribus restrictions, 238, 247–49, 250, 252–55, 268. *See also* assumptions; axioms; causal explanation; domain restrictions; mechanism
Chalmers, Alan, 179
Chapra, M. Umer, 117, 128, 129, 131, 132, 133
Choudhury, Masudul, 117, 128, 132, 133
Christian. *See* Judeo-Christian
Christian Reformed tradition, 118
Church. *See* Catholic Church; Protestant
circular causation, 345–47
Clark, Charles M. A., 218, 241
closedness of socio-economic systems, 211, 234
Co-operative Health Care Network, 55
cointegration, 264
collective bargaining, 44
common belief, 271
common good, 27–28, 30, 42, 124, 126–27, 353–54, 358
common sense, 174, 231, 235, 270–71, 274, 282–83, 290, 331
common sense analysis, 258, 276, 277
common sense reasoning, 273, 278, 359
communitarian democratic capitalism, 94
community, 92, 112, 126, 351, 353, 355; agencies, 38; identity, 356; local support, 50; religious, 59, 62; values, 341; work, 28–29, 39, 47, 354
companies: organization, 40–49; ownership and control by workers, 42–48
competing theories, 96, 148, 175, 225, 229–30, 263–67, 289
competition, 84, 101, 107, 121, 131, 313, 354; between family units, 100; between workers, 28, 54
competitive markets, 158, 159, 282
complexity, 191, 223, 241, 249–50, 256–58

constructivism, 135, 214, 221, 230, 244, 307. *See also* postmodernism; relativism
context dependent, 241, 245, 291. *See also* domain restrictions
contradiction, 60, 198, 310, 333, 347, 352
convention, 80, 151, 236, 293, 294
conventional economics, 69, 81, 95, 106, 116, 331, 339
cooperatives, 129; producers, 46, 52, 54, 100; workers, 51–55, 100, 106–7, 110, 153, 230
cost-benefit analysis, 122
Cramp, Anthony, 164
critical rationalism, 184
critical realism, 161, 213–14
critical theory, 184
cults, 272, 273
cultural relativism, 344, 356

Darwinian theory, 262, 311
debt forgiveness, 71
debt release, 70
decision making: decentralized, 126; in employment, 44, 130
deductions, 50, 64, 99, 100, 162, 165, 253, 257, 344
demarcation, 155, 205, 349; of science, 201
democratic decision making in employment, 46–47
democracy: economic, 73; of ownership, 38, 46
derivative social principles, Judeo-Christian, 60, 168, 176, 320
desires, 158, 159, 222, 225, 232, 240. *See also* preferences
didactic message, 18, 338
disadvantaged. *See* non-able-bodied; poor
dispersion of ownership, 38
distribution: economic intentions under Mosaic Law, 64–75; equality, 90, 130–32; equality in economic, 80; equality in outcomes, 77; inequalities, 74, 104, 355; Jesus' teachings relating to, 76–84; of financial capital, 37, 92; of income, 56–94, 104; of private property, 37–38; of wealth, 56–94, 104; policy, 57
divorce, 159, 160
domain restrictions, 245–47, 247–49. *See also* assumptions; axioms; causal explanation; *ceteris paribus* restrictions
Duhem-Quine theory, 267
dynamics, 248, 345, 346

econometric technique, 263–65
econometric testing procedures, 263–64
econometrics, 199, 205, 206, 232, 248–49, 264, 283, 331–32; predictive power of, 205; subjectivism in, 206
economic activities, 21
economic analysis, 274
economic democracy, 73
economic distribution: Biblical exegesis-based principles, 56–94; equality, 80; intentions under Mosaic Law, 64–75; normative intentions for, 57–64
economic equality in ancient Israel, Mosaic Law measures, *66,* 84
economic imperialism, 174, 230, 273
economic laws, 227, 231–32
economic life: God's normative intentions, 146; policy implications, 146–47; what is important, 144–46
economic methodologies, 143
economic principles, 124; common to Islam and Judeo-Christianity, *126*
economic theory, 6
economically disadvantaged, 73
economics, 10; as a science, 196–206; fundamentalist, 16; religious, 20
egalitarian results in distribution of wealth and income, 73

Elzinga, Kenneth, 157
empirical progress, 281, 285–87, 291, 294, 296, 298–300; definition, 283
empirical testing, 264, 265, 266, 277
empiricism, 142, 217, 263–64, 269, 272–76, 279
Employee Stock Ownership Plan (ESOP), 45–48
employment, 100, 130; applying principles to the organisation of, 40–49; full, 101, 102, 103, 110; Jude-Christian requirements, 105, 109; maintaining, 102; normative principles from evangelical sources, *33;* normative principles from papal encyclicals, *30;* opportunity, 33, 38; organization of, 25–55, 106. *See also* unemployment, work
encyclicals, 26, 27, 40, 42, 43, 47, 49, 349, 356; normative principles governing work, *30*
endogenous factor, 345
Enlightenment, 20, 135, 142, 143, 180
entropy, 114, 281
entrustedness, 124
epistemological dimensions, 216
epistemology, naturalized, 214
equal family distribution of wealth and income, Israelites, 65
equality, 90; dimensions of, 74; distribution, 80; distribution of income and wealth, 130–32; material, 77, 80, 82, 83; material distribution, 79, 84; of opportunity and outcome, 76; wealth, 105
Erickson, Millard, 17, 18
ethical investments, 34
ethically neutral. *See* value free
ethics, 121–22; job-generating investments, 33–34
ethomethodological studies of scientific practice, 191
evangelical interpretation of New Testament, 38
evangelical interpretation of Old Testament, 38
evangelical interpretation of private property, 35
evangelical Mosaic Law, 36
evangelical sources, normative principles governing work, *33,* 40, 42, 47, 49, 55
evangelicalism, 9, 15, 17–19, 31, 32
exegesis-based principles for economic distribution, Biblical, 56–94
explanation. *See* causal explanation
extended family units, 39, 65

falsicificationism, 188, 200, 201–2, 203, 204, 206
family, 159, 160
family distribution of wealth and income, equal, Israelites, 65
family life, 86; preservation of, 145
family units, 35, 40, 52, 74, 85, 100, 106, 355; extended, 36, 39, 65, 67, 71, 73, 74, 91; Israelites, 36–37
feminist approach, 160, 161
Feyerabend, P., 188, 206
financial capital, 34; distribution of, 37; ownership and control, 37, 38, 103; ownership and control by workers, 36. *See also* capital; human capital; social capital
Fitzgerald, M., 44
folk psychology, 223, 225, 226, 231, 273, 283, 290, 301
food for poor, 67
forecasting, 330, 332. *See also* prediction
formalism, 216–18, 225. *See also* abstraction
formalistic modelling, 235
Forrester, Duncan, 343
free will, 141, 142, 151
freedom, 36, 64, 94, 127, 325, 350; of belief, 90, 312; of workers, 43, 44, 46

Friedman, M., 194
full employment, 101, 102, 103, 110
fundamental forces, 244
fundamentalism, 15–20, 166, 177
fundamentalists, 15–16

game theory (GT), 159–60, 280–81, 283, 287, 291–96, 296–98
Gates, Jeff, 48, 50
Gay, Craig, 32, 35, 97, 155
General Equilibrium Analysis (GEA), 204
Giddens, Anthony, 5, 193
God, 13, 14, 20; as moral filter, 121–23; as ultimate owner of property, 34; communication with people, 149; creation (the natural environment and people), 34; deliverance of poor, 85; faith in, 121; intentions for human life, 8, 14, 78, 80, 90, 146; interrelationship with people, 21–22, 121, 140–41, 146; love for all people, 80; moral consistency, 75; normative purposes for humankind, 34, 167; norms, 79, 145–47, 319; obedience to, 74; personal relationship with, 36; plan for humankind, 121; principles, 8; redemption to people, 36, 351; refuting the revelations of, 313; revelations of, 117, 142, 149, 150, 316, 323, 337; triune, 31; truth, 12, 15
Golden Rule, 121
Goldingay, John, 31
governments, 102
Griffiths, Brian, 35, 59
Grudem, Wayne, 31, 59
Gushee, D., 23

Hands, D. Wade, 191, 286
Harris, Harriett, 15, 17, 18, 19
Hausman, D., 282
Hay, Donald, 16, 32, 39, 57, 59, 99–100, 106, 120, 122, 129, 339, 344
hermeneutics, 221–24. *See also* interpretive social science
heterodox economics, 114, 166, 171, 175, 328, 340–42, 352, 358
Heyne, Paul, 157
historical critical method, 9
holism, 345–47; Judeo-Christian methodological connections, 347–52; methodological characteristics, 346
Holy Spirit, 146
human action, 141–42, 167, 222–23
human alienation from God, 153
human behavior, 98, 139–42, 146, 167, 239, 250–52, 307–8, 319, 323–24; assumptions, 173; Biblical explanations, 348–49; interrelation with social behavior, 328, 339, 354, 356; secular understanding, 147–50
human capital, 34, 41. *See also* capital; financial capital; social capital
human choice, 324–25; predictions about, 271
human life, inseparable spiritual and material dimensions, 140–44

Iannaccone, Laurence, 16–19, 20, 157, 271–73
income: distribution, 56–94, 104; egalitarian results in distribution, 73; equal family distribution, Israelites, 65; equality of distribution, 125–26, 130–32; inequalities, 92
individual retirement account (IRA), 49
induction, 182, 188, 344. *See also* reasoning
inequalities, 47; distributional, 74, 104, 355; income, 92
inerrancy of the Bible, 15, 17–19
inexact laws, 331
inheritances, 132
injustice, 355
Institutionalist economics, 134, 146, 151, 161, 195

institutions, preservation, 145
intellectual development, 163
intellectual progress, 280–300; dimensions of, 284–85; in social sciences and economics, 283–86
intentions: economic distribution under Mosaic Law, 64–75; God's, 8, 14, 78, 80, 90, 146; of Bible in the modern world, 64
interdepedence between economics and Christian thought, 155, 157–63, 163–69
interest rates, 69; credit on, 70
interest-free nature of loans, 67, 70
intermediate bodies, 30–31
interpretive social science, 307, 309, 357. *See also* hermeneutics
investments, 47; job-generating, 33–34. *See also* assets; capital
Islamic belief, 2, 6
Islamic economics, 16, 38, 115–33, 340; norms, 117; principles common to Judeo-Christian belief, *126,* 126–27
Israelite families, 36–37, 39
Israelites, 37, 38, 60, 63–64, 66; ancient, 35; equal family distribution of wealth and income, 65
Italian Social Co-operative Societies, 55

Jesus Christ, 8, 13, 20, 76, 82, 120; intentions of Mosaic Law, 59–61, 84, 87; interpretation of principles of Mosaic Law, 36, 62, 84–90; interrelationship with people, 21; life, 146; parables, interpretation of, 81–82; teachings relating intentions of Mosaic Law, 76–84; teachings relating to distribution, 76–84
Jewish social thought, 38
job generating investments, 33
job generation strategies, 49–50
job guarantee, 100, 108, 110
job mobility, 111
job security, 100, 105, 107, 109, 110, 111
jobs, 105
joint ownership of capital, 41–43
Jubilee, 63–64, 72, 75
Judeo-Christian belief system, 1, 8–10, 19, 93, 98–99, 319; development of physical and social science, 309–13; economic principles common to Islam, *126,* 126–27; foundations in Bible, 139–40; socio-economic dimensions, 7
Judeo-Christian derivative socio-economic principles, 320
Judeo-Christian economic analysis, 155
Judeo-Christian economics, 118–19
Judeo-Christian interpretation, 9
Judeo-Christian methodological connections with holism, 347–52
Judeo-Christian perspective on economics, 134–53
Judeo-Christian response to naturalistic social science, 303–9
Judeo-Christian socio-economic analysis; circular causal explanation in, 345–47; methodological characteristics, *344;* methodology, 328–34, 342–45, 352–57
Judeo-Christian thought, 5–8, 20, 22, 117, 120–27, 155; Orthodox, 1, 3, 18, 69, 117, 118; Richardson on economic implications, 163–69
Junakar, P., 96
just wage, 29, 30, 47, 168

Kaiser Jr., Walter, 31, 36, 37
Keynes, John Maynard, 5, 269–70
Keynesianism, 263–64
Khalil, E., 284
Kincaid, Harold: causal explanation and laws in social sciences, 237–39, 242–43, 245, 247–9, 252–56, 258; characteristics of social science naturalism, *262;* social science naturalism, 259, 262–63, 267–68, 270–71, 275, 278, 302–3, 306–9, 313–14, 316–18, 321, 324, 326
kinds. *See* natural kinds; social kinds

Kline, M., 186–87
Knight, Frank, 170, 174
Kolakowski, Leszek, 172–73, 180, 181
Koran. *See* Qur'an
Kuran, Timur, 16, 19

labor managed firms (LMF), 101–2, 108, 109, 112
labor markets, 98, 102, 108, 109
labor mobility, 106
labor non-utilization, 106
labor utilization, 96
Lakatos, I., 188, 204, 283
land ownership, 37, 39, 64–65, 130; Israel, 65
land reform, 130
land sale, 71; in ancient Israel, 68; temporary, 72
law: defined, 238; interpreting, 239
Law, Old Testament. *See* Mosaic Law
laws: causal (*see* causal explanation); economic, 227, 231–32; in naturalistic social science, 237–58; inexact, 331; of logic (*see* logic); of supply and demand, 253–55, 271, 324–25; regularity, 250, 251, 332, 333; social science, 237
Lawson, Tony, 233–34
Leamer, E., 205–6, 248, 265
less developed countries, 130
lex talionis principle, 88–89
loans, 68; debt forgiveness, 71; debt release, 70; for poor, 67; interest on, 68; interest rates, 69; interest-free nature, 67, 70; redemption, 72, 73; rules for Israelites, 71
local community support, 50
logic, 190
logic positivism, 180, 184, 185, 195, 198, 201

macroeconomic theory, 264
management, 41–42, 43, 44, 47, 106, 128, 129, 130
marriage, 159, 160; preservation of, 145
Marty, Martin, 15
Marx, Karl, 39
Marxist economics, 134, 141, 146, 151, 195
Mason, John, 23, 31, 67, 68, 106, 108
Massaro, Thomas, 40, 168
material dimensions of human life, 140–44
material distribution, equality in, 84
material equality, 77, 80, 82, 83
materialist framework, 141–42
mathematical deductions, 228, 288, 289
mathematical economic modelling, 217
mathematical reality, 186
mathematics, 187
McCloskey, D., 195, 206–7
McCullagh, C., 12
McGrath, Alister, 140, 327
McIntyre, Lee, 237–39, 240–42, 245, 249–52, 256–58
mechanisms, 238, 258; causal explanation, 245–47
Meeks, Douglas, 134
metaphysical assumptions, 59, 335
metaphysical frameworks in physical and social science, 313–18
methodological approaches, 149–50, 149–52, 166
methodological characteristics of holism, 346
methodological connections with holism, 347–52
methodological implications, 144
methodological scientific research program (MSRP), 188
methodology, 42; characteristics of Judeo-Christian socio-economic analysis, *344;* holism as key feature, 345; of Judeo-Christian socio-economic analysis, 328–34, 342–44, 352–57
microeconomic reforms, 274–76
Millbank, John, 302, 312, 327, 339–40
minimum wages, 98, 110, 111–12, 117, 329–30

modernism, 195, 218. *See also* naturalism; positivism
Mondragon (Basque Spanish) system, 53, 107, 110
Mondragon Cooperative Corporation (MCC), 53–54
Montetarism, 264
morals. *See* ethics
Mosaic Law, 23, 32–35, 37, 38, 58, 91–92, 125; economic distributional intentions, 64–75, 90; evangelical, 36; intentions of Jesus, 59–61, 84, 87; interpretation of principles by Jesus, 36, 62, 84–90; Jesus' teachings relating intentions of, 76–84; measures, 84; measuring economic equality in ancient Israel, 65–74, *66;* normative socio-economic principles, *75,* 76; observance, 74–75; relevance to Christians for contemporary life, 59–60
Mott, Stephen, 64
multiple realization, 251–52
Munby, Denys, 57, 170
Muslem countries, 116, 117, 128, 130, 131

National Center of Employee Ownership (NCEO), 45
nationalist conceptions, 141
natural kinds, 239–42, 244–45, 251, 256, 257, 268; terms, 269
natural language, 228, 235, 236, 270, 271, 292
natural laws, 167, 168, 219, 315
natural reality, 240
natural science, 12, 22, 166. *See also* science
naturalism, 136, 184, 211–16, 234–36, 260–61, 270, 273–75, 278; characteristics of, *304;* definition and relevance, 261; differences from non-naturalism, 224–34, *228–31;* meanings of, 303–4; ontological, 303, 308, 309, 314; relation of socio-economic phenomena, *309;* weak stance on, 261–63
naturalistic economic theory: policy implications, 274–78; predictive claims, 270–74
naturalistic social science, 216–19; causal explanation, 237–58; characteristics, *262;* Judeo-Christian response, 303–9; status of economics as, 259–79
naturalized epistemology, 214, 218, 314
Naughton, Michael, 26, 40, 107, 341
Neoclassical economics, 118, 124, 161, 195, 232, 276; as science, 196, 197; definitions, 193; Judeo-Christian perspective, 134, 137, 141, 143–44, 146, 151, 152; naturalism, 212, 214, 217–18; predictions from rational choice theory, 271; theory, 225, 266, 273
New Classical theory, 263
New Testament, 5, 20, 32, 59; evangelical interpretation, 38; principles relating to contemporary economic life, 32
nomological explanation, 237, 250, 257
nomologicality, 238
non-able-bodied, 55; protection for, 145
non-economic factors in causal explanations, 357
non-natural kinds. *See* social kinds
non-naturalism, 210, 212, 214, 234–36, 260–61, 270, 278; differences from naturalism, 224–34, *228–31;* in social science, 219–24
non-naturalistic analysis, 318–19; Christian basis, 308, 309, 326
non-naturalistic verbal reasoning, 271
noncultivator classifcation, 268
normative economics, 116, 117, 119, 120–27, 218
normative intentions for economic distribution, 57–64
normative intentions of Christian socio-economic analysis, 318–25

normative principles, 167; from encyclicals governing work, *30;* from evangelical sources governing work, *33*
normative socio-economic principles, derived from ten measures, *75,* 76
normative views, 146
norms: Christian worldview, 323; God's, 79, 145–47, 319
Novak, M., 49–50

O'Boyle, Edward, 40, 341
objective analysis, 274
objective empirical warrant, 264–66, 276, 278–79
objective scientific method, 147–48
objectivity, 217–18, 236
Old Testament, 20, 58, 85, 117, 169, 219; evangelical interpretation, 38; principles relating to contemporary economic life, 32
Old Testment Law. *See* Mosaic Law
ontological dimensions, 216
ontological naturalism, 303, 308, 309, 314
ontological reality, 213, 337
ontology, 335
openness of socio-economic systems, 233–34, 245, 257, 258; mechanisms, 249–52
organicism, 346
organization and control of economic systems, 354
orthodox economics, 157, 161–63, 166, 168–71, 173–74, 193, 195, 199
orthodox Judeo-Christian thought, 1, 3, 18, 69, 117, 118
ownership and control, 131; democracy, 38; dispersion, 38; of capital by workers, 41–42, 51; of companies by workers, 42–48; of financial capital, 37, 38, 100, 103; of land, 37, 64–65; of private property, 37; of private property by workers, 43; part-ownership, 41–42; total private job, 47
Oxford Declaration on Christian Faith and Economics, 1990 ecumenical, 38

Paige, J., 242–43, 245–47, 249, 257, 268, 269
parables, 357; interpretation of, 81–82
part-ownership of capital, 41–42
patriarchal dominance, 37
personal relationship with God, 36
philosophy of science, 190–91
physical capital. *See* capital
physical science. *See* natural science; science
policy implementations, 264
policy implications from naturalistic economic theory, 274–78
political mechanisms, 38
Pontifical Academy of Social Sciences, 95
poor, 28, 48, 50–51, 65–67, 72, 76, 80, 82, 319; 'are all around Jesus,' 82; cause of poverty, 43; food for, 67; God's deliverance of, 85; interest-free loans for, 35; loans for, 67; protection, 72; reducing inequality benefits, 105. *See also* non-able-bodied
Pope John Paul II, 6, 9, 115, 349, 356; employment organization, 26–27, 29, 30, 40–41, 43–44
Popper, Karl, 184–85, 188, 201, 204, 227
positive economics, 116, 122, 199, 217
positivism, 180–182, 186, 188, 193, 216–17, 219
Post-autistic economics (PAE), 161
Post-Enlightenment, 180
Post Keynesian economics, 134, 161, 194
post-positivism, 194–95, 199, 205, 260; objectives to prediction testing and criterion for science, 202–3; thought about science, 203
postmodernism, 11, 135, 172, 221, 312, 323. *See also* constructivism; relativism
poverty. *See* poor

power. *See* ownership and control
prayer, 4, 107, 132, 147, 149, 327, 334
predictions, 200, 201, 202–4, 206, 207, 208; naturalistic economic theory, 270–74
preferences, 152, 225–26, 240, 290, 298, 349; changes in, 123, 254. *See also* desires
preservation of institutions, 145
Preston, Ronald, 63, 64
priority of labor over capital, 47–49
private financial capital, ownership and control, 36, 103
private job ownership, total, 47
private ownership principle, 46
private property, 34–35; distribution of, 37–38; evangelical interpretation, 35; governing regulations by ancient Israelites, 35; ownership and control, 37, 40–49; ownership and control by workers, 36, 42–43, 55; principle, 41; protection, 35, 91
producers cooperatives, 46, 52, 54, 100. *See also* cooperatives; workers cooperatives
productivity, 43
profit-sharing, 129
progress of economics. *See* empirical progress; theoretical progress
property, 34; as source of financial capital and employment, 34; God as ultimate owner, 34; rights, 35. *See also* private property
Protestant evangelical theology, 2, 118, 153, 174, 344, 351; economic distribution, 56, 60, 62, 74; employment organization, 25, 31, 49; modern socio-economic life, 21, 23; unemployment, 97–98
Protestants, 16, 56, 58, 195
public policy, 275–76, 276–78

qualitative understanding, 235
quantitative analysis, 236
quantum theory, 185–86
Quiggin, J., 274–75
Qur'an, 5, 16, 117, 121, 123, 129, 133

rational choice theory (RCT), 143, 151, 255, 271–73, 280–81, 287–91, 295–300, 324
Rational Emotive Therapy, 143
Rational Political Economy, 161
rationalism, 217
rationality, 20, 149, 157–58
real world, 154, 157–162, 164, 166; laws, 227, 231
realism, 136, 212–14, 270, 335–37
reality, 137, 214, 243; natural, 240; ontological, 213, 337
reason, 149–50
reasoning, non-naturalistic verbal, 271
redemption: God's, 36, 351; loan, 72, 73
reductionism, 217–18
regularity laws, 250, 251, 332, 333
relativism, 12, 213–14, 221, 230, 270, 337; cultural, 344, 356. *See also* constructivism; postmodernism
relativity, 185
religious community, 59, 62
religious economics, 20
remunerated work, 36–37
revelations, God's, 117, 142, 149–50, 316, 323, 337, 351; refuting, 313
rich, 48, 78–79, 82, 85, 105, 132, 164, 327
rich and poor, 122, 348, 354
Richardson, J. David, 155–69, 175, 176; economic implications of Christian thought, 163–69; orthodox economics, 161–63
right to work, 99
Robbins, L., 272
Rochdale cul-de-sac, 53
Roman Catholic Church. *See* Catholic Church
Rosenberg, Alexander, 161, 205, 206, 271, 283
Rule, James, 259, 300

sabbatical year, 71
Sayer, R. Andrew, 192, 268, 359
scarcity, 169–70
Schneider, M., 48
science: anti-positivism, 183–91; assumptions, 171, 173; causal explanation, 242; comtemporary economics, 179–209; defined differently between various social sciences, 192–93; development of, 309–13; economics, 196–206; kinds, 244; metaphysical frameworks, 313–18; theories, 187; traditional view, 179–82; worldviews, 313–18
science imperialism, 314
scientific knowledge, 179–82
scientific status of economics, 196, 199, 200, 204–5
scientific truth, 189, 198, 306, 315
secular belief, 69, 91, 173–74, 339
secular democratic theory, 45
secular economics, 19, 22, 345, 346; methodologies, 137, 141–44, 145–46, 147–40; on unemployment, 98, 114
secular natural science, 147–48
secular social science, 6, 22, 147–49, 328, 334, 358
secular sociology, 148
secular thought, 115, 117, 342
self-employment, 102
self-management, 36, 42, 52
seven year loan redemptions, 72
sin, 141, 150, 153, 167; social structure, 175, 350; understanding, 139
slaves, 70
Smith, Ian, 61, 62, 154–57
social behavior: interrelation with human behavior, 328, 339, 354, 356; secular understanding, 147–50
social capital, 34. *See also* capital; financial capital; human capital
social economics, 161
social kinds, 239–45, 246, 247, 251, 256, 257; terms, 268–69
social problems, resolving, 26
social science, 1, 5; anti-positivism, 191–96; causal explanation in naturalistic, 237–58; development of, 309–13; laws, 237, 253–56; metaphysical frameworks, 313–18; naturalistic causal explanation, 237–58; naturalistic characteristics of, *262;* secular, 6, 22, 147–49, 328, 334, 358; worldviews, 313–18
socio-economic analysis, 1, 8; circular causal explanation in, 345–47; holism in, 345–47; Judeo-Christian methodological characteristics, *344;* Judeo-Christian methodology, 328–34, 342–45, 352–57; Judeo-Christian normative intentions, 318–25; non-economic factors, 357
socio-economic development, 37
socio-economic phenomena, 308, *309*
socio-economic principles, 26; Judeo-Christian derivative, 320
socio-historico-cultural context, 356–57
sociology, 10; definition, 193; of science, 190–91
solidarity, 27–28, 29, 47, 48–49, 51
spiritual dimensions of human life, 140–44, 146–47
Stackhouse, M., 134
stewardship, 34–35, 102, 124, 128, 130, 145; responsibilities, 35
stocks and shares, 48
Storkey, Alan, 118
Strong Programme, 212
subjectivism in econometrics, 206
subsidiarity, 30–31, 40, 50
supply and demand laws, 253–55, 271, 324–25

tax systems, 50
teleology, 22, 166
Temple, William, 57, 170
Ten Commandments, 356
testing, 259, 262–69, 273, 274, 278; economic theory, 265
theoretical deductions, 330

theoretical progress, 281, 285, 291, 295, 296, 298–300; definition, 283
theories, competing, 263–67
Third World, 41
thought reform, 272
Tiemstra, John, 16, 23, 32, 35, 99–100, 106, 118, 120
Tigay, J., 68
Tilghman, B., 18
trade unions, 29, 42, 44, 111, 350
Trigg, Roger, 11, 12, 20, 138, 143, 172, 190, 191, 192, 227, 315, 317
truth, 18, 38, 150–51, 187, 208, 224, 333, 336; access to, 142, 335; competing theories, 230; God's, 12, 15; intellectual progress, 284–85; scientific, 189, 198, 306, 315

unemployed, 50–51
unemployment, 28, 30, 41, 49, 95–114, 115, 168, 329–30; causal explanation, 108; cyclical, 107, 110; economic reasons, 107–13; frictional, 107–9, 110, 113, 114; insurance, 110, 111; involuntary, 108; Judeo-Christian reasons, 107–13; natural rate of (NAIRU), 113; structural, 96, 107, 109–11, 113, 114; voluntary, 108. *See also* employment; work
universal destination of goods, 48–49
unshared wealth, 78–79, 80; barrier against pursuing kingdom of God, 78
utility, 240, 242, 243, 256

value free, 115, 116, 117, 122, 172
value judgement, 258, 260, 268
value-laden economics, 218
values, 122–23, 172, 322, 352–53
verbal reasoning, non-naturalistic, 271

Wacquant, L., 217
wages, 29, 101, 105, 106, 110, 112, 113, 114; minimum, 98, 110, 111–12, 117
Waterman, Anthony, 155, 156, 157, 164, 169–74
wealth: distribution of, 56–94; egalitarian results in distribution of, 73; equal family distribution of wealth and income, Israelites, 65; equality of, 105; equality in distribution of, 93, 125–26, 130–32; inequality in distribution of, 104; tax, 50. *See also* assets; capital
Weintraub, R., 204
welfare economics, 274–75
welfare support, 39
wellbeing, 323
Western capitalism, 43
Weston, S., 116–17
Wilber, Charles, 166, 207, 223, 341, 346
Wilson, Rodney, 72, 84
Winston, C., 276
Wolff, Edward, 47, 50, 103
Word of God, 13, 17
work, 356; community, 28–29, 47; God's norms, 145; normative principles from evangelical sources, *33;* normative principles from papal encyclicals, *30;* obligatory, 124–25, 128; opportunities, 39; organization of, 25–55; purpose and direction, 125; reforms, 44, 130. *See also* employment; unemployment
worker owned managed enterprises, 106, 112, 130
workers: ownership, 49–55; ownership of capital, 41–42, 51; ownership of companies, 42–48; ownership of financial capital, 100; ownership of private property, 42–43; participation, 45–48, 102, 125, 128–29
workers cooperatives, 51–55, 100, 106–7, 110, 153, 230. *See also* cooperatives; producers cooperatives
worldviews, 138–40, 334–41; in physical and social science, 313–18
Wright, Christopher, 23, 31, 36, 59, 60, 64, 68, 75

Yahweh. *See* God
Young, H., 293

About the Authors

Clive Beed is retired Senior Lecturer in the Department of Economics, University of Melbourne. He joined the University's Department of Economic Geography in 1963, concentrating on urban geography and planning. From 1983, Clive increasingly taught economics, where his main interest focused on the methodology and philosophy of economics, after his Department merged with the Department of Economics. He has published work in a variety of academic journals, encompassing economics and theology.

Cara Beed is retired Lecturer in Sociology and Graduate Adviser in the Education Faculty, Australian Catholic University. Cara led a varied career directing arts organizations, consulting nationally on community arts for the Australia Council, researched homeless youth with Scripture Union and lectured at tertiary institutions. Cara's research focuses on autonomy in God in relation to cultures of secrecy and abuse in the structures and processes of power in organizations, the community and families, especially churches.

Cara and Clive married in 1961, have two married children and two grandsons, and enjoy a rich family and community life. Having shared their intellectual and spiritual journey, they now share research and writing. Cara and Clive are (honorary) Fellows, Centre for Applied Christian Ethics, Ridley (Anglican) Theological College, University of Melbourne.